P9-CUK-434

The 2001 World Book

YEAR BOOK

The Annual Supplement to The World Book Encyclopedia

■ ■ ■ A REVIEW OF THE EVENTS OF 2000 ■ ■ ■

World Book, Inc.

a Scott Fetzer company

Chicago

www.worldbook.com

© 2001 World Book, Inc. All rights reserved. This volume may not be reproduced in whole or in part in any form without prior written permission from the publisher. Portions of the material contained in this volume are taken from *The World Book Encyclopedia* © 2001 World Book, Inc.

World Book, Inc.
233 N. Michigan Ave.
Chicago, IL 60601

ISBN: 0-7166-0451-5
ISSN 0084-1439
Library of Congress Catalog Card Number: 62-4818

Printed in the United States of America.

Staff

▪ EDITORIAL

Editor in Chief
Darlene R. Stille

Managing Editor
Scott Thomas

Senior Editors
Al Smuskiewicz
Kristina Vaicikonis

Staff Editors
Dan Blunk
Tim Frystak
Tabitha Hostetler
Anne Marie Pecha
Lindsey Welch

Contributing Editors
David Dreier
Jennifer Parello

Editorial Assistant
Ethel Matthews

Cartographic Services
H. George Stoll, Head
Wayne K. Pichler,
    Manager,
    Cartographic Database
Don Minnick,
    Staff Cartographer

Index Services
David Pofelski, Head
Tina Trettin

Statistical Services
Ken Shenkman, Head

Permissions Editor
Janet Peterson

▪ ART

Executive Director
Roberta Dimmer

Design
Brenda B. Tropinski,
    Senior Designer,
    Year Book
Cari L. Biamonte
    Senior Designer
Don Di Sante,
    Senior Designer

Photography
Sandra M. Dyrlund
    Photography Manager
Sylvia Ohlrich
    Photographs Editor
Marc Sirinsky
    Photographs Editor

Art Production Assistants
John Whitney
Laurie Schuh

▪ RESEARCH SERVICES

**Director of Research Services
and Product Development**
Paul Kobasa

Researchers
Madolynn Cronk
Karen A. McCormack
Cheryl J. Graham
Thomas Ryan Sullivan

Library Services
Jon Fjortoft, Head

▪ PRODUCTION

Manufacturing/Pre-Press
Carma Fazio,
    Senior Manager, Prepress
    and Manufacturing
Barbara Podczerwinski,
    Manufacturing Manager
Madelyn S. Underwood
    Senior Production
    Manager
Jared Svoboda,
    Production Manager

Proofreaders
Anne Dillon
Chad Rubel

Text Processing
Curley Hunter
Gwendolyn Johnson

▪ EXECUTIVE VICE PRESIDENT AND PUBLISHER
Michael Ross

Contributors

Contributors not listed on these pages are members of the editorial staff.

- **ANDREWS, PETER J.**, B.A., M.S.; Free-lance writer. **[Chemistry]**

- **APSELOFF, MARILYN FAIN**, B.A., M.A.; Professor of English, Kent State University, Ohio. **[Literature for children]**

- **ASKER, JAMES R.**, B.A.; Washington bureau chief, *Aviation Week & Space Technology* magazine. **[Space exploration Special Report: 2001: A Space Reality; Space exploration]**

- **BARNHART, BILL**, B.A., M.S.T., M.B.A.; Financial markets columnist, *Chicago Tribune*. **[Stocks and bonds]**

- **BARRETT, NORMAN**, M.A.; Free-lance writer. **[Soccer]**

- **BAYNHAM, SIMON**, B.A., M.A., Ph.D.; Senior research associate, Centre for Defence & International Security Studies, University of Lancaster, U.K. **[Africa and African country articles]**

- **BOULDREY, BRIAN**, B.A., M.F.A.; Free-lance editor. **[Hinduism; Literature, World; Poetry; Prison; Pulitzer Prizes; San Francisco]**

- **BOYD, JOHN D.**, B.S.; News editor, *Transport Topics*. **[Economics Special Report: The New Economy; Economics; International trade; Manufacturing]**

- **BRADSHER, HENRY S.**, A.B., B.J.; Foreign affairs analyst. **[Asia and Asian country articles]**

- **BRETT, CARLTON E.**, B.A., M.S., Ph.D.; Professor of geology, University of Cincinnati. **[Paleontology]**

- **BRODY, HERB**, B.S.; Senior editor, *Technology Review* magazine. **[Internet]**

- **BUERKLE, TOM**, B.A.; Correspondent, *International Herald Tribune*. **[Europe and Western European nation articles]**

- **CAMPBELL, GEOFFREY A.**, B.J.; Free-lance writer. **[U.S. government articles]**

- **CAMPBELL, LINDA P.**, B.A., M.S.L.; Editorial board member, *Fort Worth Star-Telegram*. **[U.S. government articles]**

- **CARDINALE, DIANE P.**, B.A.; Public information manager, Toy Manufacturers of America, Incorporated. **[Toys and games]**

- **CASEY, MIKE**, B.S., M.A.; Assistant editor, *Kansas City Star*. **[Automobile]**

- **DeFRANK, THOMAS M.**, B.A., M.A.; Washington bureau chief, *New York Daily News*. **[Armed forces]**

- **DILLON, DAVID**, B.A., M.A., Ph.D.; Architecture and design editor, *The Dallas Morning News*. **[Architecture]**

- **DUCKHAM, DAVID**, Free-lance writer, marketing consultant, and former professional rugby player. **[Rugby football]**

- **ELLIS, GAVIN**, Editor, *The New Zealand Herald*. **[New Zealand]**

- **ENGLUND, STEVEN**, A.B., M.A., Ph.D.; Writer for UNAIDS and other United Nations publications. **[Africa Special Report: AIDS in Africa-A Continent in Despair]**

- **FARR, DAVID M. L.**, D.Phil.; Professor emeritus of history, Carleton University. **[Canada; Canadian provinces; Canadian territories; Canada, Prime Minister of]**

- **FISHER, ROBERT W.**, B.A., M.A.; Free-lance writer. **[Labor and employment]**

- **FITZGERALD, MARK**, B.A.; Editor at large, *Editor & Publisher* magazine. **[Newspaper]**

- **FOX, THOMAS C.**, B.A., M.A.; Publisher, *The National Catholic Reporter*. **[Roman Catholic Church]**

- **FRICKER, KAREN**, B.A., M.A.; Free-lance theater critic. **[Theater]**

- **FRIEDMAN, EMILY**, B.A.; Health-policy and ethics analyst. **[Health care issues]**

- **GADOMSKI, FRED**, B.S., M.S.; Meteorologist, Pennsylvania State University. **[Weather]**

- **GATTY, ROBERT C.**, Vice president of communications and marketing, Food Distributors International. **[Food]**

- **GOLDEN, JONATHAN J.**, B.A., M.J.; Ph.D. student, Brandeis University. **[Judaism]**

- **GOLDNER, NANCY**, B.A.; Free-lance dance critic. **[Dance]**

- **GRIFFITHS, PAUL J.**, B.A., M.Phil., Ph.D.; Professor of the philosophy of religions, University of Chicago. **[Buddhism]**

- **HARAKAS, STANLEY SAMUEL**, B.A., B. Th., Th.D.; Archbishop Iakovos Professor (Emeritus) of Orthodox Theology, Holy Cross Greek Orthodox School of Theology. **[Eastern Orthodox Churches]**

- **HAVERSTOCK, NATHAN A.**, A.B.; Affiliate scholar, Oberlin College. **[Cuba Special Report: The Cold War's Last Front: The United States and Cuba; Latin America and Latin American country articles]**

- **HELMS, CHRISTINE**, B.A., Ph.D.; Writer and Middle East analyst. **[Middle East and Middle Eastern country articles; North African country articles]**

- **HENDERSON, HAROLD**, B.A.; Staff writer, Chicago *Reader*. **[Chicago]**

- **HOFFMAN, ANDREW J.**, B.S., M.S., Ph.D.; Assistant professor of organizational behavior, Boston University. **[Environmental pollution]**

- **JOHANSON, DONALD C.**, B.S., M.A., Ph.D.; Director and professor, Institute of Human Origins, Arizona State University. **[Anthropology]**

- **JOHN, NANCY R.**, A.B., M.L.S.; Assistant university librarian, University of Illinois at Chicago. **[Library]**

- **JOHNSON, CHRISTINA S.**, B.A., M.S.; Free-lance science writer. **[Ocean]**

- **JONES, TIM**, B.S.; Media reporter, *Chicago Tribune*. **[Telecommunications]**

- **KATES, MICHAEL**, B.S.J.; Associate sports editor, *Chicago Tribune*. **[Sports articles]**

- **KENNEDY, BRIAN**, M.A.; Copy editor, *Outback* magazine. **[Australia; Australia, Prime Minister of; Australian rules football]**

- **KILGORE, MARGARET**, B.A., M.B.A.; Free-lance writer, Kilgore and Associates. **[Los Angeles]**

4

- **KING, MIKE,** Reporter, *The* (Montreal) *Gazette.* **[Montreal]**

- **KLINTBERG, PATRICIA PEAK,** B.A.; Washington editor, *Farm Journal.* **[Agriculture]**

- **KNIGHT, ROBERT,** B.A., M.M.; Freelance writer. **[Nobel Prizes; People in the news]**

- **KRONHOLZ, JUNE,** B.S.J.; Staff reporter, *The Wall Street Journal.* **[Education]**

- **LAWRENCE, ALBERT,** B.A., M.A., M.Ed.; President, OutExcel! **[Chess]**

- **LEWIS, DAVID C.,** M.D.; Professor of medicine and community health, Brown University. **[Drug abuse]**

- **LIEBENSON, DONALD,** B.A.; Freelance writer. **[Popular music]**

- **LYE, KEITH,** B.A., F.R.G.S.; Freelance writer and editor. **[Cricket]**

- **MARCH, ROBERT H.,** A.B., M.S., Ph.D.; Professor of physics and liberal studies, University of Wisconsin at Madison. **[Physics]**

- **MARSCHALL, LAURENCE A.,** B.S., Ph.D.; Professor of physics, Gettysburg College. **[Astronomy]**

- **MARTY, MARTIN E.,** Ph.D.; Fairfax M. Cone Distinguished Service Professor Emeritus, University of Chicago. **[Protestantism]**

- **MAUGH, THOMAS H., II,** Ph.D.; Science writer, *Los Angeles Times.* **[Biology]**

- **MAY, SALLY RUTH,** B.A, M.A.; Freelance art writer. **[Art]**

- **McWILLIAM, ROHAN,** B.A., M.A.; D. Phil; Senior lecturer in history, Anglia Polytechnic University, Cambridge, U.K. **[United Kingdom Special Report: The Queen Mother: Creator of the Modern Monarchy; Ireland; Northern Ireland; United Kingdom; United Kingdom, Prime Minister of]**

- **MESSENGER, ROBERT,** B.A.; Editor, *New Criterion.* **[City; Crime; Literature, American; Washington, D.C.]**

- **MINER, TODD J.,** B.S., M.S.; Meteorologist, Pennsylvania State University. **[Weather]**

- **MORITZ, OWEN,** B.A.; Urban-affairs editor, *New York Daily News.* **[New York City]**

- **MORRIS, BERNADINE,** B.A., M.A.; Free-lance fashion writer. **[Fashion]**

- **MULLINS, HENRY T.,** B.S., M.S., Ph.D.; Professor of earth sciences, Syracuse University. **[Geology]**

- **NESBITT, ELEANOR M.,** M.A., M.Phil., Ph.D.; Senior lecturer in religions and education, Institute of Education, University of Warwick, U.K. **[Sikhism]**

- **NGUYEN, J. TUYET,** M.A.; United Nations correspondent, Deutsche Presse-Agentur. **[Population; United Nations]**

- **OGAN, EUGENE,** B.A., M.A., Ph.D.; Professor emeritus of anthropology, University of Minnesota. **[Pacific Islands]**

- **PAETH, GREGORY,** B.A.; Television and radio writer, *The Cincinnati Post.* **[Radio]**

- **REINHART, A. KEVIN,** B.A., M.A., Ph.D.; Associate professor of religious studies, Dartmouth College. **[Islam]**

- **ROSE, MARK J.,** B.A., M.A., Ph.D.; Managing editor, *Archaeology* magazine. **[Archaeology]**

- **RUBENSTEIN, RICHARD E.,** B.A., M.A., J.D.; Professor of conflict resolution and public affairs, George Mason University. **[Terrorism]**

- **SARNA, JONATHAN D.,** Ph.D.; Joseph H. & Belle R. Braun Professor of American Jewish History, Brandeis University. **[Judaism]**

- **SAVAGE, IAN,** B.A., Ph.D.; Assistant professor of economics and transportation, Northwestern University. **[Aviation; Transportation]**

- **SEGAL, TROY,** B.A.; Free-lance writer. **[Television]**

- **SHAPIRO, HOWARD,** B.S.; Travel editor, *The Philadelphia Inquirer.* **[Philadelphia]**

- **SOLNICK, STEVEN L.,** B.A., M.A., Ph.D.; Associate professor of political science, Columbia University. **[Russia and other former Soviet republic articles]**

- **STEIN, DAVID LEWIS,** B.A., M.S.; Urban affairs columnist, *The Toronto Star.* **[Toronto]**

- **STOCKER, CAROL M.,** B.A.; Reporter, *The Boston Globe.* **[Gardening]**

- **STUART, ELAINE,** B.A.; Senior managing editor, Council of State Governments. **[State government]**

- **TANNER, JAMES C.,** B.S.J.; Former news editor—energy, *The Wall Street Journal.* **[Energy supply]**

- **TATUM, HENRY K.,** B.A.; Associate editor, *The Dallas Morning News.* **[Dallas]**

- **THOMAS, PAULETTE,** B.A.; Staff writer, *The Wall Street Journal.* **[Bank]**

- **von RHEIN, JOHN,** B.A.; Classical music critic, *Chicago Tribune.* **[Classical music]**

- **WALTER, EUGENE J., Jr.,** B.A.; Freelance writer. **[Conservation; Zoos]**

- **WATSON, BURKE,** B.A.; Assistant suburban editor, *Houston Chronicle.* **[Houston]**

- **WIEWEL, WIM,** Ph.D; Professor of urban planning and policy, and Professor of managerial studies, University of Illinois at Chicago. **[City Special Report: The Renaissance of American Cities]**

- **WOLCHIK, SHARON L.,** B.A., M.A., Ph.D.; Professor of political science and international affairs, George Washington University. **[Eastern European country articles]**

- **WOODS, MICHAEL,** B.S.; Science editor, *The Toledo* (Ohio) *Blade* and *Pittsburgh Post-Gazette.* **[AIDS; Computer; Drugs; Electronics; Magazine; Medicine; Mental health; Public health and safety]**

- **WRIGHT, ANDREW G.,** B.A.; Managing editor, *Design-Build* magazine. **[Building and construction]**

- **WUNTCH, PHILIP,** B.A.; Film critic, *The Dallas Morning News.* **[Motion pictures]**

Contents

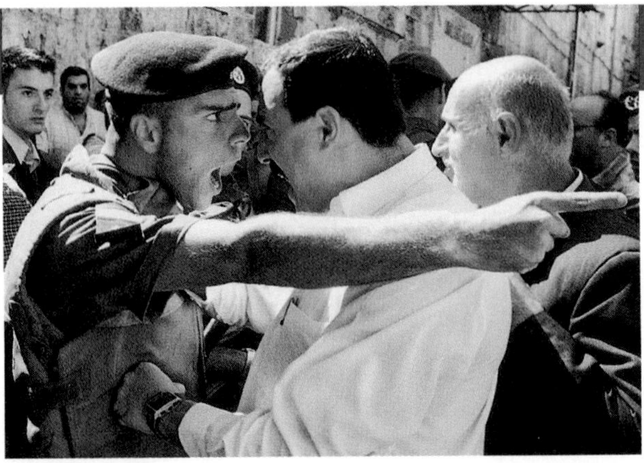

▲ Page 261

Update **36 to 448**

▲ Page 116

Special Election 2000 Supplement: War for the White House ...page 449

A down-to-the-wire battle for the presidency riveted the nation's attention and raised questions about the Electoral College.

World Book Supplement **458**

Five new or revised articles are reprinted from the 2000 edition of *The World Book Encyclopedia.*

 Page 156

Index **513**

A 15-page cumulative index covers the contents of the 1999, 2000, and 2001 editions of *The Year Book.*

◀ **Page 326**

▲ **Page 441**

From the collapse of the Middle East peace process to the presidential election crisis in the United States, 2000 was a year of memorable news events. On these three pages are stories that the editors picked as some of the most important of the year, along with details on where to find information about them in this volume.
The Editors

Work begins at space station

A U.S. astronaut and two Russian cosmonauts begin a four-month mission at the International Space Station shortly after moving into the craft in November. The station will be the first permanent human outpost in space. See **Space exploration**, page 370; **Space exploration: A Special Report,** page 372.

Sydney hosts Olympic games

Fireworks light up the harbor in Sydney, Australia, on October 1 at the concluding ceremony of the 27th Olympiad, the first Olympic Games of the new millennium. See **Australia,** page 88; **Olympics: A Special Report,** page 312; **Sports**, page 385.

PRI rule ends in Mexico

A man wearing a mask of President-elect Vicente Fox celebrates Fox's victory in July at a rally under Mexico City's Angel of Independence monument. Fox's election marked the end of 71 years of rule by the Institutional Revolutionary Party. See **Latin America,** page 272; **Mexico,** page 291; **People in the news,** page 329.

Election crisis

Republican Governor George W. Bush of Texas defeated his Democratic challenger, Vice President Al Gore, in one of the narrowest victories in U.S. history. While Gore won the popular vote, Bush captured the electoral votes needed to win the election. Questions surrounding alleged voting irregularities in Florida led to a delay in a final decision for weeks following the election. See **Courts,** page 165; **Democratic Party,** page 194; **Elections,** page 215; **Election: A Special Report**, page 449; **Republican Party**, page 349; **State government**, page 388; **Supreme Court**, page 393; **United States, Government of the**, page 431.

Elian returns to Cuba

A seven-month-long fight over custody of Elian Gonzalez ended in June when the boy flew back to Cuba from the United States with his father. The custody battle over the 6-year-old boy brought questions about relations between Cuba and the United States to the forefront of public attention. See **Cuba,** page 169; **Cuba: A Special Report,** page 170; **Miami**, page 292.

Peace process collapses

Palestinian police take cover during a shootout with Israeli soldiers in the Gaza Strip in October. Clashes between Palestinians and Israelis began in late September following the collapse of the Arab-Israeli peace process. See **Israel,** page 260; **Middle East,** page 294; **Egypt,** page 214; **United States, President of the,** page 435.

Demonstrators light torches in Belgrade, the capital of Yugoslavia, in September to celebrate the election of Vojislav Kostunica as president and to protest defeated President Slobodan Milosevic's demand for a runoff election. Massive protests helped force Milosevic to surrender the presidency in October. See **Europe,** page 222; **Yugoslavia,** page 444.

Fall of Milosevic

Korean reconciliation

The leaders of South Korea and North Korea met in Pyongyang, the North Korean capital, in June in an attempt to establish friendlier relations. The meeting was the first between North Korea and South Korea since Korea was divided between the Western and Soviet blocs at the end of World War II in 1945. See **Korea, North,** page 267; **Korea, South,** page 268.

Human genome decoded

DECODING THE BOOK OF LIFE

A Milestone For Humanity

Craig Venter of Celera Genomics Corporation (left), President Bill Clinton, and Francis Collins of the National Institutes of Health announce in June that researchers have completed rough drafts of the *human genome* (total amount of genetic information). See **Medicine,** page 289.

January February March April May June July August September

2000 YEAR IN BRIEF

A month-by-month listing of the most significant world events that occurred during 2000.

October November December

1 Vladimir Putin, who became the acting president of Russia with the resignation of Boris Yeltsin on Dec. 31, 1999, spends his first full day in office visiting Russian troops fighting in the breakaway republic of Chechnya.

3 Croatia's democratic opposition party, the Social Democrats, soundly defeats the ruling Croatian Democratic Union, party of the late president Franjo Tudjman, in parliamentary elections.

4 U.S. President Bill Clinton joins Israeli Prime Minister Ehud Barak and Syrian Foreign Minister Farouk al-Shara in West Virginia, for peace negotiations between Israel and Syria.

Nineteen people die when two passenger trains traveling in excess of 50 miles (80 kilometers) per hour collide head-on. The collision takes place approximately 100 miles (160 kilometers) north of Oslo, Norway.

5 Elian Gonzalez, a 6-year-old Cuban boy who survived the capsizing of a refugee boat that resulted in his mother's drowning, is to be returned to his father in Cuba, according to a spokesperson for the U.S. Immigration and Naturalization Service. Since being rescued by fishermen off the coast of Florida on Nov. 25, 1999, the child has been the object of a tug-of-war between relatives in Cuba, relatives and anti-Castro Cubans in Miami, Florida, and the governments of Cuba and the United States.

7 The rate of unemployment in the United States averaged 4.2 percent of the work force in 1999, its lowest level since 1969, when unemployment averaged 3.5 percent, reports the U.S. Department of Labor.

8 More than 6,000 people rally before the Statehouse in Columbia, South Carolina's capital, in defense of the Confederate flag. The flag is the emblem of the Confederacy, the 11 Southern states that *seceded* (withdrew) from the government of the United States in 1860 and 1861, resulting in the Civil War. South Carolina has flown the Confederate flag from the Capitol dome for 38 years. Defenders claim the flag represents "defiant defense of freedom and Southern heritage." Various civil rights organizations describe the banner as a symbol of slavery.

9 The Guardian Council of Iran, a body of conservative clerics that supervises government activities, bars more than 30 members of Iran's parliament from running for reelection. All are allies of Iran's moderate president, Mohammad Khatami. The council also disqualifies dozens of proreform candidates slated to run in the election scheduled for February 18.

10 The chairman of America Online (AOL), Steven M. Case, and chief executive of Time Warner, Gerald M. Levin, announce that AOL is acquiring Time Warner as part of a $165-billion merger. AOL is the world's largest Internet service provider, with more than 22 million subscribers. Time Warner is the world's largest media conglomerate.

12 The population of the United States will more than double in the next 100 years, reports the U.S. Census Bureau. According to bureau estimates, the U.S. population will climb from 275 million people in 2000 to 571 million in 2100.

13 Bill Gates, founder of Microsoft Corp., the Redmond, Washington-based software giant, steps down as chief operating officer and appoints as his successor company President Steve Ballmer.

16 A 61-year-old economist and leader of the Chilean Socialist Party is narrowly elected president of Chile. Ricardo Lagos, who took 51 percent of the vote, will be Chile's first Socialist head of state since a *coup* (overthrow) forced Salvador Allende from office in 1973.

17 U.S. Secretary of State Madeleine Albright announces that peace talks between Israeli Prime Minister Ehud Barak and Syrian Foreign Minister Farouk al-Shara have been postponed.

Nearly 48,000 protestors mark the birthday of slain civil rights leader Martin Luther King, Jr., with a march in Columbia, South Carolina. They demand that the state remove the Confederate flag from the Capitol dome.

Two rescue boats patrol near the site where Alaska Airlines Flight 261 crashed into the Pacific Ocean near Oxnard, California, northwest of Los Angeles, on Jan. 31, 2000.

18 **Helmut Kohl,** the former chancellor who presided over Germany's unification, resigns as chairman of the Christian Democratic Union party.

21 **Two car bombs** explode in Spain's capital, Madrid, killing a Spanish army officer on a walk near his residence. The government blames the Basque separatist organization ETA for breaking a cease-fire that lasted for 18 months.

22 **Vice President** Gustavo Noboa Bejarano assumes Ecuador's presidency with the backing of most of the country's armed forces and the national police.

24 **The U.S. Food and Drug** Administration (FDA) issues a new warning to physicians about the use of Propulsid, a popular heartburn medicine that was first marketed in 1993. More than 70 deaths and an additional 200 cases of irregular heartbeat have been linked to the use of the drug, according to the FDA.

26 **Officials in Beijing,** China's capital, announce new laws banning information from the Internet about the Chinese government or government officials unless the information is approved by the State Secrets Bureau.

27 **Egypt's parliament** passes legislation allowing a woman to divorce a husband without providing the court with witnesses of abuse or proof of mistreatment. Fundamentalists claim that only men have the right to initiate divorce, according to the laws of Islam, Egypt's dominant religion.

30 **The St. Louis Rams** win Super Bowl XXXIV by beating the Tennessee Titans 23 to 16 in Atlanta, Georgia.

31 **All 88 passengers** and crew members aboard Alaska Airlines Flight 261 from Puerto Vallarta, Mexico, to Seattle, Washington, are killed when the jet crashes into the Pacific Ocean near Oxnard, California.

1 **Senator John McCain** of Arizona takes 49 percent of the vote in the New Hampshire Republican presidential primary, defeating Texas Governor George W. Bush, who received 30 percent of the vote. In the Democratic primary, Vice President Al Gore collects 50 percent of the vote against former New Jersey Senator Bill Bradley, who receives 46 percent.

The leader of Austria's conservative People's Party, Wolfgang Schuessel, announces that he is forming a coalition government with the Freedom Party, an extreme anti-immigrant organization.

2 **The Federal Reserve** (the Fed), an independent government agency that oversees the U.S. banking system, raises its federal funds target rate on overnight loans among banks one-quarter of a percentage point, to 5.75 percent. The FED also raises the discount rate on Federal Reserve loans to banks by one-quarter point, to 5.25 percent.

4 **The rate of unemployment** in the United States fell to 4.0 percent, a 30-year low, in January, reports the U.S. Department of Labor.

5 **At least 50 people** are injured in clashes between demonstrators and police in the Austrian capital of Vienna. The demonstrations were staged in response to a February 4 ceremony in which members of the right-wing Freedom Party were sworn in as ministers of a coalition government.

6 **Vladimir Putin**, the acting president of Russia, announces that Russian troops have captured Grozny, the capital of the breakaway republic of Chechnya.

Hillary Rodham Clinton, the First Lady, announces that she is a Democratic candidate for the U.S. Senate from the state of New York, where she established residency in January.

7 **A hijacked Afghan jet** with approximately 150 passengers and crew members on board lands at a suburban London airport in Stansted, England. An unknown number of gunmen seized control of the state-owned Ariana Air-

lines Boeing 727 on February 6, during a flight between Kabul, Afghanistan's capital, and Mazar Sarif, a city north of Kabul.

8 **Israel bombs** targets in Lebanon for the second day in a row. On February 7, Israeli bombers destroyed power plants near the capital, Beirut, plunging much of Lebanon into darkness.

9 **Steve Forbes,** a conservative who advocates a flat income tax, drops out of the race for the Republican nomination for president of the United States.

10 **Nearly half** of the approximately 150 passengers and crew members remaining aboard a hijacked Afghan airliner that landed in Great Britain on February 7 request asylum after their captors surrender to British police.

11 **Great Britain** suspends Northern Ireland's power-sharing government of Roman Catholics and Protestants 10 weeks after it was instituted because the Irish Republican Army (IRA), a military organization that seeks to unite the independent country of Ireland with Northern Ireland, refuses to discuss establishing a timetable for disarming its members.

12 **Approximately 55 percent** of voters in Zimbabwe reject a constitution designed to increase the power of the president. The constitution would have given Zimbabwe's president the right to dissolve parliament without cause and seize white-owned farms.

13 **A Serb environmental** minister announces that Serbia will sue Romania in an international court for damages to the environment caused by a cyanide spill at a gold mine. Highly polluted water overflowed a dam at a mine in northwest Romania on January 31, pouring cyanide, which is used to separate gold from ore, into streams. The streams carried the cyanide west into the Tisza and Danube rivers in Hungary. Both rivers flow into Serbia.

15 **The U.S. prison** population reaches 2 million men and women, according to the Justice Policy Institute, a Washington, D.C.-based research organization.

18 **Iranians,** voting in record numbers, overwhelmingly elect reform-minded representatives to the Majlis, the Iranian parliament. The Majlis has been dominated by ultraconservative Islamic clergy since the 1979 revolution.

19 **Texas Governor** George W. Bush wins 53 percent of the vote in the South Carolina Republican presidential primary, defeating Arizona Senator John McCain, who takes 42 percent, and Alan Keyes, who receives 5 percent. The Democratic Party did not hold a presidential primary in South Carolina on February 19.

21 **Hundreds of people** are killed in Kaduna, a city in the north of Nigeria, in clashes between Christians and Muslims, who insist that strict Islamic law be instituted in Kaduna state. Muslims constitute a majority of the population in the region.

22 **Arizona Senator** John McCain wins the Republican presidential primary in Michigan, taking 50 percent of the vote. His opponents, Texas Governor George W. Bush and Alan Keyes, receive 43 percent and 5 percent, respectively. In the Arizona Republican primary, McCain receives 60 percent of the vote against Bush's 36 percent and Keyes's 4 percent. The Democratic Party did not hold a presidential primary in either state on February 22.

25 **The Dow Jones** average of prices of common stock of 30 U.S. industrial firms falls 230.51 points, or 2.28 percent, on the New York Stock Exchange to close below the 10,000 mark for the first time in 10 months. The Dow declined by 3.5 percent during the week of February 20 and 14.22 percent since the beginning of 2000.

29 **Governor George W. Bush** of Texas wins Republican presidential primaries in Virginia and Washington and the Republican caucus in North Dakota. Vice President Al Gore wins the Democratic primary in Washington. The Democratic Party did not hold a primary election in Virginia or a caucus in North Dakota.

Russian troops capture Grozny, the capital of the breakaway republic of Chechnya, in February. Two wars since 1994 transformed the capital city into mostly rubble.

1 Three days of riots between Muslims and Christians in the city of Aba in southeast Nigeria leave at least 400 people dead. The violence follows a similar outbreak during the week of February 19 in Kaduna, a city in the north, where hundreds of people were killed. In both cities, the clashes were triggered by Christians demonstrating against Muslim demands for an Islamic penal code.

2 Great Britain drops extradition proceedings against General Augusto Pinochet, who is allowed to return to Chile because of his failing health. The former Chilean dictator was under house arrest in England for 16 months on the possibility that he would be tried on charges of gross human rights violations.

3 An international tribunal in The Hague, Netherlands, sentences Croatian General Tihomir Blaskic to 45 years in prison for war crimes committed during the conflict in Bosnia between 1992 and 1994.

5 The Israeli cabinet votes unanimously to withdraw its troops from Lebanon. Israel established a 9-mile- (14.5-kilometer-) wide security zone in southern Lebanon in 1985 to protect settlements in northern Israel from guerrilla attack. Israel's presence in Lebanon has been a major obstacle to an Israeli-Syrian peace accord.

7 Vice President Al Gore sweeps the presidential primaries in all 16 states in which the Democratic Party held elections on Super Tuesday, against challenger Bill Bradley, a former senator from New Jersey. Gore is victorious in the delegate-rich states of California and New York as well as in Maine, Vermont, Massachusetts, Rhode Island, Connecticut, Georgia, Maryland, Ohio, and Bradley's home state of Missouri. In California, the vice president garners 81 percent of the vote, compared with Bradley's 18 percent. In the Republican presidential primaries, Texas Governor George W. Bush racks up victories in 9 of the 13 elections, beating his chief challenger, Arizona Senator John McCain, in California, Georgia, Maine, Maryland, Minnesota, Missouri, New York, Ohio, and Washington. Senator McCain captures primaries in Connecticut, Rhode Island, Vermont, and Massachusetts, where the Arizona senator took 65 percent of the vote, compared with George W. Bush's 32 percent.

8 The Chinese government executes a former provincial vice governor for taking bribes. China's premier, Zhu Rongji, has vowed to stamp out official corruption, which many experts believe extends into the highest ranks of the Communist Party.

9 Arizona Senator John McCain announces that he is withdrawing as an active candidate for president. Former New Jersey Senator Bill Bradley, running against Vice President Al Gore for the Democratic nomination for president, also announces that he is dropping out of the race.

10 Much of the United States experienced the warmest winter season— from December 1999 through February 2000—in the 105 years that records have been kept by the federal government, reports a spokesperson for the National Climactic Data Center in Asheville, North Carolina. Temperatures in the lower 48 states during the 1999- 2000 season averaged 38.4 °F (3.6 °C).

12 Pope John Paul II, attending a Mass inside Saint Peter's Basilica in Rome on the first Sunday of Lent, repents for errors committed by the "sisters and brothers" of the Roman Catholic Church over the last 2,000 years. The pope's public act of repentance, which officials characterize as a purification of memory, is unprecedented in the history of the Roman Catholic Church.

13 The Japanese economy lapsed back into recession by shrinking in the fourth quarter of 1999, announces an official of the Japanese Economic Planning Agency.

14 Vice President Al Gore and Texas Governor George W. Bush sweep the Democratic and Republican presidential primaries in Florida, Texas, Louisiana, Oklahoma, Tennessee, and Mississippi, providing each candidate with enough votes to claim his party's

Police in Taipei, Taiwan, battle Nationalist Party members protesting the party's humiliating loss in the March 18 presidential election. Thousands of members took to the streets in the days after the election.

presidential nomination in August at their party conventions.

16 **Investors** push Dow Jones Industrial Average stocks up 499 points. The point gain is the greatest in a single day of trading in the history of the New York Stock Exchange.

18 **Taiwanese voters** elect as president Chen Shui-bian, a member of the Democratic Progressive Party, ousting the Nationalist Party government after more than 50 years of rule. The Democratic Progressive Party stressed independence for Taiwan during the campaign, though Chen distanced himself from that position.

20 **Pope John Paul II** begins a pilgrimage to the Holy Land with prayers on Jordan's Mount Nebo. According to Biblical traditions, Mount Nebo is the place where Moses viewed the Promised Land.

21 **The Federal Reserve** (the Fed), an independent government agency that oversees the U.S. banking system, raises its federal funds target rate on overnight loans among banks one-quarter of a percentage point, to 6 percent. The Fed also raises the discount rate on Federal Reserve loans to banks by one-quarter point, to 5.5 percent.

26 **Acting President Vladimir Putin** is elected president of Russia in his own right, receiving a clear majority of 53 percent of the vote in national elections. Putin's greatest rival, Communist Gennady Zyuganov, comes in second with 29 percent of the vote.

28 **The Chicago Cubs** and the New York Mets open the 2000 baseball season in Tokyo, Japan. The season opener, which the Cubs win, 5 to 3, is the first to be played outside North America in major league history.

17

Elian Gonzalez is reunited with his Cuban father, Juan Miguel Gonzalez, on April 22, after federal agents seized the 6-year-old boy from relatives in Miami, Florida, during a predawn raid.

3 Microsoft, the Redmond, Washington-based software manufacturer, violated the 1890 Sherman Antitrust Act, rules Thomas Penfield Jackson, a U.S. District Court judge in Washington, D.C. The judge notes that Microsoft maintained a monopoly for its PC operating system software through anti-competitive means.

4 Japan's acting prime minister, Mikio Aoki, announces that all members of Japan's Cabinet have resigned to allow the ruling Liberal Democratic Party to form a new government. The move was necessitated by the incapacitation of Prime Minister Keizo Obuchi, who suffered a stroke.

5 Emperor Akihito of Japan presides over the swearing in of Yoshiro Mori as prime minister. Mori, who replaces the ailing Keizo Obuchi, pledges to continue Obuchi's attempts to lead the economy out of years of stagnation.

6 Former prime minister of Pakistan Nawaz Sharif is found guilty of hijacking a commercial airliner and is sentenced to life in prison. The hijacking incident, which took place on Oct. 12, 1999, occurred when then Prime Minister Sharif issued an order refusing to allow a Karachi-bound jet to land.

8 Bolivia's president, Hugo Banzer, declares a state of emergency in response to violence and police mutinies spreading across the country. The civil unrest began on April 3 in Cochabamba after the government announced it would raise the price of drinking water.

9 Incumbent Alberto Fujimori takes 49.8 percent of the vote in presidential elections in Peru, compared with opponent Alejandro Toledo's 40.3 percent. Peru's constitution specifies that a candidate needs 50 percent plus one vote to avoid a runoff election, making a second round inevitable.

10 **The government of South Korea** announces that President Kim Dae-jung will travel to Pyongyang, the North Korea capital, in June to participate in a summit conference with Kim Chong-Il, North Korea's leader. The meeting will be the first between the heads of state of the two countries.

12 **Tensions remain high** in Miami after a face-to-face meeting between 6-year-old Elian Gonzalez and his father, Juan Miguel Gonzalez, was canceled by the boy's Miami relatives, who are battling to keep Elian in the United States. Juan Miguel Gonzalez, who flew to the United States from Cuba on April 6, has not seen his son since Elian and his mother left Cuba in November 1999 to escape to the United States.

13 **The High Court of Zimbabwe** orders the country's president, Robert Mugabe, to uphold the rule of law and evict some 50,000 squatters from more than 900 farms owned by white Zimbabweans. Mugabe claims that to take any police action against the squatters, who are armed, could trigger a civil war.

14 **The Dow Jones** Industrial Average falls 617.68 points, its greatest one-day decline in history. The Nasdaq plunges 355.49 points, another historic one-day decline.

15 **Baltimore Orioles** third baseman Cal Ripken, Jr., singles to center field at the Metrodome in Minneapolis for the 3,000th hit of his career in the major leagues. Ripken is the 24th player in major league history to reach the 3,000-hit milestone.

16 **Finance ministers** from the member nations of the International Monetary Fund (IMF) and the World Bank meet in Washington, D.C., to discuss global financial stability and to set future courses for the two organizations, which are affiliated with the United Nations and provide credit to member nations. Outside the IMF headquarters, as many as 10,000 people demonstrate against IMF and World Bank policies, which protestors claim burden Third World nations with debts.

17 **Vladimir Putin** pays his first visit to the West as president of Russia, meeting with British Prime Minister Tony Blair in London.

20 **The internal structure** of the heart of a dinosaur may have been more like that of a bird or a mammal than any known reptile, announces Dale Russell, a paleontologist at the North Carolina Museum of Natural History in Raleigh. The announcement is based on a computerized imaging examination of a fossilized organ.

21 **The Duma,** the lower house of the Russian parliament, votes overwhelmingly to ratify the Comprehensive Test Ban Treaty (CTBT). The treaty bans all nuclear explosions in the hope of constraining the development and qualitative improvement of nuclear weapons.

22 **Elian Gonzalez is reunited** with his father, Juan Miguel Gonzalez, at Andrews Air Force Base in Suitland, Maryland.

23 **An Iranian court** closes five newspapers in Tehran, the capital, after imprisoning one of the country's most active proreform journalists, Akbar Ganji, for writing articles deemed in violation of "Islamic values."

24 **Ukraine's** minister of defense, Olexander Kuzmuk, announces that an April 20 explosion that left three people dead in an apartment building in Brovary, a city east of Ukraine's capital, Kiev, was caused by a Russian-made surface-to-surface missile launched by Ukraine's own military.

26 **Vermont Governor** Howard Dean signs legislation into state law creating civil unions between same-sex couples. The new law empowers justices of the peace, judges, and clergymen to certify the unions, which confer many of the rights and responsibilities enjoyed by married couples.

30 **Vietnamese veterans** march in an invitation-only parade within the walls of Ho Chi Minh City's Unification Palace as part of the government's official observance of the 25th anniversary of the end of the Vietnam War (1957-1975).

1 **South Asia** is a major hub of international terrorism, announces the U.S. State Department in a 107-page report that specifically names Pakistan and Afghanistan as havens for terrorists.

2 **The Swiss National Bank,** Switzerland's central bank, begins selling gold reserves, with an initial offering of 120 tons (108 metric tons), in the largest sale of gold in history.

3 **Executives** with the London Stock Exchange and Frankfurt's Deutsche Boerse announce plans for a merger, to create a single market on which English and German securities would be traded 24 hours a day. The combined value of the securities would exceed $5.95 trillion.

4 **A computer virus,** dubbed the "love bug" for the "I LOVE YOU" featured in the subject line of the e-mail carrying it, attacks hundreds of thousands of computers worldwide, destroying data, jamming e-mail services, and crashing programs.

Sierra Leone's Revolutionary United Front, a rebel group led by Foday Sankoh, attacks United Nations peacekeeping troops and seizes more than 500 hostages.

5 **The unemployment rate** in the United States dropped from 4.1 percent in March to 3.9 percent in April, a 30-year low, announces the U.S. Department of Labor.

Ken Livingstone is elected mayor of London in the British capital's first mayoral election in history. Previous mayors were appointed by the Crown.

7 **Vladimir Putin** is sworn in as president of Russia in the first free transfer of power in the country's 1,100-year history. In national elections held on March 26, Putin soundly defeated the Communist candidate, Gennady Zyuganov.

9 **Senator John McCain** (R., Arizona) endorses Texas Governor George W. Bush for president of the United States but insists that he will not join Bush on the Republican ticket as a candidate for vice president.

10 **A fire** that scorched more than 18,000 acres (7,284 hectares) sweeps through Los Alamos, New Mexico, forcing at least 18,000 people to evacuate their houses. Officials at the nearby Los Alamos National Laboratory, which closed on May 8 because of the fire, announce that they do not believe the fire could ignite hazardous chemicals or nuclear material stored there.

12 **Ethiopia and Eritrea** resume fighting along their disputed border two days after the collapse of peace talks brokered by the United Nations and the European Union.

15 **At least three** Palestinians are killed and more than 315 Israelis and Palestinians injured in fierce fighting between Israeli troops and Palestinian security forces on the West Bank and in the Gaza Strip. The violence was sparked by Palestinian protests over the slow pace of the Mideast peace process.

17 **Sierra Leone's** chief rebel leader, Foday Sankoh, is caught by his neighbors in Freetown, the capital, and paraded through the streets before being turned over to government authorities.

Japan's prime minister, Yoshiro Mori, apologizes for referring to Japan as a "divine country with an emperor at its core." Many believed that Mori's comment suggested emperor worship and implied that the new prime minister did not support Japan's Constitution, which guarantees a secular state.

19 **New York City** Mayor Rudolph Giuliani drops out of the race for the U.S. Senate seat from New York in which he was likely to run as the Republican candidate against First Lady Hillary Rodham Clinton. Citing health problems for his withdrawal, the mayor declares that he will devote his remaining 18 months in office to becoming a better mayor and person.

The U.S. Department of Commerce reveals that the nation's trade deficit—the shortfall between the value of a country's exports of goods and services and the value of its imports—grew to a record $30.2 billion in March. Econo-

Lebanese residents cheer along the Lebanon-Israeli border on May 24 as Israeli troops withdraw from southern Lebanon. Israeli troops had occupied the area for 22 years.

mists said that high oil prices were partially responsible for the deficit and cautioned that the deficit could threaten robust consumer spending in the United States.

20 **Fifty years** of Nationalist rule in Taiwan ends when Chen Shui-bian is sworn in as president. President Chen, leader of the Democratic Progressive Party, which has long advocated Taiwan's independence from China, succeeds Lee Teng-hui, Taiwan's first popularly elected president.

U.S. Representative Rick Lazio, a Republican from New York, announces that he will seek the nomination of his party in the New York Senate race against the Democratic candidate, First Lady Hillary Rodham Clinton.

21 **Government officials** in China announce that they have approved a plan to send two pandas to the National Zoo in Washington, D.C.

23 **Governor Jim Hodges** of South Carolina signs into law a bill that specifies the removal of the Confederate flag from the Capitol dome in Columbia, the state capital.

24 **Israel** pulls the last of its troops out of southern Lebanon, ending 22 years of occupation.

28 **Alberto Fujimori** is reelected president of Peru in a runoff election boycotted by his opponent, Alejandro Toledo.

29 **North Korean** leader Kim Chong-Il arrives in Beijing, the Chinese capital, for three days of meetings. The trip is the first the North Korean leader has taken outside of his country since 1994.

31 **Military leaders** in Fiji, who recently took control of the government, appoint Ratu Epeli Nailatikau prime minister. Nailatikau, a native Fijian, replaces Mahendra Chaudhry, Fiji's first ethnic Indian premier.

2 The United Nations war crimes tribunal refuses to launch a formal investigation into whether NATO committed war crimes during a 1999 bombing campaign in Yugoslavia. The tribunal's chief prosecutor, Carla Del Ponte, acknowledges that mistakes were made by NATO but notes that she is "very satisfied that there was no deliberate targeting of civilians."

3 Presidents Bill Clinton of the United States and Vladimir Putin of Russia meet in the Kremlin in Moscow to discuss the state of the Russian economy, conflicts in the Balkans and the Caucasus, and antimissile defense strategies.

4 Storms blowing across north Texas drop as much as 15 inches (38 centimeters) of rain in 12 hours.

5 Ukraine agrees to shut down the Chernobyl nuclear power plant in mid-December, announces Leonid Kuchma, president of Ukraine, during a meeting with U.S. President Bill Clinton. A nuclear reactor at the station exploded in 1986, spewing radioactive debris that was eventually measurable throughout the Northern Hemisphere.

Rebels demand the resignation of Solomon Islands Prime Minister Bartholomew Ulufa 'alu after seizing control of the capital, Honiara. Ulufa 'alu was detained at his residence. The rebels, known as the Malaita Eagles Force, are involved in fierce ethnic disputes involving native residents of Guadalcanal and residents originally from Malaita Island.

More than 30 giant black holes have been discovered at the centers of distant galaxies, astronomers announce at a meeting of the American Astronomical Society in Rochester, New York.

6 Approximately 10,000 veterans of World War II (1939-1945) attend the opening of the National D-Day Museum in New Orleans, Louisiana.

7 Judge Thomas Penfield Jackson, the federal judge presiding over the Microsoft antitrust case, rules that the Microsoft Corporation is to be split into two separate companies. One will be dedicated to Microsoft's Windows operating system, the second to such applications as Microsoft Office and the Internet Explorer Web browser.

J. Craig Venter of Celera Genomics Corporation (left), President Bill Clinton, and Francis Collins of the National Institutes of Health speak on June 26 prior to an announcement that the scientists had completed an initial sequencing of the human genome.

8 **Nearly two years** of war in Congo (Kinshasa) has resulted in the deaths of 1.7 million people in five eastern provinces, reveals a report commissioned by the International Rescue Committee of New York City.

9 **The Leaning Tower** of Pisa leans 5.2 inches (13 centimeters) less than it did in January 1999, announces a spokesperson for the project to save the 189-foot (57.6-meter) tower, which dates from the 1300's. Work to stabilize the monument, which has been closed to the public for 10 years, is expected to continue into 2001, when the tower is scheduled to reopen.

10 **The New Jersey Devils** beat hockey's defending champion, the Dallas Stars, 2-1, to win the Stanley Cup in a six-game series.

12 **President Vladimir Putin** of Russia appoints a Chechen Muslim cleric, Mufti Akhmed Kadyrov, governor of Chechnya. The new governor supported Russia when the Russian Army entered Chechnya on Oct. 1, 1999, to block Islamic militants from setting up an Islamic state in the Caucasus region of southern Russia.

15 **The President of South Korea,** Kim Dae-jung, and the leader of North Korea, Kim Chong-Il, culminate a historic summit with the signing of a five-point declaration aimed at peace and the eventual reunification of the two countries. The summit, held in the North Korean capital of Pyongyang, is the first ever to occur between leaders of the two nations.

17 **Members** of an upper-caste militia, Ranvir Sena, attack a low-caste village in Bihar State in northeast India and gun down 34 people, mostly women, children, and older men.

18 **Tiger Woods** wins the U.S. Open at Pebble Beach, California, by 15 strokes. The winning margin shatters golf records. The previous record at the U.S. Open was 11 strokes, held by Willie Smith since 1899. The previous record for margin of victory in the history of championship golf was 13 strokes, held by Old Tom Morris since 1862.

19 **The European Union** (EU) accepts Greece, the union's poorest nation, as the 12th member of the European Monetary Union. Greece will officially join the single currency, the euro, on Jan. 1, 2001.

22 **Liquid water** from shallow underground reservoirs may occasionally burst onto the surface of Mars, announce National Aeronautics and Space Administration (NASA) officials describing photographs taken from the Mars Global Surveyor. The photographs show features that resemble gullies and channels carved by water flowing down craters and valley walls and appear to have been created recently. While scientists have long believed that water existed on Mars billions of years ago, most researchers insisted that the planet's temperature and atmospheric pressure were currently too low to allow water to exist in a liquid state on the surface.

26 **Two groups** of researchers announce that they have each completed rough drafts of the human *genome* (total amount of genetic information). Scientists with the publicly funded Human Genome Project affirm that they had determined the order of approximately 85 percent of the 3 billion chemical building blocks, called nucleotides, that make up the genome. Researchers at Celera Genomics Corporation, a private corporation located in Rockville, Maryland, announce that they have sequenced virtually all of the nucleotides, except for a number of small gaps.

28 **The seven-month battle** over Elian Gonzalez ends when the 6-year-old Cuban shipwreck survivor arrives in Havana, Cuba, with his father, Juan Miguel Gonzalez. The Gonzalez family left the United States from Washington, D.C., only hours after the U.S. Supreme Court ended the interfamily and international conflict by refusing to hear a formal appeal from Elian's Miami relatives for custody of the child.

29 **U.S. President** Bill Clinton nominates Norman Y. Mineta as secretary of commerce for the final six months of the Clinton presidency.

Flames shoot from an Air France Concorde before it crashes into a hotel near Paris, France, on July 25. All 109 people aboard the jet and 4 people on the ground are killed.

1 **Queen Margrethe** of Denmark and King Carl XVI of Sweden officially open a 10-mile (16-kilometer), $3.5-billion bridge and tunnel that link the two countries. The bridge allows motorists to drive between Copenhagen, the Danish capital, and Malmo, Sweden.

2 **Vicente Fox Quesada,** candidate of the National Action Party, takes 43 percent of the vote in the Mexican presidential election, defeating Francisco Labastida Ochoa of the Institutional Revolutionary Party (PRI). The victory ends 71 years of PRI rule.

3 **Rebels in Chechnya** launch a series of suicide bomb attacks on Russian troops, killing at least 37 soldiers.

8 **Venus Williams** of the United States wins the women's singles title at Wimbledon with a 6-3, 7-6 (3) final victory over Lindsay Davenport at the All England Club.

9 **Pete Sampras** of the United States beats Patrick Rafter of Australia 6-7 (10), 7-6 (5), 6-4, 6-2, making tennis history by winning his 7th Wimbledon championship and the 13th Grand Slam title of his career.

10 **Ezer Weizman resigns** as president of Israel, ending a career that spanned the entire history of Israel. The resignation comes in response to a state prosecutor's report criticizing Weizman for accepting more than $300,000 in cash from private sources between 1985 and 1993.

As many as 250 people are killed when gasoline in a ruptured pipeline near Adeje in Nigeria's Niger Delta explodes, destroying buildings and crops within a 1-mile (1.6-kilometer) radius.

Two days after Venus Williams of the United States captured the women's singles title, Williams and her sister Serena take the women's doubles championship at Wimbledon.

11 **Prime Minister** Ehud Barak of Israel and Palestinian leader Yasir Arafat meet with U.S. President Bill Clinton at Camp David, the presidential retreat in Maryland, to begin extensive negotiations over "final status" issues of the Israeli-Palestinian peace process.

12 **Russia launches** the Zvezda module, the future living quarters of the new International Space Station.

13 **The Great Council of Chiefs,** the traditional Fijian governing body, appoints Josefa Iloilo president after rebels release former premier Mahendra Chaudhry and the 17 remaining hostages who were held in the nation's parliament building for nearly two months.

Bill Bradley, the former U.S. Senator from New Jersey who challenged Vice President Al Gore in the primaries for the Democratic nomination for president, gives Gore a rousing endorsement at a political rally in Green Bay, Wisconsin.

16 **More than 1 million** gallons (3.8 million liters) of crude oil spill from a state-owned refinery into Brazil's Barigui River in the state of Parana.

17 **Bashar al-Assad** is sworn in as president of Syria, replacing his father, Hafez al-Assad, who ruled Syria from 1970 until his death on June 10, 2000.

20 **Nationalist politicians** on Corsica accept a French offer that grants *autonomy* (self-government) to the island in exchange for ending 20 years of separatist violence.

21 **The existence of the tau neutrino,** building block of matter that scientists theorized existed, is verified at the Fermi National Accelerator Laboratory near Chicago.

23 **Tiger Woods** wins the 129th British Open, played at the Old Course in St. Andrews, Scotland, by eight strokes.

U.S. cyclist Lance Armstrong wins his second consecutive Tour de France bicycle race, winning by 6 minutes and 2 seconds.

24 **The Yugoslav parliament** passes new election procedures making it legal for a president to run for a second four-year term and to be elected by a simple majority in a popular vote. Both laws are designed to keep President Slobodan Milosevic in power.

25 **The Camp David summit,** which began on July 11, ends with no agreement between the Israelis and Palestinians.

An Air France Concorde en route to New York City crashes into a hotel outside Paris shortly after take-off from Charles de Gaulle airport, killing all 109 people aboard the charter flight and 4 people in the hotel.

Texas Governor George W. Bush announces that he has chosen former Defense Secretary Dick Cheney to be his running mate in the 2000 election.

28 **Peruvian** President Alberto Fujimori is inaugurated for a third five-year term, prompting wide-scale violence in the streets of Lima.

31 **Hugo Chavez** is overwhelmingly re-elected president of Venezuela with 59 percent of the vote. However, pro-Chavez parties take only 99 of 165 seats in the National Assembly, denying Chavez the absolute power he seeks to carry out his "peaceful social revolution" to reform the Venezuelan government and economy.

The Israeli parliament, the Knesset, skips over Shimon Peres, an elder statesman and former prime minister, to elect Moshe Katzav, an obscure, right-wing politician, Israel's president.

2 Delegates at the Republican Party National Convention in Philadelphia nominate Texas Governor George W. Bush for president and former Congressman Richard B. Cheney for vice president.

3 Texas Governor George W. Bush accepts the Republican nomination for president.

4 Great Britain's Queen Elizabeth the Queen Mother celebrates her 100th birthday with a carriage ride through London and an appearance on the balcony at Buckingham Palace.

5 United Airlines, the largest passenger carrier in the United States, cancels 156 flights at Chicago's O'Hare International Airport, setting off a wave of delays that inconvenience airline passengers across the nation. While United officials cite weather conditions for the cancellations, airline traffic experts claim the disruptions are caused by the refusal of United pilots to work overtime.

7 Forest fires rage in parts of 11 Western states, with a total of nearly 1 million acres (405,000 hectares) of forest ablaze. The fires threaten several national forests and parks.

8 U.S. Vice President Al Gore selects Senator Joseph I. Lieberman (D., Connecticut) as his running mate.

9 President Abdurrahman Wahid of Indonesia informs the legislature that he will turn over the daily management of the government to Vice President Megawati Sukarnoputri. The announcement comes less than 24 hours after members of parliament publicly criticized Wahid, who is nearly blind and has suffered strokes, for his mismanagement of the nation's affairs. Vice President Megawati, the daughter of Indonesia's founding father, Sukarno, has little political experience but is popular among Indonesia's poorer classes.

Bridgestone/Firestone, Inc., a Japanese-owned, U.S.-based tire manufacturer, announces that it is recalling 6.5 million tires, primarily from sport utility vehicles and light trucks. The brands slated for recall reportedly can shred at high speed. Critics maintain the tires

Texas Governor George W. Bush accepts his party's nomination for president at the Republican convention in Philadelphia on August 3.

have caused hundreds of accidents and at least 46 deaths, a claim that the U.S. government is investigating.

10 President Hugo Chavez of Venezuela meets with President Saddam Hussein of Iraq in Baghdad, the Iraqi capital. Chavez is the first head of state to pay an official visit to Iraq since the Persian Gulf War (1991).

11 The Bank of Japan raises its short-term discount interest rate to 0.25 percent, abandoning its so called "zero interest rate policy."

12 A Russian nuclear submarine, with a crew of 118 officers and sailors, sinks some 450 feet (140 meters) to the floor of the Barents Sea north of Murmansk, Russia. Russian Navy officials believe that the two nuclear reactors that power the *Kursk* are turned off.

14 The Russian Orthodox Church canonizes Russia's last czar, Nicholas II, and his wife and five children. They are elevated to sainthood for their "humbleness, patience, and meekness" during the 16 months between the czar's abdication in March 1917 and their execution in July 1918 by the Bolsheviks.

15 **The governments** of North and South Korea allow 100 family members from each country to cross into the other country to visit relatives they have not seen since the Korean War (1950-1953).

16 **The Democratic Party,** meeting in Los Angeles, nominates Vice President Al Gore for president of the United States and U.S. Senator Joe Lieberman (D., Connecticut) for vice president.

17 **U.S. Vice President** Al Gore accepts the Democratic Party's nomination for president.

18 **Ice that has covered** the North Pole for an estimated 50 million years is melting, report scientists with the Intergovernmental Panel on Climate Change (IPCC), a United Nations-sponsored organization that investigates consequences of marked changes in climate. According to a coleader of the IPCC, oceanographer James McCarthy, a 1-mile- (1.6-kilometer-) wide patch of ocean at the North Pole is ice free. In adjacent waters, ice is thin enough for sunlight to penetrate it, allowing plankton to grow.

20 **A car bomb** kills two police officers, a man and a woman, in Sallent de Gallego, in the province of Huesca in northeastern Spain. Local police blame the attack on ETA, a group of Basque separatists demanding independence.

21 **The admiral** of the Russian Northern Fleet, Vyacheslav Popov, apologizes on live television for the loss of the Russian nuclear submarine *Kursk* with its entire crew of 118 officers and sailors. The *Kursk* sank in approximately 450 feet (140 meters) of water in the Barents Sea off the northern coast of Norway. After a Russian rescue team failed to gain entry to the vessel, Norwegian divers managed to pry open an escape hatch and found the entire submarine filled with water.

23 **All 143 passengers** and crew members aboard a Gulf Air jet bound for Bahrain from Cairo, Egypt, are killed when the Airbus A320 crashes into the Persian Gulf after attempting to land at the Bahraini national airport, outside Manama, the capital.

26 **U.S. President** Bill Clinton arrives in Nigeria's capital, Abuja, to meet with President Olusegun Obasanjo. Obasanjo, a former military dictator, was elected president 15 months ago.

27 **Fire engulfs** Moscow's 1,770-foot (540-meter) Ostankino television tower, Europe's highest and the world's second-highest free-standing structure. The tower is also Russia's communications hub. At least three people are killed, two of them in an elevator that crashes 1000 feet (305 meters) to the basement.

28 **Burundi's Tutsi minority** refuses to sign a peace accord with the Hutu majority to end seven years of civil war.

31 **Clinical trials** of a vaccine to combat the most widespread strain of AIDS in Africa begin on 18 volunteers in Oxford, England. The vaccine is designed to produce T-cells that will kill HIV-infected cells before infection can take hold.

Vice President Al Gore embraces his running mate, Connecticut Senator Joe Lieberman, after accepting the Democratic nomination for president on August 17.

1 **Japan** orders the evacuation of all 3,850 residents from Miyake Island, which is part of Japan's Ise chain of islands. Frequent volcanic eruptions and earthquakes powerful enough to be felt in Tokyo, the capital, 120 miles (193 kilometers) to the north, have wracked the island for more than two months.

2 **A platoon** of nearly 200 riot police forcibly remove Myanmar's prodemocracy leader Daw Aung San Suu Kyi from her car and return her to the capital, Yangon (Rangoon). She had been detained in the car since August 22.

4 **French truckdrivers** and farmers, protesting the high cost of fuel, form barriers outside 60 of France's oil depots. The protestors demand that the government of France cut taxes on gasoline.

5 **A three-day summit** meeting, sponsored by the United Nations (UN), opens in New York City with 150 of the world's leaders in attendance.

6 **The price of crude oil** for October delivery on the New York City market rises to $35.35 a barrel, a 10-year high.

The Olympic caldron rises above torchbearer Cathy Freeman at the opening ceremony of the XXVIIth Olympiad in Sydney, Australia, on September 15.

28

7 **An enormous Mayan** palace dating from the 700's A.D. has been unearthed in a Guatemalan jungle by an international team of archaeologists. They believe the palace, which consists of 170 rooms and covers an area larger than two football fields, rivals in importance Tikal, one of the largest cities of the Maya civilization.

9 **Wimbledon** champion Venus Williams beats Lindsay Davenport, 6-4, 7-5, to take the U.S. Open women's single championship, which was won by Williams's sister, Serena, in 1999.

10 **The Palestinian Central Council** adjourns without proclaiming the existence of a new Palestinian nation. In July, Palestinian leaders announced that the council would declare sovereignty if a peace accord was not reached by September 13, the date the Israelis and Palestinians initially targeted for the agreement.

11 **U.S. film and video** producers are intentionally marketing violent R-rated movies and M-rated video games to children as young as 12 years old, report officials with the Federal Trade Commission.

12 **A blockade** by British truck, bus, and taxicab drivers halts the delivery of gasoline in the United Kingdom, forcing most gas stations to close.

13 **Officials** with the New York City-based Chase Manhattan Corporation, the third largest banking company in the United States, announce the acquisition of J. P. Morgan & Company, of New York City, for $30.9 billion. The bank was founded by financier J. Pierpont Morgan in the late 1800's and for most of its history, was a commercial institution that specialized in financing corporations and governments.

15 **The XXVIIth Summer Olympic** Games open in Sydney, Australia, with a ceremony celebrating inclusiveness with attention to reconciliation between white and indigenous Australians. The Olympic cauldron is lit by runner Cathy Freeman, an Aborigine and Australia's gold-medal hope for the 400-meter and 200-meter sprints.

16 **The president of Peru,** Alberto Fujimori, announces that he is calling for a new round of presidential elections in which he will not be a candidate. He also promises to dismantle the National Intelligence Service, a security organization that critics accuse of manipulating the last elections, held in April and May, in which Fujimori was reelected for an unprecedented third term.

19 **Members of the U.S. Senate** vote 83 to 15 to normalize trade relations with China. The legislation grants China permanent trade relations and ratifies a 1999 U.S.-China agreement that lowers tariffs and duties on various goods China imports from the United States. The legislation also opens the way for China to join the World Trade Organization.

22 **President Bill Clinton** announces that he has ordered the release of 30 million barrels of crude oil from the U.S. Strategic Petroleum Reserve in an effort to bring down the price of home heating oil in the United States.

24 **Yugoslavs** go to the polls in record numbers to vote in federal elections in which President Slobodan Milosevic faces an unprecedented challenge by Vojislav Kostunica of the multiparty Democratic Opposition of Serbia bloc. The government of Montenegro, Serbia's junior partner in the Yugoslav federation, is boycotting the elections by not running candidates for the Yugoslav parliament.

28 **Voters in Denmark** overwhelmingly reject their government's plan to adopt the euro, the European Union's single currency. International affairs experts suggest that Denmark's failed referendum is an indication of the dissatisfaction felt by many Europeans with the process of European economic and political integration.

29 **Thousands of Serbs** across Yugoslavia rally in protest of President Slobodan Milosevic and the official results of the September 24 presidential elections. According to the Federal Election Commission, Milosevic's opponent, Vojislav Kostunica, failed to win 50 percent of the vote, making a runoff election necessary.

1 **The XXVIIth Olympiad** of the modern era concludes with a spectacular fireworks display from Australia's famed Sydney Harbor Bridge. Many sports enthusiasts describe the Sydney games as among the most successful in history.

2 **The Human Rights Act,** which incorporates the European Convention on Human Rights into English law, goes into effect in the United Kingdom. Many legal experts compare the act to the U.S. Bill of Rights.

5 **The government** of Slobodan Milosevic collapses amid chaos in the streets of Belgrade, the Yugoslav capital. While tens of thousands of Serbs converge on the capital, protestors rush the steps of the federal parliament and wrench control of the burning building from state police.

6 **Yugoslav President** Slobodan Milosevic resigns in the face of a massive popular revolt against his regime.

The unemployment rate in the United States in September fell to 3.9 percent, matching a 30-year low.

7 **Vojislav Kostunica,** a 56-year-old constitutional lawyer, is sworn in as president of Yugoslavia.

Israeli Prime Minister Ehud Barak issues an ultimatum to Palestinian leader Yasir Arafat to rein in the current violent public protests by Palestinians within 48 hours or Barak would authorize Israeli troops to use "all available means" to quell the disorder.

10 **A high-ranking official** of the government of North Korea presents President Bill Clinton of the United States with a letter from North Korean leader Kim Chong-Il, outlining proposals to further ease tensions on the Korean peninsula. The meeting, which takes place at the White House, is the first between a U.S. president and any official representing North Korea.

12 **A small boat** packed with explosives rams into the side of the U.S.S. *Cole,* a U.S. Navy destroyer refueling in the Yemeni port of Aden. The explosion rips a 40-by-40 foot (12-by-12 meter) hole in the hull of the 505-foot (154-meter) ship, killing 17 U.S. sailors. Navy authorities characterize the attack as a suicide bombing carried out by unknown terrorists.

13 **President Kim Dae-jung** of South Korea is awarded the Nobel Peace Prize for his efforts to forge peace and reconciliation with North Korea.

16 **Leaders of Yugoslavia's** Socialist Party, headed by Slobodan Milosevic, agree to join in a transitional government headed by the country's new president, Vojislav Kostunica. The coalition government also includes representatives of Kostunica's Democratic Opposition of Serbia party and a third party, the Serbian Renewal Movement.

17 **Violence** between Palestinian protestors and Israeli troops continues across the West Bank and Gaza despite a cease-fire agreed to by Prime Minister Ehud Barak of Israel and Palestinian leader Yasir Arafat.

18 **The Social Security Administration** plans a 3.5-percent increase in payments in 2001, report officials with the U.S. Department of Labor. The cost-of-living increase is the largest since 1992.

19 **The U.S. House of Representatives** votes 394 to 14 to approve a $7.8-billion plan to renew the Florida Everglades, including the restoration by 2040 of the natural flow of water through the south Florida wetlands. The U.S. Senate approved a similar restoration plan in September 2000.

21 **The death toll** from an outbreak of Ebola in northern Uganda rises to 51, reports an official with Uganda's national health service.

23 **U.S. Secretary of State** Madeleine Albright meets with Kim Chong-Il, leader of North Korea, in Pyongyang, the capital. Albright is the most senior U.S. official to ever visit North Korea.

The U.S. Department of Defense places U.S. troops stationed in Turkey, Saudi Arabia, Bahrain, and Qatar on the highest state of alert due to the threat of terrorist attack.

Serbs protesting against the regime of President Slobodan Milosevic storm Yugoslavia's burning federal parliament in Belgrade on October 5.

25 **Laurent Gbagbo** declares himself president of Cote d'Ivoire after General Robert Guei, the former military dictator, flees the presidential palace in Abidjan, the capital.

26 **A note** found on the body of a seaperson recovered from the Russian nuclear submarine *Kursk,* which sank in August, reveals that 23 members of the 118-man crew survived the onboard explosions that caused the submarine to sink to the floor of the Barents Sea. The chief of the Russian Navy tells reporters that the sailors who survived the blast probably lived only hours before drowning or freezing to death.

The New York Yankees win their third consecutive World Series by beating the New York Mets, 4-2, in Game 5 of the series.

28 **The U.S. Congress** meets in an unusual Saturday session to pass a temporary spending measure to keep the government operating for another 24 hours.

29 **The U.S.S.** *Catawba,* a Navy tugboat, tows the U.S.S. *Cole* out of the port of Aden in Yemen 17 days after the Navy destroyer was attacked by terrorists.

30 **Prime Minister Ehud Barak** of Israel orders missile attacks on the offices of Palestinian leader Yasir Arafat's political organization and personal security force. Barak describes Arafat as no longer a "partner for peace."

31 **Three astronauts,** an American and two Russians, take off from the Baikonur Cosmodrome in Kazakhstan aboard a Soyuz rocket for the International Space Station.

Residents of Palm Beach County, Florida, demonstrate in front of the county elections office on November 9, protesting the disqualification of ballots from the November 7 presidential election. Hundreds of voters claimed that the butterfly style of ballot caused them to vote for the wrong candidate.

2 **U.S. Navy** Captain William M. Shepherd and Russian cosmonauts Yuri Gidzenko and Sergei Krikalev arrive at the International Space Station to launch the first permanent human outpost in space. The astronauts are scheduled to remain at the station 250 miles (400 kilometers) above Earth for four months.

3 **As many as 50,000** Angolans have crossed into Congo (Kinshasa) to escape fighting between the Angolan army and rebel groups, reports the United Nations (UN) high commissioner for refugees. UN officials are attempting to transport emergency food supplies to the refugees.

5 **The body** of the last emperor of Ethiopia, Haile Selassie, is buried with his ancestors in a crypt in Trinity Cathedral in Addis Ababa, the capital. The service is attended by thousands of

Ethiopians and Rastafarians, members of a religious group who venerate Haile Selassie as a god. Haile Selassie's rule was overthrown in 1974 by Marxist military officers, who kept the former emperor under house arrest until he died under mysterious circumstances, in 1975. His body was discovered under a slab of concrete on the grounds of the former palace.

7 **Returns are too close** for either side to claim victory in the U.S. presidential election between Vice President Al Gore, the Democratic candidate, and Texas Governor George W. Bush, the Republican candidate. In congressional contests, Republicans retain control of the House of Representatives by a slim margin.

8 **Vice President** Al Gore leads Texas Governor George W. Bush in the popular vote with a margin of approximately 97,000 votes. In Florida, Bush leads Gore by 1,784 votes, a margin of victory so close that state law mandates a recount.

9 **Republican candidate** for president George W. Bush leads Democratic candidate Al Gore by 327 votes at the conclusion of the Florida recount by machine.

10 **The Zimbabwe Supreme Court** declares the seizure of white-owned farmland by order of President Robert Mugabe illegal and instructs the government to evict black squatters from such land within 48 hours.

12 **The 11 nations** belonging to the Organization of Petroleum Exporting Countries (OPEC) will not increase production in order to cut the price of oil, announces Sheik Saud Nasser al-Sabah, oil minister of Kuwait.

13 **Florida Secretary of State** Katherine Harris declares that state law mandates that counties submit certified vote counts to officials in Tallahassee, the capital, by November 14 at 5 p.m. Absentee ballots from overseas must be submitted by November 18.

President Joseph Estrada of the Philippines is impeached by the House of Representatives on charges that he took millions of dollars in bribes from illegal gambling interests.

15 **Democrats** charge that Florida Secretary of State Katherine Harris's refusal to certify hand-recounted presidential election ballots from three Florida counties is politically motivated. All three counties are heavily Democratic. Harris, a Republican, co-chaired Texas Governor George W. Bush's presidential campaign in Florida.

16 **The first high-speed train** in the United States, the Acela Express, makes its maiden run from Washington, D.C., to New York City and on to Boston, hitting 150 miles (240 kilometers) per hour.

17 **President Bill Clinton** and First Lady Hillary Rodham Clinton, on a visit to Vietnam, meet President Tran Duc Luong after being greeted by enormous crowds thronging the streets of Hanoi, the capital.

18 **Absentee ballots** from military personnel and other Floridians living overseas triple Texas Governor George W. Bush's lead in Florida to 930 votes. The count is official but uncertified by the state of Florida.

20 **Israeli rockets** bombard Palestinian military, police, and television facilities in Gaza, cutting electricity and plunging Gaza City into darkness. The attack was in retaliation for the bombing of a bus filled with children from Israeli settlements in the Gaza Strip.

President Alberto Fujimori of Peru resigns his office in the face of mounting charges of corruption during his 10-year administration.

21 **The Florida Supreme Court** orders Florida's secretary of state to accept results of manually counted ballots from the November 7 presidential election.

23 **The Florida Supreme Court** refuses to compel Miami-Dade County to resume counting presidential election ballots by hand. The decision is a severe blow to Vice President Al Gore's efforts to overtake Texas Governor George W. Bush in the Florida presidential vote count.

27 **Canada's Liberal Party** takes 173 seats in parliamentary elections. The victory makes Prime Minister Jean Chretien Canada's first leader since World War II (1939-1945) to win majorities in three consecutive elections.

28 **The Dutch parliament** votes to legalize euthanasia, making the Netherlands the world's first nation to allow physician-assisted suicide. The new law goes into effect in 2001.

29 **Former President** Jean-Bertrand Aristide wins Haiti's November 26 presidential election with more than 90 percent of the 2.6 million votes cast. First elected to the presidency in 1990, Aristide was overthrown in 1991. He returned in 1994 but left again in 1996 because Haiti's Constitution bans presidents from serving two consecutive terms.

1 **Vicente Fox Quesada** is inaugurated as president of Mexico, bringing an end to 71 years of political dominance by Mexico's Institutional Revolutionary Party (PRI). The inauguration also marks the first transfer of power from one democratically elected party to another in Mexican history.

3 **U.S. astronauts** Joe Tanner and Carlos Noriega attach two solar wings to the International Space Station in orbit approximately 230 miles (370 kilometers) above Earth. The 240-foot- (73-meter-) long wings, the largest structures ever deployed in space, are designed to generate electricity from sunlight.

4 **The U.S. Supreme Court** orders the Florida Supreme Court to reconsider its decision to allow counties to recount votes from the November 7 election.

European Union agricultural ministers meet in an emergency session to pass measures designed to control the spread of mad cow disease as well as calm public fears.

5 **French and Kenyan scientists** have discovered fossilized bones they believe are the remains of a human ancestor dating from some 6 million years ago, announces Brigittte Senut of the National Museum of Natural History in Paris. The scientists claim that the fossils—found in the Baringo district of central Kenya—are at least 1.5 million years older than previous findings.

7 **President Bill Clinton issues** an executive order splitting the Federal Aviation Administration (FAA) into two parts, one to manage air traffic control and another to oversee safety and enforce regulations.

Some 4,000 political extremists, including Basque separatists from Spain, anarchists from France, and young Communists from Italy, stage a riot in Nice, France, during the opening of a European Union summit meeting.

8 **The Florida Supreme Court** orders an immediate state-wide manual recount of those ballots from the November 7 presidential election that had not been previously counted.

9 **The U.S. Supreme Court,** in a 5-to-4 decision, orders the Florida recount of presidential election ballots stopped, pending a Supreme Court review of a Florida Supreme Court decision to allow the recount.

Prime Minister Ehud Barak of Israel resigns, announcing he will lead a caretaker government until a special premiership election is held in early 2001.

11 **President Bill Clinton signs** into law a $7.8-billion federal project to restore the ecology of the Florida Everglades.

12 **The U.S. Supreme Court,** in a 5-to-4 decision, reverses a decision by the Florida Supreme Court to allow a manual recount of votes from the November 7 presidential election. In the opinion of the majority of the court, the recount could not be resumed because the procedures were so arbitrary that they violated the equal protection clause of the U.S. Constitution.

Executives at General Motors of Detroit announce plans to phase out the Oldsmobile, a brand that has been in existence for 103 years.

13 **George W. Bush** claims victory in the 2000 presidential election five weeks after the actual polling on November 7. Bush's opponent in the race, Vice President Al Gore, conceded approximately an hour before Bush's television address in which the Texas governor asked the nation to reconcile and unite behind his leadership.

An international team of scientists announce that they had for the first time deciphered the genetic code of a plant. Thale cress, a small garden weed, is only the fourth *eukaryote* (organism with membrane-bound nuclei) to have its genetic secrets revealed.

14 **The Federal Trade Commission,** a federal agency that maintains free and fair competition in the economy, votes 5-to-0 to approve plans for the merger of America Online, Incorporated, the world's largest Internet service provider, with Time Warner, Incorporated, the largest media conglomerate in the world.

President-elect George W. Bush flashes a W sign, in reference to his middle initial, after claiming victory on December 13 in the 2000 presidential election, one of the closest in U.S. history. Bush's Democratic opponent, Vice President Al Gore, conceded five weeks after the voting took place on November 7.

15 **Engineers in Ukraine** permanently shut down the Chernobyl nuclear power plant, scene of the worst nuclear accident in history.

16 **President-elect George W. Bush** nominates Colin Powell, a retired U.S. Army general and a former chairman of the Joint Chiefs of Staff, to serve in the new Bush Cabinet as secretary of state.

18 **Popocatepetl,** a 17,886-foot- (5,450-meter-) volcano located 40 miles (60 kilometers) southeast of Mexico's capital, Mexico City, spews molten rock thousands of feet into the air during a day-long eruption that scientists say is the most violent in 1,000 years.

22 **President-elect George W. Bush** nominates Senator John Ashcroft (R., Missouri) to serve as attorney general in the new Bush Cabinet. Ashcroft was governor of Missouri from 1985 to 1993 and held a seat in the U.S. Senate from 1995 through 2000.

25 **Arkansas, Louisiana, Oklahoma,** and parts of Texas are hit by ice storms that leave tens of thousands of people without electricity.

28 **The population** of the United States on April 1, 2000, stood at 281.4 million, announce officials at the United States Census Bureau. The figure is based on the decennial census of population and housing conducted in 2000.

Ocean
Space
People in the news
Geology
Astronomy
Architecture
Biology
South Africa
Transportation
Nobel Prizes
Economics
Canada
New York City
Chemistry
Disasters
Popular music
Archaeology

2000 UPDATE

Stocks and bonds
Conservation
Australia
Classical music

The major events of 2000 are summarized in more than 250 alphabetically arranged articles, from "Afghanistan" to "Zoos." Included are Special Reports that offer in-depth looks at subjects ranging from the development of astronomy over the past 1,000 years to the tribulations of Yugoslavia. The Special Reports can be found on the following pages under their respective Update article titles.

~1900~
A MIRROR ON THE TURN OF A CENTURY

By Alfred J. Smuskiewicz

From technology to politics and international affairs, a look at the world of 1900 offers a remarkable reflection on our own time.

It's a new century, an era of amazing technological advances that are quickening the pace of life. Some people have become rich by exploiting these new technologies, while others have been left far behind. Economic inequalities and other grievances have led to war in many parts of the globe. But in the United States, a robust economy at home and growing influence abroad have generated a great deal of confidence. Even so, some maverick politicians, concerned about the influence and power of wealthy special interests, have called for reform.

Does this scenario sound familiar? It should, because these items were much in the news in 2000. As historians have long noted, however, history tends to repeat itself. This same scenario was played out at the turn of the last century, in 1900. In some cases, the parallels between the two eras are striking—almost as if they are slightly distorted mirror images of each other.

In 2000, the Internet and other computer technologies were transforming the way people live and were making multimillionaires out of a select few. In 1900, new technology—in the form of automobiles, telephones, and electricity—was also transforming society, and a handful of industrialists and financiers became multimillionaires.

Conflicts raged in many parts of the world in 2000, from Eastern Europe to Africa to the Middle East. Diplomats and military personnel from the United

Camille Clifford, model
for the Gibson Girl

States—a nation at the peak of its economic power and world influence—were key players in these international affairs. Similarly, many countries in 1900, most notably China and South Africa, were torn by war. An economically strong United States, which had just entered upon the world stage, was governing lands won from Spain in the Spanish-American War (1898).

The 2000 presidential campaign featured calls by Senator John McCain (R., Arizona) and others for reforms to curb the influence of big campaign donors. These views appealed to large numbers of voters but were opposed by many leaders in both major parties, which relied heavily on large financial contributions. Theodore Roosevelt created a tempest within the Republican Party in 1900. Roosevelt, the party's vice presidential nominee, made Republican leaders nervous by calling for a crackdown on the influence of large corporations that were the party's biggest supporters.

Of course, there were also important differences between that earlier, simpler era and the "wired" world of 2000. Nevertheless, the fast-paced, complicated world of today was set in motion in the early 1900's.

Technology brings forth wealth and change

A summer weekend in a park during 1900 reflected the tone of the times. Ladies in sweeping, ankle-length dresses and wide-brimmed hats shaded themselves from the sun under white umbrellas, while mustachioed gentlemen wearing their best Sunday suits and straw hats politely ex-

The Republican ticket in 1900—William McKinley and Theodore Roosevelt

FOR PRESIDENT FOR VICE PRESIDENT

WM. McKINLEY   THEO. ROOSEVELT

The author:
Alfred J. Smuskiewicz is a World Book senior editor.

New York City street scene, c. 1900

A 1900 Oldsmobile

changed opinions on the news of the day. But some of their discussions, no doubt, concerned the many ways in which life was changing all around them: Take those newfangled "horseless carriages," for instance.

Approximately 8,000 automobiles shared U.S. roads with 18 million horses and mules in 1900. In November, 10,000 individuals jammed Madison Square Garden in New York City for the first U.S. auto show. Other new modes of transportation also debuted that year. New Yorkers, for the first time, rode an electric bus for a five-cent fare. The first subway in Paris opened in July. During the same month in Germany, the Zeppelin airship made its maiden flight.

Nowadays, some commuters sitting in traffic jams during rush hour may wish for that time long ago when fewer automobiles were on the roads. Then again, if modern commuters are late for an important appointment, they can call ahead on their cellular telephone. In 1900, telephones, invented in the 1870's, were beginning to become an important part of everyday life, particularly for businesses. Telephone poles, on which strips of leather were fastened to prevent horses from chewing on the wooden posts, lined city streets. Over 1 million telephones were in use in the United States at the turn of the last century.

New technology created incredible wealth in 1900, just as it does today. In 2000, Bill Gates, cofounder of Microsoft Corporation in Redmond, Washington, was one of the richest men in the world. He had amassed his billions by developing and publishing software programs for computers. One of the wealthiest and most powerful Americans in 1900 was J. Pierpont Morgan, a banker and financier who controlled chunks of the electric, railroad, telephone, and agriculture-equipment industries. In early 1901, Morgan bought the huge Carnegie Steel Company from the retiring multimillionaire Andrew Carnegie, who controlled iron mines, ore ships, and railroads as well as steel production. Morgan proceeded to combine the company, which was already the leading steel manufacturer in the United States, with other steel companies. The new company, called United States Steel Corporation (now USX Corporation), was the world's first billion-dollar corporation.

J. Pierpont Morgan

General Electric logo, c. 1900

Politics-as-usual meets reform

The business practices of Morgan, Carnegie, and other barons of American industry concerned reform-minded politicians, such as Theodore Roosevelt, who believed that the *big trusts* (large corporations that dominated certain industries) restricted free enterprise and harmed consumers. Although the U.S. Congress in 1890 had passed the Sherman Antitrust Act, which prohibits any business from monopolizing any market, the act often went unenforced. Much of the public in 1900 grew increasingly concerned as the trusts forced smaller firms out of business and then limited production and raised prices. These concerns had a familiar ring to them in the late 1990's and 2000, when large corporate mergers in banking, energy, insurance, manufacturing, and other industries seemed like an almost daily occurrence. In the major antitrust case of the late 1900's, the U.S. Justice Department sued Microsoft Corporation in 1998, charging the company with using its dominance in the computer industry to crush competing software companies. In 2000, a U.S. district judge sided with the Justice Department and ordered the breakup of Microsoft.

Back in 1900, Roosevelt's antitrust sentiments and zeal for reform caused some Republicans to label him a "madman." Nevertheless, these same Republicans were well aware of Roosevelt's popularity, which stemmed from his activist record as governor of New York and his leadership of the Rough Riders, a cavalry regiment that defeated Spanish forces in Cuba during the Spanish-American War. Party leaders decided that the best way to handle the popular maverick was to "kick him upstairs" to the vice presidency, where he could do no harm. At the Republican National Convention in Philadelphia in June 1900, the party nominated Roosevelt as its vice presidential candidate under President William McKinley, who was running for reelection. Party leaders knew they could trust the probusiness McKinley.

The 1900 campaign was the most expensive in U.S. history up to that time, costing the two major parties a total of $5 million. By contrast, the presidential campaign of Texas Governor George W. Bush had spent more than $90 million by the time the Republican convention met in Philadelphia in August 2000. The Republican and Democratic parties went on to spend multimillions more, especially on advertising, before the November election.

In November 1900, the McKinley-Roosevelt team defeated the Democratic ticket. Unfortunately for the Republican's big-business wing, McKinley was assassinated in

A Zeppelin airship rolls out of the hangar.

Uncle Sam shines a spotlight on "big trusts."

September 1901. The "madman" then moved into the White House. Roosevelt immediately began implementing his feared reforms, including dissolving J. P. Morgan's Northern Securities Company and breaking up other large firms accused of abusing their economic power.

Environmental protection and nature conservation were also among President Roosevelt's top priorities in the early 1900's. The nature conservation movement had been largely inspired by naturalist John Muir, a passionate advocate of conservation who had founded the Sierra Club in 1892 to advance his goals. In 1900, Muir began writing the book *Our National Parks,* at a time when the United States had only five national parks. As president, Roosevelt added to this number, created the U.S. Forest Service, and launched many other conservation initiatives. Environmental issues were again at the forefront of presidential politics in 2000. This time, environmental protection was particularly championed by Democratic presidential candidate Vice President Al Gore, who in 1992 wrote a book on the subject called *Earth in the Balance.*

Other calls for reform in 1900 came from labor and socialist groups that were angry at hazardous working conditions, long hours, low pay, and few or no employment benefits. In February, 7,000 construction workers went on strike in Chicago. Their chief demand was an eight-hour work day. Many workers of the time labored 12 hours a day for about 22 cents per hour. Labor unrest in several other U.S. cities led to violence. American socialist Eugene Debs, who garnered about 88,000 votes in a campaign for the U.S. presidency on the Social Democratic Party ticket in 1900, warned of the growing gap between rich and poor.

Although great progress on improving wages and working conditions was made during the 1900's, by 2000 concerns had once again arisen about economic disparities. Consumer advocate Ralph Nader, the Green Party candidate for president in 2000, claimed that the wages of most workers in the United States had not grown much over the previous 10 years compared with the skyrocketing salaries of top corporate executives. The U.S. Census Bureau also noted a marked unequal distribution of

Union glorification of the working man (above)

Theodore Roosevelt and naturalist John Muir at Yosemite

wages during this period. Other observers pointed out that many workers did not have the education or skills necessary to compete in the high-technology marketplace of 2000.

A world of trouble

Economic inequalities and political frustrations in many nations boiled over into various acts of terrorism during the 1990's and 2000. Many of these terrorist acts, such as the bombing of the warship U.S.S. *Cole* in Yemen in October 2000, were directed against the United States. Militant Muslims were suspected of attacking the *Cole*. In 1900, violence was directed against the great powers of the time by *anarchists* (individuals seeking to eliminate every form of government). In April 1900, an anarchist shot at, but missed, the Prince of Wales in Brussels, Belgium. (The next year, the prince became King Edward VII of Great Britain upon the death of his mother, Queen Victoria.) In July, King Umberto of Italy was killed by an anarchist. This assassination fascinated a young man living in Ohio named Leon Czolgosz, who achieved infamy in 1901 as the assassin of President McKinley.

The key to eliminating much of the unrest in the world lies in improving economic and political conditions. And many economists believe that the surest route to better economic conditions and living standards is free trade. The large, populous nation of China was in 1900—as it remains today—an irresistible market for Western trade. Many Chinese in 1900, however, felt protective of their unique national and cultural identity and strongly objected to contacts with Western countries. In June of that year, anti-Western Chinese, led by a group called the Righteous and Harmonious Fists (dubbed "Boxers" by Western nations), began attacking *legations* (official residences of foreign diplomats) in the Chinese capital, Beijing. United States forces joined those of six European nations and Japan in an international expedition, which seized the key port city of Tientsin in July and drove the Boxers out of Beijing in August.

Imprisoned Chinese rebels after the Boxer Rebellion, c. 1900

Uncle Sam props open the door to trade in China (above).

This international action was based on the McKinley administration's "Open-Door Policy," formulated by Secretary of State John Hay in 1899. Under the policy, the United States, Great Britain, Russia, Germany, Austria, France, Italy, and Japan pledged to respect and protect the rights of all nations to trade in China on an equal basis. The final settlement of the Boxer Rebellion in September 1901 ordered China to further expand the trade privileges of these nations. Trade with China was again a major political issue in 2000, when the U.S. Congress granted China permanent normal trade relations with the United States, setting the Asian giant on the road to becoming a full-fledged member of the World Trade Organization (WTO), an international organization that regulates trade between nations.

Globalization

The outcome of the Boxer Rebellion was an early sign that *economic globalization* (interdependence of the economic affairs of different nations) was becoming more important. To some people in 2000, economic globalization, fed by the WTO and other international financial institutions, had grown out of control. Critics claimed that this "global economy" benefited mainly multinational corporations rather than average workers in developed nations or the millions mired in poverty in underdeveloped countries. Other observers countered that greater economic integration among nations would prove beneficial to people everywhere.

Growing alongside economic globalization in 2000, according to many experts, was a political form of globalization in which the domestic affairs of different nations were becoming increasingly intertwined. The countries of Western Europe, which had often been at war during the first half of the 1900's, had formed the

President McKinley measures an expanding Uncle Sam.

European Union and adopted a common currency by 2000. Virtually all the nations of the world belonged to the United Nations, formed in 1945. And various countries intervened in the internal affairs of other nations, sometimes sending in troops. The United States, by the end of the 1900's, had participated in many interventions in Africa, Europe, and the Middle East and was—by far—the world's most powerful country. Not all Americans or citizens of other countries were pleased with what they viewed as the United States acting as "policeman of the world."

The United States had, in fact, been an important participant in world affairs for more than 100 years by 2000. It became a major player in the world arena in 1898 during the Spanish-American War, in which it obtained control of the Philippines, Puerto Rico, and Guam. The degree to which the United States should exercise authority over these lands was a subject of intense controversy in 1900. Some Americans wanted the United States to act like many European powers and rule the lands directly as colonies. Other Americans, including Andrew Carnegie and William Jennings Bryan, the Democratic candidate for president, were opposed to U.S. *imperialism* (the policy of controlling colonies or dependencies). They called for the U.S. government to grant independence to the newly won lands. The McKinley administration, guided by Secretary of State Hay, sided with the imperialists.

The U.S. role in the Philippines was of special concern to many Americans in 1900. Tens of thousands of U.S. troops were engaged in a bloody conflict against Filipino insurgents, who were fighting the U.S. presence on their islands. The conflict, which cost the lives of more than 5,000 American troops and 8,000 Filipinos, lasted until the defeat of the insurgents in 1902. The United States would hold on to the Philippines for 44 more years.

While the United States was learning to use its newly found clout on the rest of the world in 1900, European countries—old hands at the game of international power—were dealing with the inevitable problems of empire. The beginning of the 20th century was the heyday of European colonialism, especially in Africa, much of which was under Europe's dominion. This dominion, however, often came at a great cost. British forces in 1900, for example, were fighting *Boers* (Africans descended primarily from Dutch colonists; today called Afrikaners) for political supremacy in South Africa. The Boer War claimed more than 28,000 lives and lasted until British forces were victorious in 1902. France, Germany, Portugal, and Italy were also fighting in various parts of Africa at the turn of the last century.

British forces during the Boer War in South Africa, c. 1900

Back on the European continent, the seeds of World War I (1914-1918) were being planted. In January 1900, Kaiser Wilhelm proclaimed that Germany intended to build up its navy so that the country would be "in position to win the place it has not yet attained." Wilhelm's aggressive actions frightened other European countries, which soon divided themselves into two armed camps and prepared for war. This was the first "arms race" of the 20th century. Although the century's most frightening arms race—between the Soviet Union and the United States—ended with the Soviet Union's collapse in 1991, other dangerous arms races, especially between the new nuclear-weapon producers of India and Pakistan, worried the world in 2000.

Social problems—old and new

During times of war, political turmoil, and economic depression, people around the world have always sought to flee their problems for new, more promising lands. The promise of freedom and a better life has made the United States a favorite destination for such individuals since the early 1800's. Immigration to the United States was booming in 1900, when an average of 100 immigrants arrived every hour at Ellis Island, the immigrant reception center in New York Harbor. Most of the new arrivals came from Europe. In the late 1990's, immigration to the United States reached its highest level since before World War I. This modern wave of new Americans came largely from Mexico and Asia.

As newcomers from other countries were trying to build better lives in the United States in 1900, large numbers of native-born Americans had little or no chance to better themselves. African Americans, for example, often ran up against barriers of prejudice, hatred, and legal *segregation* (separation of the races), blocking them from economic and social opportunities. White hostility toward African Americans led to many race riots in the South during the first decade of the 1900's.

Immigrants arrive at
Ellis Island (below).

The most prominent black leader of the day was educator Booker T. Washington, who had founded the Tuskegee Normal Industrial Institute (today called Tuskegee University), the first college for black teachers, in 1881. In 1900, Washington formed the National Negro Business League to provide assistance to black-owned business firms. Washington urged blacks to concentrate on education and economic advancement, rather than worry about racial equality or political power. Washington's approach was criticized by black sociologist W. E. B. Du Bois, who advocated the radical—for the time—notion of ending racial segregation.

Like blacks, women were often treated as second-class citizens in the United States of 1900. In some states, women were not even allowed to own property. Only four states—Colorado, Idaho, Utah, and Wyoming—allowed women to vote. Susan B. Anthony, one of the legendary figures of the women's rights movement, retired as president of the National American Woman Suffrage Association, an organization dedicated to obtaining voting rights for all American women, in 1900. She was replaced by Carrie Chapman Catt, whose tireless work for a constitutional amendment granting women the right to vote finally achieved success in 1920, with the adoption of the 19th Amendment.

By 2000, African Americans and women of all races had made giant strides toward remedying the problems of the early 1900's. Nevertheless, many political leaders believed that more needed to be done before blacks and women could achieve economic and social equality with white males in the United States.

Booker T. Washington (left)

Suffragists campaign for the vote (below).

Medicine and science

A great amount of progress was also made in the areas of health and medicine between 1900 and 2000. At the beginning of the 20th century, the infectious diseases of influenza, pneumonia, tuberculosis, diphtheria, typhoid, and malaria were all major causes of death. Such diseases held life expectancy in the United States to a mere 47 years in 1900. The development of antibiotics, vaccinations, and other medical advances during the 1900's helped control infections and boost life expectancy to more than 76 years by 2000. The major killers at the turn of the 21st century in the United States and other industrialized countries were diseases that could be traced to aging, inactivity, and high-fat foods—especially cardiovascular diseases, which affect the heart and blood vessels.

Despite the relatively primitive state of medicine in 1900, important discoveries were made during the year that would go a long way toward bettering human health. In September, Major Walter Reed, a medical officer in the U.S. Army working in Cuba, discovered that mosquitoes are the agent that transmits yellow fever. His discovery led to mosquito control programs that virtually eliminated yellow fever as a serious threat to human health. Also in 1900, Austrian immunologist Karl Landsteiner discovered the major human blood types, referred to as A, B, AB, and O. This finding put an end to the many needless deaths that had been caused by blood transfusions between individuals with incompatible blood types. Modern techniques of surgery were being introduced in the 1890's and early 1900's by American surgeons William Halsted, who pioneered the use of sterile gloves in *aseptic* (free from germs) surgery, and William and Charles Mayo, brothers who, with their father, founded the Mayo Clinic in Rochester, Minnesota.

Many important breakthroughs in science occurred in 1900. Three European botanists discovered the long-forgotten genetics work of Gregor Mendel, an Austrian monk who studied heredity in garden peas during the 1800's. Mendel's work revealed the basic principles of genetic inheritance—es-

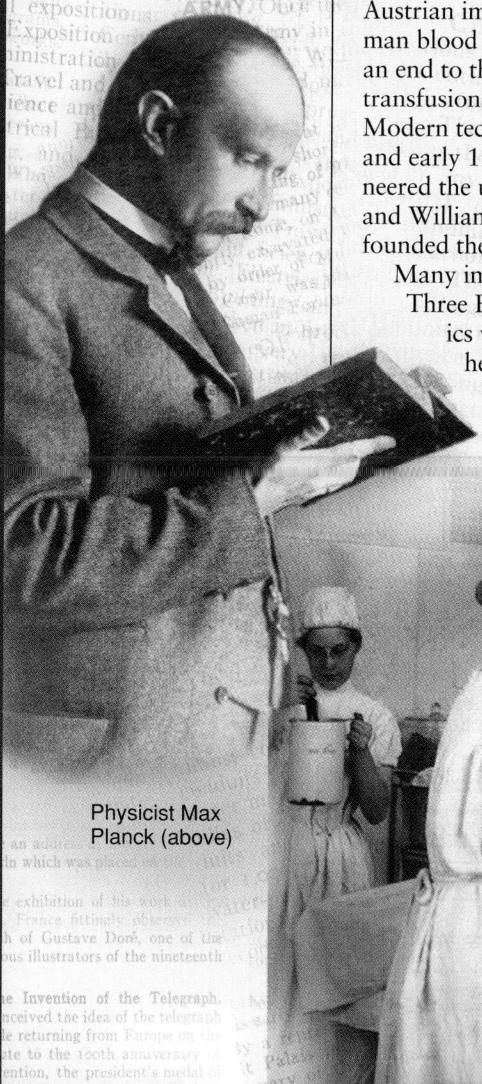

Physicist Max Planck (above)

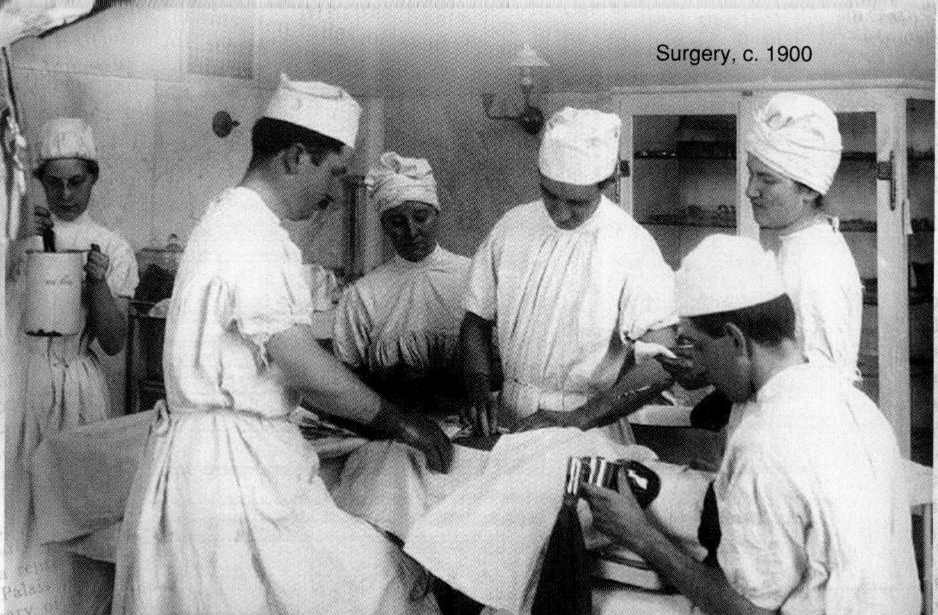

Surgery, c. 1900

sential information for researchers who were investigating genetic engineering, cloning, and the human genetic code in 2000. German physicist Max Planck formulated *quantum theory*, the branch of physics that describes the behavior of subatomic particles, in 1900. By 2000, scientists were using this complex theory to describe the origin of the universe, the fundamental nature of space, and other items of cosmic significance. The beginning of modern psychoanalysis can be traced to the 1900 publication of *The Interpretation of Dreams* by Austrian physician Sigmund Freud. In this milestone work, Freud argued that the human subconscious can be opened to scientific analysis. The book spawned a century of psychological research into dreams and other aspects of the subconscious mind.

Art and culture

Modern art in 1900 also reflected a preoccupation with delving into humanity's inner world. This was a major shift away from the Impressionist artists of the late 1800's, who focused on reproducing their impressions of surfaces and how light played across them. In 1900, the 19-year-old Pablo Picasso, who would go on to become the dominant artist of the new century, made his first visit to Paris, then the world's capital of art and culture. The young Spanish painter, who had yet to develop the first of his highly personal artistic styles, arrived in a city that was bursting with artistic energy and creativity.

Paris staged a world's fair in the summer of 1900, the Paris Universal Exposition, which was visited by more than 57 million people from around the world. The exposition awed visitors with its moving sidewalks, wireless telegraphy, the first escalator, the world's most powerful telescope, and the second Olympic Games of the modern era.

An exhibition in Paris of the work of Auguste Rodin in

Sculptor Auguste Rodin in his studio (below)

Sigmund Freud

1900 confirmed the French artist's reputation as the world's greatest living sculptor. Rodin's realistic, but often exaggerated, representations of the human figure captured the vitality of humanity and explored the intensity of human emotions.

In 1900, a new school of French painters, who would be dubbed the Fauves, or "wild beats," by an art critic, were also intent on expressing the reality of humanity's inner world, but through movement of color. Led by French painter Henri Matisse, the Fauves in 1905 staged an exhibition of their bold, brilliantly colored paintings at the Salon d'Automne. The show shocked the art world and the French *bourgeoisie* (middle class). In 2000, artists were still attempting to shock and perplex their contemporaries, though audiences—even middle-class audiences—were much harder to shock.

Many French artists at the beginning of the last century turned away from painting to explore the possibilities of the camera, including the newly invented motion-picture camera. In 1900, French director Georges Melies released *Cinderella,* a seven-minute film that astonished audiences worldwide. Until *Cinderella,* films had offered sensations—for example, locomotives barreling toward the audience—rather than stories. In 1902, Melies completed his best-known film, the science fiction adventure *A Trip to the Moon,* which inspired American cameraman Edwin S. Porter to make his own films. Although only eight minutes long, Porter's 1903 classic, *The Great Train Robbery,* was the first film made in the United States to tell a story. Hugely popular and profitable, Porter's movie launched the American motion-picture industry.

At the turn of the last century, New York City, not Hollywood, was the center of the motion picture industry, and it was also the center of the American theater. New York theater audiences in 1900 were fascinated by a new play—*Sapho*—about a woman who took a string of lovers. During one performance, New York City police arrested the star, Olga Nethersole, for "violating public decency." A jury found her innocent. Further efforts to close down the production generated more publicity, and *Sapho* played to a full house for months.

Audiences were also startled by a new style of music, "ragtime," which featured highly energetic, *syncopated* (irregularly accented) rhythms. In 1900, the "king of ragtime," Scott Joplin, published *Maple Leaf Rag,* an original composition that sold over 1 million copies of sheet music. Music critics and historians consider ragtime the forerunner of jazz, an original American art form. Like jazz, ragtime was labeled "immoral" because it sounded different and had evolved from the musical styles of honky-tonk pianists working in clubs. Later generations used the word "immoral" to describe other styles of music, such as rock 'n' roll and rap.

During the height of the ragtime craze, architects in the United States were perfecting the skyscraper, a new type of building that was also uniquely American. In 1901, a skyscraper for New York

Maple Leaf Rag and *The Wonderful Wizard of Oz* were published in 1900.

City was on the drawing board at the office of Chicago architect Daniel H. Burnham. The Flatiron building, as it came to be called, proved to be an artistic triumph, less for the details of its design, than for the triangular shape for which it was named. The building's soaring height in relation to its narrow width attracted many photographers of the day. Images by Edward Steichen and Alfred Stieglitz made the Flatiron as emblematic of New York City in the early 1900's as the Empire State Building would become later in the century.

At the same time the Flatiron was going up, magazine illustrator Charles Dana Gibson of New York was making a name for himself with his drawings of the ideal modern American woman. The "Gibson Girl," as that ideal came to be called, was a cool and sophisticated young woman. She wore her hair up and encased her hourglass figure in severe, but alluring, form-fitting outfits. In a typical illustration, Gibson tested his creation's ability to maintain her cool by placing her in difficult situations. One of these situations involved the Flatiron building, which was famous for its downdrafts that blew up the full-length skirts of the day, attracting the attention of male gawkers.

Women throughout the Western world laced themselves into torturous, tightly fitting corsets, attempting to duplicate the Gibson Girl look. A later generation of young women emulated the ideal female form of 2000—the ultrathin model of fashion magazine advertisements—by dieting, sometimes to the point of falling victim to eating disorders.

The more things change. . .

Whether the subject is fashion, entertainment, art, science, technology, medicine, world affairs, social movements, or politics, the way we are today owes a great deal to the world of 1900. So much time has passed, and so much change has occurred. Yet, when we look at the turn of the last century, we can't help but see part of ourselves staring back in a mirror. We seem to be talking about the same things today that people were talking about in 1900—new technologies that are both promising and frightening, the influence of the rich and powerful over politics and the economy, the efforts of society's underclasses to better themselves, the means by which nations may better deal with conflict, and the contributions that science and art can make to society. Perhaps these themes are timeless. What will people be talking about in 100 more years? What events will unfold between now and then? Judging from the past century, we might be safe in assuming that the more things will change, the more they will remain the same. ■■■

The Paris Universal Exposition of 1900

Afghanistan. The Taliban, a fundamentalist Muslim organization dominated by Afghanistan's largest ethnic group, the Pashtunsa, made major gains in 2000 toward destroying opposition and consolidating control over the country.

The Taliban captured many key points in the dwindling area of the northeastern corner of Afghanistan held by the United Islamic Front for the Salvation of Afghanistan, formerly known as the Northern Alliance. The Front represented various minority ethnic groups. Taliban forces, with the support of Pakistan, tried to cut off routes on which aid to the alliance from Russia, India, Iran, and Uzbekistan was transported.

International recognition. Most countries continued to deny recognition to the Taliban as the legitimate government of Afghanistan. Many governments found Taliban policies, which included the restriction of most women to their residences, disturbing. The Taliban claimed to follow Islamic law, but Islamic scholars said many rules were without a religious basis and reflected Afghan village traditions. In July, the Taliban banned Afghani women from working for international relief agencies that were in the country to help poor Afghans. International pressure led to modifications of the bans.

Terrorism. Many countries also shunned Afghanistan because of terrorism. In May, the U.S. Department of State labeled Afghanistan "a center of terrorism." The United Nations (UN) sought to stop the Taliban from sheltering Osama bin Laden, an exiled Saudi Arabian accused of backing terrorism worldwide. In December, the UN applied tough sanctions, proposed by the United States and Russia, on Afghanistan for not surrendering bin Laden for prosecution in the United States. The Taliban retaliated by boycotting all products from the United States and Russia.

In July, the Taliban issued a ban on growing opium poppies, from which morphine and heroin are made. However, Western officials were skeptical of the ban, pointing out that the group was financially dependent on the taxes collected through the narcotics trade. The UN, citing lack of cooperation by Taliban officials and declining Western aid, announced in September that it was ending its efforts to switch Afghan farmers from poppies to other crops.

Drought. A drought in southern Afghanistan, described as the worst in 30 years, caused widespread suffering and migration in 2000. The Taliban's supreme leader, Mullah Mohammad Omar, said public impiety and discontent had caused the drought, a statement that many international observers described as a rare admission that public support for the once-popular Taliban was waning. ☐ Henry S. Bradsher

See also **Asia; Terrorism.**

Africa

The United Nations (UN) Security Council declared January 2000 the "Month of Africa" at the council's first meeting of the year on January 10. The meeting's agenda focused on the many issues that continued to plague Africa throughout the year. On January 13, Sadako Ogata, UN High Commissioner for Refugees, stated that a majority of Africans had begun 2000 in "fear and despair and exhaustion," struggling just to survive. She noted that the UN was trying to protect and care for 6 million African refugees.

In 2000, wars involving rival ethnic groups affected 20 of the 53 member nations of the Organization of African Unity (OAU), an association of African nations that works to promote unity. In several countries, the violence was fueled by the trade in "blood diamonds," meaning the illegal smuggling of gems from African conflict zones to pay for war activities.

The relentless onslaught of AIDS, malaria, and other diseases, as well as rising levels of poverty and malnutrition, compounded Africa's problems in 2000. In addition, devastating floods in southern Africa and severe drought in eastern Africa left thousands of people dead and millions more facing food shortages and famine.

West Africa. Between February and May, clashes between Muslims and Christians in northern and southeastern towns in Nigeria left as many as 2,000 people dead. The violence raised fears among international observers about the stability of Africa's largest democracy. The fighting often followed the introduction or planned introduction of *sharia* (Islamic law) in 11 predominantly Muslim states in Nigeria. The proposed introduction of sharia, which mandates such penalties as amputation of a hand for theft, proved to be the most serious source of conflict in Nigeria since President Olusegun Obasanjo's inauguration in May 1999 ended 16 years of military rule.

In Sierra Leone, a July 1999 peace accord signed by rebel groups and Sierra Leone's democratically elected president, Ahmed Tejan Kabbah, broke down in May 2000. The main rebel group, the Revolutionary United Front (RUF), attacked government forces and United Nations peacekeepers. In response, British troops arrived in Sierra Leone in May to assist Kabbah's besieged government. Following this deployment, authorities captured RUF leader Foday Sankoh. The civil war in Sierra Leone had claimed more than 75,000 lives and displaced more than half of the country's 4.5 million people since it began in 1991. Rival claims to Sierra Leone's diamond

A Mozambican family stranded on an island in the Save River awaits rescue in February 2000. Severe flooding resulting from Cyclone Eline killed several hundred people and displaced more than 1 million more in southeastern Africa during the year.

Facts in brief on African political units

Country	Population	Government	Monetary unit*	Foreign trade (million U.S.$) Exports†	Imports†
Algeria	31,158,000	President Abdelaziz Bouteflika; Prime Minister Ali Benflis	dinar (78.89 = $1)	12,621	8,690
Angola	13,074,000	President Jose Eduardo dos Santos	readj. kwanza (13.29 = $1)	5,000	3,000
Benin	6,255,000	President Mathieu Kerekou	CFA franc (757.67 = $1)	389	643
Botswana	1,434,000	President Festus Mogae	pula (5.34 = $1)	2,360	2,050
Burkina Faso	11,708,000	President Blaise Compaore	CFA franc (757.67 = $1)	254	695
Burundi	5,835,000	President Pierre Buyoya	franc (793.99 = $1)	54	118
Cameroon	15,245,000	President Paul Biya	CFA franc (757.67 = $1)	1,860	1,358
Cape Verde	448,000	President Antonio Mascarenhas Monteiro; Prime Minister Antonio Gualberto do Rosario	escudo (129.48 = $1)	38	225
Central African Republic	3,731,000	President Ange Patasse	CFA franc (757.67 = $1)	195	170
Chad	7,307,000	President Idriss Deby	CFA franc (757.67 = $1)	288	359
Comoros	552,000	Head of State Assoumani Azzali	franc (568.26 = $1)	9	50
Congo (Brazzaville)	2,970,000	President Denis Sassou-Nguesso	CFA franc (757.67 = $1)	1,700	770
Congo (Kinshasa)	51,136,000	President Laurent Kabila	Congolese franc (4.50 = $1)	530	460
Cote d'Ivoire (Ivory Coast)	16,761,000	Head of State Laurent Gbagbo	CFA franc (757.67 = $1)	4,088	3,279
Djibouti	588,000	President Ismail Omar Guelleh; Prime Minister Barkat Gourad Hamadou	franc (173.80 = $1)	260	440
Egypt	69,146,000	President Hosni Mubarak; Prime Minister Atef Mohammed Obeid	pound (3.70 = $1)	3,559	16,022
Equatorial Guinea	452,000	President Teodoro Obiang Nguema Mbasogo; Prime Minister Serafin Seriche Dougan	CFA franc (757.67 = $1)	407	28
Eritrea	4,025,000	President Isaias Afworki	nafka (9.50 = $1)	53	489
Ethiopia	63,785,000	President Negasso Gidada	birr (8.15 = $1)	420	1,250
Gabon	1,227,000	President El Hadj Omar Bongo; Prime Minister Jean-François Ntoutoume-Emane	CFA franc (757.67 = $1)	3,020	1,102
Gambia	1,291,000	Head of State Yahya Jammeh	dalasi (14.50 = $1)	7	192
Ghana	20,172,000	President Jerry John Rawlings**	cedi (6,609.50 = $1)	1,788	2,555
Guinea	7,759,000	President Lansana Conte	franc (1,750.00 = $1)	695	560
Guinea-Bissau	1,192,000	President Koumba Yala	CFA franc (757.67 = $1)	49	88
Kenya	32,577,000	President Daniel T. arap Moi	shilling (79.45 = $1)	2,007	3,194
Lesotho	2,338,000	King Letsie III; Prime Minister Pakalitha Mosisili	maloti (7.48 = $1)	235	700
Liberia	3,013,000	President Charles Taylor	dollar (1 = $1)	39	142

Country	Population	Government	Monetary unit*	Foreign trade (million U.S.$) Exports[†]	Imports[†]
Libya	6,387,000	Leader Muammar Muhammad al-Qadhafi; General People's Committee Secretary (Prime Minister) Mubarak Abdullah Al-Shamikh	dinar (0.54 = $1)	6,131	5,692
Madagascar	15,020,000	President Didier Ratsiraka	franc (6,650.00 = $1)	241	511
Malawi	10,136,000	President Bakili Muluzi	kwacha (78.07 = $1)	554	667
Mali	12,559,000	President Alpha Oumar Konare; Prime Minister Mande Sidibe	CFA franc (757.67 = $1)	536	751
Mauritania	2,580,000	President Maaouya Ould Sid Ahmed Taya	ouguiya (249.11 = $1)	425	444
Mauritius	1,179,000	President Sir Cassam Uteem; Prime Minister Sir Anerood Jugnauth	rupee (26.55 = $1)	1,734	2,183
Morocco	29,637,000	King Mohamed VI; Prime Minister Abderrahmane Youssoufi	dirham (11.00 = $1)	7,367	10,788
Mozambique	18,991,000	President Joaquim Alberto Chissano; Prime Minister Pascoal Manuel Mocumbi	metical (16,050.00 = $1)	268	1,161
Namibia	1,752,000	President Sam Nujoma; Prime Minister Hage Geingob	dollar (7.43 = $1)	1,400	1,500
Niger	10,805,000	President Mamadou Tandja; Prime Minister Hama Amadou	CFA franc (757.67 = $1)	277	398
Nigeria	128,786,000	President Olusegun Obasanjo	naira (108.35 = $1)	12,082	14,142
Rwanda	7,640,000	President Paul Kagame	franc (359.03 = $1)	61	253
São Tomé and Príncipe	146,000	President Miguel Trovoada	dobra (2,390.00 = $1)	5	20
Senegal	9,495,000	President Abdoulaye Wade; Prime Minister Niasse Moustapha	CFA franc (757.67 = $1)	965	1,406
Seychelles	77,000	President France Albert Rene	rupee (5.85 = $1)	113	340
Sierra Leone	5,069,000	President Ahmad Tejan Kabbah	leone (2,250.12 = $1)	6	80
Somalia	14,470,000	Interim President Abdikassim Salad Hassan; Prime Minister Ali Khalif Galaydh	shilling (2,620.00 = $1)	187	327
South Africa	46,215,000	President Thabo Mvuyelwa Mbeki	rand (7.48 = $1)	25,901	25,890
Sudan	32,079,000	President Umar Hasan Ahmad al-Bashir	dinar (256.00 = $1) pound (2,560.00 = $1)	596	1,915
Swaziland	980,000	King Mswati III; Prime Minister Barnabas Sibusiso Dlamini	lilangeni (7.48 = $1)	825	1,050
Tanzania	31,992,000	President Benjamin William Mkapa; Prime Minister Frederick Sumaye	shilling (802.00 = $1)	540	1,634
Togo	5,198,000	President Gnassingbe Eyadema	CFA franc (757.67 = $1)	411	624
Tunisia	9,694,000	President Zine El Abidine Ben Ali; Prime Minister Mohamed Ghannouchi	dinar (1.45 = $1)	5,788	8,332
Uganda	24,618,000	President Yoweri Kaguta Museveni; Prime Minister Apollo Nsibambi	shilling (1,787.00 = $1)	516	1,340
Zambia	10,754,000	President Frederick Chiluba	kwacha (3,450.00 = $1)	914	818
Zimbabwe	12,514,000	President Robert Mugabe	dollar (53.15 = $1)	1,864	2,701

*Exchange rates as of Oct. 13, 2000, or latest available data.   †Latest available data.
**John Agyekum Kuffuor was elected president on December 28.

fields were the cause of much of the conflict.

In northern and eastern Angola, government military successes against Jonas Savimbi's rebel forces raised hopes in 2000 that the 25-year-old Angolan civil war was scaling down. The civil war had caused the deaths of more than 1 million people. However, the UN reported in 2000 that the violence and poverty in Angola made it "the worst country in the world in which to be a child."

On October 25, Cote d'Ivoire's General Robert Guei, who had seized power in a December 1999 *coup* (overthrow), was toppled in a violent popular uprising that left more than 170 people dead in the capital, Abidjan. The rebellion followed Guei's refusal to accept defeat in the Oct. 22, 2000, presidential election after which his opponent, Laurent Gbagbo, declared himself head of state.

Southern Africa. In bitterly contested elections in Zimbabwe on June 24 and 25, President Robert Mugabe's ruling Zimbabwe African National Union-Patriotic Front (ZANU-PF) narrowly defeated Morgan Tsvangirai's opposition Movement for Democratic Change (MDC). The ZANU-PF won 62 of the 120 elective parliamentary seats, while the MDC took 57 seats. One seat went to an independent. During the election campaign, illegal squatters invaded many white-owned farms, and political violence left at least 37 people dead and thousands injured. On October 25, the MDC announced it wanted Mugabe impeached for the violent campaign, which the MDC claimed was waged by ZANU-PF supporters.

South African President Thabo Mbeki's controversial insistence that poverty, rather than the HIV virus, was the cause of AIDS dominated South African politics in 2000. South Africa had the largest number of people infected with HIV of any nation in the world—4.2 million, or more than 20 percent of all adults in the country. Officials in Mbeki's African National Congress Party, as well as church leaders and trade unionists, accused Mbeki of endangering the fight against AIDS because of his unorthodox views and ineffective public health policies.

Conflict in Central Africa. A civil war in Congo (Kinshasa) continued throughout 2000 as President Laurent Kabila's government—supported by Zimbabwe, Namibia, and Angola—battled guerrillas backed by Rwanda and Uganda. An April 8 cease-fire pact, which included plans for the deployment of more than 5,000 UN peacekeepers, was not honored. The violent situation was complicated in May and June, when troops from Uganda and Rwanda fought each other for supremacy in Congo's northeast city of Kisangani, a major diamond center. Since the civil war erupted in August 1998, thousands of people had died in the fighting and at least 500,000 others

had been driven from their homes.

Security in the Great Lakes region of Central Africa was undermined in 2000 by an escalation of violence in Burundi. In January, UN Secretary General Kofi Annan predicted that the conflict could deteriorate into a repeat of the 1994 genocide in Rwanda, in which 500,000 people died. Burundi's seven-year-old civil war—between the Hutu majority and the Tutsi minority, who dominated the government—had resulted in the deaths of more than 200,000 people by 2000.

War in the Horn of Africa. A sharp escalation in fighting erupted between Ethiopia and Eritrea on May 12, when Ethiopian forces suddenly burst through Eritrean defenses and captured large sections of Eritrean territory around the capital, Asmara. The assault ended on May 30, when Ethiopia declared victory and announced a partial withdrawal from Eritrean territory. Ethiopia and Eritrea, two of the world's poorest nations, had been engaged in a border war since May 1998. The conflict concerned disputed control of the two nations' 620-mile (1,000-kilometer) common frontier.

On June 18, 2000, Ethiopian and Eritrean officials signed a cease-fire accord in Algiers brokered by Western nations and the OAU. The two countries agreed to "end all armed air and land hostilities immediately." On December 12, the two sides signed a peace agreement that formally ended the war.

Military experts estimated that more than 100,000 people on both sides had been killed in the war, and 1.5 million Eritreans had been left homeless.

Blood diamonds. International pressure grew in 2000 for a ban on the sale of so-called blood, or conflict, diamonds from war-torn areas such as Angola, Sierra Leone, and Congo (Kinshasa). According to experts in African affairs, as much as 15 percent of the $6-billion worldwide trade in rough diamonds in 2000 came from gems illegally exported from various African war zones.

Angola's rebels, according to a UN report released on March 15, continued to finance their antigovernment war in 2000 by secretly selling contraband diamonds in defiance of an international embargo. Since 1992, the rebel forces were estimated to have earned as much as $4 billion by trading in diamonds.

During 2000, Liberia remained the main route for diamonds smuggled out of rebel-held territory in neighboring Sierra Leone. The UN reported that the Liberian government provided cash, weapons, and military training to the rebels, thereby prolonging the civil war in Sierra Leone.

Seeking to end the gems-for-guns trade, the UN Security Council imposed a global embargo on illicit diamond exports from Sierra Leone on July 5. The resolution established a certificate of origin system, which allowed legitimate diamonds to be sold from Sierra Leone but inhibited the rebel trade. Experts said the resolution represented only a first step toward an international treaty outlawing the deadly trade in blood diamonds from Africa's other conflict zones.

Development issues. African nations continued to lag behind other nations that had formerly been colonies in closing the material gap with industrialized nations, according to a report issued in May by the World Bank, a UN-affiliated organization that provides short-term credit to member nations. The authors of the report, entitled "Can Africa Claim the Twenty-first Century?" argued that many African nations were poorer in 2000 than they had been upon achieving independence in the 1960's. In 2000, the joint income of all of sub-Saharan Africa's 48 countries was only slightly more than that of one European country, Belgium. The World Bank added that in order to halt the cycle of poverty and conflict, the national economies of the sub-Saharan African nations needed to grow by 5 to 7 percent annually. However, with average economic growth at only 2 percent in 2000, the African nations would likely struggle for many years to overcome developmental problems.

Health problems. On April 25, at a conference launching a "Roll Back Malaria" campaign in Abuja, Nigeria, officials with the World Health Organization (WHO), an agency of the United Nations, warned African leaders that malaria killed approximately 1 million Africans annually— 700,000 of them children. In the 1990's, more than 90 percent of the 500 million malaria cases worldwide occurred in Africa. According to WHO officials, the disease cost the nations of Africa between $3 billion and $12 billion in health care and lost economic revenues each year.

African leaders at the WHO conference resolved to ensure that at least 60 percent of Africans at risk for malaria were given access to insecticide-treated mosquito netting by 2005. According to WHO officials, only 2 percent of African children slept under such nets in 2000. Conference speakers urged development agencies to allocate at least $1 billion per year to the antimalaria campaign, which was dedicated to cutting the number of malaria deaths in half by 2010 through the use of preventive programs and low-cost drug treatments.

The human immunodeficiency virus (HIV), which causes AIDS, remained Africa's biggest single killer in 2000. Former South African President Nelson Mandela, in his closing address to the XIIIth International AIDS Conference in Durban, South Africa, on July 15, called the African AIDS epidemic a "tragedy of unprecedented proportions." UN health authorities told the delegates that more than 10 percent of the adults in 16 African countries were infected with HIV in 2000. The proportion of those infected with HIV jumped to 20 percent in 7 southern African countries and reached 35 percent in Botswana. In 2000, more than 90 percent of the world's 13 million children orphaned by AIDS lived in Africa.

Floods and drought. Catastrophic flooding in Africa began in January with storms that swelled rivers in the southeast, causing dams to overflow in South Africa. Meteorologists had believed the worst flooding was over when Cyclone Eline struck the southern African coast, including the island of Madagascar, on February 22. The cyclone, moving overland from the Indian Ocean, battered Africa with 160-mile-per-hour (260-kilometer-per-hour) winds and heavy rains that triggered the region's worst floods in 30 years. Several hundred people died and more than 1 million people lost their homes in Mozambique, South Africa, Botswana, and Zimbabwe. Many observers criticized international aid agencies for moving too slowly to help the homeless, especially in Mozambique, which was hit the hardest by the cyclone.

Three years of prolonged drought in East Africa threatened more than 12 million people with famine during 2000 as losses of food crops and livestock mounted. Thousands of people died, mainly in Ethiopia, from malnutrition and associated diseases. However, enough food aid arrived in the region to prevent the situation from reaching the proportions of the famine of 1984 and 1985, when more than 1 million people died in the Horn of Africa.

Some meteorologists traced the flooding in southern Africa and the drought in East Africa to the 1998-1999 *La Niña* (a periodic cooling of tropical Pacific waters that disrupts weather patterns).

Land management woes. Many environmentalists in Africa and elsewhere claimed that agricultural policies in South Africa were partially to blame for the floods of 2000. They argued that indiscriminate land management practices in the South African uplands had diminished the natural capacity of the country's wetlands and grasslands to absorb heavy rainfall, causing massive flooding in low-lying areas.

The UN Global Environment Outlook study reported in 2000 that African land degradation, made worse by recurrent droughts, threatened economic and physical survival. The study predicted that 25 African nations by 2025 would be subject to water shortages.   □ Simon Baynham

See also **Africa: A Special Report** and the various African country articles.

AIDS in Africa— A Continent in Despair

By 2000, AIDS had threatened the lives of tens of millions of people in sub-Saharan Africa and devastated nearly every facet of society.

By Steven Englund

A staggering 24.5 million people in sub-Saharan Africa in 1999 were living with HIV, the virus that causes AIDS. This estimated figure came from a report, published in June 2000 by the Joint United Nations Programme on HIV/AIDS (UNAIDS), on the global impact of AIDS, an incurable disease that destroys the body's immune system. While the 45 nations of sub-Saharan Africa accounted for only 10 percent of the world's population, the number of HIV infections in sub-Saharan Africa represented more than 70 percent of cases worldwide. With very limited resources for treating people with AIDS, these 45 nations also had the world's highest death rates from AIDS-related illnesses. The 2.2 million people who died of AIDS in sub-Saharan Africa in 1999 accounted for more than 78 percent of all deaths from AIDS worldwide.

The toll taken by AIDS in Africa far surpassed earlier estimates by even the most pessimistic of public health officials, who in 1990 estimated that the total number of AIDS deaths in sub-Saharan Africa would reach 5 million by the turn of the millennium. At the end of 1999, 13.7 million people in the region had died since the epidemic began in the 1980's. AIDS was no longer a fearful hypothesis or even a grim likelihood. It was a full-blown catastrophe.

By 2000, many world leaders, public health officials, and numerous nongovernmental organizations, including the United Nations Security Council, began to view the AIDS epidemic in Africa as not only a health crisis but a threat to economic development and political stability in the region. In July, at the XIII International AIDS Conference in Durban, South Africa, reports addressed the wide-reaching impact of AIDS in Africa and underscored the urgency to control an epidemic that could easily engulf more than 100 million people in the next 10 years.

The scope of the AIDS epidemic

In most African nations, the rate of infections rose continuously throughout the 1990's. By 1999, approximately 11,000 people per day were becoming infected with HIV. The rate of infection was greatest in the southern end of the continent. More than 35 percent of the adults in Botswana were infected. In Lesotho, Namibia, South Africa, Swaziland, Zambia, and Zimbabwe, more than 20 percent of the adults were HIV-positive. (UNAIDS statistics on adults include men and women, ages 15 to 49.) In countries with lower rates of infection, mostly in the western and eastern regions of the continent, the impact of the disease was still considerable. In Nigeria, the most populous nation in Africa, more than 5 percent of the adults—2.6 million men and women—were HIV-positive.

The high AIDS infection rates in Africa reversed decades of progress in economic development, education, and health care, which had resulted in longer lives for many Africans. In Kenya, for example, the mortality rate among children under the age of five declined by 10 percent from 1981 to 1986. Between 1986 and 1996, the mortality rate in that age range increased by more than 20 percent. Public health officials attributed that increase primarily to the transmission of HIV from mothers to children, either during pregnancy, delivery, or breast-feeding.

The AIDS epidemic drove the life expectancy of adults in Africa down even more dramatically. According to the United States Bureau of the Census, average life expectancy in Botswana in 1990 was 63.8 years. By 2000, the AIDS epidemic had reduced average life span in Botswana to 39.3 years. Census experts predicted that life expectancy in Botswana would drop to as low as 29 years in 2010.

The far-reaching impact of AIDS

Most public health officials agreed that no matter how alarming such statistics were, they did not adequately measure the precise impact of HIV and AIDS on Africa. While many infectious diseases afflict young children and older adults, the victims of AIDS are mostly young adults. UNAIDS noted in its 2000 report that more than half of the Africans who had died of AIDS were infected by age 25 and were dead before age 35. The disease most affected people who were raising families and who were, by and large, the most productive people in the work force. These conditions have resulted in dire consequences for many African families, communities, health care systems, local and national economies, and governments.

The most immediate impact of the disease occurs in families. When one or both parents become ill and cannot attend work regularly, family income decreases dramatically. In many of the sub-Saharan nations, as many 80 percent of the population depend on farming for a living. When a member of the family contracts AIDS, the family spends more time caring for the sick person and less time cultivating crops, tending livestock, and marketing their goods. At the same time, health care expenses overwhelm family resources, draining funds from other areas of the family budget. A study of urban areas of Cote d'Ivoire revealed that when a member of a family had AIDS, family expenditures for health care increased by 400 percent. At the same time, outlay for education decreased by 50 percent and food consumption fell by more than 40 percent.

Children are the most vulnerable victims of the AIDS epidemic. When parents become ill, the oldest children are often forced to leave school and find jobs in order to care for their parents and younger siblings. Eventually, the disease leaves many children orphaned. Since the epidemic began in Africa, more than 12 million children under the age of 15 lost one or both parents to the disease. In Zimbabwe, one of the hardest hit countries, there were more than 620,000 orphans in 1999. Some of these children lived with grandparents and other members of the extended family, but many children lived in households led by older siblings or ended up in the streets.

The challenges confronting these children were enormous. UN agencies reported in 1999 that AIDS orphans are at a greater risk than other children for malnutrition, illnesses, and sexual ex-

The author:
Steven Englund is a writer for UNAIDS and other United Nations publications.

Sub-Saharan Africa

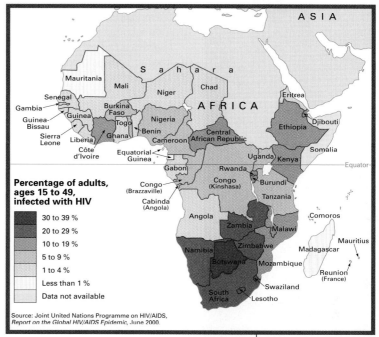

Percentage of adults, ages 15 to 49, infected with HIV

- 30 to 39 %
- 20 to 29 %
- 10 to 19 %
- 5 to 9 %
- 1 to 4 %
- Less than 1 %
- Data not available

Source: Joint United Nations Programme on HIV/AIDS, *Report on the Global HIV/AIDS Epidemic*, June 2000.

ploitation. The laws in many countries do not protect the inheritance rights of children, leaving them destitute. Many of these children also face the public's fears about the disease and the disgrace associated with having a family member die of AIDS. Consequently, orphans are often denied health care, education, and other basic social services.

While the disease has had a direct impact on individuals and families, it also extracted a heavy toll on Africa's education and health care systems. UNAIDS Executive Director Peter Piot, commenting on the far-reaching effect of the disease, stated, "HIV does to society what it does to the human body. It undermines the very institutions that are meant to defend society—its teachers, its doctors."

The greatest problem facing education systems in Africa is loss of teachers through AIDS. According to a study in Zambia, at least 1,300 teachers died of AIDS in the first 10 months of 1998. In Cote d'Ivoire, teachers were dying at a rate of six per week in the late 1990's. In most cases, the teachers could not be replaced. The disease had decimated the limited number of people in African countries who were qualified to teach. The result was overcrowded classrooms and school closings, especially in remote rural areas. Mamadou Lamine Sakho, a UNAIDS official in Cote d'Ivoire, noted information about AIDS disseminated through the educational system is essential for fighting the epidemic, but many teachers lacked adequate information about the disease and how to prevent it.

The AIDS epidemic has also crippled health care services in most African nations. While the medical profession, like the educational profession, has lost many people to the disease, the greater problem is volume of cases. The sheer number of cases of HIV infection has simply overwhelmed medical institutions. In many sub-Saharan African countries by 2000, AIDS patients occupied as many as 50 to 80 percent of all hospital beds. As a result, people with other illnesses often could not be admitted to the hospital. Hospitals in Kenya in the late 1990's reported an increase in deaths not related to HIV infection because patients

The rate of HIV infection among adults (ages 15 to 49) in the 45 nations of sub-Saharan Africa ranges from less than 2 percent in Senegal to more than 35 percent of adults in Botswana.

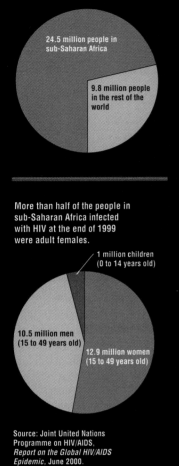

People Infected with HIV

At the end of 1999, more than 70 percent of all people infected with HIV lived in the 45 nations of sub-Saharan Africa.

24.5 million people in sub-Saharan Africa

9.8 million people in the rest of the world

More than half of the people in sub-Saharan Africa infected with HIV at the end of 1999 were adult females.

1 million children (0 to 14 years old)

10.5 million men (15 to 49 years old)

12.9 million women (15 to 49 years old)

Source: Joint United Nations Programme on HIV/AIDS, *Report on the Global HIV/AIDS Epidemic*, June 2000.

were not admitted to hospitals until their illnesses were severely advanced.

The spread of HIV also has contributed to the spread of other infectious diseases, most notably tuberculosis (TB). In Zambia, TB cases increased from 7,000 in 1984 to 40,000 in 1995. Public health officials believed 30,000 of those cases occurred because HIV had already weakened people's immune systems, making them vulnerable to the TB bacteria. Officials also concluded that the high TB rates among HIV-positive people increased the spread of the TB bacteria to people who were not infected with HIV. Consequently, a system already burdened by AIDS faced a resurgence of other diseases that would further stretch medical and financial resources.

Nations in crisis

This strain on medical services in Africa eventually overwhelmed the resources of national health programs. At a meeting of African health ministers in May 2000, Piot reported that one year of medical costs for most AIDS patients in Africa totaled two to three times the per capita gross domestic product (GDP) of most African nations. (GDP, the value of all goods and services produced in a country in a given year, is a general indicator of a nation's financial resources.) The expense of treating AIDS patients significantly reduced the amount of money that public health services could devote to other health care problems. In Rwanda, 66 percent of the nation's public health budget in the mid-1990's was devoted to treatment of people infected with HIV.

The AIDS epidemic further weakened the economics of sub-Saharan African nations by severely damaging the business sector, primarily because the disease strikes at the core of the work force. Absenteeism became rampant. Employees missed work not only because of illness, but because they needed to take care of ill family members or attend funerals. Managers at a sugar estate in Kenya, for example, noted that AIDS-related absenteeism had accounted for as many as 8,000 days of lost labor at that estate between 1995 and 1997. High absenteeism translated into lower productivity and increased costs. According to a joint report in 1999 from the UNAIDS and private business organizations, absenteeism in some East African companies accounted for 25 to 54 percent of total operational costs. Many companies spent more money paying overtime wages to healthy employees, recruiting and training new workers, and covering high insurance premiums, because of the HIV prevalence among workers.

Most economists agreed in 2000 that the impact of AIDS on businesses and industry in sub-Saharan Africa would significantly slow economic growth. At a forum in June of the International AIDS Economic Network, an organization focusing on AIDS in developing countries, researchers predicted that the GDP would decline in many nations because of the epidemic. Researchers estimated, for example, that the GDP of South Africa would be 17 percent lower in 2010 than it would have been without the AIDS crisis. UNAIDS officials noted that such predictions indicated a growing cycle of poverty and lack of government resources that could allow the disease to become an even greater threat.

Leaders from among the world's most powerful nations came to believe by 2000 that the AIDS epidemic had become the greatest threat to human security in sub-Saharan Africa. At a meeting in January, the representatives of member nations on the UN Security Council discussed this threat of AIDS in Africa—the first time in the council's history that it had addressed a health issue. UN Secretary General Kofi Annan warned that the devastating effects of the disease on families, education, health care, and national economies would "threaten political stability." Annan said, "In already unstable societies, this cocktail of disasters is a sure recipe for more conflict. And conflict, in turn, provides fertile ground for further infection."

Conditions fostering the epidemic

Experts widely agree that a key factor in the spread of HIV is denial about the disease. The most common means by which HIV is spread in Africa is through heterosexual sex. In many cultures in the sub-Saharan region, people talk very little about sexual issues and deny many of the realities of common sexual behaviors. In these countries, a sexually transmitted disease is a mark of shame—for an individual, a family, and even a whole community. Consequently, people often refuse to be tested for the virus, do not seek treatment for the disease, or do not inform sexual partners about their HIV status. Whole communities, in turn, have denied that the disease is a threat, even when rates of infection are very high.

Denial also takes place on a national level. During the 1990's, when the prevalence of AIDS was rapidly increasing throughout Africa, many political, business, and religious leaders were slow to respond to the growing crisis. Public health experts criticized African political leaders for not recognizing the severity of the problem, not providing educational programs about the disease, and spending resources inappropriately. In 2000, for example, President Thabo Mbeki of South Africa came under

Life expectancy

In many developing nations, improvements in health care, sanitation, and education have increased life expectancy. In much of sub-Saharan Africa, AIDS has reversed this progress, dramatically decreasing life expectancy.

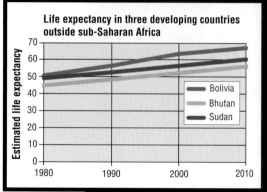

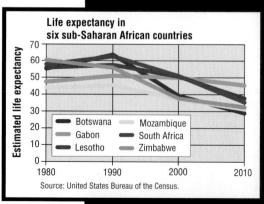

Source: United States Bureau of the Census.

harsh attacks from researchers and public health officials for questioning whether HIV was actually the cause of AIDS and spending money to reexamine theories that had been largely discredited by almost all AIDS researchers. Mbeki's critics argued that the limited resources would be better spent on prevention and health care programs.

Poverty in many sub-Saharan nations has also produced conditions that fostered the rapid spread of HIV. Because of limited job opportunities, many men leave their families to work in mines or take jobs in cities in such countries as South Africa, Zimbabwe, and Botswana, nations with the highest incidence of infection. Away from home, many of these men have casual sexual encounters, including sex with prostitutes, behaviors that increase a man's chances of becoming infected. Upon returning home, they infect their wives and other sexual partners. Poverty has also driven many young African women into prostitution, making them extremely vulnerable to HIV infection.

AIDS spread rapidly in Africa during the 1990's, in part, because of ignorance. High numbers of people did not know how HIV was transmitted and how it could be prevented. In 2000, UNAIDS reported that in a survey taken in Carletonville, South Africa, 40 percent of all adult respondents said they were unaware that an HIV-positive individual may not show any visible symptoms of AIDS for several years. Similarly, in a 1996 survey taken in Zambia, only 23.5 percent of respondents, ages 20 to 24, could name two acceptable methods of protecting against HIV infection.

There were many reasons for this lack of information. In some cases, political and religious leaders blocked efforts to inform people about AIDS, because they believed that instruction about safer sexual practices encouraged immoral sexual behaviors. In other cases, countries did not have the institutions or services in place that were needed to conduct a nationwide educational campaign. High illiteracy rates, especially among the region's poorest people, and the breakdown of the school systems prevented many people from learning about AIDS.

The AIDS epidemic created an enormous number of orphans in many of the nations of sub-Saharan Africa. An orphanage in Zambia (bottom) cares for AIDS orphans who are themselves infected with HIV.

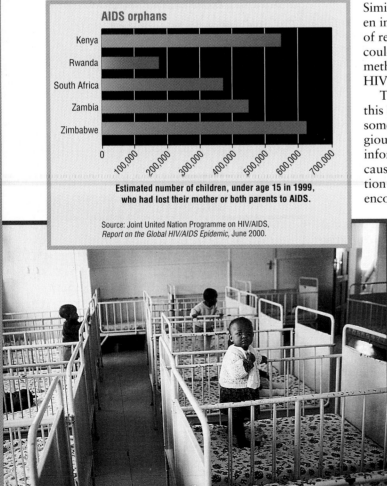

AIDS orphans

Kenya	
Rwanda	
South Africa	
Zambia	
Zimbabwe	

0   100,000   200,000   300,000   400,000   500,000   600,000   700,000

Estimated number of children, under age 15 in 1999, who had lost their mother or both parents to AIDS.

Source: Joint United Nation Programme on HIV/AIDS, *Report on the Global HIV/AIDS Epidemic*, June 2000.

The burden on marginalized people

Social standing is a major factor in the spread of HIV infections. Those least likely to have access to information about AIDS and social and medical services are those most marginalized in society—the poor; women and youth; illegal immigrants; drug users; prostitutes; and men who have sex with men. Marginalized people are not likely to engage the support and sympathies of political leaders.

In many African nations, poor women, and women in general, have a very low social standing and are subject to numerous conditions that increase their risk of HIV infection. UNAIDS officials have noted that in many African nations, violence against a wife is seen as a man's right. Many women are afraid of and often subject to physical violence if they question their husbands' extramarital encounters, ask them to use condoms, or deny them sex. Many women have not been tested for HIV nor sought treatment for fear of violent reprisals from their partners who may blame the women for being infected. Young women are often the target of sexual abuse and, therefore, more vulnerable to infection. This is especially true in war-torn regions and refugee camps, where young women are often the victims of violence and rape. Women are also more likely to be infected by a man than a man is by a woman. Consequently, infection rates among females in sub-Saharan Africa are disproportionately high, with 12 women for every 10 men infected with HIV.

Studies have shown that teen-age girls and women in their early 20's are especially vulnerable to HIV infection. A 1998 survey in Carletonville, South Africa, revealed that nearly 60 percent of women 20 to 24 years old were infected with the virus. A

A girl in Uganda, studies while caring for her mother who is dying of AIDS. When the disease strikes a family, older children often leave school in order to care for parents and raise younger siblings.

A teacher with a national AIDS prevention program in Uganda instructs teen-age girls on ways to prevent HIV infection (above left). Posters on display in Kenya (above right) clarify misunderstandings about how the disease is spread. Such public campaigns have reduced infection rates in some African countries.

crucial factor in raising HIV rates among this age group is that they often have sex with older men, either because the young women are enticed by gifts and promises of financial security or because they were the targets of rape and abuse. Public health officials reported on several occasions in the 1990's that fear of HIV prompted some men in Africa to seek out young sexual partners whom they believed were less likely to be infected. The practice led to an ever-widening circle of infection.

A search for solutions

The same conditions that fostered the spread of AIDS in Africa —denial, lack of education, poverty, and social mores—have made controlling the disease a daunting task. Public health experts agree that progress in control of the disease demands political will among leaders in Africa as well as among the leaders in the developed nations of the world. Studies have shown that in countries where the leaders took action, the results were generally positive.

In Senegal, the government responded almost immediately after the first AIDS cases were reported in 1986. A UNAIDS report in 1999 concluded that the Senegalese program to educate people about how the disease was spread and about how it could be prevented slowed the spread of HIV. By 2000, the infection rate in Senegal was less than 2 percent of the adult population, compared with 35.8 in Botswana. In Uganda, AIDS prevention programs lowered the rate of infection from about 14 percent of the adult population in the early 1990's to about 8 percent in 2000.

Public health officials have agreed that the incidence of AIDS in sub-Saharan Africa cannot be lowered without the cooperation and financial backing of developed nations. On their own, the nations of Africa cannot afford to implement prevention programs, treat AIDS patients, or sustain a medical system capable of fighting the disease. Botswana, the nation with the highest infection rate, in 1996 had approximately $14 per HIV-positive person to spend on prevention programs, medical treatment, and other AIDS-related care. UNAIDS officials also have noted that the world's developed nations must find ways to lower the costs of medical treatments and services.

Several cooperative efforts were underway in 2000 to find affordable solutions to preventing the spread of the disease. One involved the antiviral drug AZT, which significantly reduces the likelihood of an infected mother passing the virus to her child during pregnancy or delivery. The treatment regimen is expensive, however, costing more than $800 per person in the United States. In 1998, researchers developed a less expensive version of the regimen, which cost about $270. Shortly thereafter, UN agencies began working with various countries in sub-Saharan Africa to develop programs with the new AZT treatment. Then in 1999, researchers from the United States and Uganda demonstrated that a different antiviral drug, nevirapine, could work as effectively as AZT, but at a cost of only $4 per treatment. Further studies on nevirapine treatment were underway in Uganda in 2000.

Researchers also hoped to develop an AIDS vaccine that could control the epidemic in Africa. In August, the first clinical trials of a vaccine particularly designed to combat the most common strain of the virus in Africa began at Churchill Hospital in Oxford, England. Researchers hoped to conduct further trials with the vaccine in Kenya in 2001. If the vaccine is effective, it will cause the body's immune system to destroy the virus when an individual is infected.

The need for affordable treatments
Meanwhile, AIDS experts, UNAIDS officials, and African leaders were looking for ways to improve treatments for people already infected with the virus. One effort was aimed at treating infections that commonly strike AIDS patients. In April 2000, officials at UNAIDS and the World Health Organization recommended the use of cotrimoxazole, a relatively inexpensive drug, to prevent some kinds of pneumonia, diarrhea, and parasitic infections. At an annual cost of between $8 to $17, the drug could prolong the life of many AIDS patients in Africa.

Treatments that attack the AIDS virus have not been available to most Africans because of high costs and lack of medical facilities to administer the treatments. The series of medications known as a drug cocktail have significantly prolonged the lives of many HIV-positive people and reduced the number of AIDS-related deaths in most developed countries. The treatment depends on the availability of equipment and staff to monitor the effect of HIV on the immune system. These conditions, by and large, do not exist in Africa. The patient on the AIDS cocktail must also be able to follow a strict schedule, taking pills at the same time every day. In addition, the cost of such treatment is prohibitive in Africa. In the United States, such treatment averaged more than

$20,000 per HIV-positive person in 2000, an expense that is unthinkable for the public health sector of sub-Saharan nations. In Botswana, in 1999, $20,000 was more than five times the per capita GDP.

Political leaders made some progress toward making the HIV treatments more readily available. In May 2000, U.S. President Bill Clinton issued an executive order declaring that the United States would not challenge countries in sub-Saharan Africa that violated U.S. patent laws in their effort to provide less expensive drugs. Under this policy, African countries could license local companies to produce generic versions of expensive American drugs. Although U.S. pharmaceutical companies publicly protested the president's policy, some took steps to reduce their prices in Africa. After Clinton issued the order, five U.S. drug manufacturers announced that they would begin negotiations with UN agen-

A hospital in Congo (Kinshasa) is overwhelmed with patients dying of AIDS (below). Most African nations in the late 1990's had less than $90 per year per HIV-positive person to spend on prevention programs, medical treatment, and other AIDS-related care.

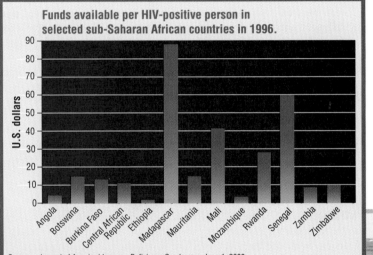

Funds available per HIV-positive person in selected sub-Saharan African countries in 1996.

U.S. dollars

Angola · Botswana · Burkina Faso · Central African Republic · Ethiopia · Madagascar · Mauritania · Mali · Mozambique · Rwanda · Senegal · Zambia · Zimbabwe

Sources: *Journal of Acquired Immune Deficiency Syndromes*, June 1, 2000; Joint United Nations Programme on HIV/AIDS; Harvard School of Public Health.

cies to sell their drugs for much less in Africa than they do in the United States. Some industry officials reported that the prices of drugs would be reduced by as much as 80 to 90 percent. Even with these efforts, most experts noted that the costs would exceed the means of most African nations.

The need for international cooperation

Education, prevention, and treatment programs all require large outlays of money. Experts on AIDS in Africa believed that the spread of AIDS could not be brought under control unless developed nations increased financial assistance to African nations. Piot in his address to the UN Security Council in January noted that effective prevention programs for sub-Saharan Africa would require between $1 billion and $3 billion annually. This estimate did not take into account numerous other expenses, such as training for health care workers, improvements in medical facilities, care for AIDS orphans, and the cost of medications.

A number of world leaders in 2000 pledged to increase aid to African countries and to offer loans for prevention and treatment programs. The World Bank, a United Nations agency that provides long-term loans to countries for development, pledged $500 million in loans to any sub-Saharan country that established a national AIDS program for preventing the spread of the disease. The U.S. government pledged to loan up to $1 billion annually to finance the purchase of medical services and drugs from pharmaceutical companies that agreed to lower the cost of AIDS medications for African nations. UNAIDS officials also called for debt relief programs that would cancel portions of national debt, allowing countries to rechannel debt payments into AIDS programs. These efforts would result in much greater resources for treatment and prevention, because African countries in 1999 paid out about four times more in debt repayment than on all national health and education programs combined.

Experts agreed that such measures were essential for altering the course of AIDS in Africa. They noted, however, that a true solution would require a well-coordinated effort among numerous international development organizations, national governments, nongovernmental organizations, religious organizations, health care systems, and community programs. In 1999, the UN set up the International Partnership Against AIDS in Africa (IPAA) to organize international, national, and local programs against HIV and AIDS. Leaders of 20 African nations endorsed the partnership, which was also supported by the Organization of African Unity, the Economic Commission for Africa, several European countries, Canada, and the United States.

The task facing IPAA was enormous, and no one believed that the battle against AIDS in Africa would be easily or quickly won. Nonetheless, those people at the forefront of the fight against the epidemic believed that they had experienced enough progress to know what must be done to alter the conditions that have created a cycle of illness, death, poverty, and despair for the people of an entire continent. ■■■

Agriculture. The world's farmers had a bountiful harvest in 2000 for the fifth consecutive year. However, sizable crops, depressed commodity prices, and growing world concern about genetically modified (GM) crops kept the United States farm sector in turmoil. Two events added a ray of hope for higher prices in the future. The ban on U.S. sales of food and medicine to Cuba was lifted in October, and the United States agreed not to oppose China's entry into the World Trade Organization.

World crop production. The global harvest of wheat, coarse grains, and rice in 2000 was down from 1999 levels. Oilseed production increased due to record crops in Argentina and Brazil. Cotton production was unchanged.

According to a U.S. Department of Agriculture (USDA) report released in November 2000, world wheat production at 580 million metric tons was down about 1 percent from 1999. Bountiful crops in Canada, Argentina, and Kazakhstan in 2000 offset a 17-percent drop in the Australian wheat crop. Small grain production, including corn, rye, grain, sorghum, barley, oats, and millet, totaled 859 million metric tons, down 2 percent. The drop was largely due to smaller corn crops in China and Eastern Europe. The 2000 world rice harvest was estimated at 401 million metric tons because of larger crops in Japan, South Korea, and the United States.

Oilseed production, including soybeans, sunflower seed, rapeseed, and peanuts, hit a record high of 304 million metric tons in 2000. Abundant crops of soybeans were harvested in the United States, Brazil, and Argentina, and sunflower seed harvests in Russia and Ukraine hit record highs. Declines in cotton production in Uzbekistan in 2000 were offset by increases in the United States to keep production at the 1999 level of 87 million bales.

U.S. crop production. In 2000, U.S. farmers harvested a record 10.1 billion bushels of corn, 7 percent more than in 1999. Soybean production also reached a record high at 2.78 billion bushels, 5 percent above the 1999 harvest. The high yield occurred despite drought-reduced crops in the western Corn Belt and the Great Plains.

Fewer acres in the United States were planted in 2000 in wheat and rice, resulting in harvests that were 7 percent smaller than in 1999. The 2000 wheat harvest was 2.23 million bushels. The rice harvest was 6.07 million metric tons. Cotton production in 2000—17.5 million bales—was up 3 percent from 1999.

Aid package. On June 20, 2000, U.S. President Bill Clinton signed a law providing farmers with $15.1 billion in assistance. Of that amount, $8.4 billion was earmarked to subsidize crop insurance for five years, making it more affordable for farmers. The remaining $6.7 billion was paid directly to U.S. farmers based on their past crop production.

The aid package, the third in three years, prompted congressional leaders in the U.S. House of Representatives to call for reforms of the 1996 Federal Agricultural Improvement and Reform Act, scheduled to expire in 2002. The law gave U.S. farmers more flexibility to plant crops in return for declining direct payments.

GM crops. America's soybean farmers planted 54 percent of their acreage in soybeans genetically modified to resist herbicides, about the same as in 1999. GM plants, also called transgenic crops, contain genes from other species that confer new traits on the crops, such as pest resistance and greater productivity. Acreage planted in corn modified to resist the corn borer pest dropped from 25 percent in 1999 to 18 percent in 2000. Acreage planted in genetically modified cotton accounted for 61 percent of total cotton plantings.

Exports. On October 28, President Clinton signed a provision into law that lifted the 40-year-old ban on sales of food and medicine to Cuba. However, USDA officials predicted that the potential $1-billion market would grow slowly. The law restricted Cuba from obtaining U.S. financing and from selling Cuban products to the United States. All U.S. exports of farm products in 2000 totaled $50.9 billion, up from $49 billion in 1999.

Antigenetically modified sentiment. The environmental group Friends of the Earth announced on Sept. 18, 2000, that gene fragments of GM corn approved only for consumption by animals had been found in U.S.food products. Federal agencies had not approved StarLink corn, the variety in question, for human use because of concerns that it might trigger allergic reactions.

The announcement caused U.S. food companies to recall products from Aventis S.A. of France that could contain StarLink corn, and the USDA began to test U.S. corn exports for StarLink.

Aventis gave up its license to sell StarLink seed in October. It also made plans to buy the 2000 U.S. harvest. Out of 79 million acres of planted in corn in the United States, only or 340,000 acres, 0.4 percent, was planted in StarLink. Because some of the crop was unaccounted for, Aventis asked that the corn be approved for human use for a four-year period. On December 5, U.S. Environmental Protection Agency officials reported that StarLink may cause allergic reactions in some people, based on a preliminary study.

Antibiotech activists suffered a setback in September when a U.S. District Court dismissed a 1998 lawsuit that challenged the FDA approval process for foods containing GM ingredients.

WTO. Negotiations on future agricultural trade began in Geneva, Switzerland, in March 2000. Positions of major exporters remained unchanged since the failed WTO meeting in Seattle in December 1999. The United States and the Cairns Group, which included Canada, Australia, and New Zealand, wanted reductions in export subsidies and domestic farm supports. The European Union wanted to continue strong monetary support for its farm sector. Between the mid-1980's and 2000, the number of farms in France, Europe's most agriculturally productive country, fell by 50 percent to 700,000 properties. No real progress was expected on agriculture until WTO member countries agreed to a global round of talks that included all economic sectors.

Bilateral disputes. In October, officials with the U.S. Trade Representative's Office agreed to investigate the Canadian Wheat Board. U.S. wheat producers charged that the Wheat Board, by controlling Canadian wheat sales, distorted world wheat prices. The U.S. action followed an October 10 decision by the Canadian International Trade Tribunal that U.S. corn imports harm Canada's corn producers. On November 7, the Canada Customs and Revenue Agency imposed a duty of $1.58 a bushel on U.S. corn imports to Western Canada. The Manitoba Corn Growers Association, an area where corn production had doubled since 1996, brought the case. (Corn production had doubled in Manitoba since 1996). The duty was to either be made permanent or lifted in 2001. Canadian purchases of U.S. coarse grains totaled $134 million in 2000.

China. In October, President Clinton signed legislation that allowed China to join the WTO. In return, China agreed to reduce barriers to imports of U.S. farm products, including beef, grapes, wine, corn, rice, and cotton. Officials with the U.S. Trade Representative's Office predicted that U.S. farm exports to China will climb to $2 billion annually by 2005.

Mad cow disease. On December 4, the European Union banned feed containing animal protein for six months. In 2000, the number of cattle with mad cow disease, or bovine spongiform encephalopathy (BSE), rose to about 120 in France compared with 31 in 1999. Germany and Spain reported their first cases of BSE in 2000 as well. Scientists believed that people who eat beef from cattle with mad cow disease may be susceptible to the human equivalent—Creutzfeldt-Jakob disease. They also thought that cattle contracted BSE by ingesting feed containing protein from diseased sheep or cattle. There were no cases of BSE in the United States in 2000. The FDA banned feed containing animal protein in June 1997.

☐ Patricia Peak Klintberg

See also **Biology; Europe; Food.**

AIDS. The Joint United Nations Programme on HIV/AIDS (UNAIDS) reported in 2000 that the global epidemic of acquired immune deficiency syndrome (AIDS) continued to affect people in Africa more severely than on any other continent. UNAIDS, based in Geneva, Switzerland, works to prevent and treat AIDS worldwide.

UNAIDS officials reported in June that 5.4 million people became infected in 1999 with HIV, the virus that causes AIDS. About 4 million of those people lived in sub-Saharan Africa. The estimated number of people worldwide with HIV or AIDS totaled 34.3 million in 1999, about 24.5 million of whom lived in sub-Saharan Africa. About 2.8 million people worldwide died of AIDS in 1999, raising total deaths to 18.8 million since the epidemic began in 1981. In July 2000, officials at the XIII International AIDS Conference in Durban, South Africa, reported that illness and deaths from AIDS caused social and economic problems in Africa.

Lower drug prices. Five pharmaceutical firms promised in May to reduce prices for anti-HIV drugs sold in Africa. Officials of Boehringer Ingelheim of Ridgefield, Connecticut; Bristol-Myers Squibb of New York City; Hoffman-La Roche of Nutley, New Jersey; Glaxo Wellcome of New York City; and Merck and Company of White House Station, New Jersey, agreed that lower prices could permit wider use of HIV drugs and prevent infection of infants born to mothers with HIV.

U.S. epidemic. In July, officials of the United States Centers for Disease Control and Prevention (CDC), a federal agency based in Atlanta, Georgia, reported that little progress was made in 1999 in the fight against AIDS and HIV. Introduction of antiviral drugs in 1995 had caused a sharp decrease in AIDS deaths and cases between 1995 and 1998. However, the CDC reported no further declines in 1999, because antiviral drugs were less effective than previously believed.

Stop-and-start therapy. In July 2000, officials reported that a new method of highly active antiretroviral therapy (HAART), which combines several antiviral drugs, could improve HIV treatments. The new approach gives patients periodic drug holidays. They take no medicine for one week, resume therapy the next week, and take a break again in the third week. Officials at the National Institute of Allergy and Infectious Diseases in Bethesda, Maryland, reported that the new method could reduce treatment time by 30 to 50 percent, reduce side effects, and decrease treatment costs—which may exceed $10,000 annually—by 50 percent. ☐ Michael Woods

See also **Africa: A Special Report; South Africa; United States, Government of the; West Indies.**

Air pollution. See Environmental pollution.

Alabama. See State government.

Alaska. See State government.

Albania. In elections in Albania in October 2000, the ruling Socialist Party won 252 seats for local councils, while the Democratic Party won 188 seats. Smaller parties split the remaining 28 seats. The elections were the first since 1996. International watchdog groups criticized the nationalist rhetoric used by both the Socialist Party and the Democratic Party against an ethnic Greek candidate in the elections.

Domestic affairs. The government of Albania continued to remove corrupt judges from the bench in 2000. In March, Italian legal experts visited Albania to discuss methods of fighting organized crime, which had become rampant, and Albanian officials pledged to take stronger steps to control smuggling.

Economy. Officials with the International Monetary Fund (IMF), a United Nations-affiliated organization that provides short-term credit to member nations, approved a $13-million credit for Albania in January. While unemployment averaged approximately 17 percent in August 2000, European economists reported that the Albanian economy was stabilizing after a series of collapses in the late 1990's.

Trade. Albanian leaders agreed in January 2000 to increase trade with neighboring Macedonia and Montenegro. In February, the only border crossing between Albania and Montenegro, which had been closed by Yugoslavia in 1998, was reopened. Albanian officials pledged in February 2000 to cooperate with neighboring countries in programs funded by various international organizations to increase trade.

Foreign affairs. In January, the United States reopened its embassy in the Albanian capital of Tirane. The embassy had been closed since 1998 due to fear of terrorist attacks. U.S. officials began issuing visas to Albanians in September 2000.

In March, Foreign Minister Paskal Milo criticized the Balkan Stability Pact, an agreement between the European Union (EU) and Balkan nations promoting peaceful relations and increased economic development. Milo also called for additional financial aid from the West.

Greek soldiers, who had been stationed in Albania since 1997 to help the Albanian government reestablish order, began pulling out in August 2000. Observers considered the move to be a step toward creating political stability and reestablishing the government's authority.

In August, Albanian leaders called for an end to violence in Kosovo and urged the international community to support Montenegro in its bid to become more independent of Serbia. The parliament called for Serbian leaders to apologize for atrocities committed by military and police units in Kosovo in 1998.   □ Sharon L. Wolchik

See also **Europe.**

Algeria. President Abdelaziz Bouteflika's "civil concord" initiative to end the civil war between Algeria's military-backed government and Islamic militants produced mixed results in 2000. The civil war, which began in 1992 when the military canceled parliamentary elections that the Islamic Salvation Front (FIS) was slated to win, had claimed more than 100,000 lives by 2000. Bouteflika's initiative, announced in 1999, offered partial amnesty to rebels who surrendered by Jan. 13, 2000.

Algerian officials claimed that some 80 percent of the Islamic militants accepted amnesty. According to government officials, at least 2,400 members of the Islamic Salvation Army (AIS), the armed wing of the banned FIS, surrendered. Furthermore, the AIS agreed in January to disband. About 1,500 other militants from two hardline groups—the Armed Islamic Group (GIA) and the Salafist Group for Preaching and Combat (GSPC)—also accepted amnesty.

Despite the surrenders, more than 1,000 civilians were killed in 2000, and large numbers of GIA and GSPC militants remained active. In late January, the Algerian military launched a major assault to "eradicate" rebel holdouts. In May, GIA attacks on Moroccan villages near Algeria led to rare cooperation between the Algerian and Moroccan armed forces to contain the militants. However, a sharp upsurge of violence occurred in October and in December.

Government. In August, Bouteflika appointed his chief of staff Ali Benflis prime minister after Prime Minister Ahmed Benbitour resigned. Benbitour's resignation followed rumors of a rift with Bouteflika over the war, the economy, and other issues within the ruling coalition cabinet. Benflis appointed Abdelaziz Belkhadem, an Islamic conservative with strong ties to Persian Gulf leaders, as foreign minister. Algerians hoped that Belkhadem would help lure foreign investment from Gulf nations.

Relations with Iran. Bouteflika and Iranian President Mohammed Khatami agreed in September to renew diplomatic relations between Algeria and Iran. The agreement came as the two leaders were attending the United Nations Millennium Summit in New York City. Algeria had broken relations with Iran in 1993 after Algeria accused Iran of supporting the FIS.

Travel. Bouteflika embarked on extensive foreign travel during 2000 to attract foreign investment and seek relief from the burden of a $28-billion debt. In June, he visited France, Algeria's former colonial ruler. The French trip was the first by an Algerian leader in 17 years.

□ Christine Helms

See also **Africa; Middle East.**

Angola. See Africa.

Animal. See Biology; Conservation; Zoos.

Anthropology. Two teams of geneticists in 2000 reported evidence that Neanderthals did not interbreed with modern humans, who are known to have existed in Europe 40,000 years ago. Neanderthals were a type of human that lived in Europe and the Middle East from approximately 130,000 years ago to as recently as 28,000 years ago. The scientists obtained their evidence by comparing *DNA* (deoxyribonucleic acid, the molecule that makes up genes) extracted from Neanderthal skeletons with DNA from modern humans.

Geneticist William Goodwin of the University of Glasgow in Scotland and his associates analyzed mitochondrial DNA—DNA that is found in *mitochondria* (tiny structures in cells that provide the cells with energy)—from the ribs of a 29,000-year-old fossil of an infant Neanderthal. The fossil had been found in a cave in the northern Caucasus Mountains in Russia. Goodwin announced in March that he had determined that the Neanderthal DNA was very different from that of modern humans.

In June, geneticist Lutz Bachmann of the Field Museum in Chicago announced that he and his colleagues had analyzed nuclear DNA—DNA found in the *nucleus* (central part) of a cell—from two Neanderthal fossils. One fossil was 50,000 years old and the other was 110,000 years old. The team compared the Neanderthal DNA with DNA from a 35,000-year-old specimen of a modern human by measuring how closely the samples chemically bonded. A close bond would suggest a strong relationship. The scientists reported that the DNA samples did not bond closely, indicating that Neanderthals were a different species than modern humans.

These two studies supported a 1997 study of Neanderthal DNA that found that Neanderthals and modern humans were distinct species that did not interbreed. However, this conclusion contradicted evidence from certain fossils that suggests that the two types of humans belonged to the same species and did interbreed.

South African paleontologist Andre Keyser examines the most complete skull ever found of *Australopithecus robustus*, a relative of early humans that lived more than 1.5 million years ago. Keyser reported the discovery of the skull in April 2000.

Neanderthal diet. Results of a chemical analysis of bones from a 28,000-year-old Neanderthal fossil led scientists to conclude in June 2000 that Neanderthals ate mostly meat. This report contradicted a common image of Neanderthals as plant-eaters who occasionally scavenged meat from abandoned animal kills.

Archaeologist Michael P. Richards of the University of Oxford in England led a group that examined Neanderthal bones found in Croatia for the occurrence of nitrogen and carbon. A heavy concentration of carbon in fossils suggests that plants constituted the majority of food in the diet, while large amounts of nitrogen indicate a significant amount of meat in the diet. The analysis revealed that the level of nitrogen in the bones was similar to that found in saber-toothed cats and other ancient predatory animals. The scientists said this indicated that Neanderthals must have been accomplished and organized hunters.

Out of Africa. In May, a team headed by anthropologist Leo Gabunia of the Republic of Georgia National Academy of Sciences reported the discovery of the oldest undisputed human fossils outside of Africa. The fossils—two skulls from Dmanisi, Republic of Georgia, that are at least 1.7 million years old—challenged the view of some anthropologists that human ancestors first left Africa approximately 1 million years ago as the species *Homo erectus.*

The skulls have large brow ridges above the eye orbits, and the braincase is sharply angled at the back. Although these characteristics are similar to traits seen in *H. erectus* fossils reported from China and Java, other features of the new finds resemble fossils of a more ancient African ancestor known as *H. ergaster.*

More than 1,000 simple stone tools found with the Georgian skulls have flaking on only one side, rather than the two-sided flaking that is typical of more advanced hand axes. The scientists said the finding suggested that humans migrated out of Africa before they had developed efficient tool technology.   □ Donald C. Johanson

See also **Archaeology.**

Archaeology.

On Aug. 8, 2000, archaeologists raised the Confederate submarine *H.L. Hunley* from 30 feet (9.1 meters) below the surface of the Atlantic Ocean. The submarine sank off Charleston Harbor on Feb. 17, 1864, for unknown reasons after it had rammed the Union warship *Housatonic* with an explosive device, causing that ship to sink. The United States Civil War (1861-1865) sea battle was the first case in which a submarine sank a warship.

Archaeologist Robert Neyland of the United States Navy directed the recovery effort, in which salvagers first lowered an elaborate steel framework over the *Hunley.* Divers then passed foam-filled slings beneath the 40-foot- (12-meter-) long submarine and attached the slings to the steel framework, forming a flexible carriage. A crane hoisted the carriage onto a barge for transport to a laboratory at the former Charleston naval base.

Conservators said restoration of the *Hunley* would probably take 7 to 10 years. They planned to display the sub in the Charleston Museum.

Maya palace. Archaeologist Arthur Demarest of Vanderbilt University in Nashville, Tennessee, reported in September 2000 that he had discovered one of the largest Maya palaces ever found. The Maya were an American Indian people whose civilization arose in southern Mexico and Central America before 1,000 B.C. and lasted

until the A.D. 1500's, when the Maya were conquered by the Spanish. The palace, in Cancuen, Guatemala, dates from the Maya Classic Period, which lasted from approximately A.D. 250 to 900.

Demarest's excavations through the dense jungle cover revealed an immense limestone structure with more than 170 rooms arranged around 11 courtyards. He reported that the structure was spread over 270,000 square feet (25,110 square meters). Demarest noted that the palace is representative of the great wealth of Cancuen during the Classic Period. The archaeologists speculated that the city's wealth was derived from its control over mineral resources.

Black Sea flood? Renowned explorer Robert Ballard announced in September 2000 that photographs taken by an underwater, remote-controlled camera revealed evidence that a great flood filled the Black Sea basin more than 7,000 years ago. The flood, according to Ballard, destroyed an inhabited region that was located on a site that today is off Turkey's northern coast. The photographs showed what appeared to be stone tools and the worked timbers of a house resting about 300 feet (90 meters) below the surface of the Black Sea.

The discovery by Ballard, who achieved fame in 1985 by locating the wreck of the *Titanic,* lent support to a 1997 theory of geologists William Ryan and Walter Pitman of the Lamont-Doherty Earth Observatory in Palisades, New York. Ryan and Pitman proposed that a natural dam once existed in the area of the Bosporus strait, separating the Aegean Sea from a freshwater lake that filled part of the basin occupied today by the Black Sea. According to the geologists, this dam was breached as melting ice caused sea levels to rise after the last *ice age* (a period when ice sheets cover vast regions of land), which ended about 11,000 years ago. As the seawater poured into the Black Sea basin, said the geologists, the water level rose, and the area covered by the water expanded, wiping out any cities that then existed in the area.

Ballard suggested that this flood may have inspired the story of Noah and other ancient flood stories. However, many archaeologists thought that the links between the Black Sea evidence and the Biblical account of Noah were too weak to draw such a conclusion.

Race to rescue Zeugma. An international team of archaeologists raced against the rising waters of the Euphrates River in southeastern Turkey to rescue ancient Greek and Roman ruins in 2000. The scientists finished their work in October, before a new dam flooded about 10 percent of Zeugma, a key trading center from its founding in approximately 300 B.C. until the early centuries of the Byzantine Empire (A.D. 395-1453).

The 6,000-year-old ruins of Tell Hamoukar in Syria lie exposed after being excavated by archaeologists from the University of Chicago in 2000. The scientists announced in May that sophisticated pottery and other recovered items provided evidence that civilization may have begun earlier than previously thought.

During their excavations, the archaeologists recovered numerous mosaics that show such mythological figures as Poseidon, Medusa, and Achilles. The archaeologists described some of the mosaics as among the most beautiful and elaborate ever found from ancient times. They also uncovered a cache of 65,000 *bullae* (clay stamps that were used to seal bundles of goods), the most ever found at a single site. Artifacts that could not be removed were carefully reburied by the archaeologists to protect them underwater.

Shipwrecks. A U.S. federal court in Norfolk, Virginia, ruled in July 2000 that foreign countries retain ownership of sunken warships in U.S. waters. The ruling prevented private treasure hunters from salvaging valuables from shipwrecks.

The case involved two Spanish frigates that had sunk off the coast of Virginia in 1750 and 1802. A private U.S. company planned to salvage them for possible caches of coins and precious metals, but the Spanish government sought to stop the company. Spain was backed by the United States and the United Kingdom, hoping to protect their own sunken naval ships from private salvaging efforts. Spanish officials said they intended to recover artifacts from the frigates for display in museums. ☐ Mark Rose

See also **Anthropology; Geology; Latin America; News bytes.**

Architecture. The June opening of the Experience Music Project (EMP) in Seattle was the most anticipated architectural event of 2000. Designed by Frank Gehry and funded by Microsoft billionaire Paul Allen, the building celebrated guitarist Jimi Hendrix and American pop music. EMP is packed with sophisticated interactive exhibits, including a sound lab where the musically challenged can play a piano or learn the basics of editing music. Gehry's exterior is a collage of organic shapes derived from musical instruments and midway rides and covered in multicolored aluminum panels. The building is similar stylistically to Gehry's celebrated Guggenheim Museum in Bilbao, Spain, but a number of critics assailed it as disjointed and self-indulgent.

The Rose Center for Earth and Space, architect James Polshek's $210-million addition to the American Museum of Natural History in New York City, opened in February. The structure resembles a glass gift box with a gigantic spherical ornament suspended inside. The box houses the center's major exhibits, while the ornament is a planetarium. From the lobby, visitors ascend a swirling ramp for a tour of the galaxy narrated by actor Tom Hanks. The bottom half of the sphere contains the Big Bang Theater, which leads to the curving Cosmic Pathway that traces 13 billion years of change in the universe.

Visitors explore the Forum, a glass-roofed open plaza, at Sony Corporation's new European headquarters on Berlin's Potsdamer Platz during the center's formal opening on June 14. Seven buildings surround the Forum in the $1-billion office, residential, and entertainment complex designed by Chicago architect Helmut Jahn.

Houston museum. The March 25 opening of the $85-million Audrey Jones Beck Building, designed by Rafael Moneo, concluded 25 years of expansion by the Museum of Fine Arts in Houston. The limestone exterior is heavy and blank, like a suburban department store, but inside visitors find a sequence of spaces that reflect the depth and variety of the museum's collections. There are square, cubic, and rectangular galleries, painted in subtle colors, with ceiling heights ranging from 12 feet (3.6 meters) to 80 feet (24.3 meters), all illuminated by natural light from an intricate system of roof lanterns. At night, these lanterns glow like a miniature skyline.

Women's history museum. The Women's Museum: An Institute for the Future opened September 29 in Dallas. It is the first comprehensive center for women's history in the United States. The $23-million project, designed by New York City architect Wendy Evans Joseph, contains more than two dozen exhibits—all thematic and many interactive. The exhibits sit within the renovated shell of a 1909 coliseum.

Federal architecture took a giant step forward on Oct. 16, 2000, with the opening of Richard Meier's U.S. Courthouse in Central Islip, New York. Like most of the architect's work, the building is clad in white metal panels and is as meticulously engineered as a computer chip. The public lobby is a dramatic tilted cone, and the brilliantly illuminated interiors erase all memories of the dense and dark courthouses of the 1800's, of which Islip is a contemporary reinterpretation.

The baseball park boom continued in 2000 with ball parks opening in Houston, Detroit, and San Francisco. Enron Field in Houston, designed by Hellmuth, Obata, & Kassabaum (HOK) of Kansas City, is the most technologically ambitious of the group, with its retractable roof and a miniature steam locomotive that chugs across the left-field wall whenever an Astro hits a home run. Yet in the use of brick, steel, natural grass, and quirky field dimensions, all three reflect the prevailing nostalgia for old-time ball parks.

The Oklahoma City Memorial was dedicated April 19, five years after the Murrah Federal Building bombing that claimed 168 lives. Designed by Hans and Torrey Butzer and Sven Berg, the memorial features a sloping lawn of bronze-and-glass chairs—one for each victim—that are illuminated at night. The chairs face a shallow reflecting pool and a lone "survivor tree." The entire site is framed by two monumental bronze gates that mark the exact time of the explosion.

World War II memorial. Ground was broken on November 11 in Washington, D.C., for a controversial memorial to commemorate U.S. soldiers who fought in World War II (1939-1945). Designed by Friedrich St. Florian and located on the National Mall midway between the Lincoln Memorial and the Washington Monument, the memorial was to consist of a vast sunken plaza framed by angular columns. St. Florian's design focuses on a wall of gold stars representing the war's dead and missing. Supporters of the memorial argued that the design is appropriately grand and solemn. Critics decried it as a monumental violation of the integrity of the mall.

Architectural prizes. In January, the American Institute of Architects based in Washington, D.C., awarded its Gold Medal to Mexican architect Ricardo Legorreta, whose buildings combine simple geometric forms with planes of intense color and a calculated asymmetry that recalls the rambling plans of haciendas in his homeland.

The 2000 Pritzker Prize was awarded in April to Dutch architect and planner Rem Koolhaas. His work integrates elements of modernism, deconstructionism, and space technology into edgy confrontational designs. Instead of the formal geometry of Greece and Rome, Koolhaas's inspiration is the Internet. His projects range from apartment buildings in Japan to a new student center for the Illinois Institute of Technology in Chicago and the Seattle Public Library.

☐ David Dillon

See also **Baseball; Building and construction; New York City; News Bytes.**

Argentina. During 2000, President Fernando de la Rua of the Alliance coalition juggled the demands imposed by the International Monetary Fund (IMF), a Washington, D.C.-based United Nations agency that provides short-term credit to member nations, against those of blue-collar Argentines caught up in recession and high unemployment. On April 26, the opposition-controlled Senate approved a controversial labor reform bill. The pro-business measure, which easily passed in the Chamber of Deputies on May 11, weakened trade federations by permitting contract negotiations at the local or company level. This enabled businesses to exploit cheaper labor costs in regions with high unemployment. The law also reduced the payroll taxes that businesses must pay for new employees from 17.5 to 12 percent.

Labor unrest. On June 9, several million workers conducted the largest strike in four years to protest a $938-million cut in public spending announced in May. The cut, which followed another for $1.4 billion shortly after de la Rua took office, was mandated by the IMF, in order to make Argentina eligible to draw on a multibillion dollar emergency line of credit. De la Rua urged Argentine blue-collar workers to be patient and pleaded for more time for his program, which was aimed at increasing the nation's competitiveness and restoring investor and consumer confidence. However, with unemployment at 14.5 percent nationally and as high as 20 percent in some provinces, Argentine workers were not easily dissuaded from protesting. On December 18, the IMF and private banks pledged $39.7 billion to help reduce the burden of Argentina's debt.

Vote scandal. As the workers were making their case, a bribery scandal unfolded around the circumstances of the Senate's passage of the labor reform law. In July, Senator Antonio Cafiero of the opposition Peronist Party charged that some members of his party had taken bribes for their votes on the labor bill. In the ensuing month, Carlos Daniel Liporaci, a federal judge, alleged that he had evidence that the amount of the bribes had been as much as $4 million. By September, the leaders of both parties in the Senate had been forced to resign their posts because of the scandal. Judge Liporaci asked the Senate to strip 11 senators of their official immunity so that he could prosecute them.

Military cuts. De la Rua cut the defense budget by $150 million to $3.75 billion, despite complaints from military officers. In February, he presided over the firing or forced retirement of more than 1,500 military officers and civilian intelligence agents, who allegedly had killed and tortured thousands of civilians during the "dirty war" of 1976 to 1983, when the military controlled the government. Fernando de Santibanes, the head of a new State Intelligence Secretariat, announced after the firings that his agency would devote itself to such problems as money laundering, tax evasion, and drug trafficking.

Graves of dissidents. On April 14, 2000, more than 90 bodies buried for more than 20 years in mass graves at a forgotten cemetery were identified as victims of the military dictatorship of 1976 to 1983. The graves were found in Lomas de Zamora, a town south of Buenos Aires.

Apology. On June 13, 2000, de la Rua apologized at a news conference in Washington, D.C., for Argentina's role in harboring fugitive Nazi war criminals following World War II (1939-1945). He also vowed to get to the bottom of two anti-Jewish bomb attacks in 1992 and 1994.

Surgeon's suicide. In July 2000, Rene G. Favaloro, Argentina's esteemed surgeon and a pioneer in heart bypass operations, took his own life, apparently in despair over government cutbacks in support for the heart institute he had founded in Buenos Aires. The suicide triggered a massive outpouring of grief, reflecting frustration over persistently high unemployment, recession, and the inaccessibility of health care for the poor.   □ Nathan A. Haverstock

See also **Latin America.**

Arizona. See State government.

Arkansas. See State government.

Armed forces. Explosives packed into a small boat were detonated alongside the U.S.S. *Cole,* a U.S. Navy destroyer, on Oct. 12, 2000. The explosion killed 17 sailors on board the destroyer and injured 39 others. It also ripped a hole 40 feet (12 meters) high and 40 feet (12 meters) wide into the side of the 505-foot- (154-meter-) long vessel.

The U.S.S. *Cole* was docked and refueling in the Port of Aden, Yemen, when the small boat, carrying two men, maneuvered alongside and exploded. Investigators described the incident as a terrorist attack. In November, Yemeni officials announced that they had arrested six people in connection with the blast. Officials expected a trial to begin in early 2001.

Missile defense postponed. On Sept. 1, 2000, U.S. President Bill Clinton announced that he would leave the decision on whether to deploy a national missile defense system to his successor. The president said that he postponed his decision because he was unable to conclude whether the system's technology and operational effectiveness was advanced enough to continue. President Clinton said that technical problems with the system have delayed initial deployment from 2005 to 2007 at the earliest.

The national missile defense program was an outgrowth of President Ronald Reagan's Strategic Defense Initiative of the 1980's—a plan for thousands of space-based interceptor missiles forming a nuclear space shield. President Clinton's proposal was more limited in concept, beginning with 100 interceptor missiles based at a single launch site in Alaska and eventually expanding to 250 missiles at two sites.

Critics of the plan argued that it violated a 1972 antiballistic missile treaty between the United States and the then-Soviet Union. Critics also maintained that the project was prohibitively expensive. A Congressional Budget Office report published in April 2000 estimated that the full 250-missile plan would cost $60 billion and would not be fully operational until 2015.

U.S. military strength by the end of 2000 stood at 1.383 million soldiers. U.S. military personnel were involved in peacekeeping or humanitarian operations in several countries. Approximately 16,000 U.S. troops were still stationed in the Middle East almost 10 years after the end of the Persian Gulf War (1991). About 5,500 troops were on peacekeeping duty in the Yugoslav province of Kosovo and another 4,600 in Bosnia-Herzegovina, a former Yugoslav republic.

Military preparedness. A U.S. General Accounting Office (GAO) report released in July 2000 concluded that the U.S. armed forces suffered from a serious personnel shortage that hampered military readiness. The report said the

U.S. Air Force lacked the 40 crews needed to operate surveillance aircraft that would be necessary in the event of a war. The GAO report revealed that only 27 crews were trained to operate such aircraft.

A separate GAO report concluded that the military was so short of aerial tankers and transport aircraft that it would be unable to implement its long-standing strategy of simultaneously waging war in the Middle East and Asia.

The preparedness of U.S. military forces for war became a major campaign issue in the 2000 presidential election, as Texas Governor George W. Bush, the Republican candidate, contended that neglect by the Clinton administration had produced a military unable to fulfill its combat mission in the event of conflict. U.S. Secretary of Defense William Cohen, also a Republican, disputed such charges. Cohen said that the U.S. military was prepared to meet its worldwide security obligations and that all U.S. Army divisions were ready for combat.

Personnel developments. All the military services met their recruiting goals in 2000 for the first time since 1997. The Navy announced on Aug. 24, 2000, that it was lowering its quotas by 1,000 sailors because its retention rates had improved. Even so, Navy officials said the service was having trouble meeting its long-term goals

for keeping highly skilled pilots and technicians.

In August, the Air Force launched a $28-million advertising campaign in which that branch of the military for the first time ran advertisements on theater screens and prime-time television and cable programs. The campaign was the latest in a series of initiatives, including cash bonuses, to stem the flow of skilled airmen, particularly pilots, out of the Air Force and into jobs within the private sector.

U.S. reserve forces were unable to meet their retention needs in 2000. U.S. Defense Department officials attributed the shortfall to the steadily increasing use of reserve and National Guard units in peacekeeping missions throughout the world. In hopes of remedying the situation, the Department of Defense cut the maximum length of overseas deployments for reserve and guard units from 270 days to 180 days.

Sexual harassment. The Army rescinded the appointment of Major General Larry G. Smith as deputy inspector general in May following an accusation of sexual harassment by another officer. In September 1999, Lieutenant General Claudia J. Kennedy, the Army's highest-ranking female officer, alleged that Smith had kissed her and touched her inappropriately following a 1996 meeting in her Pentagon office. Kennedy said that she had not reported it to her superiors to spare

Investigators examine a hole in the hull of the U.S.S. *Cole*, a U.S. Navy destroyer severely damaged in a terrorist attack on October 12 in the Port of Aden, Yemen. Two suicide bombers pulled up beside the *Cole*, which was refueling, and detonated explosives loaded onto their small boat.

the Army embarrassment but went public with her charges after Smith was named the Army's deputy inspector general, a job in which he would deal with allegations of sexual harassment and other improper conduct by soldiers.

Smith denied any wrongdoing, but an Army investigation concluded in May 2000 that Kennedy's charges were credible. Army officials gave Smith a letter of reprimand. He retired in September. Kennedy retired from the Army in June.

"Don't ask, don't tell" policy. The Army's Inspector General's office concluded in July that a homophobic climate did not exist at Fort Campbell, Kentucky, where a soldier was clubbed to death in 1999 by a fellow soldier who shouted antihomosexual epithets during the assault.

The Army's report found that, while some members of Private Barry Winchell's unit had homophobic attitudes, superior officers did not encourage or tolerate antihomosexual harassment. Officials did reprimand the unit's first sergeant, however, because he was aware of homophobic behavior but had not intervened. A military court-martial in December 1999 convicted Private Calvin Glover of Winchell's murder and sentenced him to life in prison.

The incident rekindled controversy over how well the Clinton administration's "don't ask, don't tell" policy toward homosexuals in the military worked. The U.S. military policy was intended to make it easier for homosexuals to serve in the armed forces. The report concluded that the Army needed to expand and improve its training about the policy, especially among new soldiers.

Bombing resumes. The U.S. Navy resumed gunnery training exercises on the Puerto Rican island of Vieques in January 2000. The aerial and ship-to-shore training missions had been suspended in 1999, after a civilian was killed when Navy bombs landed off the target. Under a 1999 agreement with Puerto Rico, the Navy would continue using its Vieques range but without live ammunition. Puerto Ricans were scheduled to vote in 2002 on whether the Navy should continue the controversial firing exercises, which the Navy had claimed were essential to maintain combat proficiency.

Helicopter crashes. A V-22 Osprey tilt-rotor airplane crashed on April 7, 2000, during a training mission near Tucson, Arizona, killing 19 Marines. In May, Marine Corps investigators concluded that the crash was caused because the plane had descended too rapidly.

Marine officials said there was no evidence of mechanical failure but did not rule out pilot error as a possible cause of the crash. The 11 remaining Ospreys resumed flying in June, but the aircraft was grounded again on August 27 after it was discovered that a piece on the drive shaft of one of the V-22's had failed. On December 11, another V-22 Osprey crashed in North Carolina, killing four Marines who were on board. On December 12, the Marine Corps grounded the remaining fleet of V-22's, while officials investigated the cause of that crash.

Defense budget. The Department of Defense budget for fiscal year 2001, which began Oct. 1, 2000, was released on February 7. The budget requested $291.1 billion, $11.2 billion more than in fiscal year 2000. It included $60 billion for weapons funding, a record high, as well as sizable increases in military health and housing programs.

The Defense Department requested $8.8 billion for strategic missile defense programs, $4.4 billion for the last Nimitz-class nuclear aircraft carrier, $4 billion for 10 F-22 Raptor air superiority fighters, $3.4 billion for three Burke-class missile cruisers, $3.1 billion for 42 F/A-18 jet fighters, $3.1 billion for 12 C-17 jet cargo planes, $2 billion for the first in a new class of attack submarines, and $1.8 billion for 20 V-22 Osprey tilt-wing helicopter planes.

In August, President Clinton signed a $288-billion defense spending bill. The legislation provided a 3.7-percent military pay raise and funding for all of the weapons systems, including the first 10 production models of the F-22 jet fighter. A $6.5-billion supplemental appropriations bill contained funds for ongoing U.S. peacekeeping operations in Kosovo and Bosnia-Herzegovina.

New destroyer class. President Clinton announced on July 4 that the Navy's new DD-21 class of destroyers would be named for Admiral Elmo R. Zumwalt, Jr., the former chief of naval operations and the youngest four-star admiral in the history of the U.S. Navy. Zumwalt, who died on January 2, led the Navy from 1970 to 1974 and won a reputation as a reformer and innovator. The Zumwalt-class destroyer can be operated by a smaller crew yet fire shells more accurately. The Navy estimated that each destroyer would cost approximately $750 million.

Staff changes. Air Force General Joseph R. Ralston, vice chairman of the Joint Chiefs of Staff, was sworn in as commander in chief of North Atlantic Treaty Organization (NATO) forces in Europe on May 2, 2000. He succeeded Army General Wesley K. Clark. Ralston was the first Air Force officer to serve as the supreme commander of allied forces in Europe since 1962. On July 31, 2000, Admiral Vernon E. Clark became chief of naval operations, succeeding Admiral Jay Johnson.

☐ Thomas M. DeFrank

See also **Congress of the United States; Deaths; Middle East; Puerto Rico; Terrorism; United States, Government of the.**

Armenia. See Asia.

The Legend of the True Cross, a fresco cycle painted by Italian Renaissance artist Piero della Francesca between 1452 and 1466, is unveiled in April 2000 after undergoing a 15-year restoration. The paintings decorate the church of San Francesco in Arezzo, Italy.

Art. In 2000, various European countries and museums in Europe and the United States continued to pursue the problem of art treasures plundered during World War II (1939-1945). Most of the art had been seized by the Nazi government in Germany from Jewish collectors, many of whom were later killed during the *Holocaust* (the systematic execution during World War II of millions of Jews and other people considered undesirable by the Nazis). Prompted by international guidelines adopted in December 1998, American and European institutions continued in their efforts to identify Nazi-plundered art and return it to its rightful owners. Heirs of Holocaust victims continued to mount lawsuits to recover family possessions.

The governments of France, the United Kingdom, and Germany released information on Nazi-looted art during 2000 and set up departments to handle future claims. On March 1, a group of British art museums and galleries, in cooperation with the government, published an online list of more than 350 works of art whose history of ownership during the period around World War II was unclear. In April, several major American museums published information about works of art with questionable histories on their Web sites.

Experts cautioned, however, that even with this information, claimants still faced difficulties in obtaining evidence sufficient to prove ownership. Many wartime records were missing, closed to the public, or, because art transactions were often informal, never existed in the first place.

Kann claim. The Museum of Modern Art (MOMA) in New York City continued working in 2000 with heirs of Alphonse Kann, one of France's most important prewar Jewish art collectors. Their aim was to determine ownership of a painting hanging in MOMA that the heirs suspected was among the more than 1,000 works seized when the Nazis raided Kann's residence in 1940. The painting, by Spanish artist Pablo Picasso, was among 15 works with questionable histories MOMA listed on its Web site in April 2000.

Kann heirs also filed lawsuits or initiated claims for the return of allegedly stolen artwork against European and other American museums during 2000. Two paintings were returned to the estate by French and Swiss collectors.

Schiele dispute. A U.S. Federal District Court judge ruled in July that a painting by Austrian artist Egon Schiele that was taken by the Nazis from a Jewish art dealer in Vienna in 1938 could no longer be considered stolen. The painting, therefore, could not be seized by the U.S. government to be returned to the heirs of its prewar owner. The heirs had been trying to reclaim it and another Schiele painting since 1997, when the works were loaned to MOMA by the Leopold Foundation of Vienna for an exhibition. The July 2000 decision allowed the Leopold Foundation to keep the painting, which had been recovered by U.S. forces in 1945 and mistakenly handed over to the family of another Jewish collector before it was sold to the Leopold. The July 2000 ruling, a turning point in an ongoing legal battle over the question of ownership, stated that the painting could not be considered stolen after it had passed through the hands of U.S. forces, even though it was handed over to the wrong party. Federal prosecutors were challenging the ruling.

"Trophy art" returned. On April 29, Russia and Germany made their first official exchange of "trophy art," works each country stole from the other during and after World War II. The exchange took place during a ceremony outside St. Petersburg, Russia. Russia returned 101 artworks that Soviet troops stole from Nazi Germany during the war. In exchange, Germany returned two objects stolen from Russia by the Nazis in 1941.

Art sales online. The increase of online auction sales of art during 2000 highlighted the potential for problems in these types of transactions. In May, the online auction house eBay voided the April sale of a painting after the seller had entered bids on his own offering in order to artificially inflate the price, a practice forbidden on eBay. The price of the painting had soared from 25 cents to $135,805 before bidding closed. The escalation in price was spurred by speculation that the painting, which was signed "R. D. '52," was a 1952 work by the noted California artist Richard Diebenkorn.

Museum guidelines. In July 2000, the American Association of Museums, a professional body that represents more than 3,000 art museums in North America, adopted guidelines concerning the borrowing and display of art from private collections. The guidelines urged adherence to certain ethical standards, avoidance of conflicts of interest in the borrowing of artworks for exhibition, and maintenance of full curatorial control over exhibitions. The association expected that failure by museums to follow the guidelines would lead to denial of accreditation by the association and loss of funding from governments and foundations.

A controversial 1999 exhibition at the Brooklyn Museum of Art in New York City, "Sensation: Young British Artists from the Saatchi Collection," provoked the creation and adoption of the guidelines. The exhibit consisted of contemporary art from the private collection of Charles Saatchi, a British advertising executive. Ethical questions arose when news accounts revealed that the Brooklyn Museum had not disclosed the fact that the exhibition's largest financial backer was

Saatchi, who also had exercised significant conceptual control over the exhibition. The provocative nature of some of the artwork in "Sensation" triggered a battle over freedom of expression and public funding of the arts. New York City Mayor Rudolph W. Giuliani cut off city funding to the museum in September 1999 and began a state lawsuit to dismiss the museum's board of directors and to evict it from its city-owned building. In response, the museum initiated a federal lawsuit accusing the mayor of violating the constitutional right to free speech. A federal judge restored funding in November, and a settlement ending both lawsuits was reached in March 2000.

Museum news. The Solomon R. Guggenheim Foundation in New York City and the State Hermitage Museum in St. Petersburg, Russia, signed an agreement in June to share their collections and resources across a network of existing and planned museum sites. The collaboration was expected to be one of the most extensive ever to take place between major museums.

An average of 20,000 visitors a day flocked to the new Tate Modern after it opened in London in May. The $200-million, free-to-the-public museum, housed in a former power plant, featured international art of the 1900's. The original Tate Gallery was renamed Tate Britain and reserved for exhibitions of British art.

The Tate and MOMA announced an agreement in April 2000 to form a joint for-profit Internet site, making them the first museums to form a profit-making company. The site would offer educational programs, specially designed products, and archival material on art.

Major exhibitions. The Whitney Museum of American Art in New York City unveiled "Biennial 2000," the largest in a series of surveys of contemporary art held by the museum every two years. "The Splendor of 18th-Century Rome" at the Philadelphia Museum of Art and the Museum of Fine Arts in Houston showcased Rome as a cultural mecca. Old master paintings, Russian icons, classical antiquities, and palace furnishings were among the treasures exhibited in "Stroganoff: The Palace and Collections of a Russian Noble Family" at the Portland Art Museum in Oregon and the Kimbell Art Museum in Fort Worth, Texas. Other major exhibitions in 2000 included "Van Gogh: Face to Face," at the Detroit Institute of Arts, the Philadelphia Museum of Art, and the Museum of Fine Arts, Boston, and "Norman Rockwell: Pictures for the American People," at the High Museum of Art in Atlanta, the Chicago Historical Society, the Corcoran Gallery of Art in Washington, D.C., and the San Diego Museum of Art.   ☐ Sally-Ruth May

See also **Architecture; United Kingdom.**

Asia

Adverse weather triggered death, destruction, and suffering across Asia during 2000. The worst drought in 50 years stretched in an arc from Syria to Iran, into Afghanistan, Tajikistan, and Pakistan and parts of India, China, and Mongolia. Southeast of the drought area, heavy rains caused some of the worst flooding on record in India, Bangladesh, Bhutan, Thailand, Laos, Cambodia, Vietnam, and China.

The drought produced famine conditions as rivers dried up, irrigation systems failed, and crops withered. In Mongolia, the drought followed on the heels of the hardest winter in 30 years.

Unusually heavy rains hit northeast India, Bhutan, and Bangladesh in early August, killing more than 300 people. In late September, more than 1,000 people died and millions of people were left homeless when rains ravaged the region for a second time. During the same period, the worst floods in decades surged down the Mekong River, killing more than 350 people in Laos, Cambodia, and Vietnam.

Floods in Indonesia's West Timor in May killed 125 people, while typhoons caused flooding in the Philippines, Taiwan, and China during August and September.

The United Nations (UN) Economic and Social

The swollen waters of the Mekong River flood Buddhist temples in Phnom Penh, capital of Cambodia, in September. Floods in Cambodia in 2000 left more than 90 people dead and vast areas of cropland underwater.

Facts in brief on Asian countries

Country	Population	Government	Monetary unit*	Foreign trade (million U.S.$)	
				Exports[†]	Imports[†]
Afghanistan	26,674,000	No functioning government	afghani (4,750.00 = $1)	80	150
Armenia	3,813,000	President Robert Kocharian	dram (540.17 = $1)	232	800
Australia	19,222,000	Governor General William Deane; Prime Minister John Howard	dollar (1.88 = $1)	56,087	69,135
Azerbaijan	7,969,000	President Heydar A. Aliyev	manat (4,456.00 = $1)	781	794
Bangladesh	134,417,000	President Shahabuddin Ahmed; Prime Minister Sheikh Hasina	taka (54.00 = $1)	3,919	7,687
Bhutan	1,842,000	King Jigme Singye Wangchuck	ngultrum (46.37 = $1)	111	136
Brunei	312,000	Sultan Sir Hassanal Bolkiah	dollar (1.76 = $1)	2,307	1,741
Cambodia (Kampuchea)	11,637,000	King Norodom Sihanouk; Prime Minister Hun Sen	riel (3,900.00 = $1)	821	1,200
China	1,284,597,000	Communist Party General Secretary and President Jiang Zemin; Premier Zhu Rongji	renminbi yuan (8.28 = $1)	195,150	165,788
Georgia	5,527,000	President Eduard Shevardnadze	lari (1.96 = $1)	192	878
India	1,022,021,000	President Kocheril Raman Narayanan; Prime Minister Atal Behari Vajpayee	rupee (46.37 = $1)	36,310	44,889
Indonesia	212,731,000	President Abdurrahman Wahid; Vice President Megawati Sukarnoputri	rupiah (8,910.00 = $1)	48,665	24,004
Iran	74,644,000	Supreme Leader Ayatollah Ali Hoseini-Khamenei; President Mohammed Khatami-Ardakani	rial (1,747.50 = $1)	22,391	16,274
Japan	126,472,000	Emperor Akihito; Prime Minister Yoshiro Mori	yen (107.87 = $1)	417,623	310,012
Kazakhstan	16,288,000	President Nursultan Nazarbayev	tenge (142.65 = $1)	5,592	3,683
Korea, North	21,935,000	Korean Workers' Party General Secretary Kim Chong-il	won (2.20 = $1)	680	954
Korea, South	47,149,000	President Kim Dae-jung; Prime Minister Lee Han-dong	won (1,121.50 = $1)	144,745	119,750
Kyrgyzstan	4,683,000	President Askar Akayev	som (47.60 = $1)	454	600
Laos	5,602,000	President Khamtai Siphandon; Prime Minister Sisavat Keobounphan	kip (7,565.00 = $1)	311	525
Malaysia	22,299,000	Paramount Ruler (King) Sultan Tuanku Ja'afar ibni Al-Marhum Tuanku Abdul Rahman; Prime Minister Mahathir bin Mohamad	ringgit (3.80 = $1)	84,451	64,962

Commission for Asia and the Pacific reported in September that deforestation greatly contributed to the severity of the flooding. The area of land in Asia covered by forests dropped from 70 percent in 1945 to 25 percent in 2000. During the same period, the population of Asia tripled.

Forest fires on Indonesia's Sumatra and Kalimantan islands created smog in Malaysia and Singapore in July. The Indonesian government reported that the fires were caused by plantation owners and timber companies clearing the land by burning. The fires in 2000 were not as bad as they had been in 1997, when burning caused

health problems in the region. However, the Indonesian government in 2000 remained unable to control planters and loggers despite promises made to the angry leaders of countries downwind of the fires.

Civil unrest. No wars were fought between nations in Asia, but unrest plagued many areas during 2000. Civil wars continued in Afghanistan and Sri Lanka, involving well-organized armies and extensive military equipment. The Muslim fundamentalist Taliban Militia movement in Afghanistan made gains toward destroying opposition forces. The Taliban captured the town of

Country	Population	Government	Monetary unit*	Foreign trade (million U.S.$)	
				Exports[†]	Imports[†]
Maldives	285,000	President Maumoon Abdul Gayoom	rufiyaa (11.77 = $1)	64	402
Mongolia	2,661,000	President Natsagiyn Bagabandi; Prime Minister Namburiin Enkhbayar	tugrik (1,086.00 = $1)	763	1,010
Myanmar (Burma)	48,866,000	Prime Minister, State Peace and Development Council Chairman Than Shwe	kyat (6.58 = $1)	1,125	2,301
Nepal	24,842,000	King Birendra Bir Bikram Shah Dev; Prime Minister Girija Prasad Koirala	rupee (71.87 = $1)	474	1,243
New Zealand	3,759,000	Governor General Sir Michael Hardie-Boys; Prime Minister Helen Clark	dollar (2.50 = $1)	12,452	14,301
Pakistan	145,246,000	President Mohammad Rafiq Tarar; Chief Executive General Pervez Musharraf	rupee (58.58 = $1)	8,383	10,159
Papua New Guinea	4,809,000	Governor General Sir Silas Atopare; Prime Minister Sir Mekere Morauta	kina (2.88 = $1)	1,880	1,191
Philippines	74,575,000	President Joseph Estrada	peso (47.50 = $1)	32,188	31,168
Russia	145,552,000	President Vladimir Putin	ruble (27.87 = $1)	74,663	40,429
Singapore	3,777,000	President Sellapan Rama Nathan; Prime Minister Goh Chok Tong	dollar (1.76 = $1)	114,691	111,062
Sri Lanka	19,504,000	President Chandrika Kumaratunga; Prime Minister Ratnasiri Wickramanayake	rupee (79.52 = $1)	4,593	5,884
Taiwan	22,322,000	President Chen Shui-bian; Vice President Annette Lu	dollar (31.31 = $1)	121,600	101,700
Tajikistan	6,260,000	President Emomali Rahmonov; National Assembly Chairman Makhmadsaidi Ubaydulloyev	ruble (1,550.00 = $1)	602	771
Thailand	61,909,000	King Phumiphon Adunyadet; Prime Minister Chuan Likphai	baht (43.58 = $1)	58,392	41,575
Turkmenistan	4,551,000	President Saparmurat Niyazov	manat (5,200.00 = $1)	1,100	1,250
Uzbekistan	25,383,000	President Islam Karimov	som (775.00 = $1)	3,528	3,289
Vietnam	82,648,000	Communist Party General Secretary Le Kha Phieu; President Tran Duc Luong; Prime Minister Phan Van Khai	dong (14,624.00 = $1)	9,361	11,494

*Exchange rates as of Oct.13, 2000, or latest available data.
[†]Latest available data.

Taloqan from the opposition Northern Alliance in September. Later that month, Taliban leaders asked the UN for recognition as the official government in Afghanistan. Fighting and suicide bombings carried out by the Liberation Tigers of Tamil Eelam, a group seeking independence for the Tamil minority, resulted in the deaths of hundreds of people in Sri Lanka in 2000.

Guerrilla fighting by groups seeking *autonomy* (self rule) or complete independence flared in India's states of Kashmir and Assam, in Nepal, eastern Myanmar, northeastern Laos, the southern Philippines, and parts of Indonesia. Clashes between Muslims and Christians in 2000 left hundreds of people dead in eastern Indonesia.

Economy. Despite turbulent weather and unrest, most of the nations of Asia achieved economic growth in 2000, though growth in national economies was insufficient to lift hundreds of millions of people out of poverty.

During the annual meeting of the Asian Development Bank in Chiang Mai, Thailand, in May, Japan, China, and South Korea agreed to help stabilize the currencies of the nations of Southeast Asia. The move was designed to avoid a regional economic downturn similar to the one that occurred when the value of Thailand's currency, the baht, declined significantly in 1997.

Trade among the nations of Southeast Asia increased significantly in 2000, after decades in which trade in the region was oriented toward Europe and North America. In 2000, a report by the Association of Southeast Asian Nations warned that falling trade barriers around the world would create increased competition between regional economies.

During 2000, foreign investment continued to shift from Southeast Asia to other developing Asian countries, while exports from China to the United States increased faster than those from Southeast Asia. The economies of North Asia also grew faster in 2000 than the economies of the nations of Southeast Asia.

Piracy continued to increase in 2000 in the seas around Southeast Asia. The Maritime Bureau of the International Chamber of Commerce reported that attacks on ships rose 40 percent during the first half of 2000. Most of the attacks occurred in Indonesian waters. Pirates typically boarded ships, tied up or killed the crews, and stole cargo or entire vessels.

In April, the leaders of various Asian countries met in Tokyo to define ways to stop piracy in international waters. Japan, which depended on the Indonesian sea routes for its supply of crude oil, offered armed coast guard boats as part of an antipiracy plan, but other nations held back.

Illegal immigrants. Australian officials reported that more than 250 people died in March while trying to enter the country illegally. Most of the victims had paid smugglers to transport them from Iraq or Iran to Australia. They drowned when the dilapidated and overcrowded boats they were in sank.

Boat people. On May 30, Hong Kong officials closed the last camp for the "boat people" who had fled South Vietnam after the Communist takeover in 1975. Many of the people had lived in Hong Kong camps for nearly 25 years, because officials refused to allow them to settle permanently in Hong Kong. In 2000, Hong Kong officials finally relented and offered residency to the more than 1,000 people left in the camps.

East Timor. The UN Transitional Administration for East Timor worked throughout 2000 to prepare the former Portuguese colony for self-government. Elections for a constituent assembly were scheduled for August 2001. The assembly was to decide the new nation's name, political structure, and constitution. In order to help the nation escape poor economic conditions, UN officials also aided in rebuilding the infrastructure and increasing the production of rice and the arabica coffee grown in the region. The Indonesian army and local supporters of Indonesia had devastated East Timor in 1999 after the East Timorese people voted for independence on August 30. Indonesia had seized East Timor in 1975. In 2000, local supporters continued to harass East Timor from bases in Indonesian West Timor.

The National Council of Timorese Resistance, an umbrella group for East Timor's political factions, met in Dili, the East Timorese capital, on August 21, to discuss the nation's future. The meeting focused on choosing either Portuguese or English as the second language. Only 8 percent of East Timor's 800,000 people spoke Portuguese, but the language had cultural roots in the area. Nevertheless, many people believed English would be more helpful in international affairs.

The day before the National Council of Timorese Resistance meeting, 53-year-old Jose Alexandre "Xanana" Gusmao resigned as commander-in-chief of the National Liberation Armed Forces of East Timor. Many observers believed he would become East Timor's first president in 2001.

Nepal. Girija Prasad Koirala began his fourth nonconsecutive term as prime minister of Nepal in March 2000. He succeeded Krishna Prasad Bhattarai, who was ousted by a rebellion in the Nepali Congress Party. Koirala said Nepal faced a difficult period because of increased crime and corruption, poverty, and the decline of foreign tourism, which was vital to the economy. Nevertheless, the economy grew by 6 percent in 2000 because of growth in manufacturing.

Mongolia. The Mongolian People's Revolutionary Party, the former Communist Party that controlled Mongolia as a satellite of the former Soviet Union for 70 years, returned to power in 2000. Facing a divided Democratic Alliance Party during elections in July, the Communists won 72 of the 76 seats in the Great Hural, the *unicameral* (single house) parliament. The party's chairman, Namburiin Enkhbayar, became prime minister. The party promoted socialist welfare policies to overcome the hardships caused by Mongolia's bad weather, limited economic development, and isolation from foreign markets.

Brunei, an oil-rich nation that provided its 300,000 citizens free medical care without taxing their incomes, began looking for ways to save money in 2000. The Brunei Economic Council reported in July that the old economic system was no longer sustainable. To reduce dependence on oil and gas, Brunei officials hoped to become a world financial center for Muslims.

In May, the government of Brunei settled a lawsuit out of court against Prince Jefri, younger brother of Sultan Hassanal Bolkiah. The lawsuit had charged that Prince Jefri had misused more than $40 billion in state funds.

☐ Henry S. Bradsher

See also the various Asian country articles.

Astronomy. In 2000, astronomers studied an asteroid, detected evidence of recently flowing water on Mars, and discovered a new moon of Jupiter. Outside the solar system, astronomers found more extrasolar planets, solved one of the mysteries of X-ray background radiation, and helped confirm that the universe will continue to expand.

The secrets of Eros. On February 14, a spacecraft called the Near Earth Asteroid Rendezvous (NEAR-Shoemaker, named for the late planetary geologist Eugene Shoemaker) reached the asteroid Eros and trained a series of cameras and other measuring instruments on it. The mission was the first long-term, close-up study of an asteroid, one of the thousands of tiny bodies that orbit the sun.

Images from NEAR-Shoemaker revealed that Eros was peanut-shaped and about 21 miles (34 kilometers) long and 8 miles (13 kilometers) thick. Its surface was heavily scarred from impacts with meteorites. Astronomers determined that Eros is composed of rocks very much like the oldest known meteorites. This finding implied that the asteroid was probably formed over 4.5 billion years ago, when the sun and all the planets were forming.

Water flow on Mars. Researchers working with the Mars Global Surveyor spacecraft reported in June 2000 that flowing water may have flowed across the Martian surface within the past few hundred thousand years and may still occasionally flow today. Images taken by the Global Surveyor showed gullies similar to those produced by liquid water on Earth. The extreme cold on Mars, together with an atmospheric pressure 100 times less than the pressure on Earth, causes liquid water to evaporate when exposed at the Martian surface. For the gullies to form, the liquid water thought to lie several hundred feet below the Martian surface must burst through the surface in a process that researchers do not yet understand.

New Jovian moon. In July 2000, astronomers at the Spacewatch project of the University of Arizona at Tucson announced the discovery of the 17th moon of Jupiter. The moon—about 3 miles (5 kilometers) in diameter—completed an orbit around Jupiter every two years.

Channels in a Martian crater, in an image taken in 2000 by the Mars Global Surveyor, suggest to scientists that liquid water may have flowed across the surface of Mars in recent times.

It is the smallest known moon orbiting any of the nine planets in our solar system.

More extrasolar planets. In 2000, several groups of astronomers announced the discovery of planets circling stars beyond the sun, bringing the number of known extrasolar planetary systems to more than 50 by year's end. The first such system was discovered in 1995.

The new planetary systems include a planet circling the star Epsilon Eridani, only 10.5 *light-years* from Earth, making it the nearest solar system beyond our sun. (A light-year is the distance light travels in one year, about 5.9 trillion miles

[9.5 trillion kilometers].) Astronomers also discovered the two smallest extrasolar planets yet detected. One, only 80 percent of the mass of Saturn, circles the star HD 46375, 109 light-years away. Another planet is 70 percent of the mass of Saturn and orbits the star 79 Ceti, about 117 light-years from our sun. Previously, the only extrasolar planets known were approximately the same mass as Jupiter, which is three times the mass of Saturn. Planets the size of the Earth are too small to be detected by current methods.

The discovery of an asteroid about one-fourth the size of Pluto was reported by Venezuelan and American astronomers in October 2000. EB173, as the ball of rock and ice was named, circles the sun in an orbit beyond Neptune. Although it is too small to be considered a planet, EB173 is the second-largest asteroid found within the solar system.

The mystery of the X-ray background. Astronomers since the 1960's have attempted to uncover the source of X rays detected coming from all directions in space. In 2000, researchers working with a new X-ray telescope announced that they had found the source of the radiation—the active *nuclei* (centers) of very distant galaxies.

Astronomers using earlier X-ray telescopes had discovered hot spots of X rays coming from the centers of nearby galaxies. They believed that the radiation was produced by hot gas falling into black holes within the galactic nuclei. They could not, however, identify the distant sources of the X-ray background, because the sources blurred into a continuous fog. In July 1999, the U.S. National Aeronautics and Space Administration launched the Chandra X-ray telescope, the most powerful telescope of its kind ever built. Using Chandra, astronomers resolved the fine detail of the individual sources of radiation throughout the sky and determined that these sources were black holes at the centers of active galaxies.

The cosmic microwave background. In 2000, two international teams of astronomers flew balloons high in the stratosphere to measure the *cosmic microwave background,* the fading remnants of radiation from the *big bang,* the monumental explosion during which most astronomers believe the universe began. One balloon flew over Antarctica; the other over Texas. Both carried instruments to detect variations—or ripples—in the temperature of the radiation in different areas of the sky. The ripples, which reflect variations in the density of the early universe, eventually contracted to form galaxies, stars, and planets. According to reports by the two teams in May, the data from both balloon missions matched predictions that the universe will continue to expand.

□ Laurence A. Marschall
See also **Chemistry; Space exploration.**

Australia

Australia hosted the 27th Olympiad of the modern era in September 2000, a 17-day, international event that many observers described as nearly flawless. The reconciliation of Australians of European heritage and Aborigines, the original inhabitants of Australia, continued to dominate Australian politics in 2000. During a tour of Australia in 2000, Queen Elizabeth II of Great Britain made it clear that Australia's future, whether as a monarchy or a republic, was a matter for Australians to decide.

The 2000 Olympic Games in Sydney took seven years of preparation. In all, the total cost of staging the Olympics was an estimated $3.5 billion (all amounts in Australian dollars), including the contributions of both the New South Wales government and the private sector. The preparation and planning of the games involved a certain amount of controversy. Kevan Gosper, the vice president of the International Olympic Committee

The 2000 Olympic Games, the 27th Olympiad of the modern era, end in Sydney, Australia, on October 1 in a spectacular display of fireworks staged from the Sydney Harbor Bridge above the city's famed opera house.

(IOC), triggered a storm of media criticism in May when he allowed his daughter, Sophie, to become the first Australian to carry the Olympic torch at Olympia in Greece. Gosper apologized on May 12 to Yianna Souleles, the Sydney Greek-Australian schoolgirl originally selected to be the torch bearer. Controversy subsided after the torch began its 100-day journey around Australia at Uluru (Ayers Rock) in the Northern Territory on June 8. The torch relay ended with the lighting of the Olympic flame at Stadium Australia in Sydney on September 15.

The opening ceremony began with the entry of a lone rider on horseback, followed by a spectacular entertainment depicting Australian history and environment. The games were held in a spirit of friendliness and good will as 47,000 volunteers greeted people at airports and provided transportation for athletes and officials.

The largely Australian crowds bought up al-most all available tickets to events both popular and obscure. They cheered on U.S. track and field superstars Michael Johnson and Marion Jones. They even applauded Dutch swimmer Pieter van den Hoogenband when he beat the local swimming hero, Ian Thorpe, in the 200-meter freestyle final. For most Australians, Aboriginal runner Cathy Freeman, who lit the Olympic flame, was the star of the games. She later went on to justify her selection for this honor by winning the 400-meter sprint. She followed her victory by taking a lap of honor with the Australian and Aboriginal flags entwined.

Australian swimmers Ian Thorpe, Grant Hackett, and Susie O'Neill won gold medals, and the Australian men's team enjoyed a memorable victory over the United States in the 4 x 100 freestyle relay. The victory by the Australian women's hockey team was not unexpected. Equestrian Andrew Hoy, who won three Olympic

Members of the Australian House of Representatives

The House of Representatives of the 39th Parliament convened on Nov. 10, 1998. As of Dec. 12, 2000, the House of Representatives consisted of the following members: 66 Australian Labor Party, 64 Liberal Party of Australia, 16 National Party of Australia, 2 independents. This table shows each legislator and party affiliation. An asterisk (*) denotes those who served in the 38th Parliament.

Australian Capital Territory
Annette Ellis, A.L.P.*
Bob McMullan, A.L.P.*

New South Wales
Tony Abbott, L.P.*
Anthony Albanese, A.L.P.*
John Anderson, N.P.*
Peter Andren, Ind.*
Larry Anthony, N.P.*
Bruce Baird, L.P.
Kerry Bartlett, L.P.*
Bronwyn Bishop, L.P.*
Laurie Brereton, A.L.P.*
Alan Cadman, L.P.*
Ross Cameron, L.P.*
Ian Causley, N.P.*
Janice Crosio, A.L.P.*
John Fahey, L.P.*
Laurie Ferguson, A.L.P.*
Timothy Fischer, N.P.*
Joel Fitzgibbon, A.L.P.*
Joanna Gash, L.P.*
Jill Hall, A.L.P.
Michael Hatton, A.L.P.*
Kelly Hoare, A.L.P.
Joe Hockey, L.P.*
Colin Hollis, A.L.P.*
Bob Horne, A.L.P.
John Howard, L.P.*
Kay Hull, N.P.
Julia Irwin, A.L.P.
Jackie Kelly, L.P.*
Mark Latham, A.L.P.*
Tony Lawler, N.P.
Michael Lee, A.L.P.*
Jim Lloyd, L.P.*
Stephen Martin, A.L.P.*
Robert McClelland, A.L.P.*
Leo McLeay, A.L.P.*
Daryl Melham, A.L.P.*
Allan Morris, A.L.P.*
Frank Mossfield, A.L.P.*
John Murphy, A.L.P.
Gary Nairn, L.P.*
Garry Nehl, N.P.*
Brendan Nelson, L.P.*
Tanya Plibersek, A.L.P.
Roger Price, A.L.P.*
Philip Ruddock, L.P.*
Stuart St. Clair, N.P.
Alby Schultz, L.P.
Andrew Thomson, L.P.*
Mark Vaile, N.P.*
Danna Vale, L.P.*

Northern Territory
Warren Snowdon, A.L.P.

Queensland
Arch Bevis, A.L.P.*
Mal Brough, L.P.*
Kay Elson, L.P.*
Craig Emerson, A.L.P.
Warren Entsch, L.P.*
Teresa Gambaro, L.P.*
Gary Hardgrave, L.P.*
David Jull, L.P.*
Robert Katter, N.P.*
De-Anne Kelly, N.P.*
Cheryl Kernot, A.L.P.
Peter Lindsay, L.P.*
Kirsten Livermore, A.L.P.
Ian Macfarlane, L.P.
Margaret May, L.P.
John Moore, L.P.*
Paul Neville, N.P.*
Bernie Ripoll, A.L.P.
Kevin Rudd, A.L.P.
Con Sciacca, A.L.P.
Bruce Scott, N.P.*
Peter Slipper, L.P.*
Alexander Somlyay, L.P.*
Kathy Sullivan, L.P.*
Wayne Swan, A.L.P.
Cameron Thompson, L.P.
Warren Truss, N.P.*

South Australia
Neil Andrew, L.P.*
David Cox, A.L.P.
Alexander Downer, L.P.*
Trish Draper, L.P.*
Martyn Evans, A.L.P.*
Christine Gallus, L.P.*
Christopher Pyne, L.P.*
Rodney Sawford, A.L.P.*
Patrick Secker, L.P.
Andrew Southcott, L.P.*
Barry Wakelin, L.P.*
Trish Worth, L.P.*

Tasmania
Dick Adams, A.L.P.*
Duncan Kerr, A.L.P.*
Michelle O'Byrne, A.L.P.
Harry Quick, A.L.P.*
Sid Sidebottom, A.L.P.

Victoria
Kevin Andrews, L.P.*
Fran Bailey, L.P.*
Phillip Barresi, L.P.*
Bruce Billson, L.P.*
Anna Burke, A.L.P.
Anthony Byrne, A.L.P.
Bob Charles, L.P.*
Ann Corcoran, A.L.P.
Peter Costello, L.P.*
Simon Crean, A.L.P.*
Michael Danby, A.L.P.
Martin Ferguson, A.L.P.*
John Forrest, N.P.*
Petro Georgiou, L.P.*
Steve Gibbons, A.L.P.
Julia Gillard, A.L.P.
Alan Griffin, A.L.P.*
David Hawker, L.P.*
Harry Jenkins, A.L.P.*
David Kemp, L.P.*
Louis Lieberman, L.P.*
Jenny Macklin, A.L.P.*
Stewart McArthur, L.P.*
Peter McGauran, N.P.*
Peter Nugent, L.P.*
Gavan O'Connor, A.L.P.*
Neil O'Keefe, A.L.P.*
Peter Reith, L.P.*
Michael Ronaldson, L.P.*
Nicola Roxon, A.L.P.
Bob Sercombe, A.L.P.*
Sharman Stone, L.P.*
Lindsay Tanner, A.L.P.*
Andrew Theophanous, Ind.*
Kelvin Thomson, A.L.P.*
Michael Wooldridge, L.P.*
Christian Zahra, A.L.P.

Western Australia
Kim Beazley, A.L.P.*
Julie Bishop, L.P.
Graham Edwards, A.L.P.
Jane Gerick, A.L.P.
Barry Haase, L.P.
Carmen Lawrence, A.L.P.*
Jann McFarlane, A.L.P.
Judi Moylan, L.P.*
Geoffrey Prosser, L.P.*
Stephen Smith, A.L.P.*
Wilson Tuckey, L.P.*
Mal Washer, L.P.
Kim Wilkie, A.L.P.
Daryl Williams, L.P.*

golds in previous years, lost the gold to U.S. equestrian David O'Connor. Other Australian victories brought many lesser-known sports to public attention. These included gold medals for Simon Fairweather (archery), Lauren Burns (tae kwon do), and Kerri Pottharst and Natalie Cook (beach volleyball). The Russian-born athlete Tatiana Grigorieva became a household name overnight after she won a silver medal for Australia in the women's pole vault. Altogether, Australia won 16 gold, 25 silver, and 17 bronze medals. A record total of 58 medals earned Australia fourth place behind teams from much larger countries—the United States, Russia, and China.

Director of Ceremonies Ric Birch chose to end the 2000 Olympic Games with a salute to Australian pop culture. Actor Paul Hogan, who starred in the film *Crocodile Dundee*, appeared in a parade along with the Australian golfer Greg Norman and model Elle Macpherson. The indigenous group Yothu Yindi, whose song "Treaty" contained sharp political criticism, continued the Aboriginal theme that was evident in the opening ceremony. The youngest entertainer was 13-year-old Nikki Webster, who had stolen the show at the opening and appeared again at the closing ceremony. The oldest performer was veteran country singer Slim Dusty, aged 73, who concluded the closing ceremony with "Waltzing Matilda." "Waltzing Matilda" is the most famous of Australian songs. The expression means to carry a bag of belongings.

Many Australians felt the actual games were a bit anticlimactic. The building of the venues had all been completed ahead of schedule. No terrorists or even any serious Aboriginal protests marred the games. The doomsayers who predicted transportation chaos were proven wrong. Even the spring weather was fine for the most part. On October 1, at the end of the games, IOC president Juan Antonio Samaranch praised the Sydney Olympic games as "the best ever."

Aborigines. In 2000, reconciliation continued to dominate political debate in Australia, as Aboriginal leaders met with leading figures from the general community to work out details of a final agreement between the two groups. A special ceremony billed as Corroboree 2000 was held at the Sydney Opera House on May 27 to hand over a document entitled "A Declaration Towards Reconciliation." Prime Minister John Howard was present at this ceremony. In the past, Howard had gone as far as expressing "sincere regret" but had steadfastly refused to use the word "sorry" or

Queen Elizabeth II of the United Kingdom watches traditional dancers in Bourke during a royal tour of Australia in March 2000. The queen's 16-day visit was her 13th since becoming Australia's head of state in 1952.

to apologize on behalf of the general community for injustices committed before most present-day Australians were born. He reiterated his continued support for the concept of reconciliation, but several delegates demanded he apologize and turned their backs on him when he rose to speak.

Howard was notably absent on May 28, when a crowd of between 150,000 and 250,000 people streamed across Sydney Harbor Bridge in an emotional expression of support for reconciliation. The march enjoyed the enthusiastic support of both the minister for Aboriginal affairs, John Herron, and the minister for reconciliation, Philip Ruddock. They were the only two ministers whom Howard did not bar from the event. However, Ruddock rejected as inappropriate the notion of signing a treaty between members of the same nation. Ruddock had defended his government's treatment of Australia's 200,000 Aboriginal citizens when it was called into question in

The Ministry of Australia*

John Howard—prime minister

John Anderson—minister for transport and regional services; deputy prime minister

Peter Costello—treasurer

Mark Vaile—minister for trade

Robert Hill—minister for the environment and heritage; leader of the government in the Senate

Richard Alston—minister for communications, information technology, and the arts; deputy leader of the government in the Senate

Peter Reith—minister for employment, workplace relations, and small business; leader of the House

Jocelyn Newman—minister for family and community services

Alexander Downer—minister for foreign affairs

John Moore—minister for defence

Michael Wooldridge—minister for health and aged care

John Fahey—minister for finance and administration

David Kemp—minister for education, training, and youth affairs; vice president of the Executive Council

Nick Minchin—minister for industry, science, and resources

Daryl Williams—attorney general

Philip Ruddock—minister for immigration and multicultural affairs

Warren Truss—minister for agriculture, fisheries, and forestry

*As of Dec. 12, 2000.

Premiers of Australian states

State	Premier
New South Wales	Bob Carr
Queensland	Peter Beattie
South Australia	John Olsen
Tasmania	Jim Bacon
Victoria	Steve Bracks
Western Australia	Richard Court

Government leaders of Australian mainland territories

Australian Capital Territory	Gary Humphries
Northern Territory	Denis Burke

March by a United Nations committee in Geneva, Switzerland. Ruddock pointed out that more than $2 billion was being spent on Aboriginal programs annually. Ruddock also insisted that Aborigines owned or controlled more than 15 percent of Australia's land mass—an area equivalent to Spain and France combined.

Herron found himself the center of a storm of media controversy in April when he claimed that the phrase "the stolen generation" was an exaggeration. He was referring to the now discontinued practice of taking children, especially children who were of mixed Aboriginal and European descent, from Aboriginal parents and handing them over to adoptive families, most of whom were white. The practice occurred between 1910 and 1970. Herron claimed that this affected only about 10 percent of Aboriginal children rather than a whole generation. He maintained that many of these children were taken away for their own welfare, just as contemporary children, black and white, are taken away by government authorities to protect them from abusive or neglectful parents. Aboriginal leaders claimed that Herron's remarks had severely set back the cause of reconciliation.

Mandatory sentencing in the Northern Territory and Western Australia and its effect on Aborigines continued to stir controversy in 2000. Many legal authorities claimed that the compulsory use of prison sentences for repeated offenses, even for minor ones, discriminated against Aborigines, who make up a disproportionate number of prisoners in Australian jails—about 70 percent. In February, the suicide of a young Aborigine who held been imprisoned for stealing some writing materials highlighted the use of mandatory sentencing laws. Another case that attracted media attention involved an older man from a remote area, sentenced to a year in jail for stealing food and drink worth $23. John Howard said he was personally against mandatory sentencing as a legal concept. Despite pressure from some members of his own Liberal Party, however, he refused to exercise the powers of the federal government to override state and territory legislation. Instead, he had discussions in April with the chief minister of the Northern Territory, Denis Burke. They worked out a compromise whereby territory police would exercise their own judgment about arresting young Aboriginal offenders. In return, Howard promised extra financial help for the territory to tackle some of the social problems that brought Aborigines into conflict with the law in the first place.

The royal tour. Leaders of the Australian Republican Movement viewed the visit by Queen Elizabeth II to Australia in March as controversial. They pointed out that while a 1999 referendum had failed to gain a majority, almost half the voters had wanted to replace the monarchy with a republic. The group urged people to differentiate between their affection for the queen as a person and the controversy over her role as Australia's head of state. The queen's 16-day tour proved to be a fairly low-key affair, attracting small but enthusiastic crowds in the state's capital cities and comparatively larger numbers in country centers. The overall welcome contrasted with the enormous attention Queen Elizabeth received in Australia when she made her first tour as a young monarch in 1954. Nevertheless, monarchists, who included the prime minister John Howard, pronounced the visit a great success, and the queen made it clear that the future of Australia—whether as a monarchy or a republic—was a matter for Australians to decide. In October 2000, Kim Beazley, who as leader of the Labor Party opposition supported Australia becoming a republic, announced that he would hold another referendum if he became prime minister at the next election.

The economy. For most Australians, 2000 was a prosperous year. The budget, presented by Treasurer Peter Costello on May 9, forecasted a cash surplus of $2.8 billion and projected growth at the rate of 3.75 percent for 2000-2001. Economists expected inflation to stay below 2.5 percent and unemployment to fall to around 6.25 percent.

The long-awaited goods and services tax (GST) went into effect on July 1, 2000. Most political commentators expected it to be highly unpopular despite being offset by cuts in personal income tax and increases in social welfare pensions. The introduction of Australia's first consumption tax proved to be something of an anticlimax. Most small businesses coped well with the new regulations, and in general, few people complained about increases from the additional tax on goods and services. The one exception was soaring fuel prices, but the government was quick to indicate that these increases were caused largely by overseas oil producers, rather than the GST.

Despite Australia's generally healthy economy in 2000, the Australian dollar continued to fall steadily throughout the year, reaching record low levels when it dropped below 52 cents to the U.S. dollar in October. Costello blamed the weakness of the Australian dollar on the strength of the U.S. dollar, which had adversely affected most other major currencies.

In April, 80 percent of the members of the National Roads and Motorists Association (NRMA) voted "yes" to a proposal to end the existence of Australia's largest motorist association and the country's largest insurer. Members of the old mutual association were given shares in a new company, which were then floated on the stock exchange.

Conservation. On October 6, Bob Carr, the premier of New South Wales, and Steve Bracks, the premier of Victoria, met at Jindabyne Dam in the Snowy Mountains to launch an important conservation initiative. Under the agreement, the Snowy River was to be restored to almost a third of its natural flow during the next 15 years.

The flow of the Snowy River was reduced to a trickle by dams constructed between 1949 and 1974 as part of the Snowy Mountains Scheme to provide water for hydroelectricity and irrigation. The extra water was to come from cutting waste in other parts of the system, meaning irrigation and power generation would not be affected.

On Oct. 10, 2000, John Howard announced that the federal government would spend more than $7 million over the next seven years to combat dry-land *salinity* (saltiness). Howard pointed out that salinity was already affecting more than 5 percent of Australia's cultivated land and that the water provided to the city of Adelaide, South Australia, would be undrinkable within 20 years unless action was taken. Conservationists criticized the amount of money allocated by the government for the program, claiming that it would take more than $1.5 billion to fix the problem.

☐ Brian Kennedy

See also **Asia; Olympics: A Special Report—Olympics 2000; United Kingdom.**

Australia, Prime Minister of.

John Howard, leader of the Liberal-National Party coalition, was publicly embarrassed when the National Textile Company in the Hunter Valley of New South Wales declared bankruptcy in February 2000. The prime minister's brother, Stanley Howard, was chairman of the company, which collapsed, owing money to its 342 employees. The federal government of Australia and the state government of New South Wales bailed National Textile out with a $2-million package (all amounts in Australian dollars), which allowed the company to pay its former employees. Prime Minister Howard rejected media claims that the bailout had been arranged to aid his brother.

Howard successfully introduced a 10-percent goods and services tax (GST) on July 1. The tax proved to be neither as complicated nor as unpopular as critics had predicted.

On July 26, Howard indicated that the parliamentary elections scheduled for 2001 might be his last. However, Howard retracted this statement on Aug. 3, 2000, insisting that he would be happy to continue to serve as Australia's prime minister. However, opposition leader Kim Beazley and other critics claimed that Howard had already retired in his mind and lacked the heart to continue as prime minister.   ☐ Brian Kennedy

See also **Australia.**

Australian rules football.

More than 96,000 fans packed the Melbourne Cricket Ground in Melbourne, Australia, on Sept. 2, 2000, to watch the Essendon Bombers defeat the Melbourne Demons by 60 points in the Australian Football League (AFL) grand final. The win gave the Bombers their 16th *premiership* (championship), tying the Carlton Blues' record. The premiership was coach Kevin Sheedy's fourth.

The Bombers had already gained a place in the record books with 24 wins during the 2000 season. The team's single defeat at the hands of the Western Bulldogs prevented them from becoming the first team in history to make a clean sweep. The Bombers scored 19 goals and 21 behinds for a total of 135 points. The young Melbourne side managed only 11 goals and 9 behinds, totaling 75 points. The Bombers' James Hird won the Norm Smith medal for the best player on the ground. Melbourne's Shane Woewodin took the coveted Brownlow Medal for the best and fairest player of the season.

Local premierships. In South Australia, Central Districts beat Eagles 8.13 (61) to 5.9 (39). In Western Australia, East Perth 18.11 (119) defeated East Fremantle 11.14 (80). In Tasmania, Clarence defeated Northern Bombers 15.15 (105) to 8.8 (56) to win the Statewide League.

□ Brian Kennedy

Austria

endured political turmoil through much of 2000 as the inclusion of the far-right Freedom Party in a new government proved divisive at home and prompted the European Union (EU) to impose diplomatic sanctions. The difficulties grew out of the inconclusive election of October 1999. In that election, the Freedom Party finished second and the governing Social Democratic Party and conservative People's Party suffered a significant drop in support.

New government. After months of negotiations failed to revive the previous coalition, People's Party leader Wolfgang Schuessel agreed to form a government with the Freedom Party. The decision was controversial because of remarks Freedom Party leader Joerg Haider had made in the past, defending Nazi Germany's labor policies as "sound." The Freedom Party's anti-immigrant stance and its opposition to EU expansion into Eastern Europe also alarmed Austria's European partners.

Austria's President, Thomas Klestil, swore in the new government led by Schuessel as chancellor on Feb. 4, 2000, but only after Schuessel and Haider pledged to fight *xenophobia* (hatred or fear of foreigners), racism, and anti-Semitism. Haider did not serve in the government in 2000.

EU sanctions. The EU imposed sanctions that barred any bilateral political meetings between

More than 100,000 Austrians protest in the streets of Vienna in February 2000 after the conservative People's Party formed a coalition government with the far right Freedom Party.

EU governments and Austrian ministers and downgraded the role of Austrian ambassadors in EU capitals. To defuse the opposition, Schuessel said the government would compensate people who were forced to perform slave labor in Austrian factories during World War II (1939-1945). In 1938, German troops seized Austria, which then became part of Nazi Germany. In May 2000, the government agreed to pay $400 million to an estimated 150,000 surviving laborers.

The government also presented plans to cut taxes and speed up the sale of government-owned companies. The policies reflected the Freedom Party's economic positions. The party claimed that decades of rule by the Social Democrats and the People's Party had stifled Austria with heavy bureaucracy and high taxes.

Sanctions lifted. Opposition to the EU sanctions grew in Europe during 2000, particularly among smaller EU countries that resented the EU's interference in the domestic politics of a member nation. EU countries also feared Austria could block agreement on constitutional changes in the EU if the sanctions stayed in place. On September 12, the EU lifted the sanctions after a panel of experts reported that the Austrian government had respected human rights and democracy.   □ Tom Buerkle

See also **Europe**.

Automobile industry analysts in late 2000 predicted that the sales of light trucks and cars in the United States were on a pace to break the record of 16.9 million vehicles set in 1999. By the end of September 2000, sales of new vehicles totaled 13.5 million, compared with 12.9 million vehicles for the same period in 1999. For the first nine months of 2000, motorists increasingly favored pickup trucks, sport utility vehicles (SUV's), and minivans, as sales of light trucks rose to 6.5 million units—an increase of 6 percent over the same period in 1999. Analysts reported that through the end of September 2000, the sales of cars rose to 7 million units, 4 percent more than in the first nine months of 1999.

Top sellers in the United States remained unchanged in 2000 from the previous year. Toyota and Ford again outsold other manufacturers. For the 2000 model year, Toyota Camry sales reached more than 425,000 units. Ford held the light-truck title with its 2000 F-series truck, which sold more than 897,000 units in 2000.

Shifting sales trend. Strong competition between automobile makers continued during 2000 with Asian and European manufacturers whittling away at U.S. market share. Officials at Ford Motor Company of Dearborn, Michigan, General Motors Corporation (GM) of Detroit, and the U.S. division of DaimlerChrysler AG of Germany

watched their total market share drop to 67.3 percent through September 2000, marginally better compared with the 70.2 percent drop sustained during the same period in 1999.

Meanwhile, the sales of Asian and European car models in the United States rose to 32.7 percent of the market in the first nine months of 2000, compared with 29.8 percent in the same period in 1999. Top sellers from Asia included Honda with a market share of 6.7 percent, Toyota with 9.1 percent market share, and Germany's Volkswagen with a 2.5-percent market share.

Domestic auto companies. Ford's sales through September 2000 totaled 3.3 million units, 3.2 percent ahead of the same period in 1999. The increase came with the help of better sales of the F-series pickup truck, Taurus, and Explorer. Despite the increase, the automaker's overall market share dropped to 24.2 percent.

During 2000, Ford continued to expand its purchase of overseas companies. In June, Ford purchased Land Rover from BMW AG of Germany for $2.7 billion. Through September, Ford's net income totaled $2.4 billion, compared with $5.4 billion for the same period in 1999.

GM's sales increased 0.7 percent to 3.8 million units sold through the end of September 2000. Analysts credited the increase in part to better sales of the company's Pontiac Bonneville and Chevrolet Silverado pickup truck. However, GM's market share fell 28.4 percent in the first nine months of 2000 compared with 29.7 percent for the same period in 1999. The company's net income was reported at $4.4 billion for the first three quarters of 2000 compared with $4.8 billion for the same period in 1999.

On December 12, GM announced plans to phase out the Oldsmobile, a brand that has been in existence for 103 years. GM also planned to eliminate more than 9,000 jobs, including 6,600 white-collar positions. Between 1980 and 2000, the Oldsmobile's U.S. market share had dropped from 7.3 percent to 1. 6 percent.

In March 2000, GM officials announced a deal with the Italian automobile manufacturer Fiat SpA. Under the agreement, GM acquired 20 percent of Fiat's automotive branch while Fiat received a 5.6 percent stake in GM. Although the two companies continued to compete for customers, they cooperated in some areas such as purchasing and technology. Officials from both companies reported that the agreement would save billions of dollars.

The U.S. brands of German car manufacturer DaimlerChrysler were not, for the most part, highly successful in 2000. Through September, DaimlerChrysler reported that sales were off 2.5 percent compared with the 2 million units sold in 1999. The group's market share also declined to

Distinctive new cars of 2000 included hybrid vehicles combining gasoline engines with electric motors and the uniquely designed PT Cruiser by Chrysler.

The 2000 Honda Insight (above) combines a 63-horsepower, 3-cylinder internal combustion engine and a 7-horsepower battery-powered electric motor to enhance fuel performance and pollution control.

Chrysler introduced the PT Cruiser (below), a combination minivan and sedan, in 2000. The car, inspired by automobile stylings of the 1930's and 1940's, proved so successful that buyers waited several months for delivery.

The Toyota Prius (right) also offered consumers a cleaner-running and more efficient car with a 1.5-liter, 58-horsepower internal combustion engine coupled with a 30-horsepower electric motor powered by a battery.

14.6 percent for the first nine months of 2000. Although sales of the Jeep Cherokee and Dodge Ram were down, the company managed to find a huge success with the Chrysler PT Cruiser. Buyers faced a lengthy waiting period for their PT Cruisers to be delivered. By the end of September, DaimlerChrysler's net income rose to $5.7 billion.

In March, DaimlerChrysler agreed to take a 34 percent equity in Mitsubishi Motors of Japan and later agreed to take a 10-percent stake in the Hyundai Motor Company of South Korea.

Massive tire recall. In August 2000, officials from Bridgestone/Firestone Inc., a Japanese-owned tire company located in Nashville, Tennessee, announced a recall of 6.5 million tires. The tires were installed as original equipment on light trucks and SUV's, including the Ford Explorer and the Ford Ranger.

Federal safety officials investigated the tires and reported that they could shred at high or low speeds. Officials said that the tires may have caused accidents that resulted in more than 100 deaths. Officials did not know what caused the tires to separate. In September, Jacques A. Nasser, Ford's president and chief executive officer, testified before a Congressional hearing that the company had taken steps to replace defective tires and would work with the tire industry to develop an early warning system to spot tire defects.

Hybrid vehicles. Both Honda and Toyota offered motorists mass-produced hybrid vehicles in 2000. The Honda Insight and Toyota Prius combined gasoline-powered engines with battery-powered electric motors to create more fuel-efficient cars. The electric motor enhanced the performance of the gasoline engine, which enabled it to get more miles out of each gallon of gas. The gasoline engine recharged the electric motor's battery, which eliminated the need to plug the battery into an electrical outlet to recharge it.

Manufacturers also said that the electric motors emitted no pollutants, unlike gasoline-powered engines. The Insight averaged 70 miles (113 kilometers) per gallon. The Prius averaged 52 miles (84 kilometers) per gallon.

Airbag safety. In May, the National Highway Traffic Safety Administration (NHTSA) announced new airbag safety standards designed to better protect children and small adults. The NHTSA sets and enforces safety requirements for automobiles and related products. The new regulations overhauled the federal government's standards for airbag safety. Under the new guidelines, airbags must inflate in crash tests at 25 miles (40 kilometers) per hour. The new standards were to be phased in over three years, beginning with model-year 2004 vehicles.   □ Mike Casey

See also **Germany; Public health and safety.**

Automobile racing. The rivalry between the Indy Racing League (IRL) and the Championship Auto Racing Teams (CART) took a twist in 2000 when CART's 1999 champion, Juan Montoya of Colombia, won the IRL's highest-profile event, the Indianapolis 500, on May 28, 2000. The dispute between the organizations, which began in 1996 with the formation of the IRL, showed no signs of slowing in 2000, with the IRL announcing three new races for 2001.

Indianapolis 500. Juan Montoya on May 28, 2000, became only the seventh rookie to win the Indianapolis 500. Montoya took the lead on the 27th lap and, after a brief duel with Greg Ray, led for a total of 167 laps, losing the lead only for brief periods following pit stops. Montoya's team owner, Chip Ganassi, bought cars equipped for IRL competition in order to make the first appearance at the Indy 500 by a major CART team since 1995.

The 2000 Indianapolis 500 also featured two women drivers for the first time in the race's history. In the 74th lap, the two women—53-year-old veteran Lyn St. James and 19-year-old rookie Sarah Fisher—collided. Neither of the women was seriously injured.

NASCAR. Tragedy plagued the NASCAR circuit in 2000. NASCAR's first family, the Pettys, lost both their patriarch and their hope for the future. Lee Petty, 86, a NASCAR pioneer who had won 55 races during his long career and who was the father of Richard Petty, NASCAR's all-time winningest driver, died on April 5 of complications from a stomach aneurysm. On May 12, Adam Petty, 19, grandson of Richard Petty, died of head injuries after crashing into a concrete wall at New Hampshire International Speedway in Louden while taking practice laps for the Busch 200 race.

On July 7, driver Kenny Irwin, 30, died in a crash at the same track, just yards from where Adam Petty had died two months earlier.

Bobby Labonte took the NASCAR Winston Cup Series Championship on November 20 when he finished fifth at the NAPA 500, the final race of the season, at the Atlanta Motor Speedway in Atlanta. Dale Earnhardt, Jr., finished in second place and Jeff Burton in third.

IRL. Buddy Lazier took the IRL Championship after finishing fourth in the Excite 500 at Texas Motor Speedway in Fort Worth, Texas, on October 16. Lazier, who only needed to finish 14th or better in the last race of the IRL season to win the championship, completed the race ahead of Scott Goodyear and Eddie Cheever.

CART. Gil de Ferran of Brazil took the 2000 CART series championship with 168 points. He won 2 of the 20 races held in the United States, Canada, Australia, Brazil, and Japan. De Ferran managed to finish among the top five in six of the last eight races of the season. He won the title on October 30 by taking third at the rain-delayed Marlboro 500 at the California Speedway in Fontana, California.

Formula One. Michael Schumacher of Germany won the world driver's title in 2000, taking 9 races on the 17-race Formula One circuit. He clinched the title with 108 points.

Endurance. In the Rolex 24-hour race held February 6 in Daytona, Florida, a Dodge Viper fielded by the French Oreca team overtook the defending champions, the Dyson Racing Riley & Scott Mark III-Ford, two hours from the end of the race to win. The Viper, shared by drivers Karl Wendlinger, Olivier Beretta, and Dominique Dupuy, won by just 30.879 seconds after completing 2,574 miles (4,142 kilometers), the closest finish in the race's history. On June 18, Audi dominated the Le Mans 24 Hours, taking the top three spots. The team of Frank Biela of Germany, Tom Kristensen of Denmark, and Emmanuele Piro of Italy averaged 128.34 miles (206.54 kilometers) per hour to win the race.

Dragsters. The National Hot Rod Association sponsored a 24-race series in 2000, with Gary Scelzi champion in the top fuel division, John Force in the funny car division, and Kurt Johnson in the pro stock division.   □ Michael Kates

Aviation. Labor disputes, poor weather, and air traffic control problems contributed to numerous flight cancellations and delays throughout 2000, leading to greater oversight of the airline industry by the U.S. government.

Passengers flying with United Airlines of Elk Grove Village, Illinois, endured many delays and cancellations through much of the summer because of labor disputes, including the United pilots' refusal to fly overtime. United's contract with its pilots expired on April 12. The dispute ended in August, but only after U.S. Secretary of Transportation Rodney E. Slater described United as the "poster child for what is wrong" with the airline industry. United countered that the government-owned air traffic control system was antiquated and caused delays.

Members of Congress held hearings in September to investigate the flight cancellation problem. Secretary Slater later informed airline officials that a task force would begin monitoring their performance. In November, the task force, composed of representatives from the government, the airline industry, labor unions, and consumer-advocacy groups, unveiled a program that required U.S. carriers to explain the cause of delayed or canceled flights to the general public.

Federal Aviation Authority. President Bill Clinton issued an executive order on December 7

Jerry Nadeau drives to victory in the NAPA 500 final at the Atlanta Motor Speedway on Nov. 20, 2000. While Nadeau won the race, Bobby Labonte, who finished fifth, ended the race as the NASCAR Winston Cup champion.

splitting the Federal Aviation Authority (FAA) into two parts, one to manage air traffic control and another to oversee safety and enforce regulations. A chief operating officer was to lead the air traffic segment with the guidance of a board of directors. The president also suggested a new pricing structure for airline tickets to discourage individuals from flying during peak hours.

The Concorde. The future of supersonic passenger air travel was struck a hard blow on July 25, when an Air France Concorde jet crashed near Paris. The crash, which left all 109 passengers and crew members and 4 people on the ground dead, occurred shortly after takeoff. A strip of metal on the runway caused one of the plane's tires to burst, according to investigators. Tire fragments punctured a fuel tank in the wing, and the leaking fuel ignited.

Officials at Air France immediately withdrew the airline's five Concordes from service. British Airways, the other operator of supersonic jets, grounded its Concordes after British government regulators revoked the aircraft's safety license in August. Many aviation experts suggested that modifying the design of the Concorde to reduce the danger of such crashes could prove so expensive that the jet may never fly again. The Concorde is the only passenger aircraft that flies at a greater velocity than the speed of sound, approximately 760 miles (1,225 kilometers) per hour.

Airline mergers. On May 23, UAL Corp. of Elk Grove Village, Illinois, parent company of United Airlines, made an offer to buy US Airways of Arlington, Virginia. In an effort to appease regulators, UAL proposed to sell certain of the company's operations to Robert L. Johnson, chairman and chief executive of Black Entertainment Television. Johnson planned to develop the first major airline owned by an African American.

In January, Montreal-based Air Canada purchased Canada's only other major carrier, Calgary-based Canadian Airlines, for $63 million. To compete with Air Canada, Royal Airlines, previously a charter carrier out of Montreal, launched regular service on some of Air Canada's main routes in September.

Airbus, a European-based manufacturer of passenger jets, announced a corporate change in June. Three Airbus partners—Aerospatiale Matra of France, DaimlerChrysler Aerospace (Dasa) of Germany, and state-owned Construcciones Aeronauticas (Casa) of Spain—merged to form the European Aeronautic Defense and Space Company (EADS), which controlled 80 percent of Airbus. The original consortium's fourth partner, BAE Systems of Great Britain, owned 20 percent of the company. EADS officials issued shares to the public in July. Airbus simultaneously announced that they planned to go ahead with construction of the proposed 550-seat, twin deck A3XX jet.

The chief rival of Airbus, the Boeing Company of Seattle, Washington, responded that it planned to build a stretched version of its successful 747-400 aircraft, to be called the 747-X. Boeing had dominated the large jet market since the 1970's.

Crash investigation. A Boeing MD83 operated by Alaska Airlines of Seattle plunged into the Pacific Ocean off southern California on Jan. 31, 2000, killing all 88 people aboard. The National Transportation Safety Board (NTSB), an independent government agency that investigates civil aviation accidents in the United States, concluded that the most likely cause of the accident was a mechanical malfunction of the stabilizer on the tail, which controls the movement of an aircraft's nose. In February, the Federal Aviation Administration (FAA) ordered all U.S. airlines to inspect similar aircraft. Some airlines found wear and damage to the plane's jack-screws, long rods in the tail that drive a plane's horizontal stabilizers and help control the up-and-down direction of a plane. The FAA had been investigating allegedly falsified maintenance and repair records at Alaska Airline's maintenance base in Oakland, California, since 1998.　　　　□ Ian Savage

See also **France; Labor and employment; Transportation.**

Azerbaijan. President Heydar Aliyev's New Azerbaijan Party (NAP) won a majority in parliamentary elections on Nov. 5, 2000. With the victory, Aliyev's son, Ilham, who topped the candidate list, was poised to become speaker of the new parliament. Many observers also mentioned Ilham as a likely successor to his father, who underwent heart surgery in 1999.

In early August 2000, Azerbaijan's two main opposition parties—the Azerbaijan Popular Front and the Muslim Democratic Party, also known as Musavat—joined an alliance of other parties to contest the NAP in the parliamentary elections. Popular Front leader Ebulfez Elcibey, whom Aliyev ousted from the presidency in 1993, died on Aug. 22, 2000. By September, the alliance disintegrated because of internal rivalries.

Negotiations over a permanent peace treaty with Armenia remained stalled for most of 2000. Armenian troops continued to occupy 20 percent of Azerbaijan's territory, including the Armenian enclave of Nagorno-Karabakh. In November, diplomats from the United States tried to renew negotiations in the wake of Aliyev's parliamentary victory.　　　　□ Steven L. Solnick

See also **Asia.**

Bahamas. See West Indies.
Bahrain. See Middle East.
Ballet. See Dance.

Hundreds of rickshaw drivers defy a general strike on February 16 and remain on the streets of Dhaka, capital of Bangladesh. The drivers' refusal to strike handicapped Bangladesh's opposition leaders, who called more than 60 such strikes, attempting to retake control of the government.

Bangladesh. The World Health Organization, a United Nations affiliate in Geneva, Switzerland, reported on Sept. 8, 2000, that Bangladesh faced the largest mass poisoning of a population in history. At least 7,000 people had died since 1990 from ingesting arsenic, which occurred naturally in groundwater seeping into wells.

Nearly 5 million wells were dug in Bangladesh between 1971 and 2000 to reduce the use of surface water carrying disease-causing germs. With aid from the World Bank, a UN agency that loans money to countries for development, and UNICEF, a UN agency that aids children, officials stored uncontaminated rain water and treated pond water to improve the water supply.

River flooding in Bangladesh in September killed more than 130 people and displaced more than 1 million people. Coastal storms on August 29 left some 60,000 others homeless on Sandwip Island, southeast of the capital, Dhaka.

Politicians called general strikes throughout 2000 in an effort to oust Prime Minister Hasina Wajed. Wajed had used strikes to force the elections in 1996 that defeated Prime Minister Khaleda Ziaur Rahman. Between 1996 and late 2000, more than 60 general strikes shut down nearly all urban activity in Bangladesh, causing the economy to suffer. □ Henry S. Bradsher

See also **Asia; India.**

Bank. Two of the oldest and most influential banks in the United States merged on Sept. 12, 2000, in the largest banking transaction of the year. Chase Manhattan Corporation of New York City acquired J.P. Morgan & Company, Incorporated, also of New York City, for more than $30 billion. J.P. Morgan traced its history back to 1871 when it was founded by financier John Pierpont Morgan. The company halted a national panic in 1907 by loaning money to other banks to keep them from closing. Chase Manhattan Bank was formed in 1855 from the Manhattan Company, which was founded by Aaron Burr in 1799. David Rockefeller was the chief executive officer (CEO) of Chase Manhattan from 1969 to 1980.

According to the agreement between the boards of directors of the two companies, the former CEO of Chase, William Harrison, was appointed president and CEO of the new firm, J.P. Morgan Chase & Company. Former J.P. Morgan chairman and CEO Douglas A. Warner was appointed chairman of the new firm, which became the third-largest financial institution in the United States. With $660 billion in combined assets, J.P. Morgan Chase ranked only behind Citigroup of New York City, which had $800 billion in assets, and Bank of America Corporation of Charlotte, North Carolina, which had $680 billion in assets.

The J.P. Morgan-Chase merger was the latest in a rapidly consolidating industry. Just a decade earlier, in 1990, J.P. Morgan was the biggest bank in the United States focusing on investment banking—the buying and selling of securities. It served the wealthiest individuals in the United States. As other big banks merged, grew, and diversified, officials found that J.P. Morgan needed to grow as well.

Many financial and banking experts viewed the J.P. Morgan-Chase merger as further proof of the waning power of banks in the United States. In the 1980's and 1990's, corporations in the United States were more likely to raise capital by selling stock in their companies than by borrowing from banks. The Morgan-Chase merger in 2000 followed a trend of combining long-established U.S. financial institutions such as Travelers Insurance Group Incorporated and Citicorp, which merged in 1998.

Steep rate hike. The U.S. Federal Reserve System (the Fed), an independent government agency that oversees the U.S. banking system, on May 16, 2000, raised the *federal funds rate* (the rate the Fed's member banks charge one another for overnight loans) by one-half percentage point. Officials pushed the rate up to 6.5 percent. It was the first time since February 1995 that the Fed raised the federal funds rate by a half-point. The move in 2000 followed five one-quarter-point increases over the previous 11 months. Many people closely watch the Fed's actions on interest rates because the rates strongly influence stock exchanges and the broader economy.

Historically, the Fed has tended to raise interest rates when its officials feared that strong economic growth—when demand for goods, services, and employees is greater than supply—could lead to inflation, with prices rising steadily. Economic growth, as measured by the *gross domestic product* (the measure of all goods and services in a country in a given year) was 4.8 percent in the first quarter of 2000 and 5.6 percent in the second quarter. By the third quarter, economic growth was slower, estimated at 2.7 percent. The May interest rate increase was the last change in the Fed rate through November 2000.

Earnings. Strong economic growth in the United States made 2000 a profitable year for banks. According to the Federal Deposit Insurance Corporation (FDIC), a government agency that insures deposits at financial institutions in the United States, the more than 8,000 commercial banks in the United States reported $19.5 billion in net income in the first quarter of the year. In the second quarter, the industry reported earnings of $14.7 billion. The second quarter results were the lowest quarterly earnings since the second quarter of 1997, and banks set aside some of their earnings to hold against future losses.

The 1,600 savings and loans (S&L's) in the United States reported earnings of $2.9 billion in the first quarter of 2000—the second-highest quarterly earnings ever reported. In the second quarter of 2000, S&L's reported earnings of $2.8 billion. Earnings were lower primarily because of higher loan-loss provisions and expenses, the FDIC reported.

New regulations proposed. U.S. federal banking regulators proposed on November 3 to create simpler rules for how much capital noncomplex institutions should be required to hold. Noncomplex institutions are ones with assets of $5 billion or less that use depositors' funds to invest in simple assets, such as mortgages and small business loans, rather than outside financial instruments tied to stocks or interest rate changes.

In a joint statement, the Board of Governors of the Fed, the Comptroller of the Currency, the FDIC, and the Office of Thrift Supervision announced they had concluded that many community institutions would benefit from a simpler capital framework, which would relieve some of the burden of complying with complicated regulations made for larger, more complex institutions. The announcement reflected a growing movement among government officials toward a split regulatory system that would ease burdens on smaller institutions. Such institutions invest in less risky assets. The regulations would concentrate resources on large banks, which have complex operations.

Insurance increase proposed. FDIC officials proposed in August to increase insurance coverage for deposits in banks and S&L's in the United States. Starting in 1980, depositors were covered up to $100,000. If an institution failed, the U.S. government made certain that depositors could receive up to $100,000. From 1974 to 1980, the coverage limit was $40,000.

FDIC Chairwoman Donna Tanoue noted in 2000 that inflation since 1980 had cut the value of the $100,000 coverage limit in half. Banking officials lobbied for a higher limit, but some government banking officials, including Senate Banking Committee Chairman Phil Gramm, FED Chairman Alan Greenspan, and Treasury Secretary Lawrence Summers, opposed the proposal as adding unnecessary risk to the financial system. In the 1980's, many banks and especially S&L's used depositors' funds for risky investments. Several hundred institutions failed, and insurance payments cost billions of dollars. If FDIC coverage were extended it would expose the government—and U.S. taxpayers—to more losses. The FDIC said that it would send insurance proposals to Congress in 2001. □ Paulette Thomas

See also **Economics.**

Baseball. The first World Series between two New York City teams since 1956 capped an exciting 2000 baseball season. In the series, the New York Yankees crushed the New York Mets, taking their third straight World Series crown and their fourth in five years. However, despite the excitement in the New York area over the well-publicized *subway series* (between teams located in the same city), the matchup garnered the lowest television ratings in World Series history. The home-run race, which had captivated many baseball fans during the 1998 and 1999 seasons, sputtered in July 2000 when Mark McGwire, the major league single-season home-run record holder, was sidelined with tendinitis in his right knee.

Regular season. The Chicago White Sox stunned fans in 2000 by jumping out to a double-digit lead over the Cleveland Indians, a perennial powerhouse in the American League (AL) Central Division. The Sox had taken a 10-game lead by the All-Star break in mid-July. The team flirted with the best record in baseball for much of the summer but played only slightly better than .500 baseball in the second half. Despite the downturn, the Sox took the Central Division title.

The Yankees struggled during the regular season, limping into the play-offs after losing 14 of their last 17 games. However, the Yankees still managed to win the AL East Division crown with a record of 87-74, the worst among playoff qualifiers. The results of the AL West Division race were in question until the final day of the regular season, when the Oakland Athletics slipped past the Seattle Mariners by a half game to win the division. Seattle earned a wild-card berth.

In the National League (NL), the Atlanta Braves edged the New York Mets for the NL East Division title, but the Mets still qualified for the play-offs as a wild card. The St. Louis Cardinals romped to the NL Central Division title, ending the regular season 10 games ahead of the Cincinnati Reds. The San Francisco Giants posted the best record in baseball (97-65) on their way to winning the NL West Division title.

Play-offs. The Yankees struggled against the Athletics in the first round of the AL Division Series play-offs but survived with a 7-5 victory in Game 5 to win the series 3 games to 2. The Mariners swept the White Sox in three games but could not keep up with the Yankees in the AL championship series. After losing the first game at home, the Yankees won the series 4 games to 2. In the NL division series, the Cardinals swept the Braves three games to none while the Mets defeated the Giants 3 games to 1. In the NL championship series, the Mets easily defeated the Cardinals 4 games to 1 to win the pennant.

The 2000 World Series. The World Series was a hard-fought, exciting affair in 2000, with three games decided by just one run and the rest decided by two runs. The Yankees won the first two games against the Mets to extend their World Series winning streak, dating back to the 1996 series, to a record 14 games. The Mets won Game 3, but the Yankees took Game 4 by a score of 3-2, thanks to great relief pitching by Mariano Rivera. The Yankees won Game 5 by a score of 4-2 after scoring two runs in the top of the ninth inning on a single by Luis Sojo.

Yankee shortstop Derek Jeter won the World Series Most Valuable Player award, batting .409, slugging two home runs, and driving in two runs. Jeter set a five-game World Series record with 19 total bases.

Television ratings for the 2000 World Series were the lowest in history, 12 percent below the previously lowest-rated World Series, in 1998. Game 1 lasted 4 hours, 51 minutes, the longest series game on record. The previous record of 4 hours, 17 minutes was set on Oct. 23, 1996, when the Yankees defeated the Atlanta Braves.

Transactions. The Chicago Cubs placed slugger Sammy Sosa on the trading block in June 2000, and many teams with play-off hopes expressed interest in acquiring the 31-year-old outfielder. The Yankees appeared to be the team with the most interest but did not consummate the trade because they believed the Cubs were asking for too much in return. The Yankees then traded for outfielder David Justice of the Cleveland Indians on June 29. Sosa and his agents declared in early July that Sosa would reject any proposed trade. This option was available to Sosa because he had been in the major leagues for 10 years and with the same team for 5 years.

In December 2000, star shortstop Alex Rodrigues signed a $252-million, 10-year contract with the Texas Rangers.

Home-run race. On May 24, Mark McGwire, of the St. Louis Cardinals, hit his 30th home run of the 2000 season, achieving that mark at an earlier point in the season than any player in history. However, a sore knee sidelined him in early July, when he was leading the major leagues with 30 home runs. He played only sparingly the rest of the season.

Sammy Sosa crushed the competition in the All-Star home-run contest held on July 10, hitting 26 homers in 56 swings. Sosa continued his power-hitting in the second half of the season, joining Mark McGwire as the only players in history to hit 50 or more home runs in three straight seasons. Sosa finished the season leading the major leagues with 50 home runs, one more than San Francisco's Barry Bonds.

Hall of Fame. Carlton Fisk, Tony Perez, and Sparky Anderson were inducted into the Baseball Hall of Fame on July 23. Fisk caught a record

BASEBALL

Fans gather outside Enron Field, the new home of the Houston Astros (left). The stadium, which opened on March 30, 2000, featured a roof that could be retracted in less than 20 minutes.

Detroit Tiger fans ride the new carousel on opening day—April 11, 2000—at the team's stadium, Comerica Park, in Detroit (below). The $290-million facility replaced Tiger Stadium, which had been the oldest stadium in the major leagues.

Three new ballparks open for the beginning of the 2000 baseball season.

Boaters wait outside Pacific Bell Park for a homer to be hit into San Francisco Bay (bottom). On April 11, 2000, the San Francisco Giants played their first home game in the new $319-million stadium.

Final standings in Major League Baseball

American League

American League champions—
New York Yankees (defeated Seattle Mariners, 4 games to 2)
World Series champions—
New York Yankees (defeated New York Mets, 4 games to 1)

Eastern Division	W.	L.	Pct.	G.B.
New York Yankees	87	74	.540	—
Boston Red Sox	85	77	.525	2½
Toronto Blue Jays	83	79	.512	4½
Baltimore Orioles	74	88	.457	13½
Tampa Bay Devil Rays	69	92	.429	18

Central Division	W.	L.	Pct.	G.B.
Chicago White Sox	95	67	.586	—
Cleveland Indians	90	72	.556	5
Detroit Tigers	79	83	.488	16
Kansas City Royals	77	85	.475	18
Minnesota Twins	69	93	.426	26

Western Division	W.	L.	Pct.	G.B.
Oakland Athletics	91	70	.565	—
Seattle Mariners*	91	71	.562	½
Anaheim Angels	82	80	.506	9½
Texas Rangers	71	91	.438	20½

Offensive leaders

Batting average	Nomar Garciaparra, Boston	.372
Runs scored	Johnny Damon, Kansas City	136
Home runs	Troy Glaus, Anaheim	47
Runs batted in	Edgar Martinez, Seattle	145
Hits	Darin Erstad, Anaheim	240
Stolen bases	Johnny Damon, Kansas City	46
Slugging percentage	Manny Ramirez, Cleveland	.697

Leading pitchers

Games won	David Wells, Toronto; Tim Hudson, Oakland (tie)	20
Earned run average (162 or more innings)—		
	Pedro Martinez, Boston	1.74
Strikeouts	Pedro Martinez, Boston	284
Saves	Todd Jones, Detroit; Derek Lowe, Boston (tie)	42
Shut-outs	Pedro Martinez, Boston	4
Complete games	David Wells, Toronto	9

Awards†

Most Valuable Player	Jason Giambi, Oakland
Cy Young	Pedro Martinez, Boston
Rookie of the Year	Kazuhiro Sasaki, Seattle
Manager of the Year	Jerry Manuel, Chicago

National League

National League champions—
New York Mets (defeated St. Louis Cardinals, 4 games to 1)

Eastern Division	W.	L.	Pct.	G.B.
Atlanta Braves	95	67	.586	—
New York Mets*	94	68	.580	1
Florida Marlins	79	82	.491	15½
Montreal Expos	67	95	.414	28
Philadelphia Phillies	65	97	.401	30

Central Division	W.	L.	Pct.	G.B.
St. Louis Cardinals	95	67	.586	—
Cincinnati Reds	85	77	.525	10
Milwaukee Brewers	73	89	.451	22
Houston Astros	72	90	.444	23
Pittsburgh Pirates	69	93	.426	26
Chicago Cubs	65	97	.401	30

Western Division	W.	L.	Pct.	G.B.
San Francisco Giants	97	65	.599	—
Los Angeles Dodgers	86	76	.531	11
Arizona Diamondbacks	85	77	.525	12
Colorado Rockies	82	80	.506	15
San Diego Padres	76	86	.469	21

Offensive leaders

Batting average	Todd Helton, Colorado	.372
Runs scored	Jeff Bagwell, Houston	152
Home runs	Sammy Sosa, Chicago	50
Runs batted in	Todd Helton, Colorado	147
Hits	Todd Helton, Colorado	216
Stolen bases	Luis Castillo, Florida	62
Slugging percentage	Todd Helton, Colorado	.698

Leading pitchers

Games won	Tom Glavine, Atlanta	21
Earned run average (162 or more innings)—		
	Kevin K. Brown, Los Angeles	2.58
Strikeouts	Randy Johnson, Arizona	347
Saves	Antonio Alfonseca, Florida	45
Shut-outs	Greg Maddux, Atlanta; Randy Johnson, Arizona (tie)	3
Complete games	Randy Johnson, Arizona; Curt Schilling, Arizona (tie)	8

Awards†

Most Valuable Player	Jeff Kent, San Francisco
Cy Young	Randy Johnson, Arizona
Rookie of the Year	Rafael Furcal, Atlanta
Manager of the Year	Dusty Baker, San Francisco

*Qualified for wild-card play-off spot.
†Selected by the Baseball Writers Association of America.

2,226 games for the Boston Red Sox and the White Sox, hitting 351 home runs, a record for catchers. Perez, formerly with the Cincinnati Reds, batted .279 with 2,723 hits, 379 home runs, and 1,652 RBI's (18th on the all-time list) in his 23-year career. Anderson totaled 2,194 wins in 26 years as a manager, including nine seasons and two World Series championships with the Reds. Two other former players were selected for the Hall of Fame. Former Cincinnati Reds infielder Bid McPhee, one of the last second basemen to play bare-handed, was selected from a category for players and personnel from the 1800's. Power-hit- ting outfielder Norman "Turkey" Stearnes was selected from the Negro League, a black league that existed until the 1950's.

Colleges. Louisiana State University at Baton Rouge beat Stanford University at Stanford, California, 6-5 on June 17, 2000, in Omaha, Nebraska, to take its fifth college championship since 1991.

Youth. A team from Maracaibo, Venezuela, defeated a team from Bellaire, Texas, 3-2, on Aug. 26, 2000, in Williamsport, Pennsylvania, to win the Little League World Series title. The championship was Latin America's fifth overall and the second in six years.   □ Michael Kates

Basketball. The Los Angeles Lakers won the 2000 National Basketball Association (NBA) championship under the leadership of Phil Jackson, who had coached the Chicago Bulls to six NBA titles in the 1990's. In college basketball, the Michigan State Spartans won their first National Collegiate Athletic Association (NCAA) championship since 1979. In women's professional basketball, the Houston Comets remained the only team to ever win the title in the four-year-old Women's National Basketball Association (WNBA). In women's college basketball, the University of Connecticut (UConn) took the NCAA crown, which it had last won in 1995. The biggest story off the court in college basketball was the dismissal of Indiana University's legendary and controversial coach, Bob Knight, in September 2000.

Professional men. The Los Angeles Lakers dominated the regular season in the NBA, posting a 67-15 record under Jackson, who had taken a year off after leaving the Chicago Bulls in 1998. Jackson was able to mesh the various egos and talents on what had been a consistently underachieving Lakers team to finish eight games ahead of the Portland Trailblazers in the Western Conference chase.

Despite the Lakers' overpowering regular-season success, the team was less than impressive in the first round of the NBA play-offs, barely surviving the challenge from the eighth-seeded Sacramento Kings. Sacramento won the third and fourth games of the series, forcing a deciding fifth game. Los Angeles won that contest by 27 points, taking the series 3 games to 2. After dispatching the Phoenix Suns 4 games to 1, the Lakers battled the Trail Blazers, who were led by forward Scottie Pippen. Pippen had played for Jackson during his time in Chicago. Portland won games 5 and 6 to tie the series at three games each. In the final game, the Lakers managed to erase a 15-point deficit in the fourth quarter, coming back to win the deciding game 89-84 to take the series.

In the championship, the Lakers faced the Indiana Pacers, coached by NBA Hall-of-Famer Larry Bird. The Lakers took a 2-games-to-1 lead and went on to take the final series 4 games to 2. The Lakers captured the championship in game 6 on June 19. Shaquille O'Neal scored 41 points in the 116-111 win. His average of 38 points and 16.7 rebounds per game in the series earned him the Finals Most Valuable Player (MVP) trophy by unanimous vote.

O'Neal collected 120 of 121 first-place votes to capture the regular season MVP award with the most votes given to one player since the media began voting on the award in 1980-1981. Seattle Supersonics guard Gary Payton, Phoenix Suns guard Jason Kidd, Minnesota Timberwolves for-

---

The 1999-2000 college basketball season

College tournament champions

NCAA	(Men)	Division I:	Michigan State
		Division II:	Metro State (Colorado)
		Division III:	Calvin College (Michigan)
	(Women)	Division I:	Connecticut
		Division II:	Northern Kentucky
		Division III:	Washington (Missouri)
NAIA	(Men)	Division I:	Life (Ga.)
		Division II:	Embry-Riddle (Fla.)
	(Women)	Division I:	Oklahoma City
		Division II:	University of Mary (N.D.)
NIT	(Men)	Wake Forest (North Carolina)	

Men's college champions

Conference	School
America East	Hofstra*
Atlantic Coast	Duke*
Atlantic Ten	
Eastern Division	Temple*
Western Division	Dayton
Big East	Syracuse–Miami (Fla.) (tie)
	St. John's (tournament)
Big Sky	Montana–Eastern Washington (tie)
	Northern Arizona (tournament)
Big South	Radford
	Winthrop (tournament)
Big Ten	Michigan State*–Ohio State (tie)
Big Twelve	Iowa State*
Big West	
Eastern Division	Utah State*
Western Division	Long Beach State (California)
Colonial	James Madison–George Mason (tie)
	UNC Wilmington (tournament)
Conference USA	Cincinnati
	Saint Louis (tournament)
American Division	Cincinnati
National Division	Tulane–South Florida (tie)
Ivy League	Pennsylvania†
Metro Atlantic	Siena
	Iona (tournament)
Mid-American	
East Division	Bowling Green
West Division	Ball State (Ind.)*–Toledo (tie)
Mid-Continent	Oakland
	Valparaiso (tournament)
Mid-Eastern	S. Carolina State*
Midwestern	Butler*
Missouri Valley	Indiana State
	Creighton (tournament)
Mountain West	UNLV*–Utah (tie)
Northeast	Central Connecticut State*
Ohio Valley	SE Missouri St.*–Murray St. (tie)
Pacific Ten	Stanford†–Arizona (tie)
Patriot League	Lafayette*–Navy (tie)
Southeastern	Arkansas (tournament)
Eastern Division	Tennessee–Kentucky–Florida (tie)
Western Division	LSU
Southern	
North Division	Appalachian State*
South Division	College of Charleston
Southland	Sam Houston
	Lamar (tournament)
Southwestern	Alcorn State
	Jackson State (tournament)
Sun Belt	Louisiana–Lafayette*–S. Alabama (tie)
Trans America	Troy State–Georgia State (tie)
	Samford (tournament)
West Coast	Pepperdine
	Gonzaga (tournament)
Western Athletic	Tulsa
	Fresno State (tournament)

*Regular season and conference tournament champion.
†No tournament played.
Sources: National Collegiate Athletic Association (NCAA);
National Association of Intercollegiate Athletics (NAIA);
National Invitation Tournament (NIT).

Los Angeles Lakers head coach Phil Jackson speaks to fans during a rally celebrating the Lakers winning of the 2000 NBA Championship. Jackson led Los Angeles to the title after coaching the Chicago Bulls to six NBA championships in the 1990's.

National Basketball Association standings

Eastern Conference

Atlantic Division	W.	L.	Pct.	G.B.
Miami Heat*	52	30	.634	—
New York Knicks*	50	32	.610	2
Philadelphia 76ers*	49	33	.598	3
Orlando Magic	41	41	.500	11
Boston Celtics	35	47	.427	17
New Jersey Nets	31	51	.378	21
Washington Wizards	29	53	.354	23

Central Division	W.	L.	Pct.	G.B.
Indiana Pacers*	56	26	.683	—
Charlotte Hornets*	49	33	.598	7
Toronto Raptors*	45	37	.610	11
Detroit Pistons*	42	40	.512	14
Milwaukee Bucks*	42	40	.512	14
Cleveland Cavaliers	32	50	.390	24
Atlanta Hawks	28	54	.341	28
Chicago Bulls	17	65	.207	39

Western Conference

Midwest Division	W.	L.	Pct.	G.B.
Utah Jazz*	55	27	.671	—
San Antonio Spurs*	53	29	.646	2
Minnesota Timberwolves*	50	32	.610	5
Dallas Mavericks	40	42	.488	15
Denver Nuggets	35	47	.427	20
Houston Rockets	34	48	.415	21
Vancouver Grizzlies	22	60	.268	33

Pacific Division	W.	L.	Pct.	G.B.
Los Angeles Lakers*	67	15	.817	—
Portland Trail Blazers*	59	23	.720	8
Phoenix Suns*	53	29	.646	14
Seattle Supersonics*	45	37	.549	22
Sacramento Kings*	44	38	.537	23
Golden State Warriors	19	63	.232	48
Los Angeles Clippers	15	67	.183	52

Individual leaders

Scoring	G.	F.G.	F.T.	Pts.	Avg.
Shaquille O'Neal, L.A. Lakers	79	956	432	2,344	29.7
Allen Iverson, Philadelphia	70	729	442	1,989	28.4
Grant Hill, Orlando	74	696	480	1,906	25.8
Vince Carter, Toronto	82	788	436	2,107	25.7
Karl Malone, Utah	82	752	589	2,095	25.5
Chris Webber, Sacramento	75	748	311	1,834	24.5
Gary Payton, Seattle	82	747	311	1,982	24.2
Jerry Stackhouse, Detroit	82	619	618	1,939	23.6
Tim Duncan, San Antonio	74	628	459	1,716	23.2
Kevin Garnett, Minnesota	81	759	309	1,857	22.9

Rebounding	G.	Off.	Def.	Tot.	Avg.
Dikembe Mutombo, Atlanta	82	304	853	1,157	14.1
Shaquille O'Neal, L.A. Lakers	79	336	742	1,078	13.6
Tim Duncan, San Antonio	74	262	656	918	12.4
Kevin Garnett, Minnesota	81	223	733	956	11.8
Chris Webber, Sacramento	75	189	598	787	10.5
Shareef Abdur-Rahim, Vancouver	82	218	607	825	10.1
Elton Brand, Chicago	81	348	462	810	10.0
Dale Davis, Indiana	74	256	473	729	9.9
David Robinson, San Antonio	80	193	577	770	9.6
Jerome Williams, Detroit	82	277	512	789	9.6

NBA champions—Los Angeles Lakers (defeated Indiana Pacers, 4 games to 2)

*Made play-offs

ward Kevin Garnett, and San Antonio Spurs for-ward Tim Duncan joined O'Neal on the All-NBA first team. Miami Heat center Alonzo Mourning won the defensive player of the year award while the Orlando Magic's Doc Rivers won coach of the year honors. Chicago Bulls forward Elton Brand and Houston Rockets guard Steve Francis shared rookie of the year honors.

Professional women. The Houston Comets, led by league MVP Sheryl Swoopes, maintained their stranglehold on the WNBA title. Swoopes scored 31 points as the Comets won 79-73 on August 26 and swept the New York Liberty two games to none in the championship series. Swoopes also led the league in scoring and was named defensive player of the year. Former Los Angeles Laker star Michael Cooper won coach of the year honors for turning the Los Angeles Sparks into a threat for the WNBA title.

College men. The Michigan State Spartans, led by senior guard Mateen Cleaves, defeated the Florida Gators 89-76 on April 3 in Indianapolis to win the 1999-2000 NCAA men's tournament. The championship was Michigan State's first national men's title since 1979. Cleaves injured his ankle in the second half of the final game and hobbled off the floor with his team leading 50-44 with 16 minutes to play. Cleaves returned with 12 minutes to play and his team leading by 9 points. Cleaves finished with 18 points and secured Final Four MVP honors.

To advance into the final game, Michigan State (32-7), the top seed from the Midwest Regional, outlasted the Wisconsin Badgers (22-14). The Spartans defeated Wisconsin 53-41, holding the Badgers to the lowest point total in a Final Four match since the NCAA adopted the shot clock in 1986. Wisconsin, the eighth seed in the West, had gained its first Final Four berth since 1941 by stringing together impressive upsets, topping sixth-ranked Purdue in the regional final after beating top-seeded Arizona in the second round.

College women. UConn battered its way through its six opponents in the 64-team NCAA women's tournament in 2000. UConn won every game convincingly, the smallest margin of victory being a 15-point win over Louisiana State University in the Eastern Regional finals. In the championship game on April 2 in Philadelphia, UConn's defense overwhelmed Tennessee, the top seed from the Mideast Region in a 71-52 rout. UConn (35-1) held Tennessee to just 6 points in the first 12 minutes and led 32-19 at the half. With 15 minutes to play, the lead grew to 24 points. Tennessee, which had a regular season record of 33-4, was led by Tamika Catchings, women's NCAA player of the year. Catchings was hobbled by an ankle injury she suffered in the Mideast Regional

final against Texas Tech. Tennessee coach Pat Summitt made her 12th trip to the Final Four, tying legendary UCLA coach John Wooden's mark for most appearances by a coach.

UConn, the top seed in the East, earned its place in the final game by throttling Penn State in the national semifinals by 22 points. Penn State, the second seed in the Midwest Region, upset top-seeded Louisiana Tech in the regional final 86-65, snapping the Techsters 21-game winning streak. Tennessee, which defeated third-seeded Texas Tech by 13 to advance to the Final Four in the Mideast Regional final, edged Rutgers in the other national semifinal.

Knight dismissed. On September 10, Indiana University President Myles Brand dismissed men's basketball coach Bob Knight, a Hall-of-Fame coach who developed a large following of fans during his 29 years at the university. Brand said Knight had repeatedly violated a "zero-toler-ance" conduct policy established in May, after the university investigated allegations that Knight had physically and verbally abused players. Brand's announcement of Knight's dismissal came three days after Knight had allegedly held a 19-year-old Indiana freshman by the arm at Assembly Hall when the student addressed him in a manner Knight felt was disrespectful.

□ Michael Kates

Belarus. A parliamentary election on Oct. 15, 2000, produced a lopsided victory for President Aleksandr Lukashenko but failed to cleanse his reputation as the last remaining nondemocratic ruler in Europe. The Belarusian parliament had retained few powers under the constitutional reforms introduced in 1996. Opposition parties, whose leaders had faced arrest and severe harassment for years, boycotted the election in 2000. Election officials kept 200 additional candidates off the ballot. Officials for the United States denounced the elections and continued to recognize the Supreme Soviet, which had been disbanded by Lukashenko in 1996, as the legitimate parliament.

The Belarus economy continued to decline in 2000 with little or no reform of a system of central control by the state. More than 75 percent of Belarusian citizens lived below the poverty level in 2000, and inflation ran at close to 200 percent.

The economic crisis endangered implementation of the unification treaty signed with Russia in December 1999. In April 2000, newly elected Russian President Vladimir Putin visited Belarus and warned that political and military unification of the two countries could not go forward until Belarus restructured its economy.

□ Steven L. Solnick

See also **Europe; Russia.**

Belgium experienced a resurgence of extreme right-wing politics in 2000. The right-wing party Vlaams Blok, or Flemish Bloc, made significant gains in local elections in Antwerp, Belgium's second-largest city, in October. Vlaams Blok won 33 percent of the vote and 20 seats on the 55-seat city council, up from 28 percent and 18 seats in the previous election in 1994. The party increased its overall share of the vote from 7 percent in 1994 to more than 10 percent across Flanders, the northern region of Belgium. Vlaams Blok called for returning immigrants to their country of origin, contending that they were taking jobs from Belgians. The party also demanded independence for Flanders. Other major parties banded together, as they had in 1994, and agreed not to cooperate with Vlaams Blok, effectively freezing the party from power.

The parties in Belgium's coalition government —the Liberal Party of Prime Minister Guy Verhofstadt, the Socialist Party, and the Green Party— did well in local elections outside of Antwerp. The French and Flemish Christian Democratic parties, which were voted out of power at the national level in 1999 for the first time in 40 years, saw their share of the vote drop sharply. Concern about the extreme right prompted Verhofstadt's government to lead demands that the European Union impose diplomatic sanctions against Austria in February 2000, after the far-right Freedom Party joined that country's government.

Truckers' protest. Road traffic in Belgium, as well as much of the country's economic activity, came to a standstill for several days in September, as truckdrivers protested the high cost of diesel fuel. Joining in a protest that touched several other European countries, Belgian truckers blockaded main roads into Brussels, Antwerp, and Ghent and blocked traffic at the border with Germany. The truckers called off their protest after the government offered compensation worth around $90 million to offset high fuel prices.

Sabena. The Belgian government agreed on April 26 to allow the owner of Swissair to take majority control of Sabena SA, the Belgian airline. SAirGroup, the Swiss airline company that bought 49.5 percent of Sabena in 1995, wanted to increase its stake to gain complete operating control and take measures to restore profitability at Sabena. SAirGroup paid $345 million to increase its stake to 85 percent. The deal made Belgium the first European country to give up control of its national airline to a foreign carrier. The Belgian government received a 3 percent stake in SAirGroup as part of the deal. □ Tom Buerkle

See also Europe.

Belize. See Latin America.
Benin. See Africa.
Bhutan. See Asia.

Biology. The world's largest-known living organism is a fungus in the Malheur National Forest in eastern Oregon, scientists with the United States Forest Service reported in August 2000. The "humongous fungus," a tree-killing specimen called *Armillaria ostoyae*—popularly known as the honey mushroom—is approximately 3.5 miles (5.6 kilometers) across and extends into the ground about 3 feet (0.9 meter). The fungus is about 700 acres (283 hectares) larger than a specimen of *A. ostoyae* in Washington state that was previously identified as the largest organism.

The only signs of the fungus on the surface are clumps of small golden mushrooms that emerge from the ground every autumn. Beneath the surface, a web of threadlike filaments called a mycelium spreads from tree to tree, drawing water and nutrients. The scientists said the fungus is at least 2,400 years old.

Forest Service officials said that while they are seeking ways to control *A. ostoyae*, the fungus plays an important role in forest ecology. When trees that the fungus robs of nutrients die, gaps in forest cover are opened that can be filled in by other plant species. In addition, dead trees serve as shelter for many species of wild animals.

Old worms. Giant tubeworms at the bottom of the Gulf of Mexico live at least 250 years, making them the oldest-known individual *invertebrates* (animals without a backbone), researchers from Pennsylvania State University in University Park reported in February 2000. The worms live next to *cold seeps,* cracks in the ocean floor from which *hydrocarbons* (compounds of hydrogen and carbon) and other nutrients flow into the ocean. Discovered in the 1980's, the tubeworms, called *Lamellibrachia,* live in clusters of millions of worms covering several acres of ocean floor. Each worm grows up to 9.8 feet (3 meters) in length and is protected by a thin, flexible, shell-like tube.

Marine biologist Charles Fisher and his colleagues descended to the bottom of the Gulf of Mexico in a submarine and used the vehicle's robot arms to mark the tubes with a stain. The scientists returned regularly for four years to measure how much the tubes had grown. They concluded, based on the observed growth rate, that the worms require centuries to reach their mature length. Some colonies of coral live longer than the worms, but no other single invertebrate is known to survive for such a length of time.

Cold bacteria. Bacteria could be living and multiplying deep within the East Antarctic Ice Sheet, a large glacial area in eastern Antarctica, according to a February 2000 report by physicist Buford Price of the University of California at Berkeley. Price based his conclusion on an analysis of an ice *core* (cylindrical sample) drawn from

11,775 feet (3,590 meters) below Russia's Vostok Station. At that depth, the ice sample was only about 500 feet (150 meters) above Lake Vostok, a body of water that lies below the ice sheet. The finding suggested that the lake itself may contain living bacteria that have been isolated from the rest of life on Earth for roughly 1 million years—the last time the lake waters were in contact with the ocean or atmosphere.

The existence of bacteria in the ice core was reported in December 1999 by a team headed by biologist John Priscu of Montana State University in Bozeman. In later tests at the University of Hawaii in Honolulu, the bacteria reproduced in laboratory culture media. However, the scientists could not say whether the microbes had been reproducing or lying *dormant* (inactive) while in the frozen, low-nutrient conditions of Antarctica.

Price's analysis found a pattern of dissolved *ions* (electrically charged atoms) in the ice core that indicated that a network of water veins, each roughly the diameter of a human hair, permeated the ice. These ions, he said, could function like salt on an icy road, keeping the water in the veins in a liquid state. Price speculated that the bacteria could be living and reproducing in the liquid veins. Because of the extreme cold, he added, the bacteria's metabolism would be slowed to such an extent that they would need very few nutrients to survive. Researchers planned further investigation of the Lake Vostok area to learn more about the bacteria.

Oldest organism? In October 2000, Pennsylvania and Texas scientists reported reviving and growing a bacterium that had lain dormant in a salt crystal for 250 million years. If verified, the harmless microbe, which is related to modern *Bacillus* bacteria, would be, by far, the oldest living organism in the world.

Russel Vreeland of West Chester University in Pennsylvania explained that he and colleagues had found the dormant bacterium in a 250-million-year-old salt crystal from 1,850 feet (564 meters) below the New Mexico desert. The scientists placed the microbe in a laboratory culture, where it reproduced and multiplied. The researchers said they planned to compare the genetic material of the revived prehistoric bacterium to that of modern, related bacteria to gain insights into the evolution of microbes.

Some scientists raised doubts about the age of the bacterium, claiming that the salt sample may have become contaminated with younger—perhaps even modern—microbes. Such problems had caused many scientists to dismiss a number of earlier claims to have brought ancient dormant microbes back to life.

Vanishing amphibians. The world's frogs, toads, and other amphibians began disappearing at an alarming rate long before the 1980's, when biologists became seriously concerned about the problem. This was the conclusion of the first large survey of amphibian decline, reported in April 2000. After analyzing data on more than 150 species in 37 countries, zoologist Jeff Houlahan of the University of Ottawa in Canada found that the overall number of amphibians dropped 15 percent per year between 1960 and 1966. The decline continued at a rate of about 2 percent per year until 1997, the last year for which data was available.

Scientists suspect that a combination of factors is responsible for the loss of amphibians. These factors include the destruction of wetlands; pollution caused by fertilizers and pesticides; illnesses caused by infectious microorganisms; and the introduction of non-native predators to amphibian habitats. Biologists are also concerned about a large number of physical deformities, such as extra legs, observed in amphibians since the mid-1990's. Several studies of these problems were ongoing in 2000.

How geckos get a grip. The age-old mystery of how *geckos* (small tropical lizards) are able to stick to walls and ceilings was solved by a team of scientists that included biologists Robert J. Full of the University of California at Berkeley and Kellar Autumn of Lewis and Clark College in Portland, Oregon. The researchers reported in June 2000 that the key is a phenomenon known as *van der Waals forces* (the electrical forces that hold molecules together in a compound).

Researchers had previously proposed a variety of mechanisms, including glue, friction, static electricity, and suction cups, to explain the gecko's uncanny ability to climb upside down. All such proposals have been eliminated by researchers over the years.

The gecko's feet, explained the scientists, have a multitude of tiny hairs, called seta. Each of the animal's toes contains at least 100,000 of these microscopic hairs. The end of each setae is split into hundreds of spatula-shaped tips. The flat ends of the tips get so close to whatever surface the gecko is on that they can be held in place by van der Waals forces, which operate at distances of no greater than the size of an atom.

The tip of each hair generates only a minute force. Collectively, however, they are so strong that a gecko can hang from a ceiling by just one toe. Artificial versions of the hair might be developed for use as a reusable adhesive tape, according to the researchers. The scientists also noted that the gecko's secret could be used to make sticky feet that would allow robots to climb—a problem that has long vexed robot builders.

☐ Thomas H. Maugh II

See also **Conservation.**

A New Zealand crew sails the yacht *Black Magic* to victory in the finals of the America's Cup off the coast of New Zealand in March 2000, making New Zealand the only country other than the United States to successfully defend the 149-year-old America's Cup trophy.

Boating. New Zealand scored a historic victory in March 2000 by becoming the first country other than the United States to defend the America's Cup trophy. In other events, sailing ace Randy Smyth won his fourth consecutive Worrell 1000, and powerboat pilot Dave Villwock won his fourth Gold Cup race in five years.

America's Cup. The New Zealand crew aboard *Black Magic* swept the Italian crew of *Luna Rossa* five races to none in the America's Cup finals on March 2, held for the first time off the coast of Auckland, New Zealand. The finals were plagued by insufficient winds, with four racing days being canceled. New Zealand rose above the weather to successfully defend the oldest trophy in sports. In a dramatic move, veteran

New Zealand skipper Russell Coutts, who had won nine consecutive America's Cup finals races, allowed 26-year-old Dean Barker to captain the final race of the series. Barker, a native of Auckland, completed the sweep of *Luna Rossa* when *Black Magic* won by 48 seconds in the closest race of the finals.

By stepping aside for the final race, Coutts sacrificed an opportunity to make history by becoming the first skipper to win 10 straight America's Cup finals races. Instead, he tied the record set by Charlie Barr of the United States, who from 1899 to 1903 recorded nine straight America's Cup finals wins. Coutts watched as the New Zealanders sailed to their second straight World's Cup finals sweep, assuring that the 149-year-old

America's Cup trophy would remain at Auckland's Royal New Zealand Yacht Squadron for three more years.

Sailboats. Randy Smyth and Matt Struble sailed to victory in the Worrell 1000 aboard *Blockade Runner* on May 20, 2000. The 1,000-mile (1,600-kilometer) catamaran race from Ft. Lauderdale, Florida, to Virginia Beach, Virginia, began on May 8 with 26 two-person teams participating. Brett Dryland and Rod Waterhouse, sailing *Team Rudee's*, won the final segment of the race but failed to gain enough of a lead to take the overall victory. *Blockade Runner* finished in 77 hours and 30 seconds, the second-fastest time in the history of the Worrell 1000. The crew of *Team Rudee's* took second place, finishing 28 minutes, 20 seconds later. The victory was Smyth's fourth consecutive Worrell 1000 win and his sixth overall.

Powerboats. Dave Villwock piloted *Miss Budweiser* to victory in the Gold Cup race on July 9, 2000, in Detroit. He finished ahead of *Miss DYC*, piloted by Mark Weber. The annual race features Unlimited Hydroplanes, the fastest boats on the American Powerboat Association circuit. Despite windy conditions, Villwock averaged 139.42 miles (224.37 kilometers) per hour. The victory was Villwock fourth Gold Cup in five years.

.   □ Michael Kates

Bosnia-Herzegovina ended 2000 without a functioning national government after no single party or coalition of parties was able to put together a majority following the parliamentary elections in November. Bosnia-Herzegovina consists of two semiautonomous regions: the Serb-controlled Republika Srpska and the Muslim-controlled Muslim-Croat Federation. The two regions share power, but each elects its own parliament and president.

The multi-ethnic Social Democrat Party (SDP), which supported democratic reforms in 2000, took nine seats—the most of any single party—in the Bosnia-Herzegovina Parliamentary Assembly, the nation's main political body. The nationalist parties—the Muslim SDA, the Croat HDZ, and the Serb SDS—won 19 out of 42 seats but could not form a government without support from other parties, which they failed to get. Disagreements about race and ethnicity among the three nationalist parties in Bosnia-Herzegovina led to a bloody war that lasted from 1992 to 1995.

Many international observers, who had expressed hope that the Social Democrat Party would win a majority and form a government, considered the relative success of the nationalist parties in the elections to be a severe setback to a timely introduction of democratic reforms in Bosnia-Herzegovina.

Refugees. Refugees from the 1992 to 1995 war returned to Bosnia at a faster rate in 2000 than in previous years. However, hundreds of thousands of former residents remained outside the country, fearful that they would be attacked by other ethnic groups if they returned. The United Nations reported in November 2000 that only about 10 percent of minority refugees who had been living in Bosnia-Herzegovina before the war had returned to their original places of residence.

Foreign affairs. In February, the European Bank for Reconstruction and Development extended a $34.4-million credit to Bosnia to rebuild railroads. Also in February, leaders from Bosnia and Montenegro signed an agreement to improve cooperation in several areas, including promoting tourism, transportation, and trade between the two countries.

United States Secretary of State Madeleine Albright visited Sarajevo, the Bosnian capital, in March and committed the United States to revealing the extent of U.S. military assistance to the Muslim-Croat Federation.

In November, Bosnia-Herzegovina began the process of reestablishing diplomatic ties with Yugoslavia after Vojislav Kostunica replaced Slobodan Milosevic as president.   □ Sharon L. Wolchik

See also **Europe.**

Botswana. See Africa.

Bowling. Four players, Norm Duke, Ryan Shafer, Chris Barnes, and Walter Ray Williams, Jr., dueled for the 2000 Professional Bowlers Association (PBA) Player of the Year award in one of the closest races in the history of the title. In 2000, Wendy Macpherson of Henderson, Nevada, became the second player in history to surpass $1 million in career earnings on the Professional Women's Bowling Association (PWBA) tour.

PBA. Duke captured the Brunswick ProSource Don Carter Classic in Dallas in January and the MSN Open in Tucson, Arizona, in July. In February, Duke won a major title at the PBA National Championship, held in Toledo, Ohio. He led the tour in tournament earnings in 2000 with $136,900.

Barnes, who led the tour in every category except earnings, posted an average of 220.93. Shafer won two titles and finished second in the World Tournament of Champions in November. He finished second to Duke in earnings, with $123,600.

Jason Couch of Clermont, Florida, defeated Ryan Shafer 198-166 on November 7 in Lake Zurich, Illinois, to win the World Tournament of Champions. With the victory, Couch became the first player in the 35-year history of the tournament to successfully defend his title.

PWBA. Wendy Macpherson, the tour's best

bowler in the 1990's, led the tour in earnings in 2000 with $108,525. She also had the best average, 214.9. In October, Macpherson became only the second PWBA bowler to win over $1 million.

Dede Davidson of Las Vegas, Nevada, defeated Tiffany Stanbrough of Oklahoma City, Oklahoma, 182-179 to win the Sam's Town Invitational in Las Vegas, Nevada, on November 11. Davidson was only the fourth woman to win a career Triple Crown (U.S. Open, WIBC Queens, and Sam's Town Invitational). Davidson also led the tour with four games of 300 in 2000.

Seniors. Bob Glass of Lawrence, Kansas, established himself as a leading candidate for 2000 PBA Senior Tour Player of the Year, finishing first in every statistical category except earnings. He finished second on the money list with $66,650. Roger Workman of Kenova, West Virginia, finished first on the money list, with tournament earnings of $145,275.

Glass's average of 222.69 was more than two pins higher than his closest competitor. He qualified for the championship round finals in 6 of the tour's 12 events. He also finished in the money in all 12 events. Glass captured a "major" on October 13, winning the Senior National Championship in Jackson, Michigan, defeating Rohn Morton of Vancouver, Washington, 246-236 in the title match. □ Michael Kates

Boxing. Evander Holyfield in 2000 became the first boxer in history to win a heavyweight title four different times. The sport also teetered on the edge of the bizarre in 2000, with Mike Tyson's verbal attacks on opponent Lennox Lewis, of Great Britain, and Oscar de la Hoya's retirement that lasted less than a week.

In the ring. Evander Holyfield won a unanimous 12-round decision on August 12 over John Ruiz to become the first boxer in history to win a heavyweight title four times. By winning the bout with Ruiz, Holyfield claimed the World Boxing Association (WBA) heavyweight title that had been vacated by Lennox Lewis in April when a U.S. district judge in New York City granted the WBA permission to strip Lewis of his title. Lewis lost his belt because of his decision to fight Michael Grant, who had not been approved by the WBA as Lewis's next challenger.

Lennox Lewis successfully defended his World Boxing Council heavyweight title on November 11, in Las Vegas, Nevada. Lewis soundly defeated David Tua, of Samoa, setting the stage for a possible bout with Mike Tyson.

After knocking out Lou Savarese in only 38 seconds on June 24 in a heavyweight bout in Glasgow, Scotland, Mike Tyson responded to a question about fighting Lewis with bizarre verbal attacks that left the media shocked and puzzled.

On October 20, Tyson won a fight in Auburn Hills, Michigan, by technical knockout when his opponent, Andrew Golota, quit before the third round. Golota was pelted with beer and garbage from angry fans as he left the ring. On October 22, Golata checked into a Chicago hospital and was diagnosed with a concussion, a fractured left cheekbone, and a neck injury.

Welterweight champion Oscar de la Hoya announced he was planning to retire after losing a split-decision bout on June 17 to Shane Mosley in Los Angeles. The loss was de la Hoya's second narrow defeat in less than a year. However, the retirement lasted less than a week, after which a rematch with Mosley was scheduled for early 2001.

IBF scandal. A federal jury on Aug. 17, 2000, acquitted International Boxing Federation (IBF) founder Robert W. Lee of charges he had taken bribes from promoters and managers to manipulate boxers' ratings. However, Lee was found guilty of six felony counts, including tax evasion, money laundering, and interstate travel in aid of racketeering. Lee faced up to 20 years in prison.
□ Michael Kates

World champion boxers

World Boxing Association

Division	Champion	Country	Date won
Heavyweight	Evander Holyfield	U.S.A.	8/00
	Lennox Lewis	United Kingdom	11/99
Light heavyweight	Roy Jones	U.S.A.	7/98
	Lou del Valle	U.S.A.	9/97
Middleweight	William Joppy	U.S.A.	1/98
	Julio Cesar Green	U.S.A.	8/97
Welterweight	Vacant	——	
	James Page	U.S.A.	10/98
Lightweight	Takanori Hatakeyama	Japan	6/00
	Gilbert Serrano	Venezuela	11/99
	Stefano Zoff	Italy	8/99
	Julien Lorcy	France	4/99
Featherweight	Derrick Gainer	U.S.A.	9/00
	Fred Norwood	U.S.A.	5/99
Bantamweight	Paul Ayala	U.S.A.	6/99
	Johnny Tapia	U.S.A.	12/98
Flyweight	Eric Morel	Puerto Rico	8/00
	S. Pisnurachank	Thailand	9/99
	Leo Gamez	Venezuela	3/99

World Boxing Council

Division	Champion	Country	Date won
Heavyweight	Lennox Lewis	United Kingdom	2/97
Light heavyweight	Roy Jones	U.S.A.	8/97
Middleweight	Keith Holmes	U.S.A.	4/99
	Hassine Cherifi	U.S.A.	5/98
Welterweight	Shane Mosley	U.S.A.	6/00
	Oscar de la Hoya	U.S.A.	2/00
Lightweight	Jose Luis Castillo	Mexico	6/00
	Steve Johnston	U.S.A.	2/99
Featherweight	Guty Espadas	Mexico	4/00
	Vacant	——	
	Naseem Hamed	United Kingdom	10/99
	Cesar Soto	Mexico	5/99
Bantamweight	Veeraphol Nakhonluang	Thailand	12/98
	Joichiro Tatsuyoshi	Japan	11/97
Flyweight	Malcolm Tunacao	Philippines	5/00
	Medgoen Singsurat	Thailand	9/99

Brazil commemorated the 500th anniversary of the country's discovery on April 22, 2000, with official celebrations in Porto Seguro, the coastal city where Portuguese navigator Pedro Alvares Cabral made landfall in 1500. An economic upswing gave many Brazilians cause to celebrate in 2000. However, not all Brazilians shared in the country's new-found bounty.

During the celebrations, some 2,000 Brazilian Indians—who viewed the occasion as a commemoration of the beginning of centuries of oppression—clashed with police in Porto Seguro. Poor farmers belonging to the leftist Movement of the Landless (MST) marked the anniversary by occupying 500 ranches and farms left idle by absentee landowners. In October, President Fernando Henrique Cardoso of Brazil met MST demands that poor farmers be granted low-interest loans.

Economic growth. According to August figures from Brazil's National Statistics Institute, the nation would post a 4-percent economic growth rate in 2000. Furthermore, the institute expected that Brazil's exports would increase 18 percent over 1999.

During the first six months of 2000, foreign companies unveiled plans for $138 billion in new investments in Brazil. Of this total, $40 billion was to go into the telecommunications sector, in which there was fierce competition to supply Brazil with computers, cellular telephones, and Internet access.

Foreign investment enabled Brazil's automotive industry to expand in 2000. In July, General Motors Corporation of Detroit opened a $600-million plant in the southern state of Rio Grande do Sul to produce subcompact cars. In September, Toyota Motor Corporation of Japan announced a $300-million expansion of its plant in Sao Paulo. Toyota expected to triple the production of its popular Corolla sedan at the larger facility.

Petrobras expansion. To reduce Brazil's dependency on foreign sources of oil, the state-owned petroleum company, Petroleo Brasileiro, began a five-year plan in 2000 to boost its production by 10 percent each year through 2005. To realize this goal, the company planned to invest $32.9 billion over that period.

Spaceport. United States and Brazilian officials signed an agreement in April 2000 that permitted U.S.-made satellites and rockets to be launched at Alcantara, a spaceport on the eastern edge of the Amazon basin near the equator. More than 275 launches had taken place at Alcantara since the facility was built in the early 1980's. Space-mission planners consider Alcantara a highly desirable site because rockets launched from the equatorial region reach orbit faster and can carry heavier payloads than rockets launched

Marching past police on April 22, 2000, Brazilian Indians protest celebrations to mark the 500th anniversary of Brazil's discovery. The Indians viewed the occasion as commemorating the beginning of centuries of oppression.

from other latitudes. In addition, the spaceport's remote location means there is little chance that debris will fall on populated areas in an accident.

Former First Lady Rosane Collor de Mello was sentenced to an 11-year prison term in May 2000 for misuse of public funds, including diverting money from a relief agency she headed during her husband's presidency. Collor, who lived in Miami, Florida, was not present for the trial. Her husband, Fernando Collor de Mello, resigned the presidency in 1992 after being impeached.

Senator expelled. In June 2000, the Brazilian Senate expelled one of its members for the first time in history. Luis Estevao, a prominent real estate developer and member of the ruling coalition, had been accused of embezzling $93 million that was intended for the construction of a federal courthouse in Sao Paulo. Estevao was arrested two days after being expelled.

Woman nominated for high court. In November, President Cardoso nominated federal court judge Ellen Gracie Northfleet to the Brazilian Supreme Court. Northfleet was the first woman ever to be appointed to the high court.

☐ Nathan A. Haverstock

See also **Latin America**.

British Columbia. See Canadian provinces.

Brunei. See Asia.

Buddhism. On Jan. 5, 2000, Ugyen Trinley Dorje, the 17th Karmapa, joined thousands of fellow Tibetans living in exile in the northern Indian city of Dharamsala. The Karmapa, who was recognized by Tibetan Buddhists and Chinese authorities as Tibetan Buddhism's third-ranking spiritual leader, had left Tibet secretly in December 1999. In April 2000, monks at the Rumtek monastery in the state of Sikkim, the traditional seat in India for the Karmapa, submitted a request to the Indian government asking that he be granted asylum. These events marked another stage in a continuing conflict between Tibetan Buddhists and the Chinese government, which annexed Tibet in the 1950's. The Dalai Lama, the Panchen Lama, and the Karmapa—Tibetan Buddhism's three foremost spiritual leaders—continued to reject Chinese authority over Tibet.

Falun Gong. Tensions between the Chinese government and the Chinese spiritual movement Falun Gong continued in 2000. The movement, which gained millions of adherents during the 1990's, united elements of Taoism and Buddhism with meditation and exercise. In 1999, China had banned the group. In 2000, Falun Gong regularly staged peaceful demonstrations in Beijing's Tiananmen Square, protesting the government's efforts to suppress the movement. Chinese authorities arrested thousands of the sect's members

A China Religious Affairs Bureau official congratulates a 2-year-old Tibetan boy after the child's ordination in January 2000. China proclaimed the boy the Seventh Reting Lama, though many Buddhists did not recognize him as a reincarnation of the spiritual leader.

in 2000, some of whom died while in detention.

The U.S. Commission on International Religious Freedom said in a report issued in May that China violated internationally recognized human rights in blocking the free exercise of religion by Falun Gong members and Tibetan Buddhists.

Chinese authorities also persecuted followers of Zhong Gong, a Chinese spiritual movement that blended elements of Buddhism and Taoism with meditative practices, in 2000. In September, a U.S. federal judge denied asylum in the United States to the group's leader, Zhang Hongbao, who had fled to Guam in February. The judge, however, allowed Zhang to remain on Guam, a U.S. territory.

Peace summit. The Millennium World Peace Summit of Religious and Spiritual Leaders met in New York City in August. Buddhists were well represented, though the Dalai Lama did not attend. His invitation to participate had been withdrawn as a result of pressure from the Chinese government.

In Sri Lanka, the civil war between the Hindu Tamil minority and the Buddhist Sinhalese majority continued in 2000. Buddhist Sinhalese monks were involved in forcing President Chandrika Kumaratunga to withdraw his constitutional reform bill, which was aimed at ending the conflict.

□ Paul J. Griffiths

See also **China; Human rights.**

Building and construction. The
London Eye, an "observation wheel" that was 450 feet (137 meters) tall, opened to the public in February 2000 on the south bank of the River Thames in London. The Eye resembled a Ferris wheel but was made with capsules firmly attached to the outside structure, rather than hanging gondolas. Thirty-two glass-enclosed cars, each large enough to carry 25 people, gave passengers a 25-mile (40-kilometer) view of London.

The wheel was constructed in a horizontal position on a series of pillars in the Thames. It was lifted into an upright position in October 1999 by a large crane and attached to two 100-ton (90.7-metric ton) restraining towers. The hoist required four miles (6.4 kilometers) of cable connected to the 80 spokes of the wheel. The first attempt to lift the wheel failed when a cable came loose. Safety inspectors then delayed the wheel's debut from its scheduled opening on New Year's Eve 1999.

Although mocked by some critics, the London Eye proved to be an immediate hit with the public. British Airways PLC, which sponsored the Eye, had only a five-year operating permit for the wheel, but its popularity led airline officials to seek a 20-year operating license and refinance the structure. The 1,600-ton (1,451-metric ton) structure was designed by London-based, husband-and-wife architects David Marks and Julia Barfield. Delays and redesigns to address safety concerns escalated the cost from a projected $40 million to $111 million.

Major league ballparks. Three new Major League Baseball (MLB) stadiums opened at the start of the 2000 baseball season. San Francisco's Pacific Bell Park, Detroit's Comerica Park, and Houston's Enron Field were the latest of several ballparks constructed in the 1990's.

Pacific, or Pac, Bell Park was built within walking distance of downtown San Francisco, continuing a trend to erect big-league venues near city centers. The park replaced the Giants' previous field, 3Com Park, which was notorious for its cold winds blowing off San Francisco Bay. Though Pac Bell Park was also located on the waterfront, the Kansas City, Missouri-based architectural firm Hellmuth, Obata, & Kassabaum, Inc. (HOK) rotated the stadium 90 degrees from 3Com's position to block the chilly breezes. The $319-million structure was the first privately financed MLB park since Dodger Stadium opened in 1962.

Comerica Park, another HOK-designed stadium, was a joint public-private venture that cost $290 million. The park, with a view of downtown Detroit beyond the outfield fences, featured a carousel and Ferris wheel. Comerica Park also was built with the largest scoreboard in the major leagues. It included a computerized lighting display to mark Tiger home runs.

Enron Field, yet another HOK design, was a $248-million project that replaced the Astrodome, which was the first covered ballpark, finished in 1965. Enron Field was covered with a three-paneled retractable roof 204 feet (62.2 meters) above the playing field. The roof could be opened or closed within 20 minutes.

Bethlehem brownfield. Bethlehem Steel Corporation of Bethlehem, Pennsylvania, began construction on BethWorks, a family-oriented theme park and retail complex, in 2000. The development, which was to include ice rinks, movie cinemas, and the National Museum of Industrial History, took place on part of the firm's abandoned 1,800-acre (729-hectare) complex in Pennsylvania's Lehigh Valley.

During World War II (1939-1945), the complex employed 30,000 workers making armaments and steel plates for warships. By the time the plant closed its coke furnaces in 1995, the site had become a symbol of urban decay. In 1999, Bethlehem Steel embarked on a $1-billion remodeling program at the complex. The program put the company at the forefront of a national trend focusing on new uses for *brownfields,* old industrial properties. The facilities of BethWorks were scheduled to open in stages beginning in 2001.

More than 50,000 people on June 10, 2000, walk across the Oresund Fixed Link, a 10-mile (16-kilometer) bridge and tunnel system connecting Malmo, Sweden, and Copenhagen, Denmark. The first physical connection between the two countries opened to rail and automobile traffic in July.

The Cape Hatteras Lighthouse, on North Carolina's Outer Banks, reopened to the public on May 26, 2000, after being moved to prevent beach erosion from toppling the 130-year-old structure into the Atlantic Ocean. The National Park Service spent some $10 million to save the 199-foot (60.6-meter) lighthouse.

The project began in June 1999, when workers with International Chimney Corporation in Buffalo, New York, removed the 4,400-ton (3,991-metric ton) structure from its foundation and lifted it onto a huge transport platform. They then used a hydraulic jacking system to move the lighthouse 2,900 feet (884 meters) inland on rails to a new concrete foundation. The journey took 23 days.

The Oresund Fixed Link, a 10-mile (16-kilometer) bridge and tunnel combination connecting Malmo, Sweden, and Copenhagen, Denmark, opened to rail and automobile traffic in July 2000. The $3.5-billion project, which spans the Oresund Strait, was the first physical connection between Sweden and Denmark.

The structure consists of a double-decker bridge with a four-lane highway on top and rail line on the bottom. The bridge descends to an artificial island, 2.5 miles (4 kilometers) in length, that engineers constructed in the middle of the strait. A tunnel then extends 2.3 miles (3.7 kilometers) beneath the sea to the Danish side.

☐ Andrew Wright

See also **Baseball; Transportation.**

Bulgaria. The government of Prime Minister Ivan Kostov survived a no-confidence vote in May 2000. The vote was called after opposition groups accused Kostov of fostering corruption.

In April, the World Bank, a United Nations agency that provides long-term loans to countries for development, loaned Bulgaria $7.5 million to fight corruption in the government. In July, parliament enacted a bill to fight money laundering.

Bulgarian leaders reaffirmed their willingness to negotiate entrance requirements with the European Union (EU) in 2000. They also appealed to the EU for aid after 2,500 forest fires damaged farms in August.

Bulgaria's *gross domestic product* (the value of all goods and services produced in a country in a given year) grew by 5.2 percent in the first half of 2000. Unemployment averaged approximately 18 percent through the year.

In February, the state television station began broadcasting a weekly news program in the Turkish language, a service long requested by Bulgaria's Turkish minority. ☐ Sharon L. Wolchik
See also **Europe.**

Burkina Faso. See **Africa.**

Burma. See **Myanmar.**

Burundi. See **Africa.**

Business. See **Bank; Economics; Labor; Manufacturing.**

Cabinet, U.S. Secretary of Commerce William M. Daley resigned his Cabinet position in July 2000 to become chairman of Vice President Al Gore's presidential campaign. Daley had served in President Bill Clinton's administration since 1997.

President Clinton selected Norman Y. Mineta, a former Democratic congressman from California, to fill the vacant post at the Commerce Department. Mineta served 21 years in the U.S. House of Representatives. He resigned from the House in 1995 to join the Teaneck, New Jersey-based Lockheed Martin Corporation, the largest U.S. defense contractor, as senior vice president of its transportation systems and services division. The Senate voted unanimously in July to confirm Mineta.

Mineta became the first Asian-American to serve in a Cabinet post. During World War II (1939-1945), he and his family were among the 120,000 Americans of Japanese descent placed in an internment camp.

Secretary of State Madeleine K. Albright met with Kim Chong-Il, the leader of North Korea, on Oct. 23, 2000. Albright was the first U.S. secretary of state and the most senior U.S. official to ever visit North Korea.

Cabinet nominees. In December 2000, President-elect George W. Bush nominated the follow-

ing people for his Cabinet: Colin Powell, a retired four-star U.S. Army general and the former chairman of the Joint Chiefs of Staff, as secretary of the Department of State; Don Evans, Bush's campaign chairman in the 2000 presidential election, as secretary of the Department of Commerce; Florida county official Mel Martinez as secretary of the Department of Housing and Urban Development; California agriculture official Ann Veneman as secretary of the Department of Agriculture; Paul O'Neill, chairman of Pittsburgh, Pennsylvania-based Alcoa Corp., as secretary of the Department of the Treasury; former Missouri Governor and U.S. Senator John Ashcroft as attorney general; Donald Rumsfeld, defense secretary in the Gerald R. Ford administration, as secretary of the Department of Defense; Houston school superintendent Rod Paige as secretary of the Department of Education; Wisconsin Governor Tommy Thompson as secretary of the Department of Health and Human Services; former Colorado Attorney General Gale Norton as secretary of the Department of the Interior; and Anthony Principi, a former deputy secretary of the Department of Veterans Affairs, as the secretary of Veterans Affairs.
☐ Linda P. Campbell and Geoffrey A. Campbell
See also **Korea, North; United States, Government of the; United States, President of the.**

California. See **State government.**

Cambodia enjoyed peace in 2000 after decades of war and civil strife. Political murders and human rights violations were less blatant than in past years.

Some abuses of power continued, however, under Prime Minister Hun Sen, who enjoyed the title of "strongman." Hun Sen said Cambodia's economic growth was dependent on foreign aid, which accounted for nearly half of the annual budget in 2000. Only 2 percent of domestic economic output was spent on education, health, and rural development, while 86 percent of the national budget was spent in the capital, Phnom Penh, where only 10 percent of the population lived.

Cambodia continued to negotiate with the United Nations over trials for leaders of the Khmer Rouge. The Khmer Rouge was a Communist organization that controlled Cambodia between 1975 and 1979, when more than 1.5 million people were killed. Hun Sen and other officials, who had been members of the Khmer Rouge, resisted internationally supervised trials.

Monsoon rains started in July 2000, nearly a month and a half early. The Mekong River reached its highest level in 40 years, cresting at 36.5 feet (11.13 meters), causing extensive damage to houses and crops. ☐ Henry S. Bradsher
See also **Asia.**

Canada

Canadians went to the polls on Nov. 27, 2000, and gave the Liberal Party government of Prime Minister Jean Chretien a resounding victory. The Liberals won their third majority government in seven years. They also increased their majority to 172 seats from 161 in the 301-member House of Commons, taking 41 percent of the popular vote.

The normal term of a Canadian administration is four years, but Chretien, for the second time since taking office in 1993, chose to go to the voters after only 3½ years. Political analysts widely agreed this was a risk, since voters have punished governments in the past for calling what they considered a premature election. However, Chretien's instincts proved correct.

Liberal sweep. The Liberals counted on a solid base of support in Ontario, Canada's largest province, and they were not disappointed. For the third time in a row, they captured all but a handful of the province's 103 seats, 100 in the 2000 election. In addition, they won back seats they had lost in the 1997 election in the Atlantic provinces of New Brunswick, Newfoundland, Nova Scotia, and Prince Edward Island. The Liberals also made considerable gains in Quebec, long the domain of the separatist Bloc Quebecois (BQ). Only in the four Western provinces of Alberta, British Columbia, Manitoba, and Saskatchewan did the Liberals fare poorly, winning 13 of the 88 seats in that region.

Disappointment for the Alliance. The Canadian Alliance, a new party formed in March 2000 to combine the forces of the right against the centrist Liberals, was the biggest loser in the election. It took a total of 66 seats in the House of Commons.

The Alliance was the creation of Preston Manning, an Albertan who had built up the Reform Party, a western protest party, into the official opposition in Parliament. The Reform Party, however, had never managed to win a seat east of Manitoba, and Manning was determined to build a broader base to give his party a national appeal.

In January, Manning persuaded the members of the Reform Party to merge into a new organization called the Canadian Reform Conservative Alliance. He then called for a vote to determine the leadership of the Alliance. In the contest that followed, conducted by telephone polls, he lost to a newcomer in federal politics, Stockwell Day, also of Alberta.

New conservative leader. Day was 49 years old in January, 10 years younger than most of Canada's other national political leaders, and an experienced member of the Progressive Conservative Party (PCP) government of Alberta. He had held the post of provincial treasurer, where he had successfully managed the province's books. Under his supervision, Alberta had become the first province in Canada to declare a surplus on its public accounts.

A fiscal conservative, Day had railed against the high level of taxation in Canada and the burdensome national debt. He believed strongly in the equality of the provinces and rejected a special status for Quebec in the federation. Day also held conservative views on social questions. However, he made it plain that he would not impose his views on the new party.

Chretien caught the other political parties off guard with his early election call. The prime minister immediately launched an offensive against Day and the Alliance, claiming that the party had a hidden agenda that would damage Canada's prized public health system and weaken the authority of the central government. Forced on the defensive, Day found it difficult to put forward his own policy alternatives.

Ontario voters decided that the familiar Liberal program was preferable to the incomplete agenda of the Canadian Alliance. They returned only two Alliance members, both from voting districts in eastern Ontario. The Alliance failed to win seats in Atlantic Canada and Quebec, though its popular vote rose markedly in these areas. In the West, the Alliance won 64 of 88 seats, with an especially strong showing in Alberta and British Columbia. Its popular vote across Canada rose to 25 percent. Day consoled his supporters by saying that the Alliance's time as a conservative alternative to the Liberals had not yet come.

PCP losses. Canada's historic party of the right, the PCP, fared even more poorly in the 2000 election. Beginning in 1999, Manning and then Day had urged the PCP to join forces with the Alliance in a common front. However, the PCP's leader, Joe Clark, a former prime minister, had rejected these overtures. He concentrated instead on rebuilding his seriously weakened party. Clark himself was not elected to Parliament until September 2000 and so was hampered in moving into an election mode when Chretien called the contest on October 22.

The PCP picked up some seats in Atlantic Canada, and Clark won his own seat in Calgary, Alberta, in the heart of Alliance territory. Overall, however, the PCP claimed victory in only 12 districts.

Canadians pay their final respects to former Prime Minister Pierre Elliott Trudeau at Montreal City Hall in October 2000. Trudeau, who died on September 28, at age 80, had served as prime minister for 15 years.

The Trans Canada Trail

The Trans Canada Trail, a 10,000-mile (16,000-kilometer) recreational path designed for hiking, bicycling, horseback riding, and skiing, is the longest trail in the world. The pathway, stretching across Canada, opened in September 2000.

Quebec provided the biggest surprise in the election. Chretien and the Liberals severely cut into the separatist support that had gone to the BQ. The Liberals won 37 seats, 10 more than in 1997. The BQ also won 38 seats. The PCP won 1 seat.

Chretien, who was not popular in Quebec, found the results highly gratifying. He suggested that the vote reflected growing support for his policy of national unity in a province that had flirted with secession for many years. The Liberals gained seats not only in English-speaking areas around Montreal, where the party had always been strong, but also in the province's French-speaking districts. For the first time in more than a decade, the Liberals' share of the popular vote exceeded that of the BQ.

Campaign issues. Election 2000, which Chretien stressed should be about values, turned out to be a bitter, negative campaign. The Liberals characterized their Alliance opponents as narrow-minded bigots who would let market forces destroy Canada's social fabric. Chretien's opponents accused him of political favoritism in appointments, the mismanagement of public funds through job creation programs, and a centralized, dictatorial governing style. Chretien stoutly defended his government's record, pointing to a prosperous economy, federal budget surpluses, and increased funding for the beleaguered health care system.

Regional divisions. The election results clearly demonstrated that Canada's political system remained in a state of flux. Before the election, the country's political parties had been regionally based to a degree unprecedented in the country's history. After the election, the regional basis appeared less marked. The Liberals were beginning to achieve a national reach in line with their historic past. The separatist forces in Quebec appeared weakened, and the prospect of a future referendum on independence seemed unlikely. The Alliance had won sizable voter support across the country, even though its representation in Parliament did not reflect this support. Analysts suggested that the Alliance might benefit from a further decline in the PCP's appeal. Canada's social democratic party of the left, the New Democratic Party (NDP), seemed a spent force in national politics, taking only 13 seats countrywide, down 7 seats.

Hard line on secession. In 2000, the Chretien government, which had treated Quebec's separatist movement cautiously since taking office, maintained a hard line adopted in 1999. On March 15, 2000, the House of Commons, after a stormy debate, overwhelmingly approved legislation setting out the procedures for a referendum and negotiations on secession. The provisions of the Clarity Act embodied conditions for any attempt at separation (also known as sovereignty) by Quebec set out in a 1998 decision by the Supreme Court of Canada.

The Clarity Act provided that the House would have to approve the wording of any referendum question on secession. It also gave the House the power to reject the referendum if it was not approved by a clear majority of Quebec voters. In the two previous secession votes in Quebec, in 1980 and 1995, the phrasing of the question had been ambiguous, linking secession with a partnership with the rest of Canada.

Although the Clarity Act met bitter resistance from the BQ, the measure attracted enthusiastic approval outside of Quebec and, to the surprise of many, support from a majority of Quebeckers. Opinion poll results revealed that the support for independence in the province had dropped to its lowest level in five years.

Debate over medical care. Canadians worried about the future of their $80-billion public health system in 2000. (All monetary figures are in Canadian dollars unless otherwise noted.) The pressures of an expanding and aging population, as well as outmoded technology and inadequate facilities strained the 26-year-old program, which is funded by the federal and provincial governments but administered by the provinces.

When the Liberals took office in 1993, they drastically reduced grants to the provinces for health, arguing the need to get Canada's federal budget deficits under control. However, the federal government insisted that its duty to ensure universal access to the health care system, mandated by the Canada Health Act of 1984, entitled it to retain oversight of health care programs. The provinces responded that if the federal government was unwilling to fund medical care to the extent it had previously, it should not lay down principles for its operation.

On Sept. 11, 2000, Chretien and the premiers of Canada's provincial and territorial governments met to discuss the deadlock over financing. The federal government agreed to provide an additional $23.4 billion in health and social grants over the next five years, a 35-percent increase. The government also promised a one-time payment of $2.3 billion for high-tech diagnostic equipment. The federal government wanted a national accounting of how the provinces spent health care funds, but the provinces resisted, stating that they would issue separate assessments.

Earlier in 2000, Alberta and Quebec had liberalized their rules against private health care by permitting the operation of private, for-profit magnetic resonance imaging clinics. The provinces claimed that the private facilities would relieve the burden on the public system. The move, however, triggered strong criticism from the

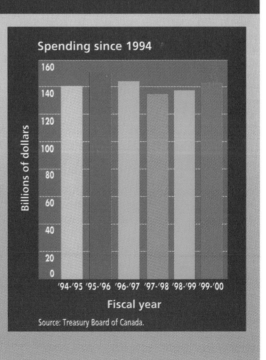

Federal spending in Canada
Estimated budget for fiscal 2000-2001*

Department or agency	Millions of dollars†
Agriculture and agri-food	2,591
Canada customs and revenue agency	2,808
Canadian heritage	2,771
Citizenship and immigration	964
Environment	583
Finance	64,461
Fisheries and oceans	1,333
Foreign affairs and international trade	3,524
Governor general	14
Health	2,394
Human resources development	27,545
Indian affairs and northern development	4,806
Industry	3,918
Justice	1,013
National defence	11,199
Natural resources	861
Parliament	325
Privy Council	302
Public works and government services	4,167
Solicitor general	3,037
Transport	901
Treasury board	1,732
Veterans affairs	2,005
Total	**143,254**

* April 1, 2000, to March 31, 2001.
† Canadian dollars; $1 = U.S. $0.66 as of Oct. 13, 2000.

Spending since 1994

Billions of dollars

160
140
120
100
80
60
40
20
0

'94-'95 '95-'96 '96-'97 '97-'98 '98-'99 '99-'00

Fiscal year

Source: Treasury Board of Canada.

Members of the Canadian House of Commons

The House of Commons of the first session of the 37th Parliament convened on Jan. 29, 2001. As of Dec. 28, 2000, the House of Commons consisted of the following members: 172 Liberal Party, 66 Canadian Alliance, 38 Bloc Québécois, 13 New Democratic Party, 12 Progressive Conservative Party, and 0 Independents. This table shows each legislator and party affiliation. An asterisk (*) denotes those who served in the 36th Parliament.

Alberta
Diane Ablonczy, C.A.*
Rob Anders, C.A.*
Leon E. Benoit, C.A.*
Rick Casson, C.A.
David Chatters, C.A.*
Joe Clark, P.C.
Ken Epp, C.A.*
Peter Goldring, C.A.*
Deborah Grey, C.A.*
Art Hanger, C.A.*
Grant Hill, C.A.*
Rahim Jaffer, C.A.*
F. Dale Johnston, C.A.*
Jason Kenney, C.A.*
David Kilgour, Lib.*
Preston Manning, C.A.*
Anne McLellan, Lib.*
Rob Merrifield, C.A.
Bob Mills, C.A.*
Deepak Obhrai, C.A.*
Charlie Penson, C.A.*
James Rajotte, C.A.
Monte Solberg, C.A.*
Kevin Sorenson, C.A.
Myron Thompson, C.A.*
John Williams, C.A.*

British Columbia
Jim Abbott, C.A.*
David Anderson, Lib.*
Andy Burton, C.A.*
Chuck Cadman, C.A.*
John Cummins, C.A.*
Libby Davies, N.D.P.*
Stockwell Day, C.A.
Herb Dhaliwal, Lib.*
John Duncan, C.A.*
Reed Elley, C.A.*
Paul Forseth, C.A.*
Hedy Fry, Lib.*
Jim Gouk, C.A.*
Gurmant Grewal, C.A.*
Dick Harris, C.A.*
Jay Hill, C.A.*
Betty Hinton, C.A.
M. Sophia Leung, Lib.*
Gary Lunn, C.A.*
James P. Lunney, C.A.
Keith Martin, C.A.*
Philip Mayfield, C.A.*
Grant McNally, C.A.*
Val Meredith, C.A.*
James Moore, C.A.
Stephen Owen, Lib.
Joe Peschisolido, C.A.
John Reynolds, C.A.*
Svend J. Robinson, N.D.P.*
Werner Schmidt, C.A.*
Darrel Stinson, C.A.*
Chuck Strahl, C.A.*
Randy White, C.A.*
Ted White, C.A.*

Manitoba
Reg Alcock, Lib.*
Bill Blaikie, N.D.P.*

Rick Borotsik, P.C.*
Bev Desjarlais, N.D.P.*
Ronald J. Duhamel, Lib.*
John Harvard, Lib.*
Howard Hilstrom, C.A.*
David Iftody, Lib.*
Inky Mark, C.A.*
Pat Martin, N.D.P.*
Anita Neville, Lib.
Rey D. Pagtakhan, Lib.*
Brian Pallister, C.A.
Vic Toews, C.A.
Judy Wasylycia-Leis, N.D.P.*

New Brunswick
Claudette Bradshaw, Lib.*
Jeannot Castonguay, Lib.
Yvon Godin, N.D.P.*
John Herron, P.C.*
Charles Hubbard, Lib.*
Dominic LeBlanc, Lib.
Andy Scott, Lib.*
Greg Thompson, P.C.*
Elsie Wayne, P.C.*

Newfoundland
George S. Baker, Lib.*
Gerry Byrne, Lib.*
Norman Doyle, P.C.*
Loyola Hearn, P.C.
Bill Matthews, Lib.*
Lawrence D. O'Brien, Lib.*
Brian V. Tobin, Lib.

Northwest Territories
Ethel Blondin-Andrew, Lib.*

Nova Scotia
Scott Brison, P.C.*
Bill Casey, P.C.*
Rodger Cuzner, Lib.
Mark Eyking, Lib.
Gerald Keddy, P.C.*
Wendy Lill, N.D.P.*
Peter MacKay, P.C.*
Alexa McDonough, N.D.P.*
Geoff Regan, Lib.
Peter Stoffer, N.D.P.*
Robert Thibault, Lib.

Nunavut
Nancy Karetak-Lindell, Lib.*

Ontario
Peter Adams, Lib.*
Sarkis Assadourian, Lib.*
Jean Augustine, Lib.*
Sue Barnes, Lib.*
Colleen Beaumier, Lib.*
Réginald Bélair, Lib.*
Mauril Bélanger, Lib.*
Eugène Bellemare, Lib.*
Carolyn Bennett, Lib.*
Maurizio Bevilacqua, Lib.*
Raymond Bonin, Lib.*

Paul Bonwick, Lib.*
Don Boudria, Lib.*
Bonnie Brown, Lib.*
John Bryden, Lib.*
Sarmite Bulte, Lib.*
Charles Caccia, Lib.*
Murray Calder, Lib.*
John Cannis, Lib.*
Elinor Caplan, Lib.*
M. Aileen Carroll, Lib.*
Marlene Catterall, Lib.*
Brenda Chamberlain, Lib.*
David M. Collenette, Lib.*
Joe Comartin, N.D.P.
Joe Comuzzi, Lib.*
Sheila Copps, Lib.*
Roy Cullen, Lib.*
Paul DeVillers, Lib.*
Stan Dromisky, Lib.*
Arthur C. Eggleton, Lib.*
John Finlay, Lib.*
Joe Fontana, Lib.*
Cheryl Gallant, C.A.
Roger Gallaway, Lib.*
John Godfrey, Lib.*
Bill Graham, Lib.*
Herb Gray, Lib.*
Ivan Grose, Lib.*
Albina Guarnieri, Lib.*
Mac Harb, Lib.*
Tony Ianno, Lib.*
Ovid L. Jackson, Lib.*
Joe Jordan, Lib.*
Jim Karygiannis, Lib.*
Stan Keyes, Lib.*
Bob Kilger, Lib.*
Gar Knutson, Lib.*
Karen Kraft Sloan, Lib.*
Walt Lastewka, Lib.*
Derek Lee, Lib.*
Judi Longfield, Lib.*
Paul H. Macklin, Lib.
Steve Mahoney, Lib.*
Gurbax Singh Malhi, Lib.*
John Maloney, Lib.*
John Manley, Lib.*
Diane Marleau, Lib.*
John McCallum, Lib.
Larry McCormick, Lib.*
John McKay, Lib.*
Dan McTeague, Lib.*
Peter Milliken, Lib.*
Dennis J. Mills, Lib.*
Maria Minna, Lib.*
Andy Mitchell, Lib.*
Lynn Myers, Lib.*
Robert D. Nault, Lib.*
Pat O'Brien, Lib.*
John O'Reilly, Lib.*
Carolyn Parrish, Lib.*
Janko Peric, Lib.*
Jim Peterson, Lib.*
Beth Phinney, Lib.*
Jerry Pickard, Lib.*
Gary Pillitteri, Lib.*

David Pratt, Lib.*
Carmen Provenzano, Lib.*
Karen Redman, Lib.*
Julian Reed, Lib.*
Scott Reid, C.A.
John Richardson, Lib.*
Allan Rock, Lib.*
Benoît Serré, Lib.*
Judy Sgro, Lib.*
Alexander Shepherd, Lib.*
Bob Speller, Lib.*
Brent St. Denis, Lib.*
Paul Steckle, Lib.*
Jane Stewart, Lib.*
Paul Szabo, Lib.*
Andrew Telegdi, Lib.*
Tony Tirabassi, Lib.
Alan Tonks, Lib.
Paddy Torsney, Lib.*
Rose-Marie Ur, Lib.*
Tony Valeri, Lib.*
Lyle Vanclief, Lib.*
Joseph Volpe, Lib.*
Tom Wappel, Lib.*
Susan Whelan, Lib.*
Bryon Wilfert, Lib.*
Bob Wood, Lib.*

Prince Edward Island
Arnold Easter, Lib.*
Lawrence MacAulay, Lib.*
Joe McGuire, Lib.*
Shawn Murphy, Lib.*

Quebec
Carole-Marie Allard, Lib.
Mark Assad, Lib.*
Gérard Asselin, B.Q.*
André Bachand, P.C.*
Claude Bachand, B.Q.*
Eleni Bakopanos, Lib.*
Michel Bellehumeur, B.Q.*
Stéphane Bergeron, B.Q.*
Robert Bertrand, Lib.*
Bernard Bigras, B.Q.*
Gérard Binet, Lib.
Diane Bourgeois, B.Q.
Pierre Brien, B.Q.*
Serge Cardin, B.Q.*
Jean Guy Carignan, Lib.
Martin Cauchon, Lib.*
Yvon Charbonneau, Lib.*
Jean Chrétien, Lib.*
Denis Coderre, Lib.•
Irwin Cotler, Lib.•
Paul Crête, B.Q.*
Madeleine Dalphond-Guiral, B.Q.*
Odina Desrochers, B.Q.*
Stéphane Dion, Lib.*
Nick Discepola, Lib.*
Claude Drouin, Lib.*
Antoine Dubé, B.Q.*
Gilles Duceppe, B.Q.*
Claude Duplain, Lib.
Georges Farrah, Lib.
Raymonde Folco, Lib.*

Ghislain Fournier, B.Q.*
Alfonso Gagliano, Lib.*
Christiane Gagnon, B.Q.*
Marcel Gognon, B.Q.
Michel Gauthier, B.Q.*
Jocelyne Girard-Bujold, B.Q.*
Monique Guay, B.Q.*
Michel Guimond, B.Q.*
André Harvey, Lib*.
Marlene Jennings, Lib.*
Mario Laframboise, B.Q.
Francine Lalonde, B.Q.*
Robert Lanctot, B.Q.
Raymond Lavigne, Lib.*
Ghislain Lebel, B.Q.*
Clifford Lincoln, Lib.*
Yvan Loubier, B.Q.*
Richard Marceau, B.Q.*
Serge Marcil, Lib.
Paul Martin, Lib.*
Réal Ménard, B.Q.*
Gilbert Normand, Lib.*
Pierre Paquette, B.Q.
Denis Paradis, Lib.*
Bernard Patry, Lib.*
Gilles-A. Perron, B.Q.*
Pierre S. Pettigrew, Lib.*
Pauline Picard, B.Q.*
Louis Plamondon, B.Q.*
David Price, Lib.*
Marcel Proulx, Lib.*
Lucienne Robillard, Lib.*
Yves Rocheleau, B.Q.*
Jean-Yves Roy, B.Q.
Jacques Saada, Lib.*
Benoît Sauvageau, B.Q.*
Hélène C. Scherrer, Lib.
Caroline St-Hilaire, B.Q.*
Diane St-Jacques, Lib.*
Guy St-Julien, Lib.*
Yolande Thibeault, Lib.*
Stéphan Tremblay, B.Q.*
Suzanne Tremblay, B.Q.*
Pierrette Venne, B.Q.*

Saskatchewan
David Anderson, C.A.
Roy Bailey, C.A.*
Garry Breitkreuz, C.A.*
Brian Fitzpatrick, C.A.
Ralph E. Goodale, Lib.*
Rick Laliberte, Lib.*
Lorne Nystrom, N.D.P.*
Jim Pankiw, C.A.*
Dick Proctor, N.D.P.*
Gerry Ritz, C.A.*
Carol Skelton, C.A.
Larry Spencer, C.A.
Maurice Vellacott, C.A.*
Lynne Yelich, C.A.

Yukon Territory
Larry Bagnell, Lib.

The Ministry of Canada*

Jean Chrétien—prime minister
Lawrence MacAulay—solicitor general of Canada
Don Boudria—leader of the government in the House of Commons
Lloyd Axworthy—minister of foreign affairs
Jane Stewart—minister of human resources development
Arthur Eggleton—minister of national defence
Herb Dhaliwal—minister of fisheries and oceans
Lyle Vanclief—minister of agriculture and Agri-Food
Alfonso Gagliano—minister of public works and government services
Robert Daniel Nault—minister of Indian affairs and Northern development
David Anderson—minister of the environment
J. Bernard Boudreau—leader of the government in the Senate
Herb Gray—deputy prime minister
Sheila Copps—minister of Canadian heritage
Elinor Caplan—minister of citizenship and immigration
John Manley—minister of industry
Allan Rock—minister of health
Paul Martin—minister of finance
David Michael Collenette—minister of transport
Lucienne Robillard—president of the Treasury Board;
minister responsible for infrastructure
Stéphane Dion—president of the Queen's Privy Council for Canada;
minister of intergovernmental affairs
Ralph Goodale—minister of natural resources and minister
responsible for the Canadian Wheat Board
Anne McLellan—minister of justice; attorney general of Canada
Hedy Fry—secretary of state (multiculturalism/status of women)
Gilbert Normand—secretary of state (science, research, and development)
Ethel Blondin-Andrew—secretary of state (children and youth)
George Baker—minister of veterans affairs; secretary of state
(Atlantic Canada Opportunities Agency)
David Kilgour—secretary of state (Latin America and Africa)
Raymond Chan—secretary of state (Asia-Pacific)
Ronald Duhamel—secretary of state (Western economic
diversification/Francophonie)
Jim Peterson—secretary of state (international financial institutions)
Claudette Bradshaw—minister of labour
Martin Cauchon—minister of national revenue; secretary of state
(Economic Development Agency of Canada for the Regions of Quebec)
Andrew Mitchell—secretary of state (rural development/federal economic
development initiative for Northern Ontario)
Pierre Pettigrew—minister for international trade
Maria Minna—minister for international cooperation
Denis Coderre—secretary of state (amateur sport)

*As of Dec. 31, 2000.

Premiers of Canadian provinces

Province	Premier
Alberta	Ralph Klein
British Columbia	Ujjal Dosanjh
Manitoba	Gary Doer
New Brunswick	Bernard Lord
Newfoundland	Brian Vincent Tobin
Nova Scotia	John Hamm
Ontario	Mike Harris
Prince Edward Island	Patrick George Binns
Quebec	Lucien Bouchard
Saskatchewan	Roy Romanow

Government leaders of territories

Northwest Territories	Stephen Kakfwi
Nunavut	Paul Okalik
Yukon Territory	Patricia Jane Duncan

federal government. On November 13, Chretien threatened to withhold federal funding from the two provinces if they did not "review" their policy of allowing the clinics to operate.

Trouble over job grants. The Chretien government in 2000 faced charges of mismanagement of the Canada Job Grants program. The plan, established in 1996, was intended to target areas of high unemployment and represented an expenditure of between $1 billion and $3 billion. Government audits revealed serious problems in the administration and monitoring of the grants.

The opposition relentlessly criticized the government on this issue, charging that money had been funneled to areas represented by Liberal members of Parliament, even though these areas did not suffer from high unemployment. Although the scandal dominated the House of Commons for several months, it did not raise the outcry across the country that the opposition parties had desired. On June 22, 2000, however, the government shut down the Jobs Fund.

A nation mourns. An outpouring of respect and affection swept Canada following the death on September 28 of former Prime Minister Pierre Elliott Trudeau at age 80. A sophisticated and articulate political figure, Trudeau had served as prime minister from

1968 to 1979 and from 1980 to 1984. Though a native of Quebec, he had passionately opposed separatism for that province, putting forward instead his vision of a united bilingual Canada, founded on the basis of individual rather than collective rights. Under his leadership, Canada began playing a larger role in world affairs and the Canadian Parliament passed the Constitution Act of 1982. The act eliminated the need for British approval of Canadian constitutional amendments and included a wide-ranging bill of rights.

A booming economy. Canada's economy recorded impressive growth in 2000. Propelled by manufacturing, telecommunications, and computer-related industries, the *gross domestic product* (the value of all goods and services produced in a given year) moved ahead by almost 5 percent, Canada's highest growth rate since 1988. In the autumn of 2000, steeply higher energy costs worried economists, but leading economic indicators remained strong. Though the *consumer price index* (a statistical measurement of changes in the prices of goods and services) stood at 2.8 percent in October, the Bank of Canada argued that various economic factors that might contribute to inflation remained unaffected by rising energy costs. The unemployment rate hovered around 6.9 percent for most of 2000.

Residents in Newfoundland welcome the *Islendingur*, a replica of a Viking ship, in a July 2000 recreation of the arrival, approximately 1,000 years ago, of the first Europeans in North America.

A "good news" budget. Tax cuts for both wage earners and businesses and increased spending for health care, education, and other social programs highlighted the $162-billion budget for fiscal year 2000 (April 1, 2000, to March 31, 2001) presented on Feb. 28, 2000, by Finance Minister Paul Martin. Martin proposed $40 billion in tax cuts for lower- and middle-level earners and a reduction in corporate tax rates from 28 percent to 21 percent over the next five years. He also announced a reduction in the tax on investment earnings. In addition, Martin reported the government would adjust tax rates periodically to account for the effects of inflation.

In spite of the tax cuts, Martin reported that higher revenues, the result of Canada's prosperity, had again produced a substantial budget surplus, the third in a row. Later in 2000, Martin had to revise his budget estimates, after projecting a record surplus of $12 billion for the year. A second budget, announced on October 18, just before the election call, doubled the tax cuts announced earlier.

Turmoil in the lobster fishery. Conflict between native and nonnative fishermen over the lucrative lobster fishery continued to disturb the Atlantic provinces in 2000. Native groups claimed that a 1999 Supreme Court decision granted them the right to earn a moderate livelihood from fishing. In a later decision, the court qualified this ruling by stating that native fishermen, as well as their nonnative counterparts, had to obey federal regulations designed to conserve fish stocks.

In summer 2000, the Mi'kmaq, a native community at Burnt Church, on Miramichi Bay on the east coast of New Brunswick, defied federal authority by establishing their own fishing program. The plan included fishing out of the federally mandated season and setting more lobster traps than were permitted under federal regulations. High prices for lobster and a plentiful harvest intensified the dispute. Confrontations occurred when federal fisheries inspectors moved in to seize Mi'kmaq traps. The situation eased after the Mi'kmaq pulled their traps on October 7, the end of the tribe's fishing season.

Security. In March, Canada's Department of National Defence announced the establishment of a $637-million surveillance system to keep watch on objects in space. The system was designed to complement the North American Aerospace Defense Command (NORAD), established by Canada and the United States in 1957 and renewed in 2000.

Diamonds and war. Canada in 2000 played a major role in efforts by the United Nations (UN) to curb the sale of so-called conflict diamonds, stones sold by rebel groups in Angola, Sierra Leone, and Congo (Kinshasa) to finance violent uprisings. Robert Fowler, Canada's ambassador to the UN, undertook fact-finding missions to the disturbed areas. In July, he helped persuade the UN Security Council to approve an 18-month ban on the export of all diamonds from Sierra Leone. On August 9, the UN agreed to lift the ban after approving a plan by the Sierra Leone government to certify all diamonds sold abroad.

□ David M. L. Farr

See also **Canada, Prime Minister of; Canadian provinces; Canadian territories; Montreal; Toronto.**

2000 Canadian population estimates

Province and territory populations

Alberta	3,023,600
British Columbia	4,048,100
Manitoba	1,149,000
New Brunswick	756,500
Newfoundland	536,600
Northwest Territories	42,100
Nova Scotia	943,500
Nunavut	27,600
Ontario	11,644,700
Prince Edward Island	139,000
Quebec	7,367,900
Saskatchewan	1,030,400
Yukon Territory	29,600
Canada	30,758,600

City and metropolitan area populations

	Metropolitan area	City
Toronto, Ont.	4,776,500	2,569,900
Montreal, Que.	3,453,600	1,046,800
Vancouver, B.C.	2,034,200	575,400
Ottawa-Hull	1,074,200	
Ottawa, Ont.		342,600
Hull, Que.		66,100
Calgary, Alta.	965,000	824,900
Edmonton, Alta.	944,200	629,200
Quebec, Que.	689,600	172,800
Winnipeg, Man.	677,100	623,400
Hamilton, Ont.	672,900	333,100
Kitchener, Ont.	421,800	189,200
London, Ont.	421,500	337,500
St. Catharines-Niagara	391,900	
St. Catharines, Ont.		133,200
Niagara Falls, Ont.		78,500
Halifax, N.S.	356,400	117,800
Victoria, B.C.	315,500	77,100
Windsor, Ont.	304,400	207,800
Oshawa, Ont.	298,300	147,600
Saskatoon, Sask.	233,200	199,600
Regina, Sask.	199,100	181,800
St. John's, Nfld.	173,600	103,000
Chicoutimi-Jonquière	162,100	
Chicoutimi, Que.		62,900
Jonquière, Que.		56,400
Sudbury, Ont.	158,900	93,400
Sherbrooke, Que.	154,100	79,700
Trois-Rivières, Que.	141,700	49,500
Saint John, N.B.	126,900	72,400
Thunder Bay, Ont.	125,700	114,100

Source: World Book estimates based on data from Statistics Canada.

Canada, Prime Minister of. Jean

Chretien led his Liberal Party government to a third consecutive victory in a general election held on Nov. 27, 2000. The victory—which made Chretien the first Canadian prime minister since World War II (1939-1945) to win a third successive mandate—was especially sweet for Chretien. While the prime minister is a Quebecker, he has been a strong supporter of a united Canada. The election results also maintained the domination of the centrist Liberal Party, in power for 70 of the last 100 years, over Canadian politics.

Since taking office in 1993, Chretien has been a pragmatic leader who encouraged a flourishing economy and established conditions that imposed a check on Quebec separatism. Despite the quality of his leadership and the success of the Liberal Party in the 2000 election, many Canadians viewed Chretien as unwilling to listen to colleagues in Parliament and overly devoted to political patronage. Opinion polls taken in 2000 showed that a majority of Canadians believed that Chretien, 67 years old and in public life since 1963, should retire.

After the election, Chretien faced two major challenges: Did he possess the vision to help Canada adapt to the demands of a technological age; and would he know when to step aside in favor of a younger leader?   □ David M. L. Farr

Canadian provinces. Despite differ-

ences, Canada's 10 provinces showed a common concern in 2000 with the national health care system. The provinces joined in urging greater federal support for a program beset by rising costs and increasing demand. Some provinces experimented with new forms of health care delivery while questioning the federal government's control over national standards. The federal government met most of the provinces' financial demands, while continuing to assert its leadership in a national health care program.

Alberta. In 2000, Alberta basked in prosperity resulting from higher oil and gas prices. The provincial budget for fiscal year 2000-2001 (April 1, 2000, to March 31, 2001), introduced by Treasurer Stockwell Day on Feb. 24, 2000, included the largest spending increases since the mid-1980's. The increases included an additional $1.1 billion (all amounts in Canadian dollars) for the health care system over a three-year period.

Day predicted a surplus of $733 million, most of which was earmarked for paying down the provincial debt. By September 2000, the surplus had swelled to $5 billion, and the Progressive Conservative Party (PCP) government of Premier Ralph Klein promised to send a $150-energy-rebate check to every taxpayer in the province in November and another in spring 2001. Later in

September 2000, the government announced tax cuts totaling more than $1 billion for corporations and small businesses as well as a reduction in the education property tax for homeowners.

The 2000-2001 budget was Stockwell Day's last as provincial treasurer. On July 8, 2000, he was elected leader of the Canadian Alliance, a new national party formed by the merger of the Reform Party and other conservative groups.

A fierce tornado, with winds of more than 185 miles (300 kilometers) per hour, struck a crowded campsite at Pine Lake, southeast of Red Deer, on July 14. Eleven people died as trailers were hurled into the lake.

British Columbia. Ujjal Dosanjh was sworn in as British Columbia's 33rd premier on February 24. He was the first premier born in India. Earlier in February, Dosanjh had been chosen leader of the governing New Democratic Party (NDP).

Dosanjh had served for four years as attorney general in the Cabinet of Premier Glen Clark, who resigned in August 1999 amid allegations of influence peddling. The NDP held 40 seats in the 75-seat provincial legislature in 2000 but stood 30 points behind the opposition Liberal Party in public opinion polls.

Despite political uncertainties and the province's flat economy, the Dosanjh government on March 27 introduced a budget that boosted spending by $900 million. Wage and benefit hikes accounted for about two-thirds of the increase. The $22.3-billion budget projected a deficit of $1.28 billion, the ninth in a row since the NDP won office in 1991. As a result, British Columbia stood in sharp contrast to most other provinces in Canada, which enjoyed budget surpluses in 2000.

A landmark treaty between the native Nisga'a and British Columbia went into effect on May 11, after a stormy passage through the federal Parliament in April. The treaty, which had been approved by the British Columbia legislature in April 1999, gave the Nisga'a about 750 square miles (2,000 square kilometers) of land in the northwestern part of the province and the right to limited self government.

On May 15, 2000, the Supreme Court of British Columbia began hearing a challenge to the treaty brought by the opposition Liberal Party. The Liberals argued that the treaty was unconstitutional, because it established a third level of government in the province and that the third level enjoyed powers equal to or exceeding the powers of the provincial and federal governments. The setback to the land claims process, and to other Indian land cases, posed a serious drawback to the province's economic development in 2000, especially in the area of natural resources.

Manitoba. The NDP government of Premier Gary Doer followed a cautious course during 2000, its first year in office. Doer's slow pace triggered grumbling among NDP supporters, who expected more dramatic action after the party's success in breaking the PCP's 11-year grip on the province's government in September 1999. The NDP's first provincial budget, presented on May 10, 2000, included a small surplus on expenditures of $6.5 billion. The government promised modest personal income tax cuts over three years as well as reductions in property taxes and levies on small business. The budget also boosted spending on health and education.

In June, the Doer government introduced legislation banning political contributions from both corporations and labor unions. The bill also limited individual donations to $3,000. The opposition PCP objected strongly to the legislation, which passed in August.

The government struck a popular chord in June 2000 with a victims' rights bill. It required prosecutors to consult victims at every stage of a court's proceedings, including hearings to release an offender from custody. This new law went further than any other victim's law in Canada.

New Brunswick. Premier Bernard Lord, who had led the PCP to victory over the Liberal Party in June 1999, angered the province's public service employees in 2000 with his plans to eliminate 750 positions to help reduce government spending. Lord declared the cuts were needed because the Liberals, who had controlled the province since 1987, had provided an overly rosy picture of New Brunswick's finances.

The PCP's first budget, presented on March 28, 2000, outlined expenditures of $4.68 billion, while cutting government spending by $238 million. The budget also included a 10-percent tax cut for individuals and businesses over a four-year period and funding increases for health and education. Public employees vigorously protested the cuts and briefly shut down a discussion of the budget in the legislature on April 17.

Newfoundland. The planned construction of a huge nickel-mining and refining project using ore mined from Voisey's Bay in Labrador remained in doubt at the end of 2000. In 1996, Inco Limited of Toronto, one of the world's largest nickel producers, had paid the province $4.3 billion for the right to exploit the bay's rich reserves. The Newfoundland government had insisted that the ore be smelted at a new refinery to be built in the province, even if that facility would be unprofitable. Inco had balked at the demand, and talks ended on Jan. 11, 2000. The refusal of the 6,700 Indian and Inuit inhabitants of the region to cooperate in the project unless their land claims were settled first further compli-

cated the Voisey's Bay scheme. Some analysts blamed the delay on an unwillingness by Brian Tobin, premier of Newfoundland, to negotiate with the company. Tobin resigned in October, leading some analysts to speculate the project would move ahead in 2001.

A modern version of a Viking long ship landed at L'Anse aux Meadows, near St. Anthony, on July 28, 2000, in commemoration of the arrival of the Vikings on Newfoundland in about A.D. 1000. Dignitaries from Newfoundland, Iceland, and Canada as well as representatives of three Native groups welcomed the long boat and a fleet of 13 other ships to the site where the first Vikings had established a temporary settlement.

Waves of anger swept through Newfoundland's fishing communities on June 15, when federal Fisheries Minister Herb Dhaliwal announced that for the first time fishers from Prince Edward Island would be given licenses to enter the lucrative shrimp fishery off the eastern and northern coasts of Newfoundland. In the past, other provinces, including Quebec and New Brunswick, shared about 30 percent of the shrimp quota from the area. Under the new plan, Newfoundland retained control over 70 percent of the fishery. However, the province's fishing industry, badly hurt by years of shrinking cod and crab stocks, expressed outrage that any outside interest would be allowed to fish in its waters.

Nova Scotia. The PCP government of Premier John Hamm, faced with the highest per capita provincial debt in Canada, took determined steps in 2000 to curb government spending. In March, it announced a massive restructuring of government operations, reducing the number of departments by one-third. The budget, presented by Finance Minister Neil LeBlanc on April 11, cut 1,200 jobs from the civil service. However, a $268-million deficit for fiscal year 2000-2001 remained, despite slashed expenditures. LeBlanc proposed no tax increases but raised user fees by a total of $20 million on a variety of services.

The budget triggered widespread protests by nurses, teachers, and other public employees. Hamm defended the cutbacks, contending that 80 percent of provincial expenditures went for salaries. Massive demonstrations took place outside the legislature in Halifax in April 2000. Teachers were particularly vocal as the debate continued over three stormy weeks. Eventually, the government backed away from cuts in teaching personnel.

In 2000, both the federal government and the provincial government of Nova Scotia attempted to reduce the 20-percent unemployment rate on Cape Breton Island. The federal government helped to lure a Texas-owned electronic customer-service center to Sydney from North Carolina. Union leaders, however, pointed out that the call center jobs paid less than those in the province's key industries, coal mining and steelmaking. Hopes for higher employment rose in October when the union representing workers at a provincially owned steel mill in Sydney reached a tentative pact with a Swiss company that agreed in June to purchase the unprofitable mill.

Ontario. One of the worst environmental disasters in Ontario's history occurred in May when two often-lethal strains of bacteria infected the water supply of Walkerton, a farm town of 4,800 people in the western part of the province. At least 7 people died and another 2,000 residents were made ill. Public indignation turned on the PCP government of Premier Mike Harris, which was accused of harming the quality of Ontario's drinking water by transferring responsibility for the monitoring of water safety to local municipalities. Heavy public pressure led Harris to launch an independent investigation of the incident.

The Harris government, reelected to a second term in 1999 and boosted by a booming economy, announced sweeping tax cuts in a budget presented on May 2, 2000. Finance Minister Ernie Eves announced that a rebate of up to $200 would be sent to every provincial taxpayer. The budget outlined 67 new tax-cutting measures. Eaves also announced that Ontario would establish its own tax-collection agency instead of relying on the federal government. Expenditures increased, especially for health care, which accounts for one-third of provincial outlays. The Harris government announced that it would lease the Bruce nuclear power station near Georgian Bay to British Energy PIC as an initial step in *privatizing* (selling to private industry) the province's nuclear power systems.

Prince Edward Island. The PCP administration of Premier Pat Binns won reelection in an April 17 poll marked by high voter turnout. The PCP, which won 26 of 27 seats in the provincial legislature, had campaigned on its success in promoting strong economic growth. Since 1996, when the PCP took office, the province's unemployment rate had dropped from 16 percent to 11 percent.

The province's potato industry, which supplies

Rescue workers search for survivors at a wrecked campsite north of Calgary, Saskatchewan, on July 15, the day after one of the deadliest tornadoes in Canadian history killed 11 people.

one-third of Canada's potatoes, faced two threats from pests in 2000. The reappearance of the potato leafroll virus led provincial farmers to import seed potatoes to maintain the quality of their crop. In November, the United States, which buys about 10 percent of the province's potato harvest, placed a quarantine on all potatoes from Prince Edward Island after the discovery of potato wart fungus in a field in New Annan. Spores from the fungus, which spreads by means of infected soil and potatoes, can contaminate soil for decades.

Quebec. Long-awaited tax cuts highlighted the province's fiscal 2000-2001 budget of $48.3 billion, presented on March 14, 2000, by Finance Minister Bernard Landry. The Parti Quebecois government offered a total of $4.5 billion in tax cuts, to be made over a three-year period. Landry, however, refused to link the tax rates to the inflation rate, which meant that some of the benefits would be lost with any increase in the cost of living.

Montreal announced on April 26 that the Nasdaq Composite Index was establishing a branch in Montreal to serve the Canadian market. The New York City-based Nasdaq consists of more than 3,000 stocks traded electronically on the system operated by the National Association of Securities Dealers. The news came as a blow to Toronto, home of Canada's dominant stock exchange, which also had been negotiating with Nasdaq.

On May 24, Montreal announced the creation of a 3.5-million-square-foot (325,000-square-meter) office complex for companies in the telecommunications and information technology fields. In 2000, approximately 2,000 high-tech communication companies operated in the province.

Saskatchewan. Premier Roy Romanow, Canada's longest-serving premier, announced his retirement on September 25. His nine years in office were marked by a successful drive to restore Saskatchewan's financial health.

The provincial budget, presented on March 29, provided balanced accounts for the seventh consecutive year and tax cuts for the fifth consecutive year. However, an increase in the number of products and services subject to the provincial sales tax compensated for the cuts. Saskatchewan also announced that it would set up a tax system independent of the federal government. The plan was to be fully implemented by 2003. In an effort to stem the loss of educated young people, the province offered a tax benefit of $350 to college graduates willing to work in Saskatchewan.

The federal government in February gave Saskatchewan and Manitoba $240 million in assistance to compensate for lost revenue claimed by wheat farmers. The farmers had claimed that their income declined because of bad weather and subsidies, which they charged were unfair, given to U.S. and European grain producers. In 1999, farmers in Saskatchewan won $1 billion in federal aid over three years. Farmers had characterized that aid as inadequate.

☐ David M. L. Farr

See also **Canada; Canadian Territories; Montreal; Toronto.**

Canadian territories. The search for diamonds and the construction of an oil pipeline made news in the Northwest Territories in 2000. Canadians in Nunavut celebrated the first anniversary of the new territory. In the Yukon, residents rejected the sitting territorial government in favor of new leadership.

The Northwest Territories' Legislative Assembly elected Stephen Kakfwi premier in January 2000. Kakfwi previously served as Cabinet member and president of the Dene Nation.

Diamonds ranked as the hottest segment of the Territories' economy in 2000. In May, the Territories' first diamond mine, at Ekati, northeast of Yellowknife, reported producing 2.51 million carats valued at U.S. $168 per carat during its first full year of production ending January 31. This output gave the owner of the mine, Dia Met Minerals Ltd., of Vancouver, a profit of $47.5 million. Work continued in 2000 on two additional diamond mines in the Territories. In addition, the search for more diamond deposits extended as far north as the Arctic coastline.

In November, the territorial government filed suit against diamond manufacturer Sirius Diamonds Ltd. of Vancouver to stop the company from using the image of a polar bear as a trademark on diamonds cut in its Yellowknife plant. Sirius had used the image of a three-legged, east-facing polar bear since 1998. The Territories, which had used the same image for tourism purposes since 1968, also wanted to use the image in a government certification program for all diamonds mined, cut, and polished in the Territories. Sirius announced its willingness to use the image of a four-legged, west-facing bear on its diamonds but wanted exclusive rights to a bear image as a trademark.

In January 2000, the chiefs of all 30 native tribes in the Territories agreed in principle to the construction of a pipeline to carry natural gas from the MacKenzie River Delta in the Arctic south to the rest of North America. In February, four major oil companies launched a one-year study to determine the feasibility of tapping into natural gas reserves worth an estimated $200 billion in the delta. Opposition from native groups and environmentalists in the late 1970's had scuttled plans to drill in the area. However, in the intervening years, native tribes have settled a series of land claims with the federal government, granting the tribes the right to share in the management and profits of resource development projects.

In May 2000, the territorial public library system received a windfall grant of $323,000 from the Bill and Melinda Gates Foundation, a charitable organization established by the cofounder of Microsoft Corporation of Redmond, Washington, and another $92,000 in software from Microsoft Canada. The Territories planned to use the funds to create "virtual libraries" in the sparsely populated North by installing computer terminals in 15 remote communities.

Nunavut celebrated its first anniversary as a Canadian territory in April. The Nunavut government spent its first year devising policies to provide services to its scattered population of 25,000. The territory's first budget, introduced on March 24, totaled $639 million, about 90 percent of which came from the federal treasury. Health, social services, education, and housing accounted for half of expenditures.

According to a court challenge filed in June 2000, Nunavut Inuit should not be bound by the federal Firearms Act of 1995, which requires the registration of all firearms, including shotguns and rifles. Nunavut Tunngavik Inc., which represents the territory's Inuit in the administration of a 1993 land-claims agreement with the Canadian government, contended that the law was inappropriate to conditions in the North and that the government had no right to place limitations on guns used for the livelihood of native peoples. The organization contended that a 1993 agreement guaranteed the Inuit's right to "hunt and harvest without any form of license or permit."

Law enforcement officials in Nunavut in 2000 noted the appearance in the territory of criminal gangs involved in the drug trade. Extensive construction in Iqaluit, Nunavut's capital, had attracted highly paid construction workers, who had provided a market for drug dealers.

Yukon. The need for diversification of the economy and more jobs were the central issues in territorial elections held on April 17. Voters decisively rejected the sitting New Democratic Party government of Piers McDonald, giving the Liberal Party, led by Pat Duncan, 10 seats in the 17-member Legislative Assembly. Duncan became the first Liberal to head Yukon's government.

Duncan's elevation to premier gave Yukon the highest concentration of women in high government posts of any Canadian province or territory. The group included the mayor of the capital, Whitehorse; Yukon's two members of the federal Parliament; and the territory's commissioner (federally appointed, honorary head of government).

In February, Aliy Zirkle of Alaska became the first woman to win the Yukon Quest, a 1,000-mile (1,600-kilometer) dog sled race. Twenty *mushers* (sled dog drivers) competed against Zirkle, who endured bitter cold and rugged terrain for nearly 11 days to win the $30,000 prize.

☐ David M. L. Farr

See also **Canada.**
Cape Verde. See Africa.

Census. The United States Census Bureau conducted its decennial census of population and housing in 2000, updating the nation's changing social profile. According to figures released on December 28, the population of the United States as of April 1, 2000, stood at 281.4 million, a growth of 33 million since the 1990 census. The bureau was scheduled to release detailed results on a state-by-state basis in 2001 and post the information on its Web site at www.census.gov.

Growing ethnicity. Preliminary figures released by the Census Bureau on Aug. 30, 2000, revealed that Asians and Hispanics were the fastest-growing minorities in the United States. Between July 1, 1990, and July 1, 1999, the nation's Asian and Pacific Islander population grew 43 percent, to 10.8 million people. The Hispanic population grew 38.8 percent, to 31.3 million people. The white population in the United States increased 7.3 percent between 1990 and 1999, to 224.6 million. Blacks remained the largest minority group in the United States, with the black U.S. population increasing 13.8 percent to 34.8 million people. The Census Bureau reported that the American Indian and Alaska Native population increased 15.5 percent, to 2.3 million people.

Growing cities. New York City, Los Angeles, and Chicago remained the most populous cities in the United States, according to preliminary census figures released in October 2000. The population of New York City totaled 7.4 million people, followed by Los Angeles with 3.6 million people, and Chicago with 2.7 million people.

Other cities, particularly in the South and Southwest, underwent major growth since the 1990 census. Estimates released by the bureau in October 2000 showed that Las Vegas, Nevada, was the fastest-growing metropolitan area during the 1990's, growing 62 percent between April 1990 and July 1999, to nearly 1.4 million people.

Poverty in the United States declined during the 1990's, the Census Bureau reported in September 2000. The poverty rate fell from 12.7 percent in 1998 to 11.8 percent in 1999. This was the lowest recorded poverty rate since 1979. The bureau also reported that real median household income in 2000 reached $40,816, the highest income recorded since the agency began tracking such data in 1967.

High response rate. A larger percentage of U.S. residents responded to the 2000 census than to the 1990 census. Sixty-seven percent of U.S. households completed census forms in 2000, compared with a total of 65 percent of U.S. households in 1990.

☐ Geoffrey A. Campbell and Linda P. Campbell
See also **City; Population.**
Central African Republic. See Africa.
Chad. See Africa.

Chemistry. In 2000, chemists made many new discoveries. They found sugar molecules in space and developed a chemical compound containing argon. Chemists also developed jet fuel from coal and created a new way to visualize the chemical composition of smells.

Sugar in space. Evidence that sugar molecules exist in *interstellar* (between stars) space was reported in June by astrochemists Jan Hollis of the Goddard Space Flight Center in Greenbelt, Maryland; Frank J. Lovas of the University of Illinois Urbana-Champaign; and Philip R. Jewell of the National Radio Astronomy Observatory (NRAO) in Green Bank, West Virginia. Hollis, Lovas, and Jewell pointed the NRAO 12 Meter Telescope on Kitt Peak, southwest of Tucson, Arizona, toward a large cloud of gas and dust in interstellar space near the center of the Milky Way Galaxy. They found combinations of radio waves that were characteristic of glycolaldehyde, an eight-atom sugar molecule made up of carbon, oxygen, and hydrogen. Like all molecules, glycolaldehyde emits characteristic radio waves as it rotates.

The astrochemists' discovery suggested that the chemical conditions required for life are fairly common in the universe. Glycolaldehyde is the simplest type of sugar, a key component of living things. Hollis said that the chemical building blocks to life probably are formed in interstellar clouds long before planets develop around stars. Since sugar and other carbon compounds are present where new stars are being formed, they may be available to give rise to life forms even as the planets take shape. Learning more about the kinds of molecules in interstellar clouds helps scientists understand more about the chemistry of the Earth before life began.

Scientists have discovered about 120 different kinds of molecules in interstellar clouds. With the discovery of the glycolaldehyde molecules, astrochemists may learn more about how large molecules like those found on Earth are formed from smaller molecules in space.

Looking at smells. In August, chemists Neal A. Rakow and Kenneth S. Suslick of the University of Illinois at Urbana-Champaign reported that they had designed a new way to visually recognize the chemical compositions of odors. Odors come from molecules of gas that have been released into the air from many different substances. To visualize odors, Rakow and Suslick used dyes called metalloporphyrins, which can change color when they are exposed to different kinds of molecules. Metalloporphyrins are *organic* (carbon-containing) molecules that also contain atoms of metallic elements. They are the chemical cousins of hemoglobin, which makes blood red, and chlorophyll, which makes plants green.

Rakow and Suslick painted a pattern of metalloporphyrin dye dots onto specially coated glass plates. Each dot contained a dye that was sensitive to a slightly different odor. When exposed to different odors, the metalloporphyrin dyes changed colors. Each odor produced a "fingerprint"—a particular color pattern.

Rakow's and Suslick's technique offered a fast, inexpensive, and portable way to detect a wide variety of chemicals in very small concentrations. Suslick said that for some substances like gasoline and alcohol, the lab technique is 10 to 100 times more sensitive than the human nose. Possible applications include detecting toxins in the workplace, analyzing foods for spoilage, and mechanically sniffing out illegal drugs. To take advantage of their newly developed visualization technique, Rakow and Suslick developed a model digital camera to take "photographs" of odors.

Argon compound. In August, University of Helsinki chemists Leonid Khriachtchev, Mika Pettersson, Nino Runeberg, Jan Lundell, and Markku Rasanen reported that they had made a compound that contained argon. Previously, chemists believed that argon was *inert* (an element that could not be combined with any other element). The new compound was made up of argon, fluoride, and hydrogen atoms. The scientists isolated it in frozen argon below −410 °F (−250 °C).

Coal-fired jets. The same fuel that polluted Charles Dickens's London in the 1800's could be remade as a cleaner, hotter-burning, and safer power source for jet engines, according to fuel chemists John M. Andresen, Chunshan Song, James Strohm, and Harold Schobert, all of Pennsylvania State University in State College. In March 2000, Andresen reported on research indicating that liquid fuel made from coal can withstand heat much better than fuels made from petroleum.

Andresen tested coal-based fuel in a flow reactor that imitated a ramjet engine, a type of engine used in jets that fly 300 miles (480 kilometers) per hour or more. Coal-based fuel withstood temperatures approaching 1,500 °F (800 °C). By contrast, traditional petroleum-based jet fuels start to break down at 750 °F (400 °C). Coal-based fuels are more stable because their molecules form strong ring shapes. Since the molecules in petroleum-based fuels are linear, they break more easily.

The heat limitations of petroleum-based fuel did not cause problems for jet engines in 2000, which operated below 570 °F (300 °C). However, as speed technology progresses, engine temperatures could reach 900 °F (480 °C), Andresen predicted.   □ Peter J. Andrews

See also **Medicine**.

Chess. Garry Kasparov of Russia, long considered the world's greatest chess player, lost a championship match to a former pupil, Vladimir Kramnik of Russia, on Nov. 2, 2000. Kasparov lost 8.5 to 6.5. Kramnik won $1.33 million for his victory, while Kasparov took home $666,000. The defeat ended Kasparov's 15-year reign as champion. Brain Games Network, an Internet company that focuses on chess, sponsored the event.

Kasparov was the best-known chess world champion of modern times. Outgoing and dynamic, he promoted chess throughout the world, even appearing on popular U.S. television shows, such as "Late Night with David Letterman." Kasparov became World Chess Federation (FIDE) champion in 1985 by defeating Anatoly Karpov, of Russia.

In 1993, Garry Kasparov, displeased with FIDE's handling of its world championship matches, broke with the organization, refusing to play in its events. The match between Kasparov and Kramnik, therefore, was not an official title match sanctioned by FIDE. However, Kasparov's reputation as one of the best chess players in history lent credibility to Kramnik's victory.

Olympiad. At the 34th biennial Chess Olympiad held in Istanbul, Turkey, from Oct. 28 to Nov. 12, 2000, the Russian team won the gold medal, Germany took the silver, and Ukraine captured the bronze.

Tournaments. Joel Benjamin of New York City won the U.S. Championship for the third time in 2000. The event was held in Seattle from September 25 to October 6. At a separate tournament also held in Seattle, Camilla Baginskaite, of San Francisco, won the U.S. Women's Championship title.

Young champions. In April, Vinay Bhat, at the age of 15, became the youngest U.S. player in history to earn the International Master title. At separate events involving more than 4,500 players from all over the United States, Masterman High School of Philadelphia won the National High School Championship, Renaissance Junior High School of Detroit took the Junior High title, and Phoenix Country Day School won its third consecutive Elementary School title.

World Chess Museum. Construction began in 2000 on the World Chess Hall of Fame and Sidney Samole Museum in Miami, Florida. The museum was named after Sidney Samole, the inventor of chess games that could be played on personal computers. The museum, designed with an entry shaped like a 45-foot- (13.7-meter-) tall chess rook (or castle), was scheduled to open in early 2001, offering interactive displays, photos and memorabilia of famous players, and a theater.

☐ Al Lawrence

Chicago. In May 2000, Chicago's Field Museum of Natural History unveiled the largest and most complete skeleton yet discovered of the dinosaur *Tyrannosaurus rex*. The 67-million-year-old carnivore was named "Sue " after its discoverer, Susan Hendrickson, a field collector at Black Hills Institute of Geological Research in Hill City, South Dakota.

Law. On February 18, the Chicago City Council passed a revised version of its antigang loitering ordinance. The United States Supreme Court ruled in 1999 that an earlier version of the law, passed in 1992, gave too much discretion to the police. Chicago police began making arrests under the revised law in August 2000, targeting 86 locations as "hot spots."

Schools. More than one-third of Chicago Public Schools elementary students were able to read at or above the national average in 1999, according to a study of test results released on Sept. 7, 2000, by Northwestern University in Evanston, Illinois. The study also revealed that the pace of student improvement had slowed and was uneven among schools citywide.

Building. In May, the city embarked on a $3.2-billion renovation of O'Hare International Airport, which was to include building two new terminals and increasing the number of boarding gates by 25 percent. The project was expected to take eight years to complete.

The city of Chicago installed a garden on the roof of City Hall in May. The garden contained 20,000 plants and two full-sized trees, which were expected to cool and clean the air and reduce energy bills. Chicago Mayor Richard M. Daley hoped the roof garden would serve as an example to the owners of other buildings in the Loop, Chicago's central business district.

City of Chicago and Illinois state officials announced in September that they would jointly pay to convert a portion of the city's famous North Michigan Avenue Water Tower and Pumping Station into a home for the Lookingglass Theatre ensemble. The project was expected to cost $6.5 million and be completed in 2002.

Utilities. Commonwealth Edison, the city's electricity provider, continued to be plagued by brief downtown power outages in 2000, while in the midst of a $1.9-billion infrastructure improvement program. On September 14, an electrical short caused a fire in a vault and cut power to downtown buildings. On October 8, an explosion and fire at a power station blacked out downtown and surrounding neighborhoods for hours.

Environment. Chicago's ozone pollution levels were lower in the summer of 1999 than in previous years with similar weather, according to an Illinois Environmental Protection Agency report issued in July 2000. The improvements in air

Patrons of Chicago's Field Museum of Natural History enjoy a close look at a 41-foot- (12.5-meter-) long dinosaur named Sue at a special unveiling on May 17 of the most complete *Tyrannosaurus rex* fossil found to date.

quality were attributed to regulations on vehicle emissions and industrial pollution.

Preservation. On Sept. 21, 2000, the Metropolitan Pier and Exposition Authority began demolishing the nearly 100-year-old, four-story Platt Luggage building in the south Loop, despite protests by preservationists. The authority eventually agreed to save the building facade by incorporating it into a new parking garage.

In August, the city revealed plans to provide $12.5 million in subsidies to preserve the historic Medinah Temple, a Moorish-style structure built in 1912. The plans included renovation of the adjacent Tree Studios building, the oldest permanent residence for artists in the United States.

Theater. In December 2000, the Goodman Theater company moved into a new $46-million, 856-seat theater complex in Chicago's North Loop. Located at Dearborn and Randolph streets, the new complex includes two theaters, a traditional proscenium-style main stage and a more flexible courtyard space.

Deaths. Sidney Yates, a Democrat who represented the city's north lakeshore in the U.S. Congress for 24 terms, died October 5 at age 91.

☐ Harold Henderson

See also **Baseball.**

Children's books. See Literature for children.

Chile. On March 11, 2000, Ricardo Lagos Escobar, the former public works minister in the governing Concertacion coalition, was sworn in for a six-year term as president. Lagos was the first Socialist to hold this post since 1973, when President Salvador Allende was killed in a military *coup* (overthrow).

Economic policies. The 62-year-old Lagos took office in the midst of a *recession* (economic downturn). Lagos pledged to create 200,000 new jobs and remedy gross economic disparities between Chile's rich and poor. He also said he would continue the economic policies followed by the centrist coalitions that had governed Chile since 1990.

Women appointees. Lagos appointed four women to his cabinet, including Soledad Alvear as minister of foreign affairs. Alvear was the highest-ranking female official in Chilean history.

Armed forces. Lagos quickly moved to curb the power of Chile's armed forces. Four days after taking office, he said he would seek a constitutional amendment to grant Chile's president the power to appoint top military commanders. In June 2000, Chile's military leadership bowed to his demand to search for the remains of 1,200 dissidents who had disappeared during the 1973-1990 dictatorship of General Augusto Pinochet Ugarte.

Pinochet returns. Pinochet returned to Chile on March 3, 2000, after being under house arrest in London for 16 months. British authorities had detained him in October 1998 due to a warrant from Spain requesting his *extradition* (surrender of a wanted individual) to face murder and torture charges stemming from his years as Chile's dictator. However, British Home Secretary Jack Straw ruled that the 84-year-old Pinochet was too ill to be extradited. On Dec. 1, 2000, a Chilean judge ordered Pinochet to stand trial on kidnapping charges stemming from his reign, but an appeals court later dismissed these charges.

Severance scandal. Press reports in September revealed that several dozen former top executives of state-owned companies had accepted higher-than-normal severance payments. Most of the executives were members of the Christian Democratic Party, a major partner in the Concertacion coalition. President Lagos demanded that those who received the severance packages and remained working in the public sector to return the payments or resign.

Joaquin Lavin, a rightist who had narrowly lost the presidential race to Lagos, won election on October 29 as mayor of Santiago. Right-wing opposition candidates also scored victories in other municipal races. ☐ Nathan A. Haverstock

See also **Latin America.**

China. Communist Party officials in China admitted in 2000 that corruption had become a threat to national stability. Many of China's 1.3 billion people were reported to be angry that the party, which came to power in 1949 with a clean image of fighting widespread corruption in the government that it defeated, had sunk into the same political corruption after 50 years of rule.

Political corruption. Premier Zhu Rongji told the National People's Congress (NPC), China's almost powerless parliament, in March 2000, that "corruption and undesirable practices have not been brought under control." Some congress delegates complained that the party did not listen to delegates or the public and that corruption thrived because of the government's lack of accountability.

Defending its right to continue absolute control, the Communist Party publicized its efforts to fight corruption. A number of officials were prosecuted in 2000. However, Chinese citizens told Western reporters that they believed several well-connected government officials were being protected from prosecution while other, lower-ranking officials were used as scapegoats.

Several Chinese officials were put to death on charges of corruption during 2000. Former vice chairman of the NPC and chairman of Guangxi province Chang Kejie, was executed in September

A woman in Beijing attempts to protect herself with a plastic bag over her head during an April dust storm, described as the worst in 10 years. Winds of 44 miles (70 kilometers) per hour blew powdered top soil from China's drought-stricken northern regions into the capital.

for extorting $4.7 million in a widespread bribery scandal. He was the most senior party member to be put to death since the founding of the People's Republic of China in 1949.

Corruption trials in the Fujian province in November 2000, concerning billions of dollars worth of smuggled goods, resulted in 14 death sentences. Along China's southern coast, most official corruption involved bureaucrats extending protection to smugglers. A crackdown in 1999 hit mid-level officials, raising questions about special treatment for senior officials. One of the people implicated in the smuggling was Lin Youfang, wife of Jia Qinglin, Beijing's Communist Party chief and former Fujian party leader.

Chinese President Jiang Zemin's public displays of friendship with Jia in 2000 were widely understood to mean that Jia had protection from blame for any activities of his wife, whom he quietly divorced in December 1999.

Jia's predecessor, Chen Xitong, was reportedly released from prison in 2000 on medical parole. He had been sentenced in 1998 to 16 years of imprisonment for corruption, supposedly for stealing 39 million yuan (U.S. $36.5 million).

Audits. The head of the National Audit Office, Li Jinhua, said in July 2000 that government units were directing cash earmarked for flood control and poverty relief into fancy office buildings and hotels. Li disclosed plans in August to bring senior officials under a year-old system of auditing the assets of county-level officials and state enterprise bosses when they leave their positions.

Economic problems. Premier Zhu—for the first time in the history of the Communist regime in China—failed to set a precise target for economic growth in his March NPC report. The rate of growth had fallen in recent years, and goals had not been met. However, by late 2000, China had rebounded from effects of the Asian economic setback that began in 1997. Exports spurred faster growth. Most gains were in urban areas, while rural incomes scarcely rose.

Exports were expected to surge as a result of China's introduction to the World Trade Organization (WTO). United States President Bill Clinton signed a bill on Oct. 10, 2000, allowing permanent trade benefits for China, paving the way for its membership in the WTO. Some U.S. officials worried that opening China to more imports under WTO rules would hurt U.S. industries by reducing the number of jobs available and lowering worker wages.

Major problems remained hidden in 2000 behind China's improved economic status. The combination of people being driven off farms by rural reforms, the firing of unneeded workers in shrinking state industries, and population growth meant nearly 18 million new urban jobs had to be created annually in China. Expansion of private enterprises, allowed by a 1999 constitutional change, created some jobs but not enough to reduce the high unemployment rate.

Riots. Economic change, compounded by corruption, fostered unrest. The government cut subsidies for inefficient state industries, resulting in workers being fired or industries being closed. In China's Communist system, housing, medical care, schools, and pensions are provided by employers. Therefore, when workers lose their jobs, many become homeless.

In February 2000, some 20,000 people rioted in northeastern China after the closure of a state-owned mine. In Tianjin, laid-off workers held six foreign managers hostage in August. In Fengcheng City, in Jiangxi province, thousands of farmers smashed government offices and looted houses of the rich in protest over high local taxes and administrative fees. Similar disturbances were reported from many areas as poor farmers complained that Communist Party officials had become an oppressive class.

Workers also complained of unsafe work conditions. While China produced one-fourth of the world's coal, it had four-fifths of all coal mining fatalities, according to a statistics compiled at the Chinese University of Mining. Chinese officials reported that more than 5,350 people were killed in coal mine accidents in China in 2000.

Drought and floods added to economic trouble in China in 2000. North China suffered the worst drought in 40 years. Water rationing and higher prices for water led farmers to riot. In Shandong province, a policeman was killed and 100 people were injured during a riot in July. In Shaanxi province, floods and landslides killed 213 people in July, raising the number of national flood deaths to more than 600 during 2000.

Repression. The Communist Party continued to use government police in 2000 to repress anything the government considered a challenge to its political authority and its right to be the only voice for public attitudes. The government arrested members of Falun Gong, a spiritual movement that combines exercises, meditation, and breathing techniques with ideas from Buddhism and Taoism. The movement, which claims 70 million members, came to public prominence in 1999.

In September 2000, criminal charges were brought against more than 80 evangelical Christians whose worship services in "house churches" were termed illegal by the government. The Christians refused to accept the authority of state-controlled religious organizations.

In 2000, Chinese officials shut down the first China-based dissident Web site. The government also cracked down on liberal intellectuals, who had become increasingly assertive in comments concerning public affairs issues. The government forbade newspapers from printing their articles, closed publishing houses that issued their books, and tried to restrict use of the Internet.

Regional unrest. A truck carrying explosives blew up in September, killing 60 people and wounding 173 people in Xinjiang's capital, Urumqi. Premier Zhu was in Urumqi at the time of the explosion. However, officials labeled the explosion an accident. Xinjiang is a large western province with 8 million minority Muslim Uighurs among its 17 million people. Opposition to Chinese rule festered in the province in 2000, particularly among separatists, after 11 Uighurs had been shot on charges of murder and separatism in March, and 13 more were executed by August.

In August, Chinese officials banned an international agency that restores old Buddhist Tibetan monasteries. The government feared the agency's activities supported Tibetan nationalism, which drew its strength from the religious system. In January, one of the most revered Tibetan religious leaders, the 14-year-old Karmapa Lama, escaped Chinese rule in Tibet by crossing the Himalayans into India, where another leader, the Dalai Lama, was already living in exile.

Hong Kong. Three years after China took over the former British colony of Hong Kong, complaints grew of arbitrary rule by the chief executive, Tung Chee-hwa, who was selected by Beijing. Two Hong Kong University officials resigned in September 2000 after an investigation found that Tung's senior special adviser had suppressed university surveys of public opinion that were critical of the chief executive.

International observers noted growing discontent when only 43 percent of Hong Kong's registered voters cast ballots in the September elections. Hong Kong's prodemocracy candidates won most of the 24 elected seats in the 60-seat legislature, which was dominated by Tung's appointed supporters.

Foreign relations. Beijing applied strong verbal pressure on Taiwan in an effort to discourage the election of Chen Shui-bian as president. After Chen's victory, China cautiously moderated comments on Taiwan, over which China claims control. A U.S. Defense Department study reported that the modernization of China's armed forces increased the threat to Taiwan. The authors of the study did not expect China to invade the island in the near future and reported that China would not be able to militarily challenge the United States.   □ Henry S. Bradsher

See also **Asia; Human rights; International trade; Korea, North; Taiwan; United States, Government of the.**

City. Seven of the world's top 10 most expensive cities were in Asia in 2000, according to January rankings by the William M. Mercer Companies LLC (formerly the Corporate Resources Group), an international consultancy firm based in New York City. Each year, the company ranks some 150 cities throughout the world by pricing numerous goods and services and comparing these costs to those in New York City, which is assigned a baseline rating of 100.

Tokyo, with a rating of 164.9, topped the rankings in 2000, as it did in 1999. This figure meant that it cost almost two-thirds more to live in Tokyo than in New York City. Osaka, Japan, with a score of 143.6, moved into second place in 2000 from fourth place in 1999. Next in the rankings were Hong Kong (141.5); Beijing (138.3); and Moscow (136.1)—the only non-Asian city to make the top five. Rounding out the top 10 were Shanghai (128); Seoul, South Korea (111.1); St. Petersburg, Russia (109.7); Guangzhou, China (107.9); and London (106.9). The least expensive city in the survey was Quito, Equador (32.1).

Quality of life. In January 2000, Mercer also released a survey of the quality of life in more than 200 cities. The company examined 39 categories, including political stability, crime rates, economic issues, individual freedom, air pollution, quality of medical services, education, transportation, recreation, and availability of consumer goods and housing. As with the cost-of-living survey, each city was assigned a numerical rating in comparison with New York City's 100.

Six cities tied for the title of best-overall city, each with a rating of 106: Vancouver, Canada; Zurich, Geneva, and Bern in Switzerland; Vienna, Austria; and Sydney, Australia. A total of 68 cities were ranked within six points (between 106 and 94) of New York City. The survey found few differences in the quality of life in these developed cities, with minor variations in such areas as public transportation and education. However, there were major differences between the cities at the top of the survey and those at the bottom. Some of the lowest-ranking cities, such as Brazzaville, Congo (23), and Khartoum, Sudan (33), had long been menaced by civil war or medical disasters. Citizens in other cities, including Tehran, Iran (55) and Baghdad, Iraq (33), suffered under repressive regimes in 2000.

Western Europe. International analysts found the quality-of-life survey most useful for comparing cities within continents. Twelve of the top 20 cities were located in Western Europe. Besides Switzerland's top three, other high-ranking Western European cities included Copenhagen, Denmark, and Helsinki, Finland (both scoring 105); and three German cities with scores of 104—Frankfurt, Munich, and Dusseldorf. Paris

50 largest urban centers in the world

Rank	Urban center*	Population
1.	Tokyo-Yokohama, Japan	29,957,000
2.	Mexico City, Mexico	27,803,000
3.	Sao Paulo, Brazil	25,286,000
4.	Seoul, South Korea	21,930,000
5.	Bombay, India	15,333,000
6.	New York City, U.S.	14,645,000
7.	Osaka-Kobe-Kyoto, Japan	14,286,000
8.	Tehran, Iran	14,198,000
9.	Rio de Janeiro, Brazil	14,151,000
10.	Calcutta, India	14,080,000
11.	Buenos Aires, Argentina	12,907,000
12.	Manila, Philippines	12,826,000
13.	Jakarta, Indonesia	12,777,000
14.	Cairo, Egypt	12,498,000
15.	Lagos, Nigeria	12,453,000
16.	Delhi, India	11,817,000
17.	Karachi, Pakistan	11,261,000
18.	Moscow, Russia	11,118,000
19.	Los Angeles, U.S.	10,714,000
20.	Lima, Peru	9,219,000
21.	Istanbul, Turkey	8,855,000
22.	Paris, France	8,804,000
23.	London, U.K.	8,573,000
24.	Taipei, Taiwan	8,501,000
25.	Bogota, Colombia	7,915,000
26.	Bangkok, Thailand	7,576,000
27.	Shanghai, China	7,539,000
28.	Madras, India	7,375,000
29.	Essen, Germany	7,240,000
30.	Bangalore, India	6,742,000
31.	Pusan, South Korea	6,686,000
32.	Chicago, U.S.	6,567,000
33.	Dhaka, Bangladesh	6,465,000
34.	Santiago, Chile	6,289,000
35.	Beijing, China	5,992,000
36.	Hong Kong, China	5,956,000
37.	Lahore, Pakistan	5,848,000
38.	Kinshasa, Congo	5,619,000
39.	Nagoya, Japan	5,302,000
40.	Tianjin, China	5,296,000
41.	Baghdad, Iraq	5,229,000
42.	Belo Horizonte, Brazil	5,111,000
43.	Madrid, Spain	5,103,000
44.	Milan, Italy	4,838,000
45.	Barcelona, Spain	4,832,000
46.	Ahmadabad, India	4,827,000
47.	Hyderabad, India	4,756,000
48.	St. Petersburg, Russia	4,739,000
49.	Shenyang, China	4,682,000
50.	Ho Chi Minh City, Vietnam	4,476,000

*The U.S. Bureau of the Census defines an urban center as a continuous built-up area, similar to a metropolitan area, having a population density of at least 5,000 persons per square mile (1,900 per square kilometer).
Source: 2000 estimates based on data from the U.S. Bureau of the Census.

50 largest cities in the United States

Rank	City	Population*
1.	New York, N.Y.	7,439,717
2.	Los Angeles, Calif.	3,650,548
3.	Chicago, Ill.	2,800,916
4.	Houston, Tex.	1,863,811
5.	Philadelphia, Pa.	1,400,905
6.	San Diego, Calif.	1,254,805
7.	Phoenix, Ariz.	1,241,753
8.	San Antonio, Tex.	1,166,333
9.	Dallas, Tex.	1,084,465
10.	Detroit, Mich.	958,543
11.	San Jose, Calif.	878,087
12.	San Francisco, Calif.	749,432
13.	Indianapolis, Ind.	739,728
14.	Jacksonville, Fla.	703,300
15.	Columbus, Ohio	675,349
16.	El Paso, Tex.	625,570
17.	Baltimore, Md.	622,839
18.	Memphis, Tenn.	604,695
19.	Austin, Tex.	600,218
20.	Milwaukee, Wis.	566,763
21.	Boston, Mass.	553,213
22.	Seattle, Wash.	539,537
23.	Charlotte, N.C.	533,560
24.	Washington, D.C.	510,638
25.	Fort Worth, Tex.	509,123
26.	Nashville, Tenn.	508,467
27.	Portland, Ore.	505,652
28.	Denver, Colo.	503,607
29.	Cleveland, Ohio	501,272
30.	Oklahoma City, Okla.	478,966
31.	Tucson, Ariz.	472,760
32.	New Orleans, La.	457,226
33.	Las Vegas, Nev.	447,080
34.	Virginia Beach, Va.	438,422
35.	Kansas City, Mo.	438,056
36.	Long Beach, Calif.	435,607
37.	Albuquerque, N. Mex.	424,644
38.	Fresno, Calif.	410,293
39.	Sacramento, Calif.	408,255
40.	Atlanta, Ga.	402,619
41.	Honolulu, Hawaii	397,479
42.	Omaha, Nebr.	390,223
43.	Tulsa, Okla.	383,233
44.	Mesa, Ariz.	379,916
45.	Miami, Fla.	370,320
46.	Oakland, Calif.	361,680
47.	Colorado Springs, Colo.	359,421
48.	Minneapolis, Minn.	351,824
49.	Wichita, Kan.	338,806
50.	Pittsburgh, Pa.	333,513

*2000 World Book estimates based on data from the U.S. Bureau of the Census.

50 largest metropolitan areas in the United States

Rank	Metropolitan area*	Population[†]
1.	Los Angeles-Long Beach, Calif.	9,441,949
2.	New York, N.Y.	8,747,450
3.	Chicago, Ill.	8,064,567
4.	Philadelphia, Pa.-N.J.	4,954,817
5.	Washington, D.C.-Md.-Va.-W.Va.	4,820,579
6.	Detroit, Mich.	4,479,089
7.	Houston, Tex.	4,095,199
8.	Atlanta, Ga.	3,972,810
9.	Dallas, Tex.	3,359,037
10.	Boston, Mass.	3,310,390
11.	Riverside-San Bernadino, Calif.	3,287,003
12.	Phoenix-Mesa, Ariz.	3,098,079
13.	Minneapolis-St. Paul, Minn.-Wis.	2,915,191
14.	San Diego, Calif.	2,877,261
15.	Orange County, Calif.	2,799,601
16.	Nassau-Suffolk, N.Y.	2,705,037
17.	St. Louis, Mo.-Ill.	2,576,736
18.	Baltimore, Md.	2,501,219
19.	Oakland, Calif.	2,383,954
20.	Seattle-Bellevue-Everett, Wash.	2,358,283
21.	Pittsburgh, Pa.	2,317,348
22.	Tampa-St. Petersburg-Clearwater, Fla.	2,303,229
23.	Cleveland-Lorain-Elyria, Ohio	2,216,739
24.	Miami, Fla.	2,201,742
25.	Denver, Colo.	2,022,529
26.	Newark, N.J.	1,960,535
27.	Portland, Ore.-Vancouver, Wash.	1,871,682
28.	Kansas City, Mo.-Kan.	1,775,214
29.	San Francisco, Calif.	1,687,333
30.	Fort Worth-Arlington, Tex.	1,668,314
31.	San Jose, Calif.	1,652,361
32.	Cincinnati, Ohio-Ky.-Ind.	1,637,274
33.	Sacramento, Calif.	1,617,138
34.	San Antonio, Tex.	1,589,988
35.	Norfolk-Virginia Beach-Newport News, Va.	1,575,136
36.	Orlando, Fla.	1,567,239
37.	Fort Lauderdale, Fla.	1,563,106
38.	Indianapolis, Ind.	1,555,105
39.	Columbus, Ohio	1,505,871
40.	Milwaukee-Waukesha, Wis.	1,465,347
41.	Charlotte-Gastonia, N.C.-Rock Hill, S.C.	1,452,647
42.	Las Vegas, Nev.-Ariz.	1,444,616
43.	Bergen-Passaic, N.J.	1,346,142
44.	New Orleans, La.	1,304,174
45.	Salt Lake City-Ogden, Ut.	1,286,552
46.	Greensboro-Winston-Salem-High Point, N.C.	1,191,178
47.	Austin-San Marcos, Tex.	1,189,600
48.	Nashville, Tenn.	1,188,160
49.	Hartford, Conn.	1,152,094
50.	Middlesex-Somerset-Hunterdon, N.J.	1,144,159

*The U.S. Bureau of the Census defines a metropolitan area as a large population nucleus with adjacent communities having a high degree of economic and social integration.

[†]2000 World Book estimates based on data from the U.S. Bureau of the Census.

(103) and London (102) scored out of the top 20 because of their high costs of living.

Eastern Europe. Three Eastern European cities had high quality-of-life ratings—Budapest, Hungary (91); Prague, Czech Republic (88); and Warsaw, Poland (83). In contrast, Moscow (58); St. Petersburg, Russia (58); and Belgrade, Yugoslavia (39), lagged far behind their Western counterparts due to continuing struggles with political stability.

North and South America. After Vancouver, the North American cities leading the quality-of-life index included Toronto, Canada; Honolulu, Hawaii; and San Francisco, California—tied with a score of 104. Mexico City at 70 points was among the lowest-ranking cities in North America. Cities in Latin America showed much more disparity, with Montevideo, Uruguay (93); Buenos Aires, Argentina (92); and Santiago, Chile (83), ranking much higher than Managua, Nicaragua (55); San Salvador, El Salvador (53); and Port au Prince, Haiti (47).

Asia and Africa also exhibited extremes in quality of life. In Asia, Sydney ranked at the top, followed by Auckland, New Zealand (105); Tokyo (103); Kobe, Japan (101); Singapore (100); and Hong Kong (93). At the bottom were Beijing (65); Jakarta, Indonesia (64); and Hanoi, Vietnam (54)—areas where political instability and social repression continued to be major problems in 2000. Middle Eastern cities ranked low for the same reasons, though Tel Aviv, Israel (86); and Amman, Jordan (71), scored relatively high. Africa was the all-around lowest ranked continent, with many cities scoring in the 30's or 40's. Two of South Africa's cities—Cape Town (84) and Johannesburg (83)—were exceptions.

U.S. cities. Thanks to another year of nationwide economic prosperity in 2000, the urban economies of the United States continued booming. The National League of Cities (NLC), a Washington, D.C.-based organization that seeks to improve the quality of life in U.S. cities, reported in July that 2000 was the seventh straight year that the majority of U.S. cities had improved fiscal health. Of the 353 cities surveyed, 73 percent reported that they were better able to meet their financial needs in 2000 than in 1999. Of these, 64 percent also increased their municipal spending, and 50 percent increased their municipal workforce. According to the NLC, these were strong numbers, but slightly down from the 1999 survey, suggesting that urban economies may have started to level off in 2000 after their fast growth during the 1990's.

Municipalities in Transition, a report issued by the NLC in July 2000, expressed concern over how the "new economy," which is based on the rapid growth in high-technology industries and the development of the Internet, is affecting U.S. cities. The report noted that city revenue has traditionally been tied to taxes on the sale of goods and property. However, the new economy is dominated by services and information, both of which are more mobile and less taxable. The report predicted that the way cities respond to these changes will be the "most important influence on public finance" in the coming years.

The U.S. Conference of Mayors took its concerns to Washington, D.C., in February for meetings with President Bill Clinton and the U.S. Congress. The chairman of the group of mayors, Wellington Webb of Denver, outlined an "Agenda for America's Cities," which recognized "four cornerstones to building successful communities and keeping the metro economies moving." Webb said these cornerstones included "public safety, kids and schools, public amenity priorities (such as cultural and sporting facilities), and economic justice for all citizens."

The conference pointed to several other areas of major concern to cities in 2000, including *e-commerce* (the selling of items over the Internet) and the 2000 *census* (a counting of the U.S. population by the U.S. Bureau of the Census). Many mayors said they were worried that as the Internet, which was not subject to local taxation in 2000, gained popularity as a place to purchase goods, cities may see a serious decrease in revenues. The census was a big issue for the mayors in 2000 because its results were to set the levels of federal aid to cities over the next decade. The conference attendees hoped for a more accurate count in 2000 than in 1990, when many mayors felt the census had underestimated the number of people living in cities by as many as 4 million.

The Entrepreneurial City, a highly praised collection of articles by leading U.S. mayors published in December 1999, had a major impact on presidential politics in 2000. Former Indianapolis Mayor Stephen Goldsmith, chairman of The Center for Civic Innovation at The Manhattan Institute in New York City—the publisher of the book—was the domestic policy adviser to Republican presidential candidate Governor George W. Bush of Texas. Another former mayor featured in the book, Ed Rendell of Philadelphia, was the chairman of the Democratic Party in 2000. Both Bush and Vice President Al Gore, the Democratic presidential candidate, regularly campaigned with the nation's mayors, reflecting the popularity of local governments over the national one. Many political analysts hoped that the new presidential administration taking office in 2001 would learn lessons in pragmatic politics from the success of the U.S. mayors.   □ Robert Messenger

See also **Cities: A Special Report.**

Civil rights. See Human rights.

The Renaissance of American Cities

By Wim Wiewel

FROG POND PAVILION

Many of the largest cities in the United States entered the new millennium undergoing what some social scientists have described as a renaissance, or rebirth. Substantial numbers of middle-class people were moving into inner-city neighborhoods, particularly the neighborhoods closest to downtown centers. This "back-to-the-city movement," as it came to be called, was quickly picked up by the media with television features and newspaper and magazine articles celebrating such urban changes as the conversion of empty warehouses and factory lofts into apartments on Chicago's long-neglected near West Side; the rehabilitation of Victorian townhouses in neighborhoods adjacent to downtown Cincinnati; and the rebirth of New York City's fabled Times Square as a center of first-rate entertainment.

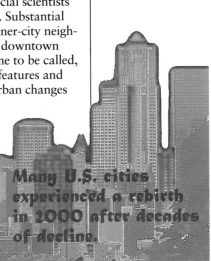

Many U.S. cities experienced a rebirth in 2000 after decades of decline.

This apparent rebirth was particularly striking since U.S. cities had been in decline for decades and were often said to be beyond saving. As late as 1991, the editors of *Newsweek* posed the question "Are Cities Obsolete?" in a cover story on the problems plaguing cities. High crime rates, loss of industry and jobs, eroding tax bases, low-quality public schools, and decaying infrastructure appeared to have turned cities into dinosaurs lumbering toward extinction.

The long decline

The period of significant decline began in most large U.S. cities in the 1930's. This decline coincided with a period of tremendous social and economic upheaval. The Great Depression of the 1930's and World War II (1939–1945) depressed demand for housing among young adults. In addition, many people during this period lacked the money to adequately maintain property. This generally reduced the quality and value of existing housing in large cities.

After the war, the birth rate in the United States soared during what became known as the "baby boom years"—1946 to 1964. The increase in population, coupled with the lack of quality housing, produced a housing shortage. Urban landlords, in many instances, responded to the shortage by dividing apartments into smaller units. Crowding more people into the same space further debased the quality of housing. Developers responded to the shortage with low-cost, high-quality housing, generally built in large developments in suburbs away from city centers. Given the burgeoning demand for housing and an increasing supply of new housing in the suburbs, those who were able——typically white, middle-class families—chose to leave urban neighborhoods.

Two major federal programs also reinforced the movement from the cities to the suburbs. Much of the suburban housing was made possible by the Federal Housing Administration (FHA), a U.S. government agency that works with private industry to provide good housing. The FHA provided low-down payment, long-term, fixed-rate mortgages to help raise home owner-

The author:
Wim Wiewel is Professor of Urban Planning and Policy, and Professor of Managerial Studies at the University of Illinois at Chicago.

CITY

■ SPECIAL REPORT

ship rates, particularly among World War II veterans. Such mortgages were only available for housing that met FHA standards. New houses in suburban developments met standards, while neglected older houses in inner-city neighborhoods did not.

However, the exploding popularity and availability of automobiles and the passage of the Interstate Highway Act of 1956 played an even more significant role in the movement to the suburbs. After World War II, more families could afford automobiles, creating a need for better roads. The interstate highway system was designed in part to ease congestion caused by increased auto traffic. Instead, the new expressways provided escape paths to the suburbs. Four-to-six lane, limited-access roads cut through city neighborhoods, reducing the sense of community and displacing large numbers of residents. Eventually, the expressways became congested themselves, leading to the creation of "beltways," which allowed traffic to bypass central cities altogether. The new highway system robbed cities of residents, retail customers, and federal funds for public transportation.

Social upheaval in the 1960's and 1970's

Cities were dealt another blow in the 1960's, with the social unrest and violence of the Vietnam War (1957–1975) and the civil rights movement. Racial divides were still ingrained in the culture and the legal system of the United States at that time. Attempts at reforming the systems were often met with violent protests. Martin Luther King, Jr., the most prominent civil rights leader of the era, was assassinated on April 4, 1968. Riots immediately broke out in cities across the nation. The riots left many inner-city neighborhoods severely damaged and many local businesses ruined. In the following years, large numbers of urban middle-class families moved out of U.S. cities to the suburbs. Increasingly, cities were left with high concentrations of poor and unemployed people living amid a deteriorating infrastructure.

In the 1970's, U.S. cities began to lose industry and with it, their financial underpinning. The economy of the United States, through the 1960's, was based on heavy manufacturing industries located in major cities, primarily in the Northeast and Mid-

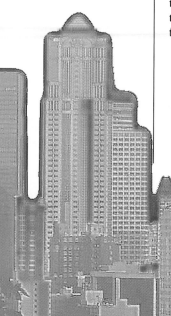

Who is moving into cities

- Single people
- Empty nesters (middle-aged couples with grown children)
- Young couples
- Immigrants

Who is moving out of cities

- The poor and the elderly
- Low-income working people
- Young couples with children starting school

west. Changes in this economy, particularly resulting from in-creased foreign competition, led to the decline of such core in-dustries as automakers and steel manufacturers. The decline of these industries often crippled smaller industries, such as foundries and tool-and-die makers, that were dependent on larg-er companies. Plant closings in cities such as Buffalo, Cleveland, and Pittsburgh resulted in the loss of thousands of well-paying jobs, both blue collar and white collar. It also left behind acres of abandoned, often contaminated industrial property. The closing down of these plants seriously eroded urban tax bases.

The U.S. corporations that did survive needed to incorporate new technology into their production methods in order to stay competitive. This often meant building new, single-story plants or warehouses, which were usually constructed in suburbs. Sub-urbs offered easy access to interstate highways and often had lower property taxes than cities. The prospect of lower costs, particularly lower labor costs, also lured manufacturers from the "Rust Belt" of Northern cities to the "Sun Belt" of the South and Southwest United States.

As U.S. corporations abandoned factories and warehouses, many large cities established urban renewal agencies, which used federal funds to buy land and demolish the old buildings. In some instances, the cities resold the land to local public housing authorities for large-scale, high-rise housing projects for the poor. These projects tended to bring together many poor people into relatively small areas of cities, creating dense pockets of poor, making cities even less attractive for those who could af-ford to leave. Urban renewal also cleared large areas of cities, leaving empty lots strewn with rubble. The empty land created gaps in the urban fabric, discouraging pedestrian traffic, which *urbanologists* (experts on cities) said hastened the decline of these neighborhoods.

Urban crime

In the late 1960's and 1970's, crime exploded in American cities. Between 1964 and 1974, the murder rate more than doubled, from 4.8 to 10.7 murders per 100,000 people. Criminologists, social scientists, and politicians came up with many explana-tions. Conservatives pointed to the liberalization of criminal laws, the court-ordered abolition of capital punishment, and to a general loosening of morality. Liberals responded that crime was a function of poverty, unemployment, and the failure of govern-ment to provide adequate educational opportunities and housing. Population experts pointed to the post-war baby boom. They noted that young males commit the majority of crimes, and that the baby boom had produced a large number of males who were then in their late teens and early 20's. According to the popula-tion experts, this large pool of young men, combined with the soaring commerce in illegal drugs, such as marijuana, cocaine, and heroine, created a set of circumstances that led to the urban crime wave of the period. Whatever the cause, crime and the fear of crime fueled the flight to the suburbs.

In Philadelphia, the Southwark public housing development is demolished (top) as part of a federal policy to break up concentrations of low-income families. Developers in Chicago convert an old factory building (above) into loft condominiums. Such conversions have turned blocks of abandoned industrial buildings into thriving neighborhoods.

Even though suburbs grew phenomenally after the 1950's, suburbs themselves were not new. Exclusive suburbs, such as Lake Forest near Chicago and Grosse Pointe near Detroit, were well-established enclaves for the wealthy by the end of the 1800's. In the late 1800's and early 1900's, upper-class people lived in these suburbs but continued to work and shop downtown. The central city remained, on the whole, a desirable place. The rapid growth of middle-class suburbs that began in the 1950's represented a significant change. When the majority of the middle class left the cities, retail and service oriented businesses followed, leaving downtown streets deserted, especially at night. In Philadelphia, Detroit, St. Louis, and many other major U.S. cities, downtown office buildings stood empty and prestigious hotels and department stores closed their doors, leaving deteriorating hulks of buildings.

American cities are reborn

In the mid-1980's, inner areas of U.S. cities began to stabilize and regain lost ground. Office development in the central business districts often led the way, but the "back-to-the-city" movement was fueled largely by "urban pioneers." Brave new residents moved into deteriorated city neighborhoods to take advantage of the low cost of property. They were usually young, middle-class adults, single or married, without children. The process of improving old buildings and old neighborhoods became known as "gentrification." Gentrification attracted more new residents.

Developers followed and began renovating apartment and factories in the late 1980's and 1990's for sale as loft condominiums. Developers also built new housing—usually townhouses or multifamily houses—often designed in a style recalling traditional architecture of the pre-World War II era. Eventually, retail and service businesses moved into city neighborhoods. City services and schools usually improved after a neighborhood had become primarily middle class. Several factors drove this process—the economy of the 1990's, changes in public policy, changes in the makeup of the population, and changes in fashion.

A booming economy

The U.S. economy broke a record at the end of February 2000 for the longest period of economic expansion in the country's history, surpassing the boom of 1961 to 1969. Economists attributed the boom of the 1990's to new technology and the ways in which that technology increased the productivity of American workers. The boom created hundreds of thousands of new jobs, many of them requiring a highly skilled work force. Many of these jobs were located in cities, and many of the people who filled them were well-educated young singles who appreciated the cultural and entertainment opportunities available in cities.

Also during the boom period of the 1990's, corporations attempting to cope

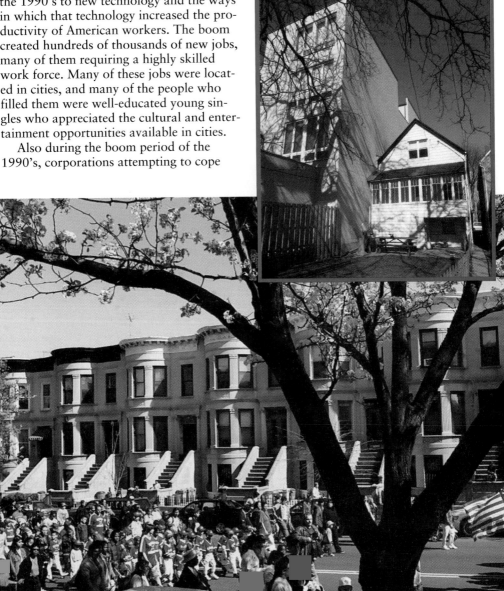

A new multifamily structure stands beside a single-family house (below) in a Chicago neighborhood undergoing "gentrification." The restoration of existing housing (bottom) gives new life to Park Slope, a Brooklyn, New York, neighborhood that dates from the 1800's.

with the new technology began hiring highly specialized experts to set up computer systems, build Web sites, and provide other technical services. These jobs created a new segment of business in the economy. Many of the new technology firms set up business in cities because of the central locations and inexpensive office space in underused and undervalued loft buildings that had formerly been factories or warehouses. For far less rent than equivalent space in normal office buildings, the lofts offered huge unobstructed spaces that could easily accept the wiring necessary for computers and Internet access.

Developers soon followed and began to renovate old factories and warehouses in such inner-city neighborhoods as New York City's SoHo, Cleveland's Flats, and Chicago's River North. People working in these areas began to see the benefits of living in them as well. Besides the advantages of being able to walk or bicycle to work, such neighborhoods were near exciting restaurants, clubs, galleries, and theaters.

Many cities in the 1980's and 1990's had ample empty land available for development because of the urban renewal programs in the 1960's and 1970's that had called for the demolition of abandoned buildings. Developers bought this vacant land and built middle-class housing in areas near central urban cores.

During the same period, the federal government actively promoted replacing high-rise public housing with mixed income housing. The idea behind the new policy was to break up the high concentrations of low-income people and redistribute individual families on sites scattered throughout the city. Plans for Chicago's Cabrini-Green public housing project located on the city's Near North Side provide a prime example of this policy change. The $1.5-billion plan called for demolishing Cabrini-Green's 51 decaying high-rises and replacing them with rows of single-family houses and townhouses to be sold to the public. Some of the homes were to be reserved for low-income residents.

Shoppers and patrons of cafes crowd a New York City sidewalk (top). The appeal of interesting and innovative restaurants and clubs helped fuel the rebirth of U.S. cities. The renovation of traditional entertainment areas, such as New York City's famed Times Square (above), attract tourists and help revitalize urban economies.

Crime rates decline

Changes in public policies toward crime also contributed to the rebirth of cities. Violent crime declined in most U.S. cities every year between 1992 and 1999. Between 1998 and 1999, violent crime declined by 10 percent and property crimes fell by 9 percent, according to statistics compiled by the Federal Bureau of Investigation (FBI). Criminologists say the reason for the decline is complex, and they point to several factors, including the economy. The 1990's boom produced a record-number of jobs, resulting in low rates of unemployment. Generally, crime diminishes in good economic times and increases during hard times.

Another factor was a tough attitude toward crime. In the 1980's, many conservative politicians called for a get-tough policy toward crime. They succeeded in getting a number of states to adopt rigorous new sentencing guidelines for judges, particularly for drug-related offenses. A "three-strikes-you're-out" policy mandated a life-in-prison sentence for persons convicted of three criminal offenses. New procedures tightened the granting of parole to prison inmates. The controversial new laws led to marked increases in U.S. prison populations in the 1990's, removing thousands of young men from the streets of U.S. cities.

The mayors and police chiefs of many major U.S. cities connected the lower crime rate to a new policy in law enforcement, which they called "community policing." Under this program, law-enforcement officers made more personal contact with the people in the neighborhoods they patrolled, building relation-

Residents and tourists take in the atmosphere at Boston's Faneuil Hall Marketplace (above, left). Such festival marketplaces draw crowds into cities on weekends and week nights. Bryant Park, restored to its original beauty (above, right), provides New Yorkers with a peaceful oasis in the center of midtown Manhattan. Beautification programs and the restoration of city parks drew residents back to cities by improving the quality of urban life.

A woman commutes to her job in downtown Philadelphia by bicycle. Increasing numbers of people in 2000 began to realize the many benefits to living near work and places of entertainment.

ships with residents, rather than simply arresting criminals. Police left their squad cars and walked, rode bicycles, and even horses through city streets. The new policing policy was not unlike the neighborhood cop of yesteryear, walking a beat.

The new urban residents

Three distinct groups of people powered the city renaissance—young adults, "empty nesters," and newly arrived immigrants. The army of young adults that filled many of the new jobs made up the largest single group of new urban residents. Initially, they created a large market for rental property, which encouraged developers to either renovate existing buildings or build new ones. As the group's income level improved with the boom, they provided much of the market for the new and renovated housing near city centers.

The baby boom generation that had contributed to the flight to the suburbs after the 1950's also contributed to the rebirth of the cities. By the 1990's, many of the baby boom generation had become "empty nesters," adults with children who have left home. Lured by the culture and entertainment available in cities and by the desire for smaller housing units, a significant number of baby boom empty nesters traded in the suburbs for city life.

The boom economy, coupled with economic stagnation and political unrest in many parts of the world, also made the United States once again a magnet for immigrants. Settling in cities, where they found familiar stores and institutions from home, immigrants swelled urban neighborhoods in the 1990's, as they had in the 1890's. Large numbers of Mexican and Asian immigrants moved to Los Angeles and Chicago, and Latin Americans moved to Miami in record numbers. Immigrants accounted for 40 percent of the population of New York City in the late 1990's—a level not seen since 1910. According to the U.S. Census Bureau estimates, the number of New Yorkers born in the former Soviet Union grew from 81,000 in 1990 to 229,000 in 1999. During the same period, the number of New Yorkers born in Mexico quadrupled to 133,000, and the number of New Yorkers born in India, Pakistan, and Bangladesh more than doubled.

The latest wave of immigrants patronized inner-city business-es and provided a relatively low-wage labor force that helped drive the economy, especially in urban service industries, such as restaurants, bars, hotels, and convention centers. American cities also attracted smaller numbers of highly skilled immigrants, helping meet a seemingly insatiable demand for computer pro-grammers, medical personnel, and other technical positions.

Cities regain popularity

The rebirth of the American city also was shaped by changing fashions. Quite simply, cities and an urban lifestyle became fash-ionable again. A generation that had grown up in suburbs, watching television, turned to cities for a different way of life. Unique night spots, ethnic restaurants, and festival marketplaces, such as Boston's Faneuil Hall Marketplace, attracted crowds on weekends and after business hours. This contributed to a new at-mosphere growing in many cities—the "24-hour downtown." By 2000, the once-empty streets of some U.S. cities were filled with people after dark, even on weeknights. After work, more people who had jobs downtown went out to restaurants, clubs, and theaters instead of going home to the sub-urbs. Following the lead of popular new bookstore chains, like Borders and Barnes & Noble, down-town stores adopted longer hours to accommodate late-night crowds.

Several U.S. cities also initiated ambitious public and private developments in the 1990's to attract shop-pers and tourists. Indi-anapolis invested millions of dollars in a downtown complex that combined Conseco Fieldhouse, built for professional basketball games, with a shopping mall and convention center.

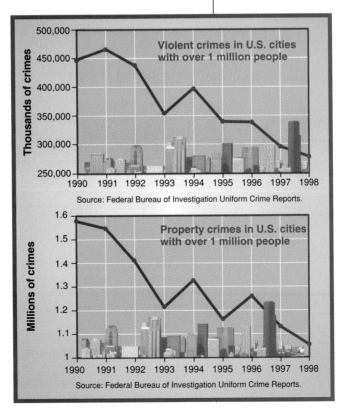

Source: Federal Bureau of Investigation Uniform Crime Reports.

Source: Federal Bureau of Investigation Uniform Crime Reports.

Cleveland, which was bankrupt in 1978, spent millions of dollars in the 1990's revamping its downtown with new retail and entertainment facilities, a performing arts complex, and the Rock and Roll Hall of Fame and Museum. The museum was constructed as part of the North Coast Harbor recreational project in a once-industrial area along the shores of Lake Erie.

The new urbanism set into motion a self-reinforcing cycle in much the same way that urban decline became self-reinforcing. As more middle-class residents moved to cities, especially in areas close to downtowns, more stores and restaurants sprang up. These new businesses attracted more middle-class residents. A highly educated work force drew companies back into cities. New housing and businesses increased tax receipts, enabling governments to improve infrastructure, school systems, and make the environment more attractive. New York City, in the late 1980's and 1990's, was able to restore much of its park system, replanting gardens that had been neglected for decades. Chicago also began restoring parks and spent some $25 million to landscape 50 miles (80 kilometers) of city streets, installing flowers in boulevards and planting tens of thousands of trees.

The future of cities

Despite the optimism generated by the back-to-the-cities movement, many U.S. cities in 2000 continued to experience serious problems, including poverty, poor schools, and aging public transportation systems. The back-to-the-city movement fueled another problem for many city residents—a rapid increase in urban real estate values. This increase displaced large numbers of lower-income residents. As real estate prices went up, property taxes increased, in some cases forcing lower-income residents, who were often elderly, to sell and move. While this imposed emotional and social costs, it also enabled sellers to reap the economic benefits of the increased property value.

Renters enjoyed no such gain from the real estate boom. As values went up, landlords raised rents or sold buildings to developers. This problem was especially evident in San Francisco's Mission District, which for generations had been home to working-class Hispanic families. High-tech Internet companies, flush with investment capital, gobbled up buildings for low prices to use as office space, making Mission District real estate more attractive and more valuable. As the buildings increased in value, landlords raised rents, sometimes astronomically. Renters simply were forced out. The displacement tended to increase the concentration of lower-income people in remaining low-cost neighborhoods or in suburbs just beyond the city limits.

Experts say that the factors that shaped the rebirth of U.S. cities—the economy, public policy, population changes, and cultural preferences—will continue to do so. Some of these factors can be predicted with reasonable accuracy. Others will change unexpectedly.

The baby boom generation, which played a major role in both the decline and resurgence of American cities, should continue to be an important component in the urban landscape until at least 2030. The aging of the baby boom generation will produce the largest number of senior citizens in history. The U.S. Census Bureau estimates that the number of U.S. citizens over the age of 65 will double by 2030 and account for 20 percent of the population. As seniors tend not to move after a certain age, the experts believe that the baby boomers who moved to cities will likely remain there into old age. The effect that this large, aging population may have on city services could be dramatic, perhaps eventually putting a strain on city services.

Minority populations will continue to play an expanding role in shaping cities. The proportion of immigrants is likely to continue to increase, particularly in large port-of-entry cities, like New York and Chicago. Other cities also are likely to experience an increase in minority populations as the United States continues to attract immigrants. Higher birth rates among younger immigrant and minority populations will translate into a much more diverse, multicultural society, the experts predict. Already in California, no single ethnic or racial group constitutes a majority of the population, according to estimates by the U.S. Census Bureau. By 2050, this may be true for most U.S. cities, if not all of the United States.

Urban and suburban lifestyles are likely to converge over the next two decades. Social scientists believe that suburbs will take on urban characteristics—developing denser populations and downtowns distinctive enough to provide a sense of community. Urbanologists, in turn, see cities becoming more suburban, with more automobile-oriented strip and parking malls, more housing designed around automobiles, and single-family housing developments. The low-density, gated communities of the suburbs may be built in or near city centers to accommodate the growing numbers of seniors. The divide between city and suburb in the metropolitan landscape of the future may, in fact, blur, offering greater variety of residential development, shopping, and places of employment sprinkled throughout metropolitan areas.   ■■■

Classical music. In 2000, the music world honored Johann Sebastian Bach on the 250th anniversary of his death. Many music lovers revere the German composer, who lived from 1685 to 1750, as the greatest composer who ever lived. Numerous Bach concerts, festivals, and symposia were held throughout 2000. In addition, two major recording projects featuring Bach's entire musical output became available to the public on compact discs.

Other anniversary tributes. Two American composers were honored on the 100th anniversary of their births. Aaron Copland created a sound that became a musical signature of American culture, while Kurt Weill was a major force in theater in the United States and Europe. Many U.S. orchestras, opera companies, and universities marked the anniversaries with tributes, retrospectives, and concerts during 2000.

Beethoven poisoned? A lock of hair snipped from Ludwig van Beethoven's head after he died in 1827 contained a concentration of lead 100 times greater than commonly found, according to a team of scientists led by William J. Walsh of the Health Research Institute in Naperville, Illinois. The researchers reported in October that tests on the hair indicated that the great German composer suffered from lead poisoning.

Grammy Award winners in 2000

Classical Album, *Stravinsky: Firebird; The Rite of Spring; Persephone;* San Francisco Symphony Orchestra and Chorus; Michael Tilson Thomas, conductor.

Orchestral Performance, *Stravinsky: Firebird; The Rite of Spring; Persephone;* San Francisco Symphony Orchestra and Chorus; Michael Tilson Thomas, conductor.

Opera Recording, *Stravinsky: The Rake's Progress;* Ian Bostridge, Bryn Terfel, Anne Sofie von Otter, Deborah York, singers; John Eliot Gardiner, conductor.

Choral Performance, *Britten: War Requiem;* Joan McFarland and Betty Scott, choir directors; The Washington Urchestra and Chorus; Robert Shafer, conductor.

Instrumental Soloist with Orchestra, *Prokofiev: Piano Concertos Nos. 1 & 3/Bartok: Piano Concerto No. 3;* Martha Argerich, piano; Montreal Symphony Orchestra; Charles Dutoit, conductor.

Instrumental Soloist without Orchestra, *Shostakovich: 24 Preludes & Fugues, Op. 87;* Vladimir Ashkenazy, piano.

Chamber Music Performance, *Beethoven: The Violin Sonatas;* Anne-Sophie Mutter, violin; Lambert Orkis, piano.

Small Ensemble Performance, *Colors of Love (Works of Thomas, Stucky, Tavener, Rands, Etc.);* Chanticleer; Joseph Jennings, conductor.

Classical Vocal Performance, *Mahler: Des Knaben Wunderhorn;* Thomas Quasthoff, baritone; Anne Sofie von Otter, mezzo soprano.

Classical Contemporary Composition, *Boulez: Repons;* Pierre Boulez, composer and conductor.

Classical Crossover Album, *Schickele: Hornsmoke;* The Chestnut Brass Company; Peter Schickele, piano and narrator.

Beethoven was deaf for much of his adult life and frequently suffered from such chronic conditions as abdominal pain, irritability, and feelings of despair. The scientists noted that these conditions are associated with lead poisoning. Though the researchers could not determine how so much lead entered the composer's system, some historians pointed out that wine was stored in lead-lined flasks at the time, and Beethoven was heavily sedated with wine in the last year of his life, as he grew increasingly ill. The discovery raised other questions, such as whether the lead affected Beethoven's personality and music, and whether it contributed to his deafness and death.

Maestros wanted. Several prominent U.S. symphony orchestras searched in 2000 for conductors willing and able to fill vacant music directorships. The Italian maestro Riccardo Muti, artistic director of Milan's La Scala Opera, refused a reported $2-million offer to become the new music director of the New York Philharmonic. Muti's decision sent orchestra executives back to square one in their search for a successor to Kurt Masur, who was scheduled to leave New York in 2002.

Robert Spano, one of the few American conductors who had been in the running for major podium positions, made his debut as chief conductor of the Atlanta Symphony Orchestra in September 2000. Also in September, the Austrian conductor Hans Graf signed on to succeed Christoph Eschenbach as head of the Houston Symphony Orchestra. In January, Paavo Jarvi, son of the Estonian conductor Neeme Jarvi, was named to lead the Cincinnati Symphony Orchestra.

Symphonies in cyberspace. In July, representatives of 66 U.S. symphony, opera, and ballet orchestras signed an accord with the American Federation of Musicians, the musicians union, that allowed the orchestras to distribute live and recorded music over the Internet. Under the terms of the pact, orchestras were permitted to make two kinds of performances available on the Web—live concerts of performances that cannot be stored on disc by listeners and prerecorded audio files that can be downloaded.

Orchestra executives and players praised the agreement as a potential means to generate new audiences and raise revenue to help financially struggling institutions survive in the new century. On August 17, the Philadelphia Orchestra gave the first live, "pay-per-listen" concert under the accord, with violinist Itzhak Perlman playing and conducting at the Saratoga Performing Arts Center in New York. Listeners paid $2 per log-in to hear the performance.

New orchestral and instrumental music. Ohio's annual Blossom Music Festival began its 2000 season in July with the first performance of American composer Augusta Read Thomas's *Song*

The Seattle Opera presents *Die Walkure* from Richard Wagner's four-part *The Ring of the Nibelung* in August 2000. The performers included Mark Baker as Siegmund (left), Margaret Jane Wray as Sieglinde (middle), and Jane Eaglen as Brunnhilde (right).

in Sorrow. Jahja Ling conducted the piece, which was commissioned by the Cleveland Orchestra and Kent State University in Kent, Ohio, in memory of four students killed on the campus in 1970 during antiwar protests. In April 2000, U.S. composer Stephen Mackey appeared as soloist with the Miami-based New World Symphony in the premiere of his *Tuck and Roll,* a concerto for electric guitar and orchestra.

Pulitzer Prize-winning composer Ellen Taaffe Zwilich saw her *Symphony No. 4 (The Gardens)* premiered in February by the Michigan State University Symphony Orchestra. In May, the Cincinnati Symphony Orchestra under James Conlon's direction premiered David Brewbaker's *Cincinnatus Psalm,* a work drawing parallels between

Cincinnatus, a statesman in ancient Rome, and David, a biblical king of ancient Israel.

New operas. The San Francisco Opera presented the premiere in October of U.S. composer Jake Heggie's *Dead Man Walking.* The opera's libretto, by Terrence McNally, was based on Sister Helen Prejean's antideath-penalty novel, which had previously been made into a film. The Houston Grand Opera in April presented *Cold Sassy Tree,* by the U.S. composer Carlisle Floyd. Set in rural Georgia, the comic opera revolves around the consequences of a prominent, older widower marrying a beautiful young woman.

Severance Hall, home of the Cleveland Orchestra, reopened in January after a $36-million renovation to provide the hall with state-of-the-art performance space and other improvements. Music director Christoph von Dohnanyi led the gala celebration concert, which premiered a fanfare by English composer Sir Harrison Birtwistle. Critics pronounced the renovation a great success, declaring that the hall's fabled warm, transparent acoustics sounded better than ever.

The Grawemeyer Award for Music Composition was presented to French composer and conductor Pierre Boulez in November. He won the top prize in international music composition for *Sur Incises,* a work for chamber ensemble.

Flat sales. The Recording Industry Association of America, the trade group representing the U.S. recording industry, reported in 2000 that the market share of classical music remained flat in 1999 compared to 1998. The stagnant market for classical recordings stood in sharp contrast to runaway sales of popular music among "baby boomers," people born between 1946 and 1964, who made up approximately one-quarter of the market. Industry experts added that thousands of stores had stopped selling classical recordings over the previous few years. □ John von Rhein

See also **Popular music.**

Clinton, Bill. See United States, President of the.

Clothing. See Fashion.

Coal. See Energy supply.

Colombia. At the request of President Andres Pastrana, U.S. President Bill Clinton signed a bill on July 13, 2000, providing Colombia with $1.3 billion in emergency military aid to fight drug trafficking. The leaders of several Latin American nations, including Colombia's neighbors Brazil and Venezuela, condemned the U.S. action as an unwarranted intervention in regional affairs. They called upon the United States to reduce what they claimed was the root cause of drug trafficking and violence in Colombia—demand in the United States for illicit drugs.

On a visit to Cartagena, Colombia, on August 30, Clinton sought to allay fears at home and abroad that the United States was becoming involved in a civil war in Colombia with unforeseeable consequences. He insisted that U.S. aid was directed exclusively at the drug fight and not to supporting the Colombian government's decades-old war against leftist guerrilla groups. "This is not Vietnam," Clinton said, referring to the Vietnam War (1957-1975), "nor is it Yankee imperialism."

Military concerns. The U.S. decision to provide stepped-up military assistance came at a time when many human rights groups in Colombia and other countries expressed concern about alleged human rights abuses by Colombian armed forces and right-wing paramilitary groups.

This concern was highlighted two weeks before Clinton's visit, when, on August 15, six children on a school field trip in rural northwestern Colombia were gunned down by Colombian soldiers. The army blamed the killings on "human error," but several witnesses reported that the soldiers had fired "directly" into the group of children.

Leftist rebels. According to public opinion polls, many Colombians in 2000 did not approve of how the Pastrana administration was handling the war against leftist guerrillas. The largest of the guerrilla groups—the 15,000-man Revolutionary Armed Forces of Colombia (FARC)—launched its campaign against the government in 1964. During 2000, FARC established its own court, tax, and land-reform system in a Switzerland-sized area in southern Colombia that Pastrana had ceded to the rebels in November 1998 in hopes of spurring peace negotiations.

In April 2000, government officials said they planned to grant a smaller area, in the northern part of the country, to the second largest guerrilla group—the 5,000-member National Liberation Army (ELN). Though the area was small, it was of great strategic importance, observers noted.

Congressman slain. Gunman killed Colombian Congressman Diego Turbay, his mother, and five other people on a highway in southern Colombia on December 29. Turbay had played a prominent role in advancing peace negotiations with both FARC and ELN.

Paramilitary leader shows face. In an extraordinary appearance on Colombian television in March, Carlos Castano, leader of the paramilitary group United Self-Defense Forces of Colombia, showed his face to the nation for the first time. Dressed as a business executive, Castano sought to win public support for his crusade against leftist insurgents following a government report that blamed the 5,500 members of paramilitary death squads for 155 massacres and 902 executions in 1999. Castano also admitted that many of his force's operations were funded by taxes on drug traffickers and coca farmers.

Exodus. During the first eight months of 2000, some 150,000 Colombians fled the troubled nation, according to government estimates. Over the previous four years, approximately 800,000 Colombians, including many engineers, architects, physicians, and other professionals, left the country. □ Nathan A. Haverstock

See also **Latin America.**

Colorado. See State government.

Common Market. See Europe.

Commonwealth of Independent States. See Asia; Azerbaijan; Belarus; Georgia; Kazakhstan; Russia; Ukraine.

Comoros. See Africa.

The Mac G4 Cube introduced by Apple Computer Incorporated in August 2000, is an 8-inch (20-centimeter) computer that is less than one-quarter the size of other personal computers.

Computers. Microsoft Corporation of Redmond, Washington, introduced Windows 2000 in February 2000. The software consisted of four different operating systems designed mainly for businesses and other organizations that have computers linked in networks. Windows 2000 replaced Windows NT, long used for networked computers. In September, Microsoft introduced Windows Millennium (ME), intended for home and business computers that previously used Windows 95 and Windows 98. Microsoft said ME would be the last in its Windows 9x family.

New Apples. In August, Apple Computer Inc., of Cupertino, California, introduced a new line of computers, including the Mac G4 Cube. Less than one-quarter the size of a regular personal computer, the silver-toned, 8-inch (20-centimeter) Cube sits suspended inside a clear plastic case. Apple also began selling four new models of its popular iMac desktop computer, available in new colors called indigo, sage, snow, and ruby.

Love Bug. A *computer virus* (a destructive computer program able to copy and transmit itself to other computers) dubbed "Love Bug" caused billions of dollars in damage to millions of computers around the world in May. Love Bug was the latest of a group of viruses, known as "worms," that hitch a ride on e-mail attachments. When the computer user opens the at-tachment, the worm infects and damages files on the computer's hard drive. Love Bug, named after the "I Love You" or "Love Letter" phrase that appeared in the subject line of the e-mails, was able to send itself to all the addresses in a computer's e-mail list. The U.S. Federal Bureau of Investigation traced the bug's origin to a *hacker* (a computer programmer who creates mischief or commits crimes) in the Philippines.

Microsoft monopoly. In June, United States District Judge Thomas Penfield Jackson ordered that Microsoft be broken into two smaller companies to keep it from violating antitrust laws designed to protect competition in the marketplace. One company would develop and sell Windows operating systems, the master control programs that coordinate the functions of 9 out of every 10 personal computers in the world. The other company would manage the rest of Microsoft's products, which include business software and the Internet Explorer Web browser.

The decision came in an antitrust suit that began in 1997, when the U.S. government accused Microsoft of using its dominance in computer operating systems to crush competing software products. Microsoft denied the charges and appealed Judge Jackson's decision.

☐ Michael Woods

See also **Internet.**

Hundreds of Congolese refugees wait in food distribution lines in eastern Congo after fleeing their homes in August 2000 to escape warring factions in a civil war that has displaced as many as 500,000 people since the war began in 1998.

Congo (Kinshasa). The civil war in Congo (Kinshasa) between the army of President Laurent Kabila and antigovernment rebels continued to rage in 2000, despite a cease-fire that was agreed to by all parties to the conflict in August 1999 and a second cease-fire agreed to by most parties in December 2000. The civil war began in August 1998. In 2000, Angola, Zimbabwe, and Namibia continued to support Kabila with direct military aid, while neighboring Rwanda and Uganda continued to back rebel combatants in Congo.

On April 8, Congo's warring parties agreed to a cease-fire. The pact specified a three-month end to hostilities, beginning April 14. More than 5,000 United Nations (UN) monitors were to be deployed in buffer zones to oversee the cease-fire. As with the 1999 cease-fire, the 2000 agreement failed to stop the fighting. By August 16, UN Secretary General Kofi Annan concluded that the complexity of Congo's security crisis made the deployment of UN peacekeepers unlikely.

Refugees. On March 17, an official with the UN-based World Food Program (WFP) announced that approximately 60,000 people had fled their residences in South Kivu, along the Rwandan and Burundian borders, where the fighting was fiercest in 2000. Approximately 200,000 residents had been displaced from the area since 1998. Humanitarian agencies estimated in 2000 that there were as many as 500,000 displaced persons in eastern Congo, which was mainly under Congolese rebel control.

Allies clash. In a series of bloody skirmishes in May and June, Rwandan and Ugandan forces—usually allies in the campaign against President Kabila's regime—battled each other in the rebel-held city of Kisangani in Congo's mineral-rich northeast. More than 500 civilians and soldiers died and more than 1,600 people were injured in what observers described as a struggle between Rwanda and Uganda for regional supremacy.

North Korean aid. During August 2000, Zimbabwean intelligence and media sources reported that North Korean military instructors, at Kabila's request, had arrived in Congo to instruct and strengthen Kabila's forces. Analysts said that Kabila eventually intended to replace troops from Zimbabwe with the North Koreans. Zimbabwe deployed approximately 11,000 soldiers in Congo in 2000, the largest foreign force in the country. Some foreign affairs experts suggested that North Korea was aiding Kabila in order to obtain Congolese uranium for North Korea's secret nuclear weapons program.   □ Simon Baynham

See also **Africa; South Africa; Uganda.**

Congress of the United States.

The Nov. 7, 2000, election left Republicans with a narrow majority in the U.S. House of Representatives and deadlocked with Democrats in the U.S. Senate. Democrats picked up two seats in the House of Representatives, cutting the Republican majority to 221 seats, compared with the Democrats' 212 seats. Independents, who usually voted with the Democrats, held two seats. A majority in the 435-seat House requires at least 218 seats. In the Senate, Democrats picked up five seats in the 2000 election, to tie Republicans at 50 to 50. Under the U.S. Constitution, the vice president, as president of the Senate, casts the deciding vote in cases of tied votes.

Major House races. Although all 435 seats in the House were up for reelection in November, there were few competitive races. Republican incumbents retained nearly all of their seats, though a close margin in some congressional races nationwide left Democratic Party leaders claiming that the balance of power may swing in their favor in 2002.

Major Senate races. The Democratic Party scored major Senate victories in the November 2000 election. In one of the year's most closely watched races, First Lady Hillary Rodham Clinton, a Democrat, won the Senate seat representing the state of New York. The seat had been held by Senator Daniel Patrick Moynihan, who retired. Clinton defeated Representative Rick Lazio. The Republican party selected Lazio to run for the position after the Republican front-runner, New York City Mayor Rudolph Giuliani, announced in May that he would drop out of the race due to health problems.

Democrats also defeated some long-time Republican senators. Thomas Carper defeated incumbent Republican Senator William Roth in Delaware. In Minnesota, Democrat Mark Dayton defeated incumbent Senator Rod Grams, a Republican. In Michigan, Democrat Debbie Stabenow defeated incumbent Republican Senator Spencer Abraham. Missouri voters elected Democrat Mel Carnahan over the Republican incumbent, John Ashcroft. Carnahan, who had been Missouri's governor, died on October 16 in an airplane crash, but his death came too close to the election to remove his name from the November ballot. Roger Wilson, who had succeeded Carnahan as governor of Missouri, announced that he would appoint Carnahan's widow, Jean, to fill the vacant seat.

Republicans gained a Senate seat in Nevada when John Ensign defeated Ed Bernstein, a Democrat, in the race to replace Democrat Richard H. Bryan. Bryan had retired from the Senate. In Virginia, Republican George F. Allen defeated incumbent Democratic Senator Charles S. Robb.

Senate leadership remained unchanged following the election. Senators from both parties met on December 5 to select leadership for the first session of the 107th Congress, which was scheduled to convene on Jan. 3, 2001. Republicans retained Trent Lott of Mississippi as majority leader and Don Nickles of Oklahoma as majority whip. Both ran unopposed. Larry E. Craig of Idaho defeated Pete V. Domenici of New Mexico to retain the position of Republican policy committee chairman.

Democratic Party leadership also remained unchanged following the December 2000 vote. Thomas A. Daschle of South Dakota was reelected minority leader. Harry M. Reid of Nevada was reelected minority whip, and Byron L. Dorgan of North Dakota was retained as chairman of the Democratic Policy Committee.

Because of the 50-50 split in the Senate, many Democrats demanded that Republicans share power when appointing senators to numerous committees at the start of the new session in 2001. While Republican leaders reported that they would "reach out to Democrats," they made it clear that they would not give up their majority rule.

In an unusual turn of events, Vice President Al Gore, who lost the bid for the presidency, continued on as president of the Senate for 17 days after Congress convened on Jan. 3, 2001, which gave Democrats a tie-breaking vote. The balance of power switched on January 20, when Republican presidential candidate George W. Bush and his running mate, Dick Cheney, took office. Cheney, as vice president, assumed the position of Senate president and tie-breaker.

Gore's running mate, Joseph I. Lieberman (D., Connecticut) also ran for the Senate. He won reelection and retained his Senate seat.

Political experts cautioned that the evenly split Senate would enable either party to filibuster committee appointments recommended by the other party. The experts said that such a strategy would paralyze the Senate.

Spending bills. Congress in 2000 failed to pass 4 of the 13 annual spending bills needed to fund the government prior to the start of fiscal year 2001, which began on Oct. 1, 2000. The proposed budget totaled $1.8 trillion. As the year drew to a close, Congress opted to wait until Republican George W. Bush took over the presidency in 2001. Leaders from the House and Senate had met with the Clinton administration through December 2000 to explore agreements on education spending, tax cuts, and other budget disputes. In order to keep federal agencies functioning during the budget crisis, the House of Representatives and the Senate approved more than a dozen stop-gap bills.

Members of the United States House of Representatives

The House of Representatives of the first session of the 107th Congress consisted of 212 Democrats, 221 Republicans, and 2 independents (not including representatives from American Samoa, the District of Columbia, Guam, Puerto Rico, and the Virgin Islands) when it convened on Jan. 3, 2001. This table shows congressional district, legislator, and party affiliation. Asterisk (*) denotes those who served in the 106th Congress; dagger (†) denotes "at large."

Alabama
1. Sonny Callahan, R.*
2. Terry Everett, R.*
3. Bob Riley, R.*
4. Robert Aderholt, R.*
5. Bud Cramer, D.*
6. Spencer Bachus, R.*
7. Earl Hilliard, D.*

Alaska
†Donald E. Young, R.*

Arizona
1. Jeff Flake, R.
2. Ed Pastor, D.*
3. Bob Stump, R.*
4. John Shadegg, R.*
5. Jim Kolbe, R.*
6. J. D. Hayworth, R.*

Arkansas
1. Marion Berry, D.*
2. Vic Snyder, D.*
3. Asa Hutchinson, R.*
4. Mike Ross, D.

California
1. Mike Thompson, D.*
2. Wally Herger, R.*
3. Douglas Ose, R.*
4. John Doolittle, R.*
5. Robert T. Matsui, D.*
6. Lynn Woolsey, D.*
7. George E. Miller, D.*
8. Nancy Pelosi, D.*
9. Barbara Lee, D.*
10. Ellen Tauscher, D.*
11. Richard Pombo, R.*
12. Tom Lantos, D.*
13. Fortney H. (Peter) Stark, D.*
14. Anna Eshoo, D.*
15. Mike Honda, D.
16. Zoe Lofgren, D.*
17. Sam Farr, D.*
18. Gary Condit, D.*
19. George Radanovich, R.*
20. Calvin Dooley, D.*
21. William M. Thomas, R.*
22. Lois Capps, D.*
23. Elton Gallegly, R.*
24. Brad Sherman, D.*
25. Howard McKeon, R.*
26. Howard L. Berman, D.*
27. Adam Schiff, D.
28. David Dreier, R.*
29. Henry A. Waxman, D.*
30. Xavier Becerra, D.*
31. Hilda Solis, D.
32. Julian C. Dixon, D.**
33. Lucille Roybal-Allard, D.*
34. Grace Napolitano, D.*
35. Maxine Waters, D.*
36. Jane Harman, D.

** Died Dec. 8, 2000.

37. Juanita Millender-McDonald, D.*
38. Steve Horn, R.*
39. Edward Royce, R.*
40. Jerry Lewis, R.*
41. Gary Miller, R.*
42. Joe Baca, D.*
43. Kenneth Calvert, R.*
44. Mary Bono, R.*
45. Dana Rohrabacher, R.*
46. Loretta Sanchez, D.*
47. C. Christopher Cox, R.*
48. Darrell Issa, R.
49. Susan Davis, D.
50. Bob Filner, D.*
51. Randy (Duke) Cunningham, R.*
52. Duncan L. Hunter, R.*

Colorado
1. Diana DeGette, D.*
2. Mark Udall, D.*
3. Scott McInnis, R.*
4. Bob Schaffer, R.*
5. Joel Hefley, R.*
6. Tom Tancredo, R.*

Connecticut
1. John Larson, D.*
2. Rob Simmons, R.
3. Rosa DeLauro, D.*
4. Christopher Shays, R.*
5. James H. Maloney, D.*
6. Nancy L. Johnson, R.*

Delaware
†Michael Castle, R.*

Florida
1. Joe Scarborough, R.*
2. Allen Boyd, D.*
3. Corrine Brown, D.*
4. Ander Crenshaw, R.
5. Karen Thurman, D.*
6. Clifford B. Stearns, R.*
7. John Mica, R.*
8. Ric Keller, R.
9. Michael Bilirakis, R.*
10. C. W. Bill Young, R.*
11. Jim Davis, D.*
12. Adam Putnam, R.
13. Dan Miller, R.*
14. Porter J. Goss, R.*
15. Dave Weldon, R.*
16. Mark Foley, R.*
17. Carrie Meek, D.*
18. Ileana Ros-Lehtinen, R.*
19. Robert Wexler, D.*
20. Peter Deutsch, D.*
21. Lincoln Diaz-Balart, R.*
22. E. Clay Shaw, Jr., R.*
23. Alcee Hastings, D.*

Georgia
1. Jack Kingston, R.*
2. Sanford Bishop, Jr., D.*

3. Mac Collins, R.*
4. Cynthia A. McKinney, D.*
5. John Lewis, D.*
6. Johnny Isakson, R.*
7. Bob Barr, R.*
8. Saxby Chambliss, R.*
9. Nathan Deal, R.*
10. Charlie Norwood, R.*
11. John Linder, R.*

Hawaii
1. Neil Abercrombie, D.*
2. Patsy T. Mink, D.*

Idaho
1. Butch Otter, R.
2. Mike Simpson, R.*

Illinois
1. Bobby Rush, D.*
2. Jesse L. Jackson, Jr., D.*
3. William O. Lipinski, D.*
4. Luis Gutierrez, D.*
5. Rod R. Blagojevich, D.*
6. Henry J. Hyde, R.*
7. Danny Davis, D.*
8. Philip M. Crane, R.*
9. Janice Schakowsky, D.*
10. Mark Kirk, R.
11. Gerald Weller, R.*
12. Jerry F. Costello, D.*
13. Judy Biggert, R.*
14. J. Dennis Hastert, R.*
15. Timothy Johnson, R.
16. Donald Manzullo, R.*
17. Lane A. Evans, D.*
18. Ray LaHood, R.*
19. David Phelps, D.*
20. John Shimkus, R.*

Indiana
1. Peter J. Visclosky, D.*
2. Mike Pence, R.
3. Tim Roemer, D.*
4. Mark Souder, R.*
5. Steve Buyer, R.*
6. Danny L. Burton, R.*
7. Brian Kerns, R.
8. John Hostettler, R.*
9. Baron Hill, D.*
10. Julia M. Carson, D.*

Iowa
1. Jim Leach, R.*
2. Jim Nussle, R.*
3. Leonard Boswell, D.*
4. Greg Ganske, R.*
5. Tom Latham, R.*

Kansas
1. Jerry Moran, R.*
2. Jim Ryun, R.*
3. Dennis Moore, D.*
4. Todd Tiahrt, R.*

Kentucky
1. Edward Whitfield, R.*
2. Ron Lewis, R.*
3. Anne Northup, R.*
4. Kenneth Lucas, D.*
5. Harold (Hal) Rogers, R.*
6. Ernie Fletcher, R.*

Louisiana
1. David Vitter, R.*
2. William J. Jefferson, D.*
3. W. J. (Billy) Tauzin, R.*
4. Jim McCrery, R.*
5. John Cooksey, R.*
6. Richard Hugh Baker, R.*
7. Chris John, D.*

Maine
1. Thomas Allen, D.*
2. John Baldacci, D.*

Maryland
1. Wayne T. Gilchrest, R.*
2. Robert Ehrlich, Jr., R.*
3. Benjamin L. Cardin, D.*
4. Albert Wynn, D.*
5. Steny H. Hoyer, D.*
6. Roscoe Bartlett, R.*
7. Elijah Cummings, D.*
8. Constance A. Morella, R.*

Massachusetts
1. John W. Olver, D.*
2. Richard E. Neal, D.*
3. James McGovern, D.*
4. Barney Frank, D.*
5. Martin Meehan, D.*
6. John Tierney, D.*
7. Edward J. Markey, D.*
8. Michael Capuano, D.*
9. John Joseph Moakley, D.*
10. William Delahunt, D.*

Michigan
1. Bart Stupak, D.*
2. Peter Hoekstra, R.*
3. Vernon Ehlers, R.*
4. Dave Camp, R.*
5. James Barcia, D.*
6. Frederick S. Upton, R.*
7. Nick Smith, R.*
8. Mike Rogers, R.
9. Dale E. Kildee, D.*
10. David E. Bonior, D.*
11. Joseph Knollenberg, R.*
12. Sander M. Levin, D.*
13. Lynn Rivers, D.*
14. John Conyers, Jr., D.*
15. Carolyn Kilpatrick, D.*
16. John D. Dingell, D.*

Minnesota
1. Gil Gutknecht, R.*
2. Mark Kennedy, R.
3. Jim Ramstad, R.*
4. Betty McCollum, D.

5. Martin O. Sabo, D.*
6. William P. Luther, D.*
7. Collin C. Peterson, D.*
8. James L. Oberstar, D.*

Mississippi
1. Roger Wicker, R.*
2. Bennie Thompson, D.*
3. Charles Pickering, R.*
4. Ronnie Shows, D.*
5. Gene Taylor, D.*

Missouri
1. William Clay, D.*
2. Todd Akin, R.
3. Richard A. Gephardt, D.*
4. Ike Skelton, D.*
5. Karen McCarthy, D.*
6. Samuel Graves, R.
7. Roy Blunt, R.*
8. Jo Ann Emerson, R.*
9. Kenny Hulshof, R.*

Montana
†Dennis Rehberg, R.

Nebraska
1. Doug Bereuter, R.*
2. Lee Terry, R.*
3. Tom Osborne, R.

Nevada
1. Shelley Berkley, D.*
2. Jim Gibbons, R.*

New Hampshire
1. John E. Sununu, R.*
2. Charles Bass, R.*

New Jersey
1. Robert E. Andrews, D.*
2. Frank LoBiondo, R.*
3. H. James Saxton, R.*
4. Christopher H. Smith, R.*
5. Marge Roukema, R.*
6. Frank Pallone, Jr., D.*
7. Mike Ferguson, R.
8. William Pascrell, Jr., D.*
9. Steven Rothman, D.*
10. Donald M. Payne, D.*
11. Rodney Frelinghuysen, R.*
12. Rush Holt, D.
13. Robert Menendez, D.*

New Mexico
1. Heather Wilson, R.*
2. Joe Skeen, R.*
3. Thomas Udall, D.*

New York
1. Felix Grucci, R.
2. Steve Israel, D.
3. Peter King, R.*
4. Carolyn McCarthy, D.*
5. Gary L. Ackerman, D.*
6. Gregory Meeks, D.*
7. Joseph Crowley, D.*
8. Jerrold Nadler, D.*
9. Anthony Weiner, D.*
10. Edolphus Towns, D.*
11. Major R. Owens, D.*
12. Nydia Velazquez, D.*
13. Vito J. Fossella, R.*

14. Carolyn Maloney, D.*
15. Charles B. Rangel, D.*
16. Jose E. Serrano, D.*
17. Eliot L. Engel, D.*
18. Nita M. Lowey, D.*
19. Sue Kelly, R.*
20. Benjamin A. Gilman, R.*
21. Michael R. McNulty, D.*
22. John Sweeney, R.*
23. Sherwood L. Boehlert, R.*
24. John McHugh, R.*
25. James Walsh, R.*
26. Maurice Hinchey, D.*
27. Thomas Reynolds, R.*
28. Louise M. Slaughter, D.*
29. John J. LaFalce, D.*
30. Jack Quinn, R.*
31. Amo Houghton, R.*

North Carolina
1. Eva Clayton, D.*
2. Bob Etheridge, D.*
3. Walter Jones, Jr., R.*
4. David Price, D.*
5. Richard Burr, R.*
6. Howard Coble, R.*
7. Mike McIntyre, D.*
8. Robin Hayes, R.*
9. Sue Myrick, R.*
10. Cass Ballenger, R.*
11. Charles H. Taylor, R.*
12. Melvin Watt, D.*

North Dakota
†Earl Pomeroy, D.*

Ohio
1. Steve Chabot, R.*
2. Rob Portman, R.*
3. Tony P. Hall, D.*
4. Michael G. Oxley, R.*
5. Paul E. Gillmor, R.*
6. Ted Strickland, D.*
7. David L. Hobson, R.*
8. John A. Boehner, R.*
9. Marcy Kaptur, D.*
10. Dennis Kucinich, D.*
11. Stephanie Jones, D.*
12. Pat Tiberi, R.
13. Sherrod Brown, D.*
14. Thomas C. Sawyer, D.*
15. Deborah Pryce, R.*
16. Ralph Regula, R.*
17. James A. Traficant, Jr., D.*
18. Bob Ney, R.*
19. Steven LaTourette, R.*

Oklahoma
1. Steve Largent, R.*
2. Brad Carson, D.
3. Wes Watkins, R.*
4. J. C. Watts, Jr., R.*
5. Ernest Jim Istook, R.*
6. Frank Lucas, R.*

Oregon
1. David Wu, D.*
2. Greg Walden, R.*
3. Earl Blumenauer, D.*
4. Peter A. DeFazio, D.*
5. Darlene Hooley, D.*

Pennsylvania
1. Robert Brady, D.*
2. Chaka Fattah, D.*
3. Robert A. Borski, Jr., D.*
4. Melissa Hart, R.
5. John Peterson, R.*
6. Tim Holden, D.*
7. W. Curtis Weldon, R.*
8. Jim Greenwood, R.*
9. E. G. (Bud) Shuster, R.*
10. Donald Sherwood, R.
11. Paul E. Kanjorski, D.*
12. John P. Murtha, D.*
13. Joseph Hoeffel, D.
14. William J. Coyne, D.*
15. Patrick Toomey, R.
16. Joseph Pitts, R.*
17. George W. Gekas, R.*
18. Michael Doyle, D.*
19. Todd Platts, R.
20. Frank Mascara, D.*
21. Philip English, R.*

Rhode Island
1. Patrick Kennedy, D.*
2. James Langevin, D.

South Carolina
1. Henry Brown, R.
2. Floyd Spence, R.*
3. Lindsey Graham, R.*
4. James DeMint, R.*
5. John M. Spratt, Jr., D.*
6. James Clyburn, D.*

South Dakota
†John Thune, R.*

Tennessee
1. William Jenkins, R.*
2. John J. Duncan, Jr., R.*
3. Zach Wamp, R.*
4. Van Hilleary, R.*
5. Bob Clement, D.*
6. Bart Gordon, D.*
7. Ed Bryant, R.*
8. John S. Tanner, D.*
9. Harold E. Ford, Jr., D.*

Texas
1. Max Sandlin, D.*
2. Jim Turner, D.*
3. Sam Johnson, R.*
4. Ralph M. Hall, D.*
5. Pete Sessions, R.*
6. Joe Barton, R.*
7. John Culberson, R.
8. Kevin Brady, R.*
9. Nick Lampson, D.*
10. Lloyd Doggett, D.*
11. Chet Edwards, D.*
12. Kay Granger, R.*
13. Mac Thornberry, R.*
14. Ron Paul, R.*
15. Ruben Hinojosa, D.*
16. Silvestre Reyes, D.*
17. Charles W. Stenholm, D.*
18. Sheila Jackson Lee, D.*
19. Larry Combest, R.*
20. Charlie Gonzalez, D.*
21. Lamar S. Smith, R.*

22. Tom DeLay, R.*
23. Henry Bonilla, R.*
24. Martin Frost, D.*
25. Ken Bentsen, D.*
26. Richard K. Armey, R.*
27. Solomon P. Ortiz, D.*
28. Ciro Rodriguez, D.*
29. Gene Green, D.*
30. Eddie Bernice Johnson, D.*

Utah
1. James V. Hansen, R.*
2. Jim Matheson, D.
3. Christopher Cannon, R.*

Vermont
†Bernard Sanders, Ind.*

Virginia
1. Jo Ann Davis, R.
2. Edward Schrock, R.
3. Robert Scott, D.*
4. Norman Sisisky, D.*
5. Virgil Goode, Jr., Ind.*
6. Robert Goodlatte, R.*
7. Eric Cantor, R.
8. James P. Moran, Jr., D.*
9. Rick C. Boucher, D.*
10. Frank R. Wolf, R.*
11. Thomas Davis III, R.*

Washington
1. Jay Inslee, D.*
2. Rick Larsen, D.
3. Brian Baird, D.*
4. Doc Hastings, R.*
5. George Nethercutt, Jr., R.*
6. Norman D. Dicks, D.*
7. Jim McDermott, D.*
8. Jennifer Dunn, R.*
9. Adam Smith, D.*

West Virginia
1. Alan B. Mollohan, D.*
2. Shelley Moore Capito, R.
3. Nick J. Rahall II, D.*

Wisconsin
1. Paul Ryan, R.*
2. Tammy Baldwin, D.*
3. Ron Kind, D.*
4. Gerald D. Kleczka, D.*
5. Thomas Barrett, D.*
6. Thomas E. Petri, R.*
7. David R. Obey, D.*
8. Mark Green, R.*
9. F. James Sensenbrenner, Jr., R.*

Wyoming
†Barbara Cubin, R.*

Nonvoting representatives

American Samoa
Eni F. H. Faleomavaega, D.*

District of Columbia
Eleanor Holmes Norton, D.*

Guam
Robert Underwood, D.*

Puerto Rico
Anibal Acevedo Vila, D.

Virgin Islands
Donna Christian-Christensen, D.

Members of the United States Senate

The Senate of the first session of the 107th Congress consisted of 50 Democrats and 50 Republicans when it convened on Jan. 3, 2001. The first date in each listing shows when the senator's term began. The second date in each listing shows when the senator's term expires.

State	Term	State	Term	State	Term
Alabama		**Louisiana**		**Ohio**	
Richard C. Shelby, R.	1987-2005	John B. Breaux, D.	1987-2005	Mike DeWine, R.	1995-2007
Jeff Sessions, R.	1997-2003	Mary L. Landrieu, D.	1997-2003	George V. Voinovich, R.	1999-2005
Alaska		**Maine**		**Oklahoma**	
Theodore F. Stevens, R.	1968-2003	Olympia Snowe, R.	1995-2007	Don Nickles, R.	1981-2005
Frank H. Murkowski, R.	1981-2005	Susan M. Collins, R.	1997-2003	James M. Inhofe, R.	1994-2003
Arizona		**Maryland**		**Oregon**	
John McCain III, R.	1987-2005	Paul S. Sarbanes, D.	1977-2007	Ron Wyden, D.	1996-2005
Jon Kyl, R.	1995-2007	Barbara A. Mikulski, D.	1987-2005	Gordon Smith, R.	1997-2003
Arkansas		**Massachusetts**		**Pennsylvania**	
Tim Hutchinson, R.	1997-2003	Edward M. Kennedy, D.	1962-2007	Arlen Specter, R.	1981-2005
Blanche Lambert Lincoln, D.	1999-2005	John F. Kerry, D.	1985-2003	Rick Santorum, R.	1995-2007
California		**Michigan**		**Rhode Island**	
Dianne Feinstein, D.	1992-2007	Carl Levin, D.	1979-2003	Jack Reed, D.	1997-2003
Barbara Boxer, D.	1993-2005	Debbie Stabenow, D.	2001-2007	Lincoln D. Chafee, R.	1999-2007
Colorado		**Minnesota**		**South Carolina**	
Ben N. Campbell, R.	1993-2005	Paul D. Wellstone, D.	1991-2003	Strom Thurmond, R.	1955-2003
Wayne Allard, R.	1997-2003	Mark Dayton, D.	2001-2007	Ernest F. Hollings, D.	1966-2005
Connecticut		**Mississippi**		**South Dakota**	
Christopher J. Dodd, D.	1981-2005	Thad Cochran, R.	1978-2003	Thomas A. Daschle, D.	1987-2005
Joseph I. Lieberman, D.	1989-2007	Trent Lott, R.	1989-2007	Tim Johnson, D.	1997-2003
Delaware		**Missouri**		**Tennessee**	
Joseph R. Biden, Jr., D.	1973-2003	Christopher S. (Kit) Bond, R.	1987-2005	Fred Thompson, R.	1994-2003
Thomas Carper, D.	2001-2007	Jean Carnahan, D.	2001-2002	Bill Frist, R.	1995-2007
Florida		**Montana**		**Texas**	
Bob Graham, D.	1987-2005	Max Baucus, D.	1978-2003	Phil Gramm, R.	1985-2003
Bill Nelson, D.	2001-2007	Conrad Burns, R.	1989-2007	Kay Bailey Hutchison, R.	1993-2007
Georgia		**Nebraska**		**Utah**	
Max Cleland, D.	1997-2003	Chuck Hagel, R.	1997-2003	Orrin G. Hatch, R.	1977-2007
Zell Miller, D.	2000-2007	Ben Nelson, D.	2001-2007	Robert F. Bennett, R.	1993-2005
Hawaii		**Nevada**		**Vermont**	
Daniel K. Inouye, D.	1963-2005	Harry M. Reid, D.	1987-2005	Patrick J. Leahy, D.	1975-2005
Daniel K. Akaka, D.	1990-2007	John Ensign, R.	2001-2007	James M. Jeffords, R.	1989-2007
Idaho		**New Hampshire**		**Virginia**	
Larry E. Craig, R.	1991-2003	Robert C. Smith, R.	1990-2003	John W. Warner, R.	1979-2003
Mike Crapo, R.	1999-2005	Judd Gregg, R.	1993-2005	George F. Allen, R.	2001-2007
Illinois		**New Jersey**		**Washington**	
Richard J. Durbin, D.	1997-2003	Robert G. Torricelli, D.	1997-2003	Patty Murray, D.	1993-2005
Peter Fitzgerald, R.	1999-2005	Jon S. Corzine, D.	2001-2007	Maria Cantwell, D.	2001-2007
Indiana		**New Mexico**		**West Virginia**	
Richard G. Lugar, R.	1977-2007	Pete V. Domenici, R.	1973-2003	Robert C. Byrd, D.	1959-2007
Evan Bayh, D.	1999-2005	Jeff Bingaman, D.	1983-2007	John D. Rockefeller IV, D.	1985-2003
Iowa		**New York**		**Wisconsin**	
Charles E. Grassley, R.	1981-2005	Charles E. Schumer, D.	1999-2005	Herbert Kohl, D.	1989-2007
Tom Harkin, D.	1985-2003	Hillary Rodham Clinton, D.	2001-2007	Russell D. Feingold, D.	1993-2005
Kansas		**North Carolina**		**Wyoming**	
Sam Brownback, R.	1996-2005	Jesse A. Helms, R.	1973-2003	Craig Thomas, R.	1995-2007
Pat Roberts, R.	1997-2003	John Edwards, D.	1999-2005	Mike Enzi, R.	1997-2003
Kentucky		**North Dakota**			
Mitch McConnell, R.	1985-2003	Kent Conrad, D.	1987-2007		
Jim Bunning, R.	1999-2005	Byron L. Dorgan, D.	1992-2005		

E-commerce. Congress took steps in 2000 to ensure the continued growth of electronic commerce, more commonly known as e-commerce, on the Internet by approving a measure that gives legal standing to the validity of electronic signatures. In sales over the Internet, purchasers are unable to sign their names for credit card purchases as they would on a sales slip at a retail store. Consequently, legal experts expressed concern that e-commerce would stagnate if electronic signatures were not held to be enforceable.

The House gave final approval to the compromise measure on June 14 by a 426-to-4 vote. The Senate approved the compromise on June 16, and President Clinton signed the legislation on June 30.

Consumer safety. Congress approved legislation in October requiring increased reporting of defects in motor vehicles and motor vehicle equipment in the wake of a massive tire recall by Bridgestone/Firestone, Incorporated, a Japanese-owned tire company located in Nashville, Tennessee. Under the measure, approved by both the House and Senate on October 11, U.S. tire manufacturers must report actual and potential defects in motor vehicle tires and related products sold in foreign countries. President Clinton signed the legislation on November 1.

Bridgestone/Firestone officials announced a recall in August of 6.5 million tires that had been installed as original equipment on light trucks and sport utility vehicles. Federal safety officials investigated and reported that the tires can shred at high or low speeds and may have caused accidents that resulted in more than 100 deaths.

IRS cleared. The General Accounting Office (GAO), the investigative branch of Congress, announced in April that it had found no evidence of misconduct or abuse by employees of the Internal Revenue Service (IRS). The GAO examination of IRS practices was spurred by hearings held in 1998 by the Senate Finance Committee. At the hearings, business owners alleged that the IRS intimidated and mistreated them during criminal investigations and enforcement actions.

Agriculture. Responding to turbulent weather conditions that ravaged crops, Congress in May 2000 approved legislation to improve the federal crop insurance program. The measure provided broader coverage for farmers at generally lower costs, included incentives for farmers to buy higher levels of coverage, and allowed farmers greater flexibility in choosing coverage that best fit their needs. President Clinton signed the bill on June 20.

Aviation. Congress approved legislation providing the U.S. Federal Aviation Administration (FAA), which regulates the airline industry and controls air traffic, with more funds to upgrade facilities and equipment in an effort to update the nation's aging air traffic control system. The legislation included funds to help small airports market and promote their air services. It also provided incentives for increased airline competition as part of an effort to lower air fares. Both the House and Senate approved the measure in March. The president signed the bill in April.

Congress approved legislation in October that sought to improve airport security by requiring more thorough background checks and extra training for airport personnel. Under the legislation, airport screeners—employees who check people and baggage entering secure areas of airports—as well as any other airport personnel with access to secure areas in airports, are required to undergo a criminal background check. President Clinton did not sign the legislation in 2000.

House chaplain. House Speaker J. Dennis Hastert (R., Illinois) in March swore in the Reverend Daniel Coughlin as chaplain of the House of Representatives. Reverend Coughlin was the first Roman Catholic priest to fill the position. The appointment ended a four-month controversy in which some Democrats had accused Hastert and House Majority Leader Richard K. Armey (R., Texas) of harboring anti-Catholic bias.

A bipartisan search committee in 1999 had recommended three candidates for the position of House chaplain, whose duties include providing a morning prayer and counseling members. Hastert initially selected the Reverend Charles Parker Wright, a Presbyterian, even though the committee's top choice was a Roman Catholic priest, the Reverend Timothy O'Brien.

Drunken driving initiative. In an effort to stem the incidence of people driving while intoxicated, Congress approved legislation in October 2000 designed to encourage states to establish by 2004 a higher standard of blood-alcohol content for legal intoxication. The legislation sets the new standard at 0.08 percent alcohol by volume of blood. The measure, included as part of a $58-billion transportation bill, allows the Department of Transportation to withhold highway funds from states that do not adopt the lower intoxication standard. Supporters of the measure claimed that the move would save 500 lives annually once all states adopt the standard. President Clinton signed the bill into law on Oct. 23, 2000.

Trade with Cuba. In October, Congress overwhelmingly approved legislation that eased sanctions against food sales to Cuba as part of a $78-billion agriculture spending bill. The United States imposed food sanctions in 1962, after Cuban President Fidel Castro's Communist government seized some 6,000 properties owned by U.S. citizens and companies.

Senator Daniel Patrick Moynihan (right) introduces First Lady Hillary Rodham Clinton as New York senator-elect during a victory rally in New York City on Nov. 7, 2000. Hillary Rodham Clinton is the only First Lady in history to be elected to office.

Under the 2000 legislation, U.S. farmers will be allowed to sell food to Cuba, though Cuba will not receive U.S. government credit or private financing to buy the food. Instead, Cuba will have to obtain funds from foreign banks or pay for the food in cash.

Debt relief. Congress on October 25 approved a $14.9-billion foreign aid spending bill for fiscal year 2001 that provided $435 million to forgive debts owed to the United States by the world's poorest nations. Supporters maintained that the legislation was a way of providing relief to poor nations so they can concentrate on feeding and educating their people.

Classified information. President Clinton on Nov. 4, 2000, vetoed legislation that would have made it a criminal offense for a government official to disclose classified information. Congress had approved the bill in October. The provision, which would have made leaks of classified information a felony punishable by fines and up to three years in prison, was included in a measure to fund the nation's intelligence agencies, including the Central Intelligence Agency.

□ Linda P. Campbell and Geoffrey A. Campbell

See also **Democratic Party; Elections; People in the news** (Lieberman, Joseph); **Republican Party; State government; Supreme Court of the United States; United States, Government of the.**

Conservation. Under pressure from an international alliance of environmental organizations, Mexico in March 2000 canceled plans with Japan's Mitsubishi Corporation to build an industrial salt factory near Punta Abrejos, Mexico. The chosen site for the factory was next to Laguna San Ignacio, a lagoon on the west coast of Baja California. Conservationists expressed concern that the factory would foul the ecosystem of the lagoon and its desert surroundings, harming whales and other wildlife. Gray whales, which were hunted in large numbers for decades until 1935 and which were on the United States Endangered Species List from 1973 to 1994, migrate to Laguna San Ignacio every year to give birth.

Environmentalists had begun the international media campaign against the proposed San Ignacio salt factory in 1995, when local residents contacted Mexican poet and activist Homero Aridjis. More than fifty Mexican conservation organizations, the Natural Resources Defense Council in New York City, and the International Fund for Animal Welfare in Yarmouth Port, Massachusetts, joined in the campaign. The group effort triggered more than 750,000 letters from the public to Mitsubishi demanding a halt to the project. The effort also led to a boycott of Mitsubishi products throughout California and convinced several U.S. mutual funds to drop Mitsubishi stock.

Oil spill survivors. A Panamanian tanker sank near Cape Town, South Africa, in June 2000, spilling more than 400 tons (360 metric tons) of oil. The oil coated miles of beaches and endangered thousands of African penguins. As the penguins' feathers became coated with oil, the birds were unable to maintain their body heat in the water. They were forced to retreat to the land, where there was insufficient food for them. The spill threatened more than 43,000 birds on nearby Dassen and Robben islands, approximately one-fourth of all the estimated 150,000 to 180,000 population of African penguins.

Tens of thousands of volunteers mobilized by the South African National Foundation for the Conservation of Coastal Birds cleaned and fed about 23,000 oil-coated birds that had been gathered into a makeshift rehabilitation center near Cape Town. Volunteers formed two-person teams and scrubbed each bird for an hour with toothbrushes and mild detergent. They hand-fed sardines to the birds, some of which needed one to two months of care.

The 20,000 uncontaminated penguins were captured and trucked about 500 miles (800 kilometers) east to Port Elizabeth, South Africa. There, the birds were released and allowed to swim back to Dassen and Robben islands while workers cleaned up the oil spill.

Because of the rapid mobilization of volunteers, the damage to wildlife was very low by comparison with similar disasters. Only about 1,000 of the 43,000 penguins died. Nevertheless, the oil spill was a setback for the penguins since the accident occurred during the middle of their breeding season, resulting in the loss of thousands of eggs and chicks.

Caribbean refuge. Officials of the Caribbean island of Dominica dedicated Morne Diablotin National Park in January. The Rare Species Conservatory Foundation, located in Loxahatchee, Florida, together with Dominica's government, raised funds to purchase a 1,300-acre (530-hectare) plot of old-growth rain forest from the Dominican Fruit Syndicate. The land was added to existing reserve land to create an 8,200-acre (3,300-hectare) park.

The new park protected 160 bird species and 55 butterfly species. Among the birds were two rare parrot species, the red-necked Amazon and the imperial Amazon. The imperial Amazon parrot, also called the sisserou, is the national bird of Dominica. In 2000, fewer than 200 imperial Amazon parrots lived in the wild.

Trading land for wildlife. In the West African nation of Gabon, conservationists, timber companies, and the government reached an agreement in July to end logging in a 1,900-square-mile (4,900-square-kilometer) reserve that

harbored the highest density of large mammals ever found in a tropical rain forest. The agreement was achieved by redrawing the boundaries of Lope Reserve, making 290 square miles (750 square kilometers) on the southeast perimeter available to loggers while adding 120 square miles (310 square kilometers) of pristine forest on the southwest. An additional 100 square miles (260 square kilometers) of land within the reserve was made off-limits to loggers.

Conservation biologists accepted the net loss of reserve land because the new addition, previously unprotected, included remote upland forests virtually unexplored by researchers. Lope was to serve as a sanctuary for lowland gorillas, elephants, mandrills, and other species.

National monuments. On January 11, U.S. President Bill Clinton signed a proclamation creating the Grand Canyon-Parashant National Monument in northern Arizona. Although a poll indicated that roughly three-fourths of Arizona's residents were in favor of creating the national monument, Arizona's Governor Jane Hull and some members of Congress, backed by hunters, off-road vehicle users, and commercial interests, protested the designation. Clinton was able to create the National Monument without congressional approval because a 1906 law called the Antiquities Act gave presidents the power to designate historic and scientific landmarks.

At the January 2000 signing, Clinton also created Agua Fria National Monument, located north of Phoenix, Arizona, and California Coastal National Monument—thousands of scattered islands, exposed reefs, and rocks along the 840-mile (1,350-kilometer) California coast. He expanded Pinnacles National Monument, located southeast of Salinas, California. In subsequent months, Clinton created five more national monuments: Grand Sequoia in California, Hanford Reach in Washington, Ironwood Forest in Arizona, Canyons of the Ancients in Colorado, and Cascade-Siskiyou in Oregon.

In December, Clinton created the largest nature preserve in the United States, the Northwestern Hawaiian Islands Coral Reef Ecosystem Reserve. The reserve protected more than 130,000 square miles (340,000 square kilometers), an area larger than Florida and Georgia combined, of coral reefs, remote islands, atolls, and submerged lagoons along the island chain that makes up Hawaii. Clinton called the reserve "a special place where the sea is a living rainbow."

California condors. The U.S. Fish and Wildlife Service (USFWS) program to boost the California condor population encountered a setback in July, when officials announced that four condors that had been released from captivity had died of lead poisoning. Lead *shot* (metal pel-

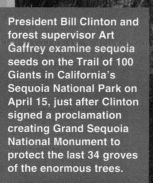

President Bill Clinton and forest supervisor Art Gaffrey examine sequoia seeds on the Trail of 100 Giants in California's Sequoia National Park on April 15, just after Clinton signed a proclamation creating Grand Sequoia National Monument to protect the last 34 groves of the enormous trees.

lets used in shotguns), which is extremely *toxic* (poisonous), was found in one bird's digestive system. A fifth bird could not be found and was presumed dead. The condors had been released near the Grand Canyon in Arizona. Condors normally feed on dead animal carcasses, and environmentalists speculated that the dead birds had eaten an animal that had been shot by hunters.

By mid-2000, the population of California condors had grown to around 170, from its lowest number of 22 in the early 1980's. About 45 condors—one-fourth of the total condor population—lived in the wild in 2000.

Everglades overhaul. Both houses of the U.S. Congress approved a 35-year, $7.8-billion federal project to correct decades of misguided water-control projects in the Florida Everglades. Clinton signed the bill in December.

The Everglades bill called for removing levees and repositioning canals to restore a natural flow of water in the Everglades. In addition to preserving threatened wetlands, the project was expected to save wildlife and cut down on water pollution while continuing to provide drinking water to the cities and towns of southern Florida. The project was expected to take 30 to 40 years to complete.

☐ Eugene J. Walter, Jr.

Costa Rica. See Latin America.

Courts. The November 2000 presidential election, one of the closest in U.S. history, became embroiled in the courts as Democrats and Republicans wrangled over Florida's 25 decisive Electoral College votes. Following the November 7 election, only a few hundred votes in Florida separated the Republican candidate, Texas Governor George W. Bush, from his Democratic challenger, Vice President Al Gore. Without Florida, neither had the 270 electoral votes necessary to claim victory.

Gore had requested hand recounts of ballots in several heavily Democratic Florida counties. Bush attorneys sued to stop the recounts. On November 21, the Florida Supreme Court ruled that manual counts would continue and should be included in the final tallies. Bush appealed to the U.S. Supreme Court, which on December 4 returned the case to the Florida court for clarification. On December 8, the Florida Supreme Court again ordered manual recounts to continue, only to have the U.S. Supreme Court stop the recount one day later. On December 12, the U.S. Supreme Court ruled that the manner in which the recounting in Florida was taking place was so arbitrary that it violated the equal protection clause of the 14th Amendment to the U.S. Constitution.

Political experts said that the court ruling left Gore with little legal recourse but to concede, which he did on December 13.

Microsoft ruling. On June 7, United States District Judge Thomas Penfield Jackson ruled that computer software giant Microsoft Corporation of Redmond, Washington, should be split into two companies for violating federal antitrust laws. Antitrust laws bar a company from blocking competition in its field. Jackson ruled that one company would control Microsoft's popular Windows *operating system* (master control program). A second company would manage other products, including *applications software* (programs for all the specific uses of computers).

Jackson ruled in April that Microsoft, the world's largest creator of computer software, discouraged competition in order to maintain a monopoly for its operating system. He also concluded that the company attempted to monopolize the *Web browser* (a program that enables computers to access the World Wide Web) software market and tried to discourage innovation by connecting its Internet Explorer Web browser to its Windows operating system. Microsoft officials appealed the ruling.

Tobacco lawsuit. A Florida jury on July 14 decided that the five largest tobacco companies in the United States should pay $145 billion in punitive damages for misleading the public for decades about possible health effects of smoking and for illnesses linked to smoking. Officials from the five companies—Philip Morris Inc. of Richmond, Virginia; R.J. Reynolds Tobacco Company of Winston-Salem, North Carolina; Brown & Williamson of Louisville, Kentucky; Lorillard Tobacco of Greensboro, North Carolina; and Liggett Group Inc. of Durham, North Carolina—planned to appeal the decision.

On November 6, Florida Circuit Court Judge Robert Kaye rejected a request from the tobacco companies to reduce the amount and upheld the record-setting verdict. Kaye also rejected a request for a new trial. However, additional appeals were expected to be filed.

Music copyright issues. During most of 2000, executives from Napster Inc., an online music-trading service headquartered in San Mateo, California, tried to fight off claims that the company was violating U.S. copyright law by allowing hundreds of thousands of computer users to trade musical recordings online. Copyright law requires that artists, such as musicians, authors, and photographers, be paid a fee when someone else uses their creative work for a profit. Napster let computer users download music or trade their song files through Napster's central computer servers for free.

In July, a federal judge in San Francisco ruled that Napster encouraged copyright infringement and should cease operation. Both the Recording Industry Association of America, a Washington,

D.C.-based trade group that represents the U.S. recording industry, and the heavy-metal rock band Metallica had filed lawsuits against the company, alleging that they violated copyright law.

The music industry claimed that Napster's services had cost the industry $300 million in lost sales by giving listeners access to songs without their purchasing tapes or compact disks (CD's). A federal appeals court ruled in July that Napster could continue its operations while the court considered the company's appeal.

MP3.com verdict. In a related lawsuit, a federal district judge in New York City ruled in September that the Internet company MP3.com violated copyright law by copying thousands of CD's produced by the Universal Music Group, the world's largest music company, headquartered in Santa Monica, California. The federal judge ruled that MP3.com should pay $25,000 in damages to Universal for each CD on which the Internet firm violated Universal's copyright. Legal experts believed that such a fine could reach as high as $250 million.

☐ Geoffrey A. Campbell and Linda P. Campbell

See also **Computer; Crime; Elections; Popular music; State government; Supreme Court of the United States.**

Cricket. In April 2000, police in New Delhi, India, charged several members of the South African cricket team, including its captain, Hansie Cronje, with cheating, fraud, and conspiracy. Cronje, who had toured India in February and March, at first denied all charges but later admitted receiving money for providing a *bookmaker* (a person who makes a living accepting bets) with information on the possible results of future matches. Cronje's dismissal as South African captain threw the cricket world into turmoil.

More inquiries. An inquiry in South Africa revealed in June that Cronje, who had by then severed his connections with cricket, had contacts with bookmakers since 1995. In March 2000, he had offered bribes to teammates Herschelle Gibbs and Henry Williams to underperform in a one-day international at Nagpur, India. Although Gibbs and Williams said they did not fulfill their promise and received no payments, they were both fined and banned from international cricket for six months.

Several distinguished Pakistani and Indian cricketers also came under scrutiny in 2000. In May, the Pakistan Cricket Board (PCB) imposed life bans on former test batsman Salim Malik, for match-fixing, and on bowler Ata-ur-Rehman, for committing perjury during the PCB investigation. Indian income tax officials raided the residences

A newspaper headline highlights U.S. District Judge Thomas Penfield Jackson's decision in June 2000 to divide the Microsoft Corporation of Redmond, Washington, into two separate companies after ruling that the software giant violated antitrust laws.

of several players, including India's greatest fast bowler, Kapil Dev, searching for undisclosed assets. Although Dev was later cleared of charges of match-fixing, he resigned as coach of the national side in September 2000. The International Cricket Council (ICC) appointed the former police commissioner of London, Sir Paul Condon, to root out corruption in international cricket competition.

Test cricket. Australia confirmed its status as the leading test-match playing country, with series victories against Zimbabwe (1-0), Pakistan (3-0), India (3-0), and New Zealand (3-0). In the first of three tests against India in March, Australian captain Steve Waugh became the first batsman to score hundreds against each of the eight test-playing nations. Shane Warne achieved another record in the first test against New Zealand when he brought his tally of test wickets to 356, beating Dennis Lillee's Australian record.

South Africa beat Zimbabwe in one test in South Africa and another in Zimbabwe, and then went on to beat England (2-1 with two drawn matches) and India (3-0). The final test between England and South Africa in January caused debate. On the final morning, after three days had been lost to rain, South African captain Hansie Cronje and English captain Nasser Hussain agreed to a double forfeiture of innings. This left England to chase a total of 249 in a minimum of 76 overs, which they achieved after an exciting tussle by two wickets. Most cricket writers applauded the decision, because it kept alive a match that would have ended in a dull draw. However, there was disagreement about whether the laws of cricket allowed the forfeiture of a first innings.

After losing to New Zealand, the West Indies recovered to beat Zimbabwe (2-0) and Pakistan (1-0, with 2 matches drawn). However, between June and September, an improving England side defeated the West Indies by 3-1, with one match drawn. Throughout this bowler-dominated series, veteran West Indian fast bowlers Curtly Ambrose and Courtney Walsh were outstanding. At the end of his final test series, Ambrose reached a test career total of 405 wickets, while Courtney Walsh finished with an all-time test record of 483 wickets. For England, fast bowler Darren Gough was the man of the series. England also beat Zimbabwe 1-0 in a two-match series which preceded the series against the West Indies.

Sri Lanka also had a mixed year, winning two away series, one against Zimbabwe (2-0, with one test drawn), and the other against Pakistan (2-1). However, Pakistan took its revenge when it visited Sri Lanka in June and July, winning two tests, with one match drawn. In July, Sri Lanka defeated South Africa by an innings, but South Africa fought back to draw the series 1-1, with one

match drawn.

Also in test cricket, the ICC in June decided to grant test match status to Bangladesh. This decision increased the number of test match-playing countries to 10.

One-day internationals. Among one-day international series, Australia won the Carlton and United series, beating India and Pakistan. New Zealand, following their test victory over the West Indies, beat the West Indians 5-0 in the one-day series. Pakistan won the Cable and Wireless Trophy against the West Indies and Zimbabwe in April. Pakistan also took the Asia Cup, a tournament held in June in Bangladesh. England had one of its most successful summers in years, winning both test series and in July taking the one-day Natwest Triangular.

The first-ever indoor one-day international series was held in the Colonial Stadium in Melbourne, Australia, in August between Australia and South Africa. The event was held in Australia's winter, and though well-attended, there was some question whether indoor cricket would be popular during the Australian summer. The Sahara Cup, due to have been played in September in Toronto, was canceled when India withdrew because the team did not want to play Pakistan due to political conflicts in Kashmir.

☐ Keith Lye

Crime. The crime rate in the United States continued to decline in 2000, according to a preliminary report released by the Federal Bureau of Investigation (FBI) in December. Serious crime fell by 0.3 percent in the first six months of 2000, compared with statistics for the same period in 1999. According to the FBI Uniform Crime Reporting Program, which gathers crime statistics from law enforcement agencies across the United States, violent crime—which includes murder, rape, robbery, and aggravated assault—and property crime—which includes motor vehicle theft, larceny, and burglary—decreased 0.3 percent in the first six months of 1999.

The murder rate decreased nationwide by 1.8 percent in the first six months of 2000, compared with the same period in 1999 statistics, according to the FBI report. Burglary decreased 2.4 percent; robbery decreased by 2.6 percent; rape increased by 0.7 percent; assault increased by 0.7 percent; larceny increased 0.1 percent; and car theft increased by 1.2 percent.

The FBI report also broke down the statistics by region. Crime decreased by 0.9 percent in the West, by 0.7 percent in the Midwest, by 1.9 percent int he Northeast, and the crime rate increased in the South by 1.2 percent. The crime rate fell in cities with populations over 250,000 and in cities with populations between 50,000

Police at the Port of Miami in Florida cut into the hull of a freighter in February 2000 looking for drugs after four massive shipments of cocaine were found hidden aboard ships arriving in Miami from Haiti.

and 99,999 people. In all other population groups, including suburban and rural counties the crime index increased during the first six months of 2000.

Officials described the increased percentages in certain crimes as a normal leveling off after decreases during the 1990's. Criminologists reported that the factors that had contributed to the decrease in violent crime were still in place in 2000, including larger police forces with proactive strategies, an increased prison population, a strong economy, and declines in the use of crack cocaine.

Campus crime. In 2000, the U.S. Department of Education for the first time published statistics on crime on college campuses in the United States. The statistics, covering 1999, appeared on the department's Web site. Since 1990, federal law has required that any college or university receiving federal funding compile a report of the crimes committed on its campus. Burglary was the most commonly committed crime on college campuses, followed by forcible sex offenses, robbery, aggravated assault, motor vehicle theft, arson, and negligent manslaughter.

Policing. The shooting of an unarmed man by a New York City police officer sparked national debate in 2000 over aggressive police tactics, particularly tactics developed by the New York

police. A number of criminologists attributed the 55-percent decrease in New York City's crime rate in the mid- to late-1990's to tactical changes made by the New York Police Department (NYPD). The tactics, which came to be widely imitated by other U.S. police departments, involved focusing police efforts on the highest-crime areas and maintaining a high level of police visibility. According to criminologists, high visibility prevents crime.

The NYPD also created a special police unit called the Street Crimes Unit (SCU), a small, elite group of officers who patrolled the city's worst neighborhoods undercover. The SCU aggressively attempted to prevent crimes, often by stopping and searching people for illegal weapons or checking for outstanding arrest warrants. SCU supporters claimed that random searches were essential to fighting crime in the worst urban areas. Critics responded that policing methods employed by the SCU were racist and led to rampant abuses of power.

Public criticism of the aggressive policing tactics used by officers in New York City grew fierce in 2000 when an SCU undercover detective shot and killed Patrick Dorismond, an unarmed security guard, in March. Dorismond was the fourth unarmed black man killed by New York City police in little more than a year. The shooting took place only weeks after a jury in Albany, New York, acquitted four New York City police officers for the 1999 shooting of Amadou Diallo. The officers, all SCU detectives, had fired 41 shots at Diallo, an immigrant from Guinea, when they mistook the man's wallet for a gun.

In the wake of the Dorismond killing, the NYPD attempted to respond to citizens' fears by showing greater leniency toward citizens committing petty offenses. However, the new policy was almost immediately called into question by a crime spree in June 2000. During the Puerto Rican National Day Parade, gangs of youths assaulted, molested, and robbed several women in Central Park. The police were accused of not doing enough to stop the assaults in the park.

25-year-old murder. In 2000, police in Greenwich, Connecticut, charged Michael Skakel with the 1975 murder of Martha Moxley, a 15 year old who had been bludgeoned with a golf club. Police had suspected that Skakel or one of his brothers had murdered the girl but were unable to find conclusive evidence. In 1998, a judge reopened the case, investigating claims that Skakel admitted to the murder while in a substance abuse center. Since Skakel's arrest, a debate has raged over whether he should be tried in an adult or a juvenile court for a crime he allegedly committed when he was a juvenile.   □ Robert Messenger

Croatia. Parliamentary elections held in January 2000 resulted in a major victory for democratic reform, when a six-party prodemocracy coalition took control of Croatia's government. The new government immediately pledged to begin economic reform and take steps to democratize Croatian politics. The coalition's victory was consolidated in February by the election of coalition candidate Stjepan Mesic as president.

Croatia's *gross domestic product* (the value of all goods and services produced in a country in a given year) increased by 3.7 percent in the second half of 2000. The unemployment rate averaged approximately 21 percent. Tourism increased by more than 50 percent from November 1999 to November 2000.

Croatian leaders improved ties with Western democracies after the January elections. Croatia joined the Partnership for Peace in May and the World Trade Organization in July. President Mesic visited the United States in August. Croatia began talks with the European Union (EU) about a stabilization and association agreement. EU representatives called for additional progress in fighting government corruption, reforming the intelligence services, democratizing the media, and creating a more favorable environment for foreign investment.   □ Sharon L. Wolchik

See also **Europe.**

Cuba. Basic questions about relations between Cuba and the United States came to the forefront of public attention on June 28, 2000, when 6-year-old Elian Gonzalez flew back to Cuba from the United States with his father. The boy had been found off the coast of Florida in November 1999 after his mother and other Cuban refugees drowned when their boat capsized. A seven-month-long fight over custody of the child pitted the boy's Miami relatives against both his father in Cuba and the U.S. government.

As the Elian case worked its way through U.S. courts, many Americans questioned their government's policy of isolation toward Cuba. When the matter was finally resolved, the U.S. government found itself on the same side of the case as the government of Cuba—the boy belonged with his father, regardless of the political issues.

U.S. trade embargo. The centerpiece of U.S. policy toward Cuba was a trade embargo that in 2000 had been in effect for 38 years. According to Congressman James Clyburn (D., South Carolina), "We are seeing different groups, like some Republicans, farm interests, church groups, and others starting to push to end the embargo." Clyburn led a fact-finding delegation of the Congressional Black Caucus to the Cuban capital, Havana, in May. "I think the only people who are suffering (from the embargo) are the seniors and the children (of Cuba)," added Clyburn.

In October, the U.S. Congress approved a measure that would ease the embargo by allowing sales of food and medicine to Cuba. However, critics noted that the bill was so weighted down with conditions that it would have little practical impact.

Venezuelan oil. On October 30, Cuban President Fidel Castro signed an agreement in Caracas, Venezuela, stipulating that Venezuela would supply Cuba with 53,000 barrels of oil a day over the next five years at reduced prices. The agreement, similar to those Venezuela had made with other Caribbean and Central American nations, permitted Cuba to pay for the oil with a combination of money, goods, and services. Cuban officials hoped the accord would help reduce Cuba's large balance-of-payment deficit.

Castro denounces globalization. At a summit of the world's poorest countries on April 12 in Havana, Castro blamed the global capitalistic system for the suffering of people in developing nations. Speaking on September 6 at the United Nations (UN) in New York City, the 74-year-old leader called for reform of the UN to make it a "true representative body of the interests of all the peoples on Earth."   □ Nathan A. Haverstock

See also **Cuba: A Special Report; Immigration; Latin America; Miami.**

Cyprus. See **Middle East.**

The Cold War's Last Front: The United States and Cuba

In 2000, many U.S. citizens voiced support for improving relations with Cuba.

By Nathan A. Haverstock

The much-publicized custody battle over a Cuban boy named Elian Gonzalez Brotons focused world attention on the continuing antagonism between Cuba and the United States—nations at odds with each other for more than 40 years. In November 1999, Elian survived a shipwreck that claimed the life of the boy's mother and several other Cuban refugees trying to reach the United States. For seven months, amid intensive coverage by the press, Elian's relatives in Miami, Florida, fought with the boy's Cuban father over custody of the child.

Tens of thousands of Cuban exiles in Miami took to the streets in flag-waving demonstrations to demand that Elian be spared a life under Communism and allowed to remain in the United States. There were scenes reminiscent of the Cold War, the intense rivalry between U.S. allies and Communist nations that began after World War II (1939-1945) and ended when the Soviet Union collapsed in 1991. In 2000, the Cold War still seemed to define relations between the Cuba and the United States.

In Cuba, President Fidel Castro seized upon the intense media coverage of the case not only to demand the boy's return, but to mount a national campaign to pressure the U.S. government to lift its 38-year-old economic embargo. In the United States, politicians of both major parties sided with the Cuban exiles, who had influenced U.S. policy toward their former homeland since Castro came to power in 1959.

The climax of the crisis came on April 22, 2000, when U.S. Attorney General Janet Reno ordered U.S. marshals forcibly to remove Elian from the house of his Miami relatives in keeping with decisions by U.S. courts. The federal agents reunited Elian and his Cuban family at Andrews Air Force Base in Maryland. On June 28, after the Gonzalez case had worked its way through the legal system, the U.S. Supreme Court decided it would hear no further appeals and awarded the boy's father permanent custody. Within hours, television cameras provided live coverage of 6-year-old Elian and his Cuban family boarding a jet to Cuba.

Rethinking Cuban-U.S. relations

By the time the custody case was resolved, most Americans, according to polls, supported the U.S. government's decision to return the boy to Cuba. Elian's case also caused people in the United States to question whether U.S. policies on Cuba made sense when compared with diplomatic relations between the United States and other Communist governments. In 2000, the U.S. Congress approved a permanent trade agreement with China, a Communist nation repeatedly cited by international observers for human rights violations. The United States also established a sweeping trade agreement with Vietnam, where U.S. troops had fought the Communist regime from 1965 to 1975. These developments led many Americans to ask: Why was the United States not doing more to improve its relations with Cuba, a small country that posed no threat to the security of the United States? A number of foreign affairs experts suggested that the resolution of

Opposite page:
A billboard depicting Elian Gonzalez, a Cuban refugee in the United States, towers over demonstrators in Pinar del Rio, Cuba, in January 2000. At several such rallies, Cubans called for the return of Elian to his father in Cuba.

United States
Florida
Atlantic
Ocean
Gulf of
Mexico
Miami
Bahamas
Havana
Mexico
CUBA
Haiti
Belize
Jamaica
Caribbean Sea
Honduras
0   200 Miles
Nicaragua
0   200 Kilometers

the Elian Gonzalez custody battle offered some hope that the many complex issues still dividing the United States and Cuba could also be resolved in the near future, even if not to everybody's satisfaction.

The Elian affair occurred during a critical period of transition in Cuba. Despite moderate concessions to improve his image abroad, Castro was grappling with the failure of the Communist system he had imposed upon the people of Cuba. Many experts believed that a constructive U.S. policy toward Cuba could help influence the people and policies that would emerge from the political and economic voids left by the Castro regime. At the same time, experts noted that U.S. policymakers would benefit from an examination of past experiences with the island neighbor.

A new nation and the United States

By 2000, the United States and Cuba shared a legacy of more than 100 years of mostly troubled relations, despite the role the United States played in Cuba's struggle for independence. The United States had declared war against Spain in 1898 out of a desire to free the island from Spanish oppression. The declaration of war included an amendment in which the U.S. government disavowed any "intention to exercise sovereignty, jurisdiction, or control" over Cuba. In the amendment, the U.S. government also pledged to occupy the island only as long as it took to establish peace. By the end of the war, however, Cubans had become skeptical of U.S. intentions. Under the Treaty of Paris, which formally ended the Spanish-American War on Dec. 10, 1898, the United States had taken possession of the Spanish colonies of Guam, the Philippines, and Puerto Rico, effectively making the United States an imperial power.

In 1901, Senator Orville H. Platt of Connecticut introduced an amendment to an Army appropriations bill that outlined conditions under which the U.S. military would turn over Cuba to a civilian government. Under the Platt Amendment, the United States reserved the right to intervene in Cuban affairs whenever necessary "for the preservation of Cuban independence [and] the maintenance of a government adequate for the protection of life, property, and individual liberty." The amendment restricted the new nation's ability to contract debts or negotiate treaties. The amendment also stipulated that a new Cuban Constitution must incorporate all the provisions of the Platt Amendment.

Cuba became self-governing on May 20, 1902. The United States secured a permanent lease for a naval base at Guantanamo Bay on the southeastern end of the island in 1903.

Invoking the Platt Amendment, the United States intervened in Cuban affairs on several occasions. Most notably, the United States governed Cuba from 1906 to 1909 after suppressing protests over disputed election results. The United States also in-

The author:
Nathan A. Haverstock is an affiliate scholar at Oberlin College in Oberlin, Ohio. Haverstock visited Cuba in 2000 to research this article.

tervened in Cuban affairs—often behind the scenes—on behalf of powerful U.S. business interests that dominated the Cuban economy. For example, by the 1920's, U.S. companies controlled about 70 percent of Cuba's sugar production, the island's most important industry.

The Batista years

The impact of the Great Depression of the 1930's sparked discontent among the Cuban people, which ultimately produced a revolution. In August 1933, a general strike and a military revolt ended the dictatorial government of President Gerardo Machado. Later in 1933, an obscure Cuban army sergeant, Fulgencio Batista y Zaldivar, led another revolt of fellow noncommissioned officers against the leaders of Cuba's armed forces. Batista and his fellow officers set up a government with a civilian president, but the new leaders of the military wielded most of the power.

Batista promoted himself to colonel, assumed command of Cuba's armed forces, restored a degree of order, and dealt harshly with his foes. In 1934, he forced the civilian president out of office and ruled Cuba, from behind the scenes, through a series of presidents who had no real power. To guarantee the support he needed to stay in power, Batista defended the interests of both U.S. citizens in Cuba and upper-class Cubans. At the same time, he won the support of the Cuban people by persuading the U.S. Congress to revoke the Platt Amendment, which the Cuban people had deeply resented.

Batista served as president of Cuba in his own right from 1940 to 1944. In 1952, he overthrew another president and governed again as dictator. Under his iron rule, Cuba appeared prosperous to American tourists who swarmed to the island. Gambling casinos, some of them run by mobsters operating out of the United States, lined the pockets of Batista and his associates. Outside the capital city of Havana and its affluent suburbs, however, most Cubans lived in poverty. Batista's government did little to improve the inadequate health and education systems in rural Cuba where most of the people worked for meager wages in the sugar industry.

These problems eventually stirred unrest. On July 26, 1953, Fi-

Important dates in Cuban-U.S. Relations

1898
The United States declares war on Spain to end Spanish rule in Cuba.

1898-1902
A U.S. military government rules Cuba.

del Castro Ruz, a 26-year-old graduate of the University of Havana School of Law, mounted a bold challenge against Batista's dictatorship. Castro led about 160 young Cubans in an attack on the Moncada army barracks in Santiago de Cuba on the island's southeast coast. The military repulsed the attack, killing more than half of Castro's group. Castro himself was jailed.

In May 1955, in response to public appeals, the government released Castro and other rebels. Castro then sought refuge in Mexico and organized another rebel force. In December 1956, the 82 members of this group landed a boat called *Granma* on Cuba's southeastern coast, where troops loyal to Batista brought them under withering fire. The dozen who survived, including Castro, sought refuge in the nearby Sierra Maestra, a mountain range on the southern end of the island. From remote hideaways, the idealistic young fighters repeatedly repulsed or escaped assaults from Batista's forces by disappearing into the jungles.

The rise of Communism

Castro's struggle against Batista's regime was reported in newspapers around the world and engaged the sympathies of people at home and abroad, including in the United States. As the Cuban revolution became the stuff of legend, it became difficult for most observers to separate fact from fiction. Viewed sympathetically by the world press, Castro was able to attract volunteers and a flow of arms that permitted his forces to mount attacks on foes, who were quickly losing public support. Amid mounting military setbacks, Batista and his circle finally fled Cuba on Jan. 1, 1959. That same day, Castro and his forces marched in triumph through the streets of a jubilant Havana.

To the dismay of many of his supporters, Castro soon assumed dictatorial powers, imposed martial law, and executed foes following trials before hastily convened military tribunals. Many Cubans, including some of Castro's closest associates, felt betrayed by the new Cuban government. When Castro declared himself a Communist and Cuba a Communist nation, there were defections from his ranks. Many of Cuba's best educated and skilled citizens sought refuge in the United States, often risking their lives attempting to flee the dictatorship.

Throughout 1960, Castro's regime seized foreign-owned properties and enterprises,

Hershey Chocolate Company of Pennsylvania, which operated a sugar refinery in Cuba (right), was one of several U.S. businesses that dominated the Cuban economy in the first half of the 1900's.

1901
The Platt Amendment, a provision of the Cuban Constitution, grants the United States the right to intervene in Cuban affairs.

1906
The United States sets up a military government in Cuba after U.S. troops suppress violent protests over disputed presidential elections.

1909
The U.S. military turns over control of Cuba to an elected civilian government.

creating a series of nationally owned companies. These measures shocked the world and cast a pall over U.S.-Cuban relations. The United States responded by imposing a trade embargo on all goods, except food and medicine. Eventually, Cuba negotiated settlements with some foreign governments for seized property, but the negotiations between the United States and Cuba broke down almost immediately.

The Cold War nears U.S. shores

Castro established close ties with the Soviet Union, and this became a major concern for the United States. The U.S. government was fearful of having a Communist satellite only 90 miles (145 kilometers) from its shores. With the approval of President Dwight D. Eisenhower, the U.S. Central Intelligence Agency developed plans to topple the Castro regime by secretly supporting an invasion of Cuba by Cuban-exile forces trained in Guatemala. The plan was carried out by the newly elected administration of President John F. Kennedy. The invasion, which was launched on Cuba's southern coast at the Bay of Pigs on April 17, 1961, was repulsed by Cuban forces in just 72 hours. The Kennedy administration, failing to overthrow Cuba's Communist government, adopted other strategies. In February 1962, the administration imposed a sweeping trade embargo intended to hurt not only Cuba but any nation trading with or offering aid to Cuba.

Later that year, at the height of Cold War tensions, U.S. surveillance planes photographed new Cuban military construction with Soviet nuclear missiles capable of striking targets in the United States. In October, Kennedy ordered a naval blockade of Cuba to prevent the arrival of Soviet ships carrying additional missiles. This crisis and the threat

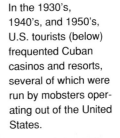

In the 1930's, 1940's, and 1950's, U.S. tourists (below) frequented Cuban casinos and resorts, several of which were run by mobsters operating out of the United States.

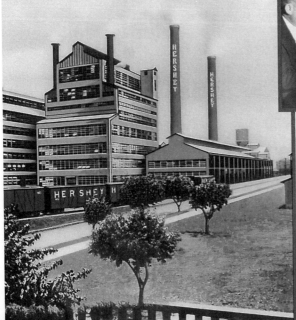

1912
The United States dispatches troops to Cuba to break up civil rights protests by black Cubans.

1917
The United States sends troops to Cuba to suppress a revolt protesting electoral fraud.

of a nuclear war was resolved when the Soviet Union withdrew its missiles from Cuba in return for a secret U.S. pledge to remove its own missiles from Turkey, which shared borders with the Soviet Union. The United States also promised not to support another invasion of Cuba.

The concessions made during the Cuban missile crisis did not prevent the United States from making further attempts to destabilize the Cuban economy. In 1963, the Kennedy administration tightened the economic embargo by prohibiting travel from the United States to Cuba, freezing Cuban-owned assets in the United States, and making it illegal for U.S. citizens to conduct any financial or commercial transaction with Cubans.

The United States also took steps to prevent the spread of Communism elsewhere in the Americas. Under this policy, the U.S. government provided military assistance to El Salvador and Nicaragua to defeat Communist insurgencies that were allegedly supported by Cuba or the Soviet Union. With U.S. support, Bolivian forces in 1967 captured and executed the Argentine-born Ernesto (Che) Guevara, one of Castro's closest associates. In Bolivia, Guevara had led a left-wing insurgency among Indians in the Andes Mountains. In 1983, U.S. military forces led an invasion of the tiny Caribbean nation of Grenada to forestall an alleged Communist takeover. On Grenada, the U.S. military briefly engaged in combat with 750 Cuban soldiers and workers who were involved in the construction of an airfield.

For its part, the Cuban government acknowledged that it sent more than 300,000 soldiers on overseas military missions from 1975 to 1992, to advise and support revolutionary movements elsewhere, mainly in Africa. Most of those troops, supported by the Soviet Union, fought on the side of left-wing rebels in Ethiopia and Angola.

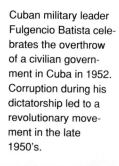

Cuban military leader Fulgencio Batista celebrates the overthrow of a civilian government in Cuba in 1952. Corruption during his dictatorship led to a revolutionary movement in the late 1950's.

The end of the Cold War

The collapse of the Soviet Union in 1991 signaled the beginning of the end of any substantial Cuban involvement in overseas revolutionary struggles. The loss of Soviet aid also proved deeply traumatic for the Cuban economy. The value of Cuba's *gross domestic product* (GDP—the total of all goods and services produced in a year) fell by more than one-third between 1990 and 1993. From 1989 to 1993, the value of Cuba's exports declined by two-thirds, the amount of imports fell by

1934

Cuba and the United States sign a treaty ending the Platt Amendment.

1934-1944

The United States supports the government of the Cuban dictator, Fulgencio Batista y Zaldivar.

1958

The United States withdraws support from a second Batista dictatorship, which began in 1952.

three-quarters, and the nation's budget deficit swelled to consume one-third of Cuba's GDP.

The Cuban government referred to the years following the loss of Soviet aid as "the special period in peacetime." With the standard of living of most Cubans drastically declining, Castro sought to refurbish his image internationally. He allowed the Cable News Network (CNN) of the United States to establish a news bureau in Havana, the first since 1969. In January 1998, Cuba hosted a visit from Pope John Paul II and granted thousands of U.S. Cuban exiles permission to attend the event. During the 1990's, the Cuban government also resumed diplomatic relations with a number of nations in an effort to improve commercial ties in Latin America.

Economic reforms in Cuba

Castro also introduced some modest economic reforms. The government by 1994 had converted 75 percent of state-owned farms into cooperatives whose members were allowed to sell one-quarter of their production at open market prices. The Cuban government also sold shares in state-owned companies to foreign investors. In July 2000, for example, a Franco-Spanish company called Altadis S.A. purchased half of the shares in Cuba's state-owned cigar company for $500 million.

In response to the Cuban government efforts to encourage foreign investment, the Sherritt International Corporation, a Toronto-based company, invested nearly $1 billion in Cuban oil production, nickel mining, power generation, agriculture, and tourism by 2000.

As tourism revived, more foreigners visited Cuba. In 1999, an estimated 1.6 million people came to the island. Citizens of Canada, which maintained diplomatic relations with Cuba, accounted for 17 percent of the visitors. Visitors from Germany, Italy, Spain, and the United Kingdom—whose business executives became increasingly active in Cuba—accounted for 55 percent of the total.

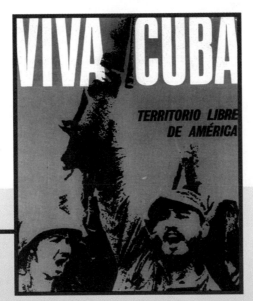

1959
The revolutionary government of Fidel Castro assumes dictatorial power in Cuba.

1960
Cuba seizes and nationalizes U.S. and other foreign-owned businesses. The United States imposes an economic embargo on all trade with Cuba, except for food and medicine.

Accommodations for tourists and business people became a booming industry. In 1999, the five-star Golden Tulip Hotel, managed by a Dutch company, opened its doors in Old Havana, the historic district of the capital. In 2000, Leisure Canada Inc. of Vancouver began construction on a 370-room hotel with a beachfront location.

The new investments and increased tourism had little impact on the lives of most Cubans who struggled to make ends meet during a time of continuing recession. The average monthly salary in 1999 remained at just over $10.00. In 2000, Cubans continued to use ration books, as they had since the 1960's, to purchase many staples: six eggs per person every 21 days and 6 pounds (2.7 kilograms) each of rice and sugar per month per person.

Ironically, the key to survival for many Cubans during the "special period" was the U.S. dollar. In 1993, the Cuban government legalized the use of U.S. dollars, though most people still received wages in Cuban pesos. The United States in 1998 granted each Cuban American household in the United States the right to send up to $300 every three months to relatives in Cuba. By 2000, the dollar had largely replaced the Cuban peso in Havana—not only in transactions with foreign visitors but also among Cubans themselves.

The predominance of the U.S. dollar came about, in part, because the Cuban government allowed some private businesses to open. Many Cubans embarked on enterprises that would allow them to do business in dollars.

The Sottolongo family of Havana, for example, gained official approval to rent out three rooms in their house to tourists at a rate of $25 per night. In return, the family paid the Cuban government a tax of $100 per room per month. According to Cuban government figures, the number of such self-employed Cubans in August 1999 was 166,000, but unofficial tallies estimated the figure to be higher.

LAUNCH POSITION

MISSILE-READY TENTS

MISSILE ERECTORS

1961

The United States breaks diplomatic relations with Cuba. Cuban exiles sponsored by the U.S. Central Intelligence Agency invade Cuba at the Bay of Pigs and are defeated by Cuban forces.

1962

The United States learns that the Soviet Union has placed nuclear missiles in Cuba; the two superpowers become embroiled in a crisis that threatens international security.

Cuban exports

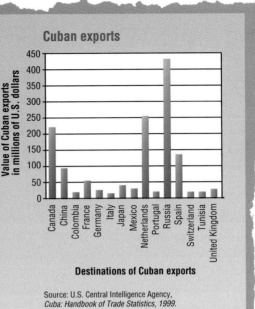

Value of Cuban exports in millions of U.S. dollars (y-axis: 0 to 450)

Destinations of Cuban exports: Canada, China, Colombia, France, Germany, Italy, Japan, Mexico, Netherlands, Portugal, Russia, Spain, Switzerland, Tunisia, United Kingdom

Destinations of Cuban exports

Source: U.S. Central Intelligence Agency,
Cuba: Handbook of Trade Statistics, 1999.

Foreign investments in the 1990's helped Cuba begin to slowly refurbish and restore beautiful structures in the historic areas of Havana (top), as an attraction for tourists. Such investments did little to ease the lives of residents of the city's neglected and poor neighborhoods (bottom).

Foreign investment in Cuba

Foreign companies invested more than $1.7 billion dollars in Cuba from January 1990 to March 1999.

Millions of U.S. dollars (y-axis: 0 to 600)

Brazil, Canada, Chile, France, Italy, Mexico, Netherlands, Portugal, Spain, United Kingdom

Source: U.S. Department of State;
U.S.-Cuba Trade and Economic Council, Inc.

1962-1963
The U.S. government adopts a strict trade embargo, prohibits U.S. citizens from traveling to Cuba, and seizes all Cuban-owned assets in the United States.

1977
The U.S. government allows U.S. citizens to travel to Cuba. Each of the two nations opens an interest section, a limited diplomatic service, in the other's capital.

1980
The Mariel boat lift brings 125,000 Cubans to U.S. shores.

Cuban-U.S. relations in transition

Changes in the Cuban economy and improved relations between Cuba and other nations did not lead to improved relations between Cuba and the United States. In 1996, Cuban MiG jet fighters shot down over international waters two small, unarmed airplanes used by Cuban exiles to search for Cubans fleeing the island. Many Americans were outraged by the incident, and the well-organized Cuban American community lobbied the U.S. Congress for tough retaliations. Senator Jesse Helms (R., North Carolina) and Representative Dan Burton (R., Indiana) co-sponsored the Cuban Liberty and Democratic Solidarity Act (Helms-Burton Act). This law, which further tightened the U.S. trade embargo, included a controversial provision enabling Americans to sue in U.S. federal courts any foreign company that profits from the use of U.S. properties expropriated by Cuba in 1960. Opponents of the law criticized it for its severity and for the imposition it placed on the role of the executive branch in setting foreign policy. In response to complaints by Canada and other nations that the Helms-Burton Act violates international law, U.S. President Bill Clinton waived enforcement of the lawsuit provision.

The Clinton administration also liberalized the rules on travel from the United States to Cuba in the late 1990's. As a result, approximately 135,000 U.S. citizens in 1999 legally visited Cuba. Most of them were members of relief organizations and religious groups or teachers and students in educational exchange programs. In that same year, the Baltimore Orioles became the first U.S. major league baseball team to play in Havana in more than 40 years. In January 2000, the Clinton administration allowed 97 U.S. companies to show medical equipment at a trade fair in Havana.

By 2000, many Americans—spokespersons for farmers and business corporations, foreign policy experts, and the public in general—voiced support for lifting the trade embargo on Cuba. They argued that the embargo had done little to promote democracy, had hurt the Cuban people, and restricted opportunities for U.S. citizens and businesses. In particular, U.S. citizens who had visited Cuba became vocal advocates of the people whom they had found welcoming and eager to restore normal relations with their neighbors to the north.

Two inescapable questions regarding better relations remained, however. How long would it take? And, does Castro

1992
The United States prohibits Cuban Americans from sending money to relatives in Cuba, U.S. citizens from traveling to Cuba, and foreign-based subsidiaries of U.S. companies from trading with Cuba.

1996
The Helms-Burton Act penalizes foreign individuals and companies doing business in Cuba.

1998
U.S. President Bill Clinton allows Cuban American households to send $300 every three months to relatives in Cuba.

1999-2000
Cuban Americans in Miami, Florida, protest to keep Elian Gonzalez in the United States.

have to go before it happens?

In 2000, many Cubans feared that the opportunity for better relations had already passed and that Castro inevitably would toughen his stance if recent reforms threatened his hold on power. They also noted that the 74-year-old Castro was unlikely to change his policies significantly.

In the United States, political experts noted that powerful leaders in Congress would not consider normalizing relations with Cuba as long as Castro remained in power. In addition, some people in the United States were unable to forgive a dictator who had brought the world to the threshold of nuclear war, caused upheaval in the lives of so many Cubans, and continued to violate human rights.

A growing number of U.S. policy experts countered that the U.S. government should begin addressing its problems with Cuba, regardless of who was in charge. Resolving difficult issues could take decades. These include finding ways to reconcile a divided people—more than 1 million exiles in the United States and more than 11 million Cubans. The two nations also needed to reach an agreement on compensation for property Castro's government had seized. Cubans, for their part, would most likely demand reparations for the loss of Cuban lives and property as a result of actions taken by the U.S. government, such as the Bay of Pigs and Grenada invasions. Nevertheless, based on public sentiments expressed after the resolution of the Elian Gonzalez case, the majority of Americans seemed ready to begin the process of resolving such issues and ending what many viewed as punishment of the Cuban people for the crimes of their leader. ■ ■ ■

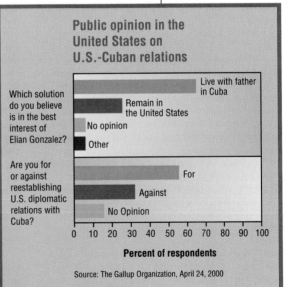

Public opinion in the United States on U.S.-Cuban relations

Which solution do you believe is in the best interest of Elian Gonzalez?
- Live with father in Cuba
- Remain in the United States
- No opinion
- Other

Are you for or against reestablishing U.S. diplomatic relations with Cuba?
- For
- Against
- No Opinion

Percent of respondents

Source: The Gallup Organization, April 24, 2000

2000

The Clinton administration, defying anti-Castro Cuban Americans, reunites Elian Gonzalez with his Cuban family.

Czech Republic. In January 2000, the governing Social Democrats and the Civic Democratic Party amended their power-sharing agreement. The amendments strengthened the agreement, addressing such issues as the state budget and election law reform, and improved communications between the two parties. Prime Minister Milos Zeman made numerous changes in the cabinet in February and March.

Domestic affairs. In January, the cabinet approved a law governing the return of property confiscated from Jews during World War II (1939-1945). The law addressed farms and farmland, which previously had been excluded from those properties subject to return. In March 2000, a commission approved rules to compensate Czech victims of the *Holocaust* (the systematic killing during World War II of millions of Jews and other people by Germany's Nazi government).

The lower house of parliament in March amended the Czech Constitution to limit the powers of the president. In July, the parliament overrode a veto by President Vaclav Havel and amended the electoral law to make it more difficult for small parties to build coalitions. Opposition groups charged that the changes unfairly favored the ruling Social Democrats and the Civic Democratic Party.

Foreign affairs. Officials of the European Union (EU) announced in August that the Czech Republic would not be excluded from joining the EU for failing to abolish the Benes Decrees, laws that had made possible the expulsion of 2.5 million Germans from Czechoslovakia in 1945. However, EU officials did criticize Czech leaders for not meeting EU standards for water quality and industrial environment policies, and for failing to enact judicial reforms.

Relations with Austria in 2000 were complicated by concerns about the safety of the Temelin nuclear power plant near Austria's border, which began operating in October. Austrian citizens protesting the plant blocked border crossings, preventing Czechs from entering Austria.

In February, the government banned the sale to Iran of construction supplies for a nuclear plant after U.S. officials threatened sanctions.

Economy. The Czech Republic's *gross domestic product* (the value of all goods and services produced in a country in a given year) grew 3.1 percent in the first half of 2000. Foreign investment increased substantially for the first time since 1997. Inflation remained low at 4.1 percent. In April 2000, the parliament passed a 40-percent increase in the minimum wage. Unemployment dropped to 8.5 percent in October.

☐ Sharon Wolchik

See also **Austria; Europe; Iran.**

Dallas. On Jan. 1, 2000, officials relit Pegasus, the flying red horse sign atop the historic Magnolia Building in dowtown Dallas. A total of $600,000 in private donations went into the restoration of one of the city's most famous landmarks. More than 45,000 people attended the ceremony. The huge neon horse, an emblem of the Mobil Oil Corporation, was erected in 1934 when the Magnolia Building was the tallest building in Dallas.

City Council member convicted. City Council member Al Lipscomb was convicted Jan. 25, 2000, on 65 counts of bribery and conspiracy in relation to payments he had accepted from taxi company owner Floyd Richards. Lipscomb resigned his council seat nine days after being convicted.

On April 28, U.S. District Judge Joe Kendall sentenced Lipscomb to 41 months of home confinement and fined him $14,000. Kendall said he had chosen not to send Lipscomb to jail because Lipscomb was in poor health. Kendall had moved the trial to Amarillo, Texas, because of Lipscomb's prominence in Dallas as a longtime civil rights activist.

Airport lawsuit resolved. On June 29, the U.S. Supreme Court enabled commercial airlines to fly from Dallas's Love Field to destinations across the country. The court refused to hear appeals against a lower court's decision that opened the municipal airport to national routes. Prior to a ruling by the U.S. Fifth Circuit Court of Appeals in New Orleans on February 1, federal law had limited Love Field flights to destinations in Texas and nearby states. Federal limits had been placed on Love Field traffic in 1979 to protect bonds issued to build Dallas-Fort Worth International Airport.

Another Cowboys coach departs. On Jan. 11, 2000, Dallas Cowboys owner Jerry Jones fired Chan Gailey after only one season as the football team's head coach. Jones named defensive coordinator Dave Campo as Gailey's replacement. Campo was the Dallas Cowboys' fourth coach since Jerry Jones purchased the team in 1989.

Tom Landry, the Cowboys' coach from 1959 until 1989, died of leukemia on Feb. 12, 2000. Landry led the team to two Super Bowl victories.

Billionaire buys Mavericks. On April 11, the National Basketball Association approved the purchase of the Dallas Mavericks professional basketball team for $280 million by Mark Cuban, an Internet entrepreneur. Ross Perot, Jr., and business associates had acquired the team in 1996 for $125 million.

Mass transit funds. On August 12, Dallas voters approved a referendum allowing Dallas Area Rapid Transit (DART) to borrow up to $2.9 billion for rail line construction and future mass transportation programs. The funds were meant to enable DART to complete a 49-mile (79-kilometer) light-rail system nearly five years ahead of schedule and finish a 22-mile (35-kilometer) commuter rail line to Dallas-Fort Worth International Airport and downtown Fort Worth. In 2000, DART served 13 cities and operated 20 miles (32 kilometers) of light rail lines, one 10-mile (16-kilometer) commuter rail line, and 1,600 miles (2,600 kilometers) of bus routes.

Change in superintendents. Dallas school board trustees voted 7 to 1 to dismiss school superintendent Waldemar Rojas in July, less than one year after he started the job. On October 9, the board hired former Texas Education Commissioner Mike Moses to replace Rojas. Moses was the leader of major educational reforms during George W. Bush's first term as governor of Texas. Moses was the sixth superintendent that the Dallas School District had appointed since 1996.

Convention center expansion. A $125-million expansion of the Dallas Convention Center was approved in March 2000. The project, which was to enlarge the center to 1 million square feet (93,000 square meters), was scheduled for completion in 2002. In 2000, convention business brought an estimated $4 billion into the Dallas economy. ☐ Henry Tatum

See also **Baseball; City; Deaths.**

Dance. The board of directors of the Martha Graham Dance Company in New York City suspended operations for the dance troupe, the junior company, and the school in May 2000. The immediate reason for the action was the company's $500,000 deficit, which prevented it from paying dancers' and administrators' salaries. The underlying cause of the crisis, however, was a long-simmering dispute between the board and the dancers, on one side, and artistic director Ron Protas on the other.

In 1999, Protas had agreed to step down as director in favor of former Graham dancer Janet Eilber, but in March 2000 he reneged, and the board removed him from the directorship. Since Protas owned the rights to Graham's work, the company still had to apply to him to perform Graham's dances. The board's decision to shut down the company was seen as a way to force Protas's hand, but at the same time it threatened the future of the company. Some dance enthusiasts feared that Graham's repertory and the very technique that she pioneered were in jeopardy.

An immediate result of the shut-down was that the Graham troupe canceled performances at the American Dance Festival in Durham, North Carolina, in June, and at the John F. Kennedy Center for the Performing Arts in Washington, D.C., in September. In July, current and former

Vera Arbuzova of the Eifman Ballet troupe of St. Petersburg, Russia, dances the lead in *Red Giselle* during a U.S. tour in April and May 2000. The *Red Giselle* choreography combines classical ballet with modern dance.

Graham dancers released a statement urging that other troupes boycott the Graham Trust as long as Protas was in control. However, such major companies as the Joffrey Ballet of Chicago (JBC) and American Ballet Theater (ABT) of New York City did perform Graham's ballets in autumn 2000.

The New York Choreographic Institute was established in 2000 to provide choreographers in New York City an opportunity to practice their craft without the pressures of public performances. The Institute was founded with a $5.5 million grant from the Irene Diamond Fund. The Diamond grant was the largest contribution to the largest fund-raising drive in the history of dance, a $50-million campaign announced by the New York City Ballet on April 24.

The Institute opened with a handful of choreographers who received free studio time and the use of dancers from the New York City Ballet. Choreographer Christopher Wheeldon, who was commissioned to create two new works for the City Ballet, was the first artist in residence.

New York City Ballet founder George Balanchine was celebrated in an unusual multicompany program at Washington's Kennedy Center from September 12 to September 24. The participating troupes included Moscow's Bolshoi Ballet, the Miami City Ballet, JBC, Suzanne Farrell Ballet of Washington, D.C., Pennsylvania Ballet of Philadelphia, and the San Francisco Ballet.

Changes in artistic leadership. Three important dance companies hired new leaders in 2000. In February, Anna-Marie Holmes announced that she planned to leave the Boston Ballet after June 2001. Holmes brought many Russian classics into the company's repertory. To succeed Holmes, officials chose Maina Gielgud, whose last post had been as artistic director of the Royal Danish Ballet. In May 2000, the United Kingdom's Royal Ballet chose Ross Stretton, who had been director of the Australian Ballet, to replace director Anthony Dowell.

In August, Russian President Vladimir Putin dismissed former Bolshoi star Vladimir Vasilyev as director of the Bolshoi Theater in Moscow. Putin once again subordinated the Bolshoi Ballet and opera companies to the Russian government's Ministry of Culture. Just prior to the shake-up, the Bolshoi Ballet had enjoyed a huge popular success while touring the United States. Many critics noted that the Moscow troupe had grown closer in style to the Kirov Ballet of Saint Petersburg, Russia, and some ballet fans missed the Bolshoi's old flamboyance.

Twyla Tharp formed a new company, Twyla Tharp Dance, in 2000. The new troupe debuted on July 6 at the American Dance Festival in Durham, North Carolina, with two premieres—*Surfer*

at the River Styx, with music by jazz composer Donald Knaack; and *Mozart Clarinet Quintet K.581*. The first dancers Tharp hired for her new venture reflected the eclectic nature of her choreography. They included modern dancers formerly with the Paul Taylor Dance Company, a Broadway dancer, and others from such groups as the New York City Ballet and ABT.

The formation of Twyla Tharp Dance ended what Tharp called a long period of "exile." She had been a free-lance choreographer since 1988. She said the new troupe would not preclude her from accepting more free-lance offers.

Tharp choreographed two major pieces for other companies before starting work with her own group. In January 2000, Tharp's *The Beethoven Seventh* premiered at the City Ballet during its winter season. Critics appreciated the ambition of mounting a ballet to Beethoven's monumental music and were especially impressed by the grandeur of the solos for dancer Nikolaj Hubbe. Tharp's other dance, set to Brahms's *Variations on a Theme by Haydn*, premiered in May at Lincoln Center's Metropolitan Opera House in New York City.

The American Ballet Theater's major commitment to classical ballet was bolstered by artistic director Kevin McKenzie's new production of *Swan Lake*, first seen on March 24 at the Kennedy Center. McKenzie added a prologue to show how Odette was transformed into a swan by the evil magician von Rothbart. He also expanded the psychological dimension of the magician by giving him two guises, as a reptilian creature and as a suave seducer. In a departure from tradition, two dancers performed the magician.

Choreographer Paul Taylor celebrated his 70th birthday with a week-long array of activity, from July 25 to July 30, at the Jacob's Pillow Dance Festival in Becket, Massachusetts. The premiere of a Taylor dance, *Fiends Angelical*, with music by contemporary composer George Crumb, highlighted the celebration. Critics noted a beguiling mix of the light and dark aspects of human life in the new work.

American debuts. Two major European companies made their debuts in the United States in 2000. The Birmingham Royal Ballet (second to the Royal Ballet) of Birmingham, England, brought artistic director David Bintley's full-length *Edward II* (based on the Christopher Marlowe play) and a mixed bill set to jazz compositions to New York City and Chicago in September and October. The Bordeaux Ballet, from France, made a three-month transcontinental tour with a program in homage to the famous Russian-born impresario Serge Diaghilev and his Ballets Russes.

☐ Nancy Goldner

See also **Classical music.**

■ Deaths

in 2000 included those listed below, who were Americans unless otherwise indicated.

Albert, Carl (1908–February 4), Oklahoma Congressman who served as speaker of the House of Representatives from 1971 to 1976.

Allen, Steve (1921–October 31), entertainer, musician, and author of more than 50 books. Allen invented television's late-night talk show format and composed such hits as "Impossible."

Assad, Hafez al- (1930–June 10), Syrian president who ruled for nearly 30 years.

Bandaranaike, Sirimavo (1916–October 10), Sri Lankan politician who was elected prime minister in 1960, becoming the first woman to head a government.

Barks, Carl (1901–August 25), animator who drew Donald Duck comics and cartoons for the Walt Disney company and created the character Scrooge McDuck in 1947.

Bassani, Giorgio (1916–April 13), Italian writer who was known for such works as *The Garden of the Finzi-Continis* (1962) and *Five Stories of Ferrara* (1971).

Beneke, Tex (Gordon Beneke) (1914–May 30), big band leader, saxophonist, and singer who provided the vocals for Glenn Miller's "Chattanooga Choo Choo" and "Don't Sit Under the Apple Tree."

Bloch, Konrad E. (1912–October 15), German chemist who won the Nobel Prize in 1964 for his explanation of how cholesterol is formed in the body.

Borge, Victor (1909–December 23), Danish pianist who combined classical music with comedy.

Bourguiba, Habib (1903–April 6), former president of Tunisia who led the country to independence from France in 1956.

Brooks, Gwendolyn (1917–December 3), poet who in 1950 became the first African American to win a Pulitzer Prize, for *Annie Allen* (1949), her second poetry collection.

Brower, David R. (1912–November 5), environmentalist who guided the Sierra Club to prominence in the 1950's and 1960's.

Carnahan, Mel (1934–October 16), two-term governor of Missouri who was considered one of the most innovative leaders in the state's history.

Cartland, Dame Barbara (1901–May 21), flamboyant British author of romantic fiction whose 723 books sold more than 1 billion copies.

Cassel, Walter (1910–July 3), baritone who sang with the Metropolitan Opera Company and originated the role of Horace Tabor in Douglas Moore's *The Ballad of Baby Doe*.

Clairborne, Craig (1920–January 22), influential *New York Times* food critic credited with coaxing Americans toward a diet fusing American food with the best of Europe, Asia, and Latin America.

Coggan, Frederick (1909–May 17), archbishop of Canterbury (1974-1980) who was the first spiritual head of the Church of England to

Al Grey, trombonist

support the ordination of women.

Comfort, Alex (1920–March 26), physician and author of 51 books who was best known for the 1970's best-seller *The Joy of Sex*.

Cooney, Barbara (1917–March 10), Caldecott Award-winning illustrator and children's book author.

Coverdell, Paul (1939–July 19), U.S. senator from Georgia who was among the inner circle of the Republican Senate leaders.

Cranston, Alan (1914–December 31), Democrat from California who served 24 years in the U.S. Senate.

Daniel, Clifton (1912–February 21), World War II-era foreign correspondent who became managing editor of *The New York Times*. Daniel was married to Margaret Truman, the daughter of President Harry Truman.

Davis, Jimmie (1899?–November 5), two-term governor of Louisiana and singer/songwriter who composed "You Are My Sunshine."

Day, Sir Robin (1923–August 6), English television broadcaster who became widely known as the "grand inquisitor" for the tough questions he posed during interviews.

Dewar, Donald (1937–October 11), Scottish politician who was appointed first minister of Scotland in 1999.

Fairbanks, Douglas, Jr. (1909–May 7), debonair screen actor decorated for distinguished naval service during World War II.

Farnsworth, Richard (1920–October 6), former

Barbara Cartland, novelist

Hedy Lamarr, actress

Dancer Harold Nicholas (right) of the Nicholas Brothers

Tito Puente, musician

movie stunt man who graduated into character parts and was nominated for Academy Awards in *Comes a Horseman* (1978) and *The Straight Story* (2000).

Fears, Tom (1922–January 4), college and pro football hall-of-fame receiver who played with the Los Angeles Rams from 1948 through 1956.

Ferebee, Thomas (1918–March 16), World War II bombardier who dropped the atomic bomb on Hiroshima, Japan, on Aug. 6, 1945.

Fitzgerald, Penelope (1916–April 28), English novelist and biographer who won the 1998 National Book Critics Circle Award for *The Blue Flower*.

Freund, Gisele (1908–March 31), German-born French photographer who was best known for her portraits of French artists and intellectuals.

Fryer, Robert (1920–May 28), Broadway producer of *Wonderful Town* (1953), *Auntie Mame* (1956), and *Sweeney Todd* (1979).

Gielgud, Sir John (1904–May 21), English actor whose career spanned eight decades and extended from the role of Hamlet, which he played more than 500 times, to *Arthur* (1981), for which he received an Academy Award.

Gilruth, Robert (1913–August 17), aeronautical engineer who oversaw the development of the Mercury spacecraft and directed the Johnson Space Center during the Gemini project and the Apollo lunar landings.

Gonzalez, Henry B. (1916–November 28), congressman from Texas who served 37 years in the U.S. House of Representatives.

Gordon, Elizabeth (1906–September 3), influential *Good Houskeeping* and *House Beautiful* editor-in-chief who championed modern American design and architecture.

Gorey, Edward (1925–April 15), author and artist—including more than 100 books and the animated prelude to the PBS "Mystery" series—who delighted while horrifying visitors to his macabre, Victorian world.

Gray, Charles (1928–March 9), British actor who was most widely known for playing the villainous Ernst Blofeld in the James Bond film *Diamonds Are Forever* (1971) and the no-neck narrator in *The Rocky Horror Picture Show* (1975).

Grey, Al (1925–March 24), jazz trombonist who

recorded nearly 100 albums, playing with such headliners as Count Basie, Ella Fitzgerald, Dizzy Gillespie, and Lionel Hampton.

Guinness, Sir Alec (1914–August 5), Academy Award-winning British actor who was known for his range and quietly powerful presence in such films as *Kind Hearts and Coronets* (1949), *The Bridge on the River Kwai* (1957), *Lawrence of Arabia* (1962), and *Star Wars* (1977).

Hall, Gus (1910–October 13), leader of the American Communist Party and presidential candidate in 1972, 1976, 1980, and 1984.

Hamilton, William (1936–March 7), British biologist who applied Mendelian genetics to unify Charles Darwin's principles of natural selection.

Hawkins, Screamin' Jay (Jalacy J. Hawkins) (1929–February 11), rock-'n'-roll singer and composer best known for "I Put a Spell on You."

Hebert, Anne (1916–January 22), French-Canadian writer who was best known for her book of poetry *Le Tombeau des Rois* (1954) and novel *Klamouraska* (1970).

Henning, Doug (1947–February 7), Canadian-born magician of the 1970's and 1980's.

Hernandez, Amalia (1917–November 4), Mexican dancer who founded the internationally successful Ballet Folklorico de Mexico.

Hinton, Milt (1910–December 19), bass player who was the first great bass solosit in jazz and one of the most recorded musicians in history.

Holcomb, Benjamin H. (1889–December 2), 111-year-old man who, according to the *Guinness Book of World Records*, was the world's oldest living man.

Ingrid (1910–November 7), Swedish-born Queen Mother of Denmark who was the queen consort of King Frederik IX and mother of Queen Margrethe II.

Jeronimo, Carmo (1871–June 14), Brazilian woman who was born into slavery and, according to baptismal records, lived to be 129 years old.

Johnson, Gus (1913–February 6), drummer who played with many of the great jazz bands of the 1930's and 1940's.

Jones, Jonah (1909–April 29), swing trumpeter of the Big Band Era who developed a new audience in the 1950's with his muted renditions of such standards as "On the Street Where You Live."

Kane, Gil (1926–January 31), comic-book artist who created the look of the highly muscled superhero in his 1960's reinterpretations of characters such as Captain Marvel and Spiderman.

Kazan, Michel (1908?–May 13), Russian-born hairstylist who was credited with creating the pageboy, French twist, and bouffant.

Kedrova, Lila (1918?–February 16), Russian-born actress who received an Academy Award in 1964 and a Tony Award in 1983 for her portrayal of Madame Hortense in *Zorba the Greek*.

Kelly, Fred (1916–March 18), Tony Award-winning Broadway dancer who invented the Cha-cha and taught his older brother, Gene, how to tap dance.

Kenner-Jackson, Doris (1941–February 4), a founding member of the female pop group the Shirelles who was inducted into the Rock and Roll Hall of Fame in 1996.

King, "Pee Wee" (Julius Frank Kuczynski) (1914–March 7), country-music band leader who introduced electric instruments to the Grand Ole Opry and cowrote "Tennessee Waltz" and "You Belong to Me."

Kirby, Durward (1912–March 15), radio broadcaster and television personality who appeared in three versions of the "Garry Moore Show" and was an early host of "Candid Camera."

Kleindienst, Richard G. (1923–February 3), Nixon administration attorney general who took office in June 1972 and resigned in April 1973, when it became apparent that members of his

Elmo R. Zumwalt, Jr.,
U.S. admiral

John Gielgud,
actor

Carl Albert,
former House Speaker

Gwen Verdon,
dancer

Loretta Young,
actress

Justice Department staff were involved in the Watergate scandal.

Klemperer, Werner (1920–December 6), German-born actor who played Colonel Klink on the television series "Hogan's Heroes" in the 1960's.

Lamarr, Hedy (Hedwig Kiesler) (1913–January 19), Austrian-born film actress who was billed as the "world's most beautiful woman."

Landry, Tom (1924–February 11), Dallas Cowboys head coach for the team's first 29 seasons. Landry led the team to 270 victories, including two Super Bowl wins.

Lardner, Ring, Jr. (1915–October 31), Academy Award-winning screenwriter for *Woman of the Year* (1942) and *M*A*S*H* (1970).

Lawrence, Jacob (1917–June 9), artist whose intensely colored narrative paintings chronicled the African American experience.

Lemon, Bob (1920–January 11), baseball player with the Cleveland Indians in the late 1940's and 1950's who was inducted into the Hall of Fame in 1976.

Lewis, Joseph H. (1907–August 30), director of such classic "B" movies as *Cry of the Hunted* (1953).

Lindsay, John V. (1921–December 19), mayor of New York City from 1966 to 1973.

Linville, Larry (1939–April 10), actor who played Major Frank Burns on the hit television series "M*A*S*H," from 1972 until 1977.

London, Julie (1926–October 18), actress on the 1970's television series "Emergency!" and singer who became known for her sultry version of "Cry Me a River."

MacNelly, Jeff (1947–June 8), political cartoonist who created the comic strip "Shoe" and won three Pulitzer Prizes for his editorial cartoons.

MacRae, Meredith (1944–July 14), actress and daughter of Gordon and Sheila MacRae who appeared on the television series "My Three Sons" and "Petticoat Junction."

Marchand, Nancy (1928–June 18), stage and television character actress who found fame playing imperious authority figures, including Margaret Pynchon on the TV series "Lou Grant" and the scheming Livia on "The Sopranos."

Walter Matthau, actor

Martin, Don (1931–January 6), cartoonist billed as "MAD's maddest artist" who helped define the look and style of MAD magazine.

Martin, Helen (1910?–March 25), stage and screen character actress who played the mouthy Pearl Shay in "227."

Matthau, Walter (Walter Mtuschanskayasky) (1920–July 1), stage and motion-picture actor who achieved stardom as a smart aleck curmudgeon in such films as *The Fortune Cookie* (1966), *The Odd Couple* (1968), *A New Leaf* (1971), and *I'm Not Rappaport* (1996).

Maxwell, William (1908–July 31), fabled fiction editor at *The New Yorker* magazine whose own restrained, subtle fiction earned him a place in American letters.

Merrick, David (1911–April 26), Broadway showman who produced such blockbusters as *Gypsy* (1959), *Hello, Dolly!* (1964), *Promises, Promises* (1968), and *42nd Street* (1980).

Morris, Eva (1885–November 2), 114-year-old English woman who, according to the *Guinness Book of World Records,* was the world's oldest living woman.

Morse, Roger A. (1927–May 12), Cornell University professor of entomology who was one of the world's foremost experts on bees and author of *The Complete Guide to Beekeeping.*

Mulligan, Richard (1932–September 26), Emmy-award winning actor who was best known for his television roles in "Soap" and "Empty Nest."

Nagako, Empress Dowager (1903–June 16), consort and widow of Emperor Hirohito of Japan and mother of the current emperor, Akihito.

Neal, James V. (1915–February 1), geneticist who led research on the effects of atomic bomb radiation

Alec Guinness, actor

Pierre Trudeau, prime minister of Canada

Tom Landry, football coach

Edward Gorey,
author and artist

and helped unlock the genetic basis of sickle cell anemia.

Neel, Louis (1904–November 17), French physicist who was awarded the Nobel Prize in 1970 for his research on magnetic fields and applications of that research on solid-state physics.

Nicholas, Harold (1921–July 3), legendary tap dancer and younger half of the Nicholas Brothers, whose careers stretched from vaudeville to 50 film musicals, including *Stormy Weather* (1943) and *The Pirate* (1948).

O'Brian, Patrick (Richard Patrick Russ) (1915?–January 2), English author who wrote a series of critically acclaimed novels involving the British Navy during the Napoleonic Wars.

Obuchi, Keizo (1937–May 15), Japanese prime minister, elected in 1998, whose massive public spending program helped boost Japan's depressed economy.

O'Connor, Cardinal John (1920–May 3), Roman Catholic archbishop of New York and one of the most influential religious leaders in the United States.

Oliphant, Marcus (1901–July 14), Australia's leading nuclear physicist. Oliphant played a key roll in the creation of the first atomic bomb but later became a vocal opponent of all nuclear weapons.

Pastore, John (1907–July 15), Rhode Island Democrat who was the first Italian American to be elected a state governor (1945-1950) and the first to be elected to the U.S. Senate (1950-1976).

Patterson, Frank (1941–June 10), Irish tenor whose repertory of light classics and sentimental ballads earned him a worldwide following.

Peters, Jean (1926–October 13), 1950's actress and wife of billionaire Howard Hughes who starred in such films as *Viva Zapata!* (1952) and *Three Coins in the Fountain* (1954).

Petty, Lee (1914–April 5), champion stock car racer of the 1950's who won the first Daytona 500 in 1959 and founded a racing dynasty.

Powell, Anthony (1905–March 28), English novelist who wrote *A Dance to the Music of Time,* a 12-volume work that critics hailed as one of the great literary achievements of the post-World War II era.

Puente, Tito (Earnest Anthony Puente, Jr.) (1923–May 31), band leader known as "El Rey," or "The King," of Latin music who wrote such hits as "Oye Como Va" (1963) and popularized the mambo in the United States.

Purdy, Al (1918–April 21), Canadian poet hailed as his country's unofficial poet laureate.

Rampal, Jean-Pierre (1922–May 20), French flutist and conductor who many critics credited with reintroducing the flute as a solo instrument.

Rankin, John Morris (1959–January 16), Canadian-born fiddler and pianist who organized his siblings into first The Rankin Family and then the Rankins.

Reeves, Steve (1926–May 1), bodybuilder turned movie actor who starred in a number of "sword-and-sandal" epics, including *The Labors of Hercules* (1957) and *The Last Days of Pompeii* (1960).

Richard, Maurice (1921–May 27), Canadian hockey legend known as "The Rocket" who many considered one of the greatest players of all time.

Richards, Beah (1926–September 14), stage, screen, and television actress who won an Emmy award in 2000 for her guest appearance on the television drama "The Practice."

Robards, Jason (1922–December 26), Academy Award winning actor who was best known for his interpretations of roles by Eugene O'Neill.

Robinson, Vicki Sue (1955–April 27), pop-gospel singer and songwriter whose "Turn the Beat Around" (1976) became one of the anthems of the disco era.

Rowan, Carl T. (1925–September 23), nationally syndicated columnist and television commentator who was considered one of the most influential journalists of his time.

Ruge, Arthur C. (1905–April 10), earthquake specialist who invented the SR-4 strain gauge, a device to measure stress that contributed greatly to the design of World War II armaments.

Runcie, Lord Robert (1921–July 11), reform-minded archbishop of Canterbury (1980–1991) who championed Britain's working class during the Conservative Thatcher government.

Schmirler, Sandra (1963–March 2), Canadian athlete who won a gold medal in women's curling at the 1998 Olympics in Nagano, Japan.

Schulz, Charles M. (1922–February 12), cartoonist who created *Peanuts,* the bittersweet comic strip.

Segal, George (1926–June 9), influential sculptor whose figurative works explored the isolation of modern, urban society.

Shapiro, Karl (1913–May 14), poet who won

Lenore Knight Wingard,
Olympic swimmer

the 1945 Pulitzer Prize for "V-Letter and Other Poems."

Shepard, Mary (1909–September 4), British book illustrator who gave life to the character Mary Poppins in a series of seven books published from 1933 to 1988.

Sigman, Carl (1909–September 26), composer and lyricist who gained fame for such hits as "Pennsylvania 6-5000" (1938) and the theme for the film *Love Story* (1970).

Simon, William E. (1927–June 3), former director of the Federal Energy Office who served as secretary of the treasury during the Nixon and Ford administrations.

Siodmak, Curt (1902–September 2), novelist and prolific screenwriter who is credited with reintroducing and molding the modern image of the ancient myth of a man turned into a wolf.

Smith, Michael (1932–October 4), British scientist who in 1993 shared the Nobel Prize in chemistry for developing one of the basic tools of genetic engineering.

Starr, Mae Faggs (1932–January 27), champion sprinter who was the first U.S. woman to compete in three Olympiads, in 1948, 1952, and 1956.

Stevens, Craig (Gail Shikles, Jr.) (1918–May 10), actor who played the title role in the television series "Peter Gunn."

Thompson, Homer (1906–May 7), Canadian-born archaeologist who led the excavation of the Agora, the civic center of ancient Athens.

Titov, Gherman (1935–September 20), Soviet cosmonaut who became the second person to orbit Earth during a 25-hour flight in August 1961.

Trevor, Claire (1909?–April 8), film actress who is best remembered for portraying cynical, hard-edged women in such films as *Key Largo* (1948), for

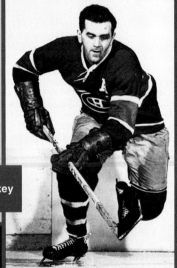

Maurice Richard, Hall-of-Fame hockey player

which she received an Academy Award for best supporting actress.

Trout, Robert (1909–November 14), pioneering broadcast journalist who coined the term "fireside chat" for President Franklin Roosevelt's radio addresses and reported on the D-Day invasion in live broadcasts during World War II.

Trudeau, Pierre Elliot (1919–September 28), Canadian statesman who served as prime minister from 1968 to 1979 and from 1980 to 1984. Trudeau implemented the Constitution Act of 1982.

Turner, Albert (1936–April 13), civil rights activist who helped lead the voting-rights march from Selma, Alabama, in 1965.

Turrentine, Stanley (1934–September 12), jazz tenor saxophonist who became a top figure in soul-jazz.

Vadim, Roger (1928–February 4), French director whose best-known films included *And God Created Woman* (1956) and *Barbarella* (1968).

Varney, Jim (1949–February 10), rubberfaced actor who played the character Ernest in television commercials and in movies.

Verdon, Gwen (1925–October 18), Broadway dancer who was best known for her roles in the musicals *Can-Can* (1953), *Sweet Charity* (1966), and *Chicago* (1975).

Walker, Edward C. (1918?–August 15), British Royal Air Force squadron leader and nudism advocate who designed the Lava Lamp, introduced in Britain in 1963.

Wechsler, Herbert (1909–April 26), Columbia University Law School professor whose work greatly influenced the U.S. legal system.

Williams, Hosea (1926–November 16), charismatic civil rights leader during the 1960's.

Wilson, Robert R. (1914–December 16), physicist who worked on the Manhattan Project to develop the atomic bomb and build the world's most powerful particle smasher.

Wingard, Lenore Knight (1911–February 9), Hall of Fame swimming champion who won medals at the 1932 and 1936 Olympics and held 21 U.S. records and 7 world records.

Windsor, Marie (1919–December 10), actress who was dubbed "Queen of the B's" for her bad-girl roles in such noir films as *Force of Evil* (1948) and *The Killing* (1952).

Yates, Sidney (1909–October 5), Illinois congressman who served 48 years in the U.S. House of Representatives.

Young, Loretta (1913–August 12), motion-picture actress who began her career in silent films and was the first woman to win both an Oscar (*The Farmer's Daughter*, 1947) and an Emmy (*A Letter to Loretta*, 1953).

Zumwalt, Elmo R., Jr. (1920–January 2), admiral who led U.S. naval forces in Vietnam and who, as chief of naval operations during the 1970's, ordered the end of racial and sexual discrimination in the U.S. Navy.

Steve Allen, entertainer

YOU'RE A GOOD MAN, Charles Schulz

By Tim Frystak

The creator of the "Peanuts" gang triggered memories of childhood, happy and bittersweet.

Cartoonist Charles Schulz died on Feb. 12, 2000. Fans of "Peanuts" and its cast of characters—Charlie Brown, Snoopy, Lucy, Linus—collectively sighed a final "Good grief" at the news. Unlike most comic strips, "Peanuts" did not survive its creator. The final daily strip ran on January 3. Sunday newspapers carried the last color strip on February 13, one day after the cartoonist's death. Schulz had drawn each of the more than 18,000 "Peanuts" that appeared during the nearly 50 years of the comic's existence, and it was his decision to end what was a cultural phenomenon.

When Schulz made that decision, "Peanuts" was syndicated in more than 2,600 newspapers. It was translated into 21 languages and published in 75 countries. Charlie Brown's "good grief," Linus's "security blanket," and "a Charlie Brown Christmas tree" were international catch phrases. The characters had been featured in a Broadway musical, films, and on more than 50 animated television specials. The first TV special, "A Charlie Brown Christmas," had become an icon of the holiday season, having been aired annually since its initial broadcast in 1965. More than 1,400 different "Peanuts" book titles had sold at least 300 million copies.

Charles Monroe Schulz was born on Nov. 26, 1922, in Minneapolis, Minnesota. He was the only child of Carl and Dena Schulz. An uncle nicknamed the boy "Sparky" after a character in the "Barney Google" comic strip of the 1920's. After skipping grades in elementary school, Schulz began having trouble with his studies. In high school, he did poorly in sports and was too shy to ask a girl for a date.

DEATHS

SPECIAL REPORT

Schulz's parents, however, nurtured their son's talent for draw-ing, and he enrolled in a cartooning course at a correspondence art school. After his discharge from the United States Army after World War II (1939-1945), Schulz accepted a job correcting the artwork of students at the same art school. He later lettered comic strips for a Roman Catholic comic magazine, where he further honed his skills. In the late 1940's, Schulz-drawn cartoons ap-peared in *The Saturday Evening Post,* a weekly magazine that en-joyed a huge readership during that period.

In 1947, Schulz sold a weekly cartoon, "Li'l Folks," with a Charlie Brown-like character to a St. Paul, Minnesota, newspaper. United Feature Syndicate, an agency that sold special features to newspapers, picked up the strip in 1950 and syndicated it to seven newspapers. Because comic strips named "Little Folks" and "Li'l Abner" already existed, United Feature executives demanded that the strip be renamed "Peanuts." Schulz reportedly regretted the new name, believing that "Peanuts" suggested "insignificance."

Charles Schulz based the "Peanuts" characters—children who make funny but wise statements—after himself, childhood friends, and family. He named the main character, Charlie Brown, after a friend but patterned the character's personality on his own. Char-lie Brown's father was a barber, like Schulz's father. Charlie Brown's dog, Snoopy, was based on the cartoonist's childhood dog, a black and white mutt named Spike. Schulz modeled Lucy on his oldest daughter, Meredith, who he described as "a fussbud-get." According to Schulz, Charlie Brown's unrequited love for a "little red-haired girl" was grounded in the creator's youthful af-fection for a young woman who rejected his proposal of marriage.

By 1953, the comic strip had become a success that provided Schulz with a handsome income and certain measure of fame. Over time, both would grow substantially until "Peanuts" blos-somed into a $1-billion-a-year industry that made Schulz the rich-est and most successful cartoonist in history. He was not, howev-er, the happiest.

In 1948, Charles Schulz married Joyce Halverson. The couple eventually had three sons and two daughters. The family left Min-nesota in 1958 for Sonoma County, California, a move that Schulz later claimed was made at his wife's insistence.

Charles Schulz disliked travel or even leaving home. He suf-fered from *agoraphobia* (fear of being in open places). According

The author:
Tim Frystak is a *World Book* staff editor.

to Schulz, nights in hotels could trigger severe anxieties, including fears that he would become so depressed that he might jump out of a window. By his own admission, the cartoonist was a loner who focused on his own shortcomings and failures, rather than his successes. He nursed ancient grudges and was, according to acquaintances, sometimes bitter about life, particularly about his lack of recognition as an artist.

In 1972, Schulz left his wife and moved to Santa Rosa, California. They divorced in 1973. Later that same year, he married Jean Forsyth Clyde, with whom he lived for the rest of his life.

"Peanuts" may have been the most studied comic strip of all time. Theologians saw Schulz as a modern moralist and compared his philosophy with that of St. Augustine. Psychiatrists claimed his humor was a Freudian device that "masked aggression." Critics pointed out connections between the strip's characters and their creator's well-known sense of inadequacy. In an interview on the CBS news program "60 Minutes," Schulz himself said, "All of my fears, my anxieties, my joys, and almost, even all of my experiences go into that strip."

In Schulz's comic world, nothing much happens. Conflicts remain unresolved. Love never triumphs. Characters fail to grow, physically or emotionally. Beset by anxieties and fears, Charlie Brown never gets to kick the football. Tests are often graded D–. And the Great Pumpkin never arrives. All the characters except one yearn for something—love or attainment—that is forever beyond their reach. The exception is Snoopy, who transcends Schulz's bleak landscape through imagination. Challenging the Red Baron to a dogfight, Snoopy wins.

Schulz's pessimism, leavened by imagination and humor, may have been at the core of the comic strip's enormous appeal. People connected with characters beset by the anxieties and insecurities of modern life. They offered children a reflection on the frustrations and joys of their own daily lives. For adults, the characters provoked bittersweet memories of childhood and offered hope. Charlie Brown stoically goes on, regardless of what obstacles life places in his path. ■■■

Democratic Party. Vice President Al Gore was unsuccessful in his attempt to keep the presidency in Democratic hands following the Nov. 7, 2000, presidential election, which was one of the closest in United States history. Gore had served as vice president for eight years under President Bill Clinton. Though Gore won the popular vote, he failed to take the 270 Electoral College votes he needed to claim the presidency, which went to the Republican challenger, Texas Governor George W. Bush. Before the election was finally resolved on December 13, both the Florida Supreme Court and the U.S. Supreme Court became involved in determining which candidate was entitled to the 25 Electoral College votes from Florida that ultimately tipped the election to Bush.

The Democratic Party nominated Gore at its convention in Los Angeles on August 16. Gore accepted the nomination the following night. Gore selected Senator Joseph Lieberman (D., Connecticut) as his vice presidential running mate. Lieberman, an Orthodox Jew, became the first Jewish major-party candidate for vice president.

Gore won the Democratic Party nomination despite an intense initial challenge from former Senator Bill Bradley of New Jersey. Bradley dropped out of the running on March 9.

Gore and Lieberman campaigned on a pledge to continue the nation's economic prosperity while safeguarding the rights and opportunities of minorities and the underprivileged.

Congressional races. Democrats failed in their attempt to regain control of Congress in the November 7 election but significantly narrowed the Republican majority in both the House of Representatives and the Senate. Following the 2000 election, Republicans held a 221-to-212 majority in the House. Independents, who usually voted with the Democrats, held two seats. A majority in the 435-seat House requires at least 218 seats. The 2000 election deadlocked the Senate 50-to-50. Under the U.S. Constitution, the vice president, as president of the Senate, casts the deciding vote in the event of a tie.

Joseph Lieberman was among the senators who won reelection. Some Democratic Party members in 2000 had suggested that Lieberman drop out of the Senate race since he was campaigning for vice president. Had Lieberman and Gore won, Connecticut Governor John G. Rowland, a Republican, presumably would have appointed a Republican to fill Lieberman's vacant Senate seat. Democrats feared that a Republican replacement would have tipped the balance of power and given Republicans a 51 to 49 majority.

In the most high-profile Democratic Party victory in 2000, First Lady Hillary Rodham Clinton

Vice President Al Gore, the Democratic candidate for U.S. president, concedes to Texas Governor George W. Bush on December 13. Gore won the popular vote in the November election, one of the closest in U.S. history, but failed to take the 270 Electoral College votes he needed to win the presidency.

defeated Rick A. Lazio, a Republican member of the House of Representatives, in a race for a U.S. Senate seat representing the state of New York. Clinton won the seat vacated by Democratic Senator Daniel Patrick Moynihan, who was retiring. Many political experts had expected that Clinton would face New York City Mayor Rudolph Giuliani in the election. In May, Giuliani announced that he was dropping out of the race because of health problems.

In an unusual turn of events, Missouri Governor Mel Carnahan, a Democrat, defeated incumbent Senator John Ashcroft, a Republican, in the U.S. Senate race, even though Carnahan had died on October 16 in an airplane crash. Carnahan's death came too close to the November election to remove his name from the ballot. On December 4, Roger Wilson, who had succeeded Carnahan as governor of Missouri, appointed Carnahan's widow, Jean, to fill the seat.

Campaign finance. The Federal Election Commission (FEC) announced in November that between Jan. 1, 1999, and Oct. 18, 2000, the Democratic Party had raised $172.7 million and spent $153.5 million. The Republican Party had raised $294.9 million and spent $252 million during the same period. Democrats raised 24 percent more in contributions than they had during the previous presidential election cycle in 1995-1996 and spent 15 percent more.

According to the FEC, soft-money contributions increased substantially for both Democrats and Republicans in 2000. Soft money refers to individual contributions made to political parties that are not subject to the same stringent restrictions placed on contributions to candidates. Democrats raised $199 million in soft money contributions, an increase of 85 percent over the previous presidential election cycle, compared with Republicans, who raised $211 million, a 74-percent increase. The FEC reported that soft money represented 53 percent of Democratic Party fundraising. It represented 42 percent of Republican Party fund-raising.

Fund-raising inquiries. Clinton administration officials disclosed in April that a U.S. Department of Justice campaign finance task force investigating fund-raising abuses by Democrats during the 1996 presidential campaign had interviewed both President Clinton and Vice President Gore. The task force was established to determine the validity of various charges, including that the Clinton-Gore campaign had accepted illegal foreign and corporate donations.

☐ Linda P. Campbell and Geoffrey A. Campbell

See also **Congress of the United States; Elections; People in the news (Lieberman, Joseph); Republican Party; State government; United States, Government of the.**

Denmark. In 2000, Danish voters rejected a proposal to adopt the euro, the single European currency. Prime Minister Poul Nyrup Rasmussen stated in March that he would call a referendum on the single currency, which 11 other European Union (EU) countries had adopted in January 1999.

Rasmussen contended that membership in the euro would benefit the Danish economy by lowering interest rates and removing any currency risk for trade with other EU countries. He also claimed that membership would enhance Denmark's influence over economic and political decisions inside the EU.

Referendum defeat. Most major political parties and most leaders of Danish industry joined Rasmussen's Social Democrats in campaigning for adoption of the euro. A loose coalition of left- and right-wing groups argued that the euro would lead toward the creation of a United States of Europe that would smother Denmark's national identity and restrict its ability to pursue independent policies, including maintenance of the country's generous welfare benefits.

Public opinion turned against the euro as the currency fell to record lows against the dollar during the summer of 2000, and voters rejected the proposal by a margin of 53.1 percent to 46.9 percent on September 28. The referendum marked the first time that any EU country had voted on the specific question of euro membership. International affairs experts suggested that the referendum's failure reflected widespread public discontent with the currency and the EU's growing influence over national affairs.

Bank merger. In October, Denmark's largest financial institution, Danske Bank, announced its plan to take over RealDanmark, the third-largest Danish bank. The merger, if approved by Danish competition authorities, would create the largest bank in the Nordic region in terms of assets.

Oresund bridge. The $3.5-billion Oresund Fixed Link opened on July 1, allowing automobile and railroad traffic across the Oresund Sound, which separates Denmark and Sweden. The link, which is 10 miles (16 kilometers) long, consists of a bridge, a tunnel, and an artificial island and connects Copenhagen, Denmark's capital, with Malmo, Sweden.

Concert deaths. Eight people were crushed to death on June 30, and a ninth later died of wounds, when crowds at a rock concert surged toward a stage on which the United States rock group Pearl Jam was playing. The deaths at Roskilde, near Copenhagen, were the first of their kind in Denmark and shocked a country known for its civility. ☐ Tom Buerkle

See also **Building and construction; Europe.**

Disabled. United States President Bill Clinton announced three new regulatory changes on July 26, 2000, in honor of the 10th anniversary of the signing of the Americans with Disabilities Act (ADA). The changes increased the amount of money Social Security disability beneficiaries can earn without losing cash and medical benefits.

Under the new regulations, the $700-per-month earnings limit beyond which a person would be ineligible for benefits will be automatically adjusted annually, based on national average wage index increases. In addition, the amount that a person can earn during a "trial month"—a period during which disabled beneficiaries can test their ability to work—will be raised from $200 to $530. Also, disabled students under the age of 22 who work and receive Supplemental Security Income will be allowed to earn up to $1,290 monthly without losing their benefits, rather than the previous limit of $400.

In February, U.S. Representatives Mark Foley (R., Florida) and E. Clay Shaw (R., Florida) introduced a bill, called the ADA Notification Act, that would require that business owners cited for noncompliance with the act receive a 90-day grace period before being assessed any penalties. ADA activists expressed concern that such legislation might dilute the power of the act.

☐ Kristina Vaicikonis

Disasters. The deadliest disasters of 2000 included torrential rains and flooding that killed an estimated 700 people in southeast Africa in February and at least 1,000 people in northern India and Bangladesh in late September and October. Disasters that resulted in 25 or more deaths during 2000 include the following:

Aircraft crashes

January 30—Cote d'Ivoire. A Kenya Airways jet en route to Lagos, Nigeria, crashes into the Atlantic Ocean shortly after take-off from the airport at Abidjan, capital of Cote d'Ivoire. At least 169 of the 179 passengers and crew aboard the Airbus A310 are killed.

January 31—Southern California. All 88 passengers and crew members aboard an Alaska Airlines jet—Flight 261 from Puerto Vallarta, Mexico, to Seattle, Washington—are killed when the McDonnell-Douglas MD-83 crashes into the Pacific Ocean near Oxnard, California, northwest of Los Angeles.

April 19—The Philippines. All 131 passengers and crew members aboard Air Philippines Flight 541 are killed when the Boeing 737-200 jet crashes on Samal Island, near the city of Davao, approximately 620 miles (1,000 kilometers) southeast of Manila, the capital, where the flight began.

July 17   India. An Alliance Air jet, owned by the Indian government, crashes into a housing complex in Patna, the capital of the Indian state of Bihar, killing 51 people aboard the Boeing 737-200 and 5 people on the ground. One of the seven survivors later died of his injuries.

July 25—Paris. An Air France Concorde en route to New York City crashes into a hotel outside Paris shortly after take-off from Charles de Gaulle airport, killing all 109 people aboard the charter flight and 4 people in the hotel.

August 23—Bahrain. All 143 passengers and crew members are killed when a Gulf Air jet crashes into the Persian Gulf after attempting to land at the Bahraini national airport, outside Manama, the capital. The jet, an Airbus A320, was arriving in Manama from Cairo, Egypt.

October 25—Georgia. All 83 passengers and crew members are killed when a Russian Ilyushin-

An emergency crew extinguishes a fire on a Singapore Airlines jumbo jet that crashed on October 31 as it tried to take off from Taipei, Taiwan. Eighty-two of the airplane's 179 passengers and crew members died in the accident, which occurred when the pilot turned onto the wrong runway.

18 military plane crashes into a mountain 12 miles (20 kilometers) northeast of Batumi, a Georgian port. The plane was carrying officers and their families to a Russian military base after a holiday trip.

October 31—Taiwan. A Singapore Airlines jumbo jet crashes and breaks apart seconds after take-off from Taipei, the capital. Eighty-two of the 179 passengers and crew members are killed, including 25 Americans. The pilot of the plane, which was en route to Los Angeles, turned onto the wrong runway.

Drought and heat

April 6—Southeastern Ethiopia. More than 400 people, most of them children, died in March from illnesses and food shortages brought on by a three-year drought in the Gode region of Ethiopia.

July 14—Southern Europe. Unusually hot temperatures, caused by a hot air mass that traveled north from the Sahara and stalled, kill at least 70 people during the first two weeks of July. The scorching heat reaches as high as 113 °F (45 °C) in some areas, igniting thousands of wildfires in Italy, Greece, Turkey, Romania, Bulgaria, Yugoslavia, and Croatia.

September 25—Northwestern Afghanistan. At least 90 people die from cholera brought on by drought in the province of Badghis. Afghan officials report that the drought, which began in April, is the worst the region has experienced in more than 30 years.

Earthquakes

June 5—Indonesia. An earthquake of magnitude 7.9 hits the island of Sumatra, leaving more than 60 people dead and thousands homeless.

Explosions and fires

March 11—Ukraine. At least 80 Ukrainian miners are killed when methane gas explodes in a coal mine, more than 2,100 feet (640 meters) deep, at Krasnodon, approximately 530 miles (853 kilometers) east of Kiev, Ukraine's capital.

April 14—Kinshasa, the Democratic Republic of Congo. Explosions involving fuel tanks and army munitions at Kinshasa's international airport topple buildings and shoot debris several miles into residential neighborhoods, killing more than 100 people and injuring at least 215.

July 10 to July 17—Nigeria. As many as 500 people are killed in Delta State in southern Nigeria during three ruptured gasoline pipeline explosions over the course of one week. Most of the victims, many of them children, were attempting to scavenge fuel from the punctured pipe. On July 10, 250 people die when the pipeline explodes near Adeje, destroying buildings and crops within a 1-mile (1.6-kilometer) radius. About 150 villagers are killed near Warri on July 16. A similar accident on July 17 near Amukpe leaves about 30 dead.

September 27—Southwestern China. A gas explosion in a coal mine at Shuicheng in Guizhou province kills 162 miners.

November 25—Bangladesh. A fire in a towel factory in Narsinghdi, Bangladesh, kills 47 people.

December 25—China. At least 300 people die in a fire at a dance hall in Luoyang, in central China.

Shipwrecks

June 29—Indonesia. Nearly 500 people drown when a ferry, licensed to carry 250 passengers, sinks in heavy seas 40 miles (64 kilometers) northwest of Sulawesi, an island in Indonesia's Greater Sunda chain. Most of the victims were Christians fleeing religion-based violence on Halmahera, one of Indonesia's Molucca Islands.

August 12—Barents Sea. The Russian nuclear-powered submarine *Kursk* sinks in the Barents Sea, 100 miles (160 kilometers) north of Murmansk. All 118 officers and sailors perish by the time divers reach them on August 21, though some had survived the initial sinking of the vessel.

September 26—Greece. A ferry traveling between Greek islands strikes a large, rocky outcrop called Piraeus and sinks near the island of Paros. At least 79 of the more than 500 passengers drown in the Aegean Sea.

Storms and floods

January 3—Brazil. At least 30 people drown in southeastern Brazil when heavy rains that began on January 1 cause massive flooding and mudslides that bury entire neighborhoods.

February—Southeast Africa. An estimated 700 people are killed and 500,000 people left homeless by floods triggered by weeks of torrential rain that began in early February in Mozambique, South Africa, Zimbabwe, and Botswana. Cyclone Eline brings even more rain to the flood-ravaged region on February 22. The people of Mozambique suffer the worst losses when, on February 27, a wall of water from opened dams in neighboring South Africa and Zimbabwe sweeps down Mozambique's Limpopo River valley.

August 4—Northeastern Brazil. At least 64 people drown in the states of Alagoas and Pernambuco in northeastern Brazil when five days of uninterrupted rain cause mudslides and the worst flooding the region has experienced in more than 25 years.

August 25—Southern India. A third day of storms accompanied by heavy downpours leaves widespread areas of southern India flooded, killing at least 162 people and damaging more than 64,000 houses and 740,000 acres (300,000 hectares) of farmland. A record-breaking 9.4 inches (23.9 centimeters) of rain fell in Hyderabad, capital of Andhra Pradesh, on August 24.

September 1—Southern China. Maria—the third typhoon to hit China in less than two weeks—kills at least 47 people and causes $233 million in damages when it strikes the southern provinces of Guangdong and Hunan.

October 2—Northern India and Bangladesh. Two weeks of flooding caused by unseasonably late and heavy monsoons leave 18 million people in India and Bangladesh homeless. The storms began in India on September 18 and in Bangladesh September 26. Government officials believe that at least 1,000 people in the two nations drowned while attempting to flee the rising waters.

October 16—Southeast Asia. Floods that began in July because of an abnormally early monsoon season leave more than 350 people dead and 4.5 million homeless in Cambodia, Vietnam, Laos, and Thailand.

October 18—Switzerland and Italy. At least 28 people are killed during four days of flooding and landslides caused by torrential rains in the Alpine region of Switzerland and Italy. An additional 43,000 people flee as the Po, Italy's longest river, and the Ticino, one of its Alpine tributaries, flood their banks.

November 29—Indonesia. Monsoon rains trigger flooding and mudslides on the Indonesian Island of Sumatra, killing at least 100 people and leaving some 100,000 people homeless.

Other disasters

March 29—Kenya. Two buses crash head-on and burst into flames near the town of Kericho,

140 miles (225 kilometers) northwest of Nairobi, the capital, killing more than 70 passengers.

April 20—Kenya. An overloaded bus attempting to pass another vehicle collides head-on with a truck at Mtito Andei, 155 miles (250 kilometers) southwest of Nairobi, killing 73 passengers and injuring 27 others.

July 6—Soria, Spain. A bus crashes head-on into a truck that crossed into the bus's lane, killing 28 people, most of whom were teen-agers enroute to a summer camp.

July 10—The Philippines. A mountain of garbage near Manila, the capital, collapses and bursts into flames, killing at least 200 people. According to Philippine officials, typhoon rains loosened the huge pile, where an estimated 80,000 people lived or scavenged. Cooking fires ignited the methane gas produced by the garbage.

November 4—Nigeria. An oil tanker truck slams into a line of vehicles stopped at a police checkpoint in southwestern Nigeria, setting off an explosion and fire that consumes everything within a 1,500-foot (457-meter) radius. At least 96 people are killed.

November 11—Austria. A cable car transporting about 180 people to ski slopes atop Kitzsteinhorn Mountain in the Austrian Alps catches fire after entering a tunnel, killing 156 passengers, many of them children and teen-agers.

Drug abuse. The overall number of Americans using illegal drugs remained constant from 1997 to 1999, though illegal drug use among children ages 12 to 17 dropped for the second year in a row in 1999, according to the National Household Survey on Drug Abuse (NHSDA). The survey, released in August 2000, is an annual report on drug use prepared by the Substance Abuse and Mental Health Services Administration (SAMHSA), part of the United States National Institutes of Health (NIH). The national trends reflected information about illegal drug use obtained from nearly 70,000 Americans ages 12 and older. The NHSDA estimated that 6.7 percent of this population group—a total of 14.8 million people—used illegal drugs at least once in the month prior to the survey.

Teen-agers. According to the NHSDA, an estimated 9 percent of children ages 12 to 17 used illegal drugs in 1999, compared with 9.9 percent in 1998 and 11.4 percent in 1997. The decline was caused in part by a drop in the number of teens who reported using marijuana, which fell to 7 percent in 1999 from 8.3 percent in 1998 and 9.4 percent in 1997. Teen use of cocaine, heroin, hallucinogens, and inhalants remained constant between 1998 and 1999.

Young adults. The NHSDA reported that an estimated 18.8 percent of U.S. adults ages 18 to 25 used illicit drugs in 1999, compared with 16.1 percent in 1998 and 14.7 percent in 1997. According to the survey, the highest rate of illegal drug use in 1999 was among adults ages 18 to 20, more than 20 percent of whom used illicit drugs.

Marijuana. Eighteen percent of the young adults in the survey said they used marijuana, the most common drug among this age group. According to the NHSDA, approximately 57 percent of all users of illegal drugs used marijuana.

Steroids. In April 2000, the National Institute on Drug Abuse (NIDA), part of the NIH, warned of an increasing use of anabolic steroids, especially among adolescents. The NIDA emphasized that steroids are not a harmless way to increase athletic prowess. Steroids are substances similar to *testosterone* (the male sex hormone) that promote the growth of muscle and the development of male secondary sexual characteristics.

The NIDA noted that although steroids may boost athletic performance, extensive research has shown that they can permanently damage a person's body. For example, steroids can permanently halt a teen-ager's growth so that the user never reaches his or her natural adult height. Steroids can also cause sexual dysfunction and difficulty in urinating in men and produce a deepened voice and excessive body hair in women.   □ David C. Lewis

Drugs. The U.S. Food and Drug Administration (FDA) approved RU-486, the so-called "French abortion pill," for use in the United States in September 2000. The drug, which is also called mifepristone, has been available in Europe since the late 1980's.

Mifepristone, produced by the Chinese firm Hua Lian Pharmaceutical Company and marketed under the brand name Mifeprex, works by causing the lining of the uterus to shed, cutting off the embryo's blood supply. FDA regulations mandate that the drug be administered in a physician's office and that it only be used within 49 days after the start of a woman's last menstrual period. The FDA also mandates two follow-up physician visits—one for the administration of a second drug, misoprostol, which causes the uterus to expel the embryo; and the second visit to verify that the abortion is complete.

Studies indicate that mifepristone is effective for 92 percent of the women to whom it has been administered. Possible side effects include severe bleeding, vomiting, and heavy cramping.

New kind of antibiotic. The first of a new family of antibiotic drugs intended for use against antibiotic-resistant strains of bacteria was approved by the FDA in April 2000. Pharmacia Corporation of Peapack, New Jersey, developed the drug, which was marketed under the brand name Zyvox. The drug, also called linezolid, was the first new antibiotic approved in more than 40 years to fight pneumonia and skin infections caused by the bacterium *Staphylococcus aureus.* Zyvox can also be used against *Enterococcus faecium,* a common bacterial cause of fatal infections in hospitals.

Since the early 1990's, physicians have noted a dramatic increase in the number of infectious microbes that have become resistant to existing antibiotics. Several new antibiotics were under development in 2000 to tackle this problem. Zyvox was the first member of the so-called oxazolidinone antibiotic class, which consists of drugs that stop the growth of bacteria, allowing the body's immune system to destroy the germs.

New diabetes drug. The FDA approved Glucovance, a pill for treating Type 2 diabetes, in August 2000. In Type 2 diabetes, which affects some 15 million people in the United States, the body's cells resist the effects of *insulin* (a hormone needed for storing glucose, or blood sugar). Type 2 diabetes occurs most commonly in people who are overweight and more than 45 years old.

Bristol-Myers Squibb Company of Princeton, New Jersey, developed Glucovance, which consists of a combination of the company's two popular antidiabetes drugs, Glucophage and a generic medicine called glyburide. Glucophage, whose active ingredient is metformin, enhances insulin's ability to remove sugar from the bloodstream. Glyburide encourages the pancreas to make more insulin. The FDA recommended that Glucovance be used along with a healthy diet and an exercise program.

Rezulin removed from market. The Warner-Lambert Company of Morris Plains, New Jersey, stopped selling its popular diabetes drug Rezulin in March after the FDA requested that it do so. The FDA made the request following a review of Rezulin that showed it to have more toxic effects on the liver than newer diabetes drugs that offered similar health benefits.

The potential liver toxicity of Rezulin was first identified in 1997, the year the drug entered the market. The FDA at the time allowed Rezulin to remain on the market but asked the manufacturer to place stronger warnings on the drug's label.

Infant vaccine. In February 2000, the FDA approved the first vaccine for preventing pneumococcal diseases in infants and toddlers. Pneumococcal diseases, which are caused by infection with the bacteria *Streptococcus pneumoniae*, are a major cause of blood infections, ear infections, and *meningitis* (an inflammation of the lining of the brain and spinal cord) in children under age 2.

The vaccine—called Prevnar—which was developed by Wyeth-Ayerst Laboratories in subur-

ban Philadelphia, protects children against seven common strains of *Streptococcus* bacteria. The FDA said that infants should receive the vaccine in a series of four shots—between 12 and 15 months and at the ages of 2, 4, and 6 .

Hair removal. The FDA in August approved the first rub-on prescription medicine to treat unwanted facial hair in women. The Gillette Company of Boston and Bristol-Myers Squibb developed the drug, eflornithine hydrochloride, to be sold under the brand name Vaniqa Cream.

Drug prices. Senior citizens were expected to spend twice as much on prescription drugs in 2000 than they did in 1992, according to a report issued in August 2000 by Families USA, a consumer-advocacy group based in Washington, D.C. According to the group, Americans aged 65 and over would spend an average of $1,205 a year for prescriptions in 2000, up from $559 in 1992. The group expected costs to rise to $2,810 by 2010.

Families USA added that prescriptions accounted for about 10 percent of senior citizens' health care expenses in 2000. To help seniors pay for drugs, the group urged Congress to provide prescription drug coverage under Medicare, the federal program that pays for many health expenses of the elderly. ☐ Michael Woods

See also **AIDS; Drug abuse; Health care issues; Medicine.**

Eastern Orthodox Churches. In

March 2000, the Orthodox Church of Serbia, under Patriarch Pavle, called on Yugoslav President Slobodan Milosevic to resign. On September 28, Pavle was among the first Serbs to recognize Vojislav Kostunica, Milosevic's chief opponent in the election, as the legally elected president of Yugoslavia. In 2000, the church continued to protest the killing of Serb civilians in Kosovo, a Serbian province, and the destruction of over 80 churches and monasteries by Albanian extremists.

In the United States. The Standing Conference of Canonical Orthodox Bishops, which represents 10 Eastern Orthodox Churches, announced in January its intention to resume an ecumenical dialogue with the Episcopal Church, a Protestant denomination in the United States that developed from the Church of England.

The Greek Orthodox Archdiocese of America awarded the Athenagoras Human Rights Award to South African Archbishop Desmond Tutu in March in recognition of the religious leader's humanitarian efforts in his country.

The Greek Orthodox Church reacted strongly to a Greek government decision in June to remove religious designations from government identity cards. Under the leadership of Archbishop of Athens Christodoulos, the church sponsored rallies in the cities of Thessaloniki and

Russian Orthodox women stand before Christ the Savior Cathedral in Moscow holding icons and portraits of Czar Nicholas II after the former czar and his family were declared saints by the Russian Orthodox Church in August 2000. The Russian ruler, his wife, and their five children were killed by Bolsheviks in 1918.

Athens and launched a petition drive protesting the action. The church asked that religious designations on identity cards be made optional.

Krystof (Pulec) was installed as archbishop of Prague on March 25 after a contested election following the death of Metropolitan Dorotej of Prague in 1999. Nikolai (Kocvar), archbishop of Michalovce-Slovakia, was elected on April 17, 2000, to the position of Metropolitan in the Orthodox Church of the Czech Lands and Slovakia.

The Russian Orthodox Church rejected a request in August from Ukrainian President Leonid Kuchma to grant fully independent status to the Ukrainian Orthodox Church. Also in August, the Russian church *canonized* (declared as saints) Czar Nicholas II and his family, who were killed by Bolsheviks in July 1918. The church canonized a total of 860 people who died under the regime of the revolutionaries who seized power in Russia in 1917.

On Aug. 19, 2000, Patriarch Alexei II dedicated Moscow's newly rebuilt Christ the Savior Cathedral. First built in the 1800's and destroyed in 1931 by Joseph Stalin, premier of the Soviet Union from 1929 to 1953, the cathedral was rebuilt to affirm the role of the Russian Orthodox Church in the new democratic era.

☐ Stanley Samuel Harakas

See also **Russia; Yugoslavia.**

Economics.
The world economy expanded in most regions in 2000, propelled in part by the powerful United States economy. Many regions that had suffered severe economic retrenchment in the late 1990's—such as East Asia, Russia, and Latin America—enjoyed improving or booming economies in 2000.

The U.S. economy was showing signs of slowing down by autumn, however, and steeply rising fuel costs were beginning to take a toll on a broad range of commercial activities. The contested outcome of the November 7 U.S. presidential election injected uncertainty into financial markets, and high-technology industries took a beating on the Nasdaq exchange and other stock markets as they had in the spring.

Millennium bug. The global economy skipped past the 1999-to-2000 year change with virtually no ill effects, despite predictions of crisis and catastrophe. The prospect of massive computer crashes triggered by the failure of old software codes to recognize the millennium date change became known and widely discussed in the late 1990's as the "millennium bug" or "Y2K" (for year 2000). The concern led to widespread updating of computer equipment and software, contributing to a late-1990's technology spending boom.

By the end of 1999, many public and private computer systems were still not fully Y2K-compliant. News organizations set up round-the-globe monitoring teams to track key government and business functions. To avoid computer glitches that might endanger flights, airlines made sure no planes were flying during the time change. When Jan. 1, 2000, came and went without major disruptions, people throughout the world heaved a sigh of relief.

Interest rates take hold. Y2K jitters even contributed to a late-1999 pause by the Federal Reserve (the Fed), the central bank of the United States, in its campaign of pushing short-term interest rates higher to cool the U.S. economy. The Fed started hiking rates in June 1999 and continued the hikes during 2000 as economic indicators showed rapid growth continuing. The U.S. economy had grown by 4.4 percent in 1998 and 4.2 percent in 1999. In the first quarter of 2000, it posted a 4.8-percent annual growth rate and a feverish 5.6-percent rate in the second quarter. In May 2000, the Fed escalated its normal quarter-point rate hikes to a half-point increase. After signs of a slowing economy at last began to emerge, the Fed took no further action through the autumn presidential election. In the third quarter of 2000, the U.S. economy slowed to a 2.4-percent annual pace.

Fuel prices surge. While the Fed fretted that the U.S. economy might be overheating, oil-producing nations limited their output of crude oil and further drove up prices that had already been rising from strong worldwide economic growth. Sharp price increases during the winter of 1999-2000 for home heating oil and diesel fuel were followed by steep price hikes for gasoline during the summer months. By September, the price for crude oil worldwide was at its highest level since the Gulf War (1991), and U.S. motor fuel prices were the highest on record.

Truckers, farmers, and cab drivers, seeking relief from high fuel prices and taxes, launched blockades of major commercial centers in September 2000, briefly shutting down cities in Europe, Asia, and Latin America. Although the United States escaped dramatic protests, some states suspended fuel taxes. On September 22, U.S. President Bill Clinton ordered the release of a record 30 million barrels of oil from the nation's Strategic Petroleum Reserve, oil stockpiled in the United States for emergency use. A production increase by the Organization of Petroleum Exporting Countries (OPEC), an association of 11 oil-producing nations, brought only mild price relief, and high fuel costs threatened worldwide economic momentum.

Around the world. Confirming the picture of a robust world economy, the International Monetary Fund (IMF)—a United Nations-affiliated organization that provides short-term credit to member nations—forecast a world economic growth rate of 4.7 percent in 2000, compared with 3.4 percent in 1999 and just 2.6 percent in 1998. The IMF's 2000 forecast included a growth rate of 5.2 percent for the U.S. economy and 4.7 percent for Canada.

The European economy posted solid growth in 2000. Like the U.S. Federal Reserve, the European Central Bank (ECB) raised interest rates periodically to keep the lid on inflation.

The European Union (EU) had launched a new common currency in January 1999 in which 11 member nations participated. The euro fell steadily in value through 1999 and continued declining during the summer of 2000. On September 22, the United States, Canada, Japan, and Great Britain finally joined the ECB in a coordinated intervention to buy euros to raise the currency's value. Though the action temporarily eased the euro's slide, the ECB was forced to engage in another series of market interventions in November to prop up the currency.

The nations of central and eastern Europe experienced considerably stronger economic growth in 2000 than in 1999. The IMF said that Russia, the region's largest economy, was on its way to a possible 7-percent growth rate in 2000, more than twice the growth of 1999.

Asia. Most Asian economies grew rapidly in 2000, with a sharp 8.8-percent gain expected for South Korea, 7.5 percent for China—which also won key trade recognition from the United States—and 6.7 percent for India. However, economic experts expected Japan's output to grow only 1.4 percent in 2000, compared with a scant 0.2 percent growth rate in 1999 and negative growth rates in the recession years of the mid-1990's.

Other world regions. A sharp economic recovery occurred in Latin America, where many countries had suffered recessions throughout 1999. Latin America's largest economy, Brazil, managed to achieve 4-percent growth during 2000 after barely missing a recession in 1999. Mexico, benefiting from its trading relationship with the United States, posted an impressive 6.5 percent rate of growth in 2000. A number of other countries in Latin America pulled out of downturns to experience solid economic growth in 2000.

Africa, long a region of weaker growth, experienced a 3.4-percent rate of growth in 2000 after just 2.2 percent in 1999. The economies of Australia and New Zealand both grew at a rate of about 4 percent in 2000.   □ John D. Boyd

See also **Economics: A Special Report; Europe; International trade; Manufacturing.**

Selected key U.S. economic indicators

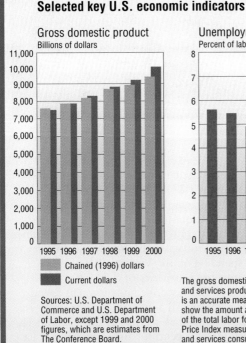

Gross domestic product
Billions of dollars

Chained (1996) dollars
Current dollars

Sources: U.S. Department of Commerce and U.S. Department of Labor, except 1999 and 2000 figures, which are estimates from The Conference Board.

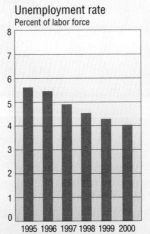

Unemployment rate
Percent of labor force

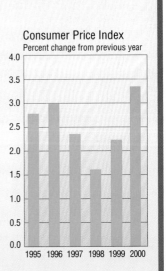

Consumer Price Index
Percent change from previous year

The gross domestic product (GDP) measures the value in current prices of all goods and services produced within a country in a year. Many economists believe the GDP is an accurate measure of the nation's total economic performance. Constant dollars show the amount adjusted for inflation. The unemployment rate is the percentage of the total labor force that is unemployed and actively seeking work. The Consumer Price Index measures inflation by showing the change in prices of selected goods and services consumed by urban families and individuals.

The New Economy

In 2000, the United States continued to enjoy unprecedented prosperity, which economists attributed to a wave of technological advances.

By John D. Boyd

The United States entered the new millennium riding a historic wave of prosperity in which rapid economic growth was accompanied by high employment and low inflation. By the end of February 2000, economic expansion, which had begun in 1991, was the longest on record, surpassing the boom of 1961 to 1969. Unlike the 1960's, when growth was fueled largely by government spending on the Vietnam War (1957-1975) and social programs, the prosperity of the 1990's took place during a time of peace and restrained government spending. It was powered by technological advances and the host of new businesses that had developed as a result of those advances.

In 1999, officials with the U.S. central bank—the Federal Reserve—feared that the economy might grow too quickly, driving up inflation. Their fears were based on experiences of the 1960's and other boom periods, which had resulted in inflation and stagnating economic growth. Federal Reserve officials, therefore, raised interest rates six times between June 1999 and May 2000, attempting to slow growth by making money more expensive to borrow. The tactic did not work quickly. On July 28, the Labor Department announced that the economy had grown by more than 5 percent in the April through June quarter—faster than in the first three months of 2000. Yet, inflation remained mild, and in some categories, consumer expenses actually dropped.

Most economists did not know what to make of the remarkable economic conditions. Experts predicted that the end to the boom inevitably was around the corner. Other economists claimed that the technology wave of the mid-1990's had created a more efficient and robust "new economy," changing the rules that had long governed commerce.

Defining the new economy

By 2000, the term "new economy" had come to represent two separate but related ideas. Initially, new economy referred to the boom of the 1990's and a set of economic conditions that appeared to defy the normal rules of economics. The term also referred to new technology, how that wave of technology affected business practices, and the variety of new businesses that were developing as a result of the new technologies.

Many economists pointed out that the economy of the late 1990's was behaving in a way they had not seen before. Steady, even dynamic, growth was driving up demand for labor without triggering inflation. In the past, when demand for labor increased, companies typically increased wages to retain employees and attract new ones. Higher wages pushed up prices of goods and services. If prices rose at a rate higher than the rate at which wages increased, purchasing power was reduced. A reduction of purchasing power reduced the value of money. At such times, most people purchased more because they preferred goods and services to money that was declining in value. This increase in demand caused prices to rise even further. If prices rose much faster than wages, purchasing power decreased rapidly, wiping out savings and producing economic stagnation.

In the late 1990's, some economists proposed that recent rapid advances in technology had created a rare economic situation in which high demand for labor coexisted with negligible inflation. According to these economists, computer manufacturers had developed faster, more powerful processors and quicker, less expensive ways of producing them. Software developers had created an array of products—from spreadsheets to inventory control systems—that revolutionized how businesses functioned and how people worked. Companies that invested heavily in new computer hardware and software enjoyed tremendous gains in efficiency. The new technology helped businesses generate more goods and services per worker. This increase in worker productivity allowed firms to grow faster without raising prices. Effi-

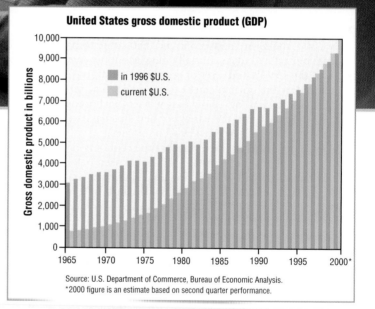

New technology, such as laptop computers (above), made workers more productive and changed the way many companies did business, pushing the U.S. *gross domestic product* (right) to new heights.

United States gross domestic product (GDP)

Gross domestic product in billions

- in 1996 $U.S.
- current $U.S.

10,000 — 9,000 — 8,000 — 7,000 — 6,000 — 5,000 — 4,000 — 3,000 — 2,000 — 1,000 — 0

1965   1970   1975   1980   1985   1990   1995   2000*

Source: U.S. Department of Commerce, Bureau of Economic Analysis.
*2000 figure is an estimate based on second quarter performance.

The author
John D. Boyd is a news editor for a transportation publication and a former economics reporter at an international financial news wire service.

ciencies built on each other to dampen inflation. In certain areas of commerce—for example, retail clothing, computers, and other electronics—competition for customers drove firms to match or exceed their competitors' cost-cutting measures, ensuring that prices were held down. New economy proponents predicted that the pattern would continue for many more years, because the boom was not just a temporary improvement in the old order. A true change in the way this economy operates had occurred.

Many economists, however, questioned this new economy model. They countered that an economy, no matter how strong and energetic, had to have limits beyond which it could not safely stretch without igniting inflation. Increases in worker productivity would eventually wind down, and the economy would overheat as it had in the past. Skeptics also pointed out that there

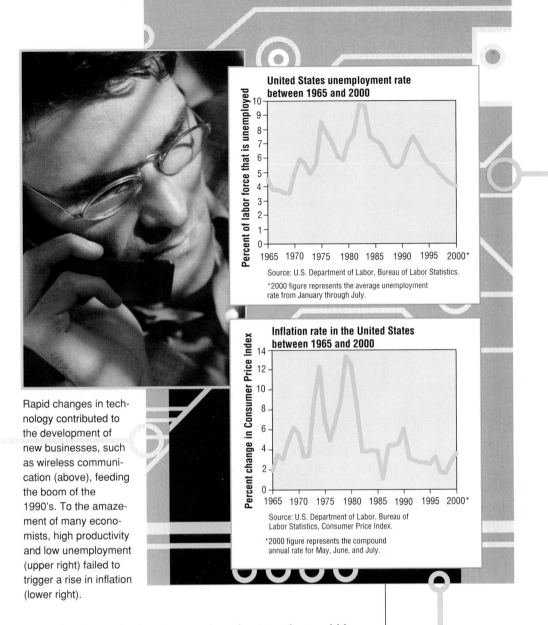

United States unemployment rate between 1965 and 2000

Percent of labor force that is unemployed

Source: U.S. Department of Labor, Bureau of Labor Statistics.

*2000 figure represents the average unemployment rate from January through July.

Inflation rate in the United States between 1965 and 2000

Percent change in Consumer Price Index

Source: U.S. Department of Labor, Bureau of Labor Statistics, Consumer Price Index.

*2000 figure represents the compound annual rate for May, June, and July.

Rapid changes in technology contributed to the development of new businesses, such as wireless communication (above), feeding the boom of the 1990's. To the amazement of many economists, high productivity and low unemployment (upper right) failed to trigger a rise in inflation (lower right).

were other factors besides increased productivity that could be responsible for the continuing prosperity. The broader world economy, for example, enjoyed tremendous capacity for growth in the recovery period following the Asian economic crisis and global slowdown of 1997 and 1998.

New economy skeptics did agree, however, that rapid technological change was generating new modes of communication that were changing how people lived and how commerce was conducted. New technology was spawning new businesses. The new businesses, which economists estimated would account for 25 percent or more of U.S. economic growth by the end of 2000, were producing an almost endless array of new products: sophisticated personal computer hardware and software, ever-faster computer chips, cellular telephones, mobile messaging and paging devices, and satellite-based navigation systems for civilian use. Economists also came to regard biotechnology discoveries as part of the new economy. Such discoveries as the mapping of the *human genome* (the total amount of genetic information) promised a wave of new medicines and medical procedures.

The Internet and the new economy

The Internet and its World Wide Web was the dominant component of the new economy. The Internet—a global, computer-based communications network—allowed people to exchange e-mail (electronic mail), offered instant news and "online" entertainment, and connected individuals with a bewildering variety of service industries—banks, travel and real estate agencies, and insurance and stock brokerages—greatly expanding choice and financial opportunities. The Internet created electronic wholesale and retail marketplaces that were truly international. For the first time, producers on one side of the world could sell directly to customers on the other side without relying on middlemen.

The Internet also allowed people to order nearly anything— groceries, books, clothing, medications, even automobiles—for home or office delivery. It increasingly made shopping in the traditional sense optional, challenging the "brick-and-mortar" retail stores of the old economy. Some Internet retailers went even further, displacing hard goods, such as books and compact music discs, completely. Customers could download stories or musical performances onto a home computer's hard drive.

The Internet, which had existed as a communication link for the government and academic research since the 1960's, did not reach a broad range of consumers until the 1990's with the development of the World Wide Web. The Web was graphical and easy to use. When Internet use exploded in popularity in the late 1990's, it pushed other technologies to change even faster. Computer makers found that the Internet was creating an ever-expanding market for faster and faster systems. Software developers rushed to create software programs for use with the Internet.

As more and more people turned to their computers for e-mail and shopping, manufacturers, such as Ford Motor Company, and traditional retailers, such as Toys R Us and Sears, rushed to build Web sites from which they could advertise and sell their wares. This rush onto the Web created vast opportunities for people who had the expertise to create and maintain Web sites. The result was more new businesses. As with major technological innovations of earlier times, such as the railroad, telephone, and automobile, the Internet produced an economic snowball effect, which grew ever larger as the number of people that were "connected" to the Internet grew.

Hundreds, perhaps thousands, of new companies were founded to exploit the possibilities of the Internet: Internet service providers, such as America Online (AOL), which offered access to the Internet and other customized services, such as e-mail; portal sites, such as Yahoo and Excite, which provided search engines, shopping, and chat rooms; search engine companies, such as Google and RagingSearch, which performed customized

Internet searches; and the "dot-coms," such as amazon.com, which only offered their services or retail products from their Web site.

Many of the new technology-based businesses were so successful that by 2000, they had generated an enormous amount of new economic output and earned vast wealth for their owners or shareholders. Some of the entrepreneurs who built these companies became instant millionaires or billionaires, when their companies "went public," when company shares initially were offered on stock markets.

The effect on the old economy

The new technology-based businesses, in many cases, eclipsed even the strongest old economy mainstays, such as consumer products giant Procter & Gamble of Cincinnati, Ohio, and automobile manufacturer General Motors of Detroit. According to a 1999 survey by *Fortune* magazine, software developer Microsoft Corporation of Redmond, Washington, enjoyed the highest profit margin—39.4 percent of revenues—among the world's top 500 companies. Neither Procter & Gamble nor General Motors were among the 50 companies with the highest profit margins.

The rapid development of technology in the 1990's affected old economy companies in both negative and positive ways. The Internet offered old economy businesses a new wholesale marketplace that proved to be a boon for many of them. In the old economy, manufacturers contracted for raw materials or developed their own, then produced goods that they shipped to retailers or stored in warehouses until customers needed them. Supply and demand estimates were based on early orders and traditional patterns, such as what goods were in demand in which season.

With the Internet, companies invited open bidding online. Online bidding allowed more suppliers to compete for their business by offering raw materials at lower costs. Companies could rapidly calculate customer demand by taking orders online. In this way firms could adjust manufacturing schedules and, therefore, schedule only the number of employees needed at any time.

The system also made it possible to ship goods directly from manufacturer to user. While online customers, in many instances, continued to buy from traditional retailers, the retailers could avoid bringing the goods they sold online to their stores. The wholesaler could hold the inventory until it was needed and then ship it directly to customers. Cutting out shipping costs to retailers further reduced the final delivered cost of products.

Some companies adjusted easily to the changes and helped lay the groundwork on the Internet for handling merchandise and

Old economy businesses, such as steel producers (top), suffered in the 1990's from a lack of capital, which was flowing into new economy companies, such as biotechnology developers (above).

Many old economy companies adapted new economy technologies—such as the Internet—to improve their efficiency in the late 1990's.

business transactions. Suppliers who were tuned into demand and could quickly adapt to changing tastes did well. So did their partners along the distribution chain, such as air-express delivery companies or trucking operations that specialized in consolidating lots of packages. FedEx corporation, based in Memphis, Tennessee, for example, had developed a fast and complex air-freight courier network and tracking system for overnight delivery of business documents and small parcels in the 1970's. With that infrastructure already in place, FedEx and similar firms were able to handle the sharp rise of small-parcel shipments that made Internet shopping so convenient. Companies that moved more slowly or that shipped in larger quantities often were less successful.

The impact of tech stocks

In the 1990's, many solid old economy companies suffered from a lack of capital, which discouraged growth and expansion. The problem was not that the old economy companies were not profitable. For the most part, they were. They simply were not sufficiently profitable to compete with the new technology-based companies. Investors liquidated holdings in old economy companies—even companies that continued to grow—and reinvested in technology-based companies, where returns grew much faster. This sent numerous older companies into mergers or in search of new types of markets in order to survive.

Many of the new technology-based companies, such as Microsoft and Dell Computer Corporation of Round Rock, Texas, were listed on the Nasdaq electronic stock exchange. Traditionally, the Nasdaq served as an incubator for companies not listed on the dominant New York Stock Exchange. As *tech stocks* (shares of technology-based companies) grew rapidly in value in the late 1990's, the Nasdaq composite index shot ahead much faster than more traditional gauges peppered with more old economy companies. The tech stocks attracted more investors, pulling more money out of the old economy stocks—another snowball effect that fed the new economy.

By the spring of 2000, however, many investors began questioning the basic financial strength of the tech stocks. Were values being matched by profits? As investor euphoria burned off, tech stocks began to tumble on Nasdaq and other markets. The values of tech stocks stayed well below their inflated highs of the late 1990's through the rest of 2000. The decline did not, however, derail the new economy itself. The technology sector continued to grow as a portion of the U.S. economy. E-commerce attracted more customers in 2000 than it had in 1999. And new high-tech products continued to roll out to meet the apparently insatiable demand for the latest gadget, such as a Palm personal digital assistant with a wireless connection to the Internet. While a natural shakeout hit many overvalued new economy stocks in 2000, the decline did not shake the underlying concept of the new economy.

A new Industrial Revolution?

Many economists have compared the rapid pace of change and accompanying benefits and upheavals brought by the new economy with the changes wrought by the Industrial Revolution, the last great age of major technological innovation. The Industrial Revolution began in Great Britain during the 1700's and spread to other parts of Europe and to North America in the early 1800's. By the mid-1800's, industrialization had become widespread in western Europe and the northeastern United States. During this period, new inventions led to entire new industries and changed the Western world from a primarily rural, agricultural society to an urban, industrial one.

The Industrial Revolution, like the new economy, produced millionaires, such as steel magnates Andrew Carnegie and Henry Clay Frick, who controlled entire industries. Government leaders, then as now, worried that so much power in so few hands hampered competition in ways that threatened the well being of the republic. In 1911, the Supreme Court of the United States ruled that Standard Oil of New Jersey stifled competition and, therefore, must be divided into separate companies. In June 2000, a U.S. federal judge ruled that Microsoft Corporation stifled competition and must be divided into two companies. As at the turn of the last century, such government action signaled to many new firms that they would have to adhere to traditional ideas of fair competition.

No country enjoyed the benefits of the new economy more than the United States. Its prosperity and rich mix of expertise in the technology fields, investment-friendly tax and regulatory policies, and emphasis on competition made it a natural incubator for New Economy companies. Other industrial nations have trailed behind. In 2000, 1 in 2 people in the United States had access to the Internet. In Germany and Japan, approximately 1 in 10 people enjoyed access. In France, the proportion of Internet users was fewer than 1 in 17. While the United States, with its propensity for change, encouraged companies fueled by dynamic ideas and risk capital, many countries, including many European countries, hindered the local development of e-commerce with rigid rules governing banking, business formation, and labor relations. The will for economic survival may force these countries to eventually catch up. However, few economists are willing to predict what form the new economy will take internationally or whether its most startling characteristic—growth with negligible inflation—can be sustained on a global basis. ■■■

Ecuador. Vice President Gustavo Noboa Bejarano was sworn in as president of Ecuador on Jan. 22, 2000, to complete the term of Jamil Mahuad Witt, who had been ousted in a military *coup* (overthrow) the previous day. The coup was sparked by thousands of angry Ecuadoran Indians, who stormed the Congress to protest Mahuad's plan to replace the *sucre,* the national currency, with the United States dollar. Indian leaders claimed that this move would be disastrous for the nation's poor.

Dollarization. Despite these concerns, Noboa signed legislation to dollarize the economy on March 9. The government completed the currency conversion on September 9. Afterwards, inflation subsided, employment increased, and Ecuadorans transferred millions of dollars they had banked abroad back into Ecuadoran banks.

Economic reform. On the day that Noboa signed the dollarization bill, the International Monetary Fund, World Bank, and other lending organizations announced that they would provide Ecuador with $2 billion to support economic reform. During 2000, Noboa won congressional approval to open the energy and mining sectors of the economy, previously controlled by government and private monopolies, to competitive foreign investment.   □ Nathan A. Haverstock

See also **Latin America.**

Education. Elementary- and secondary-school enrollment in the United States set a record for the fifth straight year in 2000, with 53 million youngsters attending the nation's public and private schools. The figure reflected an increase of 239,000 children over 1999. The U.S. Department of Education predicted that increases would continue as the grandchildren of the *baby boom generation* (the large group of people born in the United States between 1946 and 1964) and the children of recent immigrants begin school. College and university enrollment also hit an all-time high of 15.1 million students.

Presidential campaign. Education was a major issue in the U.S. presidential campaign throughout 2000. Both candidates promised more money for schools, but they also called for strict "accountability" measures to ensure that school quality improved.

Both the Democratic candidate, Vice President Al Gore, and the Republican candidate, Texas Governor George W. Bush, promised more money for after-school programs and teacher training. They also agreed that failing schools should not be allowed to continue operating, but they disagreed over what to do about them. Bush proposed that children in schools that do not improve after three years be allowed to transfer to a better public school or to use the federal mon-

ey paid to the public school on their behalf as "opportunity scholarships," to be spent on tutoring or private-school tuition, among other options. Gore proposed that a school that was still doing poorly after two years should be closed and reopened as either a charter school or a district school with new teachers and staff. The school would remain a public school, with additional funding going toward new curricula and teacher retraining.

Vouchers. Throughout 2000, the question of whether states can use *vouchers* (a system that allows children to attend private schools—including religious schools—at public expense) to educate students was frequently debated, both during the presidential campaign and in the courts. In October, an appeals court in Florida—the only state to have a state-wide voucher program—ruled that the practice did not violate the Florida constitution. The program, championed by Florida Governor Jeb Bush, George W. Bush's brother, offered a voucher to children attending any public school that failed state tests for two years out of four. Despite the victory, the Florida program faced further appeals.

In another court case in Ohio, a federal appeals court ruled in December that a voucher program that allowed low-income children in Cleveland to attend parochial schools violated the First Amendment to the U.S. Constitution, which guarantees the separation of church and state. Legal experts called the decision the most significant yet on the legality of vouchers.

Vouchers were also on the November ballot in Michigan and California in 2000. Voters in both states rejected proposals to allow state funds to be used to pay for vouchers for private schools. Vouchers had previously been on state ballots seven times and had lost every time.

Charter school enrollment in 2000 grew to 519,000 children in about 2,000 schools, according to the Center for Education Reform, a Washington, D.C.-based advocacy group. The figure represented an increase of 20 percent over 1999. Charter schools, which began to be formed in the early 1990's, are public schools that operate outside of school-district supervision. Because of their independence, many parents and educators believe that charters have more freedom to experiment with new education approaches.

In 2000, 10 percent of charter schools were managed by education-management organizations (EMO's), both profit-making and not-for-profit. Edison Schools Incorporated, the largest EMO, operated 113 schools in 2000 and began to be publicly traded on the New York Stock Exchange. A not-for-profit EMO, Aspire Public Schools, opened four California charters in 2000 with the help of local technology investors.

ESEA. By the end of its second session in late 2000, the 106th Congress had failed to renew the Elementary and Secondary Education Act (ESEA). ESEA authorizes Congress to fund about $15 billion in education programs, including about $8 billion for the Title I program for low-income children. The law, which was first enacted in 1965, must be reauthorized every five years.

Republicans wanted to change ESEA so that more money would go to states in the form of block grants free of many federal guidelines. Democrats wanted to include new programs, including one favored by U.S. President Bill Clinton to reduce class sizes nationally by giving the states money to hire 100,000 new teachers. Although ESEA was not renewed in 2000, it was to continue to be funded under its old guidelines.

Test scores improved slightly in two measures of student learning in 2000. On the SAT college-admission test administered by the College Board, the average math score rose to 514 of a possible 800 points. The score, an increase of three points from 1999, was the highest math score in 30 years. Verbal scores were flat at 505 of a possible 800 points for the fifth year in a row. According to the College Board, the fact that more students than ever before learned English as a second language or had parents who were nonnative English speakers may have affected the verbal grade.

Results from the National Assessment of Educational Progress (NAEP), given in math, science, and reading to a sample of youngsters ages 9, 13, and 17 in two-year and four-year cycles, were reported by the U.S. Department of Education in August 2000. According to the report, math scores were higher in 1999 than in any other year since 1973, when the federal government began administering the test. Nine-year-olds scored 232 points on the 500-point test, compared to 219 points in 1973. NAEP reading scores also improved but remained fairly stable since 1984, when huge federal and school-district reading programs began. Nine-year-olds scored 212 points, compared to 211 points in 1984.

Educators were concerned that both the SAT and NAEP in 2000 showed a widening gap between the scores of white students and those of minorities. Although the SAT scores of most racial groups rose in the 1990's, the scores of white and Asian American students grew more than others.

College costs. The College Board reported in October 2000 that the price of a college education continued to rise faster than the inflation rate. Tuition at four-year private colleges was up 5.2 percent to an average of $16,332 per year in the 2000-2001 academic year, while tuition at public colleges was up 4.4 percent to $3,510.

☐ June Kronholz

See also **State government.**

A home-schooled student, George Thampy, accepts the winner's trophy at the Scripps Howard National Spelling Bee in Washington, D.C., in June 2000. The second- and third-place winners in the contest were also taught at home.

French archaeologist Franck Goddio supervises the retrieval of a statue of the ancient Egyptian goddess Isis from the Mediterranean Sea in June 2000. Goddio said the statue was from one of three coastal cities that sank into the sea during a catastrophic earthquake about 1,200 years ago.

Egypt. Attempts by Egyptian President Hosni Mubarak to suppress political dissent in 2000 provoked harsh criticism from international human rights groups and increased tensions between Egypt and the United States. Many observers believed that the crackdowns were meant to consolidate the power of Mubarak's National Democratic Party (NDP). In elections held in October and November, the NDP won approximately 87 percent of 444 seats in parliament—down from 97 percent in the outgoing parliament. Many of the opposition candidates that won parliamentary seats were supported by Muslim Brotherhood, an outlawed Islamic fundamentalist party.

Prodemocracy leader charged. In June, Egyptian authorities closed the Ibn Khaldoun Center, an institution that conducted research on elections and Muslim-Christian relations. Egyptian police also detained Saad Eddin Ibrahim, the center's founder and a prominent prodemocracy advocate. Ibrahim, an Egyptian who also held a U.S. passport, was accused of defaming Egypt and spying for the United States. Ibrahim was imprisoned—despite the fact that he had not been formally charged with a crime—until he posted bail in August. He was finally charged in September, and he went on trial in November.

Labor party suspended. In July, an Egyptian public prosecutor charged opposition Labor Party leaders with being linked to banned Islamic groups and asked a special court to dissolve the party. Authorities had suspended the Labor Party in May, alleging that an article in the party's newspaper had sparked massive student riots. The article condemned the reprinting of Syrian writer Haider Haider's novel *A Banquet for Seaweed,* which some Muslims believed defamed Islam. Egyptian officials banned the book to quell the unrest.

Ambassador to Israel recalled. Following Israeli bombardment of Palestinian sites in the Gaza Strip, the Egyptian government in November recalled its ambassador from Israel. Egyptian officials said they made the move to protest Israel's "excessive use of force." The Israelis unleashed the bombardment after a bomb attack killed two Israelis and wounded several others in the Gaza Strip.

Hepatitis. Medical researchers in the United States and Egypt reported in March that a health campaign from the 1950's to the 1980's to eradicate *schistosomiasis,* an often fatal illness caused by a parasitic worm, had led to the infection of up to 20 percent of Egypt's population with the virus that causes hepatitis C. The researchers said the hepatitis virus was spread by the use of unsterilized needles to inject people with an antischistosomiasis agent.   □ Christine Helms

See also **Israel; Jordan; Middle East.**

Elections. In one of the closest elections in United States history, Republican candidate George W. Bush, the governor of Texas, defeated Democratic candidate Vice President Al Gore for the U.S. presidency. On December 13, Gore conceded the election, which took place on November 7, and Bush claimed victory. Gore's concession followed a U.S. Supreme Court decision on December 12 that prevented manual recounts of votes in certain Florida counties. Florida and its 25 electoral college votes played a pivotal role in the 2000 election.

Popular versus electoral votes. Although Gore won the popular vote—with a nationwide total of 50,996,064, compared with Bush's 50,456,167—he eventually lost in the Electoral College (source: Committee for the Study of the American Electorate). The Electoral College is a constitutionally mandated institution consisting of delegates appointed by the states. Delegates cast votes for president and vice president according to who wins the popular vote in their state. A minimum of 270 electoral votes were needed to win the 2000 presidential election. Bush and his vice presidential running mate, Dick Cheney, took the Electoral College votes of 30 states, a total of 271 electoral votes, giving Bush the presidency. Gore and his running mate, Connecticut Senator Joseph Lieberman, received 266 electoral votes.

Florida's votes. The outcome of the election remained in doubt between November 7 and December 13 because of the closeness of the vote in Florida. Without Florida's 25 Electoral College votes, neither candidate could claim victory. Early in the evening on Election Day, news networks projected Gore the winner in Florida, based on exit polls conducted throughout the day. Later, the media reversed their projections and called Florida for Bush, then reversed themselves again and declared the race too close to call. On November 8, Bush's margin of victory in Florida was so narrow—just 1,784 votes—that state law mandated a recount. At the conclusion of the recount, which was done by machine, Bush's lead had narrowed to just over 300 votes.

The Gore campaign then requested that ballots in four mostly Democratic counties be recounted by hand. In Palm Beach County, Florida, a large number of voters claimed they had been confused by the type of ballot used in the election and may have inadvertently voted for a third-party candidate, Pat Buchanan, instead of Al Gore. Buchanan had received an extraordinary number of votes in Palm Beach County, which was heavily Democratic, compared with the number of votes he had received statewide in Florida.

Controversy then erupted over the issue of manual recounts. Florida Secretary of State Katherine Harris refused to extend a November 14 deadline and accept late hand-count tallies.

Democrats charged that Harris's refusal was politically motivated. Harris, a Republican, co-chaired Bush's Florida campaign.

The Bush and Gore campaigns filed a series of legal challenges over recount issues. Gore wanted the recounts to go on. Bush wanted them to stop. Democratic voters also filed unsuccessful suits to have certain absentee ballots disqualified.

The Florida Supreme Court on November 21 ruled unanimously that Harris must accept the results of manual recounts as long as they were submitted on November 26 or early on November 27. The court set no clear standards on how to count "dimpled," or partially punched, ballots, and election officials argued whether they should be included in the tally. The Bush campaign then filed an appeal with the U.S. Supreme Court to reverse the decision of the Florida Supreme Court.

Miami-Dade County election officials stopped the manual recount after a few hours, claiming that they would be unable to finish within the time limits set by the Florida Supreme Court.

Election certification and challenge. On November 26, Florida officials certified that Bush had carried the state with a 537-vote margin over Vice President Gore. According to the official tally, Bush had 2,912,790 votes to Gore's 2,912,253. Attorneys retained by the Gore campaign challenged the results in a state circuit court.

2000 presidential election results	
Popular vote*	**Electoral College**
Gore......50,996,064	Bush 271
Bush......50,456,167	Gore 266

*Source: Committee for the Study of the American Electorate

The U.S. Supreme Court on December 4 ordered the Florida Supreme Court to review its November 21 decision to allow three Florida counties to manually recount their votes. The Florida court responded by ordering another recount. On December 9, the U.S. Supreme Court stopped the recount until it could rehear the case, which it did on December 11.

On December 12, the U.S. Supreme Court, in a 5-to-4 ruling, reversed the decision by the Florida court to allow a manual recount of votes. In the opinion of the majority on the court, the recount could not be resumed because the procedures were so arbitrary that they violated the equal protection clause of the 14th Amendment to the U.S. Constitution. According to legal experts, the decision removed all legal obstacles to Texas Governor George W. Bush claiming victory over Al Gore.

☐ Linda P. Campbell and Geoffrey A. Campbell

See also **Congress of the United States; Democratic Party; Republican Party; Special Election 2000 Supplement; State government; Supreme Court of the United States.**

Election judges in Palm Beach County, Florida, examine a punch-card ballot on November 24 during the manual recount of the 2000 presidential election. The hand-counting of votes was eventually stopped by the U.S. Supreme Court.

Electronics. Two companies that make central processing units (CPU's), the key chips in personal computers, smashed a computing speed barrier in February 2000. The companies created the first chips that could operate at one gigahertz (GHz), or 1 billion cycles per second. The more cycles a chip can process, the faster a computer can perform calculations and other work. Before the breakthrough, the fastest personal computers operated only at hundreds of megahertz (MHz). A MHz is 1 million cycles per second. The chips that achieved the new record for speed include the Pentium III, made by Intel Corporation, of Santa Clara, California, and an Athlon chip, made by Advanced Micro Devices, Inc., of Sunnyvale, California.

CPU speed, also known as "clock speed," is only one factor that determines how fast a computer can run applications and perform other functions. The amount of random access memory, or RAM, of a CPU also has a major impact on its speed. RAM is a temporary type of memory that can be accessed quickly, helping users to run applications faster. When considering performance, however, consumers often are more concerned with clock speed.

In August, Intel officials announced that the company would begin selling an even faster chip, the Pentium IV, before the end of 2000. The Pentium IV was based on an entirely new design, or architecture, made especially for running multimedia applications and accessing the Internet. Intel said the first Pentium IV's would run at 1.4 GHz.

Internet appliances. Officials at Gateway, Inc., in San Diego, and America Online, Inc., in Dulles, Virginia, announced in April that they would be offering Internet appliances that give consumers inexpensive Internet access in any room of the house without a computer. The devices were designed mainly for accessing the Internet and for sending and receiving e-mail.

The companies announced that before the end of 2000 they would offer a countertop appliance designed to be mounted to a flat surface in a high-traffic area of the house; a wireless, portable unit called the WebPad; and a desktop unit. The companies expected the units to cost less than $500.

Cell phones and radiation. The Cellular Telecommunications Industry Association (CTIA), a trade group representing cellular phone manufacturers, announced in July that it would require manufacturers to include information about the amount of radiation emitted by new cellular phones in the packaging for the phones. Manufacturers were to begin including the information in cellular phone packaging before the end of 2000.

CTIA officials said they enacted the rule be-

The i1000 Plus, introduced by Motorola in 2000, is a cellular phone that can be connected to the Internet. Mobile phones with Internet access found a wide audience in 2000.

cause of consumer concern that radiation from cellular phones might cause health problems. Cellular phones emit microwaves. If emitted close to the head, this radiation could pose health hazards. However, CTIA officials noted that cellular phone users receive very small doses of radiation.

Digital jukeboxes. The first of a new generation of audio devices called digital jukeboxes, or personal audio recorders (PAR's), went on sale in the summer of 2000. Unlike previously available portable music players that could store a few dozen songs in the digital MP3 (MPEG 1, Audio Layer 3) format, PAR's were capable of storing thousands of songs. PAR's, also called hard-disc CD changers, stored audio files on a hard-disc drive and were the size of stereo components. The first PAR, the AudioReQuest ARQ1, made by ReQuest Multimedia, sold for about $800.

Electronics and car accidents. The National Highway Traffic Safety Administration (NHTSA) in July warned that using cellular phones, navigation systems, and other electronic devices while driving was a factor in nearly a quarter of the 6.3 million motor vehicle accidents that occurred in the United States in 1999. The NHTSA said that drivers using the devices were often distracted from watching the road. ☐ Michael Woods

See also **Computers.**

El Salvador. Hector Silva of the Farabundo Marti National Liberation Front (FMLN) won re-election as mayor of El Salvador's capital, San Salvador, on March 12, 2000. The FMLN, which had its origins as a Marxist and rebel movement, also scored gains in legislative and municipal elections.

Market interventions. In May, the new Legislative Assembly raised tariffs on imported agricultural products to protect El Salvador's struggling agricultural sector. In August, the Assembly voted to limit the profits of multinational oil companies, which responded by suspending all planned investment in El Salvador.

Strike. A four-month strike by 12,500 state-employed physicians and social workers ended on March 10, when President Francisco Flores Perez scrapped plans to privatize El Salvador's public health system. Flores also agreed to negotiate with the strikers on wage demands.

Dengue fever. In September, Salvadoran health officials appealed for international assistance in coping with an outbreak of dengue fever, a mosquito-transmitted viral disease. Since January, some 100 cases of the disease, leading to the deaths of 24 people, had been reported in El Salvador.   □ Nathan A. Haverstock

See also **Latin America.**

Employment. See Economics; Labor and employment.

Endangered species. See Biology; Conservation.

Energy supply. Supplies of energy barely kept pace with demand during 2000 despite significant increases in production. A price runup in petroleum that began in 1999 accelerated in 2000, with a spillover to other energy areas. By the end of 2000, fuel prices reached their highest level in a decade.

Soaring prices kept petroleum products and natural gas at the forefront of the news in 2000. Crude oil prices surged beyond $37 a barrel in late September, but had dropped below $30 a barrel by December. As recently as 1998, during an oil glut, prices had been $10 a barrel. A barrel of oil contains 42 gallons, or 159 liters, and holds the energy equivalent of some 6,000 cubic feet (169.9 cubic meters) of natural gas.

Fuel costs reflected the rise in crude prices in 2000. In the United States, which consumes more oil than any other nation, gasoline prices jumped about 40 cents between January and mid-June, when they averaged $1.71 per gallon. By December, pump prices had dropped to approximately $1.50 per gallon. Costs of jet and diesel fuels and retail prices of home heating oil also rose sharply.

The prices of natural gas, which competes with fuel oil for industrial use and home heating and cooking, went up dramatically in 2000. The Energy Information Administration (EIA), an arm of the U.S. Department of Energy, estimated that natural gas at the wellhead averaged $4.61 per 1,000 cubic feet (28.32 cubic meters) in October

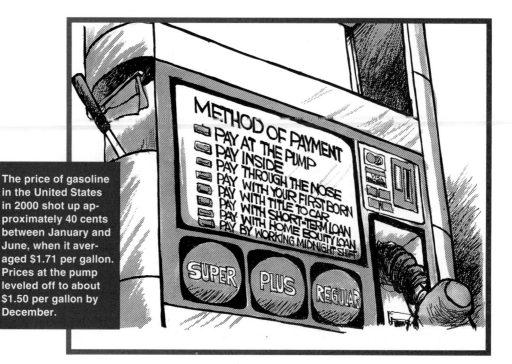

The price of gasoline in the United States in 2000 shot up approximately 40 cents between January and June, when it averaged $1.71 per gallon. Prices at the pump leveled off to about $1.50 per gallon by December.

2000, compared with $2.50 per 1,000 cubic feet in October 1999.

Strategic Petroleum Reserve. In September 2000, as concerns over energy costs rose, U.S. President Bill Clinton announced that 30 million barrels of crude oil would be released by the end of the year from the *Strategic Petroleum Reserve* (oil stockpiled in the United States for emergency use). Energy analysts, however, said the release had little overall impact on prices.

Consumption. The EIA reported that Americans burned 20 trillion cubic feet (566 billion cubic meters) of natural gas in the first 11 months of 2000, up from 19.5 trillion cubic feet (552 billion cubic meters) during the similar period in 1999. Tight supplies of natural gas triggered worries that shortages might occur during the 2000-2001 winter, which started out unusually cold.

Electric utilities in the United States burned large amounts of natural gas in 2000, partly because gas is considered a cleaner-burning form of energy than other fossil fuels. Skyrocketing electricity demand kept electricity generation at near capacity for much of the year, leading to blackouts in some cities. Bills doubled for some electricity consumers.

Among fossil fuels, only coal remained abundant and relatively cheap in 2000. Though coal was used to generate approximately one-half of the power requirements of the United States, annual production remained flat in 2000 compared with 1999. The EIA estimated that output for the first 10 months of 2000 was about 910 million tons (825 million metric tons), slightly less than the 911 million tons (826 million metric tons) produced during the first 10 months of 1999.

Americans' demand for petroleum products was up 3.3 percent between October 1999 and October 2000, according to the American Petroleum Institute (API), a Washington, D.C.-based national trade association. As a result, the above-ground stocks of crude oil in the United States plummeted to 281.7 million barrels by late October, the lowest level for autumn since the mid-1970's. The API reported inventories of heating oil and diesel fuel dropped 17.2 percent during the 12-month period ending in October 2000.

A booming economy and the popularity of large sports utility vehicles helped push U.S. demand for motor fuel to nearly 9 million barrels a day in mid-2000. Department of Energy figures showed that U.S. demand for all petroleum exceeded 20 million barrels a day in the second half of the year.

World oil demand in 2000 averaged slightly less than 76 million barrels a day. In November, the International Energy Agency (IEA), a Paris-based association of major oil-consuming nations, projected the world's consumption of oil would grow at an annual rate of nearly 2 million barrels a day over the next 20 years. According to IEA Executive Director Robert Priddle, these projections pointed to "a fossil fuel future, a continued strong role for oil as a transport fuel, and a further expansion of international oil trade."

European protests. Many economists blamed costly energy for signs of slowing in the world's robust economies in 2000. In Europe, where governments tax fuels more than in the United States, taxi, bus, and truck drivers staged several blockades of roads and petroleum refineries in 2000 to protest high fuel expenses.

OPEC boosts production. Industrial countries put pressure on the Organization of Petroleum Exporting Countries (OPEC), a group of 11 oil-producing nations, to increase production in 2000 so that prices would fall. In March, after heavy lobbying by U.S. Secretary of Energy Bill Richardson, OPEC agreed to launch a series of production boosts to hold crude prices in a $22-$28 range. Before 2000 ended, OPEC had lifted output by 3.7 million barrels a day to a total of nearly 30 million barrels—the highest level in two decades. OPEC planned to meet in early 2001 to reassess production. □ James Tanner

Engineering. See Building and construction.

England. See United Kingdom.

Environmental pollution. The 30th
anniversary of the founding of Earth Day, the annual observance to increase public awareness of environmental problems, was celebrated on April 22, 2000. In contrast to the first Earth Day in 1970, which focused on such basic, regional topics as water and air pollution, the 2000 observance highlighted broad, worldwide issues, including global climate change and the environmental responsibility of multinational corporations. Millions of people in 183 countries attended various activities to commemorate Earth Day 2000.

Record warmth. The winter of 1999-2000 was the warmest ever recorded in the United States, according to a March 2000 report by the National Climatic Data Center in Asheville, North Carolina. The center announced that the average U.S. temperature between December 1999 and February 2000 reached 38.4 °F (3.55 °C). This temperature exceeded the previous average highs of 37.8 °F (3.22 °C), established during the winter of 1998-1999, and 37.5 °F (3.05 °C), set in the 1997-1998 season. Many scientists believed the high temperatures were a sign of *global warming* (a gradual warming of Earth's surface) and that the warming was being caused by the release of carbon dioxide and other greenhouse gases from the burning of fossil fuels. These gases accumu-

A boy removes dead fish from the Tisza River in Yugoslavia after a cyanide spill at a gold mine in Romania poisoned the water in February 2000. Environmentalists predicted it would take years for the river to recover.

late in the atmosphere, where they trap heat, much like a greenhouse.

Oceans take the heat. In March 2000, scientists at the National Oceanographic Data Center in Silver Spring, Maryland, announced they had concluded that the oceans absorbed much of the heat caused by greenhouse gas emissions between the mid-1950's and mid-1990's. Measurements taken around the world revealed that temperatures in the upper 1.9 miles (3.1 kilometers) of ocean water increased an average of 0.10 °F (0.05 °C) over the 40-year period. Furthermore, the top 1,000 feet (304.8 meters) of seawater grew warmer by more than 0.50 °F (0.28 °C).

The researchers explained that the heat absorbed by the oceans would have contributed to increasing surface temperatures if it had not been absorbed. The scientists speculated that the oceans could store this heat for decades before releasing it into the atmosphere, which would delay but not stop the effects of global warming.

Good news, bad news. The average temperature in the United States may rise between 5 to 10 °F (2.8 to 5.5 °C) by 2100, according to a June 2000 report by the U.S. Global Change Research Program, an association of dozens of government agencies, universities, private groups, and corporations. The "National Assessment" report issued by the association stated that such a temperature change would produce both negative and positive consequences.

On the negative side, scientists expected that

warmer weather may lead to melting icecaps, rising sea levels, increased coastal erosion, more destructive sea storms, and water shortages resulting from less rain and snow in certain regions of the country. On the positive side, scientists expected that an increased concentration of carbon dioxide in the atmosphere would stimulate plant growth and increase agricultural and timber yields. The scientists warned that many wild plants in forests and other areas may also be spurred to grow faster, causing these environments to change in unpredictable ways.

Melting icecap. In July, climatologists at the University of Bergen in Norway projected that the Arctic icecap was melting and thinning at such an alarming rate that it might disappear entirely in summers beginning in the mid-2000's. They attributed this to a rise in Arctic temperatures since the 1970's.

In August 2000, visitors to the North Pole aboard the Russian icebreaker *Yamal* reported an ice-free patch of ocean about 1 mile (1.6 kilometer) wide. Some scientists noted that, though a small amount of polar ice probably melts every summer, the large area covered by the open water in 2000 was a possible sign of global warming. Other scientists suspected that the ice-free zone was formed by a natural combination of wind and waves and was no cause for concern.

Kyoto credits. U.S. officials proposed in August that the United States and other countries receive credit toward reducing greenhouse gas emissions by taking into account the effects of forests and farm crops in removing carbon dioxide from the atmosphere. The 1997 Kyoto Protocol required the United States to cut greenhouse gas emissions by 7 percent below 1990 levels sometime between 2008 and 2012. The international treaty also required other industrialized nations to make large cuts in emissions. The U.S. proposal was meant to take advantage of the fact that as plants grow, they absorb carbon dioxide from the atmosphere and combine it with water to make food.

Many environmental groups, which preferred that countries meet their Kyoto targets by cutting their use of coal and oil, opposed the proposal. Officials in the European Union (EU, an organization of 15 Western European countries) also spoke out against the proposal, noting that there were fewer forests, farms, and other open spaces in Europe than in North America. Some EU officials accused the United States of pushing the proposal to avoid having to make more difficult decisions on how to cut emissions.

Largest-ever ozone holes. Scientists reported in 2000 that the ozone layer over the Arctic and Antarctic regions thinned to record low levels. The ozone layer is a zone of air in the upper atmosphere that contains a form of oxygen called ozone, which shields Earth's surface from harmful ultraviolet rays from the sun. Scientists have suggested that chemical compounds called chlorofluorocarbons (CFC's)—which were formerly widely used in aerosol spray cans, refrigerants, and other products—linger in the atmosphere and break down ozone, causing an "ozone hole" to form annually above each pole during late winter. These holes allow large amounts of ultraviolet rays to reach the surface, where they can cause cancer and other serious health problems.

Scientists at a number of institutions in Europe and the United States, including the National Aeronautics and Space Administration (NASA), announced in April that the Arctic ozone hole spread across 5.7 million square miles (14.8 square kilometers) during the previous winter. In September, NASA researchers found that the ozone hole over Antarctica measured 11.4 million square miles (29.5 square kilometers). The Antarctic hole spread over Punta Arenas, Chile, marking the first time that it extended over a populated area, said scientists.

Atmospheric experts attributed the record sizes of the ozone holes to unusually cold air, which helps CFC's break down ozone, in the upper atmosphere. Some researchers noted that this cold air could be the result of global warming, which, they explained, might cool the upper atmosphere while warming the lower atmosphere. Other scientists doubted that there was a connection between global warming and ozone holes.

Corporate pledge. In July, representatives from some 50 multinational corporations joined several activist groups and labor unions at the United Nations (UN) in New York City to sign a global compact on environmental protection and worker rights. By signing the compact, the corporations agreed to maintain high environmental and labor standards throughout all of their global operations, regardless of local standards and regulations. Among the many signers were executives from the German/U.S. car company DaimlerChrysler; Nike, Incorporated of Beaverton, Oregon; and the Royal Dutch/Shell Group, headquartered in the Netherlands. Some environmental organizations, including Greenpeace, criticized the compact, noting that it had no enforcement mechanism. They also argued that many of the companies that signed the compact had poor environmental records and did not deserve the endorsement of activists and the UN.

☐ Andrew Hoffman

See also **Conservation.**

Equatorial Guinea. See Africa.
Eritrea. See Africa.
Estonia. See Europe.
Ethiopia. See Africa.

Europe

Prospects for peace and stability in the Balkans improved dramatically in 2000 with the removal of Slobodan Milosevic as president of Yugoslavia after a decade of the most severe conflict to occur in Europe since World War II (1939-1945). Economic prospects in most of the countries of Europe improved as many nations enjoyed their strongest growth in a decade. However, the value of the euro, the single currency adopted by 11 of the 15 countries of the European Union (EU) in 1999, fell steadily during most of 2000 as Europe's economic performance lagged behind that of the United States.

Milosevic era ends. In mid-2000, Milosevic ran for reelection as president of the Yugoslav federation, which consisted of Serbia and Montenegro. Opposition groups united behind the candidacy of Vojislav Kostunica, a constitutional lawyer who had not been active in politics previously. Kostunica criticized Milosevic for his role in igniting the civil war that broke up Yugoslavia in the early 1990's and for presiding over Serbia's crumbling, corruption-riddled economy.

After the Sept. 24, 2000, election, Kostunica's supporters claimed he had won outright with more than 50 percent of the vote. The government, controlled by Milosevic, claimed that neither candidate had won a majority and ordered a runoff between the two candidates in October. The opposition refused to accept the official results and organized a series of demonstrations and strikes to demand Kostunica be declared president. On October 5, several hundred thousand people from across Serbia converged on the capital, Belgrade, and stormed Parliament and the state broadcasting center. Milosevic agreed to give up power peacefully, and Kostunica was sworn in as president on October 7.

Milosevic's ouster brought an end to the last Communist-style government in Eastern Europe, completing the transition to democracy that began with the fall of the Berlin Wall in 1989. After Kostunica came to power, the United States and the EU removed economic sanctions from Serbia and restored diplomatic relations with Kostunica's government.

Kosovo. On Oct. 30, 2000, the moderate Democratic Party of Kosovo, led by Ibrahim Rugova, won control of most of the province's 30 municipalities in Kosovo's first free elections since the 1999 conflict. Rugova favored independence for Kosovo but promised to respect the rights of minorities, including ethnic Serbs and Gypsies. The moderates defeated a party headed by the leaders of the disbanded Kosovo Liberation Army, who wanted bolder moves toward independence.

Croatia moved to develop closer ties with the West after a center-left coalition defeated the nationalist Croatian Democratic Union in elections in January and February 2000. The coalition won parliamentary elections on January 3 and installed Ivica Racan, leader of the Social Democratic Party, as prime minister. On February 7, Stjepan Mesic, the last president of the former Yugoslavia, was elected president. Mesic promised a less-authoritarian presidency than Franjo Tudjman, who ruled Croatia from the time it broke away from Yugoslavia in 1991 until his death in 1999. Mesic also called for Croatia to seek membership in NATO and the EU.

European Union. EU leaders agreed to reform the bloc's governing rules to prepare the EU to accept new members from Eastern Europe. At a summit meeting in Nice, France, from Dec. 7 to Dec. 11, 2000, the leaders agreed to adjust the voting rights of member states to give the larger and most populous member nations—Germany, France, Italy, Great Britain, and Spain—a greater say over policy. In return, the large countries gave up their right to appoint a second member to the European Commission, the EU's executive agency.

The leaders also agreed to limit national veto powers by extending the number of policy areas where legislation could be adopted by a majority vote, rather than unanimously. The leaders planned another conference in 2004 to reach a permanent constitutional settlement spelling out the powers of the EU, national governments, and local authorities. In the meantime, the EU continued negotiations with 12 applicant countries with the aim of admitting the first new Eastern European members around 2004 or 2005.

Grozny, capital of the breakaway republic of Chechnya, lies in ruins after the Russian army captured the city in February. The Russian offensive in Chechnya later bogged down into guerrilla warfare.

Beef worries. An increase in the number of cases of "mad cow" disease, formally known as bovine spongiform encephalopathy (BSE), triggered a decline in beef consumption in several EU countries during 2000. BSE is a fatal brain disorder in cattle that scientists believe is related to a similar degenerative brain disease in humans called Creutzfeldt-Jakob disease.

Declining beef sales began in France, where the number of reported cases of BSE tripled to more than 100 between 1999 and 2000, partly because of increased testing of cattle. Consumer fears spread to Germany and Spain in November after those countries reported their first cases of BSE. At a meeting in Brussels, Belgium, on December 4, EU agriculture ministers agreed to ban the use of animal meat and bone meal—which is suspected of spreading BSE—in feed for cattle and other animals. The ministers also agreed to ban the sale of beef from animals over 30 months old, the age at which infected animals develop BSE. The measures were expected to cost more than $4 billion and require the destruction of 2 million cows.

Economy. Europe emerged in 2000 from a decade of sluggish growth as low interest rates fueled business confidence and gains in employment boosted consumer spending. The European Commission forecast that economic growth in the 15 EU countries would increase by almost 3.5 percent in 2000, up from 2.3 percent in 1999. The unemployment rate was expected to decline from 9.2 percent in 1999 to 8.5 percent in 2000.

A number of governments took advantage of the buoyant economy, which boosted tax revenues and reduced budget deficits, to enact the biggest tax cuts in more than 10 years. Both consumers and business leaders, who had complained that high tax rates were stifling growth and making EU countries less competitive, welcomed the cuts.

Country	Population	Government	Monetary unit*	Foreign trade (million U.S.$) Exports†	Imports†
Albania	3,624,000	President Rexhep Mejdani; Prime Minister Ilir Meta	lek (148.60 = $1)	275	1,151
Andorra	67,000	Co-sovereigns bishop of Urgel, Spain, and the president of France; Prime Minister Marc Forne Molne	French franc & Spanish peseta	58	1,077
Austria	8,148,000	President Thomas Klestil; Chancellor Wolfgang Schuessel	schilling (15.89 = $1)	63,464	68,757
Belarus	10,069,000	President Aleksandr Lukashenko	ruble (321.51 = $1)	5,922	6,664
Belgium	10,248,000	King Albert II; Prime Minister Guy Verhofstadt	franc (46.60 = $1)	176,201	160,820
Bosnia-Herzegovina	4,330,000	Chairman of the collective presidency Zivko Radisic	marka (2.26 = $1)	450	2,950
Bulgaria	8,756,000	President Petar Stoyanov; Prime Minister Ivan Kostov	lev (2.25 = $1)	3,937	5,430
Croatia	4,433,000	President Stjepan Mesic	kuna (8.70 = $1)	4,280	7,777
Czech Republic	10,346,000	President Vaclav Havel; Prime Minister Milos Zeman	koruna (40.99 = $1)	26,831	28,781
Denmark	5,207,000	Queen Margrethe II; Prime Minister Poul Nyrup Rasmussen	krone (8.61 = $1)	48,341	43,970
Estonia	1,495,000	President Lennart Meri; Prime Minister Mart Laar	kroon (18.08 = $1)	2,939	4,093
Finland	5,201,000	President Tarja Halonen; Prime Minister Paavo Lipponen	markka (6.87 = $1)	40,666	30,727
France	59,024,000	President Jacques Chirac; Prime Minister Lionel Jospin	franc (7.58 = $1)	300,171	289,943
Germany	81,700,000	President Johannes Rau; Chancellor Gerhard Schroeder	mark (2.26 = $1)	541,090	472,171
Greece	10,573,000	President Konstandinos Stephanopoulos; Prime Minister Konstandinos Simitis	drachma (392.21 = $1)	8,656	27,718
Hungary	9,940,000	President Ferenc Madl; Prime Minister Viktor Orban	forint (303.93 = $1)	24,947	27,920
Iceland	282,000	President Olafur Grimsson; Prime Minister David Oddsson	krona (84.01 = $1)	2,013	2,502
Ireland	3,689,000	President Mary McAleese; Prime Minister Bertie Ahern	pound (punt) (0.91 = $1)	70,279	46,034
Italy	57,254,000	President Carlo Azeglio Ciampi; Prime Minister Giuliano Amato	lira (2,236.52 = $1)	230,199	216,626 (includes San Marino)
Latvia	2,471,000	President Vaira Vike-Freiberga; Prime Minister Andris Berzins	lat (0.62 = $1)	1,723	2,945
Liechtenstein	33,000	Prince Hans Adam II; Prime Minister Mario Frick	Swiss franc	2,470	917

Germany led the trend toward lower taxes. The government of Chancellor Gerhard Schroeder won parliamentary approval for a five-year program of tax cuts in July 2000. The cuts were to gradually lower the top income-tax rate from 51 percent in 2000 to 42 percent in 2005 and slash the corporate tax rate from 40 percent to 25 percent in 2001. Italy and France announced tax cuts later in the summer of 2000. Most of the smaller EU countries also managed to enact some form of tax reductions.

Fuel protest. Despite the tax cuts, most EU governments were confronted in September with a rebellion over gasoline taxes. Europe's gasoline prices were among the highest in the world, with taxes accounting for more than 75 percent of the retail price in some countries. The rise in world oil prices in 2000 drove gas prices above $4 a gallon in many European countries.

The protests began in France, where truckers and farmers blocked oil refineries, cutting supplies of gasoline to retail stations. The protests then

Country	Population	Government	Monetary unit*	Foreign trade (million U.S.$)	
				Exports[†]	Imports[†]
Lithuania	3,692,000	President Valdas Adamkus; Prime Minister Rolandas Paksas	litas (4.00 = $1)	3,045	4,892
Luxembourg	425,000	Grand Duke Henri; Prime Minister Jean-Claude Juncker	franc (46.60 = $1)	7,889	10,927 (includes Belgium)
Macedonia	2,247,000	President Boris Trajkovski	denar (59.78 = $1)	1,147	1,627
Malta	377,000	President Guido De Marco; Prime Minister Eddie Fenech Adami	lira (0.46 = $1)	1,985	2,856
Moldova	4,510,000	President Petru Lucinschi; Prime Minister Dumitru Braghis	leu (12.41 = $1)	650	1,081
Monaco	34,000	Prince Rainier III	French franc	no statistics available	
Netherlands	15,995,000	Queen Beatrix; Prime Minister Wim Kok	guilder (2.55 = $1)	200,290	187,529
Norway	4,427,000	King Harald V; Prime Minister Jens Stoltenberg	krone (9.29 = $1)	44,892	34,047
Poland	38,786,000	President Aleksander Kwasniewski; Prime Minister Jerzy Buzek	zloty (4.69 = $1)	27,397	45,903
Portugal	9,807,000	President Jorge Sampaio; Prime Minister Antonio Guterres	escudo (231.57 = $1)	23,864	38,461
Romania	22,607,000	President Ion Iliescu; Prime Minister Adrian Nastase	leu (24,487.50 = $1)	8,505	10,392
Russia	145,552,000	President Vladimir Putin	ruble (27.87 = $1)	74,663	40,429
San Marino	27,000	2 captains regent appointed by Grand Council every 6 months	Italian lira	230,199	216,626 (includes Italy)
Slovakia	5,468,000	President Rudolf Schuster; Prime Minister Mikulas Dzurinda	koruna (50.65 = $1)	10,031	11,110
Slovenia	1,945,000	President Milan Kucan; Prime Minister Andrej Bajuk	tolar (242.45 = $1)	8,604	9,952
Spain	39,848,000	King Juan Carlos I; President of the Government (Prime Minister) Jose Maria Aznar	peseta (192.19 = $1)	109,966	144,438
Sweden	8,972,000	King Carl XVI Gustaf; Prime Minister Goran Persson	krona (9.86 = $1)	84,771	68,419
Switzerland	7,494,000	President Adolf Ogi	franc (1.74 = $1)	76,124	75,440
Turkey	67,748,000	President Ahmed Necdet Sezer; Prime Minister Bulent Ecevit	lira (672,770.00 = $1)	25,938	45,369
Ukraine	50,974,000	President Leonid Kuchma	hryvna (5.44 = $1)	12,637	14,676
United Kingdom	59,022,000	Queen Elizabeth II; Prime Minister Tony Blair	pound (0.68 = $1)	268,254	317,958
Yugoslavia	10,696,000	President Vojislav Kostunica; Prime Minister Zoran Zizic	new dinar (11.61 = $1)	2,604	4,622

*Exchange rates as of Oct. 13, 2000, or latest available data.   [†]Latest available data.

spread to other countries, bringing traffic to a standstill for days in many parts of Belgium and causing almost all of Great Britain's service stations to run out of fuel. The French government eventually defused the protests by reducing diesel fuel taxes for truckers and farmers, while the Belgian government granted compensation to truckers. British leaders cut truck registration taxes.

Euro weakens. The value of Europe's single currency fell during much of 2000. The euro began the year with a value of $1.03, compared with the U.S. dollar. The value of the euro then declined, hitting a low of 83 cents in October before recovering slightly in late 2000. According to economists, the euro declined because the public perceived that the European Central Bank (ECB) was not managing the currency in coordination with the governments of the 11 EU countries participating in the euro. The strength of the U.S. economy, which continued to attract a majority of international investment funds into the United States, also contributed to the decline.

Truckers block a road in the Belgian city of Eynatten, near the German border, in September. The blockade, part of a protest against the high cost of fuel, spread quickly to other European countries, where gasoline prices rose to as high as $4 a gallon.

ceive high-speed video and audio signals through mobile phones. The British government auctioned off five licenses in April for $36 billion. Germany auctioned off six licenses for $50 billion in August. Other countries received less money, as the huge sums deterred some potential bidders. However, by the end of 2000, companies had agreed to pay more than $100 billion for licenses across Europe.

The Internet took off in Europe in 2000 as more consumers went online and companies developed Internet strategies. Deutsche Telekom AG, the German telephone company, sold a 10-percent stake in its Internet service provider, T-Online AG, to raise $2.6 billion in April. T-Online also expanded by buying the French Internet service provider Club Internet for $2 billion worth of stock. Terra Networks S.A., the Internet subsidiary of Spain's Telefonica S.A., bought the U.S. Internet portal Lycos Incorporated for $12.5 billion in May. Vivendi S.A., a French utility and media company, agreed in June to buy Seagram Company, a Canadian liquor and media firm, for $34 billion. Vivendi hoped to use Seagram's Universal film studio and music business to become a global media giant able to compete with the merger of America Online Incorporated and Time Warner Incorporated.

Stock markets. Europe's many stock exchanges consolidated somewhat during 2000, but an attempt to form a pan-European market failed. The region's two biggest markets, the London Stock Exchange Plc (LSE) and Deutsche Boerse AG, which runs the Frankfurt exchange, agreed in May to merge. However, the LSE abandoned the deal in September, because many members felt the proposal would send too much business to Frankfurt. The Paris, Brussels, and Amsterdam stock exchanges merged in September to form Euronext, Europe's third-largest exchange.

International trade. Trade tensions flared after the World Trade Organization (WTO) ruled in February against a key U.S. export-promotion scheme. The WTO, acting on a complaint from the EU, ruled that a U.S. law granting companies tax breaks on exports channeled through so-called foreign sales corporations was illegal. In November, the U.S. Congress passed a law abolishing the corporations and establishing new tax breaks for exporters. The EU claimed the new provisions also violated trade rules and asked the WTO to allow the EU to impose sanctions on $4 billion worth of U.S. exports. The request was pending at the end of 2000.   □ Tom Buerkle

See also the various European country articles.

The ECB feared that the weak euro might trigger inflation in Europe, because the currency's decline made imports more expensive. In an effort to stop the decline, the ECB intervened to buy euros in global currency markets. The ECB acted in conjunction with the central banks of the United States, Japan, England, and Canada in September, then bought euros on its own in November. The weakness of the euro actually contributed to Europe's strong growth rate in 2000, because it made exports cheaper on world markets. Many governments worried, however, that the falling euro could undermine public support for the currency before euro notes and coins could be put into circulation in early 2002.

Technology surge. Europe's mobile telephone industry underwent a growth surge in 2000, prompting several major mergers. Vodafone AirTouch Plc of Great Britain acquired Mannesmann AG, owner of Germany's leading mobile telephone operator, for $160 billion in February. The deal represented the largest takeover in corporate history. On May 30, France Telecom agreed to buy Orange Plc, a British mobile telephone operator, for $40 billion.

Mobile operators also spent large sums of money on licenses to provide so-called third-generation services, which enable consumers to re-

Fashion.

Designers in 2000 failed to introduce a theme that captured the imagination of women worldwide. There was no hemline news. Trousers were accepted everywhere, and the dominant movement continued to be the American trend for casual dress.

Fashion designers had expected that the millennium celebrations would spur an interest in dressy clothes, but this failed to materialize. The main trend in luxury clothing seemed to be in the form of such pieces as leather jackets and cashmere sweaters. The trend manifested itself mainly in the development of two-piece evening clothes. For example, the same cashmere sweater might be worn with a long taffeta evening skirt or with jeans, thus extending the concept of casual dressing.

A renewed interest in suits, a form of apparel that some critics had said was vanishing, offered one sign of a renewed interest in formality. Casual Fridays in the business world did indeed extend to all days of the week, but many women still felt that a suit was appropriate at least some of the time.

Out of the office, most women generally wore casual styles, such as T-shirts and khaki pants. Capri pants, cut slightly higher than the ankle and worn with clunky mules, became a trend for women during the warmer months

Calf-length "capri pants" worn with open-toed platform shoes for women and elongated "bermuda shorts" for men highlighted summer fashions in 2000.

of 2000. Some women turned to the stiletto heels that designers were promoting, but sneakers and low-heeled sandals remained the most popular footwear. Most women were not willing to give up comfort for fashion.

The Internet. Some fashion experts believed that the Internet would make a difference in how women bought their clothes. Their expectation was based on an observation that computers were becoming increasingly attractive to women of all ages in 2000. However, most observers agreed that, while it was easy to sell books or lipsticks on the Internet, clothes were a different matter. Women wanted to feel the material and try the style on. While fashion sites multiplied on the Internet—most department stores had Web sites or planned to develop them—the Internet

did not yet make a difference in how women dressed in 2000.

Fur and the fur look. Women in 2000 wore a little bit of fur around the neck—either real or fake—to suggest luxury. Fur-print jackets and blouses provided lively accents. Similarly, beaded embroidery on sleeveless shirts and tank tops updated the casual look.

Handbags and hats. The plain black nylon tote was supplemented in 2000 by more fanciful carriers. A number of designers, including Marc Jacobs and Michael Kors, designed special handbag collections.

Hats made a minor return in 2000. The emphasis was on traditional knitted caps to keep heads warm in cold weather and floppy-brim sunshades to protect the face in the summer.

Swimwear. The minimal bikini was a favorite choice in the summer of 2000. Few women seemed to worry about the suits being revealing.

Fashion marketing. In an attempt to stimulate less-than-enthusiastic clothes shopping, stores offered a wide array of styles for larger women and more active clothes for the athletic. They also tried to spruce up styles for teen-agers.

Consolidation continued to be the major trend in fashion in both Europe and the United States in 2000. Executives aimed to bring the buying of fabrics, production facilities, and global selling under a single corporate organization. The small company headed by a designer with his or her own view of what people should wear was giving way to corporate conglomerates.

In the United States, the fashion conglomerate Pegasus Apparel Group of New York City acquired Pamela Dennis in March and Miguel Adrover and Daryl K in May in an attempt to rival Paris-based LVMH Moet Hennessy Louis Vitton SA in the luxury apparel field. In December, American designer Donna Karan agreed to sell both her Donna Karan trademarks and the public company that designed her products, Donna Karan International, Incorporated, to LVMH.

☐ Bernadine Morris

Finland elected its first woman president in 2000. Tarja Halonen, the foreign minister and candidate of the ruling Social Democratic Party, defeated Esko Aho, the former prime minister and leader of the opposition Center Party, in the election on February 6. Halonen and Aho ran well ahead of five other candidates in a first round of voting on January 16, and Halonen claimed victory by winning 51.6 percent of the votes compared with 48.4 percent for Aho in a runoff ballot three weeks later.

The election reflected gender and regional factors rather than major policy differences. Halonen, an unmarried mother and former leftist radical, won strong support from women, from voters who wanted a female president, and from a majority of voters in southern Finland, particularly in the capital, Helsinki. Aho's base of support was in the less-populated rural regions in the north. The election had little impact on policy because Halonen belonged to the same party as Prime Minister Paavo Lipponen. She took office on March 1, replacing Martti Ahtisaari, who retired from active politics.

Bank merger. Finland's leading bank, MeritaNordbanken Oyj, agreed on March 6 to buy Unidanmark A/S, the second-largest bank in Denmark, for $5 billion. On October 16, MeritaNordbanken won its year-long battle to acquire Chris-

tiania Bank ASA for $2.9 billion after the Norwegian government agreed to sell its 35 percent stake in Christiania. MeritaNordbanken also invested heavily in technology in 2000 in order to develop one of the world's largest Internet banking businesses. Approximately 1.8 million of its customers banked online in 2000.

Economy. Finland's economy boomed in 2000 because of the fast growth of such technology businesses as mobile telephony, in which Finland's Nokia Oyj remained a global market leader. The European Commission, the executive agency of the European Union, forecast that Finland's *gross domestic product* (the total amount of goods and services produced in a country in a year) would grow by 4.9 percent during 2000. The unemployment rate, which rose to nearly 20 percent during Finland's recession in the early 1990's, was expected to decline to 8.9 percent.

The strong economy enabled the government, in August 2000, to propose a budget for 2001 that would cut taxes, improve social security benefits, and still leave a large budget surplus. Labor tensions rose, however, as workers demanded a bigger share of the nation's prosperity. The paper industry suffered a major setback when 30,000 workers staged a one-week strike in April 2000 for higher pay. ☐ Tom Buerkle

See also **Europe.**

Food. Officials of the European Union (EU) took steps in 2000 to stem panic over an increase in the number of cases of "mad cow" disease, formally known as bovine spongiform encephalopathy (BSE). BSE is a fatal brain disorder in cattle that is suspected to be related to a variant of a similar degenerative brain disease in humans called Creutzfeldt-Jakob disease. Beef sales in France declined as the number of reported cases of BSE grew to more than 100 in 2000. Cases of the disease were also reported for the first time in Germany and Spain. The EU in December ordered a six-month ban on almost all animal products in livestock feed, a key suspect in spreading the disease. EU officials also banned the sale of beef from animals more than 30 months old, the age at which infected animals develop BSE.

Web stores. Most Internet-based home grocery shopping services that had hoped to tap into the busy lifestyles of consumers in the United States remained financially shaky in 2000. Priceline.com, the heavily advertised "name-your-own price" service based in Norwalk, Connecticut, was forced to close its grocery operation in October.

Peapod, headquartered in Skokie, Illinois, averted a liquidity crisis in April when the Ahold supermarket chain, based in the Netherlands, purchased 51 percent of Peapod stock for just over $70 million. Peapod reported that its 1999 sales had totaled $73 million but generated a loss of $29 million. Officials for Ahold and Peapod announced that they would roll out more than 50 "fast-pick" centers at Ahold's stores in the United States. The centers were to use existing stockroom space to pack groceries for local delivery.

In September 2000, Peapod bought operations in Chicago and Washington, D.C., from Streamline.com, Incorporated, which also serviced the Boston and northern New Jersey areas. After completing the $11.6-million deal, Streamline reported in October that it would need additional funding by 2001 to remain in business.

Webvan Group, Incorporated, of Foster City, California, merged in July 2000 with HomeGrocer.com in Kirkland, Washington. Webvan delayed opening three distribution centers in October to cut losses.

Organic standards. Officials with the U.S. Department of Agriculture in December announced the first federal regulations for producing and labeling organic foods. The rules prohibited use of synthetic chemicals and promoted sustainable farming for organic foods.

Wal-Mart Stores, Incorporated, of Bentonville, Arkansas, continued to expand its retail food businesses in 2000, increasing the competition for other companies in the supermarket industry. In October, Wal-Mart announced it would open 40 new discount stores and up to 180 new Supercenters in the fiscal year beginning in February 2001. Wal-Mart officials said the company would expand its Neighborhood Market with 15 to 20 new units. The SAM's Club division was to open 40 to 50 domestic clubs and remodel about 50 others. By September 2000, Wal-Mart owned over 3,000 stores in the United States.

Genetically modified food. Officials of the National Academy of Sciences reported in April that none of the foods on the market were unsafe to eat because of genetic modification. Scientists have created genetically modified (GM) plants, also called transgenic crops, which contain genes from other species that confer new traits on the crops, such as pest resistance and greater productivity. The academy reported that health risks from GM crops were comparable to risks from plants modified by conventional breeding.

Kraft Foods of Northfield, Illinois, recalled transgenic Taco Bell taco shells on September 22. Corn in the shells, made by Aventis S.A. of France, had been approved by the Environmental Protection Agency (EPA) for use in animal feed but not for humans. In October, Aventis agreed to cancel its license to sell the corn. The company suspended sales of the seed for the 2001 crop and agreed to reimburse the government for purchasing all of the harvest in 2000.   □ Bob Gatty

See also **Agriculture; Europe.**

Football. The Oklahoma Sooners reemerged as a national power in college football in 2000, taking the Bowl Championship Series (BCS) national title by defeating the Florida State Seminoles in the Orange Bowl on Jan. 3, 2001. In the National Football League (NFL), the St. Louis Rams stunned observers by steamrolling through the regular season and surviving a tough title game to claim the Super Bowl in January 2000.

College. On Jan. 3, 2001, the No. 1-ranked Oklahoma Sooners defeated the No. 3-ranked Florida State Seminoles, 13-2, in the Orange Bowl in Miami, Florida, to become the undisputed national champions of the 2000 season. The matchup featured a quarterback duel between Florida State's Heisman Trophy winner, Chris Weinke, and Oklahoma's Heisman Trophy runner-up, Josh Heupel. However, what was billed as an offensive showcase turned into a display of defense as Oklahoma smothered the high-octane Florida State offense.

For Oklahoma, the championship, the team's first since 1985, capped their return as a national football power. The Sooners had struggled throughout the mid-1990's. Few observers had thought that Oklahoma could beat Florida State despite being undefeated in 2000.

BCS controversy. In 2000, the BCS system ranked teams using polls of journalists and coaches, strength-of-schedule formulas, computer rankings, and other variables to determine the eight teams that would compete in the major bowls: the Rose Bowl, Orange Bowl, Sugar Bowl, and Fiesta Bowl. The National Collegiate Athletic Association (NCAA) adopted the BCS format in 1998.

The system, which was designed to assure that the best teams competed for the national title, came under fire in 2000 because of the matchup between Oklahoma and Florida State. Two teams other than Florida State—Miami and the University of Washington—could have been invited to the title game. Oklahoma was ranked No. 1 in both the coaches' and journalists' polls in December, while Florida State had been ranked third, behind Miami. However, Florida State was invited to the Orange Bowl because they had finished ahead of Miami in the overall BCS rankings.

Oklahoma's victory averted a split championship. Had Florida State defeated Oklahoma, they would have won the BCS title, but either Miami or Washington could have been voted No. 1 in the Associated Press poll of journalists, because in the regular season Miami beat Florida State and Washington defeated Miami. Because Miami defeated the University of Florida in the Sugar Bowl, 37-20, and Washington defeated Purdue in the Rose Bowl, 34-24, journalists could have chosen either team, resulting in a split title.

2000 National Football League final standings

American Conference

East Division

	W.	L.	T.	Pct.
Miami Dolphins*	11	5	0	.688
Indianapolis Colts*	10	6	0	.625
New York Jets	9	7	0	.562
Buffalo Bills	8	8	0	.500
New England Patriots	5	11	0	.312

Central Division

	W.	L.	T.	Pct.
Tennessee Titans*	13	3	0	.812
Baltimore Ravens*	12	4	0	.750
Pittsburgh Steelers	9	7	0	.562
Jacksonville Jaguars	7	9	0	.438
Cincinnati Bengals	4	12	0	.250
Cleveland Browns	3	13	0	.188

West Division

	W.	L.	T.	Pct.
Oakland Raiders*	12	4	0	.750
Denver Broncos*	11	5	0	.688
Kansas City Chiefs	7	9	0	.438
Seattle Seahawks	6	10	0	.375
San Diego Chargers	1	15	0	.062

*Made play-offs

National Conference

East Division

	W.	L.	T.	Pct.
New York Giants*	12	4	0	.750
Philadelphia Eagles*	11	5	0	.688
Washington Redskins	8	8	0	.500
Dallas Cowboys	5	11	0	.312
Arizona Cardinals	3	13	0	.188

Central Division

	W.	L.	T.	Pct.
Minnesota Vikings*	11	5	0	.688
Tampa Bay Buccaneers*	10	6	0	.625
Green Bay Packers	9	7	0	.562
Detroit Lions	9	7	0	.562
Chicago Bears	5	11	0	.312

West Division

	W.	L.	T.	Pct.
New Orleans Saints*	10	6	0	.625
St. Louis Rams*	10	6	0	.625
Carolina Panthers	7	9	0	.438
San Francisco 49ers	6	10	0	.375
Atlanta Falcons	4	12	0	.250

*Made play-offs

Team statistics

Leading offenses (yards gained)

	Total	Per game
Denver	6,567	410.4
Indianapolis	6,141	383.8
Oakland	5,776	361.0
Jacksonville	5,690	355.6
Kansas City	5,614	350.9

Leading defenses (yards allowed)

	Total	Per game
Tennessee	3,814	238.4
Baltimore	3,967	247.9
Buffalo	4,426	276.6
Miami	4,636	289.8
Pittsburgh	4,713	294.6

Team statistics

Leading offenses (yards gained)

	Total	Per game
St. Louis	7,075	442.2
San Francisco	6,040	377.5
Minnesota	5,961	372.6
New Orleans	5,397	337.3
Washington	5,396	337.3

Leading defenses (yards allowed)

	Total	Per game
Washington	4,474	279.6
New York Giants	4,546	284.1
New Orleans	4,743	296.4
Tampa Bay	4,800	300.0
Philadelphia	4,820	301.3

Individual statistics

Leading scorers, touchdowns

	TD's	Rush	Rec.	Ret.	Pts.
Edgerrin James, Indianapolis	18	13	5	0	110
Eddie George, Tennessee	16	14	2	0	96
Lamar Smith, Miami	16	14	2	0	96
Mike Anderson, Denver	15	15	0	0	92

Leading scorers, kicking

	PAT made/att.	FG made/att.	Longest FG	Pts.
Matt Stover, Baltimore	30/30	35/39	51	135
Mike Vanderjagt, Indianapolis	46/46	25/27	48	121
Al Del Greco, Tennessee	37/38	27/33	50	118
Olindo Mare, Miami	33/34	28/31	49	117

Leading quarterbacks

	Att.	Comp.	Yds.	TD's	Int.
Brian Griese, Denver	336	216	2,688	19	4
Peyton Manning, Indianapolis	571	357	4,413	33	15
Rich Gannon, Oakland	473	284	3,430	28	11
Elvis Grbac, Kansas City	547	326	4,169	28	14
Doug Flutie, Buffalo	231	132	1,700	8	3

Leading receivers

	Passes caught	Rec. yards	Avg. gain	TD's
Marvin Harrison, Indianapolis	102	1,413	13.9	14
Ed McCaffrey, Denver	101	1,317	13.0	9
Rod Smith, Denver	100	1,602	16.0	8
Keenan McCardell, Jacksonville	94	1,207	12.8	5

Leading rushers

	Rushes	Yards	Avg.	TD's
Edgerrin James, Indianapolis	387	1,709	4.4	13
Eddie George, Tennessee	403	1,509	3.7	14
Mike Anderson, Denver	297	1,500	5.1	15
Corey Dillon, Cincinnati	315	1,435	4.6	7
Fred Taylor, Jacksonville	292	1,399	4.8	12

Leading punters

	Punts	Yards	Avg.	Longest
Darren Bennett, San Diego	92	4,248	46.2	66
Shane Lechler, Oakland	65	2,984	45.9	69
Chris Gardocki, Cleveland	108	4,919	45.5	67
Hunter Smith, Indianapolis	65	2,906	44.7	65

Individual statistics

Leading scorers, touchdowns

	TD's	Rush	Rec.	Ret.	Pts.
Marshall Faulk, St. Louis	26	18	8	0	160
Randy Moss, Minnesota	15	0	15	0	92
Ahman Green, Green Bay	13	10	3	0	78
Terrell Owens, San Francisco	13	0	13	0	80

Leading scorers, kicking

	PAT made/att.	FG made/att.	Longest FG	Pts.
Ryan Longwell, Green Bay	32/32	33/38	52	131
Martin Gramatica, Tampa Bay	42/42	28/34	55	126
Joe Nedney, Carolina	24/24	34/38	52	126
David Akers, Philadelphia	34/36	29/33	51	121

Leading quarterbacks

	Att.	Comp.	Yds.	TD's	Int.
Trent Green, St. Louis	240	145	2,063	16	5
Kurt Warner, St. Louis	347	235	3,429	21	18
Daunte Culpepper, Minnesota	474	297	3,937	33	16
Jeff Garcia, San Francisco	561	355	4,278	31	10
Kerry Collins, New York Giants	529	311	3,610	22	13

Leading receivers

	Passes caught	Rec. yards	Avg. gain	TD's
Muhsin Muhammad, Carolina	102	1,183	11.6	6
Terrell Owens, San Francisco	97	1,451	15.0	13
Cris Carter, Minnesota	96	1,274	13.3	9
Joe Horn, New Orleans	94	1,340	14.3	8

Leading rushers

	Rushes	Yards	Avg.	TD's
Robert Smith, Minnesota	295	1,521	5.2	7
Marshall Faulk, St. Louis	253	1,359	5.4	18
Stephen Davis, Washington	332	1,318	4.0	11
Emmitt Smith, Dallas	294	1,203	4.1	9
James Stewart, Detroit	339	1,184	3.5	10

Leading punters

	Punts	Yards	Avg.	Longest
Mitch Berger, Minnesota	62	2,773	44.7	60
Scott Player, Arizona	65	2,871	44.2	55
John Jett, Detroit	93	4,044	43.5	59
Micah Knorr, Dallas	58	2,485	42.8	60

Florida State quarterback Chris Weinke receives the Heisman Trophy in December 10 as the outstanding college football player in the United States in 2000. At 28, Weinke was the oldest player to ever be awarded the Heisman.

Other 2000 highlights. Notre Dame rebounded from a miserable 1999 season to a 2000 record of nine wins and two losses and an invitation to the Fiesta Bowl against Oregon State on Jan. 1, 2001, in Tempe, Arizona. Oregon State defeated Notre Dame, 41-9.

Pennsylvania State University, a perennial bowl-game contender, finished with a record of five wins and seven losses, the team's worst since Joe Paterno became head coach in 1966. Penn State failed to be invited to play in a bowl game for just the fifth time under Paterno, who still managed in 2000 to record his 322nd victory, leaving him one victory short of the record held by former Alabama coach Paul "Bear" Bryant.

Heisman Trophy. On Dec. 10, 2000, Chris Weinke, quarterback at Florida State University, won a close contest for the Heisman Trophy. Weinke received 1,628 votes, compared with 1,552 votes for the runner-up, University of Oklahoma quarterback Josh Heupel. Weinke led the nation in 2000 with 4,167 yards passing, a school record, and 33 touchdown passes.

Professional. During the 1999-2000 NFL season, St. Louis quarterback Kurt Warner, who was virtually unknown at the beginning of the season, led the upstart Rams to a 23-16 victory in Super Bowl XXXIV over the Tennessee Titans. The

The 2000 college football season

National champions

NCAA Div. I-A*	Oklahoma	13	Florida State	2
NCAA Div. I-AA	Georgia Southern	27	Montana	25
NCAA Div. II	Delta State	63	Bloomsburg	34
NCAA Div. III	Mt. Union	10	St. John's (Minn.)	7
NAIA	Georgetown (Ky.)	20	NW Oklahoma State	0

Bowl games

Bowl	Result			
Alamo	Nebraska	66	Northwestern	17
Aloha	Boston College	31	Arizona State	17
Citrus	Michigan	31	Auburn	28
Cotton	Kansas State	35	Tennessee	21
Fiesta	Oregon State	41	Notre Dame	9
Gator	Virginia Tech	41	Clemson	20
Holiday	Oregon	35	Texas	30
Humanitarian	Boise State	38	Texas-El Paso	23
Independence	Mississippi State	43	Texas A&M	41
Insight.com	Iowa State	37	Pittsburgh	29
Las Vegas	UNLV	31	Arkansas	14
Liberty	Colorado State	22	Louisville	17
MicronPC.com	N. Carolina State	38	Minnesota	30
Mobile Alabama	S. Mississippi	28	Texas Christian	21
Motor City	Marshall	25	Cincinnati	14
Music City	West Virginia	49	Mississippi	38
Oahu	Georgia	37	Virginia	14
Orange*	Oklahoma	13	Florida State	2
Outback	South Carolina	24	Ohio State	7
Peach	LSU	28	Georgia Tech	14
Rose	Washington	34	Purdue	24
Sugar	Miami	37	Florida	20
Sun	Wisconsin	21	UCLA	20

* Championship decided in the Orange Bowl on Jan. 3, 2001.

Conference Champions

NCAA Division I-A

Conference	School
Atlantic Coast	Florida State
Big East	Miami
Big 10	Michigan—Northwestern—Purdue (tie)
Big 12	Oklahoma
Big West	Boise State
Conference USA	Louisville
Mid-American	Marshall
Mountain West	Colorado State
Pacific 10	Oregon—Oregon State—Washington (tie)
Southeastern	Florida
Western Athletic	Texas Christian—Texas-El Paso (tie)

NCAA Division I-AA

Conference	School
Atlantic 10	Delaware—Richmond (tie)
Big Sky	Montana
Gateway	Western Illinois
Ivy League	Pennsylvania
Metro Atlantic	Duquesne
Mid-Eastern	Florida A&M
Northeast	Robert Morris
Ohio Valley	Western Kentucky
Patriot	Lehigh
Pioneer	Dayton—Drake—Valparaiso (tie)
Southern	Georgia Southern
Southland	Troy State
Southwestern	Grambling State

All-America team (as chosen by the Associated Press)

Offense

Quarterback—Chris Weinke, Florida State
Running backs—LaDainian Tomlinson, TCU; Damien Anderson, Northwestern
Wide receivers—Marvin Minnis, Florida State; Antonio Bryant, Pittsburgh
Tight end—Brian Natkin, Texas-El Paso
Center—Dominic Raiola, Nebraska
Other linemen—Steve Hutchinson, Michigan; Leonard Davis, Texas; Chris Brown, Georgia Tech; Chad Ward, Washington
All-purpose player—Santana Moss, Miami-Florida
Place-kicker—Jonathan Ruffin, Cincinnati

Defense

Linemen—Jamal Reynolds, Florida State; John Henderson, Tennessee; Andre Carter, California; Casey Hampton, Texas
Linebackers—Dan Morgan, Miami-Florida; Rocky Calmus, Oklahoma; Keith Adams, Clemson; Carlos Polk, Nebraska
Backs—Edward Reed, Miami-Florida; Fred Smoot, Mississippi State; Dwight Smith, Akron; Jamar Fletcher, Wisconsin
Punter—Nick Harris, California

Player awards

Heisman Trophy (best player)—Chris Weinke, Florida State
Bronko Nagurski Trophy (best defensive player)—Dan Morgan, Miami-Florida
Lombardi Award (best lineman)—Jamal Reynolds, Florida State

Rams, who had finished the previous season with a record of 4-12, made a stunning turnaround and finished the 1999-2000 season with a record of 13-3, second-best in the league behind the Jacksonville Jaguars (14-2). Warner, who got the starting job when quarterback Trent Green suffered a season-ending injury in the preseason, won the NFL Most Valuable Player (MVP) award easily, completing 65 percent of his passes for 4,353 yards and 41 touchdowns.

In the American Football Conference (AFC) wild-card play-offs on January 8 and 9, the Tennessee Titans defeated the Buffalo Bills, 22-16, and the Miami Dolphins beat the Seattle Seahawks, 20-17. One week later, Jacksonville destroyed Miami, 62-7, the second highest point total in NFL postseason history, and Tennessee edged the Indianapolis Colts, 19-16. Tennessee beat Jacksonville, 33-14, in the AFC championship game on January 23.

In the National Football Conference (NFC) wild-card play-offs on January 8 and 9, the Washington Redskins defeated the Detroit Lions, 27-13, and the Minnesota Vikings defeated the Dallas Cowboys, 27-10. The next weekend, the Tampa Bay Buccaneers edged Washington, 14-13, and St. Louis outgunned Minnesota, 49-37. St. Louis edged Tampa Bay, 11-6, to win the NFC championship on January 23.

On January 30 in Atlanta, St. Louis won the Super Bowl, 23-16. The St. Louis defense stopped Tennessee wide receiver Kevin Dyson at the one-yard line as time expired, preventing what would have been Tennessee's game-tying score. Warner, a former Arena Football League player, threw for two touchdowns and 414 yards, a Super Bowl record. He was named Super Bowl MVP.

The 2000-2001 season. Injuries to two players—quarterback Kurt Warner and running back Marshall Faulk—hurt the Rams' chances of repeating as NFL champions. The Rams staggered through the late part of the season but garnered a wild-card play-off spot behind the New Orleans Saints. The Minnesota Vikings earned a play-off appearance with the best record in the NFC Central, led by quarterback Daunte Culpepper. The Washington Redskins, an early favorite, saw their record fall to 7-6 after a 9-7 loss to the New York Giants on December 3.

In the AFC, Miami Dolphins coach Dave Wannstedt had his team leading the AFC East and vying for the best record in the conference in 2000. Tennessee was locked in a tough battle with the Baltimore Ravens in the AFC Central, and the Oakland Raiders, a surprise in their own right, battled the Denver Broncos for dominance in the AFC West.

Milestones. On Oct. 22, 2000, Cincinnati Bengals running back Corey Dillon ran for an NFL-record 278 yards, breaking a record held by former Chicago Bears great Walter Payton. Payton, who died in 1999, had rushed for 275 yards against Minnesota on Nov. 20, 1977.

On Dec. 3, 2000, Green Bay quarterback Brett Favre threw for more than 3,000 yards in a single season for the ninth straight time, tying former Miami Dolphins quarterback Dan Marino.

On November 30, Minnesota Vikings wide receiver Cris Carter became the second player in NFL history after San Francisco's Jerry Rice to catch 1,000 passes in a career.

Two of the game's great quarterbacks—Steve Young of the San Francisco 49ers and Dan Marino of the Miami Dolphins—retired in 2000. Young called it quits on June 12. He won one Super Bowl as a starter, in 1995, earning Super Bowl MVP honors, and received two Super Bowl rings as a backup quarterback. Marino, who threw for 420 touchdown passes but never won a Super Bowl, retired on March 13, 2000.

Other leagues. The British Columbia Lions defeated the Montreal Alouettes, 28-26, on November 26 in Calgary to win the Canadian Football League (CFL) Grey Cup championship. The Rhein Fire won their second NFL Europe championship in three years with a 13-10 win over the Scottish Claymores on June 25 in Frankfurt, Germany. □ Michael Kates

France. Allegations of corruption and illegal party funding plagued France's political leaders in 2000. The most notorious allegation surfaced in September when the newspaper *Le Monde* published claims that President Jacques Chirac had overseen a system of illegal kickbacks to fund his party, the Rally for the Republic (RPR), while he served as mayor of Paris and prime minister during the 1980's. Chirac denied the allegations. The newspaper released a videotape made in 1996 by Jean-Claude Mery, a real-estate developer and former RPR fundraiser, in which Mery claimed to have raised over $1 million for the party from kickbacks on public housing contracts in Paris. Mery died in 1999.

The story quickly backfired against Chirac's Socialist opponents when it was discovered that the Mery tape had been kept for some time by Socialist Dominique Strauss-Kahn. Strauss-Kahn had resigned as finance minister in 1999 over unrelated corruption charges. Political insiders suggested that the tape had been held for possible blackmail instead of being turned over to prosecutors as the law demanded. Strauss-Kahn denied knowledge of the tape's contents.

Roland Dumas, the president of the Constitutional Council, France's highest legal body, resigned in March 2000 following his indictment on February 18 on charges of conspiracy and misappropriation of more than $10 million in public funds. The charges against Dumas stemmed from a long investigation of alleged corruption in the early 1990's at Elf Aquitaine, the former state-owned oil company taken over by TotalFina S.A. in 1999. Dumas, who was foreign minister at the time, denied the charges.

In April 2000, prosecutors examining the collapse in the early 1990's of the bank Credit Lyonnais S.A. began investigating the governor of the Bank of France, Jean-Claude Trichet. Trichet, as a senior finance ministry official, had supervised the government bailout of Credit Lyonnais at a cost of more than $25 billion. He denied any wrongdoing, but the inquiry raised doubts about his ability to succeed Wim Duisenberg as head of the European Central Bank around 2002, as planned.

Presidency referendum. French voters approved a constitutional change to shorten the president's term of office to five years from seven in a referendum on Sept. 24, 2000. The reform, which was to take effect in 2002, would make the president's term coincide with the five-year term of parliament.

Economy strengthens. France enjoyed its best economic performance in more than a decade in 2000, as low interest rates and rising personal incomes boosted the confidence of companies and consumers. Economists expected the *gross domestic product* (the value of all goods and services produced in a year) to grow by 3.7 percent during 2000, up from 2.8 percent in 1999. The rapid growth reduced the unemployment rate to 10 percent for the first time since 1992.

The buoyant economy also helped shrink the budget deficit and enabled the government of Prime Minister Lionel Jospin to significantly reduce taxes. In April 2000, Finance Minister Laurent Fabius announced cuts in income taxes and *value-added* taxes (a type of sales tax) totaling $5 billion for the year. On August 31, Fabius announced a three-year program of tax cuts worth $16 billion, which was to begin in 2001.

Fuel tax protests. French truckers and farmers attacked the government in September 2000 over the high price of gasoline. The protestors caused

fuel shortages across France by blocking refineries with their vehicles. They lifted the blockades after the French government agreed to provide some rebates on fuel taxes. The protests spread to other European countries, where high taxes and rises in world oil prices pushed gasoline prices above $4 a gallon.

Takeovers. Several big French companies moved in 2000 to strengthen their global positions through acquisitions. France Telecom S.A., the national telephone company, agreed on

During a July 27 memorial service at the Church of La Madeleine in Paris, a candle burns on the altar for each of the 113 victims of the July 25 crash of an Air France Concorde jet.

March 23 to buy 29 percent of MobilCom AG, a German telephone company, to gain a presence in Europe's biggest market. On May 30, France Telecom agreed to buy Orange Plc, a British mobile telephone operator, for $40 billion. Vivendi S.A., a major French utility and media company, agreed on June 20 to buy Seagram Company, a Canadian liquor and media firm, for $34 billion. Vivendi hoped that acquiring Seagram's Universal film studio and music business would transform the company into a global media giant able to rival the merger of America Online, Incorporated and Time Warner, Incorporated.

Corsica. The Jospin government made Corsica, a French island in the Mediterranean Sea, an unprecedented offer of regional autonomy in a bid to end separatist violence on the island. Violence had worsened since separatists killed the senior French official on Corsica in 1998. Under a plan agreed to by Jospin and moderate Corsican leaders on July 20, 2000, France would allow the Corsican assembly to modify French laws to fit local needs. The plan included the possibility of giving Corsica the authority to pass its own laws in 2004. Interior Minister Jean-Pierre Chevenement resigned from the government to protest the plan, saying it would fuel separatist demands in other regions.   □ Tom Buerkle

See also **Disasters; Europe.**

Gardening. Environmental issues resulting from developments in the field of genetic engineering sparked considerable controversy in 2000. Scientists began to experiment with creating longer-lasting blooms on flowers and developing slower-growing grass. The Scotts Company, a producer of lawn pesticides and fertilizers in Marysville, Ohio, in alliance with the Monsanto Company of St. Louis, Missouri, continued in 2000 to develop a lawn grass bioengineered to withstand multiple applications of potent weedkillers. The companies expected to market the product to the public in about three years.

Environmental issues. Many environmentalists feared that such genetically engineered plants might cause significant problems if they came into common use. Drifting pollen from bioengineered grass, for example, could result in the interbreeding of herbicideproof grass and wild grass, potentially creating uncontrollable weeds.

In June, the 14,000-member American Society of Landscape Architects petitioned the U.S. Department of Agriculture (USDA) to suspend field tests on new grasses. The group wanted an organization other than Scotts and Monsanto to assess the risks of bioengineered grass. In May, a group called the Anarchist Golfing Association had vandalized a Scotts Company research center in Oregon, causing $300,000 worth of damage.

The Japanese Hill-and-Pond Garden in Brooklyn, New York, reopened in 2000 after a $3-million renovation. The garden, the first public Japanese garden in the United States, was designed in 1915.

Research. Biologists at the University of California in San Diego and the Max Planck Institute for Breeding Research in Cologne, Germany, announced in 2000 that they had discovered the master genes that regulate the development of flowers. By turning on genes located in the leaves of flowers, which are normally turned off, the researchers said, they may be able to produce different varieties of plants and substitute colorful petals for normal foliage.

In May, a Brazilian team of more than 200 researchers released the first fully decoded DNA (Deoxyribonucleic acid, the molecule that carries the genetic code) for sequence of *Xylella fastidiosa*, a mysterious bacterium that attacks plants. The study was universally hailed as a gateway to advancements in controlling plant diseases.

Competition. A unique multimillion dollar horticultural competition called Mosaiculture International 2000 was presented in Montreal from June through October. The exhibit was located in Parc des Ecluses at the Port of Old Montreal. Exhibitors from 14 countries demonstrated the art of mosaiculture by creating pictures and three-dimensional sculptures using thousands of small plants of various colors and textures. A two-story dragon, made up of 3,000 begonias, created by craftsmen from China, won the top award.

Planting trees. In an attempt to promote the planting of trees, the USDA, working with the U.S. Forest Service, offered each state a hundred saplings from trees with historic associations. These included a redbud from the Maryland residence of American Red Cross founder Clara Barton; a tulip poplar George Washington had planted at Mount Vernon, Virginia; a crabapple tree from near President John F. Kennedy's gravesite at the Arlington National Cemetery; and an apple tree planted by pioneer John Chapman, known as Johnny Appleseed.

Rooftop garden. Chicago became greener in 2000 when Mayor Richard M. Daley had a garden installed on the roof of city hall in May. The garden, which contained 20,000 plants including two full-sized trees, was expected to reduce energy bills at city hall and serve as a prototype for other rooftop gardens.

Trends. Meditation gardens grew in popularity in 2000 throughout the United States. The gardens, scenic places for reflection, were usually found in cemeteries and around churches. Another popular gardening trend in 2000 included landscaping designed according to the ancient principles of fengshui, a Chinese system believed by some to balance the energy patterns of the physical environment.   □ Carol M. Stocker

Gas and gasoline. See **Energy supply.**

Genetic engineering. See **Agriculture; Biology; Medicine.**

Geology. Geologists at the Danish Center for Earth System Science reported evidence in April 2000 that low concentrations of oxygen in the Earth's atmosphere prevented animal life from diversifying until relatively late in geologic history. The atmosphere today contains about 21 percent oxygen, a gas that is vital to the survival of animal life on Earth. But when the Earth was formed, its atmosphere contained almost no oxygen. Geologists have debated for decades as to exactly when Earth's atmosphere developed enough oxygen to support complex animal life.

Geologists have found a connection between past oxygen levels and sedimentary deposits of sulfates, compounds containing sulfur and oxygen atoms. Sulfates form when certain types of bacteria process nutrients or when there is a high concentration of oxygen in the atmosphere. Scientists previously had studied sulfates in ancient sedimentary rocks but did not know whether the sulfates came from ancient bacteria or whether they indicated an oxygen-rich atmosphere. In order to better recognize properties of sulfates produced by ancient bacteria, geologists studied similar modern-day bacteria in the Gulf of California.

Donald E. Canfield, Kirsten S. Habicht, and Bo Thamdrup studied how bacteria processed sulfates in different temperatures near an active hydrothermal vent in the ocean. Canfield and his colleagues calculated that ancient sedimentary sulfates probably came from early bacteria. They then concluded that significant amounts of atmospheric oxygen did not accumulate until the late Proterozoic Era (and 700 million years ago), around the time when there was a great explosion in the diversity of animal life.

Ice ages and carbon dioxide. Geologist Nicholas J. Shackleton of Cambridge University in England reported evidence in September 2000 that atmospheric concentrations of carbon dioxide gas are closely tied to cycles of ice ages. Scientists have long been aware that Earth's Northern Hemisphere experienced cycles of ice ages, during which large ice sheets expanded and contracted across northern Asia, Europe, and North America. Throughout the past 1 million years, the great ice sheets waxed and waned about every 100,000 years in step with *eccentricity* (the shape of Earth's orbit). Geologists believed that changes in eccentricity were related to the cycle of ice ages.

Because of eccentricity, Earth would be farther from the sun at times and receive less heat. The changes in heat, however, are not great enough to directly drive the ice ages. One suggested explanation is that small changes in heat could produce small changes in the sizes of ice sheets that would, in turn, trigger even larger changes. Another hypothesis is that the ice-age

Mount Usu erupts near Abuta, Japan, on March 31, 2000, forcing residents to evacuate. The eruption spewed rocks, gas, and ash over the countryside of Hokkaido, Japan's northernmost large island.

cycle is driven directly by changes in the *green-house effect* (warming of the atmosphere caused by certain gases, including carbon dioxide).

Shackleton examined the composition of ancient Antarctic ice. He found that during the 100,000-year cycle, temperatures and atmospheric carbon dioxide changed together with eccentricity. However, changes in the size of the ice sheets lagged behind. Shackleton concluded that the 100,000-year cycle was not driven by ice sheet changes but rather by a greenhouse effect. His findings indicated a direct link between global climate cycles and atmospheric carbon dioxide concentrations, further strengthening concerns about global warming. However, geologists still do not understand why eccentricity variations were connected with changes in the concentration of atmospheric carbon dioxide.

Deep-sea burps. Geologists from the University of California at Santa Barbara and California State University in Long Beach reported in April the first direct evidence that linked global climate change to releases of methane from the ocean. Methane, made up of carbon and hydrogen atoms, is a greenhouse gas. Huge reserves of frozen methane are stored in sediments deep in the ocean.

James P. Kennett, Kevin G. Cannariato, Ingrid L. Hendy, and Richard J. Behl discovered that sediments in the Santa Barbara Basin in the ocean near California were layered in a pattern that coincided with changes in concentrations of methane found in ice cores. Methane from the atmosphere was trapped in the ice found in polar regions. The geologists documented brief, catastrophic episodes of methane release from sediments at the bottom of the basin. They found that the releases coincided with warming water temperatures that melted the frozen methane and "burped" large volumes of methane gas into the ocean and ultimately into the atmosphere.

Tsunami threat in U.S. In May, geologists warned that changes in the shape of the Atlantic Ocean floor might contribute to the creation of a *tsunami* (a large sea wave caused by an undersea earthquake) off the East Coast of the United States—anywhere from Maryland to North Carolina. Neal W. Driscoll of the Woods Hole Oceanographic Institution in Massachusetts, Jeffrey K. Weissel of Columbia University in New York City, and John A. Goff of the University of Texas in Austin mapped a system of *faults* (breaks in the Earth's crust) off the shores of North Carolina and southern Virginia. They suggested that if the cracks were the precursors of a major submarine landslide, the landslide could generate a tsunami in the Atlantic Ocean.

☐ Henry T. Mullins

Georgia. President Eduard Shevardnadze was elected to a second five-year term in April 2000. Shevardnadze won 80 percent of the vote after one of his chief rivals, Aslan Abashidze, withdrew on the eve of the election. Observers from the Organization for Security and Cooperation in Europe (OSCE), an international security group that monitors elections, charged that the election was marred by extensive fraud, including the stuffing of ballot boxes and tampering with vote totals.

Abashidze, the leader of the regional government of Adjaria, dropped out of the presidential race after Shevardnadze agreed to recognize Adjaria's autonomy in the Georgian Constitution. In June, Adjaria adopted its own constitution, a move that experts on international affairs believed could rekindle tensions within Georgia.

The International Monetary Fund (IMF), a United Nations-affiliated organization that provides short-term credit to member nations, suspended its loan programs in Georgia in June in response to continued budget shortfalls. As a result, the Georgian government cut its budget in half, and Shevardnadze launched a major anticorruption campaign in July to address the concerns of international donors and investors.

☐ Steven L. Solnick

See also **Asia.**

Georgia. See **State government.**

Germany began to emerge from nearly a decade of economic stagnation in 2000, as growth accelerated and the government initiated labor and tax reforms. The improvement enabled Chancellor Gerhard Schroeder to claim that the country was shaking off the so-called "German disease" of high tax rates, high unemployment, and an exodus of investment capital that depressed the economy throughout the 1990's.

In 2000, Germany benefited from an economic recovery across Europe that was fueled by strong consumer and business confidence at home and a weak euro, which made European goods cheaper on world markets. The country's *gross domestic product* (the value of all goods and services produced in a year) was projected to grow by 3 percent in 2000, up from 1.5 percent in 1999 and the best growth rate in a decade. The growth helped reduce the unemployment rate to 9.4 percent in 2000 from 10.2 percent in 1999.

Economic reforms. Schroeder took advantage of the recovery to pursue labor and tax reforms that were designed to sustain growth and boost Germany's competitiveness. On Jan. 9, 2000, the government reached an accord with unions and industry in which workers agreed to accept long-term wage restraint in exchange for a new system of early retirement. During the following months, the country's largest union, IG

Metall, arranged two-year wage agreements with several key industrial groups that contained pay increases averaging just over 5 percent. The settlements were a big departure from the bitter annual pay negotiations and large wage increases that many economists believed had harmed Germany's economy during the 1990's.

Schroeder then turned his attention to Germany's high tax rates, a consequence of the costly unification of the former West and East Germanies in 1990. After weeks of political jockeying with the opposition Christian Democratic Party, which controlled the upper house of parliament, Schroeder's Social Democratic government on July 14, 2000, won parliamentary approval for a five-year program of tax cuts. The cuts, which totaled around $25 billion, would gradually lower the top income-tax rate from 51 percent in 2000 to 42 percent in 2005. The measure would also slash the corporate tax rate from 40 percent to 25 percent in 2001. German companies had argued that high tax rates deterred investment.

In September 2000, Germany's labor minister, Walter Riester, proposed the first major reform of the pension system in decades. Under the proposal, the government would make modest and gradual cuts in state retirement benefits while offering tax incentives for workers to invest in their own private retirement accounts.

Opposition turmoil. Schroeder succeeded in getting his reforms adopted largely because of the weakness of the opposition Christian Democrats, who suffered from continued allegations of illegal funding under former Chancellor Helmut Kohl. The funding was first uncovered as part of a tax investigation in November 1999.

On Jan. 18, 2000, Kohl resigned from his post as honorary chairman of the Christian Democrats. Two days later, the Bundestag, or lower house of parliament, began an investigation into the affair. Kohl admitted that he had received $1 million in secret donations to the party while he served as chancellor during the 1990's, but he insisted that his government had not granted any favors in exchange for the funds. He refused to name the donors when called to testify in the Bundestag, saying it was a matter of honor to preserve their anonymity.

The Christian Democrats sought to make a clean break from the past by electing Angela Merkel, a physicist-turned-politician from the former East Germany, as its new leader on April 10, 2000. Merkel was the first senior party official to criticize Kohl over the funding scandal, and she became the first woman to lead a major German political party. The Christian Democrats suffered at the polls, however. The party, which defeated Schroeder's Social Democrats in six out of eight

On November 9, protestors in Dresden spell out "This city is tired of Nazis" in support of the government's call for a ban on the far-right National Democratic Party. The party had been implicated in a number of attacks made on foreigners and Jews in 2000.

state elections in 1999, suffered defeats in elections in the state of Schleswig-Holstein in February 2000 and North Rhine-Westphalia in May.

Racism. Germany struggled to deal with acts of racist violence throughout 2000. A number of attacks on foreigners and Jews during the year prompted the government in November to request that the Constitutional Court ban the far-right National Democratic Party. Interior Minister Otto Schily stated that the government had found evidence that implicated the party in rallying youths for the attacks.

Immigration. In May, the government approved a plan to admit as many as 20,000 foreign workers to Germany to help the country's high-tech industries. The plan, modeled on the U.S. green-card system, was designed to lure software programmers and other technology specialists from areas such as Eastern Europe and India.

Nuclear power. In June, the government reached an agreement with the electrical-generating industry to phase out Germany's nuclear power plants over a period of approximately 20 years. The agreement set the most ambitious target for closing nuclear plants of any major country. Germany's 19 nuclear plants provided one-third of the country's electric power in 2000. Their closure was the biggest environmental goal of the Green Party, which served in the coalition government with Schroeder's Social Democrats.

Merger activity. The first successful hostile takeover of a German company by a foreign firm took place in 2000. Mannesmann AG, which owned Germany's largest mobile telephone company, lost a three-month battle to remain independent by agreeing on February 3 to be acquired by Vodafone AirTouch Plc, a British mobile phone company. The record deal, worth about $160 billion, highlighted the value of Europe's fast-growing mobile telephone industry.

Other German companies moved to strengthen their global presence with take-overs. Deutsche Telekom AG, the country's largest phone company, agreed in July to acquire VoiceStream Wireless Corporation of Bellevue, Washington, for about $50 billion. Regulatory approval of the deal was pending at the end of the year. DaimlerChrysler AG agreed in March to buy 34 percent of Mitsubishi Motors Corp. of Japan for $2 billion and retain an option to gain full control in three years. Bertelsmann AG, the music and publishing company, agreed on July 20 to buy CDNow, Incorporated, the U.S. online music retailer, for $117 million.

Deutsche Bank AG agreed on March 8 to buy its German rival, Dresdner Bank AG, for $30 billion, only to see Dresdner pull out of the deal a month later because of disputes over strategy. Dresdner subsequently announced plans to cut

5,000 jobs, and in September, it agreed to buy the U.S. investment bank, Wasserstein Perella & Company, for $1.4 billion. Deutsche Boerse AG, the company that owns the Frankfurt stock exchange, agreed in May to merge with the London Stock Exchange Plc and form a pan-European exchange, but the deal collapsed in September because of opposition from members of the London exchange.

Bayerische Motoren Werke AG (BMW) agreed to sell its unprofitable British subsidiary, Rover Cars Group, in May 2000. BMW sold Rover's passenger-car operations to Phoenix, a consortium of British business leaders, for a symbolic $15. It sold Rover's profitable Land Rover unit to Ford Motor Company of Dearborn, Michigan, for $2.7 billion.

Army reform. Defense Minister Rudolf Scharping announced in October plans to overhaul the German army, making it a smaller and more mobile force. The plan called for scaling back conscription and reducing the army from 338,000 people to 282,000 people by 2004. The changes echoed similar reforms in France and Britain and reflected Europe's need to quickly respond to new types of military missions, such as peacekeeping.   □ Tom Buerkle

See also **Europe.**

Ghana. See **Africa.**

Golf. Tiger Woods dominated golf in 2000 in a way no man or woman ever had before. He captured three of the Professional Golfers' Association's (PGA) four major titles and, at age 24, became the youngest player in history to complete a career Grand Slam (winning all four majors). Karrie Webb's two major titles in the Ladies Professional Golf Association (LPGA) were also big news, but 2000 was Tiger's year.

PGA. Vijay Singh fought off David Duval, Ernie Els, and Tiger Woods to capture the Masters on April 9 at Augusta National Golf Club in Augusta, Georgia. Singh's 3-under 69 on the final day gave him a score of 10-under for the tournament, three shots better than Els.

Woods's domination over the rest of the season began when he blasted the field at the U.S. Open in Pebble Beach, California. On the final day, June 18, Woods finished 4 under par to win by a record 15 strokes. He was a record 12 under par for the tournament.

For an encore, Woods went on to dominate the British Open at St. Andrews, Scotland. He completed his career Grand Slam on July 23, firing a 3-under 69 on the final day to score a record-low 19 under par. Woods finished a commanding eight strokes ahead of Els and Thomas Bjorn.

Woods followed this victory with a gutsy performance at the PGA Championship in Louisville, Kentucky, where he engaged in a sizzling duel with relatively unknown Bob May on August 20. Woods and May battled like two heavyweight prizefighters, each sinking five birdies and shooting 31 on the back nine. May sank an 18-foot birdie putt on the 18th, but Woods responded with a six-foot birdie to tie the score at 18-under and force a play-off. Woods then won the three-hole play-off by one stroke, sealing the title with a two-foot par putt. With his victory, Woods became the first player to win three majors in a single year since Ben Hogan did so in 1953.

LPGA. Karrie Webb dominated the field in the women's first major event, the Nabisco Championship, at Mission Hills Country Club in Rancho Mirage, California. Webb connected for a hole-in-one on the fifth hole on her way to a final-round score of 2-under-par 70 on March 26. She finished 14-under for the tournament, cruising to a record 10-stroke victory and taking her fourth win in five tournaments to open the year.

Juli Inkster survived a 4-over-par final round to win the LPGA Championship on June 25 at the DuPont Country Club in Wilmington, Delaware. Inkster defeated little-known Stefania Croce on the second playoff hole to become the tournament's third-ever back-to-back winner.

Webb reclaimed her place atop the leader board in the season's third major, claiming the U.S. Open by five shots at the Merit Club in Gurnee, Illinois, on July 23. Webb struggled through the first half of her final round but finished at 6 under par to best Meg Mallon and Cristie Kerr. Webb's win assured her of enough points to qualify for the LPGA Hall of Fame.

Mallon claimed the final major of the year, winning the du Maurier Classic in Aylmer, Quebec, Canada, in August. Mallon had not won a major tournament in nine years.

Senior PGA. Tom Kite birdied the sixth hole of a play-off to beat Tom Watson in the Countrywide Tradition on April 2 in Scottsdale, Arizona. Larry Nelson made the play-off but bogeyed the second hole, leaving only Kite and Watson.

Doug Tewell captured a rain-delayed PGA Seniors' Championship on April 17 in Palm Beach Gardens, Florida. Tewell shot a final-round 5-under-par to win his first major by seven strokes.

Hale Irwin fired a 6-under-par 65 on the final day to win the U.S. Senior Open in Bethlehem, Pennsylvania. Irwin's 17-under total of 267 was the lowest in the history of the event.

Ray Floyd birdied three of his last four holes to win the Ford Senior Players Championship on July 16 in Dearborn, Michigan, with a score of 15 under par. Floyd won the title by one stroke when Dana Quigley bogeyed the 18th hole.　□ Michael Kates

Great Britain. See **United Kingdom.**

Tiger Woods tees off July 22 at the 18th hole of the Old Course at St. Andrews, Scotland, during the British Open. Woods won the tournament, shooting a record 19-under par, becoming the youngest golfer ever to win all four majors in a career.

Greece. The Socialist government of Prime Minister Costas Simitis won reelection in 2000 by promising to lead Greece into the mainstream of the European Union (EU). Simitis's Socialist Party, known by its Greek acronym PASOK, won 158 seats in the 300-seat parliament in the April 9 election. The conservative opposition party, New Democracy, took 125 seats.

The result represented a public seal of approval for Simitis's programs. Over the previous four years, the prime minister had abandoned PASOK's radical past and pursued the moderate, market-oriented policies favored by most of Europe's center-left governments. Those policies helped end the slow growth, double-digit inflation, and massive budget deficits that plagued Greece from the mid-1970's into the mid-1990's. According to EU estimates, economic growth in Greece was expected to reach nearly 4 percent in 2000. The EU estimated that inflation would be no higher than 2.3 percent and the budget deficit only 1.3 percent of gross domestic product, both close to EU averages. The EU agreed in June that Greece had fulfilled the requirements for joining the euro on schedule to adopt the single currency in January 2001.

The government continued its economic reforms in 2000, including the privatization of state-owned companies. It sold 15 percent stakes in CosmOTE, a mobile telephone company, and OPAP, the national lottery.

Ties with Turkey. Greece signed a series of agreements in 2000 aimed at improving relations with neighboring Turkey. The agreements—including measures to foster investment between the two countries, promote tourism, and protect the Aegean Sea environment—were signed in January and February. The two countries had come close to war several times since Turkey invaded the predominantly ethnic-Greek island of Cyprus in 1974, but relations improved in 1999, after earthquakes in Greece and Turkey generated waves of sympathy in both countries.

Ferry sinks. A ferry traveling between Greece's Aegean Islands sank near the island of Paros on Sept. 26, 2000, killing 66 passengers. Authorities charged the captain and several crew members with murder, alleging they had put the boat on automatic pilot to watch a soccer match on television.

Terrorism. The government of Greece promised to crack down on terrorism after the leftist guerrilla group known as November 17 murdered a British military representative on an Athens street in June. The United States had criticized Greece in the past for being lax on terrorists. ☐ Tom Buerkle

See also **Europe; Turkey.**

Grenada. See **Latin America.**

Guatemala. Alfonso Portillo Cabrera, of the right-wing Guatemalan Republican Front, was sworn to a four-year term as president of Guatemala on Jan. 14, 2000. The 48-year-old attorney and economist pledged to reduce crime and the growing gap between rich and poor.

Arrests in slaying. Guatemalan police arrested three military officers in January for the 1998 slaying of Roman Catholic Bishop Juan Gerardi Conedera. Conedera was bludgeoned to death two days after he had reported human rights abuses committed by the armed forces.

Report on missing children. The archdiocese of Guatemala issued a report in August 2000 blaming the armed forces for hundreds of abductions of children during the 36-year-long civil war that ended in 1996. According to the report, many of the children were illegally adopted by soldiers or taken to orphanages.

Televised executions. Guatemalan authorities permitted television stations to air live coverage in June 2000 of the execution by lethal injection of two convicted murderers. The men had been found guilty of the 1997 kidnapping and killing of an 80-year-old heiress to a liquor fortune. ☐ Nathan A. Haverstock

See also **Latin America.**

Guinea. See **Africa.**

Guyana. See **Latin America.**

Haiti. Former Haitian President Jean-Bertrand Aristide claimed victory in Haiti's presidential election on Nov. 26, 2000. Opposition candidates had boycotted the election, however, claiming it was a "farce." Aristide's opponents were angered by the way he allegedly rigged three sets of legislative and municipal elections earlier in 2000, beginning on May 21. To decide disputed races, Haitians went to the polls again on June 11 and July 9. By the third round of voting, the election process, according to international observers, had become hopelessly tainted.

Following the presidential election, opposition parties pledged to create an alternative "legitimate" government. Aristide had been ousted in a military coup (overthrow) in 1991, but he had been restored to power in 1994 by U.S. military forces and served through 1996.

Amid continuing turmoil in 2000, many Haitians were willing to risk their lives in order to flee the poverty and repression of their native country. In April, two Haitians died and dozens suffered dehydration and hypothermia when the boat in which they were attempting to reach the United States on ran aground in the southern Bahamas. ☐ Nathan A. Haverstock

See **Latin America.**

Harness racing. See **Horse racing.**

Hawaii. See **State government.**

Health care issues. United States President Bill Clinton announced regulations in December 2000 providing patients with greater control over and access to their health records. The rules, designed to balance the issue of privacy with public safety, established guidelines for the use and release of health care records and strengthened existing privacy protections.

The candidates and drug coverage. In 2000, public complaints about the high cost of prescription drugs became a major political issue. Both U.S. presidential candidates attempted to address the problem, which was particularly acute for people on Medicare, the federal program that pays for much of the health care used by Americans over the age of 65. Medicare did not cover costs of prescription drugs used outside of hospitals, and many people on Medicare found it difficult to pay for their prescriptions.

Vice President Al Gore, the Democratic candidate, and Texas Governor George W. Bush, the Republican candidate, both offered Medicare drug proposals that were variations of programs that had been advanced by their parties. Gore's proposal was similar to the program proposed by President Clinton in June 1999, under which seniors could pay modest premiums to Medicare, which would pay up to half the price of prescription drugs up to $5,000. Similarly, Bush offered a plan like the one that Republican leaders in Congress had earlier set forth, in which subsidies for prescription drugs would be offered to beneficiaries with incomes below a certain percentage of the federal poverty line. Bush also proposed to subsidize special prescription drug coverage sold by private insurers.

Reforming Medicare. Both candidates advocated changes in Medicare overall. Gore defended the traditional Medicare structure, which allowed seniors to join private managed care plans if they wished, but also gave them the option of staying in the original program. Bush proposed a restructuring of the entire Medicare program, featuring strong incentives for Medicare beneficiaries to buy federally subsidized private insurance. Gore and Bush and the leaders of both political parties promised to use part of the projected federal budget surplus to keep Medicare fully funded. However, the U.S. Congress made no major revisions to the Medicare program in 2000.

Reimportation. Congress did pass legislation in October that rescinded a federal ban on the reimportation of U.S.-made prescription drugs from foreign countries. Such drugs typically sell for less in Canada and Mexico than they do in the United States. U.S. citizens reimport them to save money. In late December, President Clinton terminated the program that implemented the law.

Patient protection and managed care. Critics of managed care for some time have called for federal legislation to strengthen the rights of patients who believe they have been wronged by their insurers. The House passed a bill addressing some managed care issues in 1999. The Senate passed its own version in June 2000. The bills remained unreconciled at the end of 2000.

Health insurance. The U.S. Census Bureau reported in September that fewer people in the United States were uninsured in 1999 than in 1998, reversing a long downward trend. Uninsured people in the United States totaled 42.6 million in 1999 versus 44.3 million in 1998. Officials also reported in 2000 that enrollment in Medicaid, the federal program that covers some health care costs for low-income groups, was up by 1.1 million in 1999, totaling 32 million people.

The U.S. Supreme Court made rulings in 2000 that significantly affected health care in the United States. The justices ruled in March that the U.S. Food and Drug Administration did not have the right to regulate tobacco as a drug. In June, the court struck down a Nebraska law that barred physicians from performing an abortion procedure that is usually performed late in a pregnancy. On August 29, the Court issued an emergency order overturning a 1996 California referendum allowing marijuana use for medical purposes.

☐ Emily Friedman

See also **Public health and safety.**

Hinduism. In 2000, the Hindu nationalist Bharatiya Janata Party (BJP), which led India's fractious coalition government, maintained moderation in pursuing its Hindu-centered goals. The BJP took steps to distance itself from some of the radical Hindu nationalist policies of its parent group, the Rashtriya Swayamsevak Sangh (RSS), and in September announced its intention to seek support from Muslims and other minorities. Opponents of the BJP accused the party of trying to disguise a Hindu nationalist agenda that included persecution of religious minorities.

Hindu nationalism. Hindu nationalist extremists in India continued in 2000 to condone the use of violence in the name of preserving Hindu culture. The RSS, the Vishwa Hindu Parishad (VHP), and the Bajrang Dal were among Hindu nationalist groups linked to attacks on Muslims and Christians. The states of Gujarat and Uttar Pradesh lifted bans on civil servants joining the RSS, causing concern among minority groups.

In July 2000, a court in Mumbai in Maharashtra state dismissed criminal charges against Balasaheb Thackeray, leader of the militant Hindu nationalist party Shiv Sena, for inciting riots in 1992 and 1993 in which thousands of Muslims were killed. The Maharashtra government launched an appeal of the decision in August 2000.

Canadian filmmaker Deepa Mehta was forced

by several Hindu fundamentalist groups, including the VHP and Shiv Sena, to abandon efforts to shoot a controversial film in the Hindu holy city of Varanasi in Uttar Pradesh in February 2000. The groups had staged violent demonstrations protesting the making of the film, saying it was offensive to Hinduism. The plot concerned young Hindu widows forced into prostitution.

Hindu pilgrims killed. In August, 23 Hindu pilgrims were among approximately 30 people killed in a shootout between Muslim separatists and Indian soldiers at a pilgrim camp near Pahalgam in the state of Jammu and Kashmir. The incident was one of several that took place in the region in the days following a cease-fire offer by the Hizbul Mujahideen, Kashmir's largest armed separatist group. Nearly 100 people, mainly Hindu civilians, were killed in the violence. The Kashmir region, which was claimed by both India and Pakistan, had been in dispute since 1947 and the scene of a bloody guerrilla war since 1989.

New Hindu temple in Canada. Construction began in July 2000 in Toronto, Canada, on the Shree Swaminarayan Mandir, a Hindu temple that organizers said would be the largest in Canada and one of the five largest in North America. ☐ Brian Bouldrey

See also **India**.

Hobbies. See Toys and games.

Hockey.
The National Hockey League (NHL) 1999-2000 season culminated with the New Jersey Devils winning their second Stanley Cup in six seasons. The Devils defeated the Dallas Stars, 2-1 on June 10 in Dallas, on center Jason Arnott's goal in double overtime. Arnott's goal capped a thrilling Stanley Cup finals, which New Jersey clinched, 4 games to 2. Game 5 of the series, which Dallas won, 1-0, in triple overtime, was the fourth-longest game in Stanley Cup finals history.

Season. The St. Louis Blues led the NHL with 51 victories and 114 points over the 82-game regular season. The Philadelphia Flyers posted the best record in the Eastern Conference with 105 points, just ahead of New Jersey (103) and the other divisional winners, Washington (102) and Toronto (100). Detroit had the second-best record with 108 points, while Dallas (102) and Colorado (96) also claimed division titles.

Play-offs. The Devils reached the Stanley Cup finals by sweeping the Florida Panthers in four games. They eliminated Toronto 4 games to 2 and edged the Philadelphia Flyers 4 games to 3 for the Eastern Conference title. The Flyers took an early 3-games-to-1 lead, but the Devils rallied to take the series.

The Stars beat Edmonton 4 games to 1 in the first round and defeated upstart San Jose 4 games to 1 in the conference semifinals. San Jose

National Hockey League standings

Western Conference

Central Division	W.	L.	T.	Pts.
St. Louis Blues*	51	20	11	114
Detroit Red Wings*	48	24	10	108
Chicago Blackhawks	33	39	10	78
Nashville Predators	28	47	7	70
Northwest Division				
Colorado Avalanche*	42	29	11	96
Edmonton Oilers*	32	34	16	88
Vancouver Canucks	30	37	15	83
Calgary Flames	31	41	10	77
Pacific Division				
Dallas Stars*	43	29	10	102
Los Angeles Kings*	39	31	12	94
Phoenix Coyotes*	39	35	8	90
San Jose Sharks*	35	37	10	87
Anaheim Mighty Ducks	34	36	12	83

Eastern Conference

Northeast Division				
Toronto Maple Leafs*	45	30	7	100
Ottawa Senators*	41	30	11	95
Buffalo Sabres*	35	36	11	85
Montreal Canadiens	35	38	9	83
Boston Bruins	24	39	19	73
Atlantic Division				
Philadelphia Flyers*	45	25	12	105
New Jersey Devils*	45	29	8	103
Pittsburgh Penguins*	37	37	8	88
New York Rangers	29	41	12	73
New York Islanders	24	49	9	58
Southeast Division				
Washington Capitals*	44	26	12	102
Florida Panthers*	43	33	6	98
Carolina Hurricanes	37	35	10	84
Tampa Bay Lightning	19	54	9	47
Atlanta Thrashers	14	61	7	39

*Made play-offs

Stanley Cup champions—New Jersey Devils (defeated Dallas Stars, 4 games to 2)

Leading scorers	Games	Goals	Assists	Pts.
Jaromir Jagr, Pittsburgh	63	42	54	96
Pavel Bure, Florida	74	58	36	94
Mark Recchi, Philadelphia	82	28	63	91
Paul Kariya, Anaheim	74	42	44	86
Teemu Selanne, Anaheim	79	33	52	85

Leading goalies (26 or more games)	Games	Goals against	Avg.
Brian Boucher, Philadelphia	35	65	1.91
Roman Turek, St. Louis	67	129	1.95
Ed Belfour, Dallas	62	127	2.10
Jose Theodore, Montreal	30	58	2.10
John Vanbiesbrouck, Philadelphia	50	108	2.20

Awards

Adams Award (coach of the year)—Joel Quenneville, St. Louis
Calder Trophy (best rookie)—Scott Gomez, New Jersey
Hart Trophy (most valuable player)—Chris Pronger, St. Louis
Jennings Trophy (team with fewest goals against)—Roman Turek, St. Louis
Lady Byng Trophy (sportsmanship)—Pavol Demitra, St. Louis
Pearson Award (best player as voted by NHL players)—Jaromir Jagr, Pittsburgh
Masterton Trophy (perseverance, dedication to hockey)—Ken Daneyko, New Jersey
Norris Trophy (best defenseman)—Chris Pronger, St. Louis
Ross Trophy (leading scorer)—Jaromir Jagr, Pittsburgh
Selke Trophy (best defensive forward)—Steve Yzerman, Detroit
Smythe Trophy (most valuable player in Stanley Cup)—Scott Stevens, New Jersey
Vezina Trophy (best goalkeeper)—Olaf Kolzig, Washington

had stunned top-seeded St. Louis 4 games to 3 in the first round with a 3-1 win in Game 7 at St. Louis on April 25. Dallas edged Colorado 4 games to 3 to win the Western Conference final.

Awards. Chris Pronger of the St. Louis Blues became the first defenseman since Boston Bruins great Bobby Orr in 1972 to win the Hart Memorial Trophy, the NHL's Most Valuable Player award. The award traditionally goes to an offensive player. Pronger won the award by just one vote in the closest balloting in the award's history, beating out scoring champion Jaromir Jagr of Pittsburgh and top goal-scorer Pavel Bure of Florida.

A legend dies. Maurice "Rocket" Richard, who won eight Stanley Cup titles with the Montreal Canadiens between 1944 and 1960 and was the first player to score 50 goals in 50 games, died on May 27 at the age of 78. Richard was considered the Babe Ruth of hockey. He was voted league MVP in 1947 and had 544 goals and 421 assists in 978 regular-season games. Millions of hockey fans in Canada watched his funeral live on television.

Lemieux returns. Mario Lemieux, who had retired from NHL play in 1997 for health reasons, returned to the Pittsburgh Penguins on Dec. 27, 2000. He notched one goal and two assists.

□ Michael Kates

See also **Canada; Deaths.**

Horse racing. Fusaichi Pegasus, believed by many to be the next "superhorse," briefly lived up to his impressive billing in 2000 by easily capturing the Kentucky Derby in May. However, the legend was fleeting. Despite being heavily favored, Fusaichi Pegasus lost to Red Bullet in the Preakness Stakes, missing an opportunity to be the first horse in 22 years to win the Triple Crown (Kentucky Derby, Preakness Stakes, and Belmont Stakes). Commendable won the Belmont Stakes.

Fusaichi Pegasus, who missed the Belmont due to a minor hoof injury, was sold for a reported $70 million in November to Coolmore Stud, an Irish thoroughbred breeding and racing firm.

Three-year-olds. Fusaichi Pegasus, ridden by Kent Desormeaux, won the 126th Kentucky Derby at Churchill Downs in Louisville, Kentucky, on May 6. Fusaichi Pegasus beat Impeachment by four lengths, covering the 1¼ miles in 2:01, the sixth-fastest time in Derby history.

On May 20, Red Bullet trounced Fusaichi Pegasus by more than three lengths in the Preakness Stakes at Baltimore's Pimlico Race Course.

Commendable, ridden by Pat Day and trained by Wayne Lukas, won a lackluster Belmont Stakes at Belmont Park in Elmont, New York, on June 10. Fusaichi Pegasus did not race because of an injury, and Red Bullet was held out of the race due to fatigue.

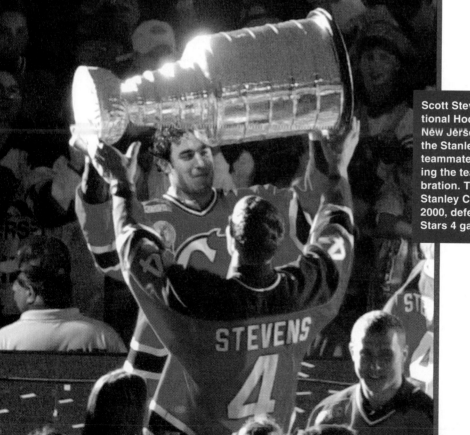

Scott Stevens, of the National Hockey League's New Jersey Devils, passes the Stanley Cup trophy to teammate Scott Gomez during the team's victory celebration. The Devils won the Stanley Cup on June 10, 2000, defeating the Dallas Stars 4 games to 2.

Major horse races of 2000

Thoroughbred racing

Race	Winner	Value to Winner
Atto Mile (Canada)	Riviera	$600,000
Belmont Stakes	Commendable	$600,000
Blue Grass Stakes	High Yield	$465,000
Breeders' Cup Classic	Tiznow	$2,438,800
Breeders' Cup Distaff	Spain	$1,040,000
Breeders' Cup Filly & Mare Turf	Perfect Sting	$629,000
Breeders' Cup Juvenile	Macho Uno	$556,400
Breeders' Cup Juvenile Fillies	Caressing	$582,300
Breeders' Cup Mile	War Chant	$608,400
Breeders' Cup Sprint	Kona Gold	$520,000
Breeders' Cup Turf	Kalanisi	$1,289,600
Canadian International Stakes	Mutafaweq	$900,000
Derby Stakes (United Kingdom)	Sinndar	$414,120
Dubai World Cup (United Arab Emirates)	Dubai Millennium	$3,600,000
Haskell Invitational Stakes	Dixie Union	$600,000
Hollywood Gold Cup Stakes	Early Pioneer	$600,000
Irish Derby (Ireland)	Sinndar	$730,000
Jockey Club Gold Cup Stakes	Albert the Great	$600,000
Kentucky Derby	Fusaichi Pegasus	$888,400
Kentucky Oaks	Secret Status	$378,696
King George VI and Queen Elizabeth Diamond Stakes (United Kingdom)	Montjeu	$295,800
Oaklawn Handicap	K One King	$360,000
Pacific Classic Stakes	Skimming	$600,000
Preakness Stakes	Red Bullet	$650,000
Prix de l'Arc de Triomphe (France)	Sinndar	$391,931
Santa Anita Derby	The Deputy	$600,000
Santa Anita Handicap	General Challenge	$600,000
Spiral Stakes	Globalize	$360,000
Stephen Foster Handicap	Golden Missile	$502,000
Travers Stakes	Unshaded	$600,000

Harness racing

Race	Winner	Value to Winner
Cane Pace	Powerful Toy	$165,675
Hambletonian	Yankee Paco	$500,000
Kentucky Futurity	Credit Winner	$214,000
Little Brown Jug	Astreos	$128,772
Meadowlands Pace	Gallo Blue Chip	$575,000
Messenger Stakes	Ain't No Stopn Him	$161,710
Woodrow Wilson	Whitefish Falls	$351,500
Yonkers Trot	Goalfish	$172,701

Sources: *The Blood Horse Magazine* and U.S. Trotting Association

Jockey Kent Desormeaux sits atop Fusaichi Pegasus in the winner's circle at the 2000 Kentucky Derby on May 6, as owner Fusao Seki-guchi (left, in sunglasses) looks on. Fusaichi Pegasus failed to win the Triple Crown, losing the Preakness to Red Bullet.

Harness racing. On August 5, Yankee Paco defeated Credit Winner in the $1-million Hambletonian at the Meadowlands race course in East Rutherford, New Jersey. In the Pacing Triple Crown, Powerful Toy won the Cane Pace on September 3; Astreos held off Gallo Blue Chip to win the Little Brown Jug on September 22; and Ain't No Stopn Him won the Messenger Stakes on October 14.

International. Dubai Millennium, a 4-year-old horse from Great Britain, claimed the $3.6-million top prize at the Dubai World Cup in the United Arab Emirates in March. Sinndar captured the Derby Stakes in Great Britain, the Irish Derby in Ireland, and the Prix de l'Arc de Triomphe in France. Papillon won the Grand National Steeplechase at Liverpool, England, in April.

Tragedies. Jockey Chris Antley, a two-time Kentucky Derby winner, was found dead in his home in Pasadena, California, on December 2. Police said it appeared that Antley, who had retired from racing, had been beaten to death.

Cam Knows Best, a world-record holder and the runner-up in the 1998 Little Brown Jug, was among 20 horses killed in a fire at Gaitway Farm in Manalapan, New Jersey, on Nov. 23, 2000.

☐ Michael Kates

Hospital. See Health care issues.
Housing. See Building and construction.

Houston. Houston took a major step toward developing a light-rail mass transit system in 2000. The Metropolitan Transit Authority (Metro) hired engineering firms to handle the final design for a 7.5-mile (12-kilometer), $300-million rail line from downtown to the Astrodome area. Light-rail cars are trolleylike and smaller than the cars typically used on commuter rail lines.

On September 7, Metro officials also took steps to acquire land for developing the line. They set a goal to open the light-rail line by 2004, when Houston was expected to host the Super Bowl for the National Football League (NFL).

United States Representative Tom DeLay (R., Texas) of Sugar Land, southwest of Houston, opposed Metro's light-rail project. In May 2000, DeLay, who helped write legislation to distribute federal transportation funds, introduced a measure that barred Metro from using any federal funds to develop light rail in the 2001 fiscal year. DeLay said he was not convinced that a rail system was the best way to meet Houston's public transit needs. He maintained that the voters should be allowed more of a voice in developing the overall transit plan.

Arena approved. On November 7, Houston voters approved a plan to build a $256-million downtown arena for the Rockets, the city's National Basketball Association (NBA) team, by a vote of more than 536,000 to just over 282,000. The result was a major turnabout from a 1999 election in which voters rejected a proposal for a $160-million arena. Rockets owner Les Alexander subsequently complained that the Compaq Center, where the Rockets played, was no longer up to NBA standards and threatened to move the team to another city. The Comets, a franchise of the Women's National Basketball Association (WNBA), and the Houston Aeros, an International Hockey League team, were also to use the new arena.

The Comets continued their run of success in 2000, winning a fourth consecutive WNBA championship in August and remaining the only champion of the four-year-old league. Led by stars Cynthia Cooper, Sheryl Swoopes, and Tina Thompson, the Comets took the championship, 2 games to 0, on August 26 by defeating the New York Liberty 79, to 73, in overtime. Cooper, who was named the most valuable player of the finals for the fourth straight year, announced that she would retire.

Enron Field opened. The Astros, Houston's Major League Baseball team, played the team's first game in Enron Field on April 7. With a retractable roof and shorter distances to the outfield corners, the downtown ball park was a home-run hitter's dream. The Astros set a National League record in 2000, hitting 249 home runs

to break the record of 239 set by the Colorado Rockies in 1997. However, the Astros finished the 2000 season with a disappointing 72-90 record after having won the Central Division championship in 1997, 1998, and 1999.

Texans stadium. In March 2000, officials broke ground for a $367-million stadium for Houston's new NFL team. Owner Bob McNair announced on September 7 that the new team would be called the Texans. The Texans were scheduled to begin playing in 2002.

The Jarvik 2000 heart implant. A major advance in the treatment of heart disease took place in Houston on April 10, 2000, when surgeons at the Texas Heart Institute implanted the Jarvik 2000, a miniature pump to assist a failing heart, into patient Lois Spiller of Houston. The surgery was performed as part of a study to assess whether the Jarvik 2000 could keep a patient alive until a donor heart could be found and transplanted.

Robert Jarvik of New York City and Houston surgeon O. H. Frazier invented the Jarvik 2000, which weighed only about 4 ounces (110 grams). Frazier implanted the device. Spiller received a donor heart in June and went home in July.

☐ Burke Watson

See also **Architecture; Baseball; Basketball; Building and construction; City.**

Human rights. An Idaho jury decided on Sept. 7, 2000, that the Aryan Nations, a white supremacist group, should pay an American Indian woman and her son $6.3 million for an assault that took place in 1998 outside the group's headquarters in northern Idaho. The award included $330,000 in compensatory damages and $6 million in punitive damages. Victoria Keenan and her son, Jason, sued the Aryan Nations after the group's security guards chased and shot at Keenan's car, forced her off the road, and physically assaulted her and her son. The Keenans said they had stopped near the group's compound to retrieve a wallet they had dropped there.

Nazi victims compensated. In July 2000, Swiss banks agreed to pay $1.25 billion to victims of Nazi persecution during World War II (1939-1945) under a class-action settlement approved by United States District Judge Edward R. Korman. The ruling stemmed from lawsuits filed against the banks by Jewish survivors of the Holocaust (the systematic murder of Jews and others by Nazis). The survivors claimed that the banks refused to turn over funds that Jews had deposited in the banks for safekeeping when the Nazis gained power. People whose assets the Nazis deposited in Swiss banks and the heirs of those forced to work as slaves for Swiss companies during the war also shared in the settlement.

In a separate action in July, government and industry officials in Germany agreed to establish a special foundation to pay $5 billion to almost 1 million people who had been forced by the Nazis to work as slaves or forced laborers. Jews and other people in Central and Eastern Europe were eligible for the payments, to which various Eastern European nations and the United States said they would contribute.

The Tulsa Race Riot Commission recommended on Feb. 4, 2000, that Oklahoma pay reparations to about 80 African American survivors of a 1921 race riot during which whites destroyed the black business district in Tulsa, Oklahoma. The Oklahoma legislature had set up the commission in 1997 to look into the incident. The commission documented that at least 40 people died in the riot, though some researchers believed that about 300 individuals had perished. On June 28, 2000, the state legislature approved $250,000 for the commission to complete its work in 2001 and to develop a memorial park.

Sexual harassment in the army. In May 2000, the U.S. Army rescinded the appointment of Major General Larry G. Smith as deputy inspector general after a fellow officer accused him of sexual harassment. In September 1999, Lieutenant General Claudia J. Kennedy, the Army's highest-ranking female officer, had alleged that Smith had kissed her and touched her inappropriately following a 1996 meeting in her Pentagon office. Kennedy said she went public with her charges after Smith had been named the Army's deputy inspector general, a job in which he would deal with allegations of sexual harassment and other improper conduct by soldiers.

Smith denied any wrongdoing, but an Army investigation concluded that Kennedy's charges were credible. Army officials gave Smith a letter of reprimand, and he retired in September 2000. Kennedy had retired from the Army in June.

Gender bias. The U.S. government agreed in March to pay $508 million to 1,100 women who said the U.S. Information Agency turned them down for jobs because of their gender. The settlement, the largest ever in a federal sex discrimination case, resolved a 23-year-old dispute involving the agency and its Voice of America broadcast system. The agency is responsible for spreading news overseas about the U.S. government.

Moves to stop death penalty. Illinois Governor George Ryan on January 31 stopped all executions in Illinois until a special commission could study problems in the state's capital punishment system. Ryan acted after evidence came to light that 13 innocent men had been sentenced to death in Illinois between 1977 and 1999. All of the men were later freed from prison.

On May 18, 2000, the New Hampshire Senate voted to ban capital punishment. Governor Jeanne Shaheen vetoed the measure on May 19.

Homosexual rights. In 2000, Vermont became the first state in the union to allow gay and lesbian couples to form "civil unions," entitling them to all of the legal rights available to married couples in such areas as taxes, inheritance, and medical decisions. Governor Howard Dean signed the legislation on April 26, and the law took effect on July 1.

British military leaders announced on January 12 that homosexuals would no longer be banned from serving in the armed forces. The government changed its policy after the European Court of Human Rights in Strausbourg, France, ruled in September 1999 that Britain had violated the European Convention on Human Rights by discharging four members of the service for being homosexual. The European Court is the legal body of the Council of Europe, an organization of European nations that seeks to promote unity.

Police inquiries. A jury in Albany, New York, on Feb. 25, 2000, acquitted four New York City police officers of murder and other charges related to the death of Amadou Diallo, a black immigrant from West Africa whom the police fatally shot on Feb. 4, 1999. The officers fired 41 shots at Diallo, hitting him 19 times as he stood outside his apartment building. During the racially charged trial, the officers, who were white, said they had mistaken a wallet in Diallo's hand for a gun.

Church bombing indictments. A grand jury in Alabama on May 16, 2000, indicted two men on murder charges for the 1963 bombing of the 16th Street Baptist Church in Birmingham. The explosion killed four black girls. The defendants, Thomas E. Blanton, Jr., and Bobby Frank Cherry, had connections to the Ku Klux Klan at the time of the incident. In 1977, a third suspect in the case was convicted of murder and sentenced to life in prison, where he died in 1985.

Alleged NATO war crimes. Amnesty International, a London-based human rights group, claimed on June 7, 2000, that the North Atlantic Treaty Organization (NATO) committed war crimes when it bombed a television facility in Belgrade, Yugoslavia, in April 1999. The group said that the bombing was illegal under international law because it "was a deliberate attack on a civilian object and as such constitutes a war crime." The air strike killed 16 people.

The Amnesty International accusations came shortly after Carla del Ponte, the chief prosecutor for the international tribunal for the former Yugoslavia, had absolved NATO of war crimes.

☐ Geoffrey A. Campbell and Linda P. Campbell
See also **Courts; Crime; New York City.**

Hungary. In June 2000, the Hungarian parliament elected Ferenc Madl, a former minister of education and culture, president of Hungary. Madl succeeded Arpad Goncz, who had served two five-year terms.

In July, Prime Minister Viktor Orban proposed further restricting property sales to non-Hungarians. Orban claimed that non-Hungarians were driving up the costs of real estate in Hungary by buying large pieces of property. However, opposition party members criticized the proposal, arguing that such restrictions would hurt Hungary's chances of joining the European Union (EU).

Hungarian officials in July filed a $47.3-million lawsuit against Esmerelda, the Australian-Romanian mining company responsible for a large cyanide spill in January. The spill, which occurred in neighboring Romania, devastated the Tisza River in Hungary, killing millions of fish.

Hungary's *gross domestic product* (the value of all goods and services produced in a country in a given year) grew by 4.6 percent in the third quarter of 2000. Unemployment remained at approximately 6 percent throughout the year.

In February, railroad workers seeking higher wages went on strike. In June 2000, farmers blocked roads to protest agricultural policies.

□ Sharon L. Wolchik

See also **Europe**.

Ice skating. Failed drug tests, an attack on a skater, and familiar faces dominated the 2000 ice skating World championships. Michelle Kwan took the women's title, becoming the first American woman since Peggy Fleming in 1968 to win three world titles. In other major competitions, Yevgeny Plushenko, of Russia, unseated two-time men's champion Russian Alexei Yagudin at the European championships, and Michael Weiss, of the United States, successfully defended his U.S. championships title.

World championships. Off-the-ice incidents took center stage at the 2000 World championships in Nice, France. Two-time Russian world pairs champions Yelena Berezhnaya and Anton Sikharulidze withdrew after being notified that Berezhnaya had tested positive for a stimulant after the pair had won the European championships in February. They were stripped of their European medal, and Berezhnaya was suspended for three months. In another incident, French pairs skater Stephane Bernadis was slashed on the arm with a razor by an unknown attacker as he opened his hotel room door.

Yagudin captured the men's title on March 30, despite falling on his final jump. Canada's Elvis Stojko took the silver medal, and Michael Weiss took the bronze medal.

Michelle Kwan performs at the ice skating World championships in Nice, France, in April 2000. The skater came from behind to capture the women's title, becoming the first American woman since Peggy Fleming to win three world titles.

On April 1, Kwan completed seven triple jumps, including a triple-toe-triple-toe combination, to win the women's title. Slutskaya won the silver, and defending champion Maria Butyrskaya of Russia took the bronze. Russians Maria Petrova and Alexei Tikhonov won the pairs gold medal, and France's Marina Anissina and Gwendal Peizerat won the ice dancing championship.

European championships. On February 10 in Vienna, Austria, Yevgeny Plushenko unseated two-time defending champion Yagudin, who settled for the silver. Third place went to Dmitri Dmitrenko, of Ukraine. On February 12, Slutskaya regained her title from Butyrskaya. Victoria Volchkova finished third, completing a sweep for the Russians. Berezhnaya and Sikharulidze won the pairs title but were later stripped of the medal. Russians Maria Petrova and Alexei Tikhonov were later awarded the gold. France's Anissina and Peizerat won the ice dancing crown.

U.S. championships. On February 12, in Cleveland, Ohio, Michael Weiss successfully defended his U.S. title, though silver medalist Timothy Goebel had landed three quadruples in the first half of his free skate, the first quadruples in a U.S. national meet.   □ Michael Kates

Iceland. See Europe.
Idaho. See State government.
Illinois. See State government.

Immigration. On June 28, 2000, 6-year-old Elian Gonzalez returned to Cuba, his homeland, after a seven-month legal battle over who should have custody of the boy. The fight over Gonzalez turned into an international furor, primarily because of the long history of strained relations between the United States and Cuba.

Gonzalez was rescued from the Atlantic Ocean and brought to the United States in Nov. 25, 1999. His mother and 10 other people had drowned attempting to flee from Cuba when their boat sank off the coast of Florida. Initially, Gonzalez stayed with a great uncle, Lazaro Gonzalez, in Miami. The U.S. Immigration and Naturalization Service (INS) decided on Jan. 5, 2000, that Elian's father, Juan Miguel Gonzalez, who lived in Cuba, should decide where his son should live. Lazaro sued to overrule the INS, but a federal court on March 21 dismissed the suit. When Lazaro refused to give up Elian, armed federal agents raided his Miami house on April 22. The agents seized Elian and reunited him with his father, who had flown to Washington, D.C. The Supreme Court of the United States turned down a final appeal of the suit on June 28, and Elian and his father returned immediately to Cuba.

Amnesty. United States Vice President Al Gore proposed on March 30 to offer legal residency to about 500,000 undocumented immigrants. A 1986 immigration law granted residency to immigrants who have lived in the United States continuously since 1972. In March 2000, Gore proposed to include immigrants living in the United States since 1986, affecting about 8 percent of an estimated 6 million undocumented immigrants.

Antislavery measure. In October 2000, Congress approved legislation to fight trafficking in human beings, especially in prostitution and other businesses. The legislation provided stiff penalties to those found guilty of trafficking in people and provided protection and assistance for victims, most of whom were immigrants.

Liberians. In September, officials for the U.S. government allowed about 10,000 Liberians to remain in the United States another year. The immigrant Liberians lived in the United States under special immigrant status but were to have lost that status on September 29. Officials determined that it was unsafe for them to return to Liberia because of the sporadic violence that continued to plague the African nation. On October 10, U.S. President Bill Clinton declared that Liberia's president, Charles Taylor, was unwelcome in the United States because of his support for rebels in neighboring Sierra Leone.

□ Linda P. Campbell and Geoffrey A. Campbell
See also **Cuba: A Special Report; Labor.**

Income tax. See Taxation.

India. Many diplomats and Indian officials had hoped that India's bloodiest internal conflict, an 11-year-old guerrilla war between groups seeking to separate the disputed Himalayan state of Kashmir from India, could be settled in 2000. However, talk of a truce soon ended, and massacres and bloodshed continued through 2000.

Kashmir separatist movement. The state of Jammu and Kashmir, known simply as Kashmir, had been in dispute since 1947, when British India was divided between predominately Hindu India and Muslim Pakistan. At the time, Kashmir's Hindu ruler chose to join India, though two-thirds of Kashmir's people were Muslims. Kashmir is India's only state with a Muslim majority.

The failure of politicians to resolve Kashmir's status led in 1989 to guerrilla warfare in the Srinagar valley and surrounding mountains. In September 2000, Indian police reported that 33,854 people had been killed in political disputes since 1989. Of those, 19,781 had been civilians; 2,316, security personnel; and 11,757, guerrillas and other militants. Separatist groups estimated that the total was much higher.

Talks with Hurriyat. In March 2000, the Indian government began releasing several leaders of Hurriyat (Freedom), an umbrella organization for 23 Kashmiri separatist groups, from prison, and suggested setting up a meeting for peace

U.S. President Bill Clinton tours the Amber Fort, a hill-top palace-fortress dating from the 1600's, near Jaipur, India, in March 2000. During his visit to India, Clinton discussed such issues as shared goals and nuclear proliferation with Prime Minister A. B. Vajpayee.

talks. Some of the leaders had been in prison since October 1999 under the Public Safety Act. On June 24, 2000, Kashmir's state assembly called for greater autonomy, leaving India with control of defense, foreign affairs, and communications, only. Fearing that other minority-dominated states would also demand autonomy, the Indian cabinet rejected the Kashmir assembly's proposal, which destroyed prospects for talks with Hurriyat.

Cease-fire. On July 24, one of India's largest guerrilla groups, Hizbul Mujahideen, announced a unilateral three-month cease-fire and proposed discussions with the government. India was receptive to talks, but other militant groups accused Hizbul of betraying the separatists' cause.

Terrorist raids by unidentified forces in early August left more than 100 people dead in Kashmir, including 33 Hindu pilgrims and 27 migrant Hindu workers. Indian officials blamed militant groups and Pakistan for the attacks, saying they were an attempt to disrupt talks with the Hizbul. Despite the raids, talks opened on August 3. They soon broke down, however, when Hizbul demanded that Pakistan be included.

Bombings and gun battles continued in Kashmir in August, killing at least 28 people. Indian officials reported in September that the number of deaths from guerrilla activities in Kashmir was higher in 2000 than in 1999.

Regional violence. Guerrilla warfare by other separatist groups smoldered in India's Assam state in 2000. The United Liberation Front of Assam sought independence for the state and fought against rival groups. The National Democratic Front of Bodoland sought to create a separate tribal state of India out of Assam.

Both groups operated illegally from bases in adjacent Bhutan, a small Himalayan kingdom unable to control its border. An Indian official reported in September that nearly 2,000 Bhutanese soldiers from the Royal Bhutan Army were being trained in India to fight the guerrillas operating out of Bhutan.

In Tripura state, near Assam, Indian officials blamed a guerrilla group seeking independence for attacking and killing 30 Bengali settlers. Indian officials estimated that more than 10,000 people have died in the past decade due to warfare in Assam.

In Bihar state, savage warfare between upper-caste Hindu militias and lower-caste militants seeking land rights flared periodically in 2000. Five hundred militiamen attacked the village of Miapurt in June, killing 34 people, mostly women, children, and old men. The incident was the eighth major caste-related attack since January. The militia said the violence was revenge for the killing of 12 upper-caste landlords a week earlier.

Violence in Bihar was also attributed to competition between caste groups for jobs and for benefits of controlling the state government, owning land, and receiving an education. Upper-caste Hindus who had long governed Bihar fought lower-caste politicians who had won political control. Some politicians and administrators were linked to gang warfare over contracts.

Christian churches bombed. Attacks on Christian churches and schools continued during 2000. Five churches were bombed in India during June and July. The All India Christian Council held India's government directly responsible for the attacks. The council accused government leaders of failing to identify and punish those people responsible for the violence.

Hindu nationalism. Two states, Gujarat and Uttar Pradesh, dropped bans on civil servants joining the Rashtriya Swayamsevak Sangh (RSS), a right-wing Hindu organization that stood behind the coalition government, led by the Bharatiya Janata Party (BJP). The RSS had been linked to several attacks against India's Muslim and Christian minorities. Opponents of the coalition government charged the BJP with a hidden agenda—making Hinduism the supreme religion of India and threatening the rights of Muslims, Christians, and other religious minorities throughout the country.

In July 2000, a judicial inquiry by the state government of Maharashtra held Balasaheb Thackeray, leader of the militant Hindu nationalist party Shiv Sena, responsible for inciting riots against Muslims in 1992 and 1993. The attacks left more than 2,000 people dead.

Thackeray's supporters in Shiv Sena—a Hindu nationalist party, in BJP's governing coalition, with a reputation for violent protests—shut down the city of Mumbai with demonstrations during July 2000. Thackeray warned that "the entire country will burn." A court in Mumbai later dismissed charges against Thackeray. The Maharashtra government launched an appeal of the decision in August.

Elections. In February state elections, both the BJP and its main rival, the Congress Party, lost ground. Many Indian observers interpreted the election as a further sign that Indian politics were splintering into state and regional political parties, making it harder to maintain a stable national coalition government. The voting results in Bihar, Orissa, and Haryana also indicated the continued decline of the Congress Party, which had governed India for 46 of the nation's 53 years of independence.

Prime Minister Atal Behari Vajpayee said the state election results showed that "it's an era of coalition." His BJP party led the national government although it held only a third of the seats in parliament.

Prime minister's health. Vajpayee's health was a subject of public concern during 2000. The 75-year-old leader appeared frail. In October, he underwent surgery to replace his left knee. Vajpayee, known by the people as a consensus builder who held together the governing coalition, was regarded as the mild face of the BJP. Many Indians worried that without him as prime minister, the party might become militant, trying to impose Hindu customs on the public.

Military spending. In February 2000, India announced a 28.2-percent increase in military spending, the largest in its history. Indian officials said the increased spending was a result of fighting in Kashmir during 1999.

Foreign relations. India accused Pakistan of sponsoring Muslim militants in Kashmir during 2000. Pakistan denied the charge. Many foreign governments agreed that the Pakistani government and fundamentalist Muslim organizations in Pakistan supported the guerrillas, but the groups also had some local support in Kashmir.

In 2000, India and Pakistan both claimed the ability to manufacture nuclear weapons. During U.S. President Bill Clinton's trips to India and Pakistan in March, he described southern Asia as "perhaps the most dangerous place in the world," because of the ongoing confrontation between the two countries.

After President Clinton visited India, Vajpayee visited the United States in September. Although relations between the two countries had improved, the two leaders failed to end differences on nuclear weapons controls. During Clinton's March visit, they signed a vision statement, which outlined shared national goals on trade, diplomacy, and environmental concerns.

Economy. India's economy remained healthy in 2000, although an inadequate infrastructure limited gains. High population growth rate also resulted in slow increases in per capita income. Government officials announced in May that India's population had surpassed 1 billion people.

In July, Vajpayee unveiled plans for a National Population Stabilization Fund, intended to promote family planning. The fund would be used in densely inhabited northern states. Vajpayee said India must reduce infant and maternal mortality rates and meet the demand for family planning supplies among poor families.

On January 25, the eve of the 50th anniversary of the adoption of the Indian Constitution, President K. R. Narayanan noted that the standard of living in India had not improved since the constitution was put into effect. Narayanan said "justice—social, economic, and political—remains an unrealized dream for millions of our fellow citizens. As a society, we are becoming increasingly insensitive and callous."

Kidnapping. In late July, India's notorious bandit, Veerappan, kidnapped the actor Rajku-mar, star of nearly 200 Indian films. Police had long characterized Veerappan as a killer.

Rajkumar's fans in Bangalore, the center of India's electronics and software industries, staged riots that resulted in millions of dollars in losses. According to government officials who negotiated with Veerappan for the release of Rajkumar, the bandit sought the release of his cohorts, who had been detained for years without a trial on charges of terrorism.

Although the government did not release Veerappan's minions, the bandit let Rajkumar go in November 2000. Rajkumar said he pretended to have a heart condition and told Veerappan that he could not be held captive for much longer and survive.

Flooding. India was hit with the worst flooding in decades during 2000. In Mumbai, a monsoon-triggered landslide in July buried nearly 100 people. The heaviest rains in nearly 50 years caused flash floods around Hyderabad in south India in late August, killing at least 160 people. In late September and October, more rains flooded large areas of West Bengal and adjacent Bangladesh, causing the deaths of more than 1,000 people and leaving more than 18 million people marooned or homeless. The flood waters began receding in October. □ Henry S. Bradsher

See also **Asia; Hinduism; Pakistan; Terrorism.**

Soldiers inspect the wreckage of a car bombed in Srinagar, India, in August 2000. Hizbul Mujahideen, a militant group seeking independence for Kashmir, claimed responsibility for the attack, which killed at least 12 people and injured more than 38 others.

Indian, American. In April 2000, the United States Bureau of Indian Affairs (BIA), a division of the Department of the Interior, finished converting the trust-fund accounts of Native Americans into an automated accounting system. The new system was one phase of an ongoing project to correct fund management problems that had plagued the BIA for decades.

In the 1800's, the U.S. government began leasing Indian property to businesses, such as oil or mining companies, and promised to turn over the fees to the owners of the property or to their descendants. Inadequate accounting systems and poor records of land ownership resulted in significant financial losses for many American Indians.

In 1996, several Native Americans filed suit seeking a court order that would compel the BIA to fix the system. In 1999, U.S. District Court Judge Royce Lamberth ordered that the lawsuit remain pending for five years, during which time the BIA must remedy problems and provide quarterly reports demonstrating progress.

According to a BIA project plan, published in February 2000, the bureau would eventually integrate the new accounting system with another automated system for handling leases, contracts, and other land management functions. A September report from the U.S. General Accounting Office also recommended that the BIA restructure its operating procedures to ensure that the new systems would be administered effectively.

Reconciliations. BIA director Kevin Gover apologized to Native Americans for the "historical conduct" of the agency toward Native Americans. At a ceremony on Sept. 8, 2000, marking the anniversary of the BIA, the director acknowledged that many past BIA policies were designed to destroy Native American cultures, languages, and religious traditions. Gover, a Pawnee, also said that the agency accepted the "moral responsibility of putting things right."

On the same occasion, the BIA dedicated a corridor at the Interior Department's main building in Washington, D.C., as the Hall of Tribal Nations to honor the 556 federally recognized American Indian and Alaska Native tribes. Gover officiated over the unveiling of more than 40 tribal flags that were put on permanent display.

Returned lands. On Jan. 14, 2000, U.S. Energy Secretary Bill Richardson signed an agreement to return 84,000 acres (34,000 hectares) of land to the Ute Indian Tribe of the Uintah and Ouray Reservation in northeastern Utah. (The tribe is also known as the Northern Ute.) The land had been a part of the reservation when it was established in 1882. The federal government took over a section of the reservation land during World War I (1914-1918), when the U.S. military was securing oil reserves. The government never ex-

tracted oil but kept the property after the war.

Under the 2000 agreement, the 84,000 acres (34,000 hectares) were returned to the sovereignty of the Northern Ute tribal government, and the tribe agreed to set aside a 75-mile (120-kilometer) strip of land along the reservation's Green River as a nature reserve. The Northern Ute also pledged 8.5 percent of royalties from potential oil or natural gas production to a federally funded environmental cleanup project in Utah.

Recognition of Cowlitz Indians. The U.S. government recognized the sovereignty of the Cowlitz Indian Tribe of southwestern Washington state in February 2000. The action grants the tribe governing authority over tribal matters and makes available federal assistance and services through the BIA.

The federal government failed to recognize the Cowlitz Indians as a sovereign nation in 1855, because the tribal leaders refused to sign a treaty requiring them to move from their ancestral lands to a reservation. The Cowlitz filed a compensation claim in 1904 for land that the U.S. government took without a treaty. The tribe won a settlement in 1973, but the BIA held the money for a final decision on tribal recognition. The latest action would allow the tribe to collect about $13 million in compensation.   □ Jay Lenn

Indiana. See **State government.**

Indonesia. President Abdurrahman Wahid apologized to the Indonesian people on Aug. 7, 2000, for failing to solve government problems during his first 10 months in office. He promised parliament, which had become increasingly critical of his erratic administrative style, that he would reorganize his cabinet.

On August 26, Wahid swore in a new 26-member cabinet and issued a decree giving Vice President Megawati Sukarnoputri the power to manage Indonesia's day-to-day affairs. Her exact role, however, remained vague. Responsibility for improving the government was given to two coordinating ministers. The mines and energy minister, Sulsilo Bambang Yudhoyono, was put in charge of political and security affairs, while Rizal Ramli, head of Indonesia's food distribution agency, was named chief economic minister.

The government changes came amid widespread violence, with some parts of Indonesia falling into anarchy. In the Moluccas, or Spice Islands of eastern Indonesia, where Christians had once been a majority, more than 3,000 people died between January 1999 and late 2000 in clashes between Muslims and Christians. The army failed to block Islamic militants from going to the Moluccas to massacre the Christians. An additional 500 Christians attempting to escape Muslim violence in the Moluccas died in June, when the overcrowded ferry they were riding in sank in the Molucca Sea.

In Irian Jaya, also known as West Papua, a 3,000-person congress called for independence in June. President Wahid rejected the declaration, claiming that it did not represent the wishes of all of the 2 million people of West Papua. The Free Papua Movement had been fighting for independence since the 1970's.

Aceh struggle. In the providence of Aceh, the separatist Free Aceh Movement, continued its fight for independence that had begun in 1976. By the end of 2000, nearly 5,000 people had been killed amid human rights abuses by the army during the Aceh struggle. In May, 24 soldiers and 1 civilian were convicted and sentenced to prison terms of up to 10 years for killing more than 50 unarmed citizens during 1999.

In May 2000, the Indonesian military and Aceh separatist rebels agreed to a cease-fire, the first formal cease-fire in 25 years. The truce failed, however. By the time a prominent local peacemaker was assassinated in September, 120 more people had been killed.

Military accused. On January 31, an Indonesian human rights panel accused high-ranking military officials of involvement in crimes against humanity in East Timor. Indonesia had seized the area in 1975 after Portugal had abandoned colonial rule, but on Aug. 30, 1999, the Timorese voted for independence, despite violent efforts by military-backed militias to stop the vote. After the voting, the militias destroyed much of the area's infrastructure and forced nearly 120,000 people into camps in West Timor, which remained under Indonesian control.

In September 2000, a militia-led mob killed three United Nations (UN) relief workers who were helping people in the West Timor camps. UN reports indicated that Indonesian soldiers had not protected the relief workers. The UN also blamed Indonesian soldiers for militia attacks along East Timor's border.

Military changes. Wahid removed General Wiranto from his position a cabinet minister after the January human rights panel accusation against the military. However Wiranto, who had

Yenni Zanuban Arifah attempts to wake her father, Indonesian President Abdurrahman Wahid, who fell asleep during a parliamentary session in Jakarta in July. Wahid later delegated management of day-to-day affairs to the vice president.

earlier been armed forces chief, was not among the 19 officials prosecuted in May for the East Timor crimes.

On February 28, Wahid reshuffled nearly 75 military officers in an effort to bring the armed forces under civilian control. The president promoted several reformers in the military in an attempt to reduce military power and prevent further human rights violations.

In September, President Wahid accused the armed forces, which had long played a key role in Indonesian politics, of instigating violence in order to destabilize his government. While some military commanders opposed Wahid, it was unclear whether the commanders had control over their troops.

Bombings. In September, a bomb explosion at the stock exchange in Jakarta, the capital, killed 15 people. The incident was one of a series of bombing attacks that Attorney General Marzuki Darusman said was intended to derail the trial of former President Suharto, whose 32-year rule ended in 1998. Wahid ordered the arrest of Suharto's youngest son and 25 others in connection with the bombings. The son evaded arrest, however.

The Indonesian Justice department abandoned trial proceedings against President Suharto in September when he was found mentally and physically unable to take part. Suharto had been charged with directing state money into charitable organizations. The organizations then distributed the money to companies controlled by Suharto's children and friends.

Economic conditions remained poor in Indonesia in 2000, and political instability discouraged most foreign investors. Despite higher prices for oil exports, the national currency remained weak and unemployment stayed high.

□ Henry S. Bradsher

See also **Asia; Australia; United Nations.**

International trade surged in 2000,

helping the world economy further recover from the economic crisis of 1997-1998. The robust economy of the United States in 2000 powered global growth, with U.S. consumers pulling in vast quantities of foreign-made goods and driving the U.S. trade deficit—the shortfall between the value of exports and imports—to new highs. The United States also concluded historic trade agreements with China and Vietnam.

By the end of 2000, rocketing fuel prices and fears of possible inflation and recession were challenging economies around the world. The euro, the common currency of 11 of the 15 members of the European Union (EU), continued its slide, and trade disputes loomed between the United States and some of its major trading partners.

China, the world's largest potential market with some 1.3 billion people, was an increasingly important player in global commerce by 2000. During the 1997-1998 Asian economic crisis, China displayed considerable clout when its centrally controlled financial system held firm and helped halt the region's economic decline. In 2000, China's export-driven economy boomed.

Yet China's restrictive economic and political system continued to hold the nation back from the full range of global trading opportunities. For years, China had sought membership in the World Trade Organization (WTO), an international body based in Geneva, Switzerland, that settles trading disputes among member nations. The United States had blocked China's entry into the WTO until China agreed to open up its markets.

Before 2000, China had received conditional U.S. treatment as a most-favored-nation (MFN) trading partner, which meant that Chinese goods were subject to the same low *tariffs* (taxes) as nations enjoying normal trade relations with the United States. However, China had to be recertified annually for MFN status, requiring an often controversial review by the U.S. Congress.

In 1999, China and the United States had negotiated a pact permitting permanent normal trade relations and supporting China's entry into the WTO. The agreement was finally approved by the U.S. Senate on Sept. 19, 2000. China also struck a trade deal with the EU in 2000. Trade experts predicted that China would gain WTO membership some time in 2001.

The United States and Vietnam signed a landmark trade agreement in July 2000. Under its provisions, Vietnam would be allowed to export to the United States under considerably reduced tariffs. In a historic visit to Vietnam in November, U.S. President Bill Clinton extended a line of credit to Vietnam to help finance investments by U.S. companies.

Fuel prices surged in 2000 to heights not seen since the Persian Gulf War (1991). As a result, oil-importing nations spent more on energy, a financial drain that began to take a toll on a wide range of economic activities.

High oil prices and the threat they posed to economic growth in Europe became yet another contributing factor to the steady decline of the euro during 2000. Because the currency's weakness made exports from the 11 euro-zone nations less expensive abroad while making imports into the euro zone more costly, the euro's declining value eventually became a global trade concern. On September 22, major industrial nations intervened to boost the euro's value on currency markets around the world. President Clinton on September 22 also ordered the release of oil from the U.S. *Strategic Petroleum Reserve* (oil stockpiled in the United States for emergency use) in an attempt to dampen rising world oil prices.

Russia. As some nations struggled to cope with escalating fuel costs, others reaped benefits from expanding revenues. With oil export revenues rising in 2000, Russia, which remained heavily in debt from the economic crises of 1997 and 1998, felt less inclined to accept dictated terms for foreign loans. A loan from the International Monetary Fund (IMF)—a United Nations-affiliated organization that provides short-term credit to member nations—failed to materialize when negotiations with Russia broke down in November 2000. However, economists and IMF officials continued to insist on loan assistance to Russia, which would need to reschedule upcoming debt payments and might see its fortunes plummet if oil prices fell in 2001.

The U.S. trade deficit ballooned in 2000, reflecting the upward spiral of oil prices and insatiable consumer demand for foreign goods. In 1999, the trade deficit grew to a record $265 billion from $167 billion in 1998.

In 2000, the deficit had already reached $270 billion by September, when the United States posted a monthly trade deficit of $34.3 billion, a new monthly record.

Trade conflicts. The United States and the European Union in 2000 continued to spar over trade issues ranging from a U.S. demand that the EU accord all banana exporters equal treatment to Europe's rejection of hormone-treated U.S. beef. The most serious conflict, however, developed over the U.S. Foreign Sales Corporation, a government-sponsored body that grants billions of dollars in tax breaks to major U.S. exporters.

EU officials charged that the tax breaks amounted to huge illegal export subsidies. In November, the EU served formal notice that it would impose sanctions against U.S. imports in retaliation. The United States protested, and the dispute went to the WTO for a ruling sometime in 2001.

The United States and Mexico, partners in the North American Free Trade Agreement (NAFTA), also became embroiled in a trade conflict in 2000. In November, a NAFTA dispute resolution panel ruled that the United States must allow Mexican trucks to carry freight throughout the United States. The U.S. Department of Transportation, the Teamsters union, and other U.S. interest groups had strongly op-

posed such a trade opening. If the United States refused to comply, it might have to pay Mexico compensation or face the possibility of retaliatory trade measures by its southern neighbor.

Protestors converged on Washington, D.C., in April 2000 to demonstrate against meetings of the IMF and the World Bank, a United Nations agency that provides long-term loans to countries for development. Various groups opposed to free

A police officer struggles to subdue an activist protesting free trade during an April 2000 demonstration in Washington, D.C. The protestors attempted to disrupt meetings of the International Monetary Fund and the World Bank.

trade had hoped to disrupt the meetings just as protestors had done when the WTO met in Seattle in late 1999. However, local police officials were able to keep the protests from spreading out of control during the conference.

□ John D. Boyd

See also **Economics; Economics: A Special Report; Manufacturing.**

Internet. The Internet continued its integration into global society in 2000. The vast interconnected network of computers became a more commonly used tool in business, education, and home life. In the United States, about 50 percent of households were plugged into the Internet, according to the Gartner Group, a leading market-research firm headquarterd in Stamford, Connecticut. However, there was a considerable "digital divide," with minorities and people in rural areas less likely to be "wired" than urban whites.

Faster access. As the number of people with access to the Internet grew, so did the demand for Internet connections that were much faster than ordinary telephone lines. In 2000, a number of Internet service providers began offering high-speed Internet connections through *cable* modems, equipment that could be used to hook computers into existing television cable lines. Also, substantial numbers of people chose to use a relatively new high-speed service available from telephone companies, called Digital Subscriber Line (DSL). A DSL service used existing telephone wire to carry both voice signals and Internet service. Both cable and DSL transmitted data at speeds of more than 1 million bits per second, compared with the 56,000 bits per second offered by standard dial-up phone connections.

In December 2000, the Federal Trade Commission, an independent federal agency that maintains free and fair competition in the economy, approved plans for the merger of Internet service provider America Online Incorporated (AOL) of Dulles, Virginia, and media company Time Warner Incorporated, of New York City. The merger enabled AOL to offer high-speed Internet services over Time Warner's vast cable systems.

The number of people with high-speed Internet access jumped from 1.8 million in 1999 to about 5.5 million in 2000, according to some estimates. Experts predicted that by 2003, between 18 million and 26 million people would opt for high-speed Internet connections.

Wireless Web. In 2000, more people began accessing the Internet through wireless devices, such as cellular phones. Because such devices had small, low-resolution screens, and because wireless connections were considerably slower than wired connections, the "wireless Web" was not as useful as the Web experienced through conventional computers and wired connections. However, Web-enabled phones did allow users to check weather forecasts and stock quotes and get driving directions.

Address shortage. A scarcity of World Wide Web addresses emerged as a serious problem for Internet users in 2000. Since the creation of the Web in 1991, only a handful of standardized suffixes were available for assignment to Web sites.

The most common of these "top level domains" (TLD's) were ".com" for companies, ".org" for nonprofit organizations, ".gov" for government agencies, and ".edu" for educational institutions. Anyone with Web access could visit a domain-name "registrar" site and claim a domain name. Because the process was so simple and inexpensive, almost every meaningful string of letters and numerals had been claimed by 2000.

As ".com" addresses were claimed, the Internet Corporation for Assigned Names and Numbers (ICANN), the nonprofit organization that governed Internet addresses, solicited proposals for new TLD's. In November, ICANN approved seven new TLD's—".info" for general use; ".biz" for businesses; ".name" for individuals; ".pro" for professionals, such as lawyers or physicians; ".museum" for museums; ".coop" for business cooperatives; and ".aero" for the aviation industry.

Dot-com shakeout. Dot-com companies, businesses that depended entirely on their Internet presence to sell products and services, experienced a difficult year in 2000. Dot-coms, so-called because of the ".com" suffix of most companies' Web addresses, had attracted huge amounts of capital from investors in the late 1990's, despite the fact that few of these firms were profitable. Investors bought stock in dot-coms hoping that the Internet's explosive growth would produce big returns. However, beginning in the spring of 2000, the high overhead and lack of profits of most dot-coms triggered anxiety in many investors, spurring a sell-off of Internet stocks. As nervous investors pulled their money out of dot-coms, many of these companies were forced to close their doors or drastically reduce their workforces. Several companies whose stock had been worth billions of dollars in 1999 lost more than 90 percent of their value in 2000.

Napster flap. The future of Napster, one of the most popular and controversial services on the Internet, came into doubt in 2000. The free service, which boasted more than 38 million users in 2000, enabled computer users to share digitized music recordings online. Several record companies filed lawsuits against Napster in December 1999, arguing that the service encouraged copyright infringement because it did not provide any mechanism to pay musicians for their work. In July 2000, a federal judge ordered Napster to shut down until the lawsuits could be heard in court, but the ruling was later reversed. In November, Napster officials announced that the company had formed a partnership with one of the major record companies. Under the agreement, Napster would charge a fee to users and pay part of that fee to the record company in return for use of musicians' music files.   □ Herb Brody

Iowa. See **State government.**

Iran. The political struggle between Iranian reformists and hard-line religious conservatives intensified in 2000 after the hard-liners lost control of parliament for the first time since the 1979 Islamic Revolution. Reformist President Mohammed Khatami urged both sides to avoid extremism. Analysts said Khatami feared a backlash by the conservatives, who maintained control of the powerful judiciary and military, as well as the broadcast media. The conservatives opposed reformist efforts to obtain greater social and political freedoms.

Elections. Reformists supporting Khatami won more than 70 percent of 290 parliamentary seats in elections held on Feb. 18, 2000. However, the Council of Guardians, composed of hard-line jurists and clerics, failed to certify some elections and voided other results for 41 seats won by reformists. By September, the parliament had ousted three conservatives who occupied seats originally won by reformists.

Press clampdown. A law passed by the previous parliament enabled the judiciary to clamp down on the proreform press in April. By November, the judiciary had banned some 30 newspapers and arrested more than 20 journalists. The reformists introduced legislation in August to block the judiciary from closing additional newspapers. The council, however, rejected the bill, claiming it was contrary to Islamic law.

In December, Ataollah Mohajerani, Iran's reformist culture minister, resigned under pressure from hard-liners. Mohajerani had played a leading role in fostering freedom of the press and developing Iran's film industry.

The attempted assassination of Iranian reformer Saeed Hajjarian in March sparked fears among Iranians that hard-liners had resorted to vigilantism to intimidate the opposition. However, law enforcement officials said that several men arrested for the shooting had no ties to political groups. Some of the eight men on trial for the crime in May said they were motivated to attack Hajjarian for religious reasons.

Trial of Jews. An Iranian appeals court in September annulled the most serious charges against 10 Iranian Jews convicted in July of spying for Israel. The court then imposed reduced prison sentences of two to nine years on the men, who were also spared the death penalty.

Khatami promised to defend the rights of Iranian Jews in August when he met with leaders of the community. Iran's Jewish population, which numbered nearly 200,000 before the Islamic Revolution, had declined to about 30,000 in 2000.

Severe drought. In August, a United Nations report warned of devastating consequences if Iran did not receive help to cope with its worst

Young Iranian women sing a campaign song in February for parliamentary candidates supporting reformist President Mohammed Khatami. Reform candidates won more than 70 percent of parliamentary seats, though some were later disqualified by the hard-line Council of Guardians.

drought in more than 30 years. The report concluded that the drought, which was in its second year in 2000, had affected half of Iran's population. According to the report, water scarcity threatened to force as much as 60 percent of Iran's rural population to migrate. Iranian officials estimated that the drought had cost the nation $3.5 billion, including the loss of hundreds of thousands of heads of livestock and millions of tons of wheat and barley crops.

U.S. relations. In March, Iran's supreme religious leader, Ayatollah Ali Khamenei, rejected an overture from U.S. Secretary of State Madeleine Albright, who said the United States regretted some past policy errors toward Iran. Albright added that the United States would end import controls on Iranian carpets and reduce tariffs on Iranian caviar and pistachios. Many Iranians criticized these U.S. trade initiatives as inadequate. The United States had maintained sanctions since 1996 against Iran's oil and gas sector, which provided the bulk of Iran's revenue.

The World Bank, an international lending organization based in Washington, D.C., approved, over U.S. objections, its first loans to Iran in seven years in May 2000. The loans, worth $232 million, were for health care and sewage treatment. ☐ Christine Helms

See also **Iraq; Middle East.**

Iraq. Efforts by the United States to isolate Iraqi President Saddam Hussein eroded in 2000 as international opposition to United Nations (UN) sanctions against Iraq mounted. The UN imposed the sanctions after Iraq's 1990 invasion of Kuwait.

United Nations. Two top UN officials resigned in February 2000 to protest the sanctions, which they claimed were having such an adverse impact on the Iraqi population that UN relief programs could not cope with the human suffering. In August, a UN subcommission issued two resolutions condemning the sanctions for causing a severe decline in living standards and health in Iraq.

In March, UN Secretary General Kofi Annan criticized the United States and Great Britain for blocking $1.7 billion in contracts to provide food, medicine, and educational and agricultural supplies to Iraq. Later in March, the United States agreed to allow Iraq to double the $300 million in oil revenues that the UN permitted the nation to spend every six months to repair its oil sector. However, the United States continued to block contracts for oil-industry spare parts.

In September, the UN Security Council agreed to reduce the amount Iraq had to pay in *reparations* (compensation) for its invasion of Kuwait from 30 to 25 percent of annual oil revenues. The council also endorsed a Kuwaiti oil company's

$15.9-billion claim against Iraq for financial losses resulting from the Persian Gulf War (1991).

International relations. In August 2000, Venezuelan President Hugo Chavez became the first head of state to visit Iraq since the Gulf War, ending Iraq's decade-long international isolation. In November, Jordanian Prime Minister Ali Abu al-Ragheb and several other Arab ministers and officials attended a trade fair in the Iraqi capital, Baghdad.

In October, Iraqi officials attended an Arab summit for the first time since the war. The Arab League, an association of Arab states, called the summit in the Egyptian capital, Cairo, to discuss the Palestinian-Israeli conflict. Iran's foreign minister flew to Iraq in October for a meeting aimed at improving relations strained by the Iran-Iraq War (1980-1988).

Air travel. In August 2000, Iraq reopened the Saddam International Airport in Baghdad, which had been closed for 10 years. Russia and France in September allowed the first international flights to Iraq since the Gulf War. By November, more than 40 international flights, including planes from at least eight Arab nations, had landed in Iraq. Iraqi Airways resumed domestic flights in November. ☐ Christine Helms

See also **Iran; Israel; Middle East; United Nations.**

Ireland. The Irish economy—which some economists have called the "Celtic tiger"—continued to boom during 2000. However, the strong economic growth caused problems for Bertie Ahern's Fianna Fail government, as it sought to maintain prosperity in the face of continued inflationary pressures.

Ireland's economic success in 2000 continued to be based on foreign investment, particularly on information technology. Foreign firms were attracted by low business tax rates, minimal regulation, an English-speaking workforce, and Ireland's participation in the single European currency. The government contributed to economic growth through grants to industry and the Programme for Prosperity and Fairness, which negotiated wage agreements with the nation's trade unions to restrain inflation and promote social inclusion.

Prosperity also brought problems, however. By October, unemployment had fallen to 3.7 percent, and business leaders began to be concerned about labor shortages. Housing prices, which had doubled between 1995 and 1999, continued to rise in 2000, causing public sector workers, such as nurses and teachers, to demand more pay.

Although inflation had been projected to rise 5.5 percent in 2000, it reached 6.8 percent by November—one of the highest rates in Europe—generating concerns that inflation would damage further economic growth. Ireland's Central Bank feared the onset of a recession unless wages, rising at a rate of 7.25 percent, could be restrained. Trade unions insisted that workers had been promised higher wages by the government.

Politics. Ireland's leaders in 2000 debated whether the Republic should move further toward a low-tax economy with limited government intervention or maintain larger state benefits with higher taxes. The Labour Party in November recommended a $3.3-billion increase in public spending. The main opposition party, Fine Gael, led by John Bruton, advocated a program of privatization. The Fianna Fail Party favored tax cuts, particularly for lower- and middle-income families but had to contend with concerns that such a move would lead to overheating of the economy.

The Moriarty tribunal, convened to investigate charges against former Fianna Fail taioseach (prime minister) Charles Haughey, reported in 2000 that Haughey had received $9.3 million in secret payments from a prominent businessman during his term in office. Haughey argued that he was too ill to stand trial and that hostile comments by Mary Harney, Ahern's deputy, who publicly suggested he should be convicted, had prejudiced his case. The opening date of his trial was deferred in June, but in November the High Court made clear that the deferral was not permanent. □ Rohan McWilliam

See also **Europe; Northern Ireland.**

Islam. The collapse of the Arab-Israeli peace process and the deadly outbreak of violence between Palestinian protesters and Israeli troops in 2000 focused the attention of Muslims worldwide on Jerusalem. In peace talks with Palestinian leader Yasir Arafat in July and August, Israeli Prime Minister Ehud Barak refused to cede *sovereignty* (control) over the Haram al-Sharif (Noble Sanctuary), a holy site in Jerusalem, to Muslim authority. The Haram al-Sharif, also known as the Temple Mount, is the third-holiest site for Muslims, after Mecca and Medina in Saudi Arabia. The site is also holy for Jews.

For many Muslims, disagreement about who would control the site had long been among the most important issues in the Arab-Israeli dispute. Religious and political leaders throughout the Muslim world continued to insist in 2000 that Islamic control over the site must be part of a final peace settlement.

In India, Hindu extremists began a campaign in 2000 to replace the Quwwat-ul-Islam mosque in Delhi with a Hindu temple. Members of the Hindu nationalist group Vishwa Hindu Parishad, which had been active in the destruction of a mosque in the town of Ayodhya in the Indian state of Uttar Pradesh in 1992, claimed that Quwwat-ul-Islam had been built on the site of an ancient Hindu temple.

A Web site offering Muslims financial advice in accordance with Islamic law was immediately swamped by visitors after debuting on the World Wide Web in March 2000. On the IslamiQ site, experts in *sharia* (Islamic law) offered advice on financial regulations and screened stocks for company conformity to Islamic norms in borrowing and what products they produce. According to a spokesperson for the site, 50 percent of all Web site hits were from residents of the United States, 20 percent from the United Kingdom, and 30 percent from the rest of the world.

United States. The Nation of Islam, led by Louis Farrakhan, reconciled in 2000 with more mainstream versions of Islam, particularly with the Sunni Islam movement of African American Muslims led by Warith Deen Muhammad. In March, Farrakhan urged his followers to observe the Muslim fasting month of Ramadan. He also revealed plans to perform the *hajj* (pilgrimage) to the holy city of Mecca. He repudiated two previous distinctive beliefs of the Nation of Islam—that Wallace D. Fard, the movement's founder, was God; and that Fard's student Elijah Muhammad was a prophet of God. Mainstream Muslims, who do not believe that God has assumed bodily form nor recognize any prophet other than Muhammad (A.D. 570?-632), found both beliefs offensive. □ A. Kevin Reinhart

Israel. The Arab-Israeli peace process foundered in 2000, as conflict worsened between Palestinians and Israelis in the face of seemingly unsolvable political differences. By December, more than 300 people, most of them Palestinians, had been killed in attacks related to the unrest.

Peace process. In May, Israel withdrew all its troops from southern Lebanon, temporarily boosting prospects for a regional peace. Israeli troops initially entered southern Lebanon in 1978 and later established a "security zone" in the area to protect Israeli border towns from attacks by the Lebanese guerrilla group Hezbollah. By 2000, the occupation had become increasingly unpopular among Israelis, who had come to view the many deadly attacks against their soldiers as too costly.

Hopes for regional peace were dashed in July, however, when Israeli Prime Minister Ehud Barak and Palestinian leader Yasir Arafat failed to reach a deal during a two-week summit hosted by United States President Bill Clinton at Camp David, the presidential retreat in Maryland. The status of Jerusalem, which both Israelis and the Palestinians claim as their capital, proved to be the key point of disagreement between the two leaders. Arafat rejected Barak's offer to grant Palestinians control over some Arab neighborhoods in Jerusalem.

An Israeli police officer orders a Palestinian to leave the grounds of a Jerusalem mosque in October 2000. Fearing that ongoing clashes between Arabs and Jews might be worsened by religious fervor, police barred thousands of Palestinians from attending services.

Uprising. On September 28, right-wing Likud Party leader Ariel Sharon visited a Jerusalem holy site—called the Temple Mount by Jews and the Noble Sanctuary by Muslims—sparking a Palestinian uprising in the Gaza Strip and West Bank, as well as unrest in some Israeli towns. On September 30, Palestinian emotions were inflamed by the broadcast of a videotape showing a 12-year-old Palestinian boy being shot to death in a gun battle between Palestinians and Israelis.

Fears of a deep social rift arose in early October, when—for the first time in Israel's history—Arab citizens of Israel joined Palestinians in violent demonstrations. In northern Israel, police killed at least 11 Israeli Arabs and wounded hundreds of other demonstrators. On October 12, Israelis were outraged by the murder and mutilation of two Israeli soldiers by a Palestinian mob.

On November 20, Israeli gunships pounded Palestinian security, political, and media sites in the Gaza Strip in retaliation for the fatal bombing of a school bus. Several attempts at establishing cease-fires to stop the violence broke down in late 2000, while Israelis and Palestinians blamed each other for the failures. On December 31, Benjamin Kahane, a prominent Israeli militant, and Thabet Thabet, a senior Palestinian official, were slain. Despite the continuing violence, halting peace negotiations resumed in late December.

Barak resigns. Barak, the Labor Party leader, saw his grip on power erode in July, when three conservative parties abandoned his coalition because of his willingness to make concessions to the Arabs. The left-wing Meretz party had defected from the coalition in June following a dispute with religious conservatives.

On December 9, in the face of declining support in the *Knesset* (Israeli parliament), Barak announced his resignation. He said he would lead a caretaker government until a special premiership election, in which he planned to be a candidate, was held in early 2001. Likud leader Sharon became Barak's main challenger for the prime minister position after former Prime Minister Benjamin Netanyahu, who had been defeated by Barak in 1999, announced he would not run in the election because of the Knesset's refusal to call new parliamentary elections. Netanyahu had been leading Barak in public opinion polls.

New president. The Knesset elected a little-known Likud candidate, Moshe Katzav, as president on July 31, 2000. Katzav's victory was a major defeat for Barak, who had supported the candidacy of former Prime Minister Shimon Peres. Katzav was the first *Sephardic* (of Middle East origin) Jew to hold the Israeli presidency.

☐ Christine Helms

See also **Lebanon; Middle East; Syria.**

The Greek National Theater stages "Oedipus Rex," a tragedy by the ancient Greek dramatist Sophocles, in the Colosseum in Rome in July. The production was the first event to be presented in the ancient Roman amphitheater in more than 1,500 years.

Italy. The center-left coalition government in Italy struggled to hold on to power in 2000 against a resurgent conservative opposition. The conservatives, led by the Forza Italia party of former Prime Minister Silvio Berlusconi, scored a major victory in regional elections on April 16, winning 52 percent of the vote and capturing 8 of 15 regional presidencies. The election reflected widespread dissatisfaction with the center-left government of Prime Minister Massimo D'Alema, a former Communist who took office in October 1998. D'Alema resigned on April 19, 2000.

The coalition turned to Guiliano Amato, who briefly served as prime minister in 1992 and as treasury minister under D'Alema, to head a new government—Italy's 58th since World War II (1939-1945). Amato took over as prime minister after winning a vote of confidence from parliament on April 28, 2000. He suffered from the same coalition divisions that had plagued D'Alema, however. In September, Amato announced that he would not lead the center-left coalition in the general election that was due to be called by spring 2001. In October 2000, the coalition chose Francesco Rutelli, the popular but relatively inexperienced mayor of Rome, as its leader.

Berlusconi strengthened the conservative opposition by campaigning in the regional elections in alliance with the Northern League. The Northern League and its leader, Umberto Bossi, agreed to abandon their demands for complete independence for northern Italy. However, Berlusconi supported votes taken in September and October in the regional assemblies of the northern states of Lombardy and Piedmont to hold referendums on autonomy in 2001. His political ambitions also received a boost when an appeals court in Milan overturned his 1998 conviction on charges of bribing tax inspectors. Berlusconi had been accused of offering bribes in return for lenient audits of his Fininvest business empire, which owns Italy's largest private television network.

Reform bid fails. A government-backed attempt to provide Italy with a stable, two-party political system failed in 2000. The government and opposition parties had agreed on a proposed constitutional amendment to abolish proportional representation, which allows numerous small parties to thrive by alloting to such groups one-quarter of the seats in the Chamber of Deputies, or lower house of parliament, according to their share of the popular vote. Most voters supported the change, but turnout in the May 21 referendum was too low for the result to be valid.

Economy. Italy's economy improved substantially in 2000, enabling the government to offer the first major tax relief after a decade of tax hikes. Economists expected the *gross domestic product* (the value of all goods and services produced in a year) to grow by 2.8 percent as Italy benefited from an increase in growth across the European Union (EU). EU officials forecast that Italy's unemployment rate in 2000 would drop below 11 percent for the first time in five years. On September 29, the Amato government took advantage of the growth to approve $5.9 billion in income-tax cuts for the remainder of 2000 and an additional $12.7 billion in cuts in 2001.

Jubilee pardon. In June 2000, President Carlo Azeglio Ciampi pardoned Mehmet Ali Agca, the Turk who shot Pope John Paul II in 1981. Agca was deported to Turkey, where he was imprisoned for the 1979 murder of a Turkish journalist. John Paul had met with Agca and expressed his forgiveness in 1983, and the Vatican had urged his release during the Roman Catholic Church's Jubilee year.

IRI closes. Istituto per la Ricostruzione Industriale (IRI), the state-owned holding company that dominated Italian industry for decades, was liquidated by the government in June 2000. Created by the fascist leader Benito Mussolini in 1933 to bail out banks in the Depression, IRI helped rebuild Italy after World War II. The corporation produced everything from airplanes and Alfa Romeos to canned tomatoes. Large losses and European pressure forced the Italian government to start selling its holdings in the 1990's. In June 2000, IRI sold its 45 percent stake in the defense contractor Finmeccanica SpA. IRI's remaining assets, including controlling interest in the airline Alitalia SpA and the broadcasting company RAI, were transferred to the Italian treasury for eventual sale to private investors.

Fiat links with General Motors. Italy's largest automaker, Fiat SpA, entered an alliance with U.S. automaker General Motors Corp. (GM) in 2000. Under the deal, which was announced on March 13, GM agreed to pay $2.4 billion for a 20-percent stake in Fiat, and Fiat agreed to buy 5.6 percent of GM's stock. The deal aimed to strengthen Fiat at a time when mergers were intensifying competition in the auto industry.

Deaths. Bettino Craxi, the prime minister of Italy from 1983 to 1987, died in Tunisia on Jan. 19, 2000. Craxi's was the longest tenure of any Italian leader since World War II. Craxi went into exile to escape corruption allegations and in 1998 was convicted in absentia for taking bribes.

Enrico Cuccia, the most powerful banker in Italy since the 1950's, died on June 23, 2000. As head of Mediobanca SpA, the Milan investment bank, Cuccia acquired small stakes in a web of companies, including the automaker Fiat SpA and the tiremaker Pirelli SpA, enabling him to exercise influence and orchestrate mergers in a wide range of Italian industries.   □ Tom Buerkle

See also **Europe; Roman Catholic Church: A Special Report.**

Ivory Coast. See Cote d'Ivoire in **Africa.**

Jamaica. See **West Indies.**

Japan. Yoshiro Mori, the secretary general of the Liberal Democratic Party (LPD), became prime minister of Japan on April 5, 2000. Mori succeeded Keizo Obuchi, who suffered a stroke in April and died on May 14. Many Japanese citizens criticized LDP leaders for hiding Obuchi's incapacitation for 22 hours and failing to name an acting prime minister.

Mori, a 62-year-old former rugby player, was known as a right-wing politician who championed *pork barrel projects* (appropriating state or federal funds for private or political advantage). He was known to have profited from stock manipulations that resulted in a 1989 financial scandal. Mori was considered a conservative at a time when a gap in the LDP between conservatives and advocates of national reforms was widening.

Controversial statements by Mori after he took office as prime minister caused public concern. In May 2000, he said Japan was a "divine nation with the emperor at its core." The statement echoed 1930's militarism and seemed to endorse emperor worship, which Japan had renounced after it lost World War II (1939-1945). After being widely criticized, Mori said he regretted any misunderstanding, but he refused to retract the statement. This and other remarks reinforced the public's initial impressions that Mori was unfit to be prime minister of Japan.

The LDP, which had ruled Japan for all but 18 months since 1955, was run by factional leaders. The last major leader, former prime minister Noboru Takeshita, who resigned in 1989 amid a financial scandal, died in June 2000. Another former prime minister, Ryutaro Hashimoto, took over the leadership in July of the faction once led by Takeshita and Obuchi. Political observers suggested that a lack of strong leaders helped Mori stay in office.

Elections. On June 2, with his popular approval rating falling and faced with an opposition motion of no confidence in the lower house of parliament, Mori dissolved the house. He then called for elections of a new lower house, four months before they were legally required.

On June 25, 62.5 percent of Japanese voters went to the polls, the second-lowest turnout in many years. In a major setback for the LDP, the party won only 233 house seats, 38 less than in the 1996 elections and 8 seats short of a majority. However, the LDP held onto a governing majority of 271 seats with the help of two coalition partners. The opposition Democratic Party, which held 95 seats before the election, won 127 seats. Mori was reconfirmed as prime minister on July 4, 2000. He selected a new cabinet but kept the same people in key positions.

Scandals developed in 2000 around LDP politicians. On June 30, a former construction minister, Eiichi Nakao, was arrested on suspicion of receiving kickbacks from a construction company. On July 30, Kimitaka Kuze, the head of the Financial Reconstruction Commission, the agency responsible for cleaning up Japan's troubled financial system, resigned after just four weeks on the job. Kuze admitted to receiving payments and benefits from Mitsubishi Trust and Banking Corporation, a bank he had supervised during 2000. Scandals continued in August when chief cabinet secretary Hidenao Nakagawa admitted receiving political donations in illegally large amounts from individuals.

Economic gains. Former Prime Minister Obuchi's stated goal had been to help Japan's economy grow after a decade-long slump. His key tool was $325 billion in public spending, which increased Japan's national debt to a point that many economists considered dangerously large. Critics accused the party of seeking votes with big construction projects and close ties to the construction industry.

In Obuchi's last months as prime minister, from January through March 2000, the economy expanded by 2.5 percent. Further growth through June, spurred not only by government spending but also by increased consumer spending, resulted in an annual growth rate of 4.2 percent. The economy seemed to be pointed toward recovery. However, unemployment remained high.

The LDP tried in 2000 to rescue Sogo, a large retail chain store, from 1.87 trillion yen ($17.3 billion) in debts. The government's efforts to arrange credit for Sogo failed, however, and in July, LDP leaders told Sogo not to expect a bailout with public money. Sogo was forced to file for bankruptcy. The public saw this as confused policymaking by Mori's cabinet.

The Bank of Japan in an effort to encourage spending that would end the recession made its first interest rate increase in 10 years—0.25 percent—in August, amid public fears that the increase might damage economic recovery. The bank had long kept interest rates near zero,

Quality questions. During 2000, several incidents raised questions about a decline in Japanese industry standards. Officials with Mitsubishi Motors of Tokyo admitted in August that for more than 20 years they had not disclosed information about manufacturing defects. Mitsubishi also failed to report 64,000 consumer complaints to the Transport Ministry, which publishes information on vehicle faults. Mitsubishi recalled 532,000 cars, buses, and trucks in July for repairs. When Japanese officials learned about the cover-up, another 88,000 vehicles were recalled in Japan and nearly 200,000 overseas. In September, Mitsubishi's president, Katsuhiko Kawasoe, was forced to resign.

Mitsubishi Electric recalled 45,000 television sets in September. Customers had been complaining since 1987 that the televisions were prone to catch on fire because of overheated parts.

Between June 2000 and December, more than 11,000 people in Japan became ill after drinking tainted milk. In late June, health officials discovered that Japan's largest dairy company, Snow Brand Milk, had been recycling milk returned from stores and falsifying freshness dates.

Nerve gas attack. In July, a Japanese court sentenced four people to death and one to life imprisonment, after they were found guilty of spraying nerve gas in a Tokyo subway in March 1995. The attack resulted in the deaths of 12 people and the injury of thousands of others. All five defendants were members of the Aum Shinrikyo sect, whose leader, Shoko Asahara, remained on trial through 2000 for masterminding the attack.

Foreign relations. Japan made little progress in 2000 in establishing relations with North Korea. In an August meeting in Tokyo, Japanese officials inquired about 10 Japanese citizens who had been abducted by North Korea during the 1970's and 1980's. North Koreans, in turn, asked for reparations for Japan's occupation of Korea from 1910 to 1945. Neither country gave in to the other's demands.

Japanese Foreign Minister Yohei Kono and China's Tang Jiaxuan met in Beijing, the Chinese capital, in August 2000, to discuss Chinese intrusion into Japanese waters. Japanese officials claimed Chinese vessels were entering Japan's 200-mile (322-kilometer) exclusion zone on espionage missions. The talks were not productive.

In September, Russian President Vladimir Putin met with Japanese Prime Minister Yoshiro Mori to discuss Japanese demands that Russia return control of islands northeast of Japan that the Soviet Union seized after World War II. Putin said Russia wanted to retain claims to the land.

Whaling. In August, Japanese officials announced a government research program involving whales. Under the program, more whales would be caught and killed than in previous years, making 2,000 to 3,000 tons (1,814 to 2,721 metric tons) of whalemeat a year available for Japanese consumption. Environmentalists protested, claiming that Japan was violating an international agreement that protected whales. In September, the United States considered issuing trade sanctions against Japan. Japanese fishing vessels were banned from U.S. waters that were open to other foreign fishing fleets in 2000. □ Henry S. Bradsher

See also **Asia; China; Conservation; Korea, North; Russia.**

Jordan. Jordanian King Abdullah II criticized "Israeli aggression" in November 2000 in the wake of a renewal of Palestinian-Israeli violence. Jordan also withheld its newly appointed ambassador to Israel. The announcement came at the same time that Egypt, the only other Arab state that had signed a peace treaty with Israel, recalled its ambassador from the Jewish state.

Fears that the conflict in Israel was spreading to neighboring states increased on December 5, when an Israeli diplomat was shot and wounded while in his car in the Jordanian capital, Amman. He was the second Israeli diplomat to be shot in Amman in less than a month.

In August, major demonstrations had rocked Jordan after United States President Bill Clinton suggested moving the U.S. embassy in Israel from Tel Aviv to Jerusalem. The thorniest unresolved issue in the Arab-Israeli conflict involved the status of Jerusalem, which both Israel and the Palestinians claim as their capital.

WTO. Jordan was admitted in April to the World Trade Organization (WTO), which is headquartered in Washington, D.C. The WTO welcomed Jordan after the National Assembly amended laws to promote foreign investment. WTO membership was expected to increase Jordan's access to world markets. □ Christine Helms

See also **Egypt; Israel; Middle East.**

Judaism. Jews in 2000 had cause to be both joyful and anxious. However, by the end of the year, hope gave way to pessimism concerning the prospects for a Middle East peace and the safety of Jews around the world.

In Israel. Pope John Paul II visited Israel in March 2000 and apologized for the Roman Catholic Church's past mistreatment of Jews. His visit elicited praise from many Jewish leaders. Other leaders responded cautiously, however, disappointed by John Paul's efforts to beatify Pope Pius XII, who had allegedly failed to speak out against the the Holocaust, and Pope Pius IX, who had defended the kidnapping and forced baptism of an Italian Jewish child in 1858.

Negotiations between Israeli and Palestinian leaders over issues in the Middle East peace process, in particular the future of Jerusalem, intensified tensions between rival parties in the Knesset, Israel's parliament, and among Jews throughout Israel. The surprise victory of Moshe Katzav, a Sephardic Jew, over Shimon Peres, the candidate supported by Israeli prime minister Ehud Barak, in Israel's July 2000 presidential election demonstrated the depth of opposition to Barak's approach to the peace process and the quest of Israel's traditionally disenfranchised Sephardic community for power. After Palestinian leader Yasir Arafat declined Israeli offers of peace and failed to reach an agreement with Barak at Camp David in the United States in July, Israelis and Palestinians clashed in the West Bank, Gaza Strip, Jerusalem, and Galilee. Each side blamed the other for the violence.

Tensions among religious and *secular* (nonreligious) Jews in Israel over the role of Judaism in public life continued in 2000. In August, Barak proposed legislation aimed at separating religion from public life. Opponents feared this "secular revolution," and in October the measures were shelved. Several Reform and Conservative synagogues in Israel were vandalized by individuals opposed to these forms of Judaism. In May, Israel's Supreme Court affirmed the right of women to pray in religious garb at the Western Wall, a Jewish holy place in Jerusalem. In November, the court decided to reexamine its decision.

Around the world. The breakdown of the Middle East peace process led to anti-Jewish sentiment and violence throughout the world in 2000. Incidents in Germany in October sparked fears of renewed anti-Semitism there. In Austria, the Freedom Party, led by Joerg Haider, who had expressed affinity for Nazism, was included in the governing coalition in February. Haider resigned as party leader after Austria was diplomatically isolated by the international community.

A trial in Iran in which 13 Jews were tried for spying for Israel concluded in July with 10 of the

Ultra-Orthodox Jewish men denounce Jewish women praying at Jerusalem's Western Wall in June 2000. In May, the Israeli Supreme Court had granted women the right to conduct organized prayers at the Jewish holy place.

defendants convicted and sentenced to prison terms. Protesters around the world insisted that the allegations were false. The sentences were reduced in September.

In Great Britain, historian David Irving lost his libel suit against American scholar Deborah Lipstadt, who had accused Irving of denying the Holocaust. The court affirmed the historical veracity of the Holocaust and vindicated Lipstadt.

In the United States. In 2000, Senator Joseph I. Lieberman (D., Connecticut) became the first Jew to be nominated for the U.S. vice presidency on a major party ticket. The selection sparked a national discussion about whether an observant Jew could fulfill such political responsibilities. Exit polls suggested that 90 percent of voters thought that Lieberman's religion made him a better candidate or would have no effect on his performance in office.

Reform Judaism passed a resolution in March permitting its clergy to officiate at gay and lesbian commitment ceremonies. Conservative and Orthodox leaders attacked the resolution.

In autumn 2000, anti-Jewish violence connected to the Middle East conflict erupted in several U.S. cities.

☐ Jonathan D. Sarna and Jonathan J. Golden
See also **Israel; Middle East; United Kingdom.**
Kansas. See State government.

Kazakhstan. The Organization for Security and Cooperation in Europe (OSCE), an international security group that monitors elections, complained in January 2000 that Kazakhstan's October 1999 elections to the *Mazhilis* (lower house of parliament) were "severely marred by widespread interference." Opposition parties won just 5 out of 77 contested seats. President Nursultan Nazarbayev defended the elections, but his opponents complained of continued harassment. A bill introduced in February 2000 would have empowered voters to elect regional governors, but Nazarbayev canceled the action, defending his power to appoint the governors.

In July, Nazarbayev signed a bill passed by parliament that granted him a lifetime seat on Kazakhstan's Security Council and lifelong immunity from prosecution. The United States Department of Justice announced in July an investigation into evidence that U.S. oil companies had illegally bribed Kazakh officials.

Rising oil prices in 2000 lifted the Kazakh economy and prompted Nazarbayev to postpone privatization of various state-owned industries. Kazakh officials estimated that the economy grew at a rate of 7.5 percent in 2000, up from 1.5 percent in 1999. ☐ Steven L. Solnick
See also **Asia.**
Kentucky. See State government.

Kenya. Millions of Kenyans faced starvation in 2000 as Kenya was gripped by its worst drought since achieving independence in 1963. The drought resulted in massive crop failure, the widespread loss of cattle, and left much of Kenya's industry crippled by lack of hydroelectric power because of water shortages.

Donor agreement. The long economic crisis endured by Kenya during the 1990's was partially alleviated by a July 28, 2000, agreement with the International Monetary Fund (IMF), a United Nations-affiliated organization that provides short-term credit to member nations. The agreement provided Kenya with a $198-million, three-year program for economic growth and the reduction of poverty. The IMF arrangement led other international organizations to resume donations and loan programs. The IMF had suspended loans to Kenya in mid-1997, because of corruption and mismanagement. Nevertheless, the Central Bank of Kenya announced in July 2000 that real *gross domestic product* (GDP), the total value of all goods and services produced within a country, had fallen to 1.1 percent by April 2000. Growth in 1999 stood at 1.4 percent compared with 1.8 percent in 1998.

Ethnic conflict. At least 100 people died in a series of interclan clashes along Kenya's remote northern border in 2000. In the worst incident, more than 40 people were killed in early May in fighting between Somali and Boran tribesmen near the town of Isiolo. Conflicts between bandits and cattle rustlers and local pastoralists along Kenya's northern frontiers with Ethiopia and Somalia had gone on for years.

Constitutional reform. Various parties and interest groups, jockeying to take power after President Daniel arap Moi's constitutionally mandated departure from office in 2002, bickered throughout 2000 over the drafting of a new constitution. Moi insisted that responsibility for reform should lie with parliament, which was dominated by his Kenya African National Union. The Ufungamano, a church-led group, argued that the reform exercise should be led by parties representing the people.

In July, members of Moi's party suggested that a national referendum could break the deadlock, but many opposition leaders believed that a referendum would be manipulated by the government in order to extend Moi's 22-year reign.

Flamingo deaths. Conservationists estimated that some 50,000 pink flamingos in Kenya's Rift Valley lakes died from a mysterious illness during the first six months of 2000. Conservationists blamed industrial and agricultural pollution.

☐ Simon Baynham

See also **Africa.**

Korea, North. In 2000, Kim Chong-il, the dictator of Communist North Korea, began to lead his tightly controlled and militarized country out of decades of self-imposed isolation. In June, Kim met with South Korean president Kim Dae-jung in Pyongyang, the capital. The North Korean leader smiled and joked with reporters during the meeting, denying various reports that described him as reclusive and unstable.

North Korea also began establishing diplomatic relations with other countries in 2000. In July, North Korea joined the Association of Southeast Asian Nations, a regional forum of 13 countries that meets annually to discuss Asian security issues.

War anniversary. The meetings between North and South Korean leaders began 12 days before the 50th anniversary of the invasion of South Korea by Soviet-trained North Korean troops. After the Korean War (1950-1953) ended without a peace treaty, relations between the two countries remained tense and highly confrontational. The U.S. Defense Department, which maintained 37,000 troops in South Korea in 2000, reported in September that North Korea remained a threat to the South, and the troops would remain in Korea. According to the report, North Korea continued to give priority to the armed forces over the needs of its citizens.

Missiles. In October, U.S. and North Korean officials met in Pyongyang. U.S. Secretary of State Madeleine K. Albright asked Kim to stop the development and testing of long-range missiles and to discontinue the sale of missiles to other countries. Reports indicated that North Korea had sold missiles to Iran, Syria, and other nations at a profit of nearly $500 million a year. Kim demanded that the United States compensate North Korea in return for discontinuing missile sales.

In November, U.S. and North Korean officials met in Malaysia, but further talks over missile sales remained unproductive. Showing caution in negotiations with North Korea, U.S. President Bill Clinton opted against visiting North Korea in 2000. Clinton did ease U.S. trade sanctions against North Korea in September.

Famine. Refugees from the famine that had plagued North Korea since 1995 continued during 2000 to attempt to escape into China. According to officials of the United Nations World Food Program, 62 percent of North Korean children were small for their age due to malnutrition. A Korean news service reported in October that North Korea had lost 1.4 million tons (1.27 metric tons) of grain to drought, heat, and typhoons in 2000, guaranteeing that food shortages would continue in 2001.

☐ Henry S. Bradsher

See also **Asia; Japan; Korea, South.**

Korea, South.

Korea, South. President Kim Dae-jung won the Nobel Peace Prize on Oct. 13, 2000, for his contributions to democracy and human rights in South Korea and for his efforts to reconcile with North Korea. Kim met with North Korean leader Kim Chong-il in Pyongyang, the North Korean capital, in June, in an attempt to establish friendlier relations. The meeting was the first between leaders of North Korea and South Korea since Korea was divided at the end of World War II in 1945.

Kim Dae-jung, a human rights campaigner who had been democratically elected, and Kim Chong-il, dictator of an economically failing Stalinist state, apparently conducted warm and cordial meetings in North Korea. However, the North kept tight media control on the visit, revealing little to its own people.

Agreements. The two leaders signed a vague agreement on the need for reconciliation and reunification of the Korean peninsula. They agreed to allow visits between members of families divided by the boundary between the two nations. They also discussed cultural exchanges and economic cooperation between the two countries. Kim Chong-il agreed to visit the South's capital, Seoul.

Reunions. A North Korean airliner brought 100 people to Seoul on Aug. 15, 2000, for four days of reunions with family members who had been separated since the Korean War (1950-1953). North and South Korea opened a liaison office in Panmunjom, the demilitarized zone between the two countries. The defense ministers from both countries met in September to discuss reducing border tensions.

Reunification. While Koreans saw the dream of reunification grow closer in 2000, it did not become a reality. The South, with twice as many people and nearly 12 times as much money per capita as the North, was wary that unity might unleash a flood of hungry northerners into the South. The cost of raising the North to a standard comparable with the South was seen as impossibly high. In addition, North Korean propaganda continued to defend the Communist system.

Troops. Kim Dae-jung quoted Kim Chong-il as having said that the 37,000 U.S. forces stationed in South Korea should remain for stability and peace in Asia. This was contrary to North Korea's decades-old demand that all U.S. troops leave the Korean peninsula. However, when South Koreans learned in July that U.S. troops were dumping untreated chemicals into the Han River, a major source of drinking water in Seoul, demonstrations were staged in the capital against the U.S. presence. Nevertheless, Kim Dae-Jung agreed with visiting U.S. Defense Secretary William Cohen on September 20 that U.S. troops should remain in South Korea.

A South Korean man meets his North Korean mother for the first time in more than 50 years, after the governments of North and South Korea agreed in August 2000 to allow visits between family members divided by the Korean War (1950-1953).

Elections. National Assembly (parliament) elections in April failed to give Kim's Millennium Democratic Party a working majority. The Grand National Party led by Lee Hoi Chang, who had narrowly lost the 1997 presidential election to Kim, won 133 out of 273 parliamentary seats. The Millennium Party won only 115. According to the South Korean political system, Kim had broad powers, but he needed legislative support.

Prime Minister Kim Chong-pil resigned in January 2000 and was succeeded by Park Tae-joon. Both men belonged to the United Liberal Democrats Party (ULD), which broke its ties with the Millennium Party in February. The link was restored in May, however, after Park resigned over a tax-evasion scandal. Kim named another ULD leader, Lee Han-dong, prime minister.

Economic growth during the first half of 2000 reached 10.9 percent, unemployment fell, and inflation was low, an improvement from the 1997 depression. As a result, in July, the World Bank, a UN agency that loans money to countries for development, closed an office that it had opened in Seoul during the depression. However, 16 of the largest business groups in South Korea had debts in 2000 of $192.5 billion—more than twice their total value. □ Henry S. Bradsher

See also **Asia; Korea, North.**

Kuwait. See **Middle East.**

Kyrgyzstan. Askar Akayev was elected to his third five-year term as president on Oct. 29, 2000. Akayev won 74 percent of the vote in a field of six candidates. Observers from the Organization for Security and Cooperation in Europe (OSCE), an international security group that monitors elections, complained that officials interfered with the election process and that the media and judiciary were strongly biased in favor of the government. The vote followed parliamentary elections in February and March in which officials banned several opposition parties, as a result, opposition parties captured only 11 of 105 contested seats.

Feliks Kulov, an opposition leader and Akayev's former vice president, lost his race for a parliamentary seat in a runoff vote in March that supporters claimed was manipulated. Kulov's defeat triggered weeks of protests by supporters in Bishkek, the capital. Kulov was arrested on March 22 and charged with corruption in his former role as minister of national security. After being acquitted, Kulov announced his intention to seek the presidency. In September, a military court annulled Kulov's acquittal and reopened the case against him. His presidential candidacy was ruled invalid after he failed to take a required Kyrgyz language exam. □ Steven L. Solnick

See also **Asia.**

Labor and employment. The United States economy in 2000 crossed a historical milestone as the period of economic expansion became the longest in U.S. history—30 quarters. The U.S. Department of Labor (DOL) reported that the year ended with over 135 million people employed and 5.5 million people unemployed. The unemployment rate was 3.9 percent in April, September, and October, the lowest in over 30 years. Jobless rates for various demographic groups also fell to historically low levels. In October, the unemployment rate was 3.2 percent for men, 3.5 percent for women, and 12.8 percent for teen-age workers. By race and ethnicity, the unemployment rate in October was 3.5 percent for white workers, 7 percent for black workers, and 5.6 percent for Hispanic workers.

The Employment Cost Index, a DOL measure of changes in wages, salaries, and benefits for all civilian workers, rose 4.3 percent from September 1999 to September 2000, compared with a rise of 3.1 percent for the same period a year earlier. Wages and salaries alone increased 4.0 percent for the year ending in September 2000, compared with 3.3 percent for 1999.

Air travel industry. Members of the Association of Flight Attendants, headquartered in Washington, D.C., voted overwhelmingly in May 2000 to approve a new contract with US Airways Incorporated of Arlington, Virginia. Under the agreement, 10,000 flight attendants were to receive an 11-percent wage increase over five years and a 5-percent signing bonus. Wages were to increase 5 percent in the first year and increase by 2 percent at intervals of 18, 30, and 42 months.

United Airlines of Elk Grove Village, Illinois, and the Air Line Pilots Association, headquartered in Washington, D.C., reached agreement on a new contract for United's pilots in August after 48 hours of continuous bargaining. United agreed to restore pilots' wages 15.7 percent above cuts that the pilots had accepted in 1994 in exchange for a 25 percent stake in the airline. United also increased pilots' benefits. On Oct. 25, 2000, more than 95 percent of the union's voting members approved the new agreement. Thousands of United Airlines flights had been canceled between May and September when many pilots refused to work overtime in protest over their contracts. Flight attendants and mechanics went on strike against United in 2000.

Aerospace. After two months of bargaining and a 40-day strike by the Society of Professional Engineering Employees in Aerospace (SPEEA), union members reached an agreement on March 19 with The Boeing Company, the world's largest aerospace company. SPEEA and Boeing are both headquartered in Seattle, Washington. The three-year contract, which covered over 22,000 engineers and technical employees, included bonuses and eliminated medical copayments and deductibles. The pact gave engineers salary increases of 8 percent in the first year and 4.5 percent the following two years.

Cleaning services. The Service Employees International Union reached an agreement in April with the Suburban Cleaning Contractors Association of Chicago after a 10-day strike. Under the pact, which covered 4,500 workers in buildings in suburban Chicago, starting wages were to increase from $6.65 to $8.00 an hour over the three-year life of the contract. In the third year, janitors were to receive family health insurance for the first time. Police in Oakbrook Terrace, Illinois, a Chicago suburb, arrested 51 SEIU janitors and supporters on April 28 in protests shortly before the agreement was reached. The agreement followed janitors' contract disputes throughout the United States, including California and New York. In Los Angeles on April 24, 8,500 SEIU janitors ended a three-week strike to gain a 26-percent raise ($1.90 more an hour) for janitors of downtown buildings and a 22-percent raise ($1.50 more an hour) for suburban janitors.

Hotel workers. The New York Hotel Trades Council reached agreement in July with the Hotel Association of New York City on a five-year contract. The pact covered 24,000 workers in 150 hotels who were to receive 4-percent pay increases each year from 2001 to 2006.

Verizon strike. Talks between Verizon Wireless of New York City and two unions—the Communications Workers of America (CWA) and the International Brotherhood of Electrical Workers (IBEW), both headquartered in Washington, D.C.—broke down on Aug. 6, 2000, idling 87,000 workers. Verizon Wireless was the offspring of the June 16 merger of Bell Atlantic Corporation of New York City and GTE Corporation of Stamford, Connecticut.

In the northeast—New England and New York—50,000 of Verizon's workers started returning to work on August 21, following a tentative contract agreement. After more than two weeks of picketing, the strike ended on August 23 in the mid-Atlantic—Pennsylvania, Delaware, New Jersey, Maryland, Virginia, West Virginia, and the District of Columbia—when 37,000 employees returned to work. Verizon agreed to boost base wages 12 percent over three years and reduce mandatory overtime from 15 hours to 8 hours, notifying workers of impending overtime at least two hours in advance.

Detroit newspapers. The long-running labor dispute involving Detroit's two daily newspapers—*The Detroit News* and *Detroit Free Press*—and six unions took another twist in January when the National Labor Relations Board (NLRB)

decided that the newspapers could not force union members to accept what the newspapers had said was their final bargaining offer. The NLRB is an independent federal agency that oversees relations between unions and employers.

In October, the newspapers submitted new final contract offers to the unions that included annual 2-percent pay raises, bonuses for increased newspaper circulation, more options for medical benefits, and optional union membership for newly hired workers. The labor dispute began on July 13, 1995, when 2,500 workers went on strike.

Seattle newspapers. About 90 percent of the more than 900 employees represented by the Pacific Northwest Newspaper Guild of Seattle went on strike November 21 against the city's two major daily newspapers—*The Seattle Times* and *The Seattle Post-Intelligencer*. On December 28, employees with the *Post-Intelligencer* accepted a $3.30-an-hour raise over six years.

Actors strike. The longest strike in Hollywood history ended on October 30 after two associations of national advertisers and two Los Angeles unions—the Screen Actors Guild and the American Federation of Television and Radio Artists—reached an agreement covering 135,000 union members. The dispute involved provisions for handling pay for residuals—money paid to performers each time commercials are played—on cable television. Pay for residuals on cable remained at a flat rate, but the union gained jurisdiction over pay for the playing of commercials on the Internet. The strike began on May 1 after advertisers announced plans to end residuals for commercials on networks.

Unions. The Bureau of Labor Statistics reported in mid-January that union membership in the United States rose slightly during 1999, to 16.5 million from 16.2 million in 1998. Just under 14 percent of the expanding U.S. labor force belonged to labor unions.

In mid-March 2000, the United Transportation Union (UTU), the largest rail-transportation union in North America, withdrew from affiliation with the American Federation of Labor and Congress of Industrial Organizations (AFL-CIO), a federation of national and international labor organizations. The UTU complained that the AFL-CIO supported a "national transportation policy that would hurt railroad employees."

Few work stoppages. The Department of Labor reported in February 2000 that U.S. work stoppages in 1999 had hit an all-time low. Only 17 major work stoppages began in 1999, half the number reported for 1998. The 1999 strikes idled 73,000 workers for 2 million workdays.

Skilled worker visas. President Bill Clinton in October 2000 signed into law legislation that increased the annual limit on immigration visas for skilled workers. High-tech companies had complained of a shortage of highly skilled workers in the United States in recent years. The U.S. Immigration and Naturalization Service allowed foreign workers with needed skills to work in the United States for prescribed periods under H-1B visas. However, these were limited to 115,000 in fiscal years 1999 and 2000 and were scheduled to decline to a 65,000 limit by fiscal year 2002. The new law increased the limit to 195,000.

International unemployment. Many of the world's industrialized nations continued in 2000 to experience higher unemployment rates than the rate in the United States. The unemployment rate in 19 major industrialized European countries—Austria, Belgium, the Czech Republic, Denmark, Finland, France, Germany, Hungary, Ireland, Italy, Luxembourg, the Netherlands, Norway, Poland, Portugal, Spain, Sweden, Switzerland, and the United Kingdom—averaged 8.8 percent in September 2000, according to the Organization for Economic Cooperation and Development (OECD), a Paris-based multinational association working to promote economic and social welfare.

The United States unemployment rate in September stood at 3.9 percent, compared with 10.5 percent in Italy; 9.5 percent in France; 8.3 percent in Germany; 6.8 percent in Canada; 5.3 percent in the United Kingdom; and 4.7 percent in Japan. Unemployment rates were lower in Luxembourg (2.1 percent), the Netherlands (2.7 percent), Austria (3.2 percent), and Portugal (3.8 percent). Spain had the highest unemployment rate at 14.5 percent.

Japan consistently experienced lower unemployment rates than the United States between 1980 and 1997. However, between 1997 and 1999, the unemployment rate in Japan, the world's second-largest industrial state, rose from 3.4 percent to 4.7 percent.

General Electric Company (GE), headquartered in Fairfield, Connecticut, and members of two unions representing 22,000 GE employees, ratified a three-year contract on July 7, 2000. The contract provided a 9.5-percent wage increase

Changes in the United States labor force

	1999	2000*
Civilian labor force	139,368,000	141,712,000
Total employment	133,488,000	135,159,000
Unemployment	5,880,000	5,653,000
Unemployment rate	4.2%	4.0%
Change in real weekly earnings of production and nonsupervisory workers (nonfarm business sector)†	1.4%	0.3%
Change in output per employee hour (nonfarm business sector)	3.2%	5.0%

*All 2000 data are through the third quarter of 2000 (preliminary data).
†Real weekly earnings are adjusted for inflation by using constant 1982 dollars.
Source: U.S. Bureau of Labor Statistics.

Customers bumped from canceled United Airlines flights wait to be rescheduled in August at Chicago's O'Hare International Airport. Disputes between United and its pilots resulted in the cancellation of thousands of flights between May and September.

over a three-year period—4 percent in the first year, 3 percent in the second year, and 2.5 percent in the third year—for members of the International Union of Electronic Workers and the United Electrical Workers.

Bridgestone/Firestone Incorporated, of Nashville, Tennessee, reached an agreement in September 2000 with the United Steelworkers of America, based in Pittsburgh, Pennsylvania. The contract, which was to last until April 2003, improved wages, pensions, and health care and clarified noneconomic issues such as seniority, attendance, and grievances for 8,000 workers.

Computers for employees. The Ford Motor Company, based in Dearborn, Michigan, announced in February 2000 that it would provide personal computers and Internet access to the company's more than 101,000 U.S. workers represented by the United Automobile Workers. The workers would pay $5 per month for the hardware and unlimited Internet access. Ford officials said they would also implement a similar program for international employees. Delta Air Lines announced in February that it would offer its 72,000 employees computers, software, and Internet access at low prices.

☐ Robert W. Fisher

See also **Aviation; Economics; Immigration; Manufacturing; Telecommunications.**

Laos. Inflation of 150 percent and the collapse of the currency, the kip, in 2000 sparked the first political demonstrations in Laos in 24 years.

In March, a bomb exploded in a restaurant in Vientiane, the capital, wounding several people. Additional bombings followed. An explosion in Vientiane's central post office on July 31 killed several more people.

Although no one claimed responsibility for the bombings, the government blamed rebels from the Hmong tribe. With the aid of the United States, the tribe had fought the Communists until they took control of the government in 1975. While the Hmong renewed guerrilla activity in northeast Laos during 2000, many observers doubted that the Hmong were to blame for the bombings. Most Hmong attacks were aimed at corrupt officials and those involved in unpopular rural resettlement policies.

Some political observers suggested that the bombings pointed to a power struggle between older Laotian leaders loyal to economically stagnant Vietnam and younger leaders who wanted to follow the more reformed economic policies of neighboring China. The Laotian economy in 2000 continued to be dependent on foreign aid and remittances by emigrants.

☐ Henry S. Bradsher

See also **Vietnam.**

Latin America

Latin America headed uncertainly into the uncharted waters of the emerging global economy in 2000. Latin America's moves in this direction followed a decade in which the region's governments had sold off many state-owned enterprises to private entrepreneurs and liberalized the rules for foreign investment in order to stimulate economic growth.

The human costs involved in attaining the higher levels of efficiency and productivity necessary to compete with nations around the world proved to be steep in many Latin American countries, as illustrated by stubbornly high unemployment rates in Argentina, Chile, and other countries. A September study by the United Nations (UN) Economic Commission for Latin America and the Caribbean (ECLAC), based in Santiago, Chile, found that most Latin Americans, especially people in the middle class, suffered from feelings of heightened "vulnerability." The study related this feeling to changes in job markets during the 1990's, which increased difficulties for unskilled workers and failed to improve the distribution of income among Latin Americans.

Many Latin Americans have been left behind economically, according to a September 2000 study, by the World Bank, an international financial organization based in Washington, D.C. This study reported that the number of Latin Americans living on less than one dollar a day had increased from 63.7 million in 1987 to 78.2 million in 1999.

Archaeologists survey the ruins of a Mayan palace that was discovered in dense jungle cover in Cancuen, Guatemala, in 2000. Archaeologist Arthur Demarest of Vanderbilt University in Nashville, Tennessee, described the structure, dating from the Mayan Classic Period (A.D. 250 to 900), as having more than 170 rooms arranged around 11 courtyards.

U.S. dominance. On April 26, 2000, the Brazilian weekly magazine *Veja* gave voice to widespread fears in the region that Latin America had become too economically dependent upon the United States. This dependency was particularly marked in the high-technology sectors, which were driving global growth, according to the *Veja* journalists. Most of the money generated by the computer industry and the Internet worldwide went into the U.S. economy.

The journalists also noted, "No one knows for sure whether the value of the $15 trillion invested in the American stock market . . . will go up or go down next week." A plunge in the value of this market, they wrote, could have devastating consequences for Latin America.

The almighty dollar. On September 9, Ecuador replaced the sucre, its national currency, with the U.S. dollar, despite protests by Ecuadoran Indians that had led to the overthrow of President Jamil Mahuad Witt in January. In November, the government of El Salvador made the U.S. dollar legal tender, to be used in addition to the Salvadoran colon, which was pegged at a 1-to-1 ratio to the dollar.

Elsewhere in Latin America, the U.S. dollar

was in increasingly widespread use in 2000. Several countries conducted the bulk of their trade in dollars, while others maintained large amounts of their foreign reserves in U.S. currency.

Moreover, money sent back home by Latin Americans living and working in the United States constituted a growing source of foreign exchange in the region in 2000. In Cuba, the dollars sent home by the more than 1 million exiles living in the United States helped to sustain the Communist island's depressed economy.

Internet growth. At a conference in Miami, Florida, in March, Bill Gates, co-founder of the computer software giant Microsoft Corporation of Redmond, Washington, and Carlos Slim Helu, head of Telefonos de Mexico (Telmex), a major player in Latin American telecommunications, announced a joint venture to create a common *portal site* (a Web site that provides search engines, shopping, and chat rooms) for Latin America. All personal computers with Microsoft software would direct users to the new portal site, according to Gates, who said, "The growth opportunities we have in Latin America are stronger than anywhere." The joint venture sought to exploit Telmex's experience in providing 6 million Mexicans with Internet access by selling them computers at affordable monthly rates charged to their telephone bills.

The announcement came at a time when the number of computers in Latin America was increasing more rapidly than in any other developing part of the world. The International Data Corporation, a high-tech consultancy group based in Framingham, Massachusetts, estimated in September that sales of personal computers in Latin America would increase 30 percent in 2000, while laptop computer sales would grow by nearly 50 percent. The group expected more than 19 million Latin Americans to have Internet access by 2003.

Morgan Stanley Dean Witter & Company, a global financial services firm headquartered in New York City, estimated in February 2000 that business-to-business *e-commerce* (financial transactions over the Internet) in Latin America would climb to $5.5 billion by 2003.

"Internet culture." In May 2000, Costa Rican President Miguel Angel Rodriguez launched a program to provide free e-mail service and limited Internet access for all Costa Ricans. The initiative was a unique partnership of the state-owned phone company and the national mail service. It relied heavily on software provided by U.S. firms.

"The idea is to create an Internet culture," explained Marco Cruz, the chief executive of the government telecommunications utility that helped make the program possible. He said the companies involved in the program expected to

recoup their investment from increased e-commerce as the number of Costa Ricans willing to pay for full Internet service climbed to an estimated 100,000 by 2001.

Rebound in growth. The economies of Latin America grew by an average of 4 percent in 2000, rebounding from a disappointing 0.4 percent in 1999, according to November 2000 estimates by the ECLAC. The UN agency reported that the Dominican Republic had the highest growth rate in the region, at 7.5 percent; followed by Chile at 6 percent; Mexico at 5.7 percent; and Brazil at 4 percent.

Income gap. "Latin America's economic success in recent years has not been associated with a reduction in inequality," said Lawrence H. Summers, secretary of the U.S. Treasury, at a March meeting of the Inter-American Development Bank (IDB), a Washington, D.C.-based financial institution. To reduce the growing gap in income between rich and poor in the region, Summers urged international aid agencies to find more effective ways of increasing education and fighting poverty.

The UN Development Program (UNDP), which provides financial support to poor nations, found that some of Latin America's larger and more productive countries failed to furnish basic human necessities in 2000. In Brazil, according to the UNDP, 21.9 percent of adults were illiterate, and 24 percent were without a source of pure drinking water. In Venezuela, 31 percent of the people lived below the poverty line, and 51 percent of the children did not attend secondary school. The agency added that nearly one-third of the houses in Argentina lacked pure water or sanitation facilities.

South American summit. The presidents of all 12 nations of South America met together for the first time in history from Aug. 31 to Sept. 1, 2000, in Brazil's capital, Brasilia. The meeting was aimed at forging South American unity on economic issues, patterned after the example of Europe, where diverse nations have forged a common market and launched a common currency.

Historic elections. In July, Mexican voters elected Vicente Fox Quesada of the center-right National Action Party as president. The inauguration of the former Coca-Cola Company executive on December 1 marked the end of 71 years of rule by the Institutional Revolutionary Party. Fox's swearing in was also the first time in Mexican history that power had been transferred from one democratically elected party to another. Many Mexicans hoped Fox's election would move Mexico away from an era of increasingly corrupt national politics that political writers referred to as "the age of the dinosaurs."

In August, voters in Paraguay elected Julio

Facts in brief on Latin America

Country	Population	Government	Monetary unit*	Foreign trade (million U.S.$)	
				Exports[†]	Imports[†]
Antigua and Barbuda	68,000	Governor General James B. Carlisle; Prime Minister Lester Bird	dollar (2.70 = $1)	38	330
Argentina	36,648,000	President Fernando de la Rua	peso (1.00 = $1)	23,309	25,538
Bahamas	295,000	Governor General Orville Turnquest; Prime Minister Hubert Ingraham	dollar (1.00 = $1)	380	1,808
Barbados	268,000	Governor General Sir Clifford Husbands; Prime Minister Owen Arthur	dollar (2.00 = $1)	229	1,021
Belize	245,000	Governor General Sir Colville Young; Prime Minister Said Musa	dollar (2.00 = $1)	169	366
Bolivia	8,329,000	President Hugo Banzer Suarez	boliviano (6.07 = $1)	1,033	1,227
Brazil	175,825,000	President Fernando Henrique Cardoso	real (1.86 = $1)	51,120	57,550
Chile	15,311,000	President Ricardo Lagos Escobar	peso (518.37 = $1)	15,616	15,137
Colombia	37,822,000	President Andres Pastrana	peso (2,183.00 = $1)	11,576	10,659
Costa Rica	3,798,000	President Miguel Angel Rodriguez	colon (314.23 = $1)	6,577	6,320
Cuba	11,385,000	President Fidel Castro	peso (1.00 = $1)	1,400	3,200
Dominica	71,000	President Crispin Anselm Sorhaindo; Acting Prime Minister Pierre Charles**	dollar (2.70 = $1)	54	141
Dominican Republic	8,495,000	President Rafael Hipolito Mejia Dominguez	peso (16.00 = $1)	795	4,897
Ecuador	12,646,000	President Gustavo Noboa Bejarano	U.S. dollar	4,451	3,017
El Salvador	5,980,000	President Francisco Flores Perez	colon (8.76 = $1)	1,164	3,130
Grenada	101,000	Governor General Daniel Williams; Prime Minister Keith Mitchell	dollar (2.70 = $1)	23	171
Guatemala	12,222,000	President Alfonso Antonio Portillo Cabrera	quetzal (7.83 = $1)	2,398	4,382
Guyana	718,000	President Bharrat Jagdeo	dollar (179.00 = $1)	574	620
Haiti	7,959,000	President Rene Preval; Prime Minister Jacques-Edouard Alexis	gourde (25.00 = $1)	199	1,035
Honduras	6,485,000	President Carlos Roberto Flores Facusse	lempira (15.00 = $1)	940	2,728
Jamaica	2,543,000	Governor General Sir Howard Cooke; Prime Minister P. J. Patterson	dollar (44.00 = $1)	1,127	2,575
Mexico	102,410,000	President Vicente Fox Quesada	new peso (9.58 = $1)	65,583	76,746
Nicaragua	5,169,000	President Arnoldo Aleman Lacayo	gold cordoba (12.67 = $1)	544	1,846
Panama	2,856,000	President Mireya Elisa Moscoso	balboa (1.00 = $1)	821	3,516
Paraguay	5,613,000	President Luis Gonzalez Macchi	guarani (3,500.00 = $1)	1,089	3,403
Peru	26,082,000	President Valentin Paniagua[††] Prime Minister Javier Perez de Cuellar	new sol (3.49 = $1)	6,841	10,264
Puerto Rico	3,522,000	Governor Pedro Rossello	U.S. dollar	34,900	25,300
St. Kitts and Nevis	41,000	Governor General Cuthbert Montraville Sebastian; Prime Minister Denzil Douglas	dollar (2.70 = $1)	36	148
St. Lucia	152,000	Governor General Perlette Louisy; Prime Minister Kenny Anthony	dollar (2.70 = $1)	61	332
St. Vincent and the Grenadines	117,000	Governor General David Jack; Prime Minister Arnhim Eustace	dollar (2.70 = $1)	49	201
Suriname	447,000	President Runaldo Ronald Venetiaan	guilder (805.50 = $1)	436	552
Trinidad and Tobago	1,380,000	President Arthur Napoleon Raymond Robinson; Prime Minister Basdeo Panday	dollar (6.24 = $1)	2,258	2,999
Uruguay	3,274,000	President Jorge Batlle	peso (11.59 = $1)	2,232	3,357
Venezuela	24,170,000	President Hugo Chavez Frias	bolivar (691.40 = $1)	14,052	14,522

*Exchange rates as of Oct. 13, 2000, or latest available data.
**Replaced Roosevelt Douglas, who died on Oct. 1, 2000.

[†]Latest available data.
[††]Interim president sworn in on Nov. 22, 2000, replacing Alberto Fujimori.

Cesar Franco of the Liberal Party vice president, replacing Luis Argana, who had been assassinated in 1999. Franco's election marked the first time since 1947 that Paraguay's long-dominant Colorado party was defeated at the national level.

Left-wing winners. Leaders on the left of the political spectrum won election in some Latin American nations in 2000 by assuring voters that they planned no radical departures in economic policy. In Chile, Ricardo Lagos Escobar of the ruling Concertacion coalition assumed the presidency on March 11 as Chile's first socialist chief executive since Salvador Allende Gossens, who was killed in a 1973 military *coup* (overthrow). Lagos emphasized free trade and foreign investment. In the Dominican Republic, Rafael Hipolito Mejia Dominguez of the center-left Dominican Revolutionary Party became president on Aug. 16, 2000, pledging to continue the policies that contributed to the booming Dominican economy. Mejia Dominguez was the first member of his party to hold the presidency since 1986.

Controversial elections. President Alberto Fujimori of Peru announced his resignation in November 2000 after months of battling charges of fraud in connection with his May election to a third term. Fujimori's bizarre resignation, which he faxed from Tokyo, was preceded by public disclosure of a video showing his closest aide, Vladimiro Montesinos, apparently bribing a congressman to switch sides to Fujimori's party.

In Venezuela, charges of election irregularities surrounded the July reelection of President Hugo Chaves Frias, who had become president in February 1999. Chaves began a six-year term on Aug. 19, 2000, in accord with a controversial new constitution that he pledged would eliminate entrenched corruption.

War in Colombia. U.S. President Bill Clinton signed legislation in July to provide $1.3 billion in military support to help Colombia curtail drug trafficking. The bill was highly controversial among Latin Americans, many of whom believed that instead of continuing to pour money into a "failed drug war," the United States should do more to curb the U.S. demand for drugs. Furthermore, many Latin Americans believed that it would be impossible for the United States to support the Colombian government's military campaign against drug traffickers without becoming involved in the country's complex civil war, which began in the early 1960's. Some U.S. politicians also expressed concern about this possibility. International observers noted in 2000 that political turmoil and drug trafficking generated by the Colombian conflict spilled across the borders into Bolivia, Peru, and Ecuador.

Genetically modified seed. In August, a Brazilian court blocked future sales in Brazil of genetically modified soybean seeds created by the Monsanto Company of St. Louis, Missouri. The laboratory-altered seed produces soybean plants resistant to a Monsanto-made *herbicide* (weed killer). Marilena Lazzarini of the Brazilian Consumer Protection Institute, a nongovernment, consumer-rights organization, called Monsanto "irresponsible" for promoting genetically altered seed "without the necessary evaluation of risks to the environment and human beings."

Victory for gray whales. On March 2, a coalition of more than 50 Mexican and international conservation groups claimed victory when the Mexican government and the Mitsubishi Corporation of Japan jointly cancelled plans to construct a $120-million salt-works plant on the shores of Laguna San Ignacio. The salt-works plant would have been the world's largest. The lagoon is located off the Pacific Ocean in a primary breeding ground for threatened gray whales.   □ Nathan A. Haverstock

See also the various Latin American countries; **Archaeology; People in the news** (Fox, Vicente; Lagos, Ricardo).

Latvia. See Europe.

Law. See Courts; Human rights; Supreme Court of the United States; United States, Government of the.

Lebanon. Arabs throughout the Middle East hailed the withdrawal of Israeli troops from southern Lebanon in May 2000 as the first Arab victory in the decades-old Arab-Israeli conflict. Israeli troops had entered southern Lebanon in 1978 and later established a "security zone" in the area to protect northern Israel from attacks by the Lebanese Muslim guerrilla group Hezbollah. Most Arabs credited the end of Israel's occupation to Hezbollah, which had waged deadly attacks against Israeli troops since 1982.

By November 2000, Lebanese military courts had tried and convicted 1,400 members of the South Lebanon Army (SLA), a Lebanese militia allied to Israel, for "collaboration." The convicted men were among some 2,500 SLA members who surrendered or were captured by Lebanese authorities after the Israeli withdrawal.

In July, the United Nations (UN) began expanding the number of its peace-keeping troops in southern Lebanon. Though the Lebanese government stationed 1,000 police and soldiers in southern Lebanon in August, the UN criticized Lebanon for not taking a more active role in ensuring security along the Lebanese-Israeli border.

Hezbollah. In October, Hezbollah guerrillas captured three Israeli sergeants in a border area known as Shabaa Farms, which was claimed by both Lebanon and Israel. Later in October,

In May 2000, a Lebanese woman carrying a portrait of Hassan Nasrallah, leader of the Islamic guerrilla group Hezbollah, salvages military equipment left behind by a pro-Israeli Lebanese militia. Israeli troops ended their 22-year occupation of southern Lebanon in May.

Hezbollah leader Sheik Hassan Nasrallah announced the capture of an Israeli army colonel, who had entered Lebanon with a false passport. The Israeli government claimed the man was a businessman, but many Lebanese speculated that he was an Israeli agent who may have been seeking information about the Israeli sergeants. In late November, Hezbollah guerrillas detonated a bomb in Shabaa Farms, injuring several Israeli soldiers. In response, Israeli warplanes bombed suspected guerrilla sites in southern Lebanon.

Domestic politics. In October, President Emile Lahoud reappointed Rafiq al-Hariri, who was prime minister of Lebanon from 1992 to 1998, to the premiership. Hariri and his supporters had won 100 of 128 parliamentary seats in August elections. His elevation surprised many observers because Hariri and Syrian President Bashar al-Assad were not on good terms. Syria, which maintained 35,000 troops in Lebanon in 2000, dominated Lebanese politics.

Many Lebanese, especially Lebanese Christians, hoped the election results and the Israeli withdrawal would reduce Syria's influence over Lebanon. However, Hariri said in early November that Lebanon and Syria would maintain close ties.

☐ Christine Helms

See also **Israel; Middle East; Syria.**

Lesotho. See Africa.

Library. The United States National Commission on Libraries and Information Science reported in September 2000 that more than 94 percent of all public libraries in the United States provided public access to the Internet in 2000, compared with 73.3 percent in 1998. Public libraries also nearly doubled their number of public-access workstations between 1998 and 2000.

In June, U.S. legislators proposed the Children's Internet Protection Act, a sweeping measure that would require all libraries receiving federal funds to equip all public computers with Internet filters. Internet filters are software programs designed to prevent children or other people from viewing sexually explicit Web sites or other subject areas deemed objectionable. Federal courts struck down two similar measures in 1997 and 1999.

Library leaders. United States President Bill Clinton named Martha B. Gould as chair of the U.S. National Commission on Libraries and Information Science. Gould succeeded Jeanne Hurley Simon, who died on Feb. 20, 2000. Simon had been active in promoting libraries and literacy.

Lynne Brindley in February was appointed chief executive of the British Library, the national library of the United Kingdom based in London. Brindley was the first professional librarian and the first woman to hold that post since the li-

Letters and characters from all the world's languages adorn the exterior of the Alexandrian Library, completed in 2000 in Alexandria, Egypt. The library was built on the site of the ancient Alexandrian Library, the most famous of ancient scroll collections.

brary separated from the British Museum in 1972.

Gifts and awards. The Institute of Museum and Library Services, an independent federal agency that grants funds to libraries in underserved communities, awarded the first four National Awards for Library Service in March 2000. The winning libraries included The Simon Wiesenthal Center Library and Archives in Los Angeles; the Urie Elementary School Library in Lyman, Wyoming; the B.B. Comer Memorial Library in Sylacauga, Alabama; and the Queens Borough Public Library in New York City.

In October, the U.S. Congress passed legislation to establish a presidential library honoring Abraham Lincoln. The library was to be built in Springfield, Illinois, where Lincoln spent most of his adult life before becoming president.

The Helsinki City Library in Finland won the Bill and Melinda Gates Foundation's first annual Access to Learning Award in July. The award included a $1-million grant for the library's programs to increase public access to computers and the Internet.

The Library of Congress announced in October that John W. Kluge would donate $60 million, the largest single gift in the library's 200-year history. The money was to be used to establish a center for scholars and a $1-million annual prize in human sciences, which included fields not cov-

ered by the Nobel Prizes—history, anthropology, sociology, and literary criticism. On April 24, the library celebrated its 200th birthday.

Books. The Chicago-based American Library Association (ALA) announced in January 2000 that Christopher Paul Curtis had won the ALA's John Newbery Medal for children's literature for his book *Bud, Not Buddy* (Delacorte Press). Curtis also received the Coretta Scott King Award, which recognized excellence among African American authors. Illustrator Simms Taback won the Randolph Caldecott Medal for illustrated children's literature for his watercolor, gouache, pencil, ink, and collage illustrations in the book *Joseph Had a Little Overcoat* (Viking).

The ALA in June issued a list of the "100 Most Challenged Books of the Decade" compiled from 5,718 challenges to library materials recorded by the ALA between 1990 and 1999. The ALA defined challenges as complaints about materials made by library patrons, parents, or administrators, usually for sexually explicit content or offensive language. The *Scary Stories* series by Alvin Schwartz was the most frequently challenged book of the 1990's. Some people charged that the book was too scary for its readers' age group.

☐ Nancy R. John

See also **Literature, American; Literature, World; Literature for Children.**

Libya. Libyan leader Muammar Muhammad al-Qadhafi's efforts to end the international isolation of Libya met with mixed results in 2000. Qadhafi was welcomed by government leaders during his tour of Arab capitals in September and October. However, Qadhafi's delegate stormed out of an Arab summit in the Egyptian capital, Cairo, on October 21, after he condemned Arab leaders for failing to sever ties with Israel. The summit had been convened to discuss the Arab-Israeli conflict. In July, Qadhafi achieved limited progress with his long campaign to create a "federation of African states" when leaders of the Organization of African Unity, a group that promotes cooperation among African nations, signed a draft agreement in Togo to begin work toward the establishment of an "African Union."

Ransom for hostages? Officials in Germany, France, and Finland praised Libya for its role in securing the release in August and September of 10 Western hostages held by Muslim rebels in the Philippines since April. Philippine officials, by contrast, charged that Qadhafi paid a $1-million ransom for each hostage, setting a precedent that would encourage more kidnapping. (The rebels had kidnapped scores of foreigners and Filipinos since March.) Libyan officials denied the charges and claimed they had merely promised to fund development projects in Muslim communities in the southern Philippines. Libya, a mainly Muslim state, had long maintained ties with Muslim rebel groups in the largely Catholic Philippines.

Pan Am trial. The trial of two Libyans charged with the 1988 bombing of Pan Am Flight 103 got underway in the Netherlands in May 2000. Qadhafi had surrendered the two Libyans in 1999. The United Nations (UN) then suspended sanctions imposed on Libya in 1992 in response to the bombing, but it said a permanent lifting of the sanctions was dependent upon Libya's full cooperation during the trial.

Deportees. Libya began deporting thousands of black African immigrant workers in early October 2000. The expulsions followed violent clashes that began in August between the African workers and young Libyan Arabs. Deportees reported that more than 130 black Africans were slain, and many houses were destroyed. The violence was centered on towns west of the capital, Tripoli.

African workers from outside Libya began flooding the job market in the mid-1990's, after Qadhafi eased immigration rules to promote African unity. By 2000, government statistics indicated that black Africans comprised 1 million of Libya's total population of 6 million. Many Libyans blamed the influx for the nation's 30-percent unemployment rate.   □ Christine Helms

See also **Africa; Israel; Middle East.**

Liechtenstein. See **Europe.**

Literature, American. Debate over the future of the printed book continued in 2000 with e-books and handheld computers, which can download and store entire books, becoming widely available. With the March publication of Stephen King's *Riding the Bullet*, which was only available online, e-books provided competition to traditional publishing for the first time. More than 500,000 people tried to download King's novella during the first two days it was offered. However, announcements of the death of the bound book were premature, as the readership for *Riding the Bullet* dropped significantly after the initial release, falling well below King's usual book sales.

The Harry Potter phenomenon produced more optimism for supporters of the traditional book as the publishing world continued to be dominated in 2000 by the astonishing success of British novelist J. K. Rowling's children's books. The publisher of *Harry Potter and the Goblet of Fire*, which came out in July, ordered a first printing of 3.8 million copies, the largest in publishing history. The sale of the Harry Potter series prompted many publishing executives to consider 2000 the strongest year for books in nearly a decade.

Dave Eggers proved to be the publishing success story of 2000. His memoir, *A Heartbreaking Work of Staggering Genius,* became one of the year's bestsellers. The book was based on Eggers's own experience at the age of 21 of becoming his 8-year-old brother's guardian after their parents had died. The story of Eggers's attempts to raise his brother, make a living, found a magazine, get on MTV's "Real World" television show, and keep child-welfare authorities from taking his brother is told with humor and cleverness. In many respects, *A Heartbreaking Work of Staggering Genius* is a parody of the popular self-aggrandizing memoirs of the 1990's.

Eggers's popularity in 2000 was facilitated by his magazine *McSweeney's*, which poked fun at the publishing industry but also included sophisticated stories and articles. Eggers's success at publishing new work, the quality of his writing, and his irreverence—he suggested that pictures of himself be captioned "Please Go Away"—provided a breath of fresh air for American literature in 2000.

The 2000 National Book Award in fiction went to Susan Sontag for *In America*, a historical novel that recreates the immigration of a Polish actress to the United States in 1876 and her founding of a utopian commune in California. Sontag describes a country rapidly expanding and becoming modern, while charting her heroine's journey from the theaters in Poland to the commune in California and eventually onto America's stages.

Four other books were nominated for the 2000 fiction award. Charles Baxter's fourth novel, *Feast of Love*, a complex narrative in which the author is at times a character in the story and in which various characters at times become the author. The novel's multiple plots concern the twists and pitfalls of love, and what sustains human beings as they search for an ideal mate. *The Diagnosis*, by Alan Lightman, is the story of a business executive who loses his memory. When his memory returns, he undergoes a battery of medical tests with inconclusive results. Lightman intertwines the story with an account of the last days of the Greek philosopher Socrates. The plots come together in an examination of contemporary obsession with speed and information. Joyce Carol Oates's *Blonde* is a fictionalized biography of Marilyn Monroe. Oates creates an inner life for the famed sex symbol, carrying her from her difficult childhood to the height of fame and tragic death. Francine Prose's 10th novel, *Blue Angel*, is an academic satire that examines university writing programs and English departments. A middle-aged novelist who teaches a creative writing class encounters a self-assured and talented student who throws his life into creative and sexual turmoil.

Important novels. In March, Saul Bellow published *Ravelstein*, a fictionalized account of the controversial teacher and writer Allan Bloom. The book was widely considered Bellow's most important work of fiction since he published *The Dean's December* in

1982. Philip Roth's productivity of the late 1990's continued in 2000 with the publication of *The Human Stain*. Roth's novel describes a teacher's hidden past and considers how we all shape our identity. John Updike's *Gertrude and Claudius* is a prequel to Shakespeare's *Hamlet*, telling the story of Hamlet's parents and his murderous uncle. In 2000, Updike also published *Licks of Love*, which added to the story of his famous character Rabbit Angstrom.

Michael Chabon's *The Amazing Adventures of Kavalier and Clay* is an epic account of two cousins, one of whom has escaped Nazi-occupied Czechoslovakia, who create a comic book during World War II (1939-1945). Chabon provides a sweeping portrait of America during the war years, with a beautiful evocation of lower class life in New York City. Julia Alvarez's *In the Name of Salome* is set in two time periods, 1960 and the late 1800's, and is the double story of a Spanish professor at a U.S. university who teaches in Cuba after the Cuban Revolution and her mother, a poet and activist in the Dominican Republic.

The 2000 National Book Award in nonfiction went to Nathaniel Philbrick for his novel *In the Heart of the Sea: The Tragedy of the Whaleship Essex*, which uses the sinking of the boat *Essex* by a sperm whale in 1820—the incident which inspired Herman Melville to write *Moby-Dick*—to examine the whaling industry of the 1800's. Four other books were nominated for the nonfiction award. Jacques Barzun's *From Dawn to Decadence: 500 Years of Western Cultural Life, 1500 to the Present* provides a pointed overview of the greatness of Western culture. David Levering Lewis's *W.E.B. Du Bois: The Fight for Equality and the American Century, 1919-1963*, is the second volume of a biography on the life of the African American sociologist and educator. The book is a chronicle of black America in the 1900's. Alice Kaplan's *The Collaborator: The Trial and Execution of Robert Brasillach* is an examination of France after its 1944 liberation from Nazi Germany through the career and trial of Brasillach, a French collaborationist writer. Patrick Tierney's *Darkness in El Dorado: How Scientists and Journalists Devastated the Amazon* is a controversial account of how Western anthropologists and physicians studied the Yanomani Indians of the Amazon River Basin.

Ravelstein, published by Nobel Laureate Saul Bellow in 2000, is a fictionalized account of the life of the prominent professor and author Allan Bloom. Bellow's depiction of his close friend sparked controversy in U.S. literary circles.

Notable nonfiction. After 10 years of research, James Atlas's biography of the 1976 Nobel Prize-winning author Saul Bellow was published in 2000. Atlas's biography was a major, although controversial, contribution to understanding Bellow and his novels. Atlas attacked the novelist for his insensitivity toward women and minorities. Catherine Clinton's *Fanny Kemble's Civil Wars* examined the life and works of the actress who became an abolitionist and writer during the 1800's. Ian Frazier's *On the Rez* is an account of the history of the Oglala Sioux and the oppressive life on the Pine Ridge Reservation in South Dakota. Frazier's tragic story is told with humor and an understanding of Native American life. *The Unabridged Journals of Sylvia Plath* were also published in 2000. The poet's journals were first published in 1982 in a heavily edited form. The 2000 volume is more than twice as long and is an exact replica of Plath's writings.

Two memoirs attracted attention in 2000—Mary Karr's *Cherry* and Joe Eszterhas's *American Rhapsody. Cherry* takes Karr into her teen years as she discovers love. *American Rhapsody* is a memoir of Hollywood frailty and the Clinton scandals. Eszterhas includes gossipy, indecent stories and a series of imagined scenes involving such figures as Kenneth Starr and President Bill Clinton.

□ Robert Messenger

See also **Literature for children; Poetry.**

Literature, World.

Chinese playwright and novelist Gao Xingjian was awarded the Nobel Prize for literature on Oct. 13, 2000, for work of "universal validity, bitter insights, and linguistic ingenuity, which has opened new paths for the Chinese novel and drama." Xingjian was best known for his novel *Soul Mountain*, in which he constructed an impressionistic account of his travels through the remote provinces of southern China. His second novel, *One Man's Bible*, continued to explore his themes of skepticism and directly confronted the damages caused by China's Cultural Revolution, a wave of radical politics in China between 1966 and 1976 during which intellectuals were persecuted.

Xingjian's plays, like his novels, used personal pronouns—"you," "he," and "she"—to make the audience concentrate on who was telling the story. The judges of the Nobel Prize, the Swedish Academy in Stockholm, Sweden, said that Xingjian's plays forced the audience "to question all confidences." Gao Xingjian left China to live in Paris in 1987.

Asian literature. Literature from Asia began to reach a wider audience in the West in 2000. Though Chinese novelist Ha Jin found an audience in the United States for the translation of *Waiting,* Chinese publishers refused to print the novel in its original language, Chinese, because they felt it slandered China. *Waiting* tells the story of a Chinese military physician who tries for years to escape an arranged marriage so he can marry the nurse he loves. The novel also presents a parable that illustrates parallels between the tyranny of love and war.

Other novels by Chinese writers published in English translations in 2000 included *Please Don't Call Me Human* by Wang Shuo and *The Republic of Wine* by Yen Mo. Shuo's story envisions a sadistic Olympic games where nations compete not on the basis of athletic prowess, but on their citizens' capacity for humiliation. Mo's tale takes place in Liquorland, where restaurant patrons eat children as a delicacy. Taiwanese writer Chang Ta-Chun's novel *Wild Kids,* published in translation in 2000, offers ironic, funny, and unsettling stories about Taiwanese teen-agers rebelling against parents in 1980's Taiwan.

Japanese writer Haruki Murakami's new novel in translation, *Norwegian Wood,* is a coming-of-age tale based on the author's college experiences. Japanese writer Junichi Wantabe's *In A Lost Paradise,* set in the political upheavals and student strikes of 1969 and 1970, focuses on past loves and the pain and pleasure of growing up.

The United Kingdom and Ireland. The highly regarded Booker Prize was given in November 2000 to Canadian author Margaret Atwood for *The Blind Assassin,* a multilayered tale of lust, death, and sibling rivalry. (The Booker Prize recognizes writers from the Commonwealth and other former British colonies.) The short list of six nominees for the 2000 Booker Prize included three obscure writers, Matthew Kneale, Brian O'Doherty, and Trezza Azzopardi, whose novels had sold only 553 copies collectively at the time of their nomination. Kneale's *English Passengers* focuses on an eclectic group of sea travelers during the 1800's on a hazardous journey to Tazmania. O'Doherty writes of the death of an Irish village and the unfolding of scandalous secrets in the clergy in *The Deposition of Father McGreevy.* Azzopardi's debut novel *The Hiding Place* depicts a young girl's experiences with the innocence and terror of childhood in a Maltese immigrant community in Cardiff, Wales. The other two nominees included authors Kazuo Ishiguro and Michael Collins. Ishiguro's *When We Were Orphans* relates the story of a British detective on a life-long search in the first half of the 1900's for his kidnapped parents. The protagonist of Collins' *The Keepers of Truth* is a reporter of a dying newspaper who has grand dreams of composing requiems on the death of the American dream.

Rose Tremain received The Whitbread Prize in January for *Music and Silence,* a historical novel about Danish royalty in the 1600's. The Whitbread is the top honor for prestigious annual awards for works published in the United Kingdom and Ireland. Tim Lott won the Best First Novel Prize for *White City Blue*, which looks with humor and pathos at male friendships.

From France and the French. The English translation of Belgian writer Amelie Nothomb's *Loving Sabotage*, a semifictional memoir of her adventures in China as a 7-year-old, received positive reviews in 2000. Michel Houellebecq's *The Elementary Particles* was also published in an English translation in 2000. The novel focuses on the lives of half-brothers abandoned by hippie parents, raised apart, then reunited during adulthood. Abandonment has destroyed both men.

Jean-Jacques Schuhl won France's coveted Prix Goncourt for *Ingrid Caven* in 2000. Schuhl's novel was a fictionalized account of the life and career of the German actress and cabaret singer Ingrid Caven, his companion in real life.

W. G. Sebald. An English translation of German expatriate W. G. Sebald's first novel, *Vertigo*, was published in 2000. Four different narratives are interwoven through the story, which revolves around a theme of memory. The author, at the age of 9, fled Nazi Germany with his family and settled in eastern England. While fluent in English and spending the majority of his life in English-speaking places, Sebald chose to write in German. He became known to non-Germans in 1996, with the translation of *The Emigrants*, a meditation on people who live a life in a foreign place.

Other European writers. Several books from past Nobel Prize recipients became available in English for the first time in 2000. Portuguese novelist Jose Saramago's *All the Names* focuses on a meek and lonely registry worker who becomes obsessed with a woman after encountering her birth, marriage, and divorce documents. German novelist Guenter Grass's *Too Far Afield* tells the story of two elderly German men encountering the unification of Germany. One man is a humanist, while the other represents political control. A new edition of Polish poet Wislawa Szymborska's *Poems New and Collected* also was issued in the United States in 2000. Italian writer Antonio Tabucchi published *Dream of Dreams* in 2000, a collection of short stories depicting the dreams of major artists. The edition includes a short work that the author entitled *The Last Three Days of Fernando Pessoa* and described as a "delirium."

Indian and African literature. Indian author Amit Chaudhuri's *A New World*, published in translation in 2000, relates the story of a divorced economics professor returning to Calcutta to spend time with his young son.

Ugandan writer Moses Isegawa impressed Western readers with *The Abyssinian Chronicles*,

an epic of life from remote villages to the urban frenzy of the Ugandan capital of Kampala.

Latin American literature. Carlos Fuentes' *The Years with Laura Diaz* outlines the story of a woman living in Mexico through the 1900's, highlighting all the changes the century brings. *Final Exam*, a novel written by Julio Cortazar in 1950, was published for the first time in English in 2000. In *Final Exam*, two pupils faced with final exams wander Buenos Aires, encountering dark and eerie happenings and pondering life in cafes. *Final Exam* is Cortazar's allegorical farewell to Argentina, which he left after finishing the novel.

Translations of classics. In 2000, W. S. Merwin completed his translation of Dante's *Purgatorio*, the second part of the *Divine Comedy*. Richard Howard produced an acclaimed translation of Stendahl's *The Charterhouse of Parma*, a story of a young man's misadventures in Napoleon's army. The late Israeli poet Yehuda Amichai's collection, *Open Closed Open*, examines the past through fragments. Stephen Mitchell, noted for his translations of spiritual writings from various religions, produced a new version of the sacred writings of Hinduism, *Bhagavad Gita*, translated as "Song of the Blessed One." □ Brian Bouldrey

See also **Literature, American; Literature for children; Nobel Prizes; Poetry.**

Literature for children.

Historical fiction, fantasy, and picture books were especially popular in 2000. Some of the outstanding books of 2000 included the following:

Picture books. *Market Day* by Lois Ehlert (Harcourt). Unusual illustrations created from folk-art objects tell the story of a typical farmers' market. All ages.

Yoshi's Feast by Kimiko Kajikawa, illustrated by Yumi Heo (DK Ink). A dispute develops when Sabu the fishmonger tries to force his neighbor, Yoshi the fan maker, to pay for the pleasure of smelling Sabu's fresh eels all day long. Ages 4 to 8.

Buttons by Brock Cole (Farrar Straus & Giroux). When a man's trouser buttons pop off, his three daughters devise schemes to replace them in this original, old-fashioned fairy tale. Ages 5 and up.

Lord of the Cranes by Kerstin Chen, illustrated by Jian Jiang Chen (North-South). The Lord of the Cranes comes down from his home in the clouds to test his subjects, only one of whom offers him food and drink and is rewarded. Ages 5 to 8.

The Secret of the Stones by Robert D. Sans Souci, illustrated by James Ransome (Phyllis Fogelman). In a folk tale based on Arkansan and Zairian legends, a childless couple find two unusual white stones. They return home each day to find their chores completed, until they finally solve the mystery. Ages 4 to 8.

Madlenka by Peter Sis (Farrar Straus & Giroux). When Madlenka feels that her tooth is loose, she must tell all the neighbors on her New York City block. The neighbors, in turn, share stories of the countries from which they came. All ages.

A Day, A Dog by Gabrielle Vincent (Front Street). Charcoal drawings capture a dog's abandonment by his family, his desperation at being alone, and his hopeful encounter with a homeless child. All ages.

Comes a Wind by Linda Arms White, illustrated by Tom Curry (DK Ink). Mama's birthday wish is that Clement and Clyde, who cannot stop trying to outdo each other, get along for a day. When a strong wind blows Mama to the rooftop, they do just that. Ages 4 to 8.

Henny-Penny retold by Jane Wattenberg (Scholastic). In this adaptation of the classic fairy tale, the story is told through wild puns in rock-and-roll rhythms and clever illustrations. All ages.

Wizzil by William Steig, illustrated by Quentin Blake (Farrar Straus & Giroux). Mean Wizzil the witch is bored and enjoys making trouble for De Witt Frimp and his family until she gets into trouble and needs to be rescued. Ages 5 to 8.

Fiction. *Peregrine* by Joan Elizabeth Goodman (Houghton Mifflin). Fifteen-year-old Lady Edith, whose child and husband have recently died, and her nurse travel on a difficult pilgrimage to the Holy Land in 1144 to escape a forced marriage to Lord Runcival. Ages 12 and up.

Nory Ryan's Song by Patricia Reilly Giff (Delacorte). Nory, whose mother is dead and whose father is away at sea, struggles to keep her family fed and to save their home from an English landlord during the 1845 potato blight in Ireland. Ages 8 to 12.

A Year Down Yonder by Richard Peck (Dial). In this sequel to *A Long Way from Chicago,* Mary Alice spends a year with her feisty Grandma in small-town Illinois during the Great Depression of the 1930's. Ages 10 and up.

The Hollow Tree by Janet Lunn (Viking). In this Canadian Governor General's Award winner set during the Revolutionary War (1775-1783), Phoebe tries to deliver a message for her beloved cousin Gideon after he is hanged as a British spy. Ages 10 to 14.

The Body of Christopher Creed by Carol Plum-Ucci (Harcourt). When class outcast Christopher Creed mysteriously disappears, 16-year-old Torey reexamines his values, his beliefs, and his attitudes toward others. Ages 12 and up.

Queen's Own Fool: A Novel of Mary Queen of Scots by Jane Yolen and Robert Harris (Philomel). The story of Mary, Queen of Scots, is told by or-

Children buy the first copies of J. K. Rowling's latest novel, *Harry Potter and the Goblet of Fire*, at a release party in Bryn Mawr, Pennsylvania, on July 8. The first printing—3.8 million copies—was the largest in book publishing history. Nevertheless, many stores were sold out before the end of the day.

phan Nicola, who, at the age of 13, becomes the queen's jester and confidant. Ages 12 and up.

Shakespeare's Scribe by Gary Blackwood (Dutton). In this sequel to *The Shakespeare Stealer*, the orphan Widge struggles to become an actor and join the Chamberlain players as the plague threatens England in the 1300's. Ages 12 and up.

Fantasy. *The Dark Portal* by Robin Jarvis (SeaStar). In the first book of the Deptford Mice trilogy, after Albert goes into the sewers of Deptford, other mice enter the perilous rat haven ruled by the evil Jupiter. Ages 10 and up.

Harry Potter and the Goblet of Fire by J. K. Rowling (Levine/Scholastic). In the fourth book of the series, Harry's wizard training and adventures with his friends continue and include his teen love for Cho Chang. All ages.

Fire Bringer by David Clement-Davies (Dutton). When evil Sgorr takes over the deer herd, changing their peaceful ways, some flee with the fawn Rannoch, who bears the mark of prophecy and is destined to return. Ages 12 and up.

Matilda Bone by Karen Cushman (Clarion). Matilda, raised as a scholar, becomes a helper to a bone-setter in medieval Blood and Bone Alley, where she begins to understand the goodness in simple people. Ages 12 and up.

Spindle's End by Robin McKinley (Putnam). A retelling of Sleeping Beauty, in which Princess Rosie, hidden in a village by one of her fairy godmothers, saves herself from the curse. Ages 12 and up.

Space Race by Sylvia Waugh (Delacorte). When the alien Thomas is hospitalized after an accident, he must decide whether to stay on Earth with a neighbor or return with his dad to the home planet he's never seen. Ages 10 and up.

Poetry. *The Mermaid's Purse* by Ted Hughes, illustrated by Flora McDonnell (Knopf). Real and mythical sea creatures, illustrated in black-and-white drawings, are depicted in original verses by the late poet laureate of England. All ages.

The Pig in the Spigot by Richard Wilbur, illustrated by J. Otto Seibold (Harcourt). In poems about creatures and objects, readers discover small words within bigger ones. All ages.

Mammalabilia by Douglas Florian (Harcourt). A new menagerie from Aardvarks to the Tiger offers poetic fun. All ages.

It's a Woman's World: A Century of Women's Voices in Poetry edited by Neil Philip (Dutton). Sixty poems from around the world highlight the lives of girls and women throughout the 1900's. Ages 10 and up.

Informational books. *Blizzard!* by Jim Murphy (Scholastic). Personal accounts, photos, and other illustrations depict the blizzard of 1888, which paralyzed the East Coast of the United States. Ages 9 and up.

Fantastic Book of Comparisons by Russell Ash (DK). Multiple-page spreads include information and illustrations about the universe, environment, human body, and more. Ages 8 and up.

Amazing Life of Benjamin Franklin by James Cross Giblin, illustrated by Michael Dooling (Scholastic). An engaging text and historically detailed oil illustrations and sketches cover Franklin's major life experiences. Ages 8 to 11.

Digging for Bird-Dinosaurs by Nic Bishop (Houghton Mifflin). A photo essay of the search by paleontologist Cathy Foster and a team of scientists for the link between dinosaurs and birds during an archeological dig in Madagascar, off the coast of Africa. Ages 8 to 11.

Too Young to Fight compiled by Priscilla Galloway (Stoddart). An anthology that explores the influence of World War II (1939-1945) on the lives of some Canadian writers of children's literature. Ages 12 and up.

The 2000 Newbery Medal was awarded to Christopher Paul Curtis for *Bud, Not Buddy*. The award is given by the American Library Association (ALA) for "the most distinguished contribution to children's literature" published the previous year. The ALA's Caldecott Medal for "the most distinguished American picture book" was awarded to Simms Taback for *Joseph Had a Little Overcoat*.

□ Marilyn Fain Apseloff

Los Angeles. The United States Department of Justice proposed in 2000 to intercede with the Los Angeles city government to monitor reform and restructuring efforts of the Los Angeles Police Department (LAPD) over a five-year period. The LAPD became the largest police department ever to be monitored by the Justice Department as a result of the federal government's authority to sue police agencies alleged to have engaged in a "pattern or practice" of civil rights violations. The LAPD was wracked by scandal, lawsuits, and police officers found guilty of violent crimes and corruption in 1999 and 2000, mainly in the downtown Rampart division of Los Angeles.

The Rampart scandal and subsequent action of the Justice Department marred Mayor Richard Riordan's final term in office and jeopardized the reappointment of police chief Bernard Parks to a second five-year term in 2002. The police scandal also contributed to prosecutor Steve Cooley's November 2000 defeat of veteran District Attorney Gil Garcetti.

Plans to expand transportation. The Metropolitan Transportation Authority (MTA) proposed in 2000 to extend the MTA subway beneath the heavily traveled Wilshire Boulevard to the populous Westside area. The MTA underscored difficulties in coping with rapid population growth and worsening traffic congestion. *Demog-*

raphers (scientists who study the statistics of human populations) projected that the population of Los Angeles County would grow from 10 million to 13 million between 2000 and 2025.

Development projects. The Port of Los Angeles spent $1 billion to expand its facilities in 2000. The Port of Long Beach, a rival for overseas trade shipments, budgeted $2 billion for larger facilities. Dust and traffic snarls caused by construction on the Alameda Corridor, a more than $2-billion, 20-mile (32-kilometer) rail system connecting the ports to downtown Los Angeles, prompted complaints from nearby property owners in 2000. Project officials reported in February that they fell short of goals to recruit workers from the many poorer cities along the rail line.

Strong economy. The Los Angeles County Economic Development Corporation (LAEDC) predicted in July 2000 that Los Angeles County would enjoy a strong, if slowing, economy through 2001. The agency cited the diversity of the county's economic base as a major factor in the economy's healthy performance and noted that international trade, technology, and tourism led the county's economic growth. LAEDC analysts predicted that nonfarm employment in 2001 would increase by 2.5 percent, offset by losses in aerospace, retailing, and apparel manufacturing.

On October 30, the longest strike in Hollywood history ended after two associations of national advertisers reached an agreement with the Screen Actors Guild and the American Federation of Television and Radio Artists. The strike, which began on May 1, involved provisions for handling pay to performers for residuals for commercials on cable television and the Internet.

Trade. The Los Angeles Customs District, all the ports and airports in the metropolitan area, estimated in 2000 that trade growth in 2001 would be just under 10 percent, down from 18 percent in 2000. High fuel prices and less foreign demand overseas for U.S. goods contributed to the projected decline. Ports reported heavy volume in late 2000 on imports of Asian-made goods slated for holiday shopping and exports of raw materials bound for Asian manufacturers.

Budgets approved. In May, Los Angeles City Council members approved a $4.4-billion annual budget that included increased spending for police and fire departments and for computer technology for government offices, schools, and libraries. The Los Angeles County Board of Supervisors approved a $15-billion budget in April that included computer technology upgrades in county offices, libraries, and schools and increased funds for law enforcement and fire department hirings.

☐ Margaret A. Kilgore

See also **City; Labor and employment.**

Louisiana. See State government.

Luxembourg. See Europe.

Macedonia. Local elections in Macedonia in September 2000 were marred by violence and irregularities. The Democratic Prosperity Party, which had the support of most ethnic Albanians, boycotted the second round because of voter intimidation and violence. One person was killed and eight others were injured during the first round of the elections.

In November, Macedonian officials signed a stabilization agreement with the European Union (EU) that was viewed as a precursor to EU membership. In March, Macedonia, Albania, and Bulgaria had agreed to support each others' requests for funding from the EU and the World Bank to improve infrastructures, particularly railroads and highways. The World Bank is a United Nations agency that provides long-term loans to countries for development.

Macedonia tightened security at its border with Kosovo in September after several Macedonian soldiers were injured when they drove over land mines. Macedonian leaders in October met with regional leaders to discuss peaceful resolution of disputes.

In July, Macedonian Albanians held protests and demanded that Tetovo University, an Albanian-language institution, receive public funding.

☐ Sharon L. Wolchik

See also **Europe.**

Magazine. Despite an overall increase in advertising revenue for magazines in 2000, the publishers of two well-known magazines announced that they would cease publication, due to declining subscriptions and low advertising volume.

Time Inc. of New York City stopped regular publication of *Life* magazine after the May issue. *Life*, which was first published in 1936, had a monthly circulation of over 1.5 million in 2000. New York City publisher Emap USA closed *Sport* magazine after the August issue. *Sport*, which covered a variety of sports, had a circulation of 1 million in 2000 and had been published monthly since 1946. Executives from both *Life* and *Sport* said that magazines dedicated to specific areas of interest were more sustainable than general-interest publications.

Ads increase. The Magazine Publishers of America (MPA), a trade group with headquarters in New York City, reported in July 2000 that magazines took in $8.4 billion in advertising revenue from January through June 2000, an increase of 17 percent over the same period in 1999. Total pages of advertising rose by 14 percent between 1999 and 2000, to just over 120,000 pages.

Boys' magazines. New general-interest magazines for teen-age boys in 2000 joined a range of publications long available for teen-age girls. In March, New York City-based Times Mirror

Television host Oprah Winfrey introduces a new magazine, *O, The Oprah Magazine*, on April 17, 2000. The magazine's inaugural issue was 318 pages long with 166 pages of ads and a distribution of 1.5 million copies.

Magazines introduced *Transworld Stance*, a 90,000-circulation bimonthly. Los Angeles publisher Joey Magazine, LLC, launched *Joey*, a quarterly magazine for gay teens with a starting circulation of 20,000. In September, *Men's Health* publisher Rodale, of Emmaus, Pennsylvania, launched *MH-18*, a bimonthly with a starting circulation of 90,000. The magazines focused on boys' fitness, fashion, sports, and relationships.

O, The Oprah Magazine. In April, Hearst Magazines of New York City introduced *O, The Oprah Magazine*, in cooperation with television talk show host Oprah Winfrey. The monthly magazine emphasized articles on spiritual well-being, health and fitness, relationships, fashion, home design, books, and food. A total of 1.5 million copies of the inaugural issue were distributed.

Online guidelines. In August, the MPA and fellow New York City-based trade group American Society of Magazine Editors (ASME) jointly issued ethical guidelines for magazines published on the World Wide Web. Like the ASME guidelines for print magazines, the guidelines for digital media emphasize the importance of keeping advertisers interests separate from news and other editorial content.　　□ Michael Woods

Maine. See **State government**.
Malawi. See **Africa**.

Malaysia. Prime Minister Mahathir bin Mohammed announced on Sept. 11, 2000, that his deputy, Abdullah Ahmad Badawi, would take over more official duties as part of a leadership transition. The 74-year-old Mahathir, who had held the office of prime minister for 19 years, said he was serving his last term.

The United Malays National Organization (UMNO), the ruling party in Malaysia, met in May and reelected party leader Mahathir. He admitted that there were still problems with corruption. Ties between the UMNO and various favored Malaysian businesses stirred numerous complaints in 2000.

Political hardball. Mahathir's government cracked down on the opposition Islamic Party of Malaysia (PAS) during 2000. This was after UMNO popularity had declined at the polls in the November 1999 parliamentary elections. In January 2000, the government accused four opposition leaders and an opposition newspaper publisher of breaking secrecy laws. In Malacca state, the UMNO government blacklisted businesses believed to support the opposition party. In September, the prime minister's regime ordered the treasury department to withhold oil royalties from Terengganu state. Terengganu, which was controlled by the opposition Islamic party, had already allocated the royalties in its state budget.

Arms theft. On July 2, several men dressed as high-ranking military officers stole a stockpile of weapons and seized four hostages at two army camps near Malaysia's border with Thailand. Two of the hostages were killed during the incident.

The government later charged 29 members of the Al-Ma'unah sect with the crime and linked the sect to Islamic opposition. Critics claimed the link was intended to harm the opposition party.

Scandal. In August, a Malaysian court found Anwar Ibrahim, a former deputy prime minister and political heir to Mahathir, guilty of sexual misconduct. He was sentenced to nine years in jail, a sentence that was to begin after Anwar served six years for a 1999 corruption conviction.

The conviction caused new protests in Malaysia and abroad. Many believed Anwar was the victim of political revenge by Mahathir. The two men had disagreed over policy in the late 1980's, and Anwar accused Mahathir of conspiring to corrupt the legal system to destroy him.

Economy. Economists estimated that Malaysia's economy grew by 8 percent in 2000. The rate of unemployment and inflation stood at less than 3 percent.　　□ Henry S. Bradsher

See also **Asia**.
Maldives. See **Asia**.
Mali. See **Africa**.
Malta. See **Europe**.
Manitoba. See **Canadian provinces**.

Manufacturing. The United States manufacturing sector began 2000 from a position of strength but weakened during the year as interest rates rose, fuel costs soared, and spring and autumn sell-offs in high-technology stocks squeezed many of the so-called new economy companies.

The Federal Reserve System (the Fed), the central bank of the United States, raised interest rates six times between June 1999 and May 2000 in an effort to slow the high-speed U.S. economy and curb inflationary pressures. The cumulative effect of these increases—amounting to 1.75 percent in all—began to show up in interest-sensitive parts of the economy during 2000. Housing starts ran behind the 1999 pace, in turn reducing consumers' appetites for new furniture and appliances. Sales of other big-ticket items such as new automobiles weakened, while sales of computers and software flattened after the 1999 year-end flurry caused by fears that old computers might not work with the century date change.

Huge jumps in the cost of fuel during 2000 pushed up manufacturers' operation costs. As demand for consumer goods slowed or even declined in some areas and competition remained tight, most companies were unable to pass on their cost increases to customers through higher prices. As a result, many manufacturers suffered financially and had to make cutbacks.

Weaker industrial trend. A closely watched monthly measure of manufacturing strength, published by the National Association of Purchasing Management (NAPM), clearly showed the industrial slowdown taking hold as the year progressed. NAPM's members are purchasing agents for major corporations. They report on a range of industrial factors, including overall factory activity, new orders, orders backlog, employment, prices, and delivery problems.

NAPM's main index of factory activity began 2000 with a strong reading of 56.3 percent in January, then edged up to 56.9 percent in February. An index reading above 50 percent indicates that the sector is still growing, while one below 50 percent points to a decline. By March, the reading slipped to 55.8 percent, still strong but harboring signals about developing weaknesses such as slower growth for new orders and a declining backlog of unfilled orders.

The index slipped downward after March. The April figure declined to 54.9 percent, followed by 53.2 percent in May and 51.8 percent in June. Economists warned at midyear that the Fed's steep May 2000 interest hike of 0.5 percent had not yet shown up in the economy. At the same time, fuel costs continued to escalate.

Downward trend continues. July's overall NAPM index also came in at 51.8 percent. However-

er, the new-orders component had fallen to just below 50 percent. The government's July reading of total industrial production—from factories, mines, and utilities—fell by a slight 0.2 percent. Another government report showed new factory orders plunging 8.1 percent during the same period. By August, the NAPM index dropped to 49.5 percent, indicating that the factory sector of the economy was no longer expanding. September's figure improved slightly to 49.9 percent, but the index slumped in October to 48.3 percent. October's new export orders also had fallen below 50 percent, "a rare occurrence, indicating concerns for a global slowdown," according to the report.

Trying to head off global retrenchment, major industrial nations on September 22 intervened in the currency markets to boost the ailing euro, the currency of the European Union. President Bill Clinton also announced on September 22 that he would release 30 million barrels of crude oil from the *Strategic Petroleum Reserve* (oil stockpiled in the United States for emergency use) in an attempt to dampen rising world oil prices.

Firestone tire recall. Fatal automobile accidents involving Firestone tires on Ford Explorer sport utility vehicles (SUV's) led to a massive Firestone recall in the United States, beginning on August 9. Bridgestone/Firestone, Incorporated., a Japanese-owned tire company located in Nashville, Tennessee, announced a recall of 6.5 million tires that had been installed on the SUV's. Safety officials reported that the tires can shred at high or low speeds. To keep up with demand for replacements, Bridgestone launched an expensive tire airlift from Japan to the United States.

A U.S. Senate subcommittee held hearings in September and examined the question of responsibility for the tire problems on the Ford Explorer. Meanwhile, the National Highway Traffic Safety Administration continued to investigate serious accidents linked with the tires.

Microsoft antitrust case. Software manufacturer Microsoft Corporation of Redmond, Washington, remained locked in antitrust litigation and appeals in 2000. U.S. District Judge Thomas Penfield Jackson had issued a finding in late 1999 that Microsoft had acted as a monopoly. The judge then ordered Microsoft and the U.S. Justice Department to negotiate a settlement or else have the court impose a judgment. On June 7, 2000, Jackson ordered Microsoft split into two companies. One company would control Microsoft's Windows *operating system* (master control system), and a second company would manage products such as *applications software* (programs for all the specific uses of a computer). Microsoft attorneys appealed the decision.

The global manufacturers. The trend toward global corporations, in which large manufacturers extend their global reach through acquisitions or partnerships, continued through 2000. Germany-based car and truck builder Daimler-Chrysler AG bought a large stake in ailing Japanese automaker Mitsubishi and added Canadian commercial truck manufacturer Western Star to its Freightliner truck unit.

As South Korea's economy underwent restructuring following the 1997-1998 Asian economic crisis, many of its manufacturers struggled with debt and threat of bankruptcy. The situation made such companies vulnerable to take-overs from abroad. Automakers General Motors (GM) of Detroit and Italy's Fiat proposed acquiring struggling Daewoo Motor, South Korea's third-largest car builder. Stability at Daewoo became even shakier in November 2000 when the company filed for *receivership* (a stage of bankruptcy), and a South Korean court froze its assets. A number of automakers, including GM, Volkswagen of Germany, and Korean competitor Hyundai, showed interest in buying off Daewoo's far-flung automotive assets in the event of a court-ordered liquidation.   ☐ John D. Boyd

See also **Economics; Economics: A Special Report; International trade.**

Maryland. See **State government.**

Massachusetts. See **State government.**

Mauritania. See **Africa.**

Masatoshi Ono, chief executive officer of the Japanese-owned Bridgestone/Firestone Inc., testifies before a U.S. Senate subcommittee about defects in Firestone tires that led to the deaths of more than 100 people.

Mauritius. The resignation of two government ministers on Aug. 7, 2000, over a corruption inquiry led Prime Minister Navinchandra Ramgoolam to call an early general election. The September 11 election, which originally had been scheduled for December, led to the defeat of Ramgoolam's ruling alliance, which included his Labor Party (LP) and Xavier-Luc Duval's small Parti Mauritian Xavier Duval (PMXD).

National elections. An opposition alliance won 54 of the 62 directly elected National Assembly seats, thoroughly beating the government coalition. Ex-Prime Minister Sir Aneerood Jugnauth's Militant Socialist Movement (MSM) and former Deputy Prime Minister Paul Berenger's Militant Mauritian Movement (MMM) led the victorious alliance. Under the terms of a pre-election pact, Jugnauth and Berenger agreed to rule for three years and two years, respectively, should their coalition win the premiership, which has a five-year mandate. Jugnauth, who ruled Mauritius for 13 years before his electoral defeat by Ramgoolam in 1995, was sworn in as prime minister on Sept. 17, 2000.

Chagos dispute. Lawyers acting on behalf of displaced islanders from the British Indian Ocean Territory, also known as the Chagos Islands, opened a High Court appeal in London on July 17. The lawyers demanded a judicial review of the British government's relocation of the population of the Chagos Archipelago. Between 1967 and 1973, the British government removed the Chagossians from the Chagos Islands, mostly to Mauritius, 1,200 miles (1,931 kilometers) to the southwest. Some 3,000 Chagossians, known as the Ilois, claimed that they had been illegally "dumped" in Mauritius and sought the right to return home. The dispute was complicated by the fact that the United Kingdom in 1966 leased one of the main islands, Diego Garcia, to the United States for 50 years for development as a huge air and naval base.

Most of the exiles never became integrated into Mauritian society. Many of the Chagos Islanders on Mauritius have suffered from unemployment and such social problems as alcoholism and drug abuse. A report commissioned by the British Foreign Office concluded in August 2000 that repatriation was "physically possible" but questioned whether it would be economically viable.

In November, the High Court of London ruled in favor of the Ilois, noting that the British government acted unlawfully in exiling the inhabitants of the 65-island Chagos archipelago. The full impact of the ruling was not immediately clear, however, since the U.S. military base still occupied Diego Garcia.   ☐ Simon Baynham

See also **Africa; United Kingdom.**

Medicine. Scientists announced in June 2000 that they had completed a first draft of the *human genome*, the total amount of genetic information in a human cell. *Genes* (basic units of heredity) are made up of molecules of deoxyribonucleic acid (DNA). Each DNA molecule contains combinations of four chemicals that spell out instructions for hereditary traits. The chemicals are known by their initial letters: adenine (A), thymine (T), cytosine (C), and guanine (G). Like letters in words, the A's, T's, C's, and G's are arranged in specific orders, or sequences, to spell out genetic instructions. Genes are located in packages, called chromosomes, found in the *nucleus* (center) of cells.

Two groups of scientists mapped the genetic instructions by working out the location and sequence of the A's, T's, C's, and G's in genes found in the chromosomes of human cells. One group—the International Human Genome Sequencing Consortium—was publicly funded. Headquartered in Bethesda, Maryland, the consortium included scientists in China, France, Germany, Japan, the United Kingdom, and the United States. The second group—Celera Genomics—was a private company located in Rockville, Maryland. Celera scientists mapped the human genome faster than previously believed possible by using different sequencing techniques than the government-funded project.

The first-draft sequences included gaps—areas in which the arrangement of A's, T's, C's, and G's were not yet determined. Experts predicted that further study of the genome would lead to better ways of diagnosing, treating, and preventing diseases.

Gene therapy safety. The U.S. Food and Drug Administration (FDA) and the National Institutes of Health (NIH) announced in March new measures to protect patients who participate in *clinical trials* (human tests) of gene therapy. The FDA regulates the safety of medical treatments while the NIH provides funding for medical research. Gene therapy involves the use of genetic manipulation to replace defective, disease-causing genes with normal genes.

The FDA and NIH cited evidence that several clinical trials of gene therapy failed to do enough to protect the safety of volunteers. In one widely publicized incident, an 18-year-old patient died in September 1999 during a clinical trial at the University of Pennsylvania in Philadelphia.

The new measures required sponsors of clinical trials to monitor experiments more carefully. In addition, the FDA required scientists to submit more detailed information about the gene therapy remedies being tested.

Made-to-order transplant. In September 2000, physicians at Fairview-University Medical Center in Minneapolis, Minnesota, infused stem cells collected from the umbilical cord blood of a newborn boy into the baby's older sister in order to replace failing bone marrow. Stem cells are cells that have the ability to develop into any of the different cell types that make up the tissues and organs of the body. The sister, 6-year-old Molly Nash of Englewood, Colorado, was born with Fanconi anemia, a rare and often fatal genetic disease that prevents the bodies of its victims from producing bone marrow. Physicians said the infusion performed on Molly Nash was unique not because of the procedure, but because of the donor. The brother had been conceived, in part, to supply his sister with the stem cells that might keep her alive.

The newborn boy, Adam, was produced through *in vitro fertilization* (the joining of egg and sperm in a test tube) to ensure that he was free of Fanconi anemia and could serve as a tissue match for his sister. Physicians tested a number of embryos before finding one with the genetic make-up needed before implanting the embryo in the mother's womb.

Medical ethicists suggested that the use of this procedure to produce a child to serve as a tissue donor was likely to spark fierce debate over genetic testing and medical ethics.

Liver transplants. In March, the United Network for Organ Sharing (UNOS) agreed to develop a new method for selecting recipients of donated livers. UNOS is a private agency in Richmond, Virginia, that supervises the distribution of donated organs in the United States.

Previously, UNOS gave priority to patients living close to a liver donor. Critics charged that the UNOS system did not place enough emphasis on the medical needs of patients on waiting lists for a liver. UNOS said it would develop a new way of ranking liver patients on waiting lists to consider medical need.

Vision treatment. A new treatment for a type of age-related macular degeneration (AMD), the leading cause of vision loss in older Americans, went into use in April. AMD is a condition in which abnormal blood vessels form in the *macula*, the central part of the *retina* (the back of the eye). In a form of AMD called wet AMD, blood vessels leak blood into the eye, causing scar tissue to form in the macula. People with wet AMD lose sharp central vision.

In the new treatment, verteporfin, a light-sensitive drug, is injected into a patient's arm. As the drug flows through blood vessels in the retina, a doctor focuses a cold laser beam onto the eye. The beam triggers a chemical reaction that stops the bleeding in the blood vessels.

☐ Michael Woods

See also **Drugs; Public health and safety.**

Mental health. The use of psychiatric drugs for childhood emotional and behavioral problems increased in 2000. In a February study headed by Julie M. Zito of the University of Maryland in Baltimore, researchers checked the medical records of 200,000 preschool children and discovered that the number of children receiving Ritalin and related medications rose drastically between 1991 and 1995. Ritalin is used to treat attention deficit hyperactivity disorder (ADHD). Children with ADHD have difficulty concentrating on tasks and may behave in ways that disrupt school classrooms and home life.

Researchers cited a trend toward diagnosing ADHD at younger and younger ages. They pointed out that many of the drugs identified in the study had not been tested widely in very young children and could have undesirable effects.

In response to the findings, scientists with the Bethesda, Maryland-based National Institute of Mental Health (NIMH) and other United States government agencies announced in March 2000 a new effort to assure appropriate treatment of behavioral problems in children. NIMH officials said the agency would launch a special $5-million study to determine how extensively Ritalin was used in preschool children and whether the medication was used appropriately. On March 20, officials with the U.S. Food and Drug Administration (FDA) announced they would order changes in the labeling of psychiatric drugs to assure that young children receive the most effective doses. The FDA, based in Rockville, Maryland, is an agency of the U.S. Department of Health and Human Services in charge of ensuring the purity of food and the safety of drugs.

ADHD in girls. Girls with ADHD are less likely to be diagnosed and treated than boys, researchers at Harvard University Medical School in Boston, Massachusetts, reported in July. The researchers found that many girls with ADHD do not have a group of symptoms called conduct disorder. The symptoms include a tendency to engage in behavior that disrupts classes in school or disturbs parents at home. Conduct disorder is one of the most common reasons why teachers and parents have children checked for ADHD.

Stephen V. Faraone, a Harvard psychiatrist who headed the study, said that girls with ADHD may attract less attention and be less likely to be treated. Girls with ADHD, however, are more likely to have short attention spans. Left untreated, such problems can affect academic performance, the researchers suggested.

Perceptions of mental illness. More people in the United States in 2000 believed they were having mental health problems than Americans did 40 years ago, according to a national survey released in July. The survey, headed by psycholo-gist Ralph Swindle, Jr., of Indiana University in Bloomington, found that 26 percent of participants in 1996 said that they felt they had a nervous breakdown at some point in life. In a similar survey in 1976, 21 percent of the population admitted feeling close to a nervous breakdown. In 1957, only 19 percent expressed this fear. Researchers defined the term nervous breakdown as "a serious mental health problem."

Swindle noted that the findings suggested that mental health problems had increased since the 1950's. However, he also noted that the stigma of mental illness may have declined, and more people may be willing to admit to having mental illnesses.

Reasons for feeling mentally ill also changed over time. In 1957, the primary reason for a nervous breakdown was worry about physical illnesses. In 1996, the main reasons for feeling mentally ill were divorce and other relationship problems.

Better adjusted. The psychological health of many people improves steadily after age 30, even for people who were well adjusted psychologically as teen-agers, according to a study reported in June 2000 by researchers at California State University at Fresno and the University of California at Berkeley. The researchers, who analyzed the psychological health of 236 people over a 50-year period, found that after age 30, most people became better adjusted, more stable, and better able to cope with life.

The study also challenged the idea that the teen-age years are a troubled time for most young people. The researchers discovered that once individuals reached adolescence, their psychological health was relatively stable. Adolescents with psychological problems also improved as they grew older, though not to the degree of those beginning adulthood with greater psychological health.

Chronic depression. A combination of antidepressant medicine and psychotherapy is more effective than either treatment is alone, according to a study released in May. The study was headed by Martin B. Keller, a psychiatrist at Brown University in Providence, Rhode Island.

Researchers studied 681 patients who were treated with either an antidepressant, psychotherapy, or a combination of the two. About 50 percent of the people receiving the antidepressant drugs or the psychotherapy groups improved after 12 weeks of treatment. However, 85 percent of the people receiving the combination of antidepressants and psychotherapy showed improvement. The researchers also concluded that at least one form of psychotherapy, called cognitive-behavioral analysis, was effective for chronic depression. □ Michael Woods

See also **Drugs; Medicine.**

A man wearing a Vicente Fox mask celebrates Fox's election as president of Mexico at a rally under Mexico City's Angel of Independence monument on July 2. Fox's election marked the end of 71 years of rule by the Institutional Revolutionary Party.

Mexico. Vicente Fox Quesada of the center-right National Action Party (PAN) was sworn to a six-year term as president of Mexico on Dec. 1, 2000. The inauguration of Fox, who had been elected in July, marked the end of 71 years of political dominance by Mexico's Institutional Revolutionary Party (PRI) and the first transfer of power from one democratically elected party to another in Mexican history.

As president, Fox moved swiftly to ease tensions among Indians living in the southwestern state of Chiapas. On December 3, after Fox withdrew some military forces from the area, Zapatista rebels offered to begin direct talks with Fox's administration on ending their seven-year revolt. The talks were to start in February 2001.

Opposition-controlled Congress. After the congressional election in July 2000, President Fox faced a Congress that was controlled by the opposition. In the Senate, PRI held 60 seats, PAN held 46, and the leftist Democratic Revolutionary Party (PRD) held 15. Minor parties won a handful of seats in both the Senate and the Chamber of Deputies, in which PRI controlled 209 seats, PAN controlled 208, and PRD controlled 52.

U.S. visit. Fox visited Washington, D.C., in August to advocate a plan whereby the United States would grant Mexican workers an additional 250,000 visas per year to work legally in the United States. Fox claimed the plan would help reduce the illegal immigration of Mexicans to the United States. Fox added that he would like to see the U.S.-Mexican border become open to all workers within 10 years.

During his U.S. visit, Fox also said his administration would encourage greater foreign investment in the Mexican economy, particularly in the energy, petrochemicals, and telecommunications sectors.

Healthy finances. In May, the Mexican government repaid $2.5 billion in debt owed to Citibank of New York City. The repayment came before it was due, saving Mexico hundreds of millions of dollars in interest payments.

Surging oil prices in 2000 permitted Mexico to collect $3 billion more in revenues from oil exports than had been anticipated by government officials. President Fox hoped to increase Mexico's crude oil production by 200,000 barrels per day between December 2000 and January 2001, using offshore production in the Gulf of Mexico.

Economists measured the growth of Mexico's *gross domestic product* (the total value of goods and services produced in a country in a given year) at 7 percent in the third quarter of 2000—down from 7.6 percent in the second quarter. Economic analysts, who had feared that rapid growth put the Mexican economy at risk of overheating in 2000, welcomed the slight decline. The Mexican automobile industry increased production by 24.9 percent between January and August, to produce a total of 1.2 million vehicles.

Reforms in law enforcement. On July 4, Fox announced plans to rebuild Mexico's federal law enforcement system along the lines of the U.S. model. He pledged to create a "Ministry of Security and Justice" that would be similar to the U.S. Federal Bureau of Investigation. The new ministry was to be responsible for all of Mexico's federal police officers, removing police functions from the heavily politicized Interior Ministry. The ministry also would remove the army from new involvement in the war on drugs.

Embezzlement scandal. In the face of charges that he had embezzled $45 million in government funds, Mexico City Mayor Oscar Espinosa Villareal resigned in August and left the country. A Mexican judge later issued a warrant for his capture and arrest. In December, Mexican authorities revealed that Espinosa was seeking *asylum* (protection) in Nicaragua. They asked Nicaraguan officials to return Espinosa to Mexico.

Student strike. On February 6, more than 2,000 federal police officers retook the Mexico City campus of the National Autonomous University of Mexico from hundreds of students who had occupied university buildings since April 1999. A planned increase in tuition had sparked the student occupation. ☐ Nathan A. Haverstock

See also **Latin America; People in the news** (Fox, Vicente).

Miami was shaken by ethnic strife, civil unrest, and political turmoil in 2000, resulting from a custody dispute over a 6-year-old Cuban boy named Elian Gonzalez. Fishermen had found the boy clinging to an inner tube off the coast of Fort Lauderdale, Florida, in November 1999. He was one of three survivors from a group of 14 refugees who had fled Cuba in a small boat. His mother was among those who drowned when the boat capsized. Upon his rescue, Elian was placed in the temporary custody of his great uncle, who wished the boy to remain with the Gonzalez family in Miami. However, Elian's father requested that the boy be returned to him in Cuba.

Hundreds of Cuban Americans in Miami took to the streets in protest on Jan. 6, 2000, after the U.S. Immigration and Naturalization Service (INS) ordered the Miami relatives to return Elian to his father. The protestors, who asserted that Elian would be better off living in the United States than under Fidel Castro's Communist regime in Cuba, disrupted traffic throughout the city and temporarily blocked access to the Port of Miami. Their actions enraged many non-Cuban residents of the city. Miami Mayor Joseph Carollo and Miami-Dade County Mayor Alex Penelas, both of Cuban ancestry, publicly sided with the city's Cuban-American community and demanded that Elian remain in the United States.

Demonstrations continued and tension built in Miami as an intense legal battle ensued over who would gain custody of Elian. On April 22, U.S. immigration agents seized Elian in a pre-dawn raid on the residence of his Miami relatives. This set off violent protests and a one-day work stoppage by Cuban Americans in Miami. Elian was returned to his father's custody in June.

Political and social fallout. On April 27, Mayor Carollo fired Miami City Manager Donald Warshaw, accusing Warshaw of mismanagement. Warshaw alleged that he was dismissed because of his refusal to fire Chief of Police William O'Brien, who reportedly angered Carollo by failing to warn him of the federal raid on the Gonzalez house. O'Brien resigned after Warshaw's dismissal.

Carollo replaced both Warshaw and O'Brien with Cuban Americans. In response, many non-Hispanic whites and blacks in Miami staged demonstrations because Cuban Americans filled nearly all of the top government positions in the city—including the posts of mayor, city manager, police chief, and three of the five city commissioners.

INS official guilty of espionage. In May, a U.S. District Court jury in Miami found INS official Mariano Faget guilty of passing classified information to a friend with connectionss to the Cuban government. Faget, an acting deputy director of the INS Miami bureau, had been arrested in February following a year-long investigation. The case also led to the expulsion of a Cuban diplomat in Washington, D.C.

Penelas reelected. Mayor Penelas narrowly avoided a runoff election in his bid for a second term when he won approximately 52 percent of the vote against nine challengers on September 5. (Miami-Dade County law requires a runoff election if no candidate for mayor receives more than 50 percent of the vote.) Miguel Diaz de la Portilla, a veteran of the Miami-Dade County commission, finished second with 21 percent of the vote. Jay Love, the owner of a popular sports bar, won 20 percent of the vote.

Citrus canker outbreak. In June, the Florida Department of Agriculture accelerated a program, begun in 1995, to protect the state's $8.5-billion citrus industry by cutting down 1 million trees in south Florida that may have been exposed to citrus canker. Citrus canker is a bacterial disease that weakens trees and causes the premature dropping of fruit. Inspectors targeted trees in both commercial and residential areas. People whose trees were cut down were promised partial compensation with state and federal funds, but several gun-wielding Miamians, determined to protect their trees from the chainsaw, chased inspectors off their property. These individuals were later arrested.   □ Alfred J. Smuskiewicz

See also **City; Cuba: A Special Report.**

Michigan. See Detroit; State government.

In April 2000, Miamians hold a prayer vigil for Elian Gonzalez beneath a mural depicting the Cuban boy before his rescue from the Atlantic Ocean in November 1999. The custody battle for the boy between Elian's Miami relatives and his father in Cuba triggered a series of demonstrations in Miami in 2000.

In 2000, renewed Palestinian-Israeli clashes, more violent than the 1987-1993 Palestinian uprising against Israel, plunged the Middle East into turmoil. The crisis began in July 2000, when Palestinian leader Yasir Arafat and Israeli Prime Minister Ehud Barak failed to conclude a comprehensive peace at a summit in Maryland sponsored by United States President Bill Clinton. Both Barak and Clinton blamed Arafat for the failure, because Arafat had rejected Barak's offer of limited control over some of Jerusalem's Arab suburbs. Arafat had sought *sovereignty* (supreme authority) over Arab-dominated eastern Jerusalem, which Palestinians wanted as the capital of an independent state. Israel claimed Jerusalem as its "undivided" capital.

Israel captured eastern Jerusalem in the 1967 Arab-Israeli war. The area contains many religious shrines, including a site known to Jews as the Temple Mount and to Muslims as the Noble Sanctuary. The mount, formerly the location of ancient Jewish temples, has for many centuries been the location of two Islamic mosques, the Dome of the Rock and the Al-Aqsa Mosque.

Al-Aqsa uprising. On Sept. 28, 2000, Likud Party leader Ariel Sharon, who was opposed to Barak's concessions regarding Jerusalem, angered Palestinians by visiting the Noble Sanctuary. On September 29, clashes at the mount between Palestinians and Israeli security forces resulted in the deaths of six Palestinians, triggering a daily cycle of violence dubbed the "Al-Aqsa uprising." By December, more than 300 people had been killed in the violence. Most of the dead were Palestinians, though some Israeli Arabs and Israeli Jews died as well.

Several cease-fire attempts failed as the intensity of the violence inflamed passions on both sides. In October, Palestinians and international human rights groups condemned Israel for excessive use of force. Israeli officials countered that Israel was on the verge of war as street battles with protestors throwing stones gave way to Palestinian gun attacks against Israeli troops and civilians.

Israeli officials condemned the October release by Palestinian authorities of jailed members of Islamic Jihad and Hamas, militant Islamic groups opposed to peace. On October 26, Islamic Jihad claimed responsibility for a failed bombing against an Israeli Army post in the Palestinian-controlled Gaza Strip. In November, Israeli gunships attacked several offices of *Fatah* (a political movement associated with Arafat) in Palestinian areas.

Israelis question policies. As the crisis unfolded, many Israelis questioned the high cost of defending Israeli settlements in Palestinian territories, where a number of Israeli settlers had been killed in recent years. Some Israelis concluded that the violence would stop only if the Arab and Jewish communities were somehow physically separated.

Barak resigns. On December 9, in the face of declining support in the *Knesset* (Israeli parliament), Barak announced his resignation. He said he would lead a caretaker government until a special premiership election, in which he planned to be a candidate, was held in early 2001. Likud leader Sharon became Barak's main challenger for the prime minister position after former Prime Minister Benjamin Netanyahu, who had been defeated by Barak in 1999, announced he would not run in the election because of the Knesset's refusal to call new parliamentary elections.

Economic costs. The Israeli Finance Ministry estimated in November 2000 that the crisis would cost Israel a 1.5-percent drop in projected economic growth through 2001. The loss included a 50-percent decline in tourism.

Some 120,000 Palestinians in the West Bank and Gaza Strip lost their jobs in Israel when Israeli authorities closed border crossings during the crisis. In Gaza, some 30,000 additional jobs were lost in the construction and textile industries, because Arabs could not import needed raw materials from Israel. Gaza's exports to Israel, which constituted 90 percent of all of Gaza's exports, were halted in 2000. A December United Nations study reported that the crisis had cost the Palestinian economy $500 million in lost wages and sales.

On December 1, Israeli authorities allowed Palestinians to reopen the airport in the southern Gaza town of Rafah for limited use. Israel had shut down the airport, which first opened in 1998, in early November 2000.

Arab reaction. On November 14, a summit in Qatar of the Organization of Islamic Conference (OIC), a group of 56 Muslim nations, urged members to break ties with Israel. The OIC also called for severing ties with any country that transferred its embassy in Israel from Tel Aviv to Jerusalem, which Israel claimed as its capital. Observers said this move was directed at the United States, because some U.S. officials had indicated that the United States might be willing to make such a move.

After a U.S. effort to broker a Palestinian-Israeli cease-fire failed in Paris on October 4, large numbers of protestors took to the streets in Arab and Islamic countries. More than 500,000 people demon-

Palestinian police take cover during a shootout with Israeli soldiers in the Gaza Strip in October 2000. Clashes between Palestinians and Israelis began in late September and left more than 300 people dead by December.

strated in Morocco. Thousands staged protests in Jordan, Egypt, and Turkey, nations that resisted pressure to sever their ties with Israel. Alarmed by growing anti-American sentiment, the U.S. government in October temporarily closed all its embassies in the Middle East and issued a heightened security alert.

Anti-Americanism. A terrorist attack crippled the U.S. Navy destroyer U.S.S. *Cole* while it was refueling in the Yemeni port of Aden on October 12. Two suicide bombers detonated an explosive after they pulled their small boat up to the destroyer. The blast killed 17 crew members, wounded 39 others, and tore a large hole in the steel hull of the *Cole.*

Some international analysts believed the bombers may have had links to Arabs sympathetic to the Palestinian uprising. Others suggested that the blame for the blast lay with Osama bin Laden, a Saudi millionaire suspected by the United States of funding such terrorist acts as the 1998 bomb-

ings of U.S. embassies in Kenya and Tanzania. Bin Laden had previously pledged to drive U.S. military forces out of the Middle East. His key supporters were so-called "Arab Afghans," Islamic militants from various Arab countries who had driven Russian troops out of Afghanistan in the late 1980's.

Yemeni authorities detained several Arab Afghans for questioning in the bombing. On Nov. 22, 2000, Yemeni Prime Minister Abd al-Karim al-Iryani announced that government investigators had concluded that the two bombers killed in the *Cole* attack had been Arab Afghans from Saudi Arabia. The prime minister said a trial would begin in January 2001 for three to six Yemenis who were suspected accomplices in the incident.

Facts in brief on Middle Eastern countries

Country	Population	Government	Monetary unit*	Foreign trade (million U.S.$)	
				Exports[†]	Imports[†]
Bahrain	633,000	Amir Hamad bin Isa Al Khalifa; Prime Minister Khalifa bin Salman Al Khalifa	dinar (0.38 = $1)	4,088	3,588
Cyprus	777,000	President Glafcos Clerides; (Turkish Republic of Northern Cyprus: President Rauf R. Denktash)	pound (0.66 = $1)	997	3,618
Egypt	69,146,000	President Hosni Mubarak; Prime Minister Atef Mohammed Obeid	pound (3.70 = $1)	3,559	16,022
Iran	74,644,000	Supreme Leader Ayatollah Ali Hoseini-Khamenei; President Mohammed Khatami-Ardakani	rial (1,747.50 = $1)	22,391	16,274
Iraq	23,753,000	President Saddam Hussein	dinar (0.31 = $1)	12,700	8,900
Israel	6,062,000	President Moshe Katzav; Prime Minister Ehud Barak	new shekel (4.12 = $1)	25,794	33,160
Jordan	4,746,000	King Abdullah II; Prime Minister Ali Abu al-Ragheb	dinar (0.71 = $1)	1,782	3,728
Kuwait	1,818,000	Amir Jabir al-Ahmad al-Jabir Al Sabah; Prime Minister & Crown Prince Saad al-Abdallah al-Salim Al Sabah	dinar (0.31 = $1)	12,192	7,617
Lebanon	3,289,000	President Emile Lahoud Prime Minister Rafiq Hariri	pound (1,514.00 = $1)	716	7,063
Oman	2,626,000	Sultan Qaboos bin Said Al Said	rial (0.39 = $1)	5,508	5,682
Qatar	605,000	Amir Hamad bin Khalifa Al Thani; Prime Minister Abdallah bin Khalifa Al Thani	riyal (3.64 = $1)	6,700	4,200
Saudi Arabia	21,257,000	King & Prime Minister Fahd bin Abd al-Aziz Al Saud	riyal (3.75 = $1)	39,775	30,013
Sudan	32,079,000	President Umar Hasan Ahmad al-Bashir	dinar (256.00 = $1) pound (2,560.00 = $1)	596	1,915
Syria	17,329,000	President Bashar al-Assad; Prime Minister Muhammad Mustafa Miru	pound (56.36 = $1)	3,464	3,832
Turkey	67,748,000	President Ahmed Necdet Sezer; Prime Minister Bulent Ecevit	lira (672,770.00 = $1)	25,938	45,369
United Arab Emirates	2,603,000	President Zayid bin Sultan Al Nuhayyan; Prime Minister Maktum bin Rashid al-Maktum	dirham (3.67 = $1)	43,307	34,745
Yemen	17,051,000	President Ali Abdallah Salih; Prime Minister Abd al-Karim al-Iryani	rial (161.46 = $1)	1,500	2,172

*Exchange rates as of Oct. 13, 2000, or latest available data.
[†]Latest available data.

Kuwaiti authorities in November arrested several men, reported to be from Kuwait, Yemen, Egypt, and Syria, on charges that they were planning attacks against U.S. military facilities in Kuwait. The United States had maintained some 5,000 troops in Kuwait since the Persian Gulf War (1991), in which U.S.-led forces drove Iraqi troops from the country.

Papal visit. On March 20, 2000, Pope John Paul II began a six-day pilgrimage to the biblical Holy Land. The visit included stops at sacred sites in Jordan, Israel, and Palestinian-controlled Bethlehem. The pope delivered a message of inter-faith healing in a strife-torn region that was the birthplace of the Judaic, Christian, and Muslim religions. He also called for a just peace between Arabs and Israelis. ☐ Christine Helms

See also **Terrorism** and the various Middle Eastern country articles.

Mining. See Energy supply.
Minnesota. See State government.
Mississippi. See State government.
Missouri. See State government.
Moldova. See Europe.
Mongolia. See Asia.
Montana. See State government.

Montreal engaged in public mourning twice in 2000—first for hockey hero Maurice Richard, then for former Canadian Prime Minister Pierre Elliot Trudeau. Richard, known to his legions of fans as "the Rocket" while he was a superstar with the Montreal Canadiens of the National Hockey League from 1942 until 1960, died on May 27, 2000, at age 78. Trudeau, who served as prime minister from 1968 to 1979 and again from 1980 to 1984, was 80 when he died on Sept. 28, 2000. The funerals for both men filled Montreal's Notre Dame Basilica and were broadcast live by every television network in the country.

Canadiens for sale. On June 27, Montreal-based Molson Incorporated announced that it intended to sell the Canadiens, which the brewing company had owned for 35 years. The announcement raised fears among Montreal sports fans that the team might be moved out of the city. However, some Montreal-based companies indicated interest in keeping the team in Montreal.

City merger. Quebec Municipal Affairs Minister Louise Harel raised the ire of suburbanites in November, when she introduced a bill to make Montreal "one island, one city" effective Jan. 1, 2002. Under the law, which was passed by the National Assembly in December 2000, the 28 municipalities of Montreal Island were to be transformed into 27 boroughs within Montreal.

Nasdaq. Montreal became the home base in 2000 for the first *satellite* (associated) market of the Nasdaq stock exchange in Canada. Officials at the U.S.-based electronic market reported that the Nasdaq would place trading terminals at qualified brokers and dealers in Quebec after the provincial government reached an agreement with the exchange in April. Government officials expected that Nasdaq, a global trading network with 5,000 listed companies, would provide Canadian firms with greater international exposure and access to capital from around the world.

Bombardier Aerospace of Montreal confirmed in August that it would build a $170-million aircraft-manufacturing plant at Mirabel Airport, north of the city (all amounts in Canadian dollars). In March, Bombardier landed a $3-billion contract to build 94 jets for regional carriers affiliated with Delta Air Lines of Atlanta, Georgia. Bombardier officials said the new factory was scheduled to be completed by 2003 and would employ up to 1,700 people.

Merck Frosst Canada & Company announced in June 2000 that it would invest $250 million to create new research laboratories and upgrade existing facilities at its headquarters in the Montreal suburb of Kirkland. Merck is one of Canada's top pharmaceutical firms and employs some 1,200 people in the Montreal area.

Big railroad merger called off. In July, Canadian National Railways of Montreal and Burlington Northern Sante Fe of Fort Worth, Texas, called off a $28-billion merger that would have created North America's largest railroad. Both companies blamed a slow U.S. regulatory process for the collapse of the deal. In March, the U.S. Surface Transportation Board had imposed a 15-month moratorium on the plan in order to conduct an extensive review. Paul Tellier, the head of Canadian National, said, "The delay and uncertainty caused by the Surface Transportation Board's moratorium and proposed rule-making made it impossible for us to continue."

Hacker charged. In April, the Royal Canadian Mounted Police arrested a 15-year-old Montreal high-school student and charged him with the February attack on CNN.com, the Web site of the U.S.-based television network CNN. In August, police filed more than 60 additional charges against the young *hacker* (a computer programmer who creates mischief or commits crimes), who was known on the Internet as "Mafiaboy." In December, a Montreal court scheduled the teen-ager's trial to begin in March 2001.

☐ Mike King

See also **Canada; Canadian provinces; City; Hockey.**

Morocco. See Africa.

Motion pictures. Enthusiastic moviegoers in early 2000 hoped that the new century would trigger a persuasive, enterprising era in American filmmaking, similar to that of the late 1960's and early 1970's, when cinema cliches were often cast aside. Film buffs and movie critics expressed optimism that the types of thoughtful, perceptive, and intellectually challenging films released in late 1999 would flourish in 2000.

The first eight months of 2000, however, offered little evidence that the hope would become a reality. Most critics agreed that from an artistic perspective, the summer was particularly barren. Escapist entertainment is always released during the summer months but frequently one film, such as *Forrest Gump* (1994) or *Saving Private Ryan* (1998), becomes an artistic success that defines the season.

Clout versus merit. Two of the biggest hits of 2000 pitted box-office clout against artistic merit. National headlines were made when *The Perfect Storm* outranked *The Patriot* as the No. 1 movie of the Independence Day weekend.

The Perfect Storm starred George Clooney in a recreation of a 1991 convergence in the North Atlantic Ocean of a tropical hurricane, a Gulf stream cold front, and a massive thunderstorm. The film contained sketchy characterizations but dazzling special effects.

Hilary Swank (far left) and Chloe Sevigny appear in *Boys Don't Cry,* the true story of a teen-age girl who passes herself off as a boy in a small rural town. Swank won the 2000 Academy Award for best actress for her portrayal.

FOCUS ON MOTION PICTURES

Academy Award-winning films in 2000 examined life in an orphanage during the Great Depression and in contemporary small-town and suburban America.

Kevin Spacey and Annette Bening (below) star in *American Beauty* which won five Academy Awards, including best picture. Spacey received the Academy Award for best actor for his role as a man going through a midlife crisis.

Michael Caine (left) portrays a physician and Tobey Maguire is his young apprentice in *The Cider House Rules.* Caine's performance won the 2000 Academy Award for best supporting actor.

The Patriot starred box-office heavyweight Mel Gibson as a reluctant soldier during the Revolutionary War in America (1775-1783). *The Patriot* eventually qualified as a box-office success, though not of the magnitude some experts had expected. Its depiction of British soldiers as merciless warriors who spared neither women nor children brought criticism from the United Kingdom, and its summation of various historical events and characters was considered simplistic.

Media coverage of how much *The Perfect Storm* earned in relation to *The Patriot* demonstrated how weekly box-office receipts have become an integral part of entertainment reporting, with a film's box-office rank playing a more important role than critical acclaim as a peg for audiences.

Summer successes. Moviegoers flocked to two summer films that were largely dismissed by critics. *Scary Movie* was an obvious, heavy-handed spoof of horror movies. The film was a collaborative effort of the comedic and energetic Wayans brothers. Keenan Ivory Wayans directed the film, while Shawn and Marlon Wayans served as screenwriters and actors. Some critics viewed the acting as the only scary thing about the movie, though teen-agers found the humor appealing, especially those who were already fans of the movies being satirized.

Many movie critics and fans of filmmaker Robert Zemeckis, who directed *Forrest Gump,* were disappointed by the eagerly awaited mystery *What Lies Beneath.* Critics viewed the film as a reworking of storylines better manipulated by Alfred Hitchcock in *Rear Window* (1954), *Vertigo* (1958), and *Psycho* (1960). However, *What Lies Beneath* boasted the box-office team of Harrison Ford and Michelle Pfeiffer and was one of the few summer films to appeal to female audiences by concentrating on the dynamics of a husband-wife relationship.

Action films gained strong audiences during 2000. Director Ridley Scott's *Gladiator* was one of the most successful films of the summer season. The film starred Russell Crowe as a wronged general who becomes a vengeful gladiator in ancient Rome. The spectacular film included digitally enhanced crowd scenes, battles, and gladiatorial combats with lions. Crowe had won praise for the critically acclaimed yet largely unseen *The Insider* (1999), but *Gladiator* elevated him to star status.

Other popular summer releases included Tom Cruise's elaborate production of *Mission: Impossible II,* directed by John Woo. Woo's large following of fans offered mixed reviews, but the film provided an effective starring role for Cruise.

X-Men, an adaptation of the influential comic books, contained strong performances from young actors Anna Paquin and Hugh Jackman. Jackman, who made an emphatic impression as the conflicted Wolverine in *X-Men,* joined Crowe and Gibson as Australian actors who made an impact on worldwide audiences.

Erin Brockovich proved to be one of the most popular releases in the first six months of 2000. Julia Roberts starred in the true story of a law office employee investigating a real estate case. Her character discovers that a public utilities firm is buying land contaminated with a toxic chemical that the firm had secretly been dumping in the area. Roberts's rambunctious, clever performance earned the popular actress some of the best reviews of her career. Venerable actor Albert Finney also won outstanding notices as her exasperated but admiring employer.

Erin Brockovich was superbly directed by Steven Soderbergh, who also triumphed later in the year with *Traffic,* a collection of vignettes dealing with urban drug traffic. Among the key players in *Traffic's* large cast were Michael Douglas, as a drug czar who discovers his daughter is a heroin addict, and Catherine Zeta-Jones, who portrayed a drug lord's trophy wife. Both films placed Soderbergh firmly in the front ranks of American filmmakers.

Academy Award winners in 2000

The following winners of the 1999 Academy Awards were announced in March 2000:

Best Picture, *American Beauty*

Best Actor, Kevin Spacey, *American Beauty*

Best Actress, Hilary Swank, *Boys Don't Cry*

Best Supporting Actor, Michael Caine, *The Cider House Rules*

Best Supporting Actress, Angelina Jolie, *Girl, Interrupted*

Best Director, Sam Mendes, *American Beauty*

Best Original Screenplay, Alan Ball, *American Beauty*

Best Screenplay Adaptation, John Irving, *The Cider House Rules*

Best Cinematography, Conrad L. Hall, *American Beauty*

Best Film Editing, Zach Staenberg, *The Matrix*

Best Original Score, John Corigliano, *The Red Violin*

Best Original Song, Phil Collins, "You'll Be in My Heart" from *Tarzan*

Best Foreign-Language Film, *All About My Mother* (Spain)

Best Art Direction, Rick Heinrichs and Peter Young, *Sleepy Hollow*

Best Costume Design, Lindy Hemming, *Topsy-Turvy*

Best Sound, John Reitz, Gregg Rudloff, David Campbell, and David Lee, *The Matrix*

Best Sound Effects Editing, Dane A. Davis, *The Matrix*

Best Makeup, Christine Blundell and Trefor Proud, *Topsy-Turvy*

Best Visual Effects, *The Matrix*

Best Animated Short Film, *The Old Man of the Sea*

Best Live-Action Short Film, *My Mother Dreams of Satan's Disciples in New York*

Best Feature Documentary, *One Day in September*

Best Short Subject Documentary, *King Gimp*

Total revenue. Despite what critics considered to be overall weak offerings from the major film studios, audiences were willing to pay top dollar to see their favorite stars on the big screen. Film receipts in 2000 totaled $2.73 billion between Memorial Day and Labor Day.

Stronger critical releases with greater artistic quality opened in the autumn of 2000. Cameron Crowe's *Almost Famous* recaptured the writer and director's own experiences as a teen-age rock journalist in the early 1970's. *Almost Famous* won some of the most enthusiastic reviews of the year and offered a star-making performance by Kate Hudson. Hudson, the daughter of actress Goldie Hawn, portrayed a rock groupie who wants to get close to the music she loved.

Two unique films of 2000 dealt with emotionally imprisoned women finding release through entertainment outlets. In *Nurse Betty,* Renee Zellweger played a naive waitress in Kansas who, after witnessing her husband's savage murder, becomes delusional and retreats into the fantasy world of her favorite daytime soap opera. For director Neil LaBute, *Nurse Betty* represented a gentler vision than was evidenced in his previous scathing films, *In the Company of Men* (1997) and *Your Friends & Neighbors* (1998).

Danish filmmaker Lars von Trier directed Icelandic singer Bjork to critical acclaim in *Dancer in the Dark,* the melodramatic story of a factory worker with a hereditary disease that will ultimately leave her blind. Bjork's character struggles to earn enough money so that her son can undergo an operation to avoid the same fate. She finds emotional release in old-time Hollywood musicals, and von Trier recreated her visions of vintage production numbers. Some critics found the film itself to be pretentious, but many were impressed with the raw power of Bjork's big screen performance.

Director Robert Altman's *Dr. T & the Women* continued the provocative filmmaker's string of controversial movies. Richard Gere starred as an overworked gynecologist who caters to wealthy women in Dallas. Some critics argued that the film contained too many familiar Texas stereotypes, while others said it put an enjoyable new spin on the cliches. Gere's performance earned him some of the warmest reviews of his career.

In *Pay It Forward,* the strong performances of Academy Award winners Kevin Spacey and Helen Hunt and young Academy Award nominee Haley Joel Osment won positive reviews. But both critics and audiences considered the film's treatment of its emotionally scarred characters to be overly simplistic.

Joel Schumacher, known for directing such polished but shallow extravaganzas as *Batman Forever* (1995) and *Batman & Robin* (1997), found

critical success with *Tigerland,* a drama about U.S. Army recruits undergoing rigorous training before being sent to Vietnam in the early 1970's.

Robert DeNiro scored one of his biggest box-office hits in recent years by mocking his intimidating presence in *Meet the Parents.* He played a suspicious, retired Central Intelligence Agency (CIA) official who is the prospective father-in-law of a character played by comedian Ben Stiller.

Director Ang Lee continued to demonstrate a remarkable versatility in 2000. In *Crouching Tiger, Hidden Dragon,* the tale of the disappearance of a magical jade sword, Lee combined operatic emotions, martial arts, and Chinese legend into one of the year's most satisfying visual and emotional experiences. Lee had previously garnered acclaim from critics and audiences for exploring such topics as the reserved traditions of Jane Austen in *Sense and Sensibility* (1995).

In 2000, box-office giant Jim Carrey continued his slide into bad movies. The summer release of *Me, Myself & Irene,* which tried to turn schizophrenia into a comedy routine, was a critical and commercial disappointment. Fans and critics alike anticipated the live-action holiday release of the Dr. Seuss tale, *How the Grinch Stole Christmas.* Many people hoped that Carrey would regain his large following with his portrayal of the mythical character from children's literature.

International successes. Australian-produced films rebounded in 2000 by targeting teen-age audiences with light-hearted romantic comedies, such as *The Wog Boy* and *Looking for Alibrandi.* The Australian comedic action film *Chopper,* about a man who dreams of being remembered as a legendary crime figure, loomed as a possible breakout worldwide hit. Critics also praised *Bootmen,* starring Adam Garcia as an Australian factory worker who uses rock music as an escape from his blue-collar world.

Polish director Juliusz Machulski won audiences with *Killer 2,* a dark satire that addressed contemporary issues, such as post-Communist freedoms, in Poland. The film was the sequel to the extremely successful comedy *Killer* (1998).

French director Leos Carax found a sizable hit with *Pola X,* a loose adaptation of Herman Melville's novel, *Pierre. Pola X,* a 1999 film released in the United States in 2000, starred Guillaume Depardieu, son of veteran French actor Gerard Depardieu, as a young man who is involved in a tragic relationship with both his mother and a woman who claims to be his half-sister.

　□ Philip Wuntch

See also **People in the news** (Spacey, Kevin; Swank, Hilary).

Mozambique. See Africa.

Music. See Classical music; Popular music.

Myanmar. Daw Aung San Suu Kyi, leader of the National League for Democracy (NLD), tried to assert political rights for the NLD in 2000. The NLD won 82 percent of the vote in the 1990 parliamentary elections, but the military rulers of Myanmar—formerly known as Burma—refused to give up power.

Suu Kyi, a 1991 Nobel Peace Prize winner, tried several times to leave the capital, Yangon, to pursue provincial political work. But police would not let her leave. On Sept. 3, 2000, police raided NLD headquarters and confined party leaders to their residences for two weeks.

Universities, which had been closed since December 1996 to prevent antigovernment student demonstrations, reopened in July 2000. The universities had only been open for a total of 30 months since 1988, when soldiers killed hundreds of students during demonstrations.

The International Labor Organization, a United Nations affiliate in Geneva, Switzerland, reported in March 2000 that the use of forced labor was common in Myanmar. The organization found that more than 800,000 people in Myanmar were virtual slaves. □ Henry S. Bradsher

See also **Asia.**

Namibia. See Africa.

Nebraska. See State government.

Nepal. See Asia.

Netherlands. In 2000, the Dutch continued to pursue some of the most liberal social policies in Europe. In September, the parliament approved a law granting gay couples the same marital status as heterosexual couples, including the right to marry at city hall, adopt children, and divorce through the courts. In November, the parliament voted to legalize *euthanasia* (mercy killing) for terminally ill patients who face unbearable suffering. Although illegal, euthanasia had been tolerated in the Netherlands for a number of years. In 1999, physicians had established guidelines for the procedure. The government hoped that by making mercy killings and assisted suicides legal, the new law would bring the practice into the open and allow authorities to regulate it. According to government statistics, 2.4 percent of all deaths in the Netherlands resulted from euthanasia. However, government officials believed that physicians reported fewer than half of all cases because of the risk of prosecution.

Economy. The Netherlands boasted one of the strongest economies in Europe in 2000, with output forecast to grow by 4.5 percent and unemployment expected to fall below 3 percent. The government, enjoying a budget surplus of about 1 percent of gross domestic product, proposed in September to increase spending by $5.8 billion in its draft budget for 2001. (The gross domestic product is the value of all goods and services produced in a year.) Most of the money was targeted for education and health care.

Lockerbie trial. The trial of two Libyans accused of placing bombs aboard Pan Am Flight 103 began in the Netherlands in May 2000 at Camp Zeist, a former U.S. air base. Pan Am Flight 103 crashed over Lockerbie, Scotland, in 1988 killing 270 people. The trial was the result of a unique agreement between the United Kingdom and the United States and Libya, which insisted on a neutral site for the trial. (Most of the victims were either British or American.) The base in the Netherlands was declared Scottish territory, and the trial was held under Scottish law with Scottish judges and attorneys.

An explosion at a fireworks factory destroyed several blocks in the Dutch city of Enschede on May 13, 2000, and killed 20 people. Authorities arrested the owners of the factory, who were charged with illegally storing fireworks. □ Tom Buerkle

See also **Europe.**

Nevada. See State government.

New Brunswick. See Canadian provinces.

New Hampshire. See State government.

New Jersey. See State government.

New Mexico. See State government.

New York. See State government.

New York City. Bernard Kerik was sworn in as New York City's 40th police commissioner on Sept. 6, 2000. A former corrections commissioner and police detective, Kerik promised to make better police and community relations a priority.

Kerik replaced Howard Safir, who resigned in August. Under Safir the police department was credited with reducing the city's crime rate. However, the department generated controversy after several confrontations with minority citizens.

In the most publicized case, four white police officers who had killed a West African immigrant in 1999 were acquitted by a racially mixed jury in February 2000. The plainclothes officers testified that they had fired 41 shots, 19 of which hit the victim, Amadou Diallo. One of the officers believed Diallo had removed a gun from his pocket, though Diallo had actually removed his wallet. The trial was held in Albany, New York, after defense lawyers argued that their clients could not receive a fair trial in the Bronx.

In March, an off-duty security guard, Patrick Dorismond, was killed during a scuffle with undercover narcotics detectives. The incident occurred outside a Manhattan bar after one of the officers asked Dorismond if he knew where to buy marijuana. A Manhattan grand jury concluded that the shooting was unintentional.

The Rose Center for Earth and Space, a division of the American Museum of Natural History, opens in New York City on Feb. 19, 2000. The 87-foot (26.5-meter) sphere at the center contains two theaters offering a virtual tour of the universe.

Politics. New York City Mayor Rudolph W. Giuliani withdrew as a candidate for the U.S. Senate from New York on May 19. Many political observers had believed Giuliani was the most likely person to beat the Democratic candidate, First Lady Hillary Rodham Clinton.

The mayor's decision to withdraw from the race came after an announcement in April that he had been diagnosed with prostate cancer. In another announcement in May, the mayor said he would seek a formal separation from his wife, actress and former news anchor Donna Hanover.

Education. In May, the Board of Education unanimously appointed Harold Levy, a New York City banking executive, as chancellor of the New York public school system. Levy assumed the $245,000-a-year post, although he had no formal training in the field of education.

Transportation. Plans for a new Second Avenue subway line were derailed on election day when voters rejected a $3.8-billion transportation bond issue. While New York City and suburban voters backed the bond issue, upstate voters were firmly against the measure.

Public health. President Bill Clinton, on October 11, declared a state of emergency in New York City because of the threat of the West Nile virus, a mosquito-borne disease. Mayor Giuliani and Governor George Pataki criticized Clinton's

$5-million pledge to battle the outbreak as inadequate. In mid-2000, the summer-long pesticide spray program was credited with limiting the outbreak. Fourteen New Yorkers and three New Jersey residents fell ill from the virus, and one person died from it. However, the virus toll in 2000 was far less deadly than in 1999, when seven people died and dozens of others became ill.

The City Council's Select Committee on Pest Control reported in May 2000 that rats had become a public health nuisance. Officials estimated that there were six rats for every person in New York City. The council cited the demolition of old buildings, poor garbage disposal, and lack of city response as factors in the current infestation. The Department of Health urged residents to put garbage in containers with a lid.

Real estate. In October, *The New York Times* selected Italian architect Renzo Piano to design a new headquarters. The newspaper planned to remain within the Times Square area, but relocate to a site on Eighth Avenue.

Subway series. In 2000, New Yorkers were treated to the first all-New York World Series since the Yankees and Brooklyn Dodgers met in 1956. The Yankees' victory over the Mets, four games to one, enthralled New Yorkers in 2000 but was a television ratings dud. □ Owen Moritz

See also **Architecture; Cities; Crime.**

New Zealand. The Labour Alliance coalition, elected in November 1999, found itself in conflict with New Zealand's business community in 2000. Business leaders were not pleased with the government's passage of legislation changing industrial law, increasing top personal tax rates by 6 percent, and renationalizing the Accident Compensation Corporation, the organization providing accident compensation to workers.

In March, New Zealand hosted the America's Cup sailing competition. Team New Zealand defeated Italy's Prada Syndicate to become the first country other than the United States to successfully defend the America's Cup trophy.

Economy. The America's Cup competition injected an estimated $640 million (all amounts in New Zealand dollars) into the economy in 2000. However, the earnings reflected only half the amount that boosters had projected the competition would produce.

By June, business confidence, as measured by a quarterly survey, had dropped sharply. Alarmed by the trend, the government worked to improve its relationship with businesses. This resulted in a national economic development forum in October, which was attended by 85 business leaders. However, business confidence remained low due to the combination of rising oil prices and the decline in September in the value of the New Zealand dollar to 39 cents to the U.S. dollar, the lowest value ever recorded.

New Zealand exporters and farmers benefited from the dollar's decline. Businesses exported more than $27.3 billion worth of products between September 1999 and September 2000, an increase of 18.3 percent over the same period in 1998 and 1999.

Defense. The government of New Zealand made significant changes in defense policy in 2000. In late 1999, officials canceled a contract for 28 F-16 fighter jets that would have replaced the Royal New Zealand Air Force's aging Skyhawk fighters. Instead, the government approved the purchase of new troop-carrying armored vehicles and radios for the army.

A New Zealand soldier who was part of the 600-member peacekeeping force on duty in East Timor was killed in July 2000 in an engagement with Indonesian militia in hill country near the border with West Timor.

Genetic engineering. In June, a royal commission headed by former Chief Justice Sir Thomas Eichelbaum began a year-long inquiry into the risks and benefits of genetic engineering technologies and their products. Scientists agreed to stop field trials involving genetically altered organisms during the inquiry, but medical experiments were not affected.   ☐ Gavin Ellis

Newfoundland. See Canadian provinces.

■ News bytes

Selected news from 2000:

Oklahoma City memorial. The Oklahoma City National Memorial, honoring the victims of the 1995 bombing of the Alfred P. Murrah Federal Building in Oklahoma City, Oklahoma, opened on April 19, 2000. The date marked the fifth anniversary of the most deadly domestic terrorist attack in U.S. history.

The memorial spans two city blocks in Oklahoma City and cost $10 million to construct. A grassy mall replaced the site where the federal building stood. On the mall are 168 sculpted stone and bronze chairs—one in tribute to each of the victims. The chairs are arranged in nine rows, symbolizing the nine floors of the federal building. Nineteen of the chairs, smaller than the rest, represent the children who died in a day-care center when the bomb exploded.

A reflecting pool 330 feet (100 meters) long covers what was once the street in front of the federal building. Two gates commemorating the moment of the explosion—9:02 a.m.—stand at opposite ends of the pool. The time 9:01 is carved at the top of the east gate while 9:03 is carved atop the west gate. Rows of trees at the memorial honor those people who helped during the rescue. The new orchard complements a nearby elm tree that survived the blast. The tree, known as the Survivor Tree, has become a symbol for those who lived through the horror.

Roller coaster ride. The Millennium Force, the world's tallest and fastest roller coaster, went into operation on May 13, 2000, at Cedar Point, an amusement park in Sandusky, Ohio. The Millennium Force stands 310 feet (95 meters)

A large pool reflects a gate at the Oklahoma City National Memorial, which opened in April 2000, in honor of the 168 victims of the bombing of the Murrah Federal Building in 1995.

high at its highest point, the approximate height of a 30-story building. Riders endure a vertical dive from a height of 300 feet (92 meters) at speeds of 92 miles (148 kilometers) per hour. The vertical dive is the steepest on record at 122 degrees.

Amusement park enthusiasts marveled at the simplicity of the blue and yellow shells of the roller coaster cars, which lacked side or shoulder harnesses. Riders were restrained by a simple seat belt and lap bar. Other riders commented on the structure's appearance as postmodern architecture, with the steel frame balanced with dramatic loops. Through the summer of 2000, visitors often waited in line for more than 3 hours for the opportunity to take the 2-minute-and-45-second ride on the Millennium Force.

Gettysburg viewing tower. A viewing tower constructed during the 1970's near Gettysburg, Pennsylvania's historic Civil War (1861-1865) battlefield, was demolished on July 3, 2000, to the delight of historians and preservationists. A Civil War reenactment company staged a mock battle the day the tower was demolished. The troop pointed two artillery pieces—one Union and one Confederate—at the tower. Moments later, 10 pounds (4.5 kilograms) of explosives planted at the base of the structure detonated, crashing it to the ground.

The National Tower at Gettysburg opened as a tourist attraction in 1974 on private property at the edge of the government-owned land that marks the site of the Battle of Gettysburg, considered to be a turning point in the Civil War. In June 2000, a federal judge ruled that the U.S. government could take the property if the owners were compensated $3 million.

The 393-foot (120-meter) observation tower consisted of a four-level octagon-shaped viewing area supported by a latticework of steel beams. Proponents of the structure argued that the tow-

er, with its displays and explanations, offered the battlefield's 2 million annual visitors an aerial view and a better understanding of the pivotal battle that occurred on the site. Critics regarded the structure as a disgrace to the memory of the Civil War dead buried nearby. They hailed the tower's destruction as an opportunity to return the Gettysburg battlefield to the way it looked in 1863.

The National Park Service, which maintains the land, announced in 2000 that it would restore fences and orchards present during the war and remove all modern buildings.

Confederate sub raised. On Aug. 8, 2000, salvage crews raised the *H.L. Hunley* from Charleston Harbor at Charleston, South Carolina. The *Hunley* was the first submarine in history to sink an enemy ship in battle. Built by the Confederacy during the Civil War, the *Hunley* sank in 1864, shortly after ramming an explosive device into the side of the Union ship *Housatonic.*

A search team found the *Hunley* in 1995, following a 15-year search. Work crews used an elaborate truss to lift the vessel from the harbor and place it on a waiting barge. The submarine was taken to a laboratory at the Old Charleston Navy Yard and immersed in fresh water cooled to 50 °F (10 °C) to aid in its preservation.

Scientists noted that treatment to conserve the *Hunley* could take as long as 10 years. Preservationists estimated the combined cost for recovering and preserving the vessel was $17 million. Historians reported that the submarine ultimately would be placed on display at the Charleston Museum.

OpSail 2000. A fleet of approximately 300 ships sailed into New York Harbor on July 4, 2000, in celebration of Independence Day. Craft of various shapes and sizes participated in the display, called Operation Sail 2000 (OpSail 2000). They included 26 tall-masted ships with huge, billowing canvas sails typical of vessels of the 1700's and 1800's. Vessels from nearly 20 countries took part in the five-hour procession of ships.

The National Tower at Gettysburg, a viewing platform that opened in 1974 near the site of a historic Civil War (1861-1865) battle, is demolished on July 3, 2000.

of New Orleans's downtown and French Quarter. Exhibits of aircraft, jeeps, tanks, and personal memorabilia, such as soldiers' diaries, maps, photographs, and uniforms, help relate the story of the D-Day invasion.

Millennium curse? British politicians and engineers attempted in 2000 to downplay what the British press was calling the "Millennium Curse"—the long series of problems that plagued all of the structures built in the United Kingdom to celebrate the dawn of the new millennium.

In June, engineers closed London's Millennium Bridge two days after it opened because the structure began swaying. An investigation revealed that pedestrian traffic on the suspension bridge, which spans the River Thames, caused the structure to sway more than expected. As the bridge swayed, pedestrians attempted to steady themselves by rocking back and forth, increasing the movement of the bridge. Engineers installed dampers—devices similar to shock absorbers on a car—under the bridge to reduce its movement.

The London Eye, a Ferris-wheel-like structure that stands 450 feet (137 meters) tall on the south bank of the River Thames, caused its engineers trouble from the day it was to open. The wheel was scheduled to go into operation on Dec. 31, 1999, in conjunction with the city's New Year's Eve celebration, but a faulty part delayed the opening until February 2000. In July, engineers closed the London Eye after a tire used to propel the wheel shredded and fell into the river.

London's Millennium Dome—an immense structure with 1 million square feet (93,000

The *Rose*, an American frigate, sails into New York Harbor on July 4 as part of Operation Sail 2000. More than 300 vessels participated in the event, a celebration of Independence Day.

D-Day museum opens. Approximately 10,000 veterans of World War II (1939-1945) attended the opening of the National D-Day Museum in New Orleans, Louisiana, on June 6, 2000. The museum, which was founded by U.S. author and historian Stephen E. Ambrose, honors the Allied forces who fought against Nazi Germany and other Axis countries during the war. The museum pays special tribute to those men who landed on the beaches of Normandy, France, on D-Day, June 6, 1944.

The museum occupies 70,000 square feet (6,503 square meters) of space in a former warehouse within walking distance

A display at the National D-Day Museum in New Orleans, Louisiana, illustrates the military power of the United States, Germany, and Japan in the late 1930's. The museum opened in June 2000.

square meters) of covered space—also had problems in 2000. In September, the chairman of the dome's operating company announced that the attraction probably should never have been built, since it attracted far fewer visitors than expected. The number of visitors, which officials originally estimated would hit 12 million people in 2000, barely reached 5 million by October. The dome was scheduled to close on December 31.

Document sold. In June 2000, television producer and director Norman Lear and Internet entrepreneur David Hayden purchased a rare, original printing of the Declaration of Independence for a record $8.1 million, the highest price ever paid for an item sold over the Internet. The duo bought the document in a live auction at the Web site of Sotheby's, a New York City-based auction company. The purchase price was also a record amount for a historical U.S. document.

The document is one of only 25 known surviving copies—and one of four copies in private hands—of the official

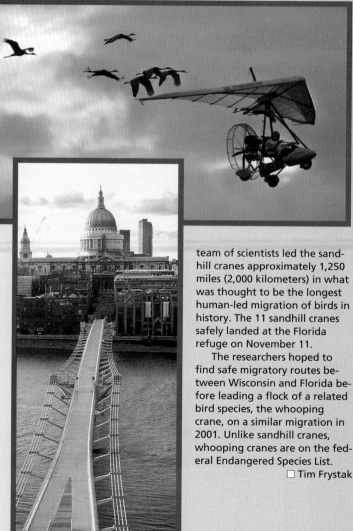

In October, sandhill cranes (right) follow an ultralight plane from the Necedah National Wildlife Refuge in Wisconsin. The flight was part of an experiment to lead the cranes southward to Florida. In London, engineers closed the Millennium Bridge (below right) in June after it began to sway.

printing of the declaration. The American Colonies used the original document to declare their freedom from the United Kingdom. It was adopted by the Continental Congress in Philadelphia on July 4, 1776.

Lear, whose credits include the 1970's television situation comedy "All in the Family," and Hayden announced that they would take the document on tour to schools and libraries around the United States.

Baseball card auction. In July 2000, a Chicago sports memorabilia collector sold a rare baseball card for a record

$1.1 million. The purchase marked the first time that a card had sold for more than $1 million. An anonymous Southern California sports memorabilia collector purchased the T206 Honus Wagner baseball card through eBay, Inc., an online auction company headquartered in San Jose, California.

The card was manufactured in 1909 and was only available in packets of cigarettes. The American Tobacco Company produced approximately 50 copies of the card depicting Wagner, who at the time was a shortstop for the Pittsburgh Pirates. According to baseball lore, the company stopped production because Wagner objected to the use of his image to promote a tobacco product. However, Wagner used chewing tobacco. He was not paid a royalty for the use of his image.

Learning to fly. Scientists flying an ultralight aircraft set out on Oct. 3, 2000, from Necedah National Wildlife Refuge in Wisconsin to lead a flock of sandhill cranes to Chassahowitzka National Wildlife Refuge in Florida for the winter. The team of scientists led the sandhill cranes approximately 1,250 miles (2,000 kilometers) in what was thought to be the longest human-led migration of birds in history. The 11 sandhill cranes safely landed at the Florida refuge on November 11.

The researchers hoped to find safe migratory routes between Wisconsin and Florida before leading a flock of a related bird species, the whooping crane, on a similar migration in 2001. Unlike sandhill cranes, whooping cranes are on the federal Endangered Species List.

☐ Tim Frystak

Newspaper. Officials of the Chicago-based Tribune Company, publisher of the *Chicago Tribune* and owner of the WGN cable television station and the Chicago Cubs baseball team, announced on March 13, 2000, that the company planned to purchase the Los Angeles-based Times Mirror Company, owner of the *Los Angeles Times,* for $8 billion. The purchase of the Times Mirror Company was finalized in June.

Other newspaper deals. A number of U.S. newspapers announced mergers and purchases in 2000. On June 28, Arlington, Virginia-based Gannett Company, the publisher of *USA Today,* agreed to pay $2.6 billion for Indianapolis-based Central Newspapers, Incorporated, the publisher of the *Arizona Republic* and *The Indianapolis* (Indiana) *Star.*

Thomson Corporation, of Toronto, Canada, announced on February 15 that the company would sell 129 of its 130 newspapers in the United States and Canada. The company retained ownership of *The Globe and Mail* in Toronto. The 129 newspapers, which were all sold by June, brought the company a total of $2.44 billion.

News World Communications, Incorporated, of Washington, D.C., announced on May 15 that it had purchased United Press International Incorporated (UPI), a news service, from Saudi Arabian-based Worldwide News, Incorporated, for an undisclosed price. News World Communications was controlled by Sun Myung Moon, founder of the Unification Church.

Joint operating agreements. On July 27, a federal judge allowed the Hearst Corporation, owner of the *San Francisco Examiner,* to end a joint operating agreement and purchase the rival *San Francisco Chronicle* for $660 million. A joint operating agreement allows rival newspapers in the same city to share business costs and revenues while still competing for news. In July, the Hearst Corporation agreed to turn over control of the *Examiner* to a local publisher and pay up to $66 million in expenses over three years.

On May 11, a century-old circulation war between two Denver, Colorado, newspapers ended when E. W. Scripps Company's *Rocky Mountain News* and MediaNews Group's *The Denver Post* agreed to a joint operating agreement.

Newspaper circulation for most of the top 10 newspapers in the United States grew slightly in 2000, the Newspaper Association of America, the industry trade group, reported in October. The circulation of *The Wall Street Journal,* the highest of any daily, increased 0.6 percent to reach 1,762,751. *The New York Times* enjoyed the top Sunday circulation, with readership jumping 1.7 percent to 1,682,208. □ Mark Fitzgerald

See also **Labor and employment; people in the news** (Thomas, Helen).

Nicaragua. The United States National Labor Committee, which investigates labor abuses in overseas factories that supply goods to U.S. markets, strongly condemned Chentex, a Taiwanese-owned textile company, in 2000 for dismissing more than 150 workers at the company's plant near the Nicaraguan capital, Managua. The workers were fired after staging a brief strike for higher wages in April.

In October, U.S. trade representative Charlene Barshefsky warned the Nicaraguan government of possible retaliatory action if labor conditions were not improved at Chentex and another Taiwanese-owned plant near Managua. Both plants supplied apparel to Wal-Mart stores in the United States, as well as to nonprofit post exchanges operated by the U.S. Defense Department on military bases.

Nicaragua faced a financial crisis in 2000 when several Nicaraguan banks struggled with possible insolvency. In August, the Nicaraguan government took control of Interbank, Nicaragua's third largest financial institution, after the bank made $40 million in unsecured loans. In September, Banco del Cafe, another large Nicaraguan bank, came under government control following $50 million in faulty loans. □ Nathan A. Haverstock

See also **Latin America.**

Niger. See **Africa.**

Nigeria. Violence between Christians and Muslims in 2000 threatened the stability of Nigeria. However, international confidence in Nigeria's new democracy was given a symbolic boost by U.S. President Bill Clinton's state visit in August, which was viewed as a turning point in relations between Nigeria and the global community.

Religious violence. In February, protests by Christians opposed to the planned introduction of *Sharia* (religious law of Islam) in the northern Nigerian state of Kaduna were met by Muslim counter-protesters, resulting in the death of several hundred people. In March, the violence spread, with Christians killing Muslims in the Christian-dominated towns of Aba, Owerri, and Umuahia. In late May, renewed religious conflict in Kaduna left at least another 300 people dead, with many mosques and churches burned. In June, officials in the state of Kano joined several other predominantly Muslim states in northern Nigeria in implementing Sharia, triggering a fresh exodus of Christians to the south.

Muslims in northern Nigeria viewed the Sharia criminal code—which includes penalties such as amputation of hands for theft and flogging or stoning for adultery—as an answer to Nigeria's widespread crime and corruption. The people of Nigeria's mainly Christian south viewed Sharia as an attempt by northerners to impose their will on the country. More than 1,000 people have died in religious clashes since President Obasanjo, a Christian, took office on May 29, 1999. In 2000, non-Muslims pressured Obasanjo to obtain a supreme court ruling on the constitutionality of Sharia in Nigeria, which is a *secular* (not connected to a state religion) nation.

Ethnic violence. In October, ethnic violence between the Yoruba and Hausa peoples in the state of Lagos left more than 100 Nigerians dead. Military personnel calmed the violence after three days of fighting.

Pipeline explosions. More than 250 people burned to death in an explosion near the town of Warri on July 10. The explosion was caused by thieves stealing gasoline from a pipe line. On November 30, a similar incident killed more than 60 people in a fishing village near downtown Lagos. Nigeria's network of crisscrossing pipe lines were frequently tapped in 2000 by fuel thieves, who sold the gasoline in a thriving black market.

Foreign affairs. President Clinton's visit to Nigeria in August 2000 stressed the importance of protecting the new democracy and provided a powerful international endorsement of Nigeria's return to democratic rule in 1999.

☐ Simon Baynham
See also **Africa; United Kingdom.**

Nobel Prizes in literature, peace, the sciences, and economics were awarded in October 2000 by the Norwegian parliament, the Storting, in Oslo and by the Royal Swedish Academy of Sciences, the Karolinska Institute, and the Swedish Academy of Literature in Stockholm. Each prize was worth almost $915,000.

The 2000 Nobel Prize for literature was awarded to Chinese novelist and playwright Gao Xingjian. Gao left his native country, where his writings were banned, for France in 1987. In announcing the award, the Swedish Academy of Literature explained that Gao "has opened new paths for the Chinese novel and drama" and cited Gao's novel *Soul Mountain* as a "singular literary creation." Gao's dramatic writing is strongly influenced by the absurdism of Irish-French playwright Samuel Beckett (1906-1989). Gao's 1983 play *Bus Stop* recalls Beckett's *Waiting for Godot.*

The 2000 Nobel Peace Prize was awarded to South Korean president Kim Dae-jung for his contributions to human rights and his efforts at achieving reconciliation with North Korea. In making the award, the Norwegian Nobel Committee, which is selected by the Storting, declined to honor Kim Chong-il, the North Korean leader. In the past, peace prizes have usually been awarded to representatives of both sides in international conflicts.

The two Koreas have been engaged in bitter hostility since the Korean War (1950-1953). After becoming president in 1998, South Korea's Kim worked to establish cordial relations with the North. In June 2000, the two Kims met in a summit in Pyongyang, North Korea's capital. Following the summit, the two governments arranged family visits and began restoring rail links.

The 2000 Nobel Prize for physiology or medicine went to Arvid Carlsson of Sweden's University of Gothenburg and Americans Eric R. Kandel of Columbia University in New York City and Paul Greengard of Rockefeller University, also in New York. These neuroscientists conducted research that clarified biochemical processes by which nerve cells in the brain communicate.

In the late 1950's, Carlsson discovered the role of the chemical dopamine as a signaling agent in parts of the brain that regulate movement. His finding led to treatment of *Parkinson disease* (a disorder that destroys brain cells) with the compound L-dopa. It also led to the development of new drugs to combat *schizophrenia* (a mental disease characterized by disturbances in thinking). Kandel worked out many of the biochemical processes of learning and memory. Greengard unraveled the sequence of molecular changes that occur inside brain nerve cells.

The 2000 Nobel Prize for economics was awarded to James J. Heckman of the University of Chicago and Daniel L. McFadden of the University of California at Berkeley. In separate research, these economists developed statistical methods that became widely used to analyze and predict various human behaviors. Incorporating such factors as personal motivation and human irrationality, their methods have been applied to studies as diverse as the motivations that affect the job choices of single mothers and incentives that encourage consumers to buy battery-powered cars.

The 2000 Nobel Prize for chemistry went to Alan J. Heeger of the University of California at Santa Barbara, Alan G. MacDiarmid of the University of Pennsylvania in Philadelphia, and Hideki Shirakawa of the University of Tsukuba in Japan. These men were honored for their pioneering work on plastics that conduct electricity like metals and semiconductors. In the early 1970's, Shirakawa was experimenting with a *polymer* (a chemical compound in which each molecule is made up of simpler molecules), when a lab mistake produced a thin, metallic-looking plastic film that turned out to be a conductor. At about the same time, Heeger and MacDiarmid were working with similar materials in the United States. Eventually, the three scientists worked together, laying the foundation for a new field of science known as polymer electronics.

The Academy of Sciences said the polymer research would likely generate a wide range of consumer products, such as inexpensive, foldable video displays and "throwaway" electronic products. By 2000, the work of these scientists had already yielded some practical applications, including antistatic coatings on photographic film.

The 2000 Nobel Prize for physics was shared by Americans Jack S. Kilby and Herbert Kroemer and Russian Zhores Alferov. The three scientists developed technologies that helped make the computer revolution possible.

In the late 1950's, Kilby was an electrical engineer at Texas Instruments, Incorporated, in Dallas. Kilby speculated that electronic components, such as transistors and capacitors, could be created out of a single block, rather than the then-current practice of making them separately and wiring them together. Acting on this speculation, he crafted a crude integrated circuit, the forerunner of the microchip. Along with U.S. engineer Robert Noyce, Kilby is regarded as the coinventor of the integrated circuit. Alferov, of St. Petersburg's Ioffe Physico-Technical Institute, and Kroemer, of the University of California at Santa Barbara, later developed refinements in microelectronic processing that proved useful in satellite communications, lasers, and compact disc players. □ Robert N. Knight

Northern Ireland. Protestant and Catholic political parties in Northern Ireland struggled in 2000 to implement the terms of the Good Friday agreement of 1998. The agreement was designed to end years of fighting between unionists, who favored the existing union of Northern Ireland with Great Britain, and nationalists, who favored the union of Northern Ireland with Ireland. The agreement introduced a cease-fire and provided for the creation of a Northern Ireland Assembly in which both sides of the religious divide would be represented. (Prior to the agreement, Northern Ireland was directly ruled by the British government.)

Decommissioning. Although the British Parliament had transferred power to the Northern Ireland Assembly on Dec. 2, 1999, the issue of the decommissioning of weapons by the Irish Republican Army (IRA)—an unofficial military group with political connections to the Sinn Fein party—caused a deadlock for much of 2000. The main Protestant party, the Ulster Unionists, refused to cooperate with the peace process as long as the IRA remained armed. On February 11, the British government suspended the assembly because the terms of the agreement over disarmament had not been met.

On May 6, the IRA agreed to put its weapons "beyond use" and to allow international officials to inspect its secret arms dumps. Nevertheless, many Ulster Unionists, unhappy over negotiations

on the formation of a new police force to replace the former—mostly Protestant—Royal Ulster Constabulary, remained unwilling to join Sinn Fein in the government. David Trimble, leader of the Unionists, persuaded his party to reconsider. On May 30, the British government allowed the Northern Ireland Assembly to reconvene. Trimble became first (prime) minister and Martin McGuiness of Sinn Fein took over as education minister.

In mid-2000, international observers Cyril Ramaphosa, of South Africa's African National Congress, and Martti Ahtisaari, a former president of Finland, visited the secret IRA arsenals. They later expressed their satisfaction that the weapons could not easily be employed.

Loyalist violence. In August, violence broke out in Belfast between Protestant paramilitary groups as they struggled to dominate loyalist areas. Troops, which had been withdrawing from the province, were recalled in an effort to keep the peace. In December, the rival groups declared an end to the feud.

New force. In November, the British Parliament passed a law creating a new police force. The Police Service of Northern Ireland replaced the Royal Ulster Constabulary. □ Rohan McWilliam

See also **Ireland; United Kingdom.**

Northwest Territories. See **Canadian territories.**

Norway. Political instability in Norway in 2000 led to the collapse of Prime Minister Kjell Magne Bondevik's government over an environmental dispute. Opposition parties had proposed legislation to allow the construction of power plants fueled by natural gas from Norway's extensive North Sea reserves. Bondevik vowed to block the initiative, claiming that gas plants would violate the country's strict environmental laws. Norway generates virtually all of its electricity from hydroelectric plants. The three-party coalition government, led by Bondevik's Christian People's Party, failed to stop the legislation. Bondevik resigned on March 10 after losing a confidence vote. The Labor Party, Norway's biggest political party, formed a new government led by Jens Stoltenberg, the new prime minister.

Economy. Stoltenberg continued Bondevik's cautious budgetary policies, restraining government spending in order to contain inflation. The government forecast the economy would grow by 3.4 percent in 2000, as high oil prices boosted revenues from North Sea oil fields. Economists also predicted a record budget surplus of $16.6 billion. The surplus was put into a savings fund to pay retirement bills after Norway's oil runs out. On October 4, the government proposed a budget for 2001 that included modest rises in welfare spending and a new 1.5 percent tax on salaries.

Train cars lie scattered along tracks near Rena, Norway, on January 5, a day after one of the worst train accidents in Norwegian history. Nineteen people died in the accident, which occurred when a local shuttle train and a regional express collided.

Labor unrest. The 86,000 members of the Norwegian Confederation of Trade Unions, Norway's largest union group, struck for six days in May 2000, demanding a greater share of Norway's prosperity. The strike shut many factories and building sites and disrupted automobile production in neighboring Sweden before employers agreed to raise wages and benefits by 4.86 percent. A national bargaining panel had recommended a 3.5-percent raise.

Mergers. Norway's national telephone company, Telenor, strengthened its position in 2000 with the purchase in August of 54 percent of Sonofon, a Danish mobile telephone operator. In October, the government approved the sale of its 35-percent stake in Christiania Bank to Nordic Baltic Holding, formed by the merger of Finland's Merita bank and Sweden's Nordbanken in 1998. The acquisition of Christiania, together with the purchase of Denmark's Unidanmark earlier in 2000, created the first pan-Scandinavian bank.

Longest tunnel. The 15.2-mile- (24.5-kilometer-) long Laerdal Tunnel, the longest in the world, opened on November 21. The tunnel connects Oslo, on the east coast, with Bergen, Norway's second-largest city, on the west.   □ Tom Buerkle

See also **Disasters; Europe.**

Nova Scotia. See Canadian provinces.
Nuclear energy. See Energy supply.
Nutrition. See Food.

Ocean researchers in May 2000 reported that the largest reef in the Northern Hemisphere, located in the Caribbean Sea off the coast of Belize, suffered a massive die-off in 1998. The scientists blamed the event on *global warming* and *El Niño.* Global warming is a gradual warming of Earth's surface. Many scientists believe that global warming is caused by a build-up of carbon dioxide and other "greenhouse gases" generated by the burning of fossil fuels. El Niño is a periodic warming of equatorial Pacific Ocean waters. The El Niño of 1997-1998 was the strongest ever recorded.

The leader of the team that conducted the Belize research, United States marine scientist Richard Aronson of the Dauphin Island Sea Laboratory in Alabama, said the coral die-off was the first to be documented on a large scale in the Caribbean. The scientists noted that corals are extremely sensitive to environmental change, and they added that their finding appeared to "justify growing concerns that global climate change is degrading coral reef ecosystems."

Open water at the pole. In August 2000, two U.S. scientists reported observing an unusual amount of open, or liquid, water at the North Pole during the previous month. They interpreted this as evidence of global warming, though some scientists disagreed.

Oceanographer James J. McCarthy, director of the Museum of Comparative Zoology at Harvard University in Cambridge, Massachusetts, and paleontologist Malcolm McKenna, of the American Museum of Natural History in New York City, said they had observed a 1-mile- (1.6 kilometer-) wide patch of open water in the Arctic Ocean. They added that the ship they were aboard, the Russian icebreaker *Yamal,* encountered thin ice or open water throughout its journey from Norway to the North Pole.

Satellite images suggested the *Yamal* was floating in a huge fracture in the Arctic ice pack. McCarthy and McKenna speculated that global warming may be weakening ice sheets, making such fractures more likely. However, other scientists noted that approximately 10 percent of the Arctic is normally free of ice during summer. They said the ice-free zone observed by McCarthy and McKenna was probably caused by a natural combination of strong winds and ocean currents.

Fertilizing the ocean. Oceanographer Edward Abraham of the Institute for Water and Atmospheric Research in New Zealand reported in October that he had shown how the greenhouse gas carbon dioxide could be removed from the air by fertilizing the ocean with iron. Abraham said that he and his colleagues had added a small amount of dissolved iron into nutrient-poor water near Antarctica. The iron encouraged the growth of an abundant amount of algae, which, through *photosynthesis* (the use of energy from the sun to combine carbon dioxide and water to make food and oxygen), removes carbon dioxide from the atmosphere.

The scientists said this process might be used to help slow down the effects of global warming. Some ecologists, however, raised concerns about possible adverse effects of the iron on ocean life.

Japanese whaling expanded. Japanese authorities revealed in May that they planned to kill up to 10 sperm whales, 50 Bryde's whales, and 100 minke whales in 2000 and in 2001. The move ended Japan's adherence to an international moratorium on whaling and sparked condemnation from other countries.

Japan had been hunting minke whales every year since the International Whaling Commission—an intergovernmental group based in Cambridge, England, and devoted to conserving whales—established the moratorium in 1986. However, until 2000, Japanese whalers respected the ban on sperm and Bryde's whales. During August and September, Japanese whalers caught a total of 88 whales in the northwest Pacific Ocean.   □ Christina S. Johnson

Ohio. See State government.
Oklahoma. See State government.
Old age. See Social security.

THE 2000 OLYMPICS

The world's best athletes gathered in Sydney, Australia, in September 2000 to compete in the XXVII Olympiad of the modern era, the first Olympic Games of the new millennium.

ARCHERY

Men's individual
GOLD   Simon Fairweather, Australia
SILVER Victor Wunderle, United States
BRONZE Wietse van Alten, Netherlands

Men's team
GOLD   South Korea
SILVER Italy
BRONZE United States

Women's individual
GOLD   Yun Mi-Jin, South Korea
SILVER Kim Nam-Soon, South Korea
BRONZE Kim Soo-Nyung, South Korea

Women's team
GOLD   South Korea
SILVER Ukraine
BRONZE Germany

BADMINTON

Men's singles
GOLD   Ji Xinpeng, China
SILVER Hendrawan, Indonesia
BRONZE Xia Xuanze, China

Men's doubles
GOLD   Tony Gunawan and Candra Wijaya, Indonesia
SILVER Lee Dong Soo and Yoo-Yong Sung, South Korea
BRONZE Ha Tae-Kwon and Kim Dong-Moon, South Korea

Women's singles
GOLD   Gong Zhichao, China
SILVER Camilla Martin, Denmark
BRONZE Ye Zhaoying, China

Women's doubles
GOLD   Ge Fei and Gu Jun, China
SILVER Huang Nanyan and Yang Wei, China
BRONZE Gao Ling and Qin Yiyuan, China

Mixed doubles
GOLD   Gao Ling and Jun Zhang, China
SILVER Tri Kusharyanto and Minarti Timur, Indonesia
BRONZE Simon Archer and Joanne Goode, Great Britain

BASEBALL

GOLD   United States
SILVER Cuba
BRONZE South Korea

Pitcher Ben Sheets, of the United States

*-World record
**-Olympic record

BASKETBALL

Men
GOLD   United States
SILVER   France
BRONZE   Lithuania

Women
GOLD   United States
SILVER   Australia
BRONZE   Brazil

BEACH VOLLEYBALL

Men
GOLD   Dain Blanton and Eric Fonoimoana, United States
SILVER   Ze Marco de Melos and Ricardo Santos, Brazil
BRONZE   Jorg Ahmann and Axel Hager, Germany

Women
GOLD   Natalie Cook and Kerri Pottharst, Australia
SILVER   Adriana Behar and Shelda Bede, Brazil
BRONZE   Sandra Pires and Adriana Samuel, Brazil

BOXING

106 lbs. (48 kg)
GOLD   Brahim Asloum, France
SILVER   Rafael Lozano Munoz, Spain
BRONZE   Maikro Romero Esquirol, Cuba, and Kim Un Chol, North Korea

112 lbs. (51 kg)
GOLD   Wijan Ponlid, Thailand
SILVER   Bulat Jumadilov, Kazakhstan
BRONZE   Jerome Thomas, France, and Vladimir Sidorenko, Ukraine

119 lbs. (54 kg)
GOLD   Guillermo Rigondeaux Ortiz, Cuba
SILVER   Raimkoul Malakhbekov, Russia
BRONZE   Serguey Daniltchenko, Ukraine, and Clarence Vinson, United States

126 lbs. (57 kg)
GOLD   Bekzat Sattarkhanov, Kazakhstan
SILVER   Ricardo Juarez, United States
BRONZE   Tahar Tamsamani, Morocco, and Kamil Dzamalutdinov, Russia

132 lbs. (60 kg)
GOLD   Mario Kindelan, Cuba
SILVER   Andriy Kotelnyk, Ukraine
BRONZE   Cristian Bejarano Benitez, Mexico, and Alexandr Maletin, Russia

140 lbs. (63.5 kg)
GOLD   Mahamadkadyz Abdullaev, Uzbekistan
SILVER   Ricardo Williams, United States
BRONZE   Mohamed Allalou, Algeria, and Diogenes Luna Martinez, Cuba

148 lbs. (67 kg)
GOLD   Oleg Saitov, Russia
SILVER   Sergey Dotsenko, Ukraine
BRONZE   Vitalii Grusac, Moldova, and Dorel Simion, Romania

156 lbs. (71 kg)
GOLD   Yermakhan Ibraimov, Kazakhstan
SILVER   Marin Simion, Romania
BRONZE   Pornchai Thongburan, Thailand, and Jermain Taylor, United States

165 lbs. (75 kg)
GOLD   Jorge Gutierrez, Cuba
SILVER   Gaidarbek Gaidarbekov, Russia
BRONZE   Vugar Alekperov, Azerbaijan, and Zsolt Erdei, Hungary

179 lbs. (81 kg)
GOLD   Alexander Lebziak, Russia
SILVER   Rudolf Kraj, Czech Republic
BRONZE   Andri Fedtchouk, Ukraine, and Sergei Mikhailov, Uzbekistan

201 lbs. (91 kg)
GOLD   Felix Savon, Cuba
SILVER   Sultanahmed Ibzagimov, Russia
BRONZE   Vladimir Tchantouria, Georgia, and Sebastian Kober, Germany

Over 201 lbs. (Over 91 kg)
GOLD   Audley Harrison, Great Britain
SILVER   Mukhtarkhan Dildabekov, Kazakhstan
BRONZE   Paolo Vidoz, Italy, and Rustam Saidov, Uzbekistan

CANOEING

MEN'S
SPRINT

500-meter canoe singles
GOLD   Gyorgy Kolonics, Hungary
SILVER   Maxim Opalev, Russia
BRONZE   Andreas Dittmer, Germany

1,000-meter canoe singles
GOLD   Andreas Dittmer, Germany
SILVER   Ledys Frank Balceiro, Cuba
BRONZE   Steve Giles, Canada

500-meter canoe doubles
GOLD   Ferenc Novak and Imre Pulai, Hungary
SILVER   Daniel Jedraszko and Pawel Baraszkiewicz, Poland
BRONZE   Florin Popescu and Mitica Pricop, Romania

1,000-meter canoe doubles
GOLD   Florin Popescu and Mitica Pricop, Romania
SILVER   Ibrahin Rojas and Leobaldo Pereira, Cuba
BRONZE   Lars Kober and Stefan Utess, Germany

500-meter kayak singles
GOLD   Knut Holmann, Norway
SILVER   Petar Merkov, Bulgaria
BRONZE   Michael Kolganov, Israel

1,000-meter kayak singles
GOLD   Knut Holmann, Norway
SILVER   Petar Merkov, Bulgaria
BRONZE   Tim Brabants, Great Britain

CANOEING, CONTINUED

500-meter kayak doubles
GOLD Zoltan Kammerer and Botond Storcz, Hungary
SILVER Daniel Collins and Andrew Trim, Australia
BRONZE Ronald Rauhe and Tim Wieskoetter, Germany

1,000-meter kayak doubles
GOLD Beniamino Bonomi and Antonio Rossi, Italy
SILVER Markus Oscarsson and Henrik Nilsson, Sweden
BRONZE Krisztian Bartfai and Krisztian Vereb, Hungary

1,000-meter kayak fours
GOLD Hungary
SILVER Germany
BRONZE Poland

SLALOM

Canoe singles
GOLD Tony Estanguet, France
SILVER Michal Martikan, Slovakia
BRONZE Juraj Mincik, Slovakia

Canoe doubles
GOLD Pavol Hochschorner and Peter Hochschorner, Slovakia
SILVER Krzysztof Kolomanski and Michal Staniszewski, Poland
BRONZE Marek Jiras and Tomas Mader, Czech Republic

Kayak singles
GOLD Thomas Schmidt, Germany
SILVER Paul Ratcliffe, Great Britain
BRONZE Pierpaolo Ferrazzi, Italy

WOMEN'S
SPRINT

500-meter kayak singles
GOLD Josefa Idem Guerrini, Italy
SILVER Caroline Brunet, Canada
BRONZE Katrin Borchert, Australia

500-meter kayak doubles
GOLD Birgit Fischer and Katrin Wagner, Germany
SILVER Katalin Kovacs and Szilvia Szabo, Hungary
BRONZE Aneta Pastuszka and Beata Sokolowska, Poland

500-meter kayak fours
GOLD Germany
SILVER Hungary
BRONZE Romania

SLALOM

Kayak singles
GOLD Stepanka Hilgertova, Czech Republic
SILVER Brigitte Guibal, France
BRONZE Anne-Lise Bardet, France

CYCLING

MEN'S
ROAD

Road race
GOLD Jan Ullrich, Germany
SILVER Alexandre Vinokourov, Kazakhstan
BRONZE Andreas Kloeden, Germany

Time trial
GOLD Viacheslav Ekimov, Russia
SILVER Jan Ullrich, Germany
BRONZE Lance Armstrong, United States

TRACK

Madison sprint
GOLD Scott McGrory and Brett Aitken, Australia
SILVER Etienne de Wilde and Matthew Gilmore, Belgium
BRONZE Marco Villa and Silvio Martinello, Italy

Keirin sprint
GOLD Florian Rousseau, France
SILVER Gary Neiwand, Australia
BRONZE Jens Fiedler, Germany

Sprint
GOLD Marty Nothstein, United States
SILVER Florian Rousseau, France
BRONZE Jens Fiedler, Germany

Individual pursuit
GOLD Robert Bartko, Germany
SILVER Jens Lehmann, Germany
BRONZE Brad McGee, Australia

Team pursuit
GOLD Germany*
SILVER Ukraine
BRONZE Great Britain

Kilometer time trial
GOLD Jason Queally, Great Britain**
SILVER Stefan Nimke, Germany
BRONZE Shane Kelly, Australia

Points race
GOLD Juan Llaneras, Spain
SILVER Milton Wynants, Uruguay
BRONZE Alexey Markov, Russia

MOUNTAIN BIKE

Men's cross-country
GOLD Miguel Martinez, France
SILVER Filip Meirhaeghe, Belgium
BRONZE Christoph Sauser, Switzerland

WOMEN'S
ROAD

Road race
GOLD Leontien Zijlaard, Netherlands
SILVER Hanka Kupfernagel, Germany
BRONZE Diana Ziliute, Lithuania

Time trial
GOLD Leontien Zijlaard, Netherlands
SILVER Mari Holden, United States
BRONZE Jeannie Longo-Ciprelli, France

TRACK

500-meter time trial
GOLD Felicia Ballanger, France**
SILVER Michelle Ferris, Australia
BRONZE Jiang Cuihua, China

Sprint
GOLD Felicia Ballanger, France
SILVER Oxana Grichina, Russia
BRONZE Iryna Yanovych, Ukraine

Individual pursuit
GOLD Leontien Zijlaard, Netherlands
SILVER Marion Clignet, France
BRONZE Yvonne McGregor, Great Britain

Points race
GOLD Antonella Bellutti, Italy
SILVER Leontien Zijlaard, Netherlands
BRONZE Olga Slioussareva, Russia

MOUNTAIN BIKE

Cross-country
GOLD Paola Pezzo, Italy
SILVER Barbara Blatter, Switzerland
BRONZE Margarita Fullana, Spain

DIVING

Men's springboard
GOLD   Xiong Ni, China
SILVER   Fernando Platas, Mexico
BRONZE   Dmitri Saoutine, Russia

Men's platform
GOLD   Tian Liang, China
SILVER   Hu Jia, China
BRONZE   Dmitri Saoutine, Russia

Women's springboard
GOLD   Fu Mingxia, China
SILVER   Guo Jingjing, China
BRONZE   Doerte Lindner, Germany

Women's platform
GOLD   Laura Wilkinson, United States
SILVER   Li Na, China
BRONZE   Anne Montminy, Canada

EQUESTRIAN

INDIVIDUAL EVENTS
Jumping
GOLD   Jeroen Dubbeldam, Netherlands
SILVER   Albert Voorn, Netherlands
BRONZE   Khaled al Eid, Saudi Arabia

Dressage
GOLD   Anky van Grunsven, Netherlands
SILVER   Isabell Werth, Germany
BRONZE   Ulla Salzgeber, Germany

Three-day event
GOLD   David O'Connor, United States
SILVER   Andrew Hoy, Australia
BRONZE   Mark Todd, New Zealand

TEAM EVENTS
Jumping
GOLD   Germany
SILVER   Switzerland
BRONZE   Brazil

Dressage
GOLD   Germany
SILVER   Netherlands
BRONZE   United States

Three-day event
GOLD   Australia
SILVER   Great Britain
BRONZE   United States

FENCING

INDIVIDUAL EVENTS
Men's foil
GOLD   Kim Young-Ho, South Korea
SILVER   Ralf Bissdorf, Germany
BRONZE   Dmitri Chevtchenko, Russia

Men's epee
GOLD   Pavel Kolobkov, Russia
SILVER   Hugues Obry, France
BRONZE   Lee Sang-Ki, Korea

Men's sabre
GOLD   Mihai Claudiu Covaliu, Romania
SILVER   Mathieu Gourdain, France
BRONZE   Wiradech Kothny, Germany

Women's foil
GOLD   Valentina Vezzali, Italy
SILVER   Rita Koenig, Germany
BRONZE   Giovanna Trillini, Italy

Women's epee
GOLD   Timea Nagy, Hungary
SILVER   Gianna Habluetzel-Buerki, Switzerland
BRONZE   Laura Flessel-Colovic, France

TEAM EVENTS
Men's foil
GOLD   France
SILVER   China
BRONZE   Italy

Men's epee
GOLD   Italy
SILVER   France
BRONZE   Cuba

Men's sabre
GOLD   Russia
SILVER   France
BRONZE   Germany

Women's foil
GOLD   Italy
SILVER   Poland
BRONZE   Germany

Women's epee
GOLD   Russia
SILVER   Switzerland
BRONZE   China

FIELD HOCKEY

Men
GOLD   Netherlands
SILVER   South Korea
BRONZE   Australia

Women
GOLD   Australia
SILVER   Argentina
BRONZE   Netherlands

Springboard diver
Fu Mingxia, of China

GYMNASTICS

Gymnast Yang Wei, of China

MEN

Team
GOLD	China
SILVER	Ukraine
BRONZE	Russia

All-around
GOLD	Alexei Nemov, Russia
SILVER	Yang Wei, China
BRONZE	Oleksandr Beresh, Ukraine

Floor exercise
GOLD	Igors Vihrovs, Latvia
SILVER	Alexei Nemov, Russia
BRONZE	Iordan Iovtchev, Bulgaria

Pommel horse
GOLD	Marius Urzica, Romania
SILVER	Eric Poujade, France
BRONZE	Alexei Nemov, Russia

Rings
GOLD	Szilveszter Csollany, Hungary
SILVER	Dimosthenis Tampakos, Greece
BRONZE	Iordan Iovtchev, Bulgaria

Vault
GOLD	Gervasio Deferr, Spain
SILVER	Alexey Bondarenko, Russia
BRONZE	Leszek Blanik, Poland

Parallel bars
GOLD	Li Xiaopeng, China
SILVER	Lee Joo-Hyung, South Korea
BRONZE	Alexei Nemov, Russia

Horizontal bar
GOLD	Alexei Nemov, Russia
SILVER	Benjamin Varonian, France
BRONZE	Lee Joo-Hyung, South Korea

Trampoline
GOLD	Alexandre Moskalenko, Russia
SILVER	Ji Wallace, Australia
BRONZE	Mathieu Turgeon, Canada

WOMEN

Team
GOLD	Romania
SILVER	Russia
BRONZE	China

All-around
GOLD	Simona Amanar, Romania
SILVER	Maria Olaru, Romania
BRONZE	Liu Xuan, China

Vault
GOLD	Elena Zamolodtchikova, Russia
SILVER	Andreea Raducan, Romania
BRONZE	Ekaterina Lobazniouk, Russia

Uneven parallel bars
GOLD	Svetlana Khorkina, Russia
SILVER	Ling Jie, China
BRONZE	Yang Yun, China

Balance beam
GOLD	Liu Xuan, China
SILVER	Ekaterina Lobazniouk, Russia
BRONZE	Elena Prodounova, Russia

Floor exercise
GOLD	Elena Zamolodtchikova, Russia
SILVER	Svetlana Khorkina, Russia
BRONZE	Simona Amanar, Romania

Trampoline
GOLD	Irina Karavaeva, Russia
SILVER	Oxana Tsyhuleva, Ukraine
BRONZE	Karen Cockburn, Canada

MODERN PENTATHLON

MEN
GOLD	Dmitry Svatkovsky, Russia
SILVER	Gabor Balogh, Hungary
BRONZE	Pavel Dovgal, Belarus

WOMEN
GOLD	Stephanie Cook, Great Britain
SILVER	Emily deRiel, United States
BRONZE	Kate Allenby, Great Britain

RHYTHMIC GYMNASTICS

Individual
GOLD	Yulia Barsukova, Russia
SILVER	Yulia Raskina, Belarus
BRONZE	Alina Kabaeva, Russia

Team
GOLD	Russia
SILVER	Belarus
BRONZE	Greece

JUDO

MEN

Extra lightweight (60 kg)
GOLD	Tadahiro Nomura, Japan
SILVER	Jung Bu-Kyung, Korea
BRONZE	Manolo Poulot, Cuba, and Aidyn Smagulov, Kyrgyzstan

Half-lightweight (66 kg)
GOLD	Huseyin Ozkan, Turkey
SILVER	Larbi Benboudaoud, France
BRONZE	Girolamo Giovinazzo, Italy, and Giorgi Vazagashvili, Georgia

Lightweight (73 kg)
GOLD	Giuseppe Maddaloni, Italy
SILVER	Tiago Camilo, Brazil
BRONZE	Anatoly Laryukov, Belarus, and Vsevolods Zelonijs, Latvia

Half-middleweight (81 kg)
GOLD	Makoto Takimoto, Japan
SILVER	Cho In-Chul, Korea
BRONZE	Aleksei Budolin, Estonia, and Nuno Delgado, Portugal

Middleweight (90 kg)
GOLD	Mark Huizinga, Netherlands
SILVER	Carlos Honorato, Brazil
BRONZE	Frederic Demontfaucon, France, and Ruslan Mashurenko, Ukraine

Half-heavyweight (100 kg)
GOLD	Kosei Inoue, Japan
SILVER	Nicolas Gill, Canada
BRONZE	Iouri Stepkine, Russia, and Stephane Traineau, France

Heavyweight (over 100 kg)
GOLD	David Douillet, France
SILVER	Shinichi Shinohara, Japan
BRONZE	Indrek Pertelson, Estonia, and Tamerlan Tmenov, Russia

ROWING

MEN

Single sculls
GOLD   Rob Waddell, New Zealand
SILVER Xeno Mueller, Switzerland
BRONZE Marcel Hacker, Germany

Double sculls
GOLD   Luka Spik and Iztok Cop, Slovenia
SILVER Olaf Tufte and Fredrik Raaen Bekken, Norway
BRONZE Giovanni Calabrese and Nicola Sartori, Italy

Lightweight double sculls
GOLD   Tomasz Kucharski and Robert Sycz, Poland
SILVER Elia Luini and Leonardo Pettinari, Italy
BRONZE Pascal Touron and Thibaud Chapelle, France

Quadruple sculls
GOLD   Italy
SILVER Netherlands
BRONZE Germany

Coxless pair
GOLD   Michel Andrieux and Jean-Christophe Rolland, France
SILVER Sebastian Bea and Ted Murphy, United States
BRONZE Matthew Long and James Tomkins, Australia

Coxless four
GOLD   Great Britain
SILVER Italy
BRONZE Australia

Lightweight coxless four
GOLD   France
SILVER Australia
BRONZE Denmark

Eight
GOLD   Great Britain
SILVER Australia
BRONZE Croatia

WOMEN

Single sculls
GOLD   Ekaterina Karsten, Belarus
SILVER Rumyana Neykova, Bulgaria
BRONZE Katrin Rutschow-Stomporowski, Germany

Double sculls
GOLD   Jana Thieme and Kathrin Boron, Germany
SILVER Pieta van Dishoeck and Eeke van Nes, Netherlands
BRONZE Birute Sakickiene and Kristina Poplavskaja, Lithuania

Lightweight double sculls
GOLD   Constanta Burcica and Angela Alupei, Romania
SILVER Valerie Viehoff and Claudia Blasberg, Germany
BRONZE Christine Collins and Sarah Garner, United States

Quadruple sculls
GOLD   Germany
SILVER Great Britain
BRONZE Russia

Coxless pair
GOLD   Georgeta Damian and Doina Ignat, Romania
SILVER Rachael Taylor and Kate Slatter, Australia
BRONZE Melissa Ryan and Karen Kraft, United States

Eight
GOLD   Romania
SILVER Netherlands
BRONZE Canada

WOMEN

Extra lightweight (48 kg)
GOLD   Ryoko Tamura, Japan
SILVER Lioubov Brouletova, Russia
BRONZE Anna-Maria Gradante, Germany, and Ann Simons, Belgium

Half-lightweight (52 kg)
GOLD   Legna Verdecia, Cuba
SILVER Noriko Narazaki, Japan
BRONZE Kye Sun Hui, North Korea, and Liu Yuxiang, China

Lightweight (57 kg)
GOLD   Isabel Fernandez, Spain
SILVER Driulys Gonzalez, Cuba
BRONZE Kie Kusakabe, Japan, and Maria Pekli, Australia

Half-middleweight (63 kg)
GOLD   Severine Vandenhende, France
SILVER Li Shufang, China
BRONZE Jung Sung-Sook, South Korea, and Gella Vandecaveye, Belarus

Middleweight (70 kg)
GOLD   Sibelis Veranes, Cuba
SILVER Kate Howey, Great Britain
BRONZE Cho Min-Sun, South Korea, and Ylenia Scapin, Italy

Half-heavyweight (78 kg)
GOLD   Lin Tang, China
SILVER Celine LeBrun, France
BRONZE Simona Marcela Richter, Romania, and Emanuela Pierantozzi, Italy

Heavyweight (over 78 kg)
GOLD   Yuan Hua, China
SILVER Daima Mayelis Beltran, Cuba
BRONZE Kim Seon-Young, South Korea, and Mayumi Yamashita, Japan

SAILING

OPEN

49er dinghy sailing
GOLD   Thomas Johanson and Jyrki Jarvi, Finland
SILVER Ian Barker and Simon Hiscocks, Great Britain
BRONZE Jonathan McKee and Charlie McKee, United States

Laser
GOLD   Ben Ainslie, Great Britain
SILVER Robert Scheidt, Brazil
BRONZE Michael Blackburn, Australia

Soling
GOLD   Jesper Bank, Denmark
SILVER Jochen Schumann, Germany
BRONZE Herman Horn Johannessen, Norway

Star
GOLD   Mark Reynolds and Magnus Liljedahl, United States
SILVER Mark Covell and Ian Walker, Great Britain
BRONZE Torben Grael and Marcelo Ferreira, Brazil

Tornado
GOLD   Hans Peter Steinacher and Roman Hagara, Austria
SILVER John Forbes and Darren Bundock, Australia
BRONZE Roland Gaebler and Rene Schwall, Germany

MEN

Finn
GOLD   Iain Percy, Great Britain
SILVER Luca Devoti, Italy
BRONZE Fredrik Loof, Sweden

SAILING, CONTINUED

Mistral (boards)
GOLD Christoph Sieber, Austria
SILVER Carlos Espinola, Argentina
BRONZE Aaron McIntosh, New Zealand

470
GOLD Tom King and Mark Turnbull, Australia
SILVER Paul Foerster and Robert Merrick, United States
BRONZE Javier Conte and Juan de la Fuente, Argentina

WOMEN
Europe
GOLD Shirley Robertson, Great Britain
SILVER Margriet Matthysse, Netherlands
BRONZE Serena Amato, Argentina

Mistral (boards)
GOLD Alessandra Sensini, Italy
SILVER Amelie Lux, Germany
BRONZE Barbara Kendall, New Zealand

470
GOLD Belinda Stowell and Jenny Armstrong, New Zealand
SILVER J. J. Isler and Pease Glaser, United States
BRONZE Olena Pakholchyk and Ruslana Taran, Ukraine

SOCCER

Men
GOLD Cameroon
SILVER Spain
BRONZE Chile

Women
GOLD Norway
SILVER United States
BRONZE Germany

SOFTBALL

GOLD United States
SILVER Japan
BRONZE Australia

**Swimmer Lenny Krayzelburg,
of the
United States**

SHOOTING

RIFLE
Men's air
GOLD Cai Yalin, China**
SILVER Artem Khadjibekov, Russia
BRONZE Evgueni Aleinikov, Russia

Men's small bore, prone
GOLD Jonas Edman, Sweden
SILVER Torben Grimmel, Denmark
BRONZE Sergei Martynov, Belarus

Men's small bore, three position
GOLD Rajmond Debevec, Slovenia**
SILVER Juha Hirvi, Finland
BRONZE Harald Stenvaag, Norway

Men's running target
GOLD Yang Ling, China
SILVER Oleg Moldovan, Moldova
BRONZE Niu Zhiyuan, China

Women's air
GOLD Nancy Johnson, United States
SILVER Kang Cho-Hyun, Korea
BRONZE Jing Gao, China

Women's small bore, three-position
GOLD Renata Mauer-Rozanska, Poland
SILVER Tatiana Goldobina, Russia
BRONZE Maria Feklistova, Russia

PISTOL
Men's air
GOLD Franck Dumoulin, France**
SILVER Wang Yifu, China
BRONZE Igor Basinsky, Belarus

Men's free
GOLD Tanyu Kiriakov, Bulgaria
SILVER Igor Basinsky, Belarus
BRONZE Martin Tenk, Czech Republic

Men's rapid fire
GOLD Serguei Alifirenko, Russia
SILVER Michel Ansermet, Switzerland
BRONZE Iulian Raicea, Romania

Women's air
GOLD Tao Luna, China
SILVER Jasna Sekaric, Yugoslavia
BRONZE Annemarie Forder, Australia

Women's free
GOLD Maria Grozdeva, Bulgaria**
SILVER Tao Luna, China
BRONZE Lolita Evglevskaya, Belarus

SHOTGUN
Men's trap
GOLD Michael Diamond, Australia
SILVER Ian Peel, Great Britain
BRONZE Giovanni Pellielo, Italy

Men's double trap
GOLD Richard Faulds, Great Britain
SILVER Russell Mark, Australia
BRONZE Fehaid al Deehani, Kuwait

Men's skeet
GOLD Mykola Milchev, Ukraine*
SILVER Petr Malek, Czech Republic
BRONZE James Graves, United States

Women's trap
GOLD Daina Gudzineviciute, Lithuania**
SILVER Delphine Racinet, France
BRONZE Gao E, China

Women's double trap
GOLD Pia Hansen, Sweden**
SILVER Deborah Gelisio, Italy
BRONZE Kimberly Rhode, United States

Women's skeet
GOLD Zemfira Meftakhetdinova, Azerbaijan**
SILVER Svetlana Demina, Russia
BRONZE Diana Igaly, Hungary

SWIMMING

MEN

50-meter freestyle
GOLD Anthony Ervin and Gary Hall, Jr.,   :21.98
      United States
BRONZE Pieter van den Hoogenband,
      Netherlands

100-meter freestyle
GOLD Pieter van den Hoogenband,   :48.30
      Netherlands
SILVER Alexander Popov, Russia
BRONZE Gary Hall, Jr., United States

200-meter freestyle
GOLD Pieter van den Hoogenband,   1:45.35*
      Netherlands
SILVER Ian Thorpe, Australia
BRONZE Massimiliano Rosolino, Italy

400-meter freestyle
GOLD Ian Thorpe, Australia   3:40.59*
SILVER Massimiliano Rosolino, Italy
BRONZE Klete Keller, United States

1,500-meter freestyle
GOLD Grant Hackett, Australia   14:48.33
SILVER Kieren Perkins, Australia
BRONZE Chris Thompson, United States

100-meter backstroke
GOLD Lenny Krayzelburg, United States   :53.72**
SILVER Matthew Welsh, Australia
BRONZE Stev Theloke, Germany

200-meter backstroke
GOLD Lenny Krayzelburg, United States   1:56.76**
SILVER Aaron Peirsol, United States
BRONZE Matthew Welsh, Australia

100-meter breaststroke
GOLD Domenico Fioravanti, Italy   1:00.46**
SILVER Ed Moses, United States
BRONZE Roman Sloudnov, Russia

200-meter breaststroke
GOLD Domenico Fioravanti, Italy   2:10.87
SILVER Terence Parkin, South Africa
BRONZE Davide Rummolo, Italy

100-meter butterfly
GOLD Lars Froelander, Sweden   :52.00
SILVER Michael Klim, Australia
BRONZE Geoff Huegill, Australia

200-meter butterfly
GOLD Tom Malchow, United States   1:55.35**
SILVER Denys Sylant'yev, Ukraine
BRONZE Justin Norris, Australia

200-meter individual medley
GOLD Massimiliano Rosolino, Italy   1:58.98**
SILVER Tom Dolan, United States
BRONZE Tom Wilkens, United States

400-meter individual medley
GOLD Tom Dolan, United States   4:11.76*
SILVER Erik Vendt, United States
BRONZE Curtis Myden, Canada

4x100-meter freestyle relay
GOLD Australia   3:13.67*
SILVER United States
BRONZE Brazil

4x200-meter freestyle relay
GOLD Australia   7:07.05*
SILVER United States
BRONZE Netherlands

4x100-meter medley relay
GOLD United States   3:33.73*
SILVER Australia
BRONZE Germany

WOMEN

50-meter freestyle
GOLD Inge de Bruijn, Netherlands   :24.32*
SILVER Therese Alshammar, Sweden
BRONZE Dara Torres, United States

100-meter freestyle
GOLD Inge de Bruijn, Netherlands   :53.83
SILVER Therese Alshammar, Sweden
BRONZE Dara Torres and Jenny Thompson,
      United States (tie)

200-meter freestyle
GOLD Susie O'Neill, Australia   1:58.24
SILVER Martina Moravcova, Slovakia
BRONZE Claudia Poll, Costa Rica

400-meter freestyle
GOLD Brooke Bennett, United States   4:05.80
SILVER Diana Munz, United States
BRONZE Claudia Poll, Costa Rica

800-meter freestyle
GOLD Brooke Bennett, United States   8:19.67**
SILVER Yana Klochkova, Ukraine
BRONZE Kaitlin Sandeno, United States

100-meter backstroke
GOLD Diana Mocanu, Romania   1:00.21**
SILVER Mai Nakamura, Japan
BRONZE Nina Zhivanevskaya, Spain

200-meter backstroke
GOLD Diana Mocanu, Romania   2:08.16
SILVER Roxana Maracineanu, France
BRONZE Miki Nakao, Japan

100-meter breaststroke
GOLD Megan Quann, United States   1:07.05
SILVER Leisel Jones, Australia
BRONZE Penny Heyns, South Africa

200-meter breaststroke
GOLD Agnes Kovacs, Hungary   2:24.35
SILVER Kristy Kowal, United States
BRONZE Amanda Beard, United States

100-meter butterfly
GOLD Inge de Bruijn, Netherlands   :56.61*
SILVER Martina Moravcova, Slovakia
BRONZE Dara Torres, United States

200-meter butterfly
GOLD Misty Hyman, United States   2:05.88**
SILVER Susie O'Neill, Australia
BRONZE Petria Thomas, Australia

200-meter individual medley
GOLD Yana Klochkova, Ukraine   2:10.68**
SILVER Beatrice Caslaru, Romania
BRONZE Cristina Teuscher, United States

400-meter individual medley
GOLD Yana Klochkova, Ukraine   4:33.59*
SILVER Yasuko Tajima, Japan
BRONZE Beatrice Caslaru, Romania

4x100-meter freestyle relay
GOLD United States   3:36.61*
SILVER Netherlands
BRONZE Sweden

4x200-meter freestyle relay
GOLD United States   7:57.80**
SILVER Australia
BRONZE Germany

4x100-meter medley relay
GOLD United States   3:58.30*
SILVER Australia
BRONZE Japan

SYNCHRONIZED DIVING

MEN'S
Platform
GOLD   Igor Loukachine and Dmitri Saoutine, Russia
SILVER Hu Jia and Tian Liang, China
BRONZE Jan Hempel and Heiko Meyer, Germany

Springboard
GOLD   Xiao Hailiang and Xiong Ni, China
SILVER Alexandre Dobroskok and Dmitri Saoutine, Russia
BRONZE Robert Newbery and Dean Pullar, Australia

WOMEN'S
Platform
GOLD   Li Na and Sang Xue, China
SILVER Emilie Heymans and Anne Montminy, Canada
BRONZE Rebecca Gilmore and Loudy Tourky, Australia

Springboard
GOLD   Vera Ilina and Ioulia Pakhalina, Russia
SILVER Fu Mingxia and Guo Jingjing, China
BRONZE Ganna Sorokina and Olena Zhupina, Ukraine

SYNCHRONIZED SWIMMING

GOLD   Russia
SILVER Japan
BRONZE Canada

TABLE TENNIS

Men's singles
GOLD   Kong Linghui, China
SILVER Jan-Ove Waldner, Sweden
BRONZE Liu Guoliang, China

Men's doubles
GOLD   Wang Ligin and Yan Sen, China
SILVER Kong Linghui and Liu Guoliang, China
BRONZE Patrick Chila and Jean-Philippe Gatien, France

Women's singles
GOLD   Wang Nan, China
SILVER Li Ju, China
BRONZE Chen Jing, Taipei

Women's doubles
GOLD   Li Ju and Wang Nan, China
SILVER Sun Jin and Yang Ying, China
BRONZE Kim Moo-Kyo and Ryu Ji-Hye, South Korea

TAEKWONDO

MEN'S
Under 58 kg
GOLD   Michail Mouroutsos, Greece
SILVER Gabriel Esparza, Spain
BRONZE Huang Chih-Hsiung, Taiwan

Under 68 kg
GOLD   Steven Lopez, United States
SILVER Sin Joon-Sik, South Korea
BRONZE Hadi Saeibonehkohal, Iran

Under 80 kg
GOLD   Angel Valodia Matos Fuentes, Cuba
SILVER Faissal Ebnoutalib, Germany
BRONZE Victor Manuel Estrada Garibay, Mexico

Over 80 kg
GOLD   Kim Kyong-Hun, South Korea
SILVER Daniel Trenton, Australia
BRONZE Pascal Gentil, France

WOMEN'S
Under 49 kg
GOLD   Lauren Burns, Australia
SILVER Urbia Melendez Rodriguez, Cuba
BRONZE Chi Shu-Ju, Taiwan

Under 57 kg
GOLD   Jung Jae-Eun, South Korea
SILVER Tran Hieu-Ngan, Vietnam
BRONZE Hamide Bikcin, Turkey

Under 67 kg
GOLD   Lee Sun-Hee, South Korea
SILVER Trude Gundersen, Norway
BRONZE Yoriko Okamoto, Japan

Over 67 kg
GOLD   Chen Zhong, China
SILVER Natalia Ivanova, Russia
BRONZE Dominique Bosshart, Canada

TEAM HANDBALL

Men		Women	
GOLD	Russia	GOLD	Denmark
SILVER	Sweden	SILVER	Hungary
BRONZE	Spain	BRONZE	Norway

TENNIS

Men's singles
GOLD   Yevgeny Kafelnikov, Russia
SILVER Tommy Haas, Germany
BRONZE Arnaud Di Pasquale, France

Men's doubles
GOLD   Sebastien Lareau and Daniel Nestor, Canada
SILVER Todd Woodbridge and Mark Woodforde, Australia
BRONZE Alex Corretja and Albert Costa, Spain

Women's singles
GOLD   Venus Williams, United States
SILVER Elena Dementieva, Russia
BRONZE Monica Seles, United States

Women's doubles
GOLD   Serena Williams and Venus Williams, United States
SILVER Kristie Boogert and Miriam Oremans, Netherlands
BRONZE Els Callens and Dominique Van Roost, Belgium

MEN

100 meters
GOLD	Maurice Greene, United States	:9.87
SILVER	Ato Boldon, Trinidad and Tobago	
BRONZE	Obadele Thompson, Barbados	

200 meters
GOLD	Konstantinos Kenteris, Greece	:20.09
SILVER	Darren Campbell, Great Britain	
BRONZE	Ato Boldon, Trinidad and Tobago	

400 meters
GOLD	Michael Johnson, United States	:43.84
SILVER	Alvin Harrison, United States	
BRONZE	Gregory Haughton, Jamaica	

800 meters
GOLD	Nils Schumann, Germany	1:45.08
SILVER	Wilson Kipketer, Denmark	
BRONZE	Aissa Djabir Said-Guerni, Algeria	

1,500 meters
GOLD	Noah Ngeny, Kenya	3:32.07**
SILVER	Hicham el Guerrouj, Morocco	
BRONZE	Bernard Lagat, Kenya	

5,000 meters
GOLD	Millon Wolde, Ethiopia	13:35.49
SILVER	Ali Saidi-Sief, Algeria	
BRONZE	Brahim Lahlafi, Morocco	

10,000 meters
GOLD	Haile Gebrselassie, Ethiopia	27:18.20
SILVER	Paul Tergat, Kenya	
BRONZE	Assefa Mezgebu, Ethiopia	

Marathon
GOLD	Gezahgne Abera, Ethiopia	2:10:11
SILVER	Eric Wainaina, Kenya	
BRONZE	Tesfaye Tola, Ethiopia	

110-meter hurdles
GOLD	Anier Garcia, Cuba	:13.00
SILVER	Terrence Trammell, United States	
BRONZE	Mark Crear, United States	

400-meter hurdles
GOLD	Angelo Taylor, United States	:47.50
SILVER	Hadi Souan Somayli, Saudi Arabia	
BRONZE	Llewellyn Herbert, South Africa	

3,000-meter steeplechase
GOLD	Reuben Kosgei, Kenya	8:21.43
SILVER	Wilson Boit Kipketer, Kenya	
BRONZE	Ali Ezzine, Morocco	

20-kilometer walk
GOLD	Robert Korzeniowski, Poland	1:18:59
SILVER	Noe Hernandez, Mexico	
BRONZE	Vladimir Andreyev, Russia	

50-kilometer walk
GOLD	Robert Korzeniowski, Poland	3:42:22
SILVER	Aigars Fadejevs, Latvia	
BRONZE	Joel Sanchez, Mexico	

4x100-meter relay
GOLD	United States	:37.6
SILVER	Brazil	
BRONZE	Cuba	

4x400-meter relay
GOLD	United States	2:56
SILVER	Nigeria	
BRONZE	Jamaica	

High jump
GOLD	Sergey Kliugin, Russia	7 ft. 8½ in. (2.35 m)
SILVER	Javier Sotomayor, Cuba	
BRONZE	Abderrahmane Hammad, Algeria	

Pole vault
GOLD	Nick Hysong, United States	19 ft. 4¼ in. (5.90 m)
SILVER	Lawrence Johnson, United States	
BRONZE	Maksim Tarasov, Russia	

Long jump
GOLD	Ivan Pedroso, Cuba	28 ft. ½ in. (8.55 m)
SILVER	Jai Taurima, Australia	
BRONZE	Roman Schurenko, Ukraine	

Triple jump
GOLD	Jonathan Edwards, Great Britain	58 ft. 1¼ in. (17.71 m)
SILVER	Yoel Garcia, Cuba	
BRONZE	Denis Kapustin, Russia	

Shot-put
GOLD	Arsi Harju, Finland	69 ft. 10 in. (21.29 m)
SILVER	Adam Nelson, United States	
BRONZE	John Godina, United States	

Discus
GOLD	Virgilijus Alekna, Lithuania	227 ft. 4½ in. (69.30 m)
SILVER	Lars Riedel, Germany	
BRONZE	Frantz Kruger, South Africa	

Hammer
GOLD	Szymon Ziolkowski, Poland	262 ft. 6½ in. (80.02 m)
SILVER	Nicola Vizzoni, Italy	
BRONZE	Igor Astapkovich, Belarus	

Javelin
GOLD	Jan Zelezny, Czech Republic	295 ft. 10 in. (90.17 m)**
SILVER	Steve Backley, Great Britain	
BRONZE	Sergey Makarov, Russia	

Decathlon
GOLD	Erki Nool, Estonia	8,641 pts.
SILVER	Roman Sebrle, Czech Republic	
BRONZE	Chris Huffins, United States	

WOMEN

100 meters
GOLD	Marion Jones, United States	:10.75
SILVER	Ekaterini Thanou, Greece	
BRONZE	Tanya Lawrence, Jamaica	

200 meters
GOLD	Marion Jones, United States	:21.84
SILVER	Pauline Davis-Thompson, Bahamas	
BRONZE	Susanthika Jayasinghe, Sri Lanka	

400 meters
GOLD	Cathy Freeman, Australia	:49.11
SILVER	Lorraine Graham, Jamaica	
BRONZE	Katharine Merry, Great Britain	

800 meters
GOLD	Maria Mutola, Mozambique	1:56.15
SILVER	Stephanie Graf, Austria	
BRONZE	Kelly Holmes, Great Britain	

1,500 meters
GOLD	Nouria Merah-Benida, Algeria	4:05.10
SILVER	Violeta Szekely, Romania	
BRONZE	Gabriela Szabo, Romania	

5,000 meters
GOLD	Gabriela Szabo, Romania	14:40.79**
SILVER	Sonia O'Sullivan, Ireland	
BRONZE	Gete Wami, Ethiopia	

10,000 meters
GOLD	Derartu Tulu, Ethiopia	30:17.49**
SILVER	Gete Wami, Ethiopia	
BRONZE	Fernanda Ribeiro, Portugal	

Sprinter Cathy Freeman, of Australia

TRACK AND FIELD, CONTINUED

Marathon
GOLD Naoko Takahashi, Japan 2:23:14
SILVER Lidia Simon, Romania
BRONZE Joyce Chepchumba, Kenya

100-meter hurdles
GOLD Olga Shishigina, Kazakhstan :12.65
SILVER Glory Alozie, Nigeria
BRONZE Melissa Morrison, United States

400-meter hurdles
GOLD Irina Privalova, Russia :53.02
SILVER Deon Hemmings, Jamaica
BRONZE Nouzha Bidouane, Morocco

20-kilometer walk
GOLD Liping Wang, China 1:29:05
SILVER Kjersti Plaetzer, Norway
BRONZE Maria Vasco, Spain

4x100-meter relay
GOLD Bahamas :41.95
SILVER Jamaica
BRONZE United States

4x400-meter relay
GOLD United States 3:22
SILVER Jamaica
BRONZE Russia

High jump
GOLD Yelena Yelesina, 6 ft. 7 in. (2.01 m)
Russia
SILVER Hestrie Cloete, South Africa
BRONZE Kajsa Bergqvist, Sweden

Pole vault
GOLD Stacy Dragila, 15 ft. 1 in. (4.60 m)**
United States
SILVER Tatiana Grigorieva, Australia
BRONZE Vala Flosadottir, Iceland

Long jump
GOLD Heike Drechsler, 22 ft. 11¼ in. (6.99 m)
Germany
SILVER Fiona May, Italy
BRONZE Marion Jones, United States

Triple jump
GOLD Tereza Marinova, 49 ft. 10¼ in. (15.20 m)
Bulgaria
SILVER Tatyana Lebedeva, Russia
BRONZE Olena Hovorova, Ukraine

Shot-put
GOLD Yanina Korolchik, 67 ft. 5¼ in. (20.56 m)
Belarus
SILVER Larisa Peleshenko, Russia
BRONZE Astrid Kumbernuss, Germany

Discus
GOLD Ellina Zvereva, 224 ft. 4¾ in. (68.40 m)
Belarus
SILVER Anastasia Kelesidou, Greece
BRONZE Irina Yatchenko, Belarus

Hammer
GOLD Kamila Skolimowska, Poland
233 ft. 5½ in. (71.16 m)**
SILVER Olga Kuzenkova, Russia
BRONZE Kirsten Muenchow, Germany

Javelin
GOLD Trine Hattestad, 226 ft. 1 in. (68.91 m)**
Norway
SILVER Mirella Maniani-Tzelili, Greece
BRONZE Osleidys Menendez, Cuba

Heptathlon
GOLD Denise Lewis, Great Britain 6,584 pts.
SILVER Yelena Prokhorova, Russia
BRONZE Natalya Sazanovich, Belarus

TRIATHLON

Men
GOLD Simon Whitfield, Canada
SILVER Stephan Vuckovic, Germany
BRONZE Jan Rehula, Czech Republic

Women
GOLD Brigitte McMahon, Switzerland
SILVER Michellie Jones, Australia
BRONZE Magali Messmer, Switzerland

VOLLEYBALL

Men		**Women**	
GOLD	Yugoslavia	GOLD	Cuba
SILVER	Russia	SILVER	Russia
BRONZE	Italy	BRONZE	Brazil

WATER POLO

MEN'S		**WOMEN'S**	
GOLD	Hungary	GOLD	Australia
SILVER	Russia	SILVER	United States
BRONZE	Yugoslavia	BRONZE	Russia

WEIGHTLIFTING

MEN'S

123 lbs. (56 kg)
GOLD Halil Mutlu, Turkey 672 lbs (305.0 kg)*
SILVER Wu Wenxiong, China
BRONZE Zhang Xiangxiang, China

137 lbs. (62 kg)
GOLD Nikolay Pechalov, Croatia 717 lbs. (325.0 kg)
SILVER Leonidas Sabanis, Greece
BRONZE Gennady Oleshchuk, Belarus

152 lbs. (69 kg)
GOLD Galabin Boevski, Bulgaria 788 lbs. (357.5 kg)**
SILVER Georgl Markov, Bulgarla
BRONZE Sergei Lavrenov, Belarus

170 lbs. (77 kg)
GOLD Zhan Xugang, China 810 lbs. (367.5 kg)
SILVER Viktor Mitrou, Greece
BRONZE Arsen Melikyan, Armenia

187 lbs. (85 kg)
GOLD Pyrros Dimas, Greece 860 lbs. (390.0 kg)
SILVER Marc Huster, Germany
BRONZE George Asanidze, Georgia

207 lbs. (94 kg)
GOLD Akakios Kakiasvilis, Greece 893 lbs. (405.0 kg)
SILVER Szymon Kolecki, Poland
BRONZE Alexei Petrov, Russia

231 lbs. (105 kg)
GOLD Hossein Tavakoli, Iran 937 lbs (425.0 kg)
SILVER Alan Tsagaev, Bulgaria
BRONZE Said Asaad, Qatar

Over 231 lbs. (Over 105 kg)
GOLD Hossein Rezazadeh, Iran 1,042 lbs. (472.5 kg)*
SILVER Ronny Weller, Germany
BRONZE Andrei Chemerkin, Russia

WRESTLING

FREESTYLE

119 lbs. (54 kg)
GOLD   Namig Abdullayev, Azerbaijan
SILVER Samuel Henson, United States
BRONZE Amiran Karntanov, Greece

128 lbs. (58 kg)
GOLD   Alireza Dabir, Iran
SILVER Yevgen Buslovych, Ukraine
BRONZE Terry Brands, United States

139 lbs. (63 kg)
GOLD   Mourad Oumakhanov, Russia
SILVER Serafim Barzakov, Bulgaria
BRONZE Jae Sung Jang, South Korea

152 lbs. (69 kg)
GOLD   Daniel Igali, Canada
SILVER Arsen Gitinov, Russia
BRONZE Lincoln McIlravy, United States

168 lbs. (76 kg)
GOLD   Brandon Slay, United States
SILVER Moon Eui Jae, South Korea
BRONZE Adem Bereket, Turkey

187 lbs. (85 kg)
GOLD   Adam Saitiev, Russia
SILVER Yoel Romero, Cuba
BRONZE Mogamed Ibragimov, Macedonia

214 lbs. (97 kg)
GOLD   Saghid Mourtasaliyev, Russia
SILVER Islam Bairamukov, Kazakhstan
BRONZE Eldar Kurtanidze, Georgia

Rulon Gardner of the United States defeats Alexandre Kareline of Russia in heavyweight Greco-Roman wrestling.

287 lbs. (130 kg)
GOLD   David Moussoulbes, Russia
SILVER Artur Taymazov, Uzbekistan
BRONZE Alexis Rodriguez, Cuba

GRECO-ROMAN

119 lbs. (54 kg)
GOLD   Sim Kwon Ho, South Korea
SILVER Lazaro Rivas, Cuba
BRONZE Kang Yong Gyun, North Korea

128 lbs. (58 kg)
GOLD   Armen Nazarian, Bulgaria
SILVER Kim In-Sub, South Korea
BRONZE Sheng Zetian, China

139 lbs. (63 kg)
GOLD   Varteres Samourgachev, Russia
SILVER Juan Luis Maren, Cuba
BRONZE Akaki Chachua, Georgia

152 lbs. (69 kg)
GOLD   Filiberto Azcuy, Cuba
SILVER Katsuhiko Nagata, Japan
BRONZE Alexei Glouchkov, Russia

168 lbs. (76 kg)
GOLD   Mourat Kardanov, Russia
SILVER Matt Lindland, United States
BRONZE Marko Yli-Hannuksela, Finland

187 lbs. (85 kg)
GOLD   Hamza Yerlikaya, Turkey
SILVER Sandor Istvan Bardosi, Hungary
BRONZE Mukhran Vakhtangadze, Georgia

214 lbs. (97 kg)
GOLD   Mikael Ljungberg, Sweden
SILVER Davyd Saldadze, Ukraine
BRONZE Garrett Lowney, United States

287 lbs. (130 kg)
GOLD   Rulon Gardner, United States
SILVER Alexandre Kareline, Russia
BRONZE Dmitry Debelka, Belarus

WOMEN'S

106 lbs. (48 kg)
GOLD   Tara Nott, United States   408 lbs. (185.0 kg)
SILVER Rumbewas Raema Lisa, Indonesia
BRONZE Indriyani Sri, Indonesia

117 lbs. (53 kg)
GOLD   Xia Yang, China   496 lbs. (225.0 kg)*
SILVER Li Feng-Ying, Taipei
BRONZE Winarni Binti Slamet, Indonesia

128 lbs. (58 kg)
GOLD   Soraya Jimenez Mendivil,   491 lbs. (222.5 kg)
        Mexico
SILVER Ri Song Hui, North Korea
BRONZE Suta Khassaraporn, Thailand

139 lbs. (63 kg)
GOLD   Chen Xiaomin, China   535 lbs. (242.5 kg)*
SILVER Valentina Popova, Russia
BRONZE Ioanna Chatziioannou, Greece

152 lbs. (69 kg)
GOLD   Lin Weining, China   535 lbs. (242.5 kg)
SILVER Erzsebet Markus, Hungary
BRONZE Malleswari Karnam, Indonesia

165 lbs. (75 kg)
GOLD   Maria Isabel Urrutia,   540 lbs. (245.0 kg)
        Colombia
SILVER Ruth Ogbeifo, Nigeria
BRONZE Kuo Yi-Hang, Taiwan

Over 165 lbs. (Over 75 kg)
GOLD   Ding Meiyuan, China   661 lbs. (300.0 kg)*
SILVER Agata Wrobel, Poland
BRONZE Cheryl Haworth, United States

Pacific Islands. Political unrest dominated developments in the Pacific during 2000. Armed forces toppled the governments of Fiji and the Solomon Islands.

Fiji. A group of armed men, led by part-Fijian businessman George Speight, invaded Parliament House on May 19. The rebels took 27 members of the parliament hostage, including Prime Minister Mahendra Chaudhry. Speight's demands included overturning the 1997 constitution, which had enabled Chaudhry and the Fiji Labour Party to gain power. Many ethnic Fijians deeply resented Chaudhry's victory because, as the first prime minister descended from indentured Indian laborers, Chaudhry symbolized threats to the rights of Fiji's original inhabitants.

Fiji's Constitution was abolished on May 29, 2000. Army leader Commodore Frank Bainimara-

ma swore in an all-Fijian interim government on July 4. Led by banker Laisenia Qarase, who assumed the prime minister's post, the interim government successfully negotiated the release of the hostages. Speight was arrested. Observers expected the interim government to write a new constitution. Australia and other neighboring countries imposed trade and travel sanctions on Fiji as a result of the incident.

Solomon Islands. Two years of ethnic violence between residents of Guadalcanal Island and people from Malaita Island, who had settled on Guadalcanal, led to a crisis when members of the self-styled Malaitan Eagle Force (MEF) seized control of the capital, Honiara, on June 5. They held Prime Minister Bartholomew Ulufa'alu hostage until he agreed to resign.

The government of the Solomon Islands re-

Facts in brief on Pacific Island countries

Country	Population	Government	Monetary unit*	Foreign trade (million U.S.$) Exports[†]	Imports[†]
Australia	19,222,000	Governor General William Deane; Prime Minister John Howard	dollar (1.88 = $1)	56,087	69,135
Fiji	845,000	President Josefa Iloilo; Prime Minister Laisenia Qarase	dollar (2.25 = $1)	590	965
Kiribati	87,000	President Teburoro Tito	Australian dollar	8	40
Marshall Islands	63,000	President Kessai Note	U.S. dollar	28	58
Micronesia, Federated States of	144,000	President Leo A. Falcam	U.S. dollar	73	168
Nauru	12,000	President Bernard Dowiyogo	Australian dollar	25	21
New Zealand	3,759,000	Governor General Sir Michael Hardie-Boys; Prime Minister Helen Clark	dollar (2.50 = $1)	12,452	14,301
Palau	19,000	President Kuniwo Nakamura	U.S. dollar	14	72
Papua New Guinea	4,809,000	Governor General Sir Silas Atopare; Prime Minister Sir Mekere Morauta	kina (2.88 = $1)	1,880	1,191
Samoa	222,000	Head of State Malietoa Tanumafili II; Prime Minister Tuila'epa Sailele Malielegaoi	tala (3.44 = $1)	20	115
Solomon Islands	444,000	Governor General Sir John Lapli; Prime Minister Mannaseh Damukana Sogavare	dollar (5.11 = $1)	173	170
Tonga	107,000	King Taufa'ahau Tupou IV; Prime Minister Lavaka ata Ulukalala	pa'anga (1.91 = $1)	11	75
Tuvalu	10,000	Governor General Sir Tomasi Puapua; Prime Minister Ionatana Ionatana	Australian dollar	1	4
Vanuatu	192,000	President Father John Bani; Prime Minister Barak Sope	vatu (141.80 = $1)	34	88

*Exchange rates as of Oct. 13, 2000, or latest available data.
[†]Latest available data.

Fijian soldiers struggle with armed rebels at a roadblock near Parliament House in Suva on May 27, 2000. Rebel leader George Speight and his supporters held members of parliament hostage from May 19 through early July.

mained at a standstill until June 30, when 44 of 50 members of the parliament chose a new prime minister in a special session. The members voted 23 to 21 for Mannaseh Sogavare, who was from Choiseul Island and had been Ulufa'alu's finance minister. The MEF and the Isatambu Freedom Movement, the militia group of the Guadalcanal people, signed a peace treaty on October 15 that called for international monitors to help restore order to the islands. Both ethnic militia groups were reported to be looting private and state property.

Papua New Guinea. On September 16, Prime Minister Sir Mekere Morauta led celebrations of the 25th anniversary of Papua New Guinea's independence. The celebrations included tribal dancing and military parades in each provinicial capital and in Port Moresby, the national capital.

Morauta's government obtained $300 million in financial aid in 2000 from the World Bank, a United Nations (UN) agency that provides long-term loans to countries for development. In June, Morauta's cabinet approved a nickel and cobalt mining project in Madang Province estimated to be worth $850 million. The mine was expected to produce 2,500 jobs.

In March, Papua New Guinea government minister Sir Michael Somare agreed to allow a referendum on independence for Bougainville island. The Bougainville Revolutionary Army (BRA) had waged armed conflict against the Papua New Guinea government from 1988 to 1997. Also in March 2000, representatives for Papua New Guinea and Bougainville independence leaders agreed to establish an interim provincial government and work toward greater autonomy for Bougainville.

Tuvalu. Tuvalu joined the United Nations in September 2000, bringing the number of Pacific Island nations represented in the UN in 2000 to 12.

Marshall Islands. Kessai Note was elected president of Marshall Islands in January. He was the first commoner to serve as president since Marshall Islands gained independence in 1986.

Kiribati. Officials in Kiribati scored a public relations coup by declaring an atoll in the islands as the first place in the world to celebrate the millennium on Jan. 1, 2000. The media flocked to the previously uninhabited atoll renamed "Millennium" for the occasion.   □ Eugene Ogan

Pakistani women search for water in the Thar Desert of south-eastern Pakistan in May 2000. Rain had not fallen in the region for at least two years, causing livestock and crop losses and forcing thousands of people to migrate.

Pakistan. General Pervez Musharraf promised on May 25, 2000, that he would honor the May 12 decision of the Pakistani Supreme Court to return Pakistan to civilian rule within three years. Musharraf had seized power in Pakistan on Oct. 12, 1999. The court, which also ruled that the army was justified to oust an incompetent civilian government riddled with corruption, gave Musharraf the power to amend the constitution.

The ruling came after the government removed Chief Justice Saeed uz Zaman Siddiqui and five other justices from the 13-member Supreme Court on January 26. Saeed had refused to swear loyalty to the military regime.

The government scheduled local elections for sometime between December 2000 and May 2001, the first step toward returning to an elected government. Major political parties, which are banned from participation in local elections, rejected the plan, calling for national elections first.

Tax trouble. The World Bank, a United Nations agency that provides long-term loans to countries for development, reported in September 2000 that efforts to reduce poverty in Pakistan during the 1990's were undermined by the deterioration of the quality of government and declining governmental revenue. In 2000, this revenue was approximately 15 to 16 percent of the national economic output, less than half of the revenue percentage in most countries. In order to qualify for foreign aid, the government ousted by Musharraf had misled various agencies by claiming that budget deficits were low.

In 2000, Musharraf tried to raise taxes, which only 1.2 million of Pakistan's 150 million people paid. According to some estimates, 70 percent of the economy of Pakistan was not officially recorded in 2000. In May, Musharraf developed a plan to enforce the collection of sales taxes. Shopkeepers, who feared sales tax records would show they owed personal taxes, responded to the plan with repeated strikes.

Sharif sentenced. In April, Nawaz Sharif, prime minister of the government overthrown by Musharraf, was sentenced to two life terms in prison for hijacking and terrorism. He had threatened a plane carrying Musharraf, ordering it diverted as the army took over. In December the government commuted Sharif's sentences and sent him into exile in Saudi Arabia.

Terrorism. A series of bombings in Pakistan in 2000 killed nearly 80 people. The worst explosion killed 16 people in a produce market in Islamabad, the capital, in September. Musharraf blamed the terrorism on an Indian intelligence agency. The bombings came amid tension between Pakistan and India over a territorial conflict in Kashmir. The Pakistan government also worried about terrorism by militants associated with Islamic parties.   ☐ Henry S. Bradsher

See also **India.**

Paleontology. North Carolina
scientists stirred excitement among paleontologists in April 2000, when they announced they had used the latest in advanced medical imaging technology to discover what they believed was a fossilized dinosaur heart.

A team from North Carolina State University in Raleigh, which included biomedical imaging expert Paul Fisher and paleontologist Dale Russell, said the supposed heart was preserved in an iron-rich *concretion* (a cemented mass of sediment) inside

the ribcage of a small, *herbivorous* (plant-eating) dinosaur. The dinosaur, called *Thescelosaurus,* lived 66 million years ago during the Cretaceous Period (145 million to 65 million years ago) in what is now South Dakota. When examined with *computed tomography* (a technique in which a computer processes X rays to produce a three-dimensional image on a video screen), the concretion revealed what appeared to be four chambers, including two large ovals divided by a partition. The researchers interpreted these ovals as being *ventricles* (the lower chambers of a heart).

The structure of the organ suggested that some dinosaurs had four-chambered hearts, a type of heart that occurs in *warm-blooded* (constant body temperature) animals, such as birds and mammals. Such animals typically have high *metabolic* (body function) rates. Reptiles, amphibians, and other *cold-blooded* (body temperature dependent on outside temperature) animals usually have two- or three-chambered hearts and a low metabolism. The scientists said the efficiency of a four-chambered heart implied that at least some small dinosaurs were warm-blooded and capable of running and other high levels of activity.

Other scientists responded that the heartlike object in the fossil was simply an *inorganic* (not

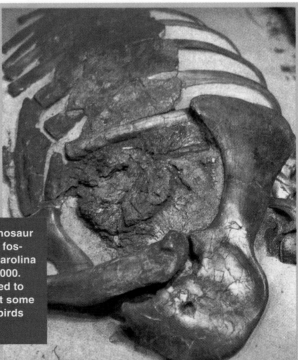

A 66-million-year-old ribcage of a dinosaur encases a solid mass identified as a fossilized heart by scientists at North Carolina State University in Raleigh in April 2000. The scientists said the heart appeared to have four chambers, suggesting that some dinosaurs were warm-blooded, like birds and mammals.

derived from a living animal or plant) concretion with mineralized features resembling heart structures. Paleontologists agreed that additional research was needed to determine the true nature of the "heart."

Flap over feathers. In June, a team of scientists led by zoologists Terry Jones and John Ruben of Oregon State University in Corvallis, reported that an ancient reptile fossil shows what appears to be feathers. The scientists said the fossil may represent an early ancestor of birds and called into question a widespread view among paleontologists that birds evolved from dinosaurs.

The fossil, found in Kyrgyzstan in central Asia dated to about 220 million years ago, is a skeleton of a small reptile called *Longisquama insignis*. The animal carried a double row of plumelike appendages down its back. The Oregon researchers found evidence that each plume had a hollow central shaft and base— like a feather. If so, these features would represent the evolution of feathers from scales almost 75 million years before the earliest known bird, *Archaeopteryx*.

Longisquama belongs to the same large group—the Archosauria—as birds, dinosaurs, and crocodiles. The researchers argued that it is unlikely that feathers would have evolved more than once in this group. *Longisquama*, which has no known link to dinosaurs, therefore, could have been an early ancestor of *Archaeopteryx* and other birds. Many paleontologists strongly criticized this view. They pointed to a large amount of skeletal evidence suggesting similarities and links between birds and *theropods*, which were small *carnivorous* (meat-eating) dinosaurs.

In November, zoologists Hans-Dieter Sues and Robert Reisz of the University of Toronto reported that their analysis of a *Longisquama* specimen indicated that the plumelike appendages were thickened scales. Paleontologists said further research would be needed to resolve this dispute.

Evolution of snakes. An Australian study completed in 2000 indicated that snakes did not evolve from ground-burrowing lizards, as had long been suspected. Instead, the finding suggested that serpents descended from creatures akin to extinct marine reptiles called mosasaurs.

In January, zoologists John Scanlon and Michael Lee of the University of Queensland in Australia reported the discovery of well-preserved fossils of the extinct snake *Wonambi*. The fossils, which were found in Queensland, dated from the Pleistocene Epoch (approximately 2 million to 11,500 years ago). The fossils showed that the skull of *Wonambi* was similar to the skulls of mosasaurs, large, predatory lizards that were related to modern monitor lizards. Mosasaurs thrived in the shallow seas of the Cretaceous Period.

Tiny primates. In March 2000, paleontologist-anthropologist Daniel Gebo of Northern Illinois University in DeKalb described discoveries of foot bones and teeth from three species of tiny primates. Gebo's team found the fossils in southern China in sediments approximately 45 million years old. One of the species, the 4-inch- (10-centimeter-) long *Eosimias centennicus,* had been described from previously found fossils, but the fragmentary nature of those fossils prevented scientists from making a firm classification of the creature. The new fossils provided convincing evidence that *Eosimias* was an early representative of *anthropoid primates,* the group of primates that includes monkeys, apes, and humans. The fossils indicated that anthropoids originated in Southeast Asia rather than Africa, where scientists had previously believed they had originated.

Gebo also outlined the discovery of the smallest known primate remains. They belonged to a creature estimated to have been only about 2 inches (5 centimeters) long, excluding the tail. ☐ Carlton E. Brett

Panama. President Mireya Elisa Moscoso de Grubar called upon Panama's Congress and business sectors to live up to their "moral obligation" and confront the "social problems" of Panamanians during a Sept. 1, 2000, address on the first anniversary of her inauguration. She said her goal was to reduce the gross inequality in the distribution of national wealth.

According to Panamanian government statistics, the *per capita* (per person) income of Panamanians was $3,000 in 2000, and 37 percent of the population lived in poverty. Economists at the University of Panama in Panama City reported in September that just 76 individuals, many linked by family and business ties, controlled $5 billion of Panama's assets. This sum was equal to half of Panama's annual *gross national product* (total amount of goods and services produced).

In June, the United States Customs Service alleged that poorly patrolled borders and ports made Panama a major transshipment point for cocaine and heroine on its way to the United States. ☐ Nathan A. Haverstock
See also **Latin America.**

Papua New Guinea. See **Asia; Pacific Islands.**

Paraguay. See **Latin America.**

Pennsylvania. See **Philadelphia; State government.**

■ People in the news

in 2000 included those listed below, who were all Americans unless otherwise indicated.

Assad, Bashar al- (1965-) became president of Syria on July 17, 2000, succeeding his father, Syrian strongman Hafez al-Assad, who died on June 10. Soon after the elder Assad's death, the Baath Party-dominated People's Council (the Syrian parliament) eased Bashar's way to the presidency by amending the nation's constitution to lower the minimum presidential age. Bashar al-Assad was made commander of the armed forces and head of the Baath Party. In a presidential referendum on July 10, he won 97 percent of the vote.

Bashar al-Assad was born in Damascus on Sept. 11, 1965. The shy, unassuming second son of the president of Syria grew up in the shadow of his outgoing older brother Basil, Hafez al-Assad's heir-apparent. Bashar studied medicine at Damascus University, becoming an ophthalmologist. Syrians call him "Dr. Bashar." When Bashar's older brother Basil died in a January 1994 car accident, Bashar assumed the role of his father's successor.

After Bashar al-Assad's election, Western journalists speculated that he might prove to be a reformer and modernizer. They were quick to observe changes of style in the new regime. Portraits of the Assads, father and son, disappeared from public places, and the Syrian media dropped exaggerated terms of presidential respect from their reports. In July 2000, Assad released dozens of political prisoners.

On the issue of Middle East peace, however, he reaffirmed Syria's position on the return of the Golan Heights, lost to Israel in the 1967 war. Middle East experts suggested that because Assad was intent on consolidating power at home, he was unlikely to offer any new peace initiatives.

See also **Syria.**

Bashar al-Assad, president of Syria

Buchanan, Patrick "Pat" (1938-), ran on the Reform Party ticket for president in 2000 after a bitter party fight and a contested nomination. Buchanan, a long-time Republican, announced in October 1999 that he would leave his party and seek the nomination of the Reform Party, founded by Ross Perot in 1992. The Reform Party's convention in Long Beach, California, in August 1999 split between Buchanan's followers and a pro-Perot faction. The Federal Election Commission eventually declared Buchanan the nominee.

Pat Buchanan was born Nov. 2, 1938, in Washington, D.C., to a Roman Catholic family that emphasized traditional conservative values. Buchanan attended Georgetown University in Washington, D.C., and Columbia University in New York City. After finishing his education, he worked for several years as a newspaper journalist. Richard Nixon later employed Buchanan as a writer. After Nixon was elected to the presidency in 1968, Buchanan became Nixon's chief speechwriter. Buchanan also worked briefly in the Reagan administration as the director of communications. In the 1980's and 1990's, he became familiar to many television audiences as a conservative panelist on several news shows.

In 1992, Buchanan challenged Republican President George Bush in the presidential primaries and took 37 percent of the New Hampshire primary vote. As a candidate, Buchanan provoked intense controversy as an opponent of abortion, feminism, and the gay rights movement. Buchanan maintained that Republicans had moved too far toward the middle of the road and should return to traditional conservative politics.

See also **Elections.**

Chen Shui-bian (1951-) won election on March 18, 2000, as Taiwan's first president from an opposition party. He took office on May 20. Chen's election marked the end of the ruling Kuomintang (KMT) Party's hold on the presidency—though the KMT still held a parliamentary majority. Chiang Kai-shek and his supporters fled mainland China and the Communists in 1949 and moved his government, the KMT, to Taiwan. The KMT, or Nationalist Party, subsequently ruled Taiwan for more than 50 years.

Chen Shui-bian was born on Feb. 18, 1951, into a poor family in a farming village in southwestern Taiwan. Unlike the KMT elite, who came to Taiwan from mainland China, Chen was Taiwanese, descending from Chinese who migrated to Taiwan centuries ago.

Chen's introduction to dissident politics came in 1980 when he defended prodemocracy demonstrators in a court case. He later served a jail term for accusing a Nationalist politician of plagiarism.

In 1985, a hit-and-run driver struck Chen's wife, leaving her permanently paralyzed. Several dissidents suspected that the driver had been a KMT hit-man, though no proof was ever found. In the mid-1990's, Chen served as mayor of Taipei, earning the reputation of a reformist.

Before Chen's election, his Democratic Progress Party had advocated formal independence for Taiwan, but Chen worked to allay mainland China's worries about Taiwan's intentions. However, his efforts to restart suspended talks with Beijing officials were unsuccessful.

See also **Taiwan**.

Collins, Francis S. (1950-), announced

jointly with J. Craig Venter of Celera Genomics Corp. at a June 26, 2000, conference at the White House that researchers had completed a working draft of the human genome, the human genetic code. Collins, a geneticist and director of the government-sponsored research effort based at the National Human Genome Research Institute in Bethesda, Maryland, said of the achievement, "We have caught the first glimpse of our own instruction book, previously known only to God." Using different methods, both the Collins team and the Venter team had sifted through more than 3 billion molecular pieces to map an estimated 80,000 human genes.

Francis Collins was born on April 14, 1950, in Staunton, Virginia. He earned a bachelor degree in molecular biology at the University of Virginia in Charlottesville and a doctorate at Yale University in New Haven, Connecticut, in 1974. After graduating

from medical school at the University of North Carolina in Chapel Hill, Collins became a genetic researcher and led research teams that identifiy genes for cystic fibrosis (1989) and neurofibromatosis, a nervous system disorder (1990). By the early 1990's, Collins was a leader in the field of genetic research. In 1993, he became director of the National Human Genome Project at the National Institutes of Health and continued research into disease-causing genes. In 1993, he headed the team that discovered the gene for Huntington's disease, a degenerative disease of the nervous system.

See also **Biology; Medicine; People in the news** (Venter, J. Craig).

Edelman, Marian Wright (1939-), received the Presidential Medal of Freedom from U.S. President Bill Clinton on Aug. 9, 2000, for her advocacy work on behalf of children and families. Edelman had headed the Children's Defense Fund (CDF), a Washington, D.C.-based advocacy organization for children's rights to health care and education, since 1973. Senator Edward Kennedy (D., Massachusetts) dubbed Edelman "the 101st senator on children's issues" because of her skill in lobbying Congress for child and family legislation. Efforts by CDF resulted in increased Medicaid funding for poor children in 1984, increased funding for Head Start in 1992, and a measure to extend health care coverage to 5 million uninsured children in 1997.

Marian Wright was born on June 6, 1939, in Bennetsville, South Carolina. She went to Spelman College in Atlanta, Georgia, and law school at Yale University in New Haven, Connecticut. In the early 1960's, she helped register African American voters in Mississippi. She returned to that state in 1963 as the legal defense fund attorney for the National Association for the Advancement of Colored People (NAACP). She also guided Senator Robert F. Kennedy on his poverty fact-finding tour of the Mississippi Delta in 1967. During the tour, she met Peter Edelman, Kennedy's legislative assistant. They married in 1968 and settled in Washington, D.C., where Marian Edelman built up the organization that became the Children's Defense Fund.

Marian Wright Edelman, Children's Defense Fund president

Vicente Fox, president of Mexico

Fox Quesada, Vicente

(1942-), won election as president of Mexico on July 2, 2000. He was inaugurated on December 1 and became the first president of Mexico in 71 years who did not belong to the Institutional Revolutionary Party (PRI), which had dominated the Mexican presidency for 13 consecutive presidential terms. The PRI's election defeat—described as a political "earthquake" by observers in Mexico—deprived the once-dominant party of control of both houses of the parliament and delivered the two contested governorships to opposition parties.

Vicente Fox Quesada was born on July 2, 1942, to a prosperous family in Guanajuato state, the "breadbasket" of Mexico. Fox attended schools in Mexico and the United States, earning a masters degree in business at Harvard University in Cambridge, Massachusetts. Fox went to work for the Coca-Cola Corporation of Atlanta, Georgia, and eventually rose to the position of chief executive for Coca-Cola Mexico. In 1979, Fox resigned from his position at Coca-Cola and returned to Guanajuato to help run the family's ranch.

Fox entered politics in the 1980's as a member of the right-of-center National Action Party (PAN). In 1995, he was elected governor of Guanajuato. In 1999, he took leave as governor to run for president. Campaigning across Mexico, the mustachioed candidate, who is 6 feet, 5 inches (1.8 meters, 12.7 centimeters) tall, often appeared in cowboy attire, earning him the nickname "the Marlboro Man." Fox ran a media-savvy campaign that convinced Mexican voters that the PRI had been in control too long.

Advocating free-market reforms, Fox promised to eliminate Mexico's budget deficit by 2004, in an effort to reduce inflation from 10 to 3 percent and to achieve a 7 percent annual growth rate. Fox was a strong supporter of the North American Free Trade Agreement (NAFTA).

See also **Mexico.**

Kostunica, Vojislav

(1944-), a constitutional lawyer and scholar, became president of Yugoslavia on Oct. 7, 2000. Kostunica's swearing-in ceremony was the culmination of a national drama that began with a presidential election on September 24 and ended in a mass uprising against president Slobodan Milosevic. Milosevic's 13-year rule had brought bloody ethnic conflict, North Atlantic Treaty Organization (NATO) bombing raids in 1999, and economic sanctions. When Milosevic attempted to void the results of the 2000 election, which gave Kostunica a clear majority, demonstrators poured into the streets of Belgrade, the capital, taking control of key government buildings. The public outcry forced Milosevic to resign on Oct. 6, 2000.

Vojislav Kostunica, born on March 24, 1944, in Belgrade, received his law degree at Belgrade University Law School in 1966 and later taught there. He was dismissed in 1974 after defending a fellow professor's criticism of constitutional changes. Kostunica, who is the head of a pro-Serbian nationalist

Julie Krone, hall-of-fame jockey

political party, has long supported democratic reforms and the rule of law. When the government changed in Belgrade, Western nations quickly ended trade sanctions against Yugoslavia.

See also **Yugoslavia.**

Krone, Julie

(1963-), was inducted into the National Racing Hall of Fame in Saratoga, New York, on Aug. 7, 2000. She was the first female jockey to be so honored.

Krone, during her career, won 3,543 racing victories, more than any other female jockey in history, and earned more than $81 million in *purses* (prize money). Krone's most prestigious victory was the 1993 Belmont Stakes in Elmont, New York. She was the first woman to win one of the three premier U.S. horse races, which include the Kentucky Derby, the Preakness, and the Belmont Stakes. In April 1999, Krone retired after a string of injuries following a riding accident.

Julie Krone was born in Benton Harbor, Michigan, on July 24, 1963. She spent her childhood in Michigan and summers working at the Kentucky Downs race track in Louisville, Kentucky. As a teen-ager, she lived with her grandparents in Tampa, Florida, to be near Tampa Bay Downs. She won her first race in 1981 at Tampa Bay Downs. At the August 2000 Hall of Fame ceremony, Krone aimed her remarks at aspiring female jockeys: "If the stable gate is closed, climb the fence."

See also **Horse racing.**

Ricardo Lagos,
president of Chile

Vojislav Kostunica,
Yugoslav president

Joseph I. Lieberman,
Democratic candi-
date for U.S. vice
president

Lagos, Ricardo (1938-), became president of Chile on March 11, 2000. He was Chile's first Socialist president since Salvador Allende, who lost his office and life in a 1973 *coup* (overthrow). Lagos was elected president on Jan. 16, 2000, in a close two-way race with Joaquin Lavin of the rightist Alliance for Chile.

Ricardo Lagos Escobar was born on March 2, 1938, into a middle-class Chilean family. He was educated at the University of Chile and Duke University in Durham, North Carolina. After serving in Allende's ill-fated government, Lagos fled to the United States in 1973 and taught Latin American Studies for several years at the University of North Carolina at Chapel Hill. In 1978, Lagos returned to Chile, where Augusto Pinochet, the general who had led the 1973 coup to oust Allende, was firmly in command as dictator. In 1988, Lagos won prominence among opposition leaders by openly criticizing Pinochet on television and working to defeat a referendum that would have extended Pinochet's power.

After Chile returned to civilian rule in 1990, Lagos participated in the coalition-led government, holding several ministerial posts. He allayed fears of a Socialist government in the business community by appointing promarket advisers.

See also **Chile.**

Lieberman, Joseph I. (1942-), was selected by Democratic presidential candidate Al Gore as his vice-presidential running mate prior to the August 2000 Democratic national convention.

Lieberman, a U.S. senator from Connecticut, became the first Jewish vice-presidential nominee of a major U.S. political party. He and Al Gore lost the election by a narrow margin.

Lieberman was born in Stamford, Connecticut, on Feb. 24, 1942, to an Orthodox Jewish family. He attended public schools in Stamford before attending Yale University in New Haven, Connecticut, where he earned a bachelors degree in 1964 and a law degree in 1967. During the 1960's Lieberman helped register African American voters in the South, participated in the 1963 civil rights march on Washington, D.C., and cochaired Robert F. Kennedy's 1968 presidential campaign in Connecticut.

Lieberman won a Connecticut state Senate seat in 1970. In 1980, he made a bid for Congress but lost. In 1982, he became the Connecticut state attorney. In 1988, he ran for the U.S. Senate and defeated Republican Lowell Weicker, Jr., who had held the seat for three terms. Lieberman was reelected to the Senate in 1994, by the widest margin in Connecticut history.

In the Senate, Lieberman earned a reputation as a bipartisan moderate. He gained notoriety for condemning President Bill Clinton's behavior in the Monica Lewinsky scandal before any other Senate Democrat had spoken on the issue. Lieberman also campaigned against violence and explicit sexual content on television and in movies and video games.

Joseph Lieberman married Hadassah Freilich Tucker in 1983. They have one daughter together. Both have children from previous marriages.

See also **Congress of the United States; Democratic Party; Elections; United States, Government of the.**

Megawati Sukarnoputri (1947-), the first female vice president of Indonesia, received new duties in a power-sharing arrangement announced by President Abdurrahman Wahid in August 2000. The arrangement, termed a "dual presidency" by some observers, was expected to continue through the end of Wahid's term in 2004. The president reserved for himself foreign affairs and humanitarian duties but delegated the day-to-day running of the government to Megawati.

Although untested as a leader, Megawati, who was the daughter of Indonesia's first president, Sukarno, enjoyed immense popularity in 2000. She gained the respect of many Indonesians for her defiance of former president Suharto, when he attempted in June 1996 to have her party leadership removed from her. The incident provoked violent riots. Megawati responded by launching lawsuits against Suharto in every Indonesian court that would take her case—230 in all.

Megawati Sukarnoputri was born on Jan. 23, 1947, in Jakarta, Indonesia's capital, to Sukarno and his first wife, Fatmawti. A life of privilege in the presidential palace ended when Sukarno was ousted by Suharto in 1966. Megawati later became a mother and homemaker, remaining out of the public spotlight until she entered politics in 1987, when she won a seat in parliament. In 1993, she was named leader of the Indonesian Democratic Party (PDI).

See also **Indonesia**.

Mori, Yoshiro (1937-), was elected prime minister of Japan on April 5, 2000, three days after Prime Minister Keizo Obuchi suffered a massive stroke. Mori pledged to continue Obuchi's policies, particularly deficit government spending to stimulate the economy, after Obuchi's death on May 14.

Mori inherited an administration troubled by scandal and an economy that remained sluggish after nearly a decade of recession. During his first weeks in power, the new prime minister stirred controversy by stating that Japan was a "divine nation centering on the emperor." The comment, which seemed to evoke the pre-World War II (1939-1945) imperial system that led Japan to defeat, provoked protest in Japan and abroad. Mori's approval rating sank to below 15 percent. In parliamentary elections on June 25, Mori's ruling Liberal Democratic Party (LDP) fared poorly, as the opposition Democratic Party gained more than 30 seats in the lower house of the Diet, the Japanese parliament.

Yoshiro Mori was born on July 14, 1937, to rice farmers in Neagari, a rural town in Ishikawa Prefecture. He attended Tokyo's Waseda University, where he met Keizo Obuchi. Mori graduated in 1960. After a brief career as a journalist, he won election to a seat in the Diet in 1969.

See also **Japan**.

Musharraf, Pervez (1943-), the military leader of Pakistan, worked in 2000 to strengthen Pakistan's fragile economy and obtain Western aid. Musharraf took power in an October 1999 *coup* (overthrow) and declared himself the nation's "chief executive."

Pakistan's debt burden in 2000 consumed more than 50 percent of the annual budget. To increase revenue, Musharraf cracked down on tax evaders, an enormous problem. According to Pakistani statistics, less than 1 percent of the population paid taxes under previous regimes, and less than 1 percent of small businesses bothered to collect sales taxes.

In September 2000, Musharraf announced that the International Monetary Fund (IMF—a United Nations-affiliated organization that provides short-term credit to member nations) was close to an agreement to extend Pakistan credits. The IMF had suspended debt aid to Pakistan in 1998.

Pervez Musharraf was born Aug. 11, 1943, in New Delhi, India. His father, a civil servant in British-ruled India, later served as a Pakistani ambassador to Turkey. The family fled to Pakistan in 1947 when British India was partitioned into predominantly Hindu India and Muslim Pakistan. Young Musharraf joined the army in 1964. In 1965, he received a medal for gallantry for his efforts during the 16-day war with India. In 1998, Musharraf became chief of the army.

See also **India; Pakistan**.

Putin, Vladimirovich (1952-), was elected president of Russia on March 26, 2000, and inaugurated on May 7. He had served as acting president of Russia since Dec. 31, 1999, when Boris Yeltsin resigned.

Vladimir Putin was born on Oct. 7, 1952, in Leningrad, (now St. Petersburg) Russia. He attended a prestigious college-preparatory high school and in 1970 enrolled at Leningrad State University, where he studied law. After graduation, Putin worked at the Soviet secret police agency, the KGB. He spent most of the 1980's serving as a KGB agent in East Germany.

In 1990, Putin returned to Russia and became deputy mayor to Anatoly Sobchak, St. Petersburg's first elected mayor. In 1997, Putin was called to

Megawati Sukarnoputri, Indonesian vice president

**Vladimir Putin,
Russian president**

Moscow for a post in the Kremlin, and he soon attracted the attention of President Boris Yeltsin. In 1998, Putin became chief of the Federal Security Service, the successor organization to the KGB. Yeltsin appointed Putin prime minister on Aug. 9, 1999. The September 1999 terrorist attacks across Russia, which authorities attributed to rebels in Chechnya, proved to be Putin's ladder to the presidency.

When Putin sent troops into the breakaway republic in October, public opinion swung strongly behind him.

In July 2000, Putin demonstrated presidential clout during a major political shakeup, extracting critical reform measures from Russia's powerful regional leaders. The 89 governors yielded to a plan that barred them from membership in the upper house of the national parliament. They also relinquished control of substantial local tax revenues and agreed to lowering personal and corporate taxes. In a single stroke, Putin strengthened the central government and achieved significant economic reforms.

Associates have described Putin as tough, focused, and disciplined. He has advocated restoring Russia to a position of strength, and his critics have questioned his commitment to democracy, noting his KGB past and his government's hostile relations with the press. Journalists in Russia have been restrained or arrested on several occasions since Putin took office.

See also **Russia**.

Rowling, J. K. (1965-), was at the center of a media and publishing frenzy in July 2000 with the publication of her eagerly awaited fourth "Harry Potter" novel for young readers. *Harry Potter and the Goblet of Fire*, which continued the adventures of an orphaned English schoolboy-wizard, shattered records for book sales. Despite a record first print run of 3.8 million copies by the U.S. publisher Scholastic, many bookstores ran out of books within 24 hours of the July 8 release date. The book sold 4 million copies through Internet preorders before July 8, and Federal Express trucks and airplanes were said to have delivered 250,000 copies of the new Harry Potter book.

British author Joanne Kathleen Rowling was born on July 31, 1965, and grew up near Bristol,

England. She was a graduate of Exeter University in the United Kingdom and became a teacher. In 1992, she married a Portugese journalist. Their marriage was short-lived and left Rowling a single mother.

Struggling to support herself, Rowling wrote her first Harry Potter book in longhand, because she could not afford a word processor. London publisher Bloomsbury Press picked up the book, publishing it as *Harry Potter and the Philosopher's Stone* in 1997 (retitled *Harry Potter and the Sorcerer's Stone* in the United States). It sold 800,000 copies. The sequel, *Harry Potter and the Chamber of Secrets*, sold 900,000 copies, becoming a best seller in the United States in 1998.

See also **Literature for children**.

Santana, Carlos (1947-) Rock music veteran Carlos Santana won eight Grammy awards on Feb. 23, 2000, tying the previous record set by Michael Jackson in 1983. Santana won the award for best song of the year for "Smooth" and best album of the year for *Supernatural*.

Santana, who had performed at the legendary 1969 Woodstock festival, made huge inroads with a younger generation of fans with the release of his *Supernatural* album in 1999. The album cleverly combined Santana's talents with those of younger performers, such as Lauryn Hill, Dave Matthews, Wyclef Jean, and Rob Thomas of Matchbox 20. By 2000, *Supernatural* had sold more than 20 million copies worldwide. One of its songs, "Smooth," became a huge hit single, outplaying all other songs on U.S. radio stations in 1999.

Carlos Santana was born in Mexico on July 20, 1947. He grew up in the bordertown of Tijuana but moved to San Francisco in 1961. In 1966, he formed the Santana Blues Band, which gained national fame and made its first album in 1969. Throughout his career, Santana experimented with various musical influences, but his fusion of Latin, African, and jazz elements proved perennially popular. The band Santana was elected to the Rock and Roll Hall of Fame in Cleveland, Ohio, in 1998, making it the first Latin group to be inducted.

See also **Popular music**.

Spacey, Kevin (1959-), received on March 26, 2000, the Academy Award for best actor for his performance in *American Beauty* (1999). Spacey had previously received an Academy Award for best supporting actor in 1996 for his role in the film *The Usual Suspects* (1995).

Kevin Spacey was born Kevin Spacey Fowler on July 26, 1959, in South Orange, New Jersey. In 1963, the family moved to Los Angeles. By his own admission, Spacey was a difficult child, who bounced from school to school. While a student at Chatsworth High School, he developed a passion for acting and set his sights on a theatrical career.

J. K. Rowling, author of Harry Potter books

Spacey made his Broadway debut in 1982 as Oswald in Henrik Ibsen's *Ghosts*, playing opposite Liv Ullman. Recognizing the young actor's talent, director Mike Nichols gave Spacey his first motion-picture break in *Heartburn* (1986). Spacey attracted more attention with his rendition of the character Jamie Tyrone in Jonathan Miller's 1986 staging of Eugene O'Neill's *Long Day's Journey Into Night*, which starred Jack Lemmon. Lemmon later worked with Spacey on several projects and became the young actor's mentor, a relationship that Spacey acknowledged by dedicating his best actor award in 2000 to Lemmon.

Spacey has performed in several major film roles, including *Glengarry Glen Ross* (1992), *Consenting Adults* (1992), *The Ref* (1994), *Seven* (1995), and *L.A. Confidential* (1997). During 1998 and 1999, he performed the role of Hickey in Eugene O'Neill's *The Iceman Cometh*, on Broadway, for which he was nominated for a Tony Award.

See also **Motion pictures.**

Swank, Hilary (1974-), received the Academy Award for best actress on March 26, 2000, for her performance in the 1999 film *Boys Don't Cry*. The role also netted her the Golden Globe Award and the New York and Los Angeles film critics awards. Swank won rave reviews for her portrayal of Teena Brandon, a small-town transgender youth who adopts a male identity. When her true identity is discovered, she is raped and murdered.

Hilary Swank was born in Lincoln, Nebraska, on July 30, 1974, but grew up in Bellingham, Washington. She excelled in athletics, participating in the Junior Olympics and Washington state swimming championship meets. In 1990, Swank and her mother, Judy Swank, moved to Los Angeles to allow Hilary to pursue a film career, and she soon began to land television roles. Her first acting job

was a guest appearance on the syndicated sitcom "Harry and the Hendersons." She also appeared on CBS's "Evening Shade" and ABC's "Growing Pains." A number of television roles followed, including a stint on the Fox Network's "Beverly Hills, 90210" during the 1997-1998 season. Swank made her feature film debut in 1992 in *Buffy the Vampire Slayer* and went on to star in *The Next Karate Kid* in 1994.

See also **Motion pictures.**

Thomas, Helen (1920-), a pioneering woman reporter and White House correspondent, resigned from United Press International (UPI) in May 2000 after the company was purchased by Rev. Sun Myung Moon, founder of the Unification Church. Millions of Americans knew Thomas as the woman who concluded presidential news conferences by saying, "Thank you, Mr. President." She had been with UPI for 57 years and covered eight presidents since 1961.

Thomas earned respect—sometimes grudgingly—from politicians and fellow journalists. Former President Gerald Ford once described her as "a fine blend of journalism and acupuncture." CBS News anchor Dan Rather called her "a hero of journalism." The determined and resourceful Thomas often scooped her colleagues. In the mid-1960's, she reported Luci Baines Johnson's engagement even before the father of the bride—President Lyndon Johnson—had been told.

Born to an immigrant Lebanese family in Kentucky on Aug. 4, 1920, Helen Thomas grew up in Detroit. After putting herself through college, she went to Washington, D.C. She joined UPI as a $24-a-week radio scriptwriter during World War II (1939-1945). The news organization assigned her to the White House in 1961 to cover the "woman's beat"— the fashions and ac-

Helen Thomas, reporter

Best actress Hilary Swank and best actor Kevin Spacey

tivities of First Lady Jackie Kennedy. Thomas took every opportunity, however, to expand her role into reporting "hard news," and by 1975, she had become UPI's White House bureau chief. Thomas also led the drive for full female membership in the National Press Club, which was finally granted in 1971.

See also **Newspapers.**

Venter, J. Craig (1946-), president and chief science officer of Celera Genomics Corporation, of Rockville, Maryland, announced at a White House conference on June 26, 2000, that researchers had completed a working draft of the human genome, the total amount of genetic information in a human cell. Venter made the announcement with Francis S. Collins, the director of the government-sponsored National Human Genome Project in Bethesda, Maryland.

Both the Collins team and the Venter team had arrived at a map of the estimated 80,000 human genes, but Venter's team had gotten there faster by using a shortcut method, which he dubbed "whole genome shotgun sequencing." The method involved breaking genetic material in a cell into millions of smaller fragments. Then sophisticated machines determined the makeup of each fragment, and high-speed computers assembled the data. Venter's detractors, including Collins, speculated that the shotgun method introduced many mistakes into the code. Critics also blasted Venter for his stake in a private corporation that was expected to patent and sell portions of the genetic code. Venter defended his, and Celera's, record.

John Craig Venter was born in Salt Lake City, Utah, in 1946 and grew up in California. He served in the medical corps in Vietnam, posting duty during the 1968 Tet Offensive. After completing a Ph.D. in physiology and pharmacology in 1976 at the University of California at San Diego, Venter joined the faculty of the State University of New York at Buffalo. In 1984, he went to the National Institute of Health to pursue genetic research. Striking out on his own in 1992, Venter cofounded Celera in 1998. In 1995, he startled the scientific community by mapping the entire genome of a bacterium, the first researcher to do so.

See also **Biology; Medicine; People in the news** (Collins, Francis S.)

Welch, John F. "Jack" (1935-), announced on Nov. 1, 1999, that he would retire as chief executive officer (CEO) of General Electric (GE) Corporation in April 2001. Welch, who had become head of GE in 1981, transformed it from a stagnating industrial giant into an immensely profitable and diversified conglomerate. Under Welch, the market value of GE rocketed from $13 billion in 1981 to

$425 billion in 1999. In November 1999, *Fortune* magazine named him "manager of the century," while some analysts compared his influence on business in the United States with that of Henry Ford.

Welch moved GE's focus from making products to selling services and realizing the importance of global business. Welch's corporate innovations stemmed from a philosophy of sharing. He championed the "boundary-less" company, in which all barriers to information flow—communication black-outs between business divisions and bureaucratic layering of management—were dismantled. Welch's program came with a cost, however. His strategy of selling off business units that were not leading in their field led to 100,000 layoffs, prompting detractors to dub him "Neutron Jack" in reference to the neutron bomb, which kills people but leaves buildings standing.

Jack Welch was born in Peabody, Massachusetts, in 1935. After obtaining a doctoral degree in chemical engineering at the University of Illinois in Urbana/Champaign, he joined GE's plastics division in 1960. In 1977, he was made a senior vice president, and in 1981 at age 45, he became the youngest CEO in GE history.

See also **Economics; Manufacturing.**

Williams, Venus (1980-), captured the Wimbledon women's singles championship on July 8, 2000, defeating defending champion Lindsay Davenport. Two days later, Venus and Serena Williams became the first sisters in history to win the Wimbledon women's doubles title.

In September 2000, Venus Williams won the U.S. Open women's singles championship, one year after Serena had taken the title. With their tennis prowess and friendly sibling competition, the Williams sisters have won numerous fans for the sport, particularly among minorities.

Venus Williams was born on June 17, 1980, in Los Angeles and was raised in Compton, California. Both Venus and Serena demonstrated unusual athletic talent while still preschoolers. Their father, Richard Williams, who was also their manager and coach, believed that his two youngest daughters would grow up to be tennis champions. In 1991, the Williams family moved to south Florida so the sisters could enroll in Ric Macci's professional tennis academy. In 1993, both girls left public school and continued their education at home.

Venus made her professional debut at the age of 14 in the Bank of the West Classic in Oakland, California. She made her Wimbledon debut in 1997. In September 2000, she won the gold medal in women's singles at the Olympics in Sydney, Australia. Venus was the first black woman to win Wimbledon, the U.S. Open, and an Olympic gold medal in the same year.   □ Robert Knight

See also **Tennis; Olympics: A Special Report.**

Peru. Valentin Paniagua, the leader of Peru's Congress, was sworn in as interim president on Nov. 22, 2000. Paniagua replaced President Alberto K. Fujimori, who had faxed his resignation to Congress on November 20 while he was visiting Japan, his ancestral homeland. In his first act as president, Paniagua named Javier Perez de Cuellar, a former secretary-general of the United Nations, as prime minister. An election for a new president was scheduled for April 2001.

Flawed election. Peru was rocked by political scandal for seven months in 2000, beginning with the presidential election on April 9, when neither Fujimori nor his principal opponent, Alejandro Toledo, were certified as having received more than 50 percent of the vote. Under Peru's Constitution, the vote made a run-off election necessary. However, critics charged the initial election was unfair and fraudulent, and Toledo boycotted the May run-off, giving Fujimori his third, five-year term as president by default.

Inauguration violence. Fujimori's inauguration on July 28 was marred by violent protests. Tear gas and smoke engulfed the capital, Lima, as police and demonstrators engaged in running battles. Protestors built bonfires at the gates of the presidential palace.

Damaging videotape. In early September, Lima television stations broadcast a videotape showing Vladimiro Montesinos, the head of Peru's powerful intelligence service and Fujimori's closest adviser, apparently bribing an opposition party member to switch to Fujimori's Peru 2000 coalition party. On September 16, as numerous other possible illegalities involving the fugitive Montesinos mounted, Fujimori surprised Peruvians by announcing that he

would call a new election for 2001 in which he would not be a candidate.

Despite this announcement, protests and strikes continued in several parts of Peru, with demonstrators calling on Fujimori to resign immediately. The demonstrations continued until Fujimori finally stepped down in November.

New trial for American. On Aug. 28, 2000, Peru's highest military court overturned the sentence of Lori Berenson, a 30-year-old native of New York City who in 1996 had been condemned to life in prison without parole by a secret military tribunal. The tribunal had found Berenson guilty of helping pro-Cuban Tupac Amaru guerrillas plan an attack on Peru's Congress. The case against Berenson, who maintained that she was neither a member nor collaborator of the guerrilla group, was moved to a civilian court for retrial.

☐ Nathan A. Haverstock

See also **Latin America.**

Petroleum and gas. See Energy supply.

Peruvian presidential candidate Alejandro Toledo holds a Peruvian flag and an Incan symbol of power as he greets supporters in Cusco, Peru, in April 2000. Toledo lost the election to President Alberto Fujimori amid charges of widespread fraud.

Philadelphia hosted the Republican National Convention from July 31 to Aug. 3, 2000, culminating years of planning and $50 million in public and private expenditures. The event was the ninth national political convention to meet in Philadelphia in United States history, though it was the city's first in 52 years. Convention delegates, meeting at the First Union Center, part of a giant sports complex in southern Philadelphia, nominated Texas Governor George W. Bush for president of the United States and former Secretary of Defense Dick Cheney as his running mate.

Approximately 35,000 visitors, including 15,000 members of the media, came to the city for the convention. Ten thousand local volunteers offered aid to conventioneers, and taxi drivers and hotel employees received special training to give visitors the best impression of Philadelphia. Billboards and banners depicting elephants—the mascot of the Republican Party—became a staple in a city where Democrats outnumbered Republicans 3-to-1.

Thousands of extra police, including Police Commissioner John F. Timoney, patrolled Philadelphia's streets, where some minor clashes occurred between officers and protestors. Many protestors were angered by their confinement to a single designated area and by a requirement that they obtain permits to march or rally. By the end of the convention, police had jailed some 390 people. Police operations related to the convention cost an estimated $10 million—twice the budgeted amount.

Police beating on TV. On July 12, a video camera in a television-news helicopter captured a group of Philadelphia police officers punching and kicking a carjacking suspect, Thomas Jones, after a high-speed car chase. The tape, widely broadcast on television, embarrassed city officials just two weeks before the start of the Republican convention.

At a preliminary hearing in October, a Philadelphia judge ordered Jones held for trial on several charges, including carjacking, aggravated assault, and purse-snatching. The officers involved in the incident faced possible disciplinary sanctions pending a police department investigation.

School chief resigns. David Hornbeck, Philadelphia's superintendent of schools, resigned on June 5 after six years in the post. Hornbeck criticized Pennsylvania legislators for failing to provide enough funding to Philadelphia's schools. He said the lack of funds prevented him from carrying out his plans, including more comprehensive testing of students' progress in learning. In October, the Philadelphia Board of Education named former Deputy Mayor Philip R. Goldsmith to the newly created post of Chief Executive Officer of the Philadelphia School District.

Teacher contract dispute. For the first time in more than three decades, Philadelphia's public school teachers reported to school in 2000 without a contract. They did so after Philadelphia Mayor John Street pledged that the city would honor the terms of their expired contract while negotiations between the teachers union and the school board continued. The teachers went on strike on October 27 but returned to work after the union and school board agreed to a new four-year contract on November 3.

Abandoned cars. Mayor John Street launched a campaign against the growing number of abandoned cars on Philadelphia streets in 2000, ordering towing companies to remove the vehicles and haul them to crushing machines. He rallied Philadelphians to help by calling in license numbers of cars that had been abandoned in their neighborhoods. In April and May, the city towed more than 32,000 abandoned cars, at a cost of $1.2 million.

New university president. David Adamany, former president of Wayne State University in Detroit, became the eighth president of Philadelphia's Temple University in August. Adamany succeeded Peter Liacouras, who retired after 19 years as university president.

☐ Howard S. Shapiro

See also **City; Republican Party.**

Philippines. The Philippines House of Representatives impeached President Joseph E. Estrada on Nov. 13, 2000, and began his trial on December 7. Estrada was accused of bribery, graft, betrayal of public trust, and violation of the constitution. The charges against Estrada had been raised by Governor Luis Singson, who accused Estrada of accepting almost $11 million in kickbacks on illegal gambling and tobacco taxes.

After Singson made the accusations, Vice President Gloria Macapagal Arroyo joined with former presidents Corazon C. Aquino and Fidel V. Ramos in calling for Estrada's resignation. Estrada refused, despite nationwide demonstrations against him.

Estrada had been widely blamed for government corruption and economic failure from the earliest days of his presidency. While Estrada claimed not to favor friends or relatives, several business agreements created the perception of special treatment for Estrada's acquaintances.

Estrada's finance minister, Edgardo Espiritu, resigned in January, criticizing what he called the government's "culture of corruption." In March, Estrada's chief of staff, Aprodocio A. Laquian, was forced to resign. Laquian claimed that the president and his cabinet participated in midnight drinking binges during which major policy decisions were made.

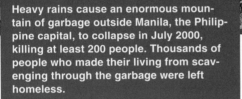

Heavy rains cause an enormous mountain of garbage outside Manila, the Philippine capital, to collapse in July 2000, killing at least 200 people. Thousands of people who made their living from scavenging through the garbage were left homeless.

Economy. In 2000, political turmoil in the Philippines, a stock market scandal, and guerrilla insurgencies added to economic troubles that discouraged foreign investment. Finance officials reported that foreign investors had pulled nearly $390 million out of the financial markets by September. Unemployment hit a nine-year high of 13.9 percent in April and stood at 11.1 percent in July. In 2000, the value of the national currency, the peso, reached its lowest level—49.6 to the U.S. dollar—since early 1998.

Hostages. Islamic guerrillas fighting for independence plagued the government and kept the southern Philippines in turmoil throughout 2000. In April, members of the Muslim extremist group Abu Sayyaf kidnapped 21 people, mostly Westerners, from a Malaysian diving resort and took them to Jolo Island in the southern Philippines. The Libyan government reportedly paid Abu Sayyaf $1 million apiece for the release of most of the hostages.

In August, Abu Sayyaf took Jeffrey C. Schilling, a U.S. Muslim convert, hostage. Schilling had apparently befriended members of the group who later kidnapped him. Frustrated by negotiation efforts while Abu Sayyaf bands seized more people for ransom, 4,000 troops attacked the rebels on Jolo Island in September. Most of the hostages were then freed.

Base captured. The 15,000-member Moro Islamic Liberation Front (MILF), another guerrilla group, also sought independence from the Philippines, which is primarily Roman Catholic. Despite peace talks in 2000, the MILF continued to fight at Mindanao Island. Islamic guerrillas had been responsible for the deaths of an estimated 120,000 people since the 1970's, a situation that stunted economic growth in the area. In July 2000, the Philippine army captured the MILF's headquarters at Camp Abubakar. President Estrada said the government would focus on rehabilitating Mindanao Island, which had been ravaged by the MILF's three-decade struggle for independence. After the capture of Camp Abubakar, MILF leader Salamat Hashim called for a holy war against the Philippine government. MILF guerrillas killed 21 Christians in a Mindanao village.

Disaster. In July, five days of heavy rains near the capital, Manila, caused a 50-foot- (15-meter-) high mountain of garbage to slide into a squatter community. Officials found the bodies of more than 200 people among the garbage. Officials believe at least 100 other victims remained buried. Nearly 80,000 people earned their living from scavenging through the garbage pile.

☐ Henry S. Bradsher

See also **Asia.**

Physics. Physicists apparently re-created a state of matter that was common only in the earliest moments of the universe, according to a February 2000 announcement by scientists at the CERN laboratory, an international research center near Geneva, Switzerland. The physicists produced a quark-gluon plasma (QGP) by slamming lead *nuclei* (the center part of atoms) together in CERN's *particle accelerator* (a device that speeds up subatomic particles).

Atomic nuclei are made of particles called protons and neutrons, which are, in turn, made up of smaller particles called quarks. Quarks are held together by a force that is transmitted by particles called gluons. Under normal conditions, quark-gluon combinations are unbreakable. However, when a nucleus is compressed to a fraction of its normal volume—as can happen when nuclei are slammed together—the force exerted by the gluons diminishes, and the quarks move freely in a "sea" of gluons. This is the QGP.

The QGP created by the CERN scientists lasted less than a trillionth of a trillionth of a second and could not be studied in detail. The physicists hoped that research using a new particle accelerator at the Brookhaven National Laboratory in Upton, New York, would produce more accurate measurements of QGP behavior.

Tau neutrino found. Physicists announced in July that they had detected evidence of the tau neutrino, a long-suspected subatomic particle that had remained the last basic building block of matter to be discovered. The scientists made the discovery using the Tevatron particle accelerator at Fermi National Accelerator Laboratory near Chicago. The finding helped confirm the Standard Model, a theory that describes the fundamental particles that make up atoms and the forces at work within the subatomic realm.

After detecting the tau neutrino, the physicists said they planned additional research to determine whether the tau neutrino and other types of neutrinos have mass—as had been hinted at by earlier research. They said this knowledge would help them unravel some deep secrets of the universe, such as whether there is enough mass in the universe to eventually halt its expansion and cause it to contract.

Newton bests exotica. At a conference in Rome in July, a team of researchers from the University of Washington in Seattle announced the results of the first test of English scientist Sir Isaac Newton's theory of gravitation at distances of less than one *millimeter* (about 1/25 of an inch). The test, according to the scientists, revealed that Newton's theory remains valid at such tiny distances and that space may not be quite as exotic as some physicists have proposed.

Newton demonstrated in the 1600's that gravity is an "inverse square force." This means that the force between two objects drops off as they move farther apart, in proportion to the *square of the distance* (the distance multiplied by itself). Gravity grows weaker with distance, according to physicists, because it spreads out over the three known dimensions of space—length, width, and depth. Some physicists have suggested that, at extremely short distances, there are more than these three dimensions of space. If this proposal were true, then Newton's inverse square law would not apply in this tiny realm, because the force of gravity would spread out over these additional dimensions and drop off more rapidly than at longer distances.

The Seattle scientists used a device called a torsion balance—which consisted of two thin metal plates, one suspended above the other—to test the effects of gravity at tiny distances. If unusual gravitational conditions existed as the plates were brought very close together, irregularities in the force of gravitational attraction between the plates would cause significant twisting in the top plate. However, if the inverse square force held, little twisting would occur. The experiment resulted in little twisting, indicating that Newton's law and the three normal dimensions of space remain valid at two-tenths of a millimeter. ☐ Robert H. March

Poetry. C. K. Williams won the Pulitzer Prize in 2000 with *Repair*, a poetry collection that in 1999 was a finalist for the National Book Award. Williams's signature style, which is immediately recognizable on the page, is characterized by long, elaborate, descriptive lines that wind along in a conversational way. Many of his poems are about the poet examining an object or scene and finding emotional or intellectual sympathies within himself. In "The Dance," the poet's description of an ordinary woman dancing with confidence with a handsome partner seems to soothe the narrator, calming all doubt.

A number of established American poets regarded the millennium as an opportunity to survey a lifetime's work by publishing a volume of selected poems. Among many fine examples was *The Collected Poems of Stanley Kunitz*, by the poet who, in October 2000, at the age of 95, became the 10th poet laureate of the United States. Taken as a whole, the work in this collection could be interpreted as a single ongoing self-portrait. Like Williams, Kunitz sees abstractions and makes discoveries in ordinary things. "I like to think that it is the poet's love of particulars, the things of this world, that leads him to universals," he writes.

The work in *Charles Simic: Selected Early Poems,* a collection released late in 1999, is full of games and idioms and everyday language, revealing the poet as a playful imagist.

The late Russian emigre poet Joseph Brodsky published *Collected Poems in English* in 2000. Some scholars criticized Brodsky, an old-fashioned formalist, for his strict adherence to meter and rhyme, because the work loses something in translation. It is easier to rhyme words in Russian than in English, and rigid rhyme schemes that have been translated from Russian into English often sound strained or childish. The poems Brodsky wrote in English have a natural formalism that suits the language better.

National Book Award contenders. Lucille Clifton won the National Book Award in 2000 for her meditations on tragedy in *Blessing the Boats: New and Selected Poems, 1988-2000*. Galway Kinnell, another U.S. poet of stature, was nominated for the award for *A New Selected Poems,* a collection spanning nearly a quarter of a century. Kim Addonizio writes about family and partners in verse rich with rhythms and traditional forms in her collection *Tell Me,* which was also short-listed for the award. In Kenneth Koch's *New Addresses: Poems,* another contender for the award, the poet directly addresses a variety of personally significant topics, creating a poetic autobiography. Bruce Smith's volume of verse *The Other Lover,* also nominated, uses improvisational jazz motifs to describe personal experience and emotion.

Short takes. If there was an unusual number of compendium volumes published in 2000, there was also a wealth of work by distinguished and upcoming poets. Marge Piercy, better known for her novels, produced *The Art of Blessing the Day: Poems With a Jewish Theme.* Martin Espada, a New York poet of Puerto Rican descent, writes about Latin Americans as well as American Indians and African Americans in his sixth collection of political verse, *A Mayan Astronomer in Hell's Kitchen: Poems.* Gjertrud Schnackenberg secured her reputation as one of the most compelling of American poets with *The Throne of Labdacus,* a lyrical retelling of the story of Oedipus. Philip Levine, born in Detroit and now living in California, produced *The Mercy,* another collection.

John Ashbery, who has built a career around seeking ways for his readers to take part in the poems, continued his exploration in 2000 with *Your Name Here: Poems.* The title refers to Spanish souvenir bullfighting posters in which the buyer's name is placed in a list of toreadors, evoking a fantasy of full participation in a fatally heroic act. "Why do I tell you these things? You are not even here," Ashbery asks in the opening poem, in a lament addressed to an absent friend, or perhaps to the reader. □ Brian Bouldrey

See also **Literature, American; Literature, World.**

Poland. In June 2000, all of the members of the Freedom Union reform party resigned from their positions in the Polish cabinet. They cited lack of progress in privatizing state assets and disagreement over budget issues as their reasons for leaving the government. The resignations dissolved the coalition that Freedom Union had formed with the Solidarity Electoral Action Party, forcing Prime Minister Jerzy Buzek to form a minority government. The resignations also opened the possibility of early elections in 2001. In October 2000, President Aleksander Kwasniewski won reelection.

Poland's *gross domestic product* (the value of all goods and services produced in a country in a year) grew 5.6 percent in the first half of 2000. Unemployment stood at between 13.5 percent and 13.8 percent between January and August. In April, Polish leaders removed trade restrictions on the Polish currency, the zloty, letting the market set the currency's value. Inflation remained at approximately 10 percent through 2000.

In February, the European Union (EU) announced that it would quadruple its aid to Poland in 2001 to $860 million. However, EU officials urged Poland to improve its environmental standards. □ Sharon L. Wolchik

See also **Europe.**

Pollution. See Environmental pollution.

Popular music. Bands with young members dominated popular music in 2000, as they continued to appeal to preteen and teen-aged audiences. 'N SYNC sold 2.4 million copies of its second album, *No Strings Attached,* in the first week of the album's release in March. Controversial rapper Eminem sold the second-highest number of albums in the United States in 2000 when he released *The Marshall Mathers LP* in May. The album sold 1.76 million copies in its first week, although many critics, feminist organizations, and parent groups criticized the album for its homophobic lyrics and portrayal of violence toward women. Other critics praised the album for such rap songs as "Stan," a chilling exploration of star worship that unfolds in a series of letters from a fan. The Backstreet Boys placed third in sales for the year with their second album, *Black and Blue,* which sold 1.6 million copies during its first week of release in November.

Out of tune. Popular music fans also proved in 2000 that fame is fleeting. *This Time Around,* a new album by teen-aged brothers band, Hanson, failed to find an audience. *This Time Around* offered a harder-edged sound than did Hanson's 1997 debut, *Middle of Nowhere* and the hit single "MMMBop," but proved unpopular with fans.

Fame also abandoned the Spice Girls in 2000. The British singers had gained a strong following, especially among young girls, as a quintet in the late 1990's. The band regrouped as a quartet after the departure of Geri Halliwell in 1998. Following a series of ill-received solo albums the Spice Girls released *Forever* in November 2000. *Forever* received poor reviews and was not a hit with fans. The album sold approximately 40,000 copies in its first week. However, a rhythm-and-blues tinged single, "Holler," did find some success on playlists of dance-rock radio stations and in dance clubs.

Long-awaited returns. After long absences, several of rock music's most influential artists released new albums in 2000. Steely Dan's *Two Against Nature* was duo Walter Becker and Donald Fagan's first record together since 1981. Paul Simon released *You're the One*, the singer-songwriter's first nonsoundtrack record of new material since *Rhythm of the Saints* in 1990. In November 2000, Enya, known for her style of music that blends New Age, pop, and classical music with traditional Celtic tunes and haunting melodies, re-

Carlos Santana wins eight Grammy Awards, including Album of the Year for *Supernatural* at the annual Grammy Awards ceremony on Feb. 23, 2000. Santana had not enjoyed such popularity since the 1970's.

Grammy Award winners in 2000

Record of the Year, "Smooth," Santana featuring Rob Thomas

Album of the Year, "Supernatural," Santana

Song of the Year, "Smooth," Itaal Shur and Rob Thomas

New Artist, Christina Aguilera

Pop Vocal Performance, Female, "I Will Remember You," Sarah McLachlan

Pop Vocal Performance, Male, "Brand New Day," Sting

Pop Performance by a Duo or Group with Vocal, "Maria Maria," Santana

Traditional Pop Vocal Performance, "Bennett Sings Ellington—Hot & Cool," Tony Bennett

Pop Instrumental Performance, "El Farol," Santana

Rock Vocal Performance, Female, "Sweet Child O' Mine," Sheryl Crow

Rock Vocal Performance, Male, "American Woman," Lenny Kravitz

Rock Performance by a Duo or Group with Vocal, "Put Your Lights On," Santana featuring Everlast

Hard Rock Performance, "Whiskey In The Jar," Metallica

Metal Performance, "Iron Man," Black Sabbath

Rock Instrumental Performance, "The Calling," Santana featuring Eric Clapton

Rock Song, "Scar Tissue," Flea, John Frusciante, Anthony Kiedis, and Chad Smith

Alternative Music Performance, "Mutations," Beck

Rhythm-and-Blues Vocal Performance, Female, "It's Not Right But It's Okay," Whitney Houston

Rhythm-and-Blues Vocal Performance, Male, "Staying Power," Barry White

Rhythm-and-Blues Performance by a Duo or Group with Vocal, "No Scrubs," TLC

Rhythm-and-Blues Song, "No Scrubs," Kevin "Shekspere" Briggs, Kandi Burruss, and Tameka Cottle

Rap Solo Performance, "My Name Is," Eminem

Rap Performance by a Duo or Group, "You Got Me," The Roots featuring Erykah Badu

New-Age Album, "Celtic Solstice," Paul Winter & Friends

Contemporary Jazz Performance, "Inside," David Sanborn

Jazz Vocal Performance, "When I Look In Your Eyes," Diana Krall

Jazz Instrumental, Solo, "In Walked Wayne," Wayne Shorter

Jazz Instrumental Performance, Individual or Group, "Like Minds," Gary Burton, Chick Corea, Pat Metheny, Roy Haynes, and Dave Holland

Large Jazz Ensemble Performance, "Serendipity 18," The Bob Florence Limited Edition

Latin Jazz Performance, "Latin Soul," Poncho Sanchez

Country Album, "Fly," Dixie Chicks

Country Vocal Performance, Female, "Man! I Feel Like A Woman," Shania Twain

Country Vocal Performance, Male, "Choices," George Jones

Country Performance by a Duo or Group with Vocal, "Ready To Run," Dixie Chicks

Country Vocal Collaboration, "After The Gold Rush," Emmylou Harris, Linda Ronstadt, and Dolly Parton

Country Instrumental Performance, "Bob's Breakdowns," Asleep At The Wheel featuring Tommy Allsup, Floyd Domino, Larry Franklin, Vince Gill, and Steve Wariner

Bluegrass Album, "Ancient Tones," Ricky Skaggs and Kentucky Thunder

Country Song, "Come On Over," Robert John "Mutt" Lange and Shania Twain

leased *A Day Without Rain,* her first album of new material since 1995.

Another notable release in 2000 was U2's *All That You Can't Leave Behind,* the first new album by the Irish rock band since 1997. Fans enjoyed the album's "back to basics" style. Madonna released *Music* in 2000. Though it was not as big a seller as past albums, it was a hit with critics.

In country music, singer Lee Ann Womack scored the biggest hit of her career so far with the title song of her album, *I Hope You Dance.* Some people in 2000 criticized country music groups for fusing a pop music style into their songs in order to appeal to a wider audience, though George Strait and Alan Jackson made a stand for traditional country music with the song "Murder on Music Row," an indictment of the commercialism of country music.

Emmylou Harris's solo album *Red Dirt Girl* was one of the year's most critically acclaimed country albums. For the first time since her 1989 concept album, *The Ballad of Sally Rose,* Harris wrote most of the songs herself.

Jazz fans celebrated the birthdate of icon Louis Armstrong in 2000 with the release of several box-set tributes. Armstrong claimed to have been born on July 4, 1900, though most sources list his birthday as 1901. This discrepancy did not dampen a centennial celebration, which included the notable Armstrong anthology, *The Complete Hot Five and Hot Seven Recordings,* a four-disc collection of Armstrong recordings made between 1925 and 1929.

Reunion tour. Singer Diana Ross tried unsuccessfully in 2000 to recapture the popularity of The Supremes, one of the most successful singing groups in the history of American rock music. Ross, one of the founding members of the group in 1961, launched the "Return to Love" tour in 2000. However, some critics maintained that the reunion had been destined for failure. Ross's original partners, Mary Wilson and Cindy Birdsong, declined to participate after they claimed they were not being offered enough money. Ross was joined by two singers who had joined the group after she had left in 1969 to pursue a solo singing career and an acting career. The trio ended the tour early after being plagued by poor ticket sales, bad publicity, and public indifference.

"Who Let the Dogs Out," a single released in 2000 by The Baha Men, a previously unknown nine-member band from the Bahamas, enjoyed surprising success when the song was used by various professional sports teams. Some Major League baseball teams, including the New York Mets, adopted the song as their anthem. "Who Let the Dogs Out" contained a catchy chorus that became a favorite when the children's cable television network, Nickelodeon, began repeatedly broadcast-

ing the music video. The company included the song on the soundtrack of the Nickelodeon-produced animated feature, *Rugrats in Paris,* released in November.

Napster, a company that has enabled a reported 38 million registered users to copy music for free over the Internet, agreed to a plan on October 31 to charge a fee for its service. Napster announced it would enter into a partnership with Bertelsmann, a Germany-based media company. Bertelsmann is the parent company of BMG music, whose roster of artists includes 'N SYNC and Christina Aguilera.

A federal judge in San Francisco had ordered Napster in July to cease operation because the Web site enabled users to exchange music files stored on their computers, a practice that some artists and the music labels considered copyright infringement because they are not compensated. An appellate court later stayed the decision.

Under the terms of the October agreement, Napster and Bertelsmann were to create a fee-based membership program that would compensate record companies and artists for the use of their music. Bertelsmann was to lend Napster the money needed to help develop the tracking technology that would permit labels and artists to be compensated for the music traded using Napster's services. Once the system was in place, Bertelsmann agreed to drop a lawsuit filed along with four other major record companies in 1999 that accused Napster of copyright infringement.

MP3.com verdict. A federal district judge in New York City ruled in September 2000 that the Internet company MP3.com, headquartered in San Diego, was guilty of copyright infringement on compact discs (CD's) sold by Universal Music Group, the world's largest music company, headquartered in Universal City, California. The judge ruled that MP3.com must pay $25,000 in damages to Universal for each CD on which the Internet firm violated Universal's copyright.

On November 14, U.S. District Judge Jed Rakoff awarded $53.4 million in damages and attorneys fees to the Universal Music Group. Legal experts recognized the case as one of the first to limit the legal boundaries of digital music distribution. Four other major record companies that had been parties to the lawsuit settled out of court prior to Rakoff's award.

MP3.com is named after the MP3 music format, which converts a digital recording into a file small enough for a computer to handle efficiently but large enough to preserve the sound quality of the music. The MP3 format makes it possible to offer high-quality audio recordings on the Web.

□ Donald Liebenson
See also **People in the news** (Santana, Carlos).

Population. The world population stood at 6.06 billion in mid-2000, growing by more than 75 million people during the year, according to estimates by the United Nations Population Fund (UNFPA). UNFPA is a United Nations (UN) agency that promotes greater access to reproductive information and services. Agency officials also reported that the vast majority of births in 2000 took place in developing countries.

UNFPA officials emphasized that global population growth is directly affected by the condition of women around the world. They called for ending discrimination against women and girls as a means of slowing global population growth. According to UNFPA officials, women usually had smaller, healthier, and better-educated families when they had a full range of lifestyle choices.

When the UNFPA released its annual report on September 20, executive director Nafis Sadik noted, "The price of inequality is too high to pay." She added that women in poverty, as well as discrimination and violence against women, affected not just women but also men, whole communities, and entire countries. Sadik said that the consequences of gender discrimination included high fertility rates, inflated population growth, and the spread of *human immunodeficiency virus* (HIV, the virus that causes AIDS).

UN officials estimated that 80 million pregnancies a year were unplanned or unwanted due to women's lack of access to health care or reproductive choices. According to UNFPA statistics, at least 500,000 women in developing countries die annually from complications during pregnancy.

The UN General Assembly met in a special session in June to review progress toward attaining goals developed at the Fourth World Conference on Women in Beijing in 1995. The five-year goals for public and private sectors addressed obstacles to women's advancement in 12 areas—poverty, education, health care, violence against women, armed conflict, gender equality in work, sharing in decision making, women in government, human rights, mass media, the environment, and discrimination against girls. At the 2000 session, assembly members found that "significant progress" had been made, but that "major obstacles" remained. Members recommended increased women's participation in national economic decisions; increased women's participation in resolution of armed conflicts; stronger legislation to end domestic violence; and strengthened programs for sexual and reproductive health.

New director. Nafis Sadik retired from her post as UNFPA executive director in late 2000. To replace Sadik, UN Secretary General Kofi Annan appointed Thorya Ahmed Obaid, the first Saudi Arabian to head a UN agency.

☐ J. Tuyet Nguyen

Portugal helped forge a new economic strategy for Europe during the first half of 2000, when it held the presidency of the 15-nation European Union (EU). At a summit meeting in Lisbon on March 24 and March 25, chaired by Prime Minister Antonio Guterres, EU leaders agreed to pursue policies aimed at making the EU the leading information-based economy in the world. The leaders hoped the strategy would enable the EU to rival the United States as a source of innovation and high-technology growth.

Under the strategy, EU leaders agreed to speed up legislation and regulatory measures to foster the growth of electronic commerce and increase competition in telecommunications. They set a goal of connecting every school in the EU to the Internet by 2001 and making basic government services available on the Internet by 2003. The leaders also committed their governments to improving and coordinating national research programs, devoting more resources to education and training, and encouraging the creation of new businesses.

The Portugese government also defused a lengthy EU argument over taxes by convincing EU leaders to allow their governments to exchange information about the investment income of nonresidents. The agreement, reached at a summit meeting on June 19 and June 20 in the town of Santa Maria da Feira, was designed to prevent citizens of EU countries from avoiding taxes by depositing money in secret bank accounts in such countries as Luxembourg and Austria.

Economy. Portugal continued to enjoy strong economic growth in 2000. The European Commission (the administrative arm of the EU) forecast that the *gross domestic product* (the value of all goods and services produced in a year) would increase by 3.6 percent, compared with an

Pilgrims at a shrine in Fatima await the arrival of Pope John Paul II on May 12. During the visit, the Pope *beatified* (the final step toward Roman Catholic sainthood) two of the children who, in 1917, reported visions of the Virgin Mary at the site.

EU average of 3.4 percent. The unemployment rate was expected to remain one of the lowest in Europe at around 4.5 percent.

Banking consolidation. The number of banks in Portugal in 2000 continued to decline as banks merged and consolidated in an effort to compete with bigger institutions elsewhere in Europe. Banco Comercial Portugues SA (BCP) became the largest bank in Portugal by buying 53 percent of Banco Pinto & Sotto Mayor SA, the country's third-largest bank, for about $2 billion on March 31. BCP had acquired two smaller financial firms, Banco Mello SA and Companhia de Seguros Imperio SA, earlier in 2000.

☐ Tom Buerkle
See also **Europe; Roman Catholic Church.**

Prison. The United States Department of Justice reported in mid-2000 that 1.37 million offenders were under federal or state jurisdiction in December 1999, an increase of 3.4 percent since December 1998. Between 1990 and 1999, the number of inmates in the United States grew an average of 5.7 percent annually. Nationally, prisons operated at 1 percent to 17 percent above expected capacity in 1999.

Local jails, which held people who awaited trial or served sentences of one year or less, contained nearly 606,000 inmates in December 1999. Inmate population growth during 1999 was significantly lower in jails and state prisons than in previous years. Inmate populations grew by 2.3 percent in jails and 2.1 percent in state prisons.

Federal Bureau of Prisons (BOP) director Kathleen Hawk Sawyer reported on April 6, 2000, that the inmate population in federal prisons in 1999 increased in record-breaking numbers for a second consecutive year. The number of inmates in federal prisons in 1999 increased by 13.4 percent, the largest 12-month gain ever reported. Federal prisons operated at 34 percent above capacity.

Much of the increase in the federal prison population in 1999 resulted because federal prisons assumed responsibility for sentenced felons from the District of Columbia. The Federal Bureau of Prisons reported funding 22 new prisons

in 2000 and sought funding for an additional nine new prisons over the next three years.

Racial disparities. In December 1999, there were 3,400 black male inmates in federal or state prisons for every 100,000 black men in the general population in the United States. There were 1,300 Hispanic male inmates in prisons for every 100,000 Hispanic men, and 400 white male inmates in prisons for every 100,000 white men in the general population.

Gender trends. The Justice Department reported that there were nearly 91,000 women under state or federal jurisdiction in the United States in 1999, 6.6 percent of the total correctional population. For the seventh time since 1990, the rate of increase in prisoners was greater for women (4.4 percent) than for men (3.3 percent). The Justice Department reported in October 2000 that of all the female violent offenders in 1998, 62 percent had prior relationships with their victims. Only 36 percent of male violent offenders committed similar crimes.

Death row inmates. Between January and mid-November 2000, 77 people were executed in the United States. In 1999, 98 people were executed, more than in any year since 1951. In July 2000, nearly 3,700 prisoners awaited execution in U.S. prisons. ☐ Brian Bouldrey

Prizes. See **Nobel Prizes; Pulitzer Prizes.**

Protestantism. Mainline Protestant churches in the United States continued to be divided in 2000 over issues involving homosexuality. A majority of voters at conferences of the Episcopal Church, the United Methodist Church, and the Presbyterian Church (U.S.A.) voted against changing existing church rules forbidding the blessing of homosexual unions by clergy. Gay-rights activists and some members of the clergy had argued that church doctrine maintaining that homosexuality is "incompatible with Christian teaching," should be revised.

Some observers suggested that the decisions by the conferences to retain the language and continue to ban the blessing of same-sex unions had created a new era of conservatism within those Protestant denominations, which historically had been seen as moderate to liberal.

Episcopal trends. At a ceremony in Singapore in January 2000, several conservative leaders of the Anglican Communion "irregularly" consecrated two U.S. priests as bishops. The Anglican leaders charged that the Episcopal Church in the United States had grown too liberal, especially over issues surrounding homosexuality. Frank T. Griswold III, presiding bishop of the Episcopal Church in the United States, said that the U.S. church could not recognize the new bishops or assign them to U.S. churches.

Nearly 200 protesters, including Methodist clergy, are arrested on May 10, 2000, outside a conference of United Methodist Church leaders in Cleveland, Ohio. The activists were protesting the church's doctrine that "homosexuality is incompatible with Christian teaching."

Church elected Vashti Murphy McKenzie as their first female bishop.

Congressional chaplain. In March, the Reverend Daniel P. Coughlin, a Roman Catholic vicar, was appointed as chaplain of the U.S. House of Representatives. The appointment ended a four-month controversy in which two Republican members of Congress, both Protestants, denied charges of anti-Catholicism. House Speaker J. Dennis Hastert (R., Illinois) and House Majority Leader Richard K. Armey (R., Texas) had chosen a Presbyterian, the Reverend Charles Wright, for the position despite a bipartisan search committee's recommendation that the position be given to Reverend Timothy O'Brien, a Catholic priest.

Elian Gonzalez. The National Council of Churches in 2000 supported returning 6-year-old Elian Gonzalez to Cuba. Elian had been part of a group of Cubans trying to immigrate to the United States in 1999 when the group's boat capsized. National Council of Churches leaders cited family values in backing Elian's return to his father in Cuba. The evangelical community opposed efforts to return Elian to his father, citing religious repression in Cuba. ☐ Martin E. Marty

Psychology. See Mental health.

Public health and safety. In August 2000, Bridgestone/Firestone, Inc., a Japanese-owned tire company located in Nashville, Tennessee, announced the recall of 6.5 million tires, primarily on sport utility vehicles (SUV's) and light trucks. Federal safety officials found evidence that the tires shred at high speeds and may have caused automobile accidents that resulted in the deaths of more than 100 people and the injury of more than 250 others.

The recall involved all size P235/75R15 Firestone radial ATX and radial ATX II tires produced in North America as well as Wilderness AT tires, which were produced at Firestone's Decatur, Illinois, facility.

Ford Motor Company of Dearborn, Michigan, also participated in the recall. Almost 3.8 million of the 6.5 million recalled tires were used as original equipment on Ford's Explorer SUV. Ford Rangers and F-150 pickups were also equipped with the tires. Nissan Motor Co. of Tokyo, Japan, Toyota Motor Corporation of Tokyo, Japan, General Motors Corporation of Detroit, and Subaru of America, a Japanese-owned company in Cherry Hill, New Jersey, also equipped vehicles with the Bridgestone/Firestone tires.

Bridgestone/Firestone blamed the tire blowout problem on Ford, which had recommended that tires be inflated at between 26 and 30

In July, representatives at the General Convention of the Episcopal Church in Denver, Colorado, voted to enter into "full communion" with the Evangelical Lutheran Church in America (ELCA). The accord allowed for cooperation between the two churches on many levels. The ELCA had approved the agreement in 1999.

Evangelical organizations. The National Association of Evangelicals (NAE), an umbrella group for theologically conservative Protestants, announced in March 2000 that it would allow churches that belonged to the more theologically liberal National Council of Churches of Christ, an organization of 32 U.S. Protestant and Orthodox denominations, to join the NAE if leaders of these churches committed themselves to the NAE's conservative statement of faith and mission.

In August, more than 10,000 evangelists—the largest assembly ever organized—gathered in Amsterdam, the Netherlands, for an international conference. The conference was organized by evangelist Billy Graham and his associates, though poor health kept Graham from attending.

Women as leaders. In June 2000, voters at the Convention of Southern Baptists in Orlando, Florida, strongly discouraged individual Southern Baptist congregations from ordaining women as pastors.

In July, the African Methodist Episcopal Zion

pounds per square inch (179 and 207 kilopascals). Bridgestone/Firestone recommended a tire inflation of 30 pounds-per-square-inch (207 kilopascals). Ford responded that many of the defective tires were produced at Firestone's Decatur plant, where temporary workers were employed due to labor disputes.

Window blinds. In November, the Consumer Product Safety Commission, an independent Federal regulatory agency in Bethesda, Maryland, announced the recall of nearly 500 million horizontal window blinds. According to the commission, at least 130 children have been strangled since 1991 after accidently getting their necks caught in the loop at the end of the pull cord. Blinds sold after 1995 do not have pull cords ending in loops.

Accident toll. Accidents injured more than 20 million people in 1999 and resulted in the loss of $500 billion according to the National Safety Council (NSC). The NSC is a nonprofit agency, located in Itasca, Illinois, that promotes policies and practices to reduce the number of unintentional injuries. The NSC reported that accidents killed 95,500 Americans in 1999.

Most accidents in 1999 occurred in residences or public places and involved falls, poisoning, fires, or choking. Approximately 30,800 accidental deaths occurred in houses during 1999, an increase of 9 percent over 1998. Accidental deaths in public places increased 6 percent in 1999 to 21,200. Highway deaths dropped by 1 percent to 40,800. The number of people killed at work remained steady in 1999 at 5,100. Overall, the number of accidental deaths rose by 4 percent between 1998 and 1999.

Life expectancy. The World Health Organization (WHO), a United Nations agency, located in Geneva, Switzerland, that sets standards for health and strengthens national health programs, ranked 191 countries according to healthy life expectancy. The rankings were based on the number of years that people in a given country can expect to live in good health. Prior to June 2000, WHO based rankings on the number of years that people could expect to live.

Japan ranked first among all nations, with a healthy life expectancy of 74.5 years. Australians have a life expectancy of 73.2 years. They were followed by the French with 73.1 years; the Swedes with 73.0 years; the Spanish with 72.8 years; and the Italians with 72.7 years.

The United States placed 24th in the ranking, with a healthy life expectancy of 70 years. WHO said the low U.S. ranking was due to poor health conditions among rural African Americans, Native Americans, and inner city poor people.

☐ Michael Woods

See also **Medicine.**

Puerto Rico. On Nov. 7, 2000, Puerto Ricans elected San Juan Mayor Sila Maria Calderon, of the antistatehood Popular Democratic Party, governor. She was the first woman to hold the office.

The government of Puerto Rico and the United States Navy reached an interim agreement on January 31 to allow Navy warships to resume training exercises on the island of Vieques but using only dummy rounds of ammunition. Training with live ammunition had been suspended after an April 1999 bombing accident in which a civilian guard was killed.

The agreement triggered massive protests by thousands of Puerto Ricans who were opposed to the exercises. Before the training could resume, U.S. agents had to expel more than 200 protestors from the island's bombing range on May 4, 2000.

The accord required the U.S. government to release $40 million in aid to boost the Vieques economy. Vieques residents were scheduled to vote in May 2001 on whether to allow the U.S. Navy to resume training with live ammunition.

On August 2000, 18 Puerto Ricans, including government officials, were indicted for allegedly accepting $800,000 in bribes during the awarding of contracts for a computerized system for collecting taxes. ☐ Nathan A. Haverstock

See also **Latin America.**

A Puerto Rican protester occupies a tank used as a bombing target by the United States Navy on the island of Vieques, off Puerto Rico's east coast, in May 2000. U.S. agents eventually expelled more than 200 protesters opposed to the naval presence on the island from the bombing range.

Pulitzer Prizes in journalism, letters, and music, were awarded on April 10, 2000, by Columbia University in New York City on the recommendation of the Pulitzer Prize Board.

Journalism. *The Washington Post* won three awards—Katherine Boo's work on problems in group homes for the mentally retarded won the public service award; the distinguished criticism prize went to Henry Allen for writing on photography; and Carol Guzy, Michael Williamson, and Lucian Perkins took the feature photography award for depicting Kosovar refugees. *The Wall Street Journal* won two awards, one for national affairs for a series on United States post-Cold War defense practices, and another for commentary, awarded to Paul A. Gigot for his political columns.

Associated Press reporters Sang-Hun Choe, Charles J. Hanley, and Martha Mendoza shared the investigative prize for revealing how U.S. soldiers killed hundreds of Korean civilians early in the Korean War (1950-1953). *The Denver Post* won the breaking news reporting award for coverage of the 1999 student massacre at Columbine High School in Littleton, Colorado. Columbine coverage also won *Denver Rocky Mountain News* the breaking news photography prize. Eric Newhouse of Montana's *Great Falls Tribune* captured the explanatory reporting award with a series on alcohol abuse.

George Dohrmann of the *St. Paul Pioneer Press* covered academic fraud in University of Minnesota men's basketball to earn the beat reporting prize. *The Village Voice's* Mark Schoofs wrote a series on AIDS in Africa, earning the international reporting prize. The feature writing prize went to J. R. Moehringer of the *Los Angeles Times* for his portrait of Gee's Bend, an isolated community in Alabama. John C. Bersia of *The Orlando* (Florida) *Sentinel* received the editorial prize for his attack on predatory lending practices. The editorial cartooning prize went to Joel Pett of the *Lexington* (Kentucky) *Herald-Leader*.

Letters and music. Jhumpa Lahiri won the fiction prize for *Interpreter of Maladies*. Donald Margulies was awarded the drama prize for *Dinner With Friends*. *Freedom From Fear: The American People in Depression and War, 1929-1945*, earned the history prize for David M. Kennedy. Stacy Schiff won the biography prize for *Vera (Mrs. Vladimir Nabokov)*. C. K. Williams received the poetry prize for *Repair*. The general nonfiction prize went to John W. Dower for *Embracing Defeat: Japan in the Wake of World War II*. The prize in music was awarded to Lewis Spratlan for *Life is a Dream, Opera in Three Acts: Act II, Concert Version*, with a libretto by James Maraniss.

□ Brian Bouldrey

Quebec. See Canadian provinces.

Radio. Indecision about a proposal for a new type of radio station in the United States created static in the radio industry in 2000. The political storm centered on the newly proposed low-power FM (LPFM) radio stations, which proponents argued would open the airwaves to more people. A new satellite radio system was put into orbit in 2000, and in July federal regulators approved a $28 billion merger between Clear Channel Communications and AMFM, Inc.

LPFM debate. The proposed LPFM stations that stirred debate in 2000 would be equipped with low-power transmitters (between 10 and 100 watts) and would not be picked up by listeners further than 3.5 miles (5.6 kilometers) from the station's broadcast tower. William Kennard, chairman of the Federal Communications Commission, the federal agency charged with regulating U.S. radio stations, led the effort to create the stations. He contended that LPFM stations would open the door to broadcasting for school, church, and community groups and organizations that had not had access to the public airwaves.

The proposal touched off a battle between LPFM supporters and numerous critics, including owners of large numbers of commercial radio stations; the National Association of Broadcasters, an industry trade group; National Public Radio, the tax-supported network of noncommercial stations; and some members of the U.S. Congress. Critics complained that the new stations would interfere with existing stations, though LPFM proponents claimed that the critics were really concerned that LPFM's would create competition for existing stations.

Late in 2000, Congress passed legislation sharply reducing the number of LPFM stations that could be licensed. Although President Bill Clinton opposed reducing the number of LPFM's and threatened to veto the bill, observers expected him to sign it into law in early 2001.

Satellite radio. Another form of competition literally blasted off the launch pad June 30 when Sirius 1, a satellite owned by Sirius Satellite Radio, of New York City, was launched into space from the Baikonur Cosmodrome in Kazakhstan. The satellite and two others launched later in 2000 were designed to be space-age transmission towers for the first pay-per-listen radio network to deliver digital radio programming to a national audience. The new service, expected to be available in 2001, was the radio equivalent of cable or satellite television. Sirius and its major competitor, XM Satellite Radio, of Washington, D.C., planned to charge subscribers $9.95 a month for access to as many as 100 channels.

Clear Channel merger. Despite the new competition on the horizon, companies in the radio industry continued to strengthen their positions in the 283 U.S. radio markets where listenership was measured by Arbitron Co., a leading media research company based in New York City. Clear Channel Communications, of San Antonio, passed the 1,000-station ownership mark after both the Department of Justice and the FCC in July 2000 approved a $23-billion merger between Clear Channel and AMFM, Inc., of Dallas. Shareholders of both companies had approved the merger in April. At the end of 2000, Clear Channel owned 1,120 U.S. radio stations.

On the air. Talk shows hosted by Laura Schlessinger, who offered no-nonsense, sometimes controversial advice, and conservative political pundit Rush Limbaugh were the most popular radio shows in the United States in 2000. Both programs were distributed by Premiere Radio Networks in Sherman Oaks, California. Another Premiere radio personality, Art Bell, stunned listeners in March 2000 when he announced while on the air that he would leave his nightly "Coast to Coast AM" show in April. The show, which dealt with issues such as government conspiracies and Unidentified Flying Objects (UFO's), remained on the air with a new host.

□ Greg Paeth

Railroad. See Transportation.
Religion. See Islam; Protestantism; Roman Catholic Church.

Republican Party. Republican Governor George W. Bush of Texas defeated his Democratic challenger, Vice President Al Gore, in one of the closest presidential elections in U.S. history. While Gore, vice president for eight years under President Bill Clinton, won the popular vote, Bush won in the Electoral College with 271 votes, one vote more than he needed. Questions surrounding alleged voting irregularities in some counties in Florida delayed the final tabulation of the November 7 election for weeks. Attorneys for both sides argued and reargued cases before both the Florida Supreme Court and the U.S. Supreme Court, which on December 9 ordered the recounting of ballots in Florida stopped.

The Republican Party nominated George W. Bush for president on Aug. 2, 2000, during the Republican National Convention in Philadelphia. Bush accepted the nomination the following night. He chose as his vice presidential running mate Dick Cheney, a former U.S. congressman from Wyoming and secretary of defense from 1989 to 1993 during the administration of George Herbert Walker Bush. Cheney had originally been selected to lead the search for a vice presidential running mate for George W. Bush.

In the primary elections, Senator John McCain (R., Arizona) had challenged Bush for the 2000 presidential nomination. McCain won stunning

Texas Governor George W. Bush, speaking in the Texas House of Representatives chamber in Austin, the state capitol, claims victory in the U.S. presidential election on Dec. 13, 2000, five weeks after the November 7 election, which was one of the closest in U.S. history.

victories in some Republican primaries, including the New Hampshire primary on February 1. However, Bush emerged as the clear front-runner after winning 9 of 13 states in the so-called Super Tuesday primaries on March 7. On March 9, McCain withdrew from the presidential race. He immediately rejected suggestions made by some Republican Party (or GOP for Grand Old Party) leaders that he accept the role of Bush's running mate if the position was offered to him.

Bush and Cheney campaigned on a platform that included improving military readiness, cutting taxes, and delegating a greater amount of federal authority to state and local governments.

Majority in Congress erodes. In the November 2000 Congressional elections, Republicans fared better in the House than in their bids for Senate seats. Republicans retained their majority in the House for the fourth consecutive election by a margin of 221 to 212 seats. Previously they held a 223 seat majority. Two additional seats were held by independents who typically voted with the Democrats. A majority in the 435-seat House requires at least 218 seats.

The 2000 election deadlocked the Senate 50-to-50. Under the U.S. Constitution, the vice president, as president of the Senate, casts a vote in the event of a tie. With a Republican vice president, the Republicans retained control of the Senate.

The GOP suffered a high-profile loss in the New York Senate. Hillary Rodham Clinton defeated Republican Representative Rick A. Lazio for the seat formerly filled by Democrat Daniel Patrick Moynihan, who retired. Lazio was a relatively late entry for the Republicans, having been tapped to run against Clinton when New York City Mayor Rudolph Giuliani dropped out of the race in May. Giuliani chose not to run after being diagnosed with prostate cancer. He said that he would spend the time concentrating on his health and his mayoral duties.

Republican Senator John Ashcroft of Missouri lost in his attempt to retain his Senate seat. Missouri Governor Mel Carnahan, a Democrat, defeated Ashcroft even though Carnahan had died on October 16 in an airplane crash. Missouri Governor Roger Wilson in December appointed Carnahan's widow, Jean, to the vacant Senate seat.

Campaign finance. The Federal Election Commission (FEC) announced in November that between Jan. 1, 1999, and Oct. 18, 2000, the Republican Party had raised $294.9 million and spent $252 million, compared with the Democratic Party, which had raised $172.7 million and spent $153.5 million. Republicans raised 6 percent more money than they had during the previous presidential election cycle in 1995-1996 but spent 7 percent less compared with the prior period.

According to the FEC, soft-money contributions increased substantially for both Republicans and Democrats. Soft money refers to individual contributions made to political parties that are not subject to the same stringent restrictions placed on contributions to candidates. Republicans raised $211 million in soft money in 2000, an increase of 74 percent over the 1996 presidential campaign. Democrats raised $199 million in soft money in 2000, an 85 percent increase. The FEC reported that soft money represented 42 percent of Republican Party fund-raising and 53 percent of Democratic Party fund-raising.

Nominating system proposed. A Republican committee in May 2000 proposed a new system in which small states would hold primaries in March, with larger states holding decisive primary votes later in the year. The entire process would be completed by June. Some Republicans maintained that the proposed system would build and create interest in the presidential nominating system and would provide voters with a longer time frame to learn about the candidates.

☐ Linda P. Campbell and Geoffrey A. Campbell

See also **Congress of the United States; Democratic Party; Elections; State government; Supreme Court of the United States; United States, Government of the.**

Rhode Island. See State government.

Roman Catholic Church.
In January 2000, 160 Asian Roman Catholic bishops gathered in Bangkok, Thailand, to chart the Roman Catholic Church's course in Asia. The meeting came shortly after Pope John Paul II, during a trip to New Delhi, India, called upon Asia's bishops to renew their efforts to spread the Christian gospel through Asia. During the gathering, the bishops discussed presenting an "Asian image" of Jesus and fostering a church sensitive to the "ancient and enduring cultures and spirituality of Asia." The bishops committed themselves to spreading the gospel by performing works of charity and assisting the poor. Most of the Asian Roman Catholic bishops headed dioceses in countries with populations that were only 2 percent Roman Catholic.

Pope John Paul II made a pilgrimage to the Middle East in February and March, fulfilling a long-expressed wish to visit sites sacred to Christianity. During the first part of his journey, he traveled to Egypt, where he called for greater justice and peace in the region and condemned all forms of violence carried out in the name of religion. In Egypt, the pope visited the 1,500-year-old St. Catherine's Monastery located near Mount Sinai, where Moses was believed to have received the Ten Commandments. John Paul prayed at the monastery for interfaith dialogue.

Mourners carry the coffin of Cardinal John Joseph O'Connor into St. Patrick's Cathedral in New York City for a requiem mass. O'Connor, Roman Catholic archbishop of the Archdiocese of New York, died on May 3, 2000.

for Jewish suffering during World War II (1939-1945). Vatican officials emphasized that the pope's 2000 trip was of a spiritual, not political, nature.

New York cardinal dies. Cardinal John Joseph O'Connor, who served as archbishop of the Archdiocese of New York for 16 years, died at the age of 80 on May 3. O'Connor often addressed current controversies in his weekly newspaper column and in *homilies* (short moral talks) at St. Patrick's Cathedral in New York City. The cardinal frequently spoke against abortion and was a strong supporter of the labor movement and of better Catholic-Jewish relations. Edward Michael Egan, previously the bishop of the Diocese of Bridgeport, Connecticut, succeeded O'Connor as Archbishop of New York.

Fatima secret revealed. On May 13, Vatican secretary of state Angelo Cardinal Sodano revealed the "third secret of Fatima," which he said seemed to refer to the 1981 assassination attempt in Vatican City on Pope John Paul II. Sodano said the third secret contained a vision of a "bishop clothed in white" who "falls to the ground, apparently dead, under a burst of gunfire." The pope had long credited the Lady of Fatima with saving his life during the attempt on his life.

Other Catholics said that the "bishop in white" could be a reference to Oscar Arnulfo Romero, Roman Catholic archbishop of El Salvador, who was killed in San Salvador in 1980 while celebrating mass.

The secret was one of three said to have been revealed by an apparition of the Virgin Mary to three children in 1917 near Fatima, Portugal. Sodano said that the Pope decided to disclose the third secret in order to put an end to speculation surrounding it. The first two secrets, which had already been revealed by the church, were said to refer to warfare in Europe and the rise and fall of Communism in the Soviet Union. In a ceremony on May 13, 2000, John Paul beatified two of the three visionaries of Fatima.

□ Thomas C. Fox

See also **Portugal; Roman Catholic Church** Special Report: **Roman Catholics Celebrate Holy Year.**

The second and final part of the pope's pilgrimage took him to Jordan, Israel, and Palestinian-administered territories and included a visit to Bethlehem, the birthplace of Jesus Christ. The pope met with both Palestinian and Israeli leaders, who continued to be involved in the Arab-Israeli conflict. "No one can ignore how much the Palestinian people have had to suffer in recent decades," the pope said. John Paul, who had overseen Vatican recognition of the Jewish state in 1993, also took pains to articulate solidarity with Israel, too, expressing grief

CLEMENS·X·PONT·MAX
ANNO IVBILEI·MDCLXXV

Pope John Paul II marks the start of Jubilee 2000 by opening the Holy Door at St. Peter's Basilica in Rome on Dec. 24, 1999. Jubilee 2000 was a year-long celebration in which Roman Catholics worldwide were encouraged to focus on forgiveness and reconciliation.

The Roman Catholic Church marks the new millennium with Jubilee 2000 and a reflection on life.

ROMAN CATHOLICS CELEBRATE HOLY YEAR

By Tim Frystak

Pope John Paul II launched Jubilee 2000 with the symbolic opening of the Holy Door at St. Peter's Basilica in Rome on Dec. 24, 1999. For Roman Catholics, a Jubilee is a *holy year*, a period during which they focus on forgiveness and reconciliation. The opening of the Holy Door, a practice that dates back to 1500, symbolized the opening of the human heart to God's word, offering an opportunity for the individual to reflect on his or her relationship with God.

Although the Roman Catholic Church has generally celebrated holy years every 25 years since 1300, many Roman Catholics viewed Jubilee 2000 as a special time because it coincided with the new millennium. John Paul II stressed that Jubilee 2000 gave all the world's peoples—regardless of religion—an opportunity to reflect on their lives.

Some Roman Catholics made a pilgrimage to Rome for spiritual, psychological, or social reasons. Vatican officials estimated that 30 million people visited Rome in 2000 to attend the nearly 100 events that commemorated Jubilee 2000. In addition to celebrations planned around Easter, *Pentecost* (a feast that marks the end of the 50-day observance of Easter), and Christmas, Vatican officials in June hosted a Eucharistic Congress, an assembly of Catholic clergy and laypeople from all countries to promote the religious way of life. During the Congress, John Paul II asked that Catholic churches worldwide commemorate Jubilee 2000 with special masses for the vast majority of Catholics who were unable to travel to Rome. Roman Catholics also celebrated several special "jubilee days" during each month, in which the faithful prayed for various groups, such as the sick and the poor of the world. Jubilee 2000 ended on Jan. 6, 2001, with a mass at St. Peter's Basilica and the closing of the Holy Door.

The author:

Tim Frystak is a *World Book* staff editor.

John Paul II hosts a lunch (below) for 200 homeless and poor residents of Rome on June 15. Throughout the year, the Church encouraged Roman Catholics to pray for various groups, including the world's poor.

On July 2, more than 1,000 motor-cyclists fill St. Peter's Square, roaring their engines and honking their horns in response to a Jubilee service for bikers.

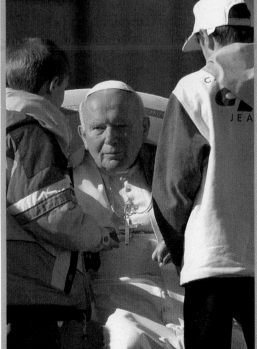

John Paul II (left) blesses children during the Children's Jubilee celebration on Jan. 2, 2000. Thousands of children from around the world attended the special mass.

John Paul II celebrates the Pardon Mass on March 12 at St. Peter's Basilica. For the first time in history, a pope asked forgiveness for errors made by the Catholic Church over the past 2,000 years.

John Paul II prays at the Western Wall, Judaism's most sacred site, in Jerusalem (right) in March 2000. The pope visited the Holy Land as part of a personal and spiritual pilgrimage. Cardinal Francis George of the Archdiocese of Chicago celebrates mass (below) for more than 30,000 people at Soldier Field on June 24, as part of a worldwide observation of Jubilee 2000.

Romania. Ion Iliescu, a former Communist who had served as president of Romania from 1990 to 1996, was reelected president on Dec. 10, 2000. Iliescu defeated nationalist hardliner Corneliu Vadim Tudor by a wide margin in a runoff election.

International political observers speculated that Iliescu would likely form a government that would pass economic and social reforms that would place Romania in a position to join the European Union and the North Atlantic Treaty Organization. Iliescu, however, faced the difficult challenge of forming a minority government because his leftist Party of Social Democracy received only 37 percent of the votes in parliamentary elections in November.

Economy. Romania's economy began growing in 2000 after several years of stagnation. Romania's *gross domestic product* (the value of all goods and services produced in a country in a given year) increased approximately 2 percent in 2000.

In December, President-elect Iliescu announced plans to step up *privatization* (selling of government-owned companies and assets) and to lend support to medium and small businesses in Romania to ease unemployment. In 2000, Romania's rate of unemployment averaged between 10 and 12 percent.

Inflation in Romania dropped to approximately 40 percent in 2000 from 54 percent in 1999. However, in September 2000, the International Monetary Fund (IMF), a United Nations-affiliated organization located in Washington, D.C., that provides short-term credit to member nations, criticized Romania for not doing enough to slow inflation. IMF officials also complained that Romanian leaders were moving too slowly in selling state-owned companies.

Cyanide spill. On January 30, workers for an Australian Romanian owned gold mine in western Romania accidentally released more than 3.5 million cubic feet (100,000 cubic meters) of cyanide-laden waste into the Somes River. The cyanide entered several other rivers, including the Tisza, an important waterway in neighboring Hungary, contaminating drinking water and killing millions of fish. Environmental experts estimated it would cost more than $20 billion to clean up the spill.

Foreign affairs. In March 2000, Romania resolved a nine-year-old dispute with Bulgaria over the building of a second bridge over the Danube River. In August, Romanian and Hungarian military leaders discussed methods of increasing cooperation, including the creation of a common peacekeeping battalion.   □ Sharon L. Wolchik

See also **Europe.**

Rowing. See Sports.

Rugby football. Australia won the 2000 Tri-Nations Series in Rugby Union (RU) and England took the historic first European Six-Nations Championship. Australia also continued its domination in Rugby League (RL), taking its 12th World Cup victory.

International Rugby Union (RU). Australia, the defending World Cup champions, won the fifth annual Southern Hemisphere Tri-Nations Series, a six-match tournament played on a home-and-away basis between New Zealand, Australia, and South Africa in July and August 2000. In the final match played on August 26, Australia narrowly defeated South Africa 19 to 18 in Durban, South Africa. The Series also determined the winner of the Bledisloe Cup, an annual two-match series between Australia and New Zealand. In the second of the two matches, held at Eden Park, Auckland, on August 5, Australia defeated New Zealand, 24-23, to retain the Cup.

England became Lloyds TSB European Champions in the first Six-Nations Tournament, following the admission of Italy. After comfortable victories against Wales, Ireland, and Italy, England survived a tense contest with France in Paris, winning, 15-9, to secure the championship.

In the Super 12 Series, contested by 12 provincial teams from the three Southern Hemisphere countries, the Canterbury Crusaders from New Zealand narrowly defeated ACT Brumbies of Australia, 20-19, in the final at Australia's capital, Canberra, in June.

Samoa won the Pacific Rim Series, which also involved Japan, the United States, Hong Kong, Canada, Fiji, and Tonga.

Fiji won a new Official World Series Seven-a-Side Competition contested at 10 separate tournaments in Hong Kong, Argentina, Dubai, South Africa, Uruguay, New Zealand, Fiji, Australia, Japan, and France. Fiji won five Tournament finals, four of them against New Zealand.

RU national competitions. In the Heineken European Cup Final, Northampton (England) narrowly defeated Munster (Ireland), 9-8, at Twickenham on May 27. In the all-French final of the European Shield, which included teams that had not qualified to compete in the Heineken Cup, Pau overcame Castres, 34-21, on May 28 in Toulouse, France. Also in France, Biarritz defeated Brive 24-13 in the French Cup Final on June 1 in Bordeaux. In the final match of the French Club Championship, Stades Francais defeated Colomiers, 28-23, in Paris on July 15.

In England, the Wasps Club retained the Tetleys Bitter Cup by defeating Northampton in the Final at Twickenham on May 13. Leicester finished at the top of the Allied Dunbar Premier Division to retain the title. The County Championship, which was once again sponsored by

Tetleys, wrapped up on June 3 at Twickenham, with Yorkshire defeating Devon, 16-9, in the championship final.

In Scotland, Caledonia won the District Championship and in the AIB All-Ireland League Final, St. Mary's College beat Lansdowne, 25-22, in Dublin. In a new Wales/Scotland League, Cardiff became champions and in the Welsh Challenge Cup Final at The Millennium Stadium in June, Llanelli defeated Swansea, 22-12.

In New Zealand national competitions, Canterbury defeated Otago, 29-26, on September 30 to take the Ranfurly Shield Final held in Christchurch, New Zealand. On October 21, Wellington beat Canterbury, 34-29, in the Air New Zealand National Provincial Championship Final, also in Christchurch.

International Rugby League (RL). In November, Australia reconfirmed its status as the leading RL nation by taking the Lincoln World Cup in England, a title it has held since 1975.

Most of the matches were poorly attended, mainly because of widespread criticism over the marketing and management of the competition. Group games began Oct. 28, 2000, when England lost, 2-22, to Australia in the first-ever rugby league international played at Twickenham, home of England Rugby Union. New Zealand easily overcame England, 49-6 in the first semifinal at Bolton. The next day, Australia defeated Wales, 46-22, at Huddersfield to go to the final match. In the final game, held on November 25 at Old Trafford, England, Australia resisted a spirited challenge from New Zealand to claim victory and the championship by a score of 40-12.

National competitions. In Great Britain, the Bradford Bulls defeated the Leeds Rhino, 24-18, in the Silk Cut Challenge Cup at Murrayfield in Edinburgh (Scotland) on April 29. On July 29 in the Northern Ford Premiership Grand final at Bury, the Rams, which had been defeated in the final game in 1999, narrowly defeated the Leigh Centurions by a score of 13-12. In the Super League Grand Final held at Old Trafford, on October 14, 2000, St. Helens again stole the honors with a victory over the Wigan Warriors by a score of 29-16.

In Australia, the Brisbane Broncos won the NRL Premiership Grand Final in Sydney on August 27 with a 14-6 victory over Sydney City. In the three-match State of the Origin Series in May and June between New South Wales (NSW) and Queensland, NSW won all three matches, easily taking the final encounter in Sydney on June 7 by a score of 56-16.

In New Zealand, the Canterbury Bulls defeated the Otahuhu Leopards, 28-24, in the National Bartercard Cup Grand Final in Auckland on September 17. □ David Duckham

Russia. Former Prime Minister Vladimir V. Putin won a landslide victory in the March 26, 2000, presidential election. Putin had become acting president of Russia after former President Boris Yeltsin resigned on the last day of 1999, transforming the landscape of Russian politics. Putin's appointment as acting president boosted his campaign for the March elections. In addition, Putin's 2000 campaign for the presidency was aided by a popular war in Chechnya, one-sided press coverage, and a recovering economy. Putin spent the second half of 2000 launching a program to rebuild the Russian state and testing the limits of his power and popularity.

Yeltsin passed the torch. Yeltsin's resignation on Dec. 31, 1999, took everyone but his closest aides by surprise. Under Russian law, the resignation forced the presidential election to be scheduled for March 2000, a full three months before Yeltsin's second term was to have ended. Putin remained prime minister while he assumed the duties of acting president, and he wasted little time in charting a new course for the Russian government.

Discussion of constitutional amendments to weaken the Russian presidency and strengthen the legislature—which had gained momentum in 1999 as Yeltsin had grown increasingly frail and erratic—was abandoned under Putin's interim government. Putin reached a power-sharing arrangement at the end of January with members of the Communist Party in the Duma, the lower house of the parliament, abandoning Yeltsin's long-standing refusal to work with the Communist Party. Putin gained a workable majority in the legislature by agreeing to split control of Duma committees between the Unity Party, which supported Putin, and the Communist Party, led by Gennady Zyuganov.

Putin. Putin's rise from political obscurity to the summit of power in Russia was extraordinarily rapid. He had joined the KGB, the intelligence service of the Soviet Union, of which Russia was the principal republic, after college in 1975 and resigned in 1991. Putin arrived at the Kremlin in 1996, after having served as the first deputy to St. Petersburg Mayor Anatoly Sobchak.

In 1998, Putin was appointed head of the Federal Security Service (FSB), the successor to the KGB. In 1999, Yeltsin chose Putin to replace Sergei Stepashin as prime minister. Focusing most of his energies on executing a military campaign against Chechen separatists, Putin was credited with the strong showing of the Unity Party in the parliamentary elections of December 1999. Though the Chechen campaign slowed in early 2000, the Russian media devoted little attention to the military setbacks suffered by the Russian troops in Chechnya.

Smoke pours from Moscow's 1,770-foot (540-meter) Ostankino television tower during a fire on Aug. 27, 2000, that left three people dead. Two of the victims were killed when an elevator crashed 1,000 feet (305 meters) into the basement.

Presidential campaign. Putin's strategy for the 2000 presidential election was to proclaim his disinterest in the campaign and to present himself as a decisive leader already grappling with Russia's grave problems. Putin repeatedly expressed open disdain for the process of campaigning and used his disdain as a reason to avoid publishing a preelection platform. With the Kremlin-dominated media giving him saturation coverage, Putin declined the free air time given to all candidates for political advertising. He condemned such advertising as an attempt to brainwash the electorate, and he compared political ads to commercials about which sort of groceries to buy. At the same time, the nightly news savaged Putin's opponents, continuing the propaganda barrage that had been launched for the Duma elections in December 1999.

Putin's potentially most serious challengers, Moscow Mayor Yuri Luzhkov and former Prime Minister Yevgeny Primakov, decided not to run for president in 2000, following a disappointing showing of their Fatherland-All Russia bloc (OVR), a centrist opposition movement in the 1999 parliamentary elections. Their exit from the field left Putin running against Communist leader Gennady Zyuganov. Zyuganov had failed to defeat an ailing Yeltsin in a runoff election in 1996, and the Communists had failed to expand their electoral base since then. In addition, the January 2000 deal to share power between the Communists and the Unity Party in the Duma undermined Zyuganov's credentials as an opposition candidate. In the absence of a credible opposition candidate, most of the regional leaders who had supported the OVR alliance in December 1999 rushed to support Putin in 2000.

Presidential election. Putin won in the first round of the election with 53 percent of the vote. Zyuganov finished in second place with 29 percent of the vote. Nine other candidates shared the remaining vote, though only two of them exceeded the 1.8-percent tally that went to "none of the above." Turnout totaled just over 68 percent of the 108 million voters in the electorate. In war-torn Chechnya, officials for the Organization for Security and Cooperation in Europe (OSCE), an international security group that monitors elections, reported that the region's 460,000 voters had limited access to media, limited freedom of movement, and that the potential for voter intimidation could not be ruled out.

Power consolidated. With his election victory secure, Putin quickly put his own stamp on the government when he took office as the elected president in May. He named respected finance minister Mikhail Kasyanov to be his prime minister and retained a number of other members of the previous cabinet. At the same time, Putin ap-

President Vladimir Putin (center) is congratulated by Russian Orthodox Patriarch Alexi II after Putin's inauguration in Moscow on May 7, 2000. Putin succeeded Boris Yeltsin (left) to become the second president of Russia.

pointed many associates from the security services and former KGB to second- and third-tier posts in the government. In the eyes of many Russian observers, Putin's appointments provided him with loyal supporters in key ministries.

After being elected, Putin moved to limit the power of certain political and business groups that had grown more independent under Yeltsin. In May, he reorganized the structure of the government into seven large districts to bring regional laws into compliance with federal law.

Over the summer, Putin introduced laws that deprived the elected heads of Russia's 89 regions of their automatic seats in the Federation Council, the upper house of the parliament, and gave the president the power to remove regional leaders if they acted unconstitutionally. A third law gave regional governors the right to remove mayors from office. Putin's reforms restored what he called the "vertical of power" in the federal system and moved Russia closer to Putin's stated aim of a "dictatorship of laws."

Putin also threatened the power of the so-called oligarchs—powerful business leaders who had provided Yeltsin with much support. In August 2000, Putin met with 18 of the most powerful business leaders in Russia and demanded that they pay taxes and abide by Russian law. For his part, Putin reportedly agreed not to overturn Yeltsin's controversial privatization sales of lucrative state property.

Several business leaders came under direct pressure from the government, especially businessmen in the mass media. Police arrested Vladimir Gusinsky, owner of the independent television network NTV, the only national network critical of Putin, on June 13 and jailed him for three days on charges of corruption. Gusinsky claimed he was only released after he agreed to sell his media holdings to the government-controlled natural gas monopoly, Gazprom. In November, after Gusinsky and Gazprom reached a sale agreement that would preserve NTV's independence, government officials issued a new arrest warrant for Gusinsky, and the sale was scuttled. In December, Spanish police acting at Russia's behest arrested Gusinsky in the resort town of Sotogrande.

Boris Berezovsky, who controlled 49 percent of the government television station ORT and who had been one of Yeltsin's most powerful supporters, was repeatedly investigated for corruption. In July, Berezovsky resigned from his post in the Duma and announced his opposition to Putin's plans to recentralize power.

The Kursk disaster. Russians were stunned by news that the nuclear-powered submarine *Kursk* sank on August 12 in the Barents Sea just

100 miles (160 kilometers) from the northern port of Murmansk. The sub, one of the most modern in the Russian fleet, carried a crew of 118 sailors, at least some of whom survived the initial descent to the ocean floor. Despite the fact that the *Kursk* was in relatively shallow water, Russian divers were unable to enter the ship and waited several days before accepting offers of help from Norway and the United Kingdom. The crew had perished by August 21 when Norwegian divers opened the hatch of the stricken ship. National mourning turned to anger over the botched rescue. Sailors' families criticized Putin for failing to interrupt his vacation when he heard news of the tragedy, while Putin lashed out at the media for its exceptionally critical coverage of the navy.

Economic recovery. Rising world oil prices boosted the Russian economy in 2000 and produced the strongest year of economic growth since the collapse of the Soviet Union in 1991. A group of economists led by economics minister German Gref produced a 10-year economic blueprint that incorporated many market reforms. The Duma passed the first stage of the Gref plan for tax reform in July 2000.

Weapons treaties. The Duma approved on April 14 the START II nuclear arms reduction treaty, which had been signed in January 1993 by Yeltsin and United States President George Herbert Walker Bush. The Duma's approval seemed to signal a desire by newly elected President Putin to improve relations with the United States, but Russian-U.S. relations deteriorated as the United States moved closer in 2000 to approving plans for a limited ballistic missile defense system. The Russians claimed that any such system would violate the antiballistic missile treaty signed in 1972 as part of the SALT I agreement.

Spy trial. FSB agents arrested suspected spy Edmond Pope, a citizen of the United States, in Moscow in April 2000. Pope was accused of illegally obtaining classified blueprints for a high-speed torpedo. President Clinton and other officials for the United States repeatedly tried to persuade Putin and the Russian government to release Pope, who suffered from bone cancer and was denied treatment from physicians from the United States. During Pope's closed-door trial in November, a defense lawyer reported that a key prosecution witness testified that the FSB had forced the witness to give false, incriminating evidence against Pope. On December 6, Pope was found guilty of espionage and sentenced to the maximum 20 years in prison. On December 14, Putin pardoned Pope, who returned to the United States. □ Steven L. Solnick

See also **Eastern Orthodox Churches; Europe; Terrorism.**

Sailing. See Boating.

San Francisco. The median cost of a three-bedroom house in San Francisco in 2000 rose to $360,000, from $305,000 in 1999, according to the United States Bureau of the Census. The increase in housing costs reflected the finite supply of space in San Francisco in relation to the demand generated by the booming economy in 2000. San Francisco's location on a peninsula allowed little room for outward expansion. Much of the city's housing was built on landfill, where seismic dangers make high-rise buildings impractical. Strict laws that limit growth, control building design, and protect scenic views added to the city's inability to expand. Some San Franciscans hoped to maintain the beauty and small-town feel of their city, while others wanted to expand to a Manhattan-style city that would accommodate an ever-growing, high-tech industry and a prosperous, highly paid citizenship.

Planning issues. The sale of Downtown Rehearsal, a large studio space in the Hunter's Point area of San Francisco, symbolized the conflict between rapid dot-com growth and cultural, nonprofit, and artistic groups. Nearly 500 musical groups shared the rehearsal space. The owners, Teryl and Greg Koch, sold the studio on August 8 for $14 million to Cupertino, California-based JMA Properties, which announced that the building would be revamped into a telecommunications high-tech complex. The owners required that all of the estimated 2,000 tenants vacate by September 25, so that the sale could close on October 6. Local musicians considered this another challenge to bands and to the arts in general. Musicians faced noise ordinances, venue closures, and general rent increases as more housing units sprung up in areas once designated for clubs.

Many of the bands had spent large amounts of their own money to furnish or outfit the studio spaces, and they refused to leave without protest. On September 30, many musicians participated in Rock Out SF, a protest that featured live performances, and the coalition called Save Local Music launched a fight for musicians' rights.

The Kochs offered the bands an estimated $750,000 to vacate, an amount the tenants later pooled to find or build a new facility. This money split the tenants' ranks and resulted in further divisiveness among artists.

In 2000, dance studios, bookstores, theaters, galleries, and other venues for the arts fell victim to demand for commercial office space, and many citizens began to rethink the problems involved with rapid growth in a contained space. By October, the city approved the construction of office space totaling 7.5 million square feet (696,773 square meters).

Propositions L and K. San Francisco voters turned down two propositions, L and K, on November 7. Proposition L would have permanently banned new offices in parts of the city. Mayor Willie Brown attempted, but failed, to file a lawsuit against the proposition before San Franciscans could even vote on it. The city's developers backed Brown in August when he drafted a competing proposition, K, described as a "slow growth" measure opposed to L's "no growth" details. The mayor's proposed law would have put a temporary moratorium on growth in some neighborhoods pending in-depth studies.

By November 22, San Francisco supervisors proposed combining key elements of the two growth-control propositions, as the issue of city growth remained unresolved.

The recovery of supervisor elections. In the November elections, San Francisco returned to a system of electing representatives to the governing board of supervisors by districts (neighborhoods). Previously, all voters selected city supervisors from a general pool of candidates. Because San Francisco was known for its clearly delineated, colorful, and often highly organized neighborhoods, many city residents hoped returning to the election-by-district system would better serve the interests of ethnic and cultural groups and help preserve neighborhood profiles.   □ Brian Bouldrey

See also **City.**

Saudi Arabia.
In September 2000, Crown Prince Abdullah of Saudi Arabia publicly called upon Palestinian leader Yasir Arafat not to compromise over the status of Jerusalem in peace negotiations with Israel. Representatives of the United States reportedly pressured Arafat during a July summit in Maryland to accept an Israeli offer of limited control over Arab suburbs rather than full sovereignty over eastern Jerusalem.

The final status of Jerusalem, which both Israeli and Palestinians claim as their capital, was the thorniest issue in the Arab-Israeli peace process. The inability to resolve this issue contributed to the collapse of the peace process and the outbreak of violence between Palestinians and Israelis in September. At an Arab summit in Cairo in October, Abdullah pledged $250 million to assist families of Palestinians killed in the violence and to maintain Islamic monuments and schools in Jerusalem.

Terrorism. The explosion of three car bombs in Saudi Arabia in November and December 2000 killed one British national and wounded five others. International affairs experts speculated that the bombings were the result of growing anti-Western animosity among many Saudis. However, Saudi Deputy Interior Minister Prince Ahmed attributed the bombings to personal, rather than political, motivations.

Foreign workers. More than 350,000 illegal workers, mostly Asians, left the Saudi kingdom in 2000 before an August deadline would have imposed fines and prison terms on their employers. Since October 1997, a Saudi campaign to expel foreign workers to create jobs in the private sector for Saudi citizens led to the departure of an estimated 1.5 million people.

Border agreements. Abdullah concluded historic border agreements with Yemen in June 2000 and Kuwait in July. Both agreements resolved long-time disputes over energy reserves.

Human rights. Amnesty International, a human rights organization based in London, condemned Saudi Arabia in March for widespread human rights abuses. The group accused the Saudi government of arbitrary arrests, torture, and failure to provide detainees with legal counsel. Human rights groups also criticized the more-than 125 beheadings carried out by Saudi authorities in 2000 for violations of Islamic law.

Hijackings. Iraqi authorities arrested two Saudi citizens on October 14 after the two hijacked a London-bound Saudi jetliner to Iraq. On September 14, Saudi officials apprehended an Iraqi who forced a Qatar jet bound for Jordan to land in Saudi Arabia.   □ Christine Helms

See also **Energy supply; Israel; Middle East.**

Senegal. See Africa.

Sierra Leone.
Sierra Leone's peace accord collapsed in May 2000, when units of the Revolutionary United Front (RUF), Sierra Leone's main rebel group, kidnapped hundreds of United Nations (UN) peacekeepers and attacked the capital, Freetown. The accord had been signed in 1999 by President Ahmed Tejan Kabbah and RUF leaders.

The renewal in rebel violence appeared to have been sparked by the final withdrawal of the Nigerian-led West African military force, the Economic Community Monitoring Group (ECOMOG), on May 2, 2000. ECOMOG left behind a largely ineffective UN contingent with limited rules of engagement. RUF rebels then abducted some 500 UN peacekeepers.

In an attempt to prevent Sierra Leone from plunging back into full-scale civil war, Kabbah requested help from the UN and the British government. The UN expanded its peacekeeping force, originally deployed in 1999, from about 8,000 troops in May 2000 to 13,000 troops by September. The United Kingdom sent a battle group of 1,500 elite troops in May to secure Freetown and its airport and to strengthen government and UN forces. The swift deployment halted the rebel assault on the capital and led, by the end of May, to the release of all UN hostages. However, dozens of peacekeepers had died during skirmishes with RUF rebels. The British task force withdrew from Sierra Leone in mid-June, leaving a team of between 400 and 500 people to stabilize the country and train Sierra Leone's army.

In August, the UN Security Council voted to establish a special court to prosecute Foday Sankoh, leader of the RUF, and other rebel leaders for crimes against humanity, including the murder, rape, and maiming of tens of thousands of civilians. Sankoh had been named Sierra Leone's vice president in the 1999 peace pact, but in early May 2000, he had renewed efforts to seize power from President Kabbah. Sankoh was arrested in mid-May after hiding for days.

On November 10, Sierra Leone's government and RUF leaders agreed to a 30-day ceasefire.

Rescue mission. On September 10, British airborne forces rescued six British soldiers and a Sierra Leonean officer who had been held hostage 40 miles (64 kilometers) east of Freetown for 16 days by the West Side Boys, a renegade militia of former government troops. The mission, in which one British soldier and at least 25 West Side Boys militiamen died, dealt a blow to rebel morale. However, in late 2000, rebel forces continued to control Sierra Leone's north and, more crucially, the eastern diamond mines, which had fueled the decade-long insurgency.

□ Simon Baynham
See also **Africa**.

Sikhism. In January 2000, Giani Puran Singh, head of the Akal Takht, Sikhism's highest seat of religious authority, excommunicated Bibi Jagir Kaur, president of the Shiromani Gurdwara Parbandhak Committee (SGPC), Sikhism's highest elected body. Singh excommunicated Kaur because she supported calendar reform. In March, the SGPC voted to replace Puran Singh as head of the Akal Takht with Giani Joginder Singh Vedhyanti. In November, the Shiromani Akali Dal, the Sikh political party in India, elected Jagdev Singh Talwandi as SGPC president to replace Kaur, who had been accused by Indian authorities of murdering her daughter.

On March 20, a group of unidentified gunmen killed more than 30 unarmed Sikhs in Chati Singhpura Mattan, in Jammu and Kashmir, a state in northern India. Many people in India believed that Islamic militants were responsible. In November, Farooq Abdullah, the chief minister of Jammu and Kashmir, announced his intention of launching an inquiry into the massacre.

The Indian Supreme Court ruled in April that the Guru Granth Sahib, the Sikhs's sacred scripture, could in certain circumstances legally be viewed as a person and could, therefore, hold property in its own name. □ Eleanor Nesbitt
See also **India**.

Singapore. In 2000, the government of Singapore designated a place where citizens could make public speeches without a police permit. Previously, authorities had tightly limited public discourse out of fears of ethnic conflicts and other civil disorders. On September 1, the government opened a "speakers' corner" in Hong Lim Park, where anyone could talk about nonsensitive issues. Discussions of race, language, and religion continued to be off limits, and libel laws continued to apply. A newspaper poll conducted in August revealed that 9 out of 10 people in Singapore said they would not publicly express disagreement with any government policy.

The salaries of civil servants raised public ire in 2000. Already among the world's best paid, Singapore civil servants received raises on July 1 averaging 13 percent. Some top officials received raises of 50 percent. Many people responded to the increases with anger, despite government explanations that the raises were necessary in order to retain workers and discourage corruption.

Singapore's economy grew by a healthy 8.8 percent in the first half of 2000. During the same period, financial disparity between Singapore's rich and poor widened, and unemployment reached 3.5 percent. □ Henry S. Bradsher
See also **Asia**.

Skating. See Hockey; Ice skating.

Skiing. Austrian skiers Hermann Maier and Renate Goetschl dominated the World Cup professional season in 2000. Daron Rahlves of the United States enjoyed unexpected success in 2000, winning two World Cup races in Kvitfjell, Norway. The victories were the first by an American male on the World Cup circuit since 1995.

Hermann Maier topped the World Cup men's standings in 2000, breaking the season scoring record with a whopping 2,000 points. He also became only the third skier to win four World Cup titles in one season. Maier won the World Cup overall, Super-G, and downhill titles before clinching the giant-slalom trophy on March 18 in Bormio, Italy. Norway's Kjetil Andre Aamodt finished second in the World Cup standings with 1,440 points.

Maier's amazing season included overtaking Franz Klammer as the most successful Austrian in the history of Alpine ski racing. On February 5 in Todtnau, Germany, Maier won the giant slalom, his 27th career World Cup victory. Only two other skiers collected four World Cup titles in a single season before Maier—Jean-Claude Killy of France in 1967 and Pirmin Zurbriggen of Switzerland in 1987.

Renate Goetschl pulled away from the rest of the World Cup pack by winning two events in three days in February 2000. She took the down-

Christian Mayer of Austria sweeps past a gate on his way to winning the World Cup giant slalom in Kranjska Gora, Slovenia, on March 8, 2000.

hill in Igls, Austria, on February 25 and the Super-G race in 1 minutes 33.42 seconds in Innsbruck, Austria, on February 27. Goetschl clinched the overall title on March 16 by winning the final Super-G race of the season at the World Cup finals in Bormio, Italy, in 1 minutes 17.98 seconds

Goetschl had clinched the Super-G title earlier in the season but failed to defend her downhill crown, losing out to Germany's Regina Haeusl by five points. Michaela Dorfmeister, who lost the women's overall title to teammate Goetschl, took the giant-slalom crown on March 18 in Bormio, Italy. Dorfmeister won the title despite finishing in second place in the giant slalom at Bormio behind Brigitte Obermoser of Austria.

Other Alpine news. Daron Rahlves won back-to-back races on March 3 and March 4, in Kvitfjell, Norway, on the same course that had hosted the 1994 Winter Olympics. Rahlves's wins were the first on the World Cup circuit by an American man in any discipline since Kyle Rasmussen won the downhill in 1995.

Nordic skiing. Finland's Samppa Lajunen edged out Norway's Bjarte Engen Vik in the World Cup circuit, capturing the individual title with 8 wins in 20 events. Lajunen capped his year by winning the final event of the season, the 15-kilometer cross-country race, on March 18, 2000, in Santa Caterina, Italy. □ Michael Kates

Slovakia. Conflict within Slovakia's coalition government continued through 2000. Threats by Hungarian members to leave endangered the future of the coalition government, which included the Christian Democratic Movement, the Hungarian Coalition Party, the Slovak Democratic Coalition, the Democratic Left Party, and the Party of Civic Understanding. The Hungarian members demanded equal treatment for the minority Hungarian population in Slovakia.

Domestic affairs. In May 2000, supporters of Vladimir Meciar, the leader of the opposition political party Movement for a Democratic Slovakia, organized protests calling for early elections. The protesters obtained more than 600,000 signatures in support of a referendum on early elections. However, on November 11, the referendum was declared invalid when less than 20 percent of Slovakian voters participated. Under Slovak law, at least 50 percent of the electorate must vote for any election to be valid.

In March 2000, protestors convinced officials in the town of Zilina to remove a memorial to Jozef Tiso, a Catholic priest who was president of the Nazi-sponsored Slovak State during World War II (1939-1945). Tiso was later executed as a war criminal.

Gypsy activists in March 2000 called for a law allowing them to speak their own language in areas in which they comprised more than 20 percent of the population. In August, a Gypsy woman was beaten to death and a Gypsy family was beaten with iron bars in their house near Bratislava, the capital. After the attacks in 2000, many Gypsies feared attack and sought asylum in other European countries, mainly in Finland and Norway.

In April, the government agreed to return property that had been taken from the Roman Catholic Church when the Communist Party ruled Czechoslovakia from 1948 to 1989.

Economy. In January 2000, the Slovak government raised prices on utilities, telecommunications, and transportation as much as 40 percent. In May, the government proposed a law creating new incentives for foreign investors. Unemployment reached 20 percent in the second half of 2000.

Foreign relations. In February, while on a state visit to Israel, Slovak President Rudolf Schuster formally apologized for the actions of the Slovak government against Jewish citizens during World War II.

In March, the European Union (EU) began membership negotiations with Slovakia. EU officials noted that to be considered for membership by 2004, Slovak officials needed to accelerate economic reforms. ☐ Sharon L. Wolchik

See also **Europe**.

Soccer.

Soccer. France confirmed its status as World Champion in soccer in 2000 by winning the European Championship in July. In Olympic competition at Sydney, Australia, in September, Cameroon won the gold medal in men's soccer and Norway took the women's gold.

European Championship. Sixteen countries took part in the finals of the 2000 European Championship, held in Belgium and the Netherlands from June 12 to July 2. France defeated Italy, 2-1, on a "golden goal" in the deciding game, staged at Feyenoord Stadium in Rotterdam. A "golden goal" is a goal scored in extra time (also called sudden death) that wins the game.

Italy took the lead in the final game on a goal by Marco Delvecchio, who volleyed in from close range at the 55-minute mark. However, at the finish, French substitute Sylvain Wiltord cut in from the left to hit the equalizer as regulation time expired. After 13 minutes of extra time, France won, thanks to the play of substitutes David Trezeguet and Robert Pires. Trezeguet scored the winning goal on Pires's crossing pass from the left.

The Gold Cup. The United States hosted the Gold Cup, a major international soccer tournament, in February 2000. However, the U.S. team was knocked out of the competition in the quar-

terfinals on penalties by the team from Colombia. Canada defeated Colombia, 2-0, in the final on February 27 at the Los Angeles Coliseum.

Olympic competition. Cameroon defeated Spain, 5-3, on penalties to win the Olympic gold medal in Sydney on September 30. The victory was Cameroon's first Olympic gold medal. Spain had taken a 2-0 lead in the first half, but Cameroon came back to tie the game. Spain then survived extra time despite having had two players dismissed. However, Cameroon won on penalty kicks. Chile beat the United States, 2-0, in the bronze-medal match. The U.S. women's soccer team went down in the gold-medal match to Norway, which scored a golden goal to win, 3-2, in extra time. Germany defeated Brazil, 2-0, for the women's bronze medal.

2002 World Cup. In the 2002 World Cup qualifying competition, the United States succeeded in making it through its zone semifinals, which concluded in November 2000. The United States, Trinidad and Tobago, Honduras, Jamaica, Mexico, and the winner of the playoff between Costa Rica and Guatemala, to be held in early 2001, will compete for three spots in the 32-team 2002 World Cup field.

International club competition. Real Madrid defeated fellow Spanish club Valencia, 3-0, to win the final of the European Champions League at Stade de France, Paris, on May 24, 2000. Boca Juniors, of Argentina, beat Palmeiras, of Brazil, on penalties on June 21 at Sao Paulo after two tied games, to win South America's Libertadores Cup.

Brazil's Corinthians won the inaugural Federation Internationale de Football Association (FIFA) World Club Championship, held in Brazil in January. The Corinthians beat Vasco da Gama on penalties after a scoreless tie on January 14 at Maracana Stadium in Rio de Janeiro.

Other championships. Cameroon won the African Nations Cup final on penalties after a 2-2 draw with Nigeria at Lagos, Nigeria, on February 13. Japan defeated Saudi Arabia, 1-0, in the Asian Cup final on October 29 in Beirut, Lebanon.

Major League Soccer (MLS). The Kansas City Wizards, having been the worst team in the MLS in 1999, defeated the Chicago Fire, 1-0, on Oct. 15, 2000, at RFK Stadium in Washington, D.C., to win their first MLS Cup. Striker Miklos Molnar scored the only goal in the 11th minute. Wizards goalkeeper Tony Meola, with 10 saves, including 3 in the last 10 minutes, was named the game's most valuable player. Meola also was named season MVP, having set league records with 16 shut-outs during the regular season and another 5 in the play-offs.

Records, rules, and awards. Germany defender Lothar Matthaus won his 144th *cap* (ap-

Real Madrid striker Nicolas Anelka (left) and teammate Christian Karembeu (right) display the European Cup during a celebration on May 24 in Paris. Real Madrid defeated Valencia, 3-0, to take their record eighth European Champions League title.

pearance in a game) in February, setting an international record. On June 20, Matthaus brought his total to 150 caps when he played his last game for his country. French midfielder Zinedine Zidane was voted FIFA World Player of the Year for 2000.

Transfer fees took another huge leap during the 2000 season, with the record broken first by Argentina striker Hernan Crespo, who was acquired by Lazio from fellow Italian club Parma for $52.5 million. Later, Portugal midfielder Luis Figo was transferred from Barcelona to Spanish rival Real Madrid for $54.4 million.

Beginning on July 1, a new law change came into force allowing goalkeepers six seconds in which to release the ball after taking possession, with no restrictions on goalkeepers' movements within the penalty area.

Brazil remained at the top of the FIFA World Rankings published in November 2000. France, the World and European champion, was second and Argentina third. The United States placed 18th, an improvement of four places since 1999.

The Confederation of North, Central American, and Caribbean Association Football (CONCACAF) changed its name to the Football Confederation. Officials reported the name change was to avoid the cumbersome CONCACAF acronym.

□ Norman Barrett

Social Security. Trustees of the Social Security and Medicare trust funds reported on March 30, 2000, that both funds would remain solvent longer than previously thought. The Social Security fund, which authorities in 1999 believed would last until 2034, was projected to have adequate revenues until 2037. The Medicare program, which authorities believed would run out of money in 2015, was expected to pay benefits until 2023. Trustees attributed the extended solvency to a booming economy and a slowdown in Medicare spending.

On April 7, 2000, United States President Bill Clinton signed into law legislation allowing most Social Security recipients to earn as much money as they wish without losing any retirement benefits. Under prior law, citizens aged 65 to 69 who earned more than $17,000 annually lost $1 in benefits for every additional $3 earned.

On October 18, Social Security Commissioner Kenneth S. Apfel announced that Social Security and Supplemental Security Income (SSI) benefits would increase 3.5 percent in 2001. For Social Security beneficiaries, the average monthly benefit would rise from $816 to $845. The maximum SSI payments to individuals would increase from $512 to $530.

□ Linda P. Campbell and Geoffrey A. Campbell
See also **United States, Government of the.**

South Africa

Thabo Mbeki, who succeeded Nelson R. Mandela as South African president in June 1999, faced considerable dissent within the ranks of his ruling African National Congress (ANC) party in 2000. The president came under fire not only for his controversial views on the nation's AIDS epidemic but also for his probusiness economic policies aimed at attracting foreign investment.

Political issues. In the most significant realignment of South African politics since the ANC won office in 1994, the opposition Democratic Party (DP) and New National Party (NNP) decided in June 2000 to join forces and form the Democratic Alliance. The historic decision placed DP

leader Tony Leon as Alliance head, with NNP leader Marthinus van Schalkwyk as his deputy leader. Leon said the need to strengthen multiparty democracy and to prevent a one-party political system from evolving in South Africa motivated the move. In the June 1999 general elections, the mainly white, liberal DP won 38 parliamentary seats, becoming the official opposition. The NNP, which had a largely white and mixed-race following, came in fourth with 28 seats. The merger in 2000 gave the Democratic Alliance 66 seats in the 400-member National Assembly, compared with 266 for the ANC, which the black majority overwhelmingly supported.

The consolidation of opposition forces in 2000 coincided with major rifts inside the three-part alliance that had existed since 1994 between the ANC, the Congress of South African Trade Unions (Cosatu), and the South African Communist Party (SACP). At its annual conference on Sept. 19, 2000, Cosatu officials warned that their support for the ANC—the dominant partner in the ruling alliance—could collapse unless the government backed down on its plans to loosen labor laws in favor of employers. The number of strikes, mostly over wages, had increased substantially in 1999 and 2000.

In nationwide local elections on Dec. 5, 2000,

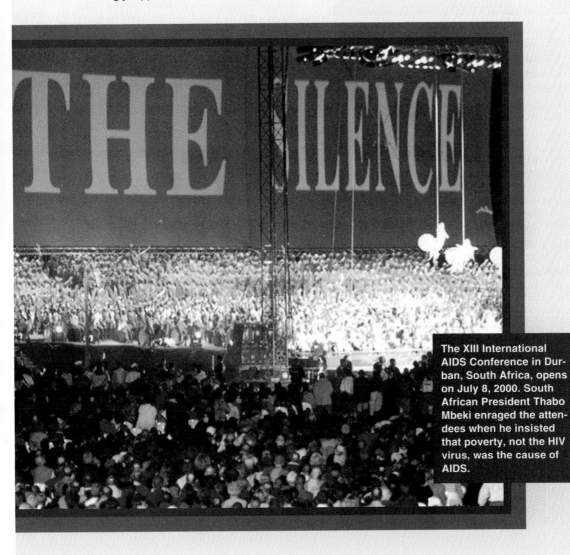

The XIII International AIDS Conference in Durban, South Africa, opens on July 8, 2000. South African President Thabo Mbeki enraged the attendees when he insisted that poverty, not the HIV virus, was the cause of AIDS.

the ANC suffered a significant decline in support when it received only 60 percent of the vote, compared with the 66 percent that it polled in the 1999 general election. The Democratic Alliance announced that "our gains are a victory for democracy," referring to the ANC'S falling popularity.

AIDS debate. In his most controversial act since becoming president of South Africa, Mbeki caused an uproar at an international AIDS conference in Durban on July 9, 2000, when he claimed that the real cause of Africa's AIDS pandemic was poverty and poor hygiene, rather than the human immunodeficiency virus (HIV). In May, Mbeki had appointed a presidential committee packed

The Ministry of South Africa*

Thabo Mvuyelwa Mbeki—president

J. G. Zuma—deputy president

A. K. Asmal—minister of education

N. Balfour—minister of sport and recreation

M. G. Buthelezi—minister of home affairs

A. T. Didiza—minister of agriculture and land affairs

N. C. Dlamini-Zuma—minister of foreign affairs

A. Erwin—minister of trade and industry

G. J. Fraser-Moleketi—minister for the public service and administration

R. Kasrils—minister of water affairs and forestry

P. Lekota—minister of defence

P. M. Maduna—minister of justice and constitutional development

T. A. Manuel—minister of finance

I. Matsepe-Casaburri—minister of communications

M. M. S. Mdladlana—minister of labour

P. Mlambo-Ngcuka—minister of minerals and energy

M. V. Moosa—minister of environmental affairs and tourism

S. D. Mthembi-Mahanyele—minister of housing

F. S. Mufamadi—minister for provincial and local government

B. S. Ngubane—minister of arts, culture, science, and technology

J. M. Nhlanhla—minister of intelligence

D. Omar—minister of transport

E. G. Pahad—minister in the presidency

J. T. Radebe—minister for public enterprises

S. N. Sigcau—minister of public works

B. Skosana—minister of correctional services

Z. S. T. Skweyiya—minister of social development

M. E. Tshabalala-Msimang—minister for health

S. V. Tshwete—minister for safety and security

*As of Dec. 31, 2000.

with scientists who held the same minority view. Despite a signed declaration from 5,000 scientists at the conference that HIV was known to be the cause of the disease, Mbeki stuck to his opinion.

During 2000, the government rebuffed offers from international pharmaceutical companies to provide South Africa with drugs at reduced prices that were known to inhibit mother-to-child transmission of HIV. On September 20, the head of South Africa's Anglican Church, Archbishop Njongonkulu Ndungane, said that the government's inaction on AIDS ranked as a crime against humanity comparable with *apartheid* (the system of racial segregation operating in South Africa before 1994). Mbeki's stance, which caused a revolt within the ranks of the ANC alliance, degenerated into a race conflict when the DP's Tony Leon accused the president of resorting to "snake-oil cures and quackery," to which Mbeki responded by accusing Leon of "entrenched white racism." On October 15, Mbeki acknowledged contributing to public confusion regarding the causes of AIDS and withdrew from public debates.

In 2000, UNAIDS, a joint program run by the United Nations, the World Health Organization, and the World Bank, reported that South Africa had the largest number of people infected with HIV in the world—4.2 million, approximately one out of every five adults in the population. Mbeki insisted that the reports were "hysterical estimates," even though an official publication of the Department of Health endorsed the UNAIDS reckoning.

Equality law. In a move to stamp out virtually all forms of discriminatory behavior, South Africa's National Assembly approved the Promotion of Equality and Prevention of Unfair Discrimination Bill on January 26. The controversial legislation banned discrimination on the basis of "race, sex, pregnancy, marital status, ethnic or social origin, color, sexual orientation, age, disability, religion, conscience, belief, culture, language and birth." It also prohibited speech that was "hurtful," "harmful," or that propagated hatred. The bill, which provided for equality courts to rule on discrimination cases, placed the burden of proof on those accused of illegal discrimination.

Attempting to end the legacy of apartheid, the law excluded from the ban "affirmative action" measures to protect or advance people previously disadvantaged by unfair discrimination. However, both black and white opponents of the bill claimed that the legislation was too far-reaching, prescribing rules on "proper" behavior to every sector of society.

Race relations. At the opening of a four-day national conference on racism organized by the South African Human Rights Commission (SAHRC) in Johannesburg on August 30, President Mbeki declared that, although black people had been the main victims of racism, "anti-white racism" by blacks should also not be tolerated. In response, Mbeki's critics claimed that the ANC had abandoned the nonracial spirit that had prevailed at the end of apartheid in favor of race-based Africanist ideologies. On August 31, F. W. de Klerk, the white president replaced by Nelson Mandela in 1994, claimed at the conference that many "members of the white, *colored* (mixed-race), and Asian minorities are demoralized and confused. They are feeling alienated and afraid." Outside the conference center, the mainly white Mineworkers' Union (MWU) demonstrated against the government's affirmative action policy, claiming that thousands of qualified whites were being sidelined on the job market by less-qualified blacks.

Military integration. On July 17, Defence Minister Mosiuoa Lekota accused white military officers of abusing their authority and "sabotaging" racial reconciliation in the South African National Defense Force (SANDF).

During May 2000, a commission of inquiry into racial tensions within the SANDF continued its work investigating a September 1999 incident in which a black lieutenant killed seven white soldiers and a woman before being shot to death. The military was engaged in the difficult task of integrating the former apartheid-era armed forces with black guerrilla units.

Urban terrorism. The government provided members of the South African judiciary with 24-hour police protection in Cape Town, the parliamentary capital, after a prominent magistrate, Pieter Theron, was shot dead on Sept. 7, 2000. The safety and security minister, Steve V. Tshwete, blamed People Against Gangsterism and Drugs (Pagad), a militant Muslim vigilante group, for what he described as "an assassination by terrorist thugs on the warpath against the state." Before being killed, Theron had been presiding in a case against Pagad members accused of a 1999 pipe-bomb attack on a police station.

Cabinet ministers indicated that special anti-terrorist legislation would be rushed through the National Assembly after seven people were injured on Sept. 12, 2000, in another bomb explosion at a political rally attended by Western Cape Premier Gerald Morkel.

Several people had been killed and hundreds injured in a series of urban terrorist attacks in Cape Town since the Planet Hollywood restaurant was bombed in August 1998. Court proceedings had been disrupted repeatedly by bomb hoaxes, and several state witnesses against Pagad members had been murdered. Pagad leaders repeatedly denied responsibility, claiming the terror campaign was organized by gangsters and drug barons to discredit them. The violence intensified with warfare between minibus and taxi operators vying for business in Cape Town's "commuter war" in August.

International relations. In a show of solidarity with Zimbabwean President Robert Mugabe, President Mbeki visited Zimbabwe in May 2000. During the visit, he refused to publicly condemn the violent election campaign then being waged by Mugabe's ruling party in the run-up to Zimbabwe's June general election.

Leading businessmen in South Africa sharply criticized Mbeki for failing to take the lead in persuading Mugabe to end the violence and illegal invasions of mainly white-owned farms. Mbeki's stance was sharply at odds with that of Nelson Mandela, who called on Zimbabwe's citizens to take up arms against Mugabe on May 6. The crisis in Zimbabwe adversely affected investor confidence in South Africa. It also highlighted the slowness of the ANC's land reform program for the resettlement of landless blacks.

South Africa's economy was hit by labor unrest, floods, and high oil prices in 2000. In July, the Reuters EconoMeter—a survey based on forecasts from 30 local and international economists—reported that while confidence in the economy remained upbeat in 2000, prospects for growth had faded, dampening hopes that jobs would be created for the large adult population who were unemployed. The survey predicted that South Africa's *gross domestic product* (the total value of all goods and services produced in a country in a given year) would grow at a rate of 2.97 percent in 2000—a sharp pickup from the 1999 figure of 1.2 percent but well below the 5- or 6- percent figure required for addressing unemployment.

Sports. The Federation Internationale de Football Association (FIFA) announced on July 6, 2000, that Germany would host the 2006 World Cup soccer championship. FIFA'S executive committee cast 12 votes for Germany, 11 for South Africa, and 1 abstention. The decision meant that South Africa was denied the chance to stage the first World Cup finals on the African continent. President Mbeki reacted bitterly to the news, attributing it to a "globalization of apartheid." Local analysts had forecast that staging the World Cup would boost the South African economy and create 130,000 jobs.

Environment. Conservationists relocated two colonies of rare penguins in the world's largest evacuations of wild birds, following the sinking of a bulk oil carrier near Cape Town in June 2000. Some 20,000 penguins from Dassen and Robben islands were removed and released into unaffected seas more than 500 miles (800 kilometers) to the east near Port Elizabeth. □ Simon Baynham

See also **Africa; South Africa, President of.**

South Africa, President of.

President Thabo Mbeki faced major opposition within the ranks of his ruling African National Congress (ANC) party in 2000 over his insistence that factors such as poverty and poor hygiene, rather than the human immunodeficiency virus (HIV), caused AIDS.

Prominent ANC figures challenged Mbeki's views, which were in sharp contrast to accepted scientific thinking on the subject. Former South African President Nelson Mandela urged Mbeki to focus on affordable treatment for the estimated 4.2 million HIV-positive South Africans in 2000. More than 20 percent of all adults in South Africa were infected with the HIV virus, a situation which Mandela described as "a tragedy."

Launching a national conference on race relations on August 30, Mbeki urged the delegates to purge South Africa of the "nightmare of racism." However, South Africa's Democratic Party claimed that Mbeki's ANC party had abandoned its previous commitment to nonracialism, in favor of *Africanism* (a political ideology favoring the native black population).   □ Simon Baynham

See also **Africa: A Special Report; South Africa.**

South America. See Latin America.
South Carolina. See State government.
South Dakota. See State government.

Space exploration. The first crew was launched to the International Space Station on Oct. 31, 2000. Two Russian cosmonauts and an American astronaut blasted off in a Soyuz spacecraft from the Baikonur Cosmodrome in Kazakhstan. Their planned 17-week mission marked the beginning of an intended permanent human presence in space.

One of the main tasks facing the Expedition 1 crew—astronaut William M. Shepherd, the mission commander, and cosmonauts Sergei Krikalev and Yuri P. Gidzenko—was to test systems and equipment on board the station so that additional components could be added. The work was not all routine, however. On November 18, an unmanned Progress cargo spacecraft approaching to dock with the station began swinging from side to side. Suspecting a problem with the spacecraft's guidance system, controllers in Moscow asked Gidzenko to fly the Progress, with the help of his crewmates, into a safe docking by remote control, using a joy stick on board the station.

Shuttle missions. The U.S. National Aeronautics and Space Administration (NASA) conducted five space shuttle missions in 2000. All but the first flew to the International Space Station.

On February 11, Endeavour and a crew of six were launched to map the Earth's surface in three dimensions (3-D). The 11-day flight was known as the Shuttle Radar Topography Mission. Endeavour carried two radars, operating at different radio frequencies, which beamed their radio waves at Earth. Each of the radars had two sets of antennas—in two different areas of the shuttle—to receive the echoes that were bounced back from Earth. The difference in the perspectives of the two receiver antennas supplied the data for a 3-D map. The topographic map was slated to be used for such diverse purposes as missile-targeting, determining the locations of sites for cellular communications towers, and geological studies.

On May 19, Atlantis and a crew of seven were launched with a cargo of supplies, batteries, and new equipment for the International Space Station. During the 10-day mission, astronauts conducted a spacewalk to install communications antennas and to secure and add parts to a crane. The crew also prepared the station for the arrival of a Russian module called Zvezda ("star" in Russian).

Zvezda, also known as the service module, originally had been scheduled for launch as early as 1998. However, Russia was contributing the module to the station, and economic difficulties and problems with the vehicle to be used to loft the Zvezda caused delays. Finally, on July 12, 2000, the 43-foot- (13-meter-) long Zvezda was launched from Baikonur, to dock at the station two weeks later.

On September 8, Atlantis and a crew of seven, including two Russians, flew to the station with supplies and equipment to prepare the Zvezda for the arrival of the first permanent space station crew. During the 12-day mission, they installed batteries, a toilet, and an exercise treadmill on the station. Astronaut Edward T. Lu and cosmonaut Yuri Malenchenko attached a *magnetometer* (an instrument to measure the Earth's magnetic field) to the outside of the station and connected cables.

Discovery and its crew of seven astronauts, including Japan's Koichi Wakata, was launched on a space station construction mission on October 11. The main cargo was a 9-ton (8-metric ton) section of truss to which arrays of solar power cells would later be added to supply electricity for the station. The truss section was also loaded with equipment for communications, cooling, and station control systems. Two pairs of astronauts alternated in spacewalks over four days to assemble the truss.

The last shuttle flight of 2000, aboard Endeavour, was launched on November 30. It carried a $600-million set of solar arrays, or solar power wings. Canadian astronaut Marc Garneau used the shuttle's manipulator arm to lift the wings out of the Endeavour's cargo bay. Two of his colleagues connected the arrays to the station during three days of spacewalks.

Mir. The Russian government struggled in 2000 with a decision on whether to abandon Mir, its aging space station launched in 1986. The govern-

The first crew of the International Space Station—Russian cosmonauts Sergei Krikalev (left) and Yuri Gidzenko (center) and mission commander U.S. astronaut Bill Shepherd (right)—test systems and equipment aboard the station on November 2. They were launched to the station on a Soyuz spacecraft on October 31.

ment had decided in 1999 to take Mir out of orbit. However, early in 2000, MirCorp was formed to revive the Mir for commercial operations. In February and April, the Russians launched spacecraft to the station to prepare Mir for further use. In response, NASA, concerned that supporting the older station would drain Russian resources from the International Space Station, pressured its Russian counterparts to scuttle the Mir. Finally, in November, the Russian Aviation and Space Agency announced that it would send a spacecraft to Mir to plunge the station into the South Pacific in late February 2001.

The Compton Gamma Ray Observatory, a satellite launched by NASA in 1991 to detect the sources of mysterious gamma rays in space, was forced from orbit by NASA in 2000. On June 4, the spacecraft landed in the Pacific Ocean, about 2,400 miles (3,862 kilometers) southeast of Hawaii. Some scientists protested that the Compton was still useful, but NASA administrators were concerned that the spacecraft soon could no longer be reliably steered and might pose a risk to human life.

Mars Global Surveyor. In December, NASA unveiled images of what seemed to be outcroppings and layers of sedimentary rocks on Mars, strongly suggesting that lakes and small seas had once existed in equatorial regions. The images were taken by the Mars Global Surveyor, in orbit around the red planet since 1997.

NASA's Near Earth Asteroid Rendezvous (NEAR) spacecraft went into orbit around the asteroid Eros on Feb. 14, 2000. Eros became the first small planetary body to be orbited by a spacecraft—no mean feat, as the gravitational field of Eros is just one-thousandth that of Earth.

Iridium, a satellite telephone system, went bankrupt in 2000. Built by Motorola Corporation engineers in the 1990's, the constellation of 66 satellites (and 8 spares) in low Earth orbit offered mobile telephone service from literally any point on the globe. However, Iridium's phones were larger and more expensive than cell phones and did not always work well inside buildings. Calls cost more than those on other systems. With too few customers, the $5-billion system failed to make a profit. In December, the U.S. Department of Defense agreed to pay Iridium $36 million per year for unlimited use of the network. Iridium's encrypted wireless service would allow Defense Department personnel to safely discuss classified information worldwide.   □ James R. Asker

See also **Astronomy.**

Exploration of space in 2001 had a long way to go to catch up to the dramatic vision of the 1968 movie _2001: A Space Odyssey_.

Back in 1968, moviegoers flocked to a new film entitled _2001: A Space Odyssey_. The movie offered a spectacular vision of the future of human space exploration, with ordinary citizens traveling into space on commercial flights aboard sleek spaceplanes. The passengers eventually arrive at an enormous space station, shaped like a rotating wheel, where they could board transport shuttles for travel to one of many outposts on the moon.

The main plot of the movie, which was based on a short story by British-born science-fiction author Arthur C. Clarke, concerns a mission of exploration to Jupiter. Before departure on the long interplanetary journey, crew members are placed in a state of hibernation. While they lie in deep sleep, their Discovery One spaceship is largely controlled by a computer, the HAL 9000, a machine so sophisticated and intelligent that it seems almost human.

However fantastic the plot, most people who saw the film in 1968 were convinced that director Stanley Kubrick had gotten the basics correct. Confidence in the United States space program was at an all-time high in the late 1960's. The National Aeronautics and Space Administration (NASA) was in the midst of the

The reality of life aboard the International Space Station—weightless and crowded (right)—contrasts with *2001* director Stanley Kubrick's dazzling vision (left) of life aboard a spaceship.

2001:
A Space Reality

By James R. Asker

ambitious Apollo program to send astronauts to the moon. It was easy for Americans and many other people to believe that by 2001—which then seemed far in the future—routine commercial space flights, colossal space stations, moon bases, human voyages to other planets, and superintelligent computers would be realities.

When 2001 actually arrived, this vision remained only a fantasy, leaving many space enthusiasts disappointed and wondering if the dream of interplanetary space flight by humans was hopelessly beyond reach. What went wrong on the way to that starry dream? Space authorities point to four main reasons why the optimistic 1960's concept of space travel failed to materialize: political factors; economic considerations; human frailties; and technical difficulties.

The *Cold War* (a period of intense rivalry between the United States and the Soviet Union between 1945 and 1991) provided the primary motivation for human space flight during the 1960's. Sending people into space was a dramatic and highly visible way for both the United States and the Soviet Union to demonstrate their technological prowess. The Soviet Union launched the first artificial satellite, Sputnik 1, in 1957, and Soviet cosmonaut Yuri Gagarin became the first human in space in 1961. When U.S. President John F. Kennedy proposed sending U.S. astronauts to the moon, most Americans agreed it was vitally important to best the Russians with such a feat. The "space race" to the moon ended on July 20, 1969, when Apollo 11 astronauts Neil Armstrong and Edwin "Buzz" Aldrin became the first humans to walk on the lunar surface.

After the United States won the moon race, technological competition between the superpowers remained a way for each country to demonstrate the superiority of its particular political and economic systems. Both nations decided to concentrate their space efforts close to Earth. These efforts included building orbiting stations and reusable shuttles.

Space stations and space shuttles

The Soviets launched the world's first space station, the single-module Salyut 1, in 1971. Six more Salyuts followed. The last operated from 1982 to 1986. In 1986, the Soviet Union launched the first module of the Mir space station. As more modules were added, Mir grew to a size of about 90 feet (27 meters) by 107 feet (33 meters).

The spaceplane featured in *2001* (top)— the sleek Orion III— was fully reusable and could take off and land as a single unit. The space shuttle (bottom) can land like a plane but must be launched attached to two rocket boosters and an external fuel tank.

The Mir program proved that humans could live and work in space for extended periods of time. In the longest mission, cosmonaut Valeri Polyakov completed 438 consecutive days aboard the small station in March 1995. By that time, Mir was beginning to show its age, and accidents and failing hardware were becoming increasingly common. In early 2000, a private company based in the Netherlands paid the Russians to continue operating Mir. However, the Russian government announced in November that it planned to let Mir fall from orbit in early 2001.

The United States launched its first space station in 1973. Skylab, a station with the volume of a three-bedroom house, served as home for a series of three small crews through Febru-

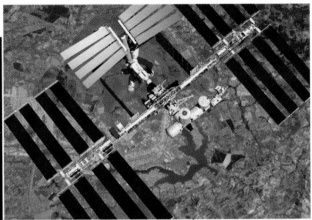

The wheel-shaped Space Station One (left) envisioned in the 1968 film rotated continuously to provide occupants with artificial gravity. Astronauts aboard the International Space Station (above) must deal with microgravity (very low gravity), which weakens muscles over time.

ary 1974. Skylab was the United States' first experience with lengthy space flights—the longest mission ran 84 days. In 1979, the station's orbit degraded, and it burned up as it reentered the atmosphere.

The space shuttle came to dominate the U.S. space program when it got off the ground in 1981. The shuttle fleet, which logged its 100th flight in 2000, served many important purposes, including carrying satellites and space probes into orbit and providing an orbiting laboratory in which scientists could conduct experiments in *microgravity* (very low gravity). The Soviets conducted an unmanned flight test with their own shuttle in the 1980's, but a shortage of funds stopped the program.

In 1984, U.S. President Ronald Reagan and Congress authorized NASA to build a large, permanent space station, which was to be named Freedom. As NASA considered a number of designs and capabilities for this ambitious project, cost estimates skyrocketed far beyond the original $8 billion. In 1985, NASA invited the European Space Agency, Japan, and Canada to become partners in the effort and share the costs.

Loss of public interest

The political motivation driving the U.S. space program came to an end in 1991, when the Soviet empire collapsed. Russia then became a virtual ally of the United States and even joined the space station project, which became known as the International Space Station (ISS). NASA gained a valuable space partner, but with no archrival, the space agency lost a compelling reason to persuade Americans of the importance of human space flight.

The author:
James R. Asker is the Washington Bureau Chief of *Aviation Week & Space Technology* magazine.

The crew of the imaginary Discovery One (above) could exercise in a clean, spacious environment totally monitored by a computer with artificial intelligence. The cluttered, confined existence aboard the Russian space station Mir (right) tested the emotional stability of its inhabitants

This was a big problem for NASA. Citizen interest in the U.S. space program had been on the decline long before the Soviet collapse. In fact, NASA managers and aerospace companies noted this decline soon after the first moon landing. Even while new crews were landing on the moon, Congress cut back funding of the Apollo program, resulting in the cancellation of some later scheduled moon missions.

From this bitter experience, NASA officials learned that while an impressive objective like landing a man on the moon could galvanize public support, once that goal is achieved, the public and its elected representatives quickly adopt an attitude of "been there, done that." The agency hoped that the permanent nature of the ISS would help rekindle and keep the public's interest.

Construction on the ISS began in space in 1998, and in November 2000, the first three-man crew took up residence in the still unfinished station. In its final design, the awkward-looking ISS, with its many connected modules and solar panels sprawling over an area the size of two football fields, bears no resemblance to the graceful, circular Space Station One depicted in the movie *2001*. Despite proclamations from NASA touting the station's potential as a site for unique scientific and commercial research, many scientists had low expectations for the ISS. They said the limited type of research to be done on the station—such as crystal growth and microgravity experiments— could never justify its cost, estimated by many experts at over $100 billion. They added that most of the work done on the ISS could be accomplished with unmanned spacecraft at a much lower cost.

The staggering costs of space

Observers note that the daunting costs of manned space travel have played an important role in dampening public interest in space and keeping humans tied to Earth. Unmanned, or robotic, spacecraft have provided the public, as well as scientists, with a more cost-efficient way to explore beyond the boundaries of Earth and its atmosphere.

Since the 1960's, numerous unmanned probes have gathered valuable scientific information about the planets. These included several Mariner craft that flew past or orbited Mars between 1965 and 1972; two Viking landers that touched down on the Martian surface in 1976; the Pioneer and Voyager probes that studied Jupiter, Saturn, Uranus, and Neptune between 1973 and 1989; the Magellan orbiter that mapped Venus in 1990; the Galileo spacecraft that reached Jupiter in 1995; and Mars Path-finder—the camera-carrying rover that wheeled across Mars in 1997. While acknowledging these successes, some scientists point out that periodic failures of unmanned craft, such as the loss of two Mars probes—the Mars Climate Orbiter and Mars Polar Lander—in 1999, highlighted the fact that unmanned probes have limits on their usefulness and reliability.

Unmanned spacecraft, though less costly than human space flight, are not cheap. The basic task of getting a satellite into low Earth orbit—an altitude of about 100 to 300 miles (161 to 483 kilometers)—is extremely expensive. With today's launch vehi-cles, transporting a payload into orbit costs a minimum of $5,000 to $10,000 per pound. With such expenses, launching a typical communications satellite costs tens of millions of dollars.

Manned spacecraft are in an altogether different league in terms of expense. To sustain a crew, such vehicles need to be larger than unmanned craft and include complicated environmental controls and life-support systems. Building another copy of the space shuttle would cost at least $2 billion, according to space experts. The cost of preparing a shuttle to fly, adding the external fuel tank, and refurbishing and refueling a set of booster rockets is also significant. There are various ways to do the accounting, but most authorities consider $350 million per shuttle mission to be a fair benchmark. That figure does not include the cost of any satellite or probe the shuttle might be carrying.

The cost of a human voyage to Mars could be truly staggering. In 1989, President George Bush proposed that the United States commit itself to sending human explorers to Mars. NASA responded to the president's call by sketching out a Mars plan that came with a price tag of $450 billion. When that figure was made public, the plan quickly died.

Limits of the human mind and body

Beside the high cost of interplanetary travel, mission planners must also take into account the physical limitations of the human body. Although Mir cosmonauts proved that humans can endure long space flights, "weightlessness" is rough on the body. Prolonged exposure to the microgravity conditions of orbit can cause muscles to *atrophy* (waste away) and bones to lose mass—even when astronauts adhere to an exercise program. Upon return to the planet's surface, the body may require days of rest to readjust to gravity.

The psychological rigors of long-duration space flight are another major challenge to mission planners. Not long after completing a 366-day mission on Mir in 1988, cosmonaut Musa Manarov was asked at a press conference whether he would like to be part of the first crew to go to Mars. Most plans for exploring the red planet call for missions of approximately two-and-a-half years. The dedicated cosmonaut surprised many in the audience when he swiftly and firmly answered, "Nyet." Perhaps Manarov's negative response should not have been so surprising. Imagine having to spend an entire year with the same handful of people locked in a house trailer full of noisy equipment. This provides a rough idea of what a long mission on Mir is like. Tempers, cliques, rivalries, and jealousies can complicate life in space, just as they do on Earth. It's no wonder the Russians have always carefully evaluated cosmonauts' psychological make-up before selecting crews for long space missions.

Long trips to reach the outer planets might be made more tolerable for astronauts if scientists were able to discover a safe mechanism to induce hibernation in humans. There have been a few small steps in this direction. In February 2000, geneticist Matthew Andrews of North Carolina State University reported that he had identified two inactive genes in humans that are similar to genes regulating body function during hibernation in ground squirrels. One of these genes allows *glucose* (a sugar that

The fully reusable launch vehicle VentureStar (left) was a concept developed in the 1990's by Lockheed Martin Corporation. VentureStar was to have been in service by 2004, but test failures of an experimental precursor vehicle called the X-33 caused the project to fall at least two years behind schedule.

is the chief source of energy for animals) stored in the body from the animal's last meal to be preserved and used by the brain and nervous system during hibernation. The other gene plays a role in the conversion of stored fatty acids into usable fuel for hibernating animals. Geneticists said they might someday learn how to activate and control such genes in humans, but it will likely take many decades to do so.

The introduction of artificial gravity could also make long space voyages more bearable, because the muscles and bones of astronauts living in conditions of artificial gravity would be protected from deterioration. Engineers know that artificial gravity can be created by making a spacecraft spin. This motion causes the craft's *centrifugal force* (a force that pulls an object outward as it moves in a circular path) to produce the equivalent of gravity. Astronauts on a spinning spacecraft would be pulled outward toward the craft's floor instead of floating, as they do aboard current spacecrafts. Artificial gravity has not yet been tried on a manned spacecraft—mainly because much of the research being performed in space is designed to take advantage of microgravity conditions.

Breakthroughs in propulsion needed

Crossing the vast distances of interplanetary space could be made a lot quicker and economical with the development of new propulsion technology. Although some engineers argue that it is not necessary for space propulsion technology to advance in order for humans to travel to Mars, most engineers agree that advances would make it faster, easier, and cheaper. Furthermore,

Mars Direct is a "live-off-the-land" plan for a mission to Mars that is based on the use of chemical processing equipment designed to produce useful materials from Martian resources. In the first step of Mars Direct (above right), an un-manned "Earth return vehicle" (ERV) extracts carbon dioxide from the Martian atmosphere and produces methane rocket fuel, drinkable water, and breathable oxygen. In the second phase (below right), a crew arrives on Mars and sets up a base. The crew will return to Earth in the fully equipped ERV.

no space-mission planner would seriously propose sending astronauts to the moons of Jupiter with the kind of rockets being used at the beginning of the 2000's.

Space propulsion encompasses two engineering problems: getting a spacecraft into orbit and making the spacecraft go to the right place. Just reaching low Earth orbit means overcoming so much gravity that the spacecraft can consume most of its fuel, leaving little for an interplanetary space flight. Consuming so much energy is extremely expensive as well as impractical.

One way to slash the cost of getting into orbit could be to stop throwing away the launch vehicle with each flight, as was done with all rockets in 2001. Even the space shuttle is not fully reusable. After the shuttle blasts off for space, its two rocket boosters are discarded (to later be recovered and refurbished), and its external fuel tank separates and burns up in the atmosphere. A fully reusable space vehicle—one that would both launch and land as a single unit—could bring the cost of a mission down considerably. Research into such a vehicle began in the early 1990's, when the U.S. Department of Defense staged a series of test flights of a small, single-stage rocket called the Delta Clipper. It was shaped roughly like a cone and used rocket engines at its base to take off and land vertically. Following the tests, NASA held a competition to build a larger, more capable reusable launch vehicle (RLV). In 1996, the space agency selected an RLV proposal by the Lockheed Martin Corporation of Bethesda, Maryland. Lockheed's spaceplane, called the X-33, was designed to take off vertically but glide to a horizontal landing. It was to lead to a commercial successor called VentureStar by 2004. By 2000, however, the X-33 project was at least two years behind schedule, having suffered serious test failures.

Several small private companies began trying to develop simpler RLV's in the late 1990's. Most of these startup firms soon found themselves struggling with serious financial or technical problems. Despite the problems of both NASA and the entrepreneurs, the RLV concept in 2001 remained one of the most promising for making space launches more efficient and economical.

Nuclear and matter-antimatter power

Space travel experts suggest that efficiency must also be improved in methods of propelling ships through space if astronauts are to make interplanetary jouneys. They note that propulsion provided by chemical rockets, the best of which are based on the reaction of hydrogen atoms with oxygen atoms, is simply too slow for long space trips. Engineers believe that transit times to the planets could be cut in half by using nuclear-powered engines. Work in nuclear propulsion goes back to the 1960's, when President Kennedy suggested it in his speech challenging Americans to go to the moon.

Early research into nuclear propulsion involved *fission* (the splitting of atomic nuclei to release energy), the same sort of reaction that is used in nuclear power plants. Fission provided power on certain robotic spacecraft, but it has not yet been used on manned missions, partly because of fears about possible nuclear accidents and releases of radioactivity. The most promising nuclear research in the early 2000's involved *fusion* (the fusing of atomic nuclei to release energy), the method by which the sun produces energy. Propulsion experts believe that fusion power could accelerate a spacecraft to much faster speeds than chemical rockets can—to 10 percent of the speed of light (18,600 miles [30,000 kilometers] per second). However, progress in nuclear fusion research has been slow. Many researchers expect that it will take many years before scientists develop a practical fusion device that can produce more energy than it consumes.

Scientists believe that another propulsion concept—matter-antimatter annihilation—could offer the fastest possible journeys to the outer planets and even to distant solar systems. Antimatter is material identical to ordinary matter but opposite in electrical charge. When matter meets antimatter, the two types of materials annihilate each other and release an enormous amount of energy. Antimatter is usually in the form of antiprotons, which have the same mass as *protons* (positively charged particles in the nucleus of an atom) but a negative electrical charge. Antiprotons do not exist in nature. Scientists create them in *particle accelerators* (large devices in which scientists speed up atoms and subatomic particles in order to discover properties of the particles and the forces that govern them). Experts believe that matter-antimatter annihilation could accelerate a spaceship to about one-third the speed of light. But as of 2001, the technology necessary to apply this kind of propulsion to space travel remained far in the future.

Living off the land

Many space scientists are convinced that if humans are to ever travel successfully to other planets, they will need to "live off the land," as American pioneers did when they moved west in the 1800's. Carrying all the supplies needed for a long space voyage places severe limits on the mission. When mission designers have tried to take the carry-it-all approach, they have found their plans tending toward giant, impractical spaceships stuffed with enormous provisions of food and fuel.

Engineers, therefore, are working on ways to extract natural resources from the moon and Mars. For example, there is strong evidence that craters at the lunar poles contain water in the form of ice. Scientists believe that the molecules of water in the ice can be split into separate hydrogen and oxygen atoms by *electrolysis* (the process of passing an electric current through a liquid to cause a chemical reaction). The resulting hydrogen and oxygen could then be used for rocket fuel and life support.

On Mars, a similar process could be used to extract oxygen from carbon dioxide, which makes up 95 percent of the Martian atmosphere. Moreover, by combining carbon and oxygen atoms from carbon dioxide with a supply of liquid hydrogen brought from Earth, a small nuclear reactor on a spacecraft on Mars could produce water and *methane*, a carbon-hydrogen compound that could be used as rocket fuel for the return flight. If natural water supplies on Mars were discovered, they too could be tapped for use by astronauts.

Some engineers have argued that all the basic technologies needed for humans to travel to Mars already exist. One such engineer is Robert Zubrin, who while working in the early 1990's at Martin Marietta Astronautics (now Lockheed Martin Astronautics) in Denver, Colorado, developed a live-off-the-land plan called Mars Direct. His plan called for large, conventional rockets to get to Mars and landers carrying chemical-processing devices to extract useful chemicals from the Martian atmosphere.

A spaceship of the future is propelled by the enormous amounts of energy released by the annihilation of matter and antimatter. Scientists believe that matter-antimatter annihilation could provide the fastest possible journeys to distant planets and stars.

Zubrin estimated that Mars Direct would cost between $20 billion and $30 billion—far less than the $450-billion price tag that NASA had previously placed on the carry-it-all approach to a Mars trip.

Although Mars Direct offered hope to those who long to see humans walking on Mars in the near future, NASA, as of 2001, had no firm plans to send astronauts to the red planet. Most space enthusiasts did not expect a manned mission to Mars to be attempted before 2030, and many observers believed such a mission would probably have to wait until a much later date.

Looking for a wild card

It is next to impossible to predict the timetable of such a turning point in history as the first human trip to another planet. However, various "wild-card" developments might speed up the timetable. In 2000, NASA scientists reported photographic evidence, obtained by the Mars Global Surveyor spacecraft, that liquid water may periodically flow on Mars. In the late 1990's, spacecraft photographs of Jupiter's moon Europa suggested that an ocean of water may exist under that moon's icy surface. Scientists noted that each of these reports raised the probability that life may exist beyond the boundaries of Earth. Further evidence of water or life on Mars or Europa could dramatically increase public interest in sending human explorers to these distant worlds. Such support might be the key element in finally turning the exciting vision of interplanetary space travel into reality. Perhaps then, a true space odyssey would begin. ■ ■ ■

Spain. The conservative government of Prime Minister Jose Maria Aznar won reelection by a substantial margin in 2000, cementing Aznar's hold on power. In the March 12 election, the prime minister's Popular Party received 45 percent of the vote and won 183 seats in the 350-seat Chamber of Deputies. The party had previously held 156 seats. The election was the first in which the conservatives won an absolute majority in parliament since Spain became a democracy in 1975. The result enabled Aznar to govern without the support of minor regional parties.

The opposition Socialist Workers' Party won 125 seats, down from 141 seats in the previous parliament. The party formed an alliance during the campaign with the Communist-led United Left, but Aznar criticized the ties and the move appeared to backfire with voters. The election result was the party's worst since the early 1980's and forced leader Joaquin Almunia to resign.

Economy. The Popular Party based its election campaign on Spain's vibrant economy, one of the strongest in Western Europe. Economists forecast that output would grow by about 4 percent in 2000, the fourth consecutive year of strong growth, and that the unemployment rate would fall to 13.8 percent, a seven-year low.

Basque terrorism. ETA, a group seeking independence for the Basque people of northern Spain, renewed its terrorist attacks in 2000, after announcing an end to a 14-month cease-fire in December 1999. The group, whose initials stand for Basque Homeland and Freedom in the Basque language, claimed responsibility for the deaths of more than 20 people in 2000. In September, Spanish police arrested 36 suspected ETA members, including the group's presumed military commander, Ignacio Gracia Arregui. On October 30, a car bomb that authorities suspected was planted by the ETA exploded, killing a Supreme Court justice, his bodyguard, and his chauffeur. Tens of thousands of people marched in the streets of Madrid to protest the attacks.

Telefonica goes global. The Spanish telephone company Telefonica S.A. expanded boldly in 2000. In July, the company completed the $4.5-billion purchase of Endemol Entertainment Holding NV, a Dutch production firm. In May, Telefonica's Internet subsidiary, Terra Networks S.A., bought Lycos Incorporated, a United States Internet portal, for $12.5 billion. Telefonica's attempted $58-billion merger with Dutch telephone company Royal KPN NV was blocked by key shareholders and the government, however, and criticism of lucrative share options for top executives forced the resignation of Chief Executive Juan Villalonga on July 26.   □ Tom Buerkle

See also **Europe.**

A car burns in the streets of Madrid in January after the explosion of a bomb planted in it by the separatist group ETA. ETA, which seeks independence for the Basque people of northern Spain, resumed terrorist attacks after a 14-month ceasefire.

Sports. In 2000, Eldrick "Tiger" Woods ensured his reputation as a golf legend, with a string of tournament wins that broke records that had stood for more than a century. In tennis, Venus Williams triumphed at Wimbledon, the U.S. Open, and the Olympics.

In professional team sports, the St. Louis Rams won the National Football League's (NFL) Super Bowl XXXIV. The New York Yankees took their third consecutive World Series title, defeating the New York Mets 4 games to 1.

Tiger's tale. In 2000, Tiger Woods became the first professional golfer to win three of the PGA's four major tournaments in one year since Ben Hogan did so in 1953. The only major Woods did not win was the Masters. His three major victories made him the youngest golfer ever to achieve a career Grand Slam (winning all four majors in a career). Woods won in commanding fashion, firing a 19-under par at the British Open. He won the U.S. Open by a record 15-shot margin, breaking a record that had stood since 1862.

The Williams sisters. The year 2000 proved to be a very good year for sister tennis stars Venus and Serena Williams of the United States. Venus had greater success, taking titles at Wimbledon in July and the U.S. Open in September. Venus, in fact, eliminated Serena in the semifinals at Wimbledon. Venus also took the gold medal in women's singles at the Olympics in Sydney, Australia, in September. However, Serena also was involved in Wimbledon history. On July 10, two days after Venus had won the singles title, Venus and Serena teamed up to beat Ai Sugiyama and Julie Halard-Decuguis 6-3, 6-2 to become the first sisters ever to win the women's doubles final at Wimbledon.

Super Bowl XXXIV. Quarterback Kurt Warner led the St. Louis Rams to victory in the Super Bowl on January 30. Warner, a former Arena Football League player, threw for a Super-Bowl record 414 yards in a 23-16 win over the Tennessee Titans.

The 2000 World Series. The first World Series between two New York City teams since 1956 capped an exciting baseball season in 2000. The well-publicized *subway series* (between teams located in the same city) between the New York Yankees and the New York Mets was a hard-fought, dramatic affair. During the best-of-seven series, three games were decided by just one run, and the rest were decided by two runs. The Yankees won the first two games to extend their World Series winning streak, dating back to the 1996 series, to a record 14 games. The Mets won Game 3, but the Yankees came back to take Game 4 by a score of 3-2, thanks to the efforts of ace Yankee relief pitcher Mariano Rivera. The Yankees then won Game 5 by a score of 4-2 after

scoring two runs in the top of the ninth inning.

Yankee shortstop Derek Jeter was named the World Series Most Valuable Player, batting .409 and slugging two home runs. Jeter set a five-game World Series record with 19 total bases.

Iron Lance. Cyclist Lance Armstrong of the United States, who had survived testicular cancer that had spread to his lungs and brain, captured his second straight Tour de France in 2000, winning by 6 minutes 2 seconds over Jan Ullrich of Germany. Armstrong, sponsored by the U.S. Postal Service, won one of 21 stages and covered the 2,275-mile (3,662-kilometer) course in 92 hours 33 minutes and 8 seconds.

Armstrong also survived two potentially fatal crashes in 2000. In May, he suffered a concussion when he fell during a training ride in France. In his second crash, on August 29, he was hit by a truck while on a training ride and fractured a vertebra in his neck. His injuries threatened his participation in the Olympics in Sydney, Australia, in September. He recovered but had to settle for a bronze medal in the Olympic individual time trial on September 30. Though disappointed with this result, Armstrong was the first cyclist ever to win the Tour de France and an Olympic medal in the same year.

Crime and punishment. In 2000, the NFL was shaken by a series of high-profile tragedies off the field. Two players were charged with murder and a third player was allegedly killed by his wife.

Former Carolina Panthers receiver Rae Carruth was put on trial for murder in November 2000. Carruth had been charged with first-degree murder in December 1999 for his alleged involvement in the death of his girlfriend, Cherica Adams, who was seven months pregnant with Carruth's child. Adams was shot four times from a passing vehicle as she drove her car near Charlotte, North Carolina. The baby was delivered by emergency Caesarean section hours after the shooting. Carruth was arrested but free on $3-million bail when Adams died in December. Authorities issued a first-degree murder warrant against Carruth who disappeared after the warrant was issued. Police found Carruth hiding in the trunk of a car in Wildersville, Tennessee.

Baltimore Ravens star linebacker Ray Lewis and two other men were charged with murder, felony murder, and aggravated assault in the Jan. 31, 2000, stabbing deaths of two men outside a Super Bowl party in Atlanta. On June 5, Lewis pleaded guilty to obstruction of justice for not cooperating with police after the murders, which occurred outside Lewis's limousine. The charges against him were then dropped, and he received probation. His two codefendants were acquitted on June 11. In August, the NFL fined Lewis

Tour de France winner Lance Armstrong (center) rides with U.S. Postal Service teammates down the Champs Elysees in Paris after winning the race on July 23, 2000. Armstrong's victory was his second Tour de France win in two years.

$250,000 for conduct detrimental to the league, but he was not suspended.

Fred Lane, a former Carolina Panther who had joined the Indianapolis Colts, was shot to death in his Charlotte, North Carolina, home on July 6. In August, prosecutors charged his wife, Deidra Lane, with first-degree murder.

Marty McSorley, a Boston Bruins defenseman, became the first National Hockey League (NHL) player since 1999 to face trial for an on-ice attack. In October 2000, McSorley was convicted of assault in a Canadian court for striking Donald Brashear of the Vancouver Canucks on the head with his stick during a game on February 21 in Vancouver, Canada. Brashear suffered a concussion. McSorley received no jail time but was sentenced to 18 months of probation, during which he would not be allowed to play against Brashear. After the incident, the NHL suspended McSorley, the third-most penalized player in league history, for the final 23 games of the season.

IOC scandal continues. Salt Lake City Olympic-bid executives Dave Johnson and Tom Welch were indicted in July 2000 for allegedly paying $1 million in favors to 15 International Olympic Committee (IOC) members to encourage them to vote to hold the 2002 Winter Olympics in Salt Lake City. The scheme, which first surfaced in 1999, also led to the resignation or dismissal of 10 members of the IOC.

In another Olympic scandal, Wade Exum, the director of drug control programs for the U.S. Olympic Committee (USOC), resigned in June 2000, three months before the Olympic Games in Sydney, Australia, were to begin. Exum charged that his bosses turned a blind eye to the use of illegal drugs by athletes. The USOC denied Exum's claims, saying Exum's job performance was under scrutiny at the time of his resignation. In July, Exum filed a lawsuit against the USOC, claiming that officials there had interfered with the anti-drug effort he was hired to lead and that he had been discriminated against because he is black.

Retirements. San Francisco 49ers quarterback Steve Young, who suffered 6 concussions during his 15 seasons in the NFL, retired on June 12. Young, who had replaced Hall of Fame quarterback Joe Montana, was the highest-rated passer of all time (minimum 1,500 attempts). He also had the highest career completion percentage (.643) and the most rushing touchdowns of any quarterback in NFL history (43). He won one Super Bowl as a starter in 1995, earning Super Bowl Most Valuable Player honors. He also received two Super Bowl rings as Montana's backup in 1989 and 1990.

Miami Dolphins quarterback Dan Marino, one of the most successful quarterbacks in NFL history, retired March 13, 2000. Marino threw a record 420 touchdown passes during his career but never won a Super Bowl. The Dolphins retired Marino's jersey number, 13, during a ceremony on September 1.

In August, Jerry West, the Los Angeles Lakers' head of basketball operations since 1982, retired. West, who joined the Lakers as a player in 1960, helped lead the Lakers to the NBA finals nine times, winning the title in the 1971-1972 season. As an executive, he was involved in six championships with the Lakers.

Deaths. Kansas City Chiefs star linebacker Derrick Thomas, who held the NFL record of seven sacks in a single game, died Feb. 8, 2000, of complications from injuries suffered in a car crash on January 23. Thomas, 33, and two companions were driving to the Kansas City airport to fly to St. Louis, Missouri, for the National Football Conference championship game.

Maurice "Rocket" Richard, who won eight Stanley Cup titles with the Montreal Canadiens and was the first player to score 50 goals in 50 games, died of cancer on May 27. He was 78.

Two NBA players died in separate car accidents in 2000. Charlotte's Bobby Phills, 30, was killed January 12 in Charlotte, North Carolina, while drag-racing with teammate David Wesley. Minnesota's Malik Sealy, 30, died in an accident on May 20 in a Minneapolis suburb.

Awards. American cyclist Lance Armstrong won the 2000 Jesse Owens International Trophy award in January in recognition of his first Tour de France win in 1999. In April 2000, Kelly and Coco Miller, identical twins who led the University of Georgia women's basketball team to the National Collegiate Athletics Association Final Four in 1999, won the James E. Sullivan Award. Each year the Amateur Athletic Union presents the award to the nation's top amateur athlete. The Miller sisters were considered one entry because of the similarity of their statistics. It was the first time in the 70-year history of the award that there were two recipients.

Among the winners in 2000 were—

Archery. The World Field Archery Championships were held in Cortina d'Ampezzo, Italy, from July 9 to July 16. Women team champions: Italy; Women's compound champion: Jahna Davis, of the United States; Men's compound champion: Morgan Lundin, Sweden.

Cricket. New Zealand defeated India by four wickets on October 15 to win the International Cricket Council Knockout Trophy.

Curling. Canadian curling teams managed to sweep the men's and women's team curling titles at the 2000 world championships, held November 15 and 16 in Glasgow, Scotland.

Fencing. Elliot Clinton, Patrick Ghattas, and Marten Zagunis of the Oregon Fencing Association won the team sabre title in the national championships in Austin, Texas.

Gymnastics. The U.S. women's gymnastics team took the title at the 2000 Pontiac International Team Championships, held November 9 and 10 at Syracuse, New York. The team from Romania won the men's division.

Modern pentathlon. Stephanie Cook of Great Britain won the women's title and Chad Senior of the United States took the men's title at the Mexico City World Cup, held March 9 to March 12.

Rowing. In July 2000, rowing crews from U.S. universities won five of 17 finals on the closing day of the 161st Henley Royal Regatta in England. Brown University in Providence, Rhode Island, took the Ladies Challenge Plate; Yale University in New Haven, Connecticut, won the Temple Cup; St. Joseph's Prep of Philadelphia took the Princess Elizabeth Cup; the University of Washington in Seattle won the Henley Prize; and Aquil Abdullah of Princeton University in Princeton, New Jersey, was awarded the Diamond Sculls. In March, Oxford University ended Cambridge University's seven-year winning streak by taking the Boat Race on the Thames River.

Sled-dog racing. On March 14, defending champion Doug Swingley of Lincoln, Montana, won the 1,100-mile (1,770-kilometer) Iditarod Trail Sled Dog Race. Swingley had won the race twice before. He completed the race in 9 days and 58 minutes, breaking his 1995 record of 9 days 2 hours and 42 minutes.

Triathlon. Michellie Jones and Chris McCormack, both of Australia, swept the Escape from Alcatraz Triathlon held in San Francisco on May 27. The event involved swimming 1.5 miles (2.4 kilometers), biking 18 miles (29 kilometers), and running 8 miles (12.9 kilometers). McCormack won the men's event by more than three minutes and Jones won by more than six minutes.

Other champions

Equestrian. World Cup Equestrian Final individual show jumping champion: Rodrigo Pessoa, Brazil.

Lacrosse. U.S. college champions: men, Syracuse University; women, University of Maryland.

Motorcycle racing. FIM Grand-Prix 500-cc champion: Kenny Roberts, United States.

Soap Box Derby. Masters champion: Cody Butler of Anderson, Indiana.   □ Michael Kates

See also **Baseball; Basketball; Football; Golf; Hockey; Olympics: A Special Report; Tennis.**

Sri Lanka elected a new parliament on Oct. 10, 2000. The results thwarted President Chandrika Kumaratunga's hopes of winning a sufficient majority in order for her People's Alliance party to enact a new constitution. The new constitution was intended to offer Sri Lanka's Tamil ethnic minority sufficient autonomy to end a 17-year-old civil war.

After a violent five-week election campaign during which more than 70 people died, the Alliance Party won only 107 out of 225 seats in parliament. The opposition United National Party (UNP), backed by Buddhist monks, won 89 seats, enough to block a new constitution.

Ratnasiri Wickramanayake was elected prime minister. Kumaratunga's estranged brother, Anura Bandaranaike, a UNP leader, became speaker of parliament, marking the first time in Sri Lankan history that an opposition member was elected to the speakership.

The war between the Sri Lankan government and the Liberation Tigers of Tamil Eelam (LTTE), whose separatist guerrilla struggle had resulted in the deaths of nearly 63,000 people since 1983, raged throughout 2000. In April, the LTTE captured the Sri Lankan army base at Elephant Pass, the only overland route to the Jaffna area in the north. Some observers believed the military loss was the army's greatest since the war began. The LTTE also threatened to take Jaffna, an important Tamil-majority city, which the army had recaptured from the LTTE in 1995.

In addition to jungle fighting, the LTTE continued in 2000 to send suicide bombers into Sinhalese ethnic majority areas. Young Tamils attached bombs to themselves and set off the explosives in close proximity to government officials. The Tamils made an attempt on the life of president Kumaratunga in December 1999, which left her blind in the right eye. In June 2000, a suicide bombing in Colombo, the capital, killed Clement V. Gooneratne, minister for Industrial Development, and 22 others.

In October, villagers attacked a camp in southern Sri Lanka and killed 27 captured Tiger guerrillas who were being held there. Officials accused police of failing to try to protect the prisoners.

Wickramanayake, who was intent on ending terrorism throughout Sri Lanka, said the government would not negotiate with the LTTE but would destroy the group in battle.

Death of former prime minister. Sirimavo Bandaranaike, mother of Kumaratunga, suffered a heart attack and died on October 10, after casting her vote on election day. In 1960, Bandaranaike became the first woman in the world to be elected prime minister of a nation.

◻ Henry S. Bradsher

See also **Asia**.

State government. The Democratic Party did well in gubernatorial races in November 2000. Of the 11 open governors' seats in the November 7 election, Democrats retained offices in each of the seven states already held by the party and took control of the governor's office in West Virginia. Republican Party candidates retained the governorship in three states.

Missouri State Treasurer Bob Holden, a Democrat, defeated Republican Jim Talent, a U.S. representative, in the race to replace Governor Mel Carnahan. Carnahan, a Democrat, died on October 16 in an airplane crash near St. Louis, while campaigning for a U.S. Senate seat. Lieutenant Governor Roger Wilson was sworn in on October 18 to complete Carnahan's term as governor.

Democrats also scored a victory in Delaware, where Lieutenant Governor Ruth Ann Minner defeated Republican John Burris, a former state representative, in the governor's race. In North Carolina, Democrat Mike Easley, the state attorney general, defeated Republican Richard Vinroot. In West Virginia, voters elected Democrat Bob Wise, a U.S. representative. Wise defeated Governor Cecil Underwood, a Republican.

Democratic governors reelected in 2000 included Frank O'Bannon of Indiana, Jeanne Shaheen of New Hampshire, Howard Dean of Vermont, and Gary Locke of Washington.

Montana voters elected Lieutenant Governor Judy Martz, a Republican, as governor. Martz, who competed in the 1964 Olympics as a speed skater, was the first woman elected governor of Montana. She defeated Democrat Mark O'Keefe. In North Dakota, Republican John Hoeven defeated state Attorney General Heidi Heitkamp to replace retiring Governor Ed Schafer, a Republican. Voters in Utah reelected Republican Governor Michael Leavitt.

Taxes. A study published jointly in January 2000 by the National Governors' Association and the National Association of State Budget Officers revealed that the majority of U.S. governors cut taxes and fees in fiscal year 1999. According to the study, 29 states reduced personal income taxes, 16 states cut business and corporate taxes, and 19 reduced sales and user taxes. The National Conference of State Legislatures reported that states cut taxes by $7.3 billion in 1999. The U.S. Census Bureau reported in 2000 that state revenues rose 5 percent in 1999 compared with 1998 figures.

CHIP funding. Forty states failed to meet a Sept. 30, 2000, federal deadline for spending all their 1998 federal funds under the Children's Health Insurance Program (CHIP). The program provides federal funds to help states expand health insurance to children whose families earn too much to qualify for traditional Medicaid, yet

Selected statistics on state governments

State	Resident population*	Governor†	House (D)	House (R)	Senate (D)	Senate (R)	State tax revenue‡	Tax revenue per capita‡	Public school expenditure per pupil§
Alabama	4,369,862	Don Siegelman (D)	68	37	24	11	$ 14,844,000,000	$ 3,400	$ 5,020
Alaska	619,500	Tony Knowles (D)	13	27	6	14	9,039,000,000	14,590	10,710
Arizona	4,778,332	Jane Dee Hull (R)	24	36	15	15	16,582,000,000	3,470	4,960
Arkansas	2,551,373	Mike Huckabee (R)	72	28	27	8	9,487,000,000	3,720	5,780
California	33,145,121	Joseph Graham (Gray) Davis (D)	50	30	26	14	144,985,000,000	4,370	5,580
Colorado	4,056,133	Bill F. Owens (R)	27	38	18	17	13,514,000,000	3,330	5,750
Connecticut	3,282,031	John G. Rowland (R)	100	51	21	15	16,520,000,000	5,030	9,900
Delaware	753,538	Ruth Ann Minner (D)	15	26	13	8	4,594,000,000	6,100	8,650
Florida	15,111,244	Jeb Bush (R)	43	77	15	25	51,752,000,000	3,420	6,070
Georgia	7,788,240	Roy Barnes (D)	#104	74	31	25	25,707,000,000	3,300	6,480
Hawaii	1,185,497	Benjamin J. Cayetano (D)	32	19	22	3	6,761,000,000	5,700	6,570
Idaho	1,251,700	Dirk Kempthorne (R)	9	61	3	32	4,705,000,000	3,760	5,610
Illinois	12,128,370	George H. Ryan (R)	62	56	27	32	40,460,000,000	3,340	6,420
Indiana	5,942,901	Frank L. O'Bannon (D)	53	47	18	32	18,508,000,000	3,110	7,240
Iowa	2,869,413	Tom Vilsack (D)	44	56	20	30	10,029,000,000	3,500	6,280
Kansas	2,654,052	Bill Graves (R)	46	79	10	30	8,444,000,000	3,180	6,840
Kentucky	3,960,825	Paul E. Patton (D)	64	36	18	20	15,989,000,000	4,040	6,670
Louisiana	4,372,035	Murphy J. (Mike) Foster (R)	71	31	26	13	17,605,000,000	4,030	5,910
Maine	1,253,040	Angus S. King, Jr. (I)	#88	62	17	17	5,690,000,000	4,540	7,850
Maryland	5,171,634	Parris N. Glendening (D)	106	35	33	14	20,559,000,000	3,980	7,520
Massachusetts	6,175,169	Paul Cellucci (R)	137	23	34	6	28,235,000,000	4,570	7,940
Michigan	9,863,775	John Engler (R)	51	59	15	23	40,069,000,000	4,060	8,150
Minnesota	4,775,508	Jesse Ventura (Reform)	65	69	#39	21	24,509,000,000	5,130	7,800
Mississippi	2,768,619	Ronnie Musgrove (D)	**86	33	34	18	10,611,000,000	3,830	4,700
Missouri	5,468,338	Bob Holden (D)	87	76	17	17	19,021,000,000	3,480	5,690
Montana	882,779	Judy Martz (R)	43	57	19	31	3,626,000,000	4,110	6,950
Nebraska	1,666,028	Mike Johanns (R)	unicameral (49 nonpartisan)				5,636,000,000	3,380	6,750
Nevada	1,809,253	Kenny Guinn (R)	27	15	9	12	7,320,000,000	4,050	6,020
New Hampshire	1,201,134	Jeanne Shaheen (D)	††143	256	11	13	4,010,000,000	3,340	6,840
New Jersey	8,143,412	Christine Todd Whitman (R)	35	45	16	24	37,007,000,000	4,540	10,500
New Mexico	1,739,844	Gary E. Johnson (R)	42	28	24	18	9,059,000,000	5,210	5,750
New York	18,196,601	George E. Pataki (R)	99	51	25	36	96,131,000,000	5,280	9,840
North Carolina	7,650,789	Mike Easley (D)	62	58	35	15	33,327,000,000	4,360	6,570
North Dakota	633,666	John Hoeven (R)	29	69	18	31	3,128,000,000	4,940	4,510
Ohio	11,256,654	Robert Taft (R)	39	60	12	21	48,133,000,000	4,280	7,150
Oklahoma	3,358,044	Frank Keating (R)	53	48	30	18	12,186,000,000	3,630	5,570
Oregon	3,316,154	John Kitzhaber (D)	27	33	14	16	15,688,000,000	4,730	7,600
Pennsylvania	11,994,016	Tom J. Ridge (R)	99	104	20	30	48,503,000,000	4,040	7,820
Rhode Island	990,819	Lincoln C. Almond (R)	84	16	44	6	4,438,000,000	4,480	8,450
South Carolina	3,885,736	Jim Hodges (D)	54	69	23	23	15,203,000,000	3,910	6,270
South Dakota	733,133	William J. Janklow (R)	20	50	12	23	2,874,000,000	3,920	5,320
Tennessee	5,483,535	Don Sundquist (R)	57	42	18	15	16,675,000,000	3,040	5,680
Texas	20,044,141	Rick Perry (R)	78	72	15	16	57,807,000,000	2,880	6,480
Utah	2,129,836	Michael O. Leavitt (R)	24	51	9	20	8,762,000,000	4,110	4,140
Vermont	593,740	Howard Dean (D)	‡‡62	83	16	14	2,373,000,000	4,000	7,950
Virginia	6,872,912	James S. Gilmore III (R)	#47	52	18	22	25,918,000,000	3,770	6,640
Washington	5,756,361	Gary Locke (D)	49	49	25	24	27,980,000,000	4,860	6,560
West Virginia	1,806,928	Bob Wise (D)	75	25	28	6	7,808,000,000	4,320	7,380
Wisconsin	5,250,446	Tommy G. Thompson (R)	43	56	18	15	21,395,000,000	4,070	8,060
Wyoming	479,602	Jim Geringer (R)	14	46	10	20	2,653,000,000	5,530	7,430

*July 1, 1999, estimates. Source: U.S. Census Bureau
† As of December 2000. Source: National Governors' Association; National Conference of State Legislatures; state government officials
§1999-2000 estimates for elementary and secondary students in average daily attendance. Source: National Education Association.

#One independent.
**Three independents.
††One libertarian.
‡1999 figures.
‡‡One independent, four progressives.

A South Carolina man expresses his opposition to the Confederate flag flying above the South Carolina statehouse in Columbia during a January 2000 rally. Critics said that the flag represented slavery and racism. On May 23, Governor Jim Hodges signed legislation that removed the flag from the dome but not from the grounds.

not enough to afford private insurance.

Under a 1997 federal law, states forfeit any unspent funds, which are then redistributed to states that have exhausted their federal grants. States that were in line to benefit from the windfall included Alaska, Indiana, Kentucky, Maine, Massachusetts, Missouri, New York, North Carolina, Pennsylvania, and South Carolina. Some state officials criticized the federal deadline as setting an unrealistic goal for putting such complicated new programs into operation.

Stronger drunken driving law. President Bill Clinton on Oct. 23, 2000, signed a new national standard for drunken driving that required states to adopt a lower legal threshold for drunk driving. Under the legislation, states were forced to adopt a blood-alcohol level of 0.08 percent as a standard by 2004 or risk losing millions of dollars in annual federal highway funds. Only 18 states had the lower level prior to the legislation.

Confederate flag controversy. On May 23, 2000, South Carolina Governor Jim Hodges signed a bill into law that removed a Confederate flag from the dome of the Capitol in Columbia, the state capital. The flag was lowered in July and a smaller version raised near a Confederate memorial in front of the Capitol.

The Confederate flag was the emblem of the 11 Southern states that seceded from the United States in 1860 and 1861, resulting in the Civil War (1861-1865). The flag had flown over the Capitol dome since 1962.

Civil rights organizations, including the National Association for the Advancement of Colored People (NAACP), claimed that the flag represented slavery. In January 2000, the NAACP launched a tourism boycott to pressure the legislature to remove the flag from the statehouse. Supporters of the flag argued that it represented Southern heritage and honored the memory of soldiers who fought for the Confederacy.

Death penalty debates. In January, Illinois Governor George Ryan said that he would temporarily halt all scheduled lethal injection executions. He expressed doubts about the fairness of capital punishment, after 13 inmates on death row in Illinois had been exonerated since 1977, when the state reinstated the death penalty.

The New Hampshire legislature tried to repeal the death penalty in 2000, but Governor Jeanne Shaheen vetoed the measure in May. Shaheen said that though she respected the views of death-penalty opponents, she believed that some crimes warrant execution.

Education. A nationwide shortage of teachers in 2000 spurred California Governor Gray Davis to propose comprehensive education changes, most of which the legislature enacted throughout the year. These included a $99.4-bil-

lion package for education and $974 million in incentives to recruit and keep teachers. The state also gave teachers personal income tax credits, bonus pay, and higher starting salaries and forgave student loans.

Florida established the nation's largest public charter school district in 2000. Charter schools are typically created and run by parents, teachers, or other groups outside a school district's authority. In July, Florida allowed Volusia County to become the first charter school district in that state.

Moment of silence. A state law in Virginia requiring public school students to daily observe a minute of silence for prayer, meditation, or reflection went into effect on July 1. The Virginia chapter of the American Civil Liberties Union (ACLU) had filed a lawsuit against the state, claiming that the law violated the separation of church and state outlined in the U.S. Constitution. The ACLU is a New York City-based, nonpartisan organization devoted to defending the rights and freedoms of people in the United States. In October, a federal judge ruled that the minute-of-silence law was constitutional because it did not promote religion in schools.

Civil unions. On July 1, a new law in Vermont went into effect, legalizing civil unions for same-sex couples. Vermont was the first state to enact such legislation. The law offered same-sex couples the same rights and protections conferred by marriage. The Vermont Supreme Court in 1999 ruled that the state must provide the same benefits to same-sex couples that it does to heterosexual couples.

Vermont officials reported that many of the couples taking advantage of the civil union ceremony were from out of state. Some experts questioned what legal significance the certification would have in the couples' home states.

Historic vote. The Mississippi House of Representatives voted 86 to 36 on Jan. 4, 2000, to select Democrat Ronnie Musgrove as governor. Neither Musgrove, who was the state's lieutenant governor, nor Republican challenger Mike Parker won a majority of the vote in a November 1999 election. Mississippi state law dictated that the state House cast the deciding votes. It was the first time in Mississippi history that an election for governor had been decided by the House.

Reform Party defection. On Feb. 11, 2000, Minnesota Governor Jesse Ventura announced that he had left the national Reform Party. The governor criticized the party as being "hopelessly dysfunctional." Ventura became the highest-ranking Reform Party member following his election in 1998. ☐ Elaine Stuart

See also **Courts; Democratic Party; Education; Elections; Health care issues; Human rights; Republican Party; Welfare.**

Stocks and bonds. Stock market investors learned in 2000 that what goes up can come down. After five years of extraordinary stock gains in areas such as computer technology and telecommunications, the growth of these popular sectors began to slow dramatically beginning in mid-March. Other sectors, including financial services, food, health care, utilities, and energy—all of which in previous years had labored in the shadow of the more popular technology and telecommunications sectors—produced winners in 2000.

The Dow Jones Industrial Average was down more than 9 percent to 10,414 by the end of November. The Dow is a composite of the stock prices of 30 major companies traded on the New York Stock Exchange and on the Nasdaq Composite Index, which consists of the more than 3,000 stocks traded electronically on the system operated by the National Association of Securities Dealers. The Nasdaq slumped 36 percent through November after an unprecedented 86-percent gain in 1999. The broader Standard & Poor's 500 (S&P 500) index of 500 major companies was down 10 percent in 2000.

Financial analysts cited two main factors for the market volatility and the pressure on stock prices. First, the U.S. Federal Reserve System (the Fed), the central bank of the United States, increased interest rates six times between June 1999 and May 2000—totaling 1.75 percentage points—in an effort to cool the fast-growing economy. Second, the analysts theorized, corporate sales and profit growth began to slow in 2000 as higher short-term interest rates began to affect the economy.

The U.S. stock market was also hampered by a continued weakness in the value of the euro, the shared monetary unit of 11 of the 15 members of the European Union. Some financial analysts noted that the euro's weakness was caused in part by the relative strength of the U.S. stock and bond markets, which attracted global capital into dollar-denominated investments.

However, the strength of the dollar in relation to the euro also diminished the dollar value of sales and profits recorded in Europe by U.S. multinational companies, whose stock prices suffered accordingly.

Winners and losers. Many investors turned away from Internet-related companies in 2000 after it became clear that sustainable profitability for many of these fledgling companies was remote. An index of Internet stocks compiled by *Interactive Week,* a Northbrook, Illinois-based weekly magazine that covers all aspects of the Internet and interactive technology, soared 168 percent in 1999 and peaked in March 2000. The index was down 45 percent at the end of November.

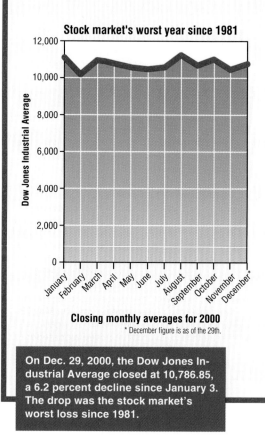

Stock market's worst year since 1981

Dow Jones Industrial Average

Closing monthly averages for 2000
* December figure is as of the 29th.

On Dec. 29, 2000, the Dow Jones Industrial Average closed at 10,786.85, a 6.2 percent decline since January 3. The drop was the stock market's worst loss since 1981.

One of the most dramatic of the technology stock slumps involved Qualcomm, Inc., of San Diego, a maker of wireless communications equipment. The company's share price skyrocketed during 1999 before reaching $200 a share on Jan. 3, 2000. The stock lost 75 percent of its value by mid-July, falling to approximately $50 per share. By the end of November, however, Qualcomm stock had recovered to $80.25 a share.

Despite the troubles that plagued technological and telecommunications stocks during 2000, other stocks performed solidly throughout the year. Biotechnology stock values increased nearly 50 percent through November 2000 after doubling in 1999. The Dow Jones Utilities Average, an index of 15 utility companies, climbed nearly 40 percent through November 2000 after losing 9 percent in 1999.

Overall in 2000, mid-sized stocks decisively beat the giant companies that comprised the S&P 500 and Dow Jones Industrial Average and dominated the Nasdaq composite index.

Bond market. The yield on 30-year U.S. Treasury bonds, which reflect changes in price to accommodate current market rates, rallied for most of 2000 as the Fed's increase in short-term interest rates slowed the economy and tamed inflation pressures. The repurchase of government bonds by the U.S. Treasury, reflecting federal budget surpluses, increased the price of the bonds and reduced their yields.

But corporate bonds, especially those bonds issued by speculative telecommunications companies within the United States, ran into trouble throughout much of 2000. Financial experts theorized that the poor return on corporate bonds reflected a slowing U.S. economy and diminished investor expectations.

International stock markets. Stock markets outside the United States struggled with generally disappointing economic conditions and the relative attractiveness of U.S. investments. The Nikkei 225 index of 225 major companies traded on the Tokyo Stock Exchange fell 23 percent through November 2000, compared with a 37-percent gain in 1999. However, on Feb. 8, 2000, the Nikkei 225 did close above the 20,000 level for the first time since 1997. The climb to 20,007.77 followed sharp gains in technology stocks during the day.

An index of 30 leading stocks at the London Stock Exchange fell 13 percent through November 2000, compared with a 17-percent gain in 1999. Leading German stocks showed little movement in 2000 following a 39-percent rally in 1999.

☐ Bill Barnhart

See also **Economics; Manufacturing.**

Sudan. President Umar al-Bashir in September 2000 ordered the arrest of 51 members of the People's National Congress (PNC), a new opposition party, for allegedly inciting riots. Bashir's archrival, Hassan al-Turabi—an advocate of strict Islamic law—formed the PNC after Bashir suspended Turabi's leadership of the ruling National Congress Party in May and closed that party's provincial offices. In late 1999, Bashir had dissolved the parliament, which Turabi headed, and declared a state of emergency after Turabi moved to reduce Bashir's powers.

Civil war. Bashir undertook several efforts in 2000 to end the civil war that began in 1983. Opposing sides in the war consisted of various groups of black Christians and *animists* (those believing that souls are present in all parts of nature) from southern Sudan who fought for self-determination against the Arab-and Muslim-dominated north. Some northern groups were allied with opposition forces.

In late September 2000, Bashir's government opened peace negotiations in Kenya with the main rebel group, the Sudan People's Liberation Army (SPLA). In June, Bashir had decreed a blanket amnesty for rebels who rejected violence and returned to Sudan from bases in Ethiopia. The government welcomed a cease-fire by rebels belonging to the Umma (Nation) Party in March.

Umma leader Sadeq al-Mahdi returned to Sudan on November 23, ending a four-year exile. Mahdi had been ousted as prime minister in 1989 after a *coup* (overthrow) that was led by Bashir. Upon his return, Mahdi was welcomed by some 100,000 supporters, who lined the streets of the Sudanese capital, Khartoum.

U.S. relations. United States diplomats in April 2000 resumed limited diplomatic activities at the U.S. embassy in Khartoum. The United States had shut the mission in 1998 after U.S. officials accused Sudan of connections to bombings of American embassies in Kenya and Tanzania. In December 2000, Sudanese authorities ordered the expulsion of a U.S. diplomat, whom they accused of discussing security issues with dissidents.

Sudan lost its bid for a seat on the UN Security Council in October. U.S. officials, who regarded Sudan as having a poor human rights record and links to terrorists, had opposed the bid.

Slavery. In September, Christian Solidarity International (CSI), a Swiss-based aid group, announced that it had purchased the freedom of 4,435 slaves in southern Sudan. CSI claimed to have bought the freedom of more than 38,000 slaves since 1995. International affairs experts said slavery had become widespread in Sudan since the civil war began.   ☐ Christine Helms

See also **Middle East; United Nations.**

Supreme Court of the United States

played a key role in the outcome of the hotly contested 2000 U.S. presidential election. On December 12, the court, voting 5 to 4, reversed a decision by the Florida Supreme Court that had allowed a manual recount of votes from the November 7 election. In the opinion of the majority on the U.S. Supreme Court, the recount in Florida could not be resumed because the procedures were so arbitrary that they violated the equal protection clause of the U.S. Constitution. According to legal experts, the decision removed all legal obstacles preventing Texas Governor George W. Bush, the Republican candidate for president, from claiming victory over his Democratic challenger, Vice President Al Gore. On December 13, Gore conceded the election.

The U.S. Supreme Court on December 4 had ordered the Florida Supreme Court to reconsider its decision allowing vote recounts in three Florida counties. The decision set aside, but did not overturn, the Florida Supreme Court decision, which extended the vote-certification deadline to allow manually counted votes to be included in the Florida results. Gore had asked for the recount.

The Florida Supreme Court on December 8 had ruled that the recount should resume, but on December 9, the U.S. Supreme Court ordered the process to stop so that it could rehear the case.

Separation of church and state. On June 28, the court ruled by a 6-to-3 vote that the federal government can loan instructional material, such as computers, to church-affiliated schools without violating the U.S. Constitution's requirement of separation of church and state. The court determined that if such programs provide materials to both public and private schools, then it does not promote religion.

Abortion decision. In another decision handed down on June 28, the court overturned a Nebraska law that barred physicians from performing an abortion procedure that is usually performed at a late state in a pregnancy. Voting 5 to 4, the court ruled that the Nebraska law violated constitutional protections allowing a woman to choose whether to have an abortion.

In a separate abortion-related case, the court ruled in June that laws forcing abortion protestors to maintain a distance of at least 8 feet (2.5 meters) from abortion clinics, personnel, and patients do not violate the Constitution's free-speech protections. The court voted 6 to 3 that the privacy rights of people seeking care at such medical facilities and their interest in avoiding unwelcome speech outweighed the rights of the protestors to make sure their message was heard.

Boy Scout verdict. In a 5-to-4 vote on June 28, the court ruled that the Boy Scouts of America did not engage in illegal discrimination by refusing to allow a homosexual man to serve as a troop leader. The decision overturned a New Jersey Supreme Court ruling against the Boy Scouts for expelling the man. The justices ruled that, as a private organization, the Boy Scouts' right of free association, as guaranteed by the First Amendment, outweighed the state's antidiscrimination law.

FDA and tobacco regulation. On March 21, the justices ruled 5 to 4 that the Food, Drug, and Cosmetic Act of 1938 did not give the federal Food and Drug Administration (FDA) the authority to regulate tobacco as a drug. In 1996, the FDA proposed guidelines to restrict the marketing of tobacco products to children and teen-agers, claiming that the 1938 legislation gave them the authority to do so. The 1996 FDA restrictions barred tobacco sales to anyone under age 18, required clerks to check photo identifications of customers who appeared to be underage, and limited vending machines to places where minors were prohibited from entering.

Cable television ruling. On May 22, 2000, the court overturned a provision of the Telecommunications Act of 1996 requiring cable television channels to show sexually explicit programs only during late-night hours. The justices voted 5 to 4 that the act restricted free speech as guaranteed by the First Amendment. The court deter-

mined that the late-night regulation was too broad since cable operators can give subscribers devices that fully scrambled the signals of sexually explicit channels.

Health care issues. The court unanimously determined on June 12, 2000, that patients cannot sue health maintenance organizations (HMO's) in federal court for paying physicians bonuses in an attempt to reduce health care costs. HMO's are a type of managed care plan. The justices ruled that only state courts can hear lawsuits that claim physicians gave their patients inadequate care because of the financial incentives to keep costs low.

School prayer. On June 19, the court ruled that student-led prayers at high school football games violate the separation of church and state as outlined in the First Amendment. By a 6-to-3 vote, the court determined that a Texas school district's pregame prayer equaled an endorsement of religion. The district had allowed student-initiated and student-led prayer to be broadcast over the public address system before school football games.

Student activity fees. In a unanimous decision, the court ruled on March 22 that public colleges and universities can use student activity fees to fund campus activities, even if some students disagree with the views of those organizations. A group of students had sued the University of Wisconsin at Madison in 1995 to stop their activity fees from going to campus organizations they found objectionable. The university students argued that the practice violated their First Amendment right of free speech by forcing them to support 18 organizations whose positions they found objectionable. The Supreme Court justices ruled that the fee system promoted free speech by funding a range of groups regardless of their views.

Miranda decision. The court on June 26, 2000, reaffirmed a 1966 ruling requiring law enforcement officials to read criminal suspects their constitutional rights before questioning them about a crime. The 1966 ruling, commonly called the Miranda decision, required that police inform suspects in custody or under arrest of their right to remain silent, their right to consult with a lawyer, and of the fact that any statement they make may be used as evidence against them. A confession to police is usually considered voluntary and admissible in court if the suspect was advised of his or her rights before making a statement.

Voting 7 to 2, the justices refused to replace the Miranda decision with a 1968 federal law allowing a voluntary confession to be admitted in court, even if police had not advised the suspect of his or her Miranda rights. The U.S. government never tried to enforce the 1968 law.

Suspects' rights. On Jan. 12, 2000, the court broadened police authority, ruling that in general, police may stop and briefly question any person who runs at the sight of an officer. The 5-to-4 decision, which was based upon the Fourth Amendment protection against unreasonable searches and seizures, reversed an Illinois Supreme Court ruling that two Chicago police officers had wrongfully stopped a man just because he fled from them. The U.S. Supreme Court justices determined that police were justified in stopping and searching a suspect who flees if other factors make the situation suspicious.

Gender-motivated crimes. The court ruled in a 5-to-4 decision on May 15 that victims of gender-motivated crimes cannot sue their attackers for monetary awards in federal court. The court determined that Congress overstepped its authority by enacting the damages provision of the 1994 Violence Against Women Act. The justices ruled that such lawsuits should be limited to the state courts. The court determined that the Constitution requires a distinction between what is a national issue and what is a local or state issue.

☐ Geoffrey A. Campbell and Linda P. Campbell
See also **Courts; Elections; Health care issues.**

Surgery. See Medicine.
Suriname. See Latin America.
Swaziland. See Africa.

Sweden continued to enjoy robust economic growth in 2000, primarily because of the success of its high-technology industries. A number of start-up companies and venture capital firms seeking to develop products and services for Europe's Internet and mobile telephone industries established offices in Stockholm during the year. Economists forecast that Sweden's *gross domestic product* (the value of all goods and services produced in a year) would grow by 3.9 percent in 2000, well above the European Union average of 3.4 percent.

Economic policy. The strong growth enabled the government to cut taxes for the second straight year. On September 20, Finance Minister Bosse Ringholm announced that income taxes would be reduced by $1.2 billion in 2001. The government hoped the cuts would improve competitiveness, though Sweden continued to have the highest tax rates of any industrial country.

The Swedish government sold a 30-percent stake in Telia AB, the national telephone company, for $7.7 billion in June 2000. The company's share price fell sharply after the sale, the largest privatization in Swedish history, and the company's president and chief executive officer resigned in October.

The euro. The ruling Social Democratic Party of Prime Minister Goran Persson agreed to support Swedish membership in the single European currency at a party congress in March. However, Persson did not set a date for a public vote on the referendum. Popular support in Sweden for the euro declined after voters in neighboring Denmark rejected the euro in a referendum in September.

World War II legacy. Persson broke with decades of tradition in January 2000 when he stated that Sweden had been wrong to remain neutral during World War II (1939-1945). The government allocated $5 million for research into Swedish actions during and after the war. The moves followed revelations in the late 1990's that Sweden had sold iron ore to Nazi Germany and allowed German troops to cross its territory to enter Finland and Norway.

Saab. General Motors Corporation (GM) of Detroit bought the remaining 50 percent of Sweden's Saab Automobile AB in January 2000 for $125 million, taking full control of the company. GM bought its initial 50-percent stake in 1989.

Oresund link. Sweden opened the $3.5-billion Oresund Fixed Link—its first road and rail link to Denmark—on July 1, 2000. The 10-mile- (16-kilometer-) long link connects Malmo, Sweden, and Copenhagen with a bridge and tunnel across the Oresund Sound. ☐ Tom Buerkle

See also **Building and construction; Europe.**

Swimming. World records fell at a furious clip in 2000 in Olympic and non-Olympic trial swimming, with Alexander Popov of Russia and Inge de Bruijn of the Netherlands making the biggest waves. The 2000 swimming season also saw the fall of the sport's oldest record—American Mary Meagher's 19-year-old mark in the 200-meter butterfly—and the introduction of a controversial new type of bodysuit.

Record-breakers. Popov, a four-time Olympic gold medalist, broke the world record in the 50-meter freestyle on June 16 in Moscow, with a time of 21.64 seconds. The previous mark had been set by Tom Jager of the United States in 1990. However, Popov's record came in a heat specifically designed to give him a chance to break the record. Popov swam with an empty lane on either side of him, resulting in less water resistance from the waves of other swimmers. A day earlier, fellow Russian Roman Sludnev set the world record in the 100-meter breaststroke with a time of 1:00.36.

In the first half of 2000, de Bruijn set records in the women's 50- and 100-meter freestyle and the 50- and 100-meter butterfly. She set the world mark in the 50-meter freestyle on June 10 at the Brazilian swimming championships in Rio de Janeiro with a time of 24.39 seconds. Two weeks earlier, in Sheffield, England, on May 27

Alexander Popov of Russia relaxes after setting a new world record in the 50-meter freestyle at a competition in Moscow in June 2000. Popov swam the event in 21.64 seconds.

and May 28, she set records in the other three events and matched the then-world record in the 50-meter freestyle.

Jenny Thompson, 26, of the United States, bettered her own world mark in the 100-meter butterfly twice in 2000. On February 12, in Paris, she finished in 56.80 seconds. She broke her own record again on March 18 at the World Short Course Championships in Athens, Greece, finishing in 56.56 seconds.

Butterfly record caught. Australian swimming star Susie O'Neill erased a piece of history at Australia's Olympic trials in Sydney on May 17 by breaking American Mary T. Meagher's 19-year-old world record in the 200-meter butterfly. O'Neill, 26, finished in a time of 2 minutes 5.81 seconds, breaking the record by .15 seconds.

New suits make splash. A new type of bodysuit that supposedly helped athletes swim up to 3 percent faster emerged in 2000. The "Fastskin" suit made by Speedo, a sports apparel company located in Los Angeles, was covered with tiny v-shaped ridges that simulated shark skin. The suit was designed to help water pass more efficiently over a swimmer's body. Though controversial, the suits were allowed to be used in competition during the 2000 Olympic games in Sydney, Australia. ☐ Michael Kates

See also **Australia; Olympics: A Special Report.**

Switzerland. Swiss voters chose to maintain an open policy to the outside world in two major ballot initiatives during 2000. On May 21, voters approved by a 2-to-1 margin agreements aimed at increasing Switzerland's economic ties with the European Union (EU). The seven agreements contained measures to expand trade and facilitate the movement of workers between Switzerland and EU countries. Opponents of closer ties with the EU had demanded the initiatives, claiming that the agreements could revive attempts to have Switzerland join the EU, an idea that Swiss voters had rejected in 1992.

On Sept. 24, 2000, voters rejected a proposition to limit the number of foreign residents in Switzerland to 18 percent of the population. Supporters of the proposition, which included the nationalist Swiss People's Party, claimed that growing numbers of foreigners threatened to overwhelm the country's identity and culture. Opponents contended that the proposal would damage the Swiss economy because many of the country's multinational companies rely on their ability to recruit an international work force. The result was seen as an affirmation of Switzerland's increasingly cosmopolitan population, which in 2000 included 19 percent foreign residents.

Banks expand. Switzerland's two leading banks made major acquisitions of firms in the

United States in 2000 in an attempt to strengthen their positions in the global investment banking industry. UBS AG agreed on July 12 to buy Paine-Webber Group, Incorporated, the fourth-largest U.S. brokerage, for $12.4 billion. On August 30, Credit Suisse Group of Zurich agreed to buy the investment bank Donaldson, Lufkin & Jenrett, Incorporated, of New York City for $12 billion.

Switzerland took aggressive steps to implement changes made in the 1990's to loosen banking secrecy policies. In January 2000, police announced that authorities had frozen $670 million in Swiss bank accounts controlled by the family and associates of former Nigerian dictator Sani Abacha. Nigeria had requested the move, claiming that Abacha illegally siphoned money out of Nigeria during his five-year reign that ended with his death in 1998. UBS and Credit Suisse helped draw up a code of conduct to deter money-laundering that was adopted by a group of major international banks in October 2000.

Economy. Switzerland benefited from an economic upturn that swept across Europe in 2000. Economists expected the *gross domestic product* (the total of all goods and services produced in a given year) to grow by more than 3.5 percent compared with 1.5 percent in 1999.

☐ Tom Buerkle

See also **Europe.**

Syria. President Hafez al-Assad, who seized power in Syria in 1970, died on June 10, 2000, at age 69. An ardent standard bearer of Arab nationalism and a bitter foe of Israel, Assad was often referred to as the "Lion of Damascus." He was a member of Alawite, a minority Muslim sect to which only 12 percent of Syrians belong. As a young man, he was active in the movement to win Syrian independence from French rule, which was achieved in 1946. Assad took power in a bloodless *coup* (overthrow) when he was the Syrian minister of defense. He subsequently held an iron grip on Syria by eliminating all rivals, building a cult of personality, and quelling dissent.

Prior to Assad's death, some analysts believed he might conclude a peace treaty with Israel to help end Syria's economic and political isolation. However, during a meeting in Geneva, Switzerland, on March 26, 2000, U.S. President Bill Clinton failed to convince Assad to resume peace talks with Israel, which had stalled in January. Assad insisted that there could be no peace without the return of the Golan Heights, Syrian land captured by Israel during the 1967 Arab-Israeli war.

Succession. On July 17, 2000, Assad's son, Bashar, a 34-year-old, British-trained ophthalmologist, was inaugurated as president after taking 97 percent of the vote in a one-candidate referendum on July 10. Bashar al-Assad was also

Pallbearers carry the casket of Hafez al-Assad, the president of Syria, through the streets of his hometown, Qardaha, in June 2000. Assad died on June 10 at age 69. He had ruled Syria for 30 years as a champion of Arab nationalism and foe of Israel. Assad was succeeded by his 34-year-old son, Bashar.

Taiwan's President Chen Shui-bian (left) and Vice President Annette Lu greet crowds in front of the Presidential Building in Taipei, the capital, after Chen's inauguration in May 2000 ended 50 years of Nationalist rule.

named head of the armed forces and secretary general of the ruling Baath Party.

Upon assuming the presidency, Bashar al-Assad promised to revitalize the economy, reform government, and uphold his father's goal of recovering the Golan Heights. The younger Assad had been groomed to succeed his father after the death of his older brother Basil in 1994. Although Bashar never held a public post, his father had given him responsibility for overseeing Lebanon, a nation in which Syria maintained 35,000 troops.

Bashar al-Assad cultivated a broader public appeal than his father by courting Syrian businessmen, expanding public access to the Internet, and assuming a low-key public profile. He also initiated an anticorruption campaign that led to the arrest of three former high-ranking Syrian officials during the first half of 2000.

Anti-Israel moves praised. In October, Fayez al-Sayegh, head of the Syrian Radio Authority, praised Morocco, Tunisia, and Oman for cutting ties with Israel. These nations blamed Israel for an outbreak of violence in Jerusalem, the West Bank, and the Gaza Strip, which between September and December had resulted in the deaths of more than 300 people, most of them Palestinians. □ Christine Helms

See also **Israel; Lebanon; Middle East; People in the news** (Assad, Bashar al-).

Taiwan. Chen Shui-bian became president of Taiwan on May 20, 2000, in the first democratic transfer of power in 5,000 years of Chinese history. Chen, the leader of the opposition Democratic Progressive Party (DPP), was elected on March 18 with only 39 percent of the vote after the long-ruling Kuomintang (KMT), or Nationalist, party split, and its official candidate came in third behind a party rebel.

Chen's predecessor, Lee Teng-hui, took responsibility for the KMT's defeat and resigned as party chairman on March 24. During his 12 years as president, Lee had transformed Taiwan into one of the most democratic states in Asia.

The 2000 election campaign focused on domestic issues and eliminating a corrupt combination of politics, business, and gangsters. However, voting was overshadowed by relations with China, which regarded Taiwan as a renegade province. The DPP had long advocated independence for the island, while the KMT considered Taiwan part of China and sought reunification.

Chinese threats. During the election campaign, Chinese officials declared Chen an unacceptable candidate because he was opposed to reunification with China. The officials tried to sway voters' opinions by threatening to use force if Taiwan refused to pursue reunification. During the election campaign, Chen said he would not declare independence or hold a referendum on reunification unless China first used force.

After taking office as president, Chen showed flexibility in relations with the mainland, and China toned down its rhetoric. To avoid criticizing Chen, China attacked his vice president, Annette Lu, for advocating independence.

China's Defense Minister Chi Haotian told visiting U.S. Defense Secretary William Cohen in July that China reserved the right to use force against Taiwan, but that it had no intention of doing so. In September, the United States announced that it would supply air combat missiles to Taiwan if China acquired a similar weapons system.

Politics. With the legislature still controlled by the KMT, Chen named KMT leader Tang Fei as prime minister. The legislature, however, blocked reforms. Citing poor health, Tang resigned in October and was replaced by Chang Chun-hsiung, a DPP leader who had been deputy prime minister.

In October, Chen canceled work on a nuclear power station favored by the KMT. The KMT responded by threatening to launch a campaign to remove Chen from the presidency.

Economics. Taiwan's gross national product in 2000 topped $316.6 billion. Taiwan remained competitive in electronics, and officials expected foreign trade to grow. ☐ Henry S. Bradsher

See also **Asia; China.**

Tajikistan. Parliamentary elections in February and March 2000 completed the peace process that had halted civil war in Tajikistan in 1997. A presidential election in November 1999 and the parliamentary elections in 2000 provided President Emomali Rahmonov with major victories. He easily won a second term in office in November 1999, and his allies in the People's Democratic Party dominated the new parliament in 2000, taking 65 percent of the party-list vote in the elections.

Members of the Islamic Revival Party (IRP), the government's chief opponents in the 1992-1997 civil war, were particularly disappointed in their showing in the 2000 election. The IRP had hoped to capture 50 percent of the 63 seats in the new parliament, but instead took just two. The IRP's image was hurt by the group's association with Islamic guerrillas who waged military operations against neighboring Uzbekistan.

The Uzbek government accused Tajikistan of allowing the guerrillas to operate from bases in Tajik territory. IRP leader Sayo Abdullo Nuri denied that Tajikistan supported the guerrillas, but the dispute led to increased tensions between Tajikistan and Uzbekistan throughout 2000.

☐ Steven L. Solnick

See also **Asia; Uzbekistan.**

Tanzania. See **Africa.**

Taxation. U.S. President Bill Clinton vetoed a bill in August 2000 that would have cut taxes for nearly all married couples in the United States. The bill would have eliminated a tax provision popularly known as the "marriage penalty." Under the U.S. tax code, many married men and women who both earn incomes pay more taxes than they would if both were single. The legislation would have lowered taxes by approximately $290 billion over 10 years. The U.S. House of Representatives voted 268 to 158 in February to approve the measure. The U.S. Senate voted 61 to 38 in favor of the bill in July.

President Clinton rejected the legislation, claiming that it gave a much larger tax cut to wealthy families than to middle-income couples. In September, the House failed to overturn the president's veto. The 270 to 158 vote was 16 fewer votes than the two-thirds majority necessary to enact the measure over President Clinton's veto.

Estate tax. On September 7, the House failed to override President Clinton's veto of a bill that would have eliminated the federal estate tax, which is a tax on inherited wealth. Representatives voted 274 to 157—14 votes shy of the necessary two-thirds majority.

The president vetoed the bill on August 31. The U.S. Congress had passed legislation to phase out the tax over 10 years, which would have resulted in a loss of an estimated $104 billion in government revenues. The House on June 9 voted 279 to 136 to approve the measure. The Senate voted 59 to 39 in favor of the legislation on July 14.

The federal estate tax is applied to the value of an estate before it has been transferred to the heirs. The tax ranges from 18 percent to 55 percent. Under current federal law, estates valued at up to $675,000 are exempt from the tax, and only about 2 percent of estates are of sufficient size to be taxed. Republicans argued that eliminating the tax was a necessity for families who operate small businesses and farms. Democrats countered that the cut would have benefited the wealthy only.

Constitutional amendment. Representatives in April failed to garner enough votes in support of a proposed amendment to the U.S. Constitution. The amendment would have made it more difficult for Congress to raise taxes. The House voted 234 to 192 in favor of the plan, 50 votes short of the necessary two-thirds majority. Under the proposal, Congress would have been unable to increase taxes unless two-thirds of both houses of Congress approved the measure. Supporters pledged that they would continue to push for the amendment, though some said the measure lacked enough serious support to pass.

☐ Linda P. Campbell and Geoffrey A. Campbell

See also **United States, Government of the.**

Telecommunications companies continued to move toward consolidation in 2000. The Federal Trade Commission (FTC), an independent federal agency that maintains free and fair competition in the economy, voted 5-to-0 on Dec. 14, 2000, to approve plans for the merger of America Online, Incorporated, of Dulles, Virginia, and Time Warner, Incorporated, a New York City-based media corporation. In 2000, AOL was the world's largest Internet service provider, with more than 22 million subscribers. Time Warner was the world's largest media conglomerate with operations in book and magazine publishing; cable television systems and channels; and the film and record industries. The merger offered AOL a means of offering subscribers high-speed Internet services over Time Warner's vast cable systems. It connected Time Warner into AOL's online service, where magazine subscriptions could be sold and films and records advertised. Under the terms of the FTC approval, the new company must abide by a series of conditions designed to ensure that it does not drive other Internet service providers and cable television companies out of business.

Trouble on the regulatory front. MCI WorldCom, Incorporated, of of Clinton, Mississippi, and Sprint Corporation of Westwood, Kansas, called off their proposed merger on July 13 after opposition had mounted in the United States and Europe. Federal Communications Commission (FCC) Chairman William Kennard had expressed concern about consumers being the ultimate losers if the two communications giants merged and drove up long-distance and Internet access rates. U.S. Attorney General Janet Reno announced shortly before the companies called off the merger that the U.S. Department of Justice would sue to block the deal on antitrust grounds.

The big get still bigger. On June 16, FCC officials approved the $65-billion merger of Bell Atlantic Corporation of New York City and GTE Corporation of Stamford, Connecticut. The union produced Verizon Wireless, the largest local phone company in the United States. Verizon controlled 63 million phone lines in 30 states—about one-third of all lines in the United States.

On June 26, regulators reported that Qwest Communications International Incorporated and US West Communications Incorporated, both of of Denver, Colorado, could complete their $36-billion merger. Qwest announced on September 7 that it would cut 11,000 jobs—about 15 percent of its workforce—as part of the merger plan.

SBC Communications Incorporated of San Antonio, Texas, and BellSouth of Atlanta, Georgia, joined wireless operations on October 5. The new company, Cingular Wireless, served customers in 42 of the top 50 markets in the United States.

Deutsche Telekom AG of Germany bid to enter the U.S. market in July with a $51-billion offer for VoiceStream Wireless Corporation of Bellevue, Washington. On August 27, VoiceStream said it would buy Powertel Inc., a West Point, Georgia, cell phone company, for $5.8 billion, after completing the Deutsche Telekom deal.

But is bigger better? State regulators from five states joined forces to demand better service from Chicago-based Ameritech Corporation, a local phone service provider. In July, Ohio officials ordered Ameritech to spend $8.7 million and threatened a $122-million fine if the company failed to improve service. Consumers in Ohio, Michigan, Indiana, Illinois, and Wisconsin had complained of lengthy delays for telephone installation and repairs. Service had deteriorated after Ameritech's $74-billion merger with SBC in 1999. State regulators had raised concerns in 1999 about the quality of customer service but did not block the merger.

In October 2000, giant AT&T Corporation came to symbolize the idea that size does not guarantee success. Amid problems in AT&T's long-distance, cable, and business telephone units, the company's stock plummeted. In October, officials announced that AT&T would break into four businesses in an attempt to improve operations and investor confidence. ☐ Tim Jones

See also **Internet; Radio; Television.**

Television. In January 2000, the National Broadcasting Company (NBC) and the American Broadcasting Company (ABC) announced agreements with the National Association for the Advancement of Colored People (NAACP), a civil rights organization headquartered in New York City. The networks pledged to increase the hiring of qualified minority candidates for positions both behind and in front of television cameras. The agreements followed criticism made in 1999 by NAACP President Kweisi Mfume that the major networks failed to foster the creation of racially integrated TV shows. He also threatened a NAACP boycott of network programming.

Although not a direct part of the agreement with the NAACP, the major networks did debut programs with more racially diverse casts in 2000. Veteran TV-show producer Steven Bochco developed "City of Angels," an urban hospital drama with a predominantly black cast, which debuted on CBS in January. In October, ABC launched "Gideon's Crossing," another medical drama, which starred actor Andre Braugher. The series was considered a critical success.

However, CBS executives announced in November that it had canceled "City of Angels" because of consistently low ratings. The series was ranked as CBS's lowest-rated prime-time series, averaging 7.4 million viewers.

Antidrug messages. Officials with the White House Office of National Drug Control Policy announced in January that they would stop previewing scripts of prime-time television programs to determine whether antidrug messages worked into story lines reduced the need for public-service announcements. The office revealed that for two years it had reviewed scripts for antidrug and alcohol abuse messages. The insertion of these messages allowed the networks to decrease the number of public service announcements they were obligated to run. The networks were then able to sell air time that would have gone to the government for half price to regular advertisers for full price.

Many critics denounced the little-known agreement, claiming that it established a precedent for the federal government to influence program content. However, network executives maintained that they had never given control over their content to any governmental office.

Network ratings. During the 1999-2000 television season, ABC became the first network in history to move from third place to first place in a single season. Viewership of the game show "Who Wants To Be A Millionaire?" helped ABC average 14.27 million viewers in prime time, a 20 percent increase over the 1998-1999 television season. During the 1999-2000 season, CBS averaged 12.42 million viewers, with NBC trailing with 12.34 million viewers. Fox's prime time average was 8.97 million; UPN averaged 3.92 million prime time viewers; and the WB network averaged 3.64 million viewers.

Cable disruption. For 39 hours in May 2000, Time Warner Inc., a New York City-based media corporation, disrupted the broadcasting of ABC programming on cable systems owned by Time Warner in seven major metropolitan areas, including New York City and Los Angeles. The disruption resulted from a dispute with the Walt Disney Company, of Burbank, California, which owns ABC. Time Warner blocked ABC's signal to approximately 3.5 million households in an effort to gain leverage in contract negotiations with Disney. Disney had demanded that Time Warner make the Disney Channel part of its system's basic cable package and carry other new Disney channels, which Time Warner refused to do. Federal regulators criticized Time Warner for the disruption.

Reality-based television grew in popularity throughout 2000. Such programs were essentially game shows in which contestants competed not by answering questions but by their real life behavior. The concepts consisted of showing ordinary people in extraordinary situations, allowing themselves to be constantly on camera for the chance to win large cash prizes. Though these shows were unscripted and unrehearsed, they of-

ten took on the excitement of a fictional series.

The most popular such program was "Survivor," which aired on CBS for 13 weeks during the summer. The show put 16 people, ages 22 to 72, on Palau Tiga, a remote island off the coast of Malaysian Borneo, for 39 days. Contestants were required to build an island society while voting one member off the island at periodic intervals. The "survivor" won $1 million.

The series attracted 30 million viewers during its run—a record amount for a summer series—and generated huge, demographically desirable ratings for CBS, which had long been seen as the network for older audiences.

The success of "Survivor" prompted the other major networks to launch similar programs. No other "reality TV" show, however, did as well. Neither the ABC series "Making the Band," which had 25 men competing for five slots in a band, nor CBS's "Big Brother," which had 10 people confined to a house under constant TV surveillance for three months, garnered the ratings of "Survivor." To increase audiences for "Big Brother," CBS offered some of the houseguests money to leave the show early, so they could be replaced with more interesting contestants.

Emmy Award winners in 2000

Comedy
Best Series: "Will & Grace"
Lead Actress: Patricia Heaton, "Everybody Loves Raymond"
Lead Actor: Michael J. Fox, "Spin City"
Supporting Actress: Megan Mullally, "Will & Grace"
Supporting Actor: Sean Hayes, "Will & Grace"

Drama
Best Series: "The West Wing"
Lead Actress: Sela Ward, "Once and Again"
Lead Actor: James Gandolfini, "The Sopranos"
Supporting Actress: Allison Janney, "The West Wing"
Supporting Actor: Richard Schiff, "The West Wing"

Other awards
Drama or Comedy Miniseries or Special: *The Corner*

Variety, Music, or Comedy Series: "Late Show with David Letterman"

Made for Television Movie: *Oprah Winfrey Presents: Tuesdays with Morrie*

Lead Actress in a Miniseries or Special: Halle Berry, *Introducing Dorothy Dandridge*

Lead Actor in a Miniseries or Special: Jack Lemmon, *Oprah Winfrey Presents: Tuesdays with Morrie*

Supporting Actress in a Miniseries or Special: Vanessa Redgrave, *If These Walls Could Talk 2*

Supporting Actor in a Miniseries or Special: Hank Azaria, *Oprah Winfrey Presents: Tuesdays with Morrie*

Richard Hatch (right) outlasted 15 other castaways to win $1 million on the reality-based CBS series "Survivor" during the summer of 2000. Millions of viewers tuned in each week to watch the 13-week series—a survival-of-the-fittest contest on a desert island.

Reality-based programs dominated the airwaves in 2000 as they took viewers from a desert island to a game show paradise.

John Carpenter (below, left) becomes the first contestant to win $1 million on the ABC game show "Who Wants to Be a Millionaire?" in November 1999. The prime-time game show, hosted by Regis Philbin, pushed ABC into first place among television networks in 2000.

In September 2000, the Court TV cable channel launched "Confessions," a controversial half-hour program consisting entirely of the confessions of convicted felons, videotaped by the police and district attorneys across the United States. Although some legal experts considered the show a good educational tool, others called the idea morbid and feared it would distort the understanding of the legal process.

Even public television succumbed to the allure of "reality" programming in 2000. In June and July, PBS aired "The 1900 House," in which a British family spent three months living as people did in 1900.

Marriage melee. On Feb. 15, 2000, the Fox network broadcast "Who Wants to Marry a Multimillionaire?" which many critics labeled one of the worst TV specials ever aired. During the live broadcast, 50 women competed in a beauty pageant-like contest to marry a man they had never met and who remained hidden through most of the broadcast. The millionaire and the winning contestant had their marriage annulled shortly after returning from their honeymoon. Approximately 22 million people watched the program. Fox network officials were embarrassed when it was later discovered that the groom had once been charged with assaulting a girlfriend.

The 2000 Summer Olympic Games, which took place in Sydney, Australia, during the last two weeks in September, proved to be a ratings

disappointment for NBC, which had paid $3.5 billion to broadcast them. The games averaged 14 ratings points (one ratings point equals approximately 1 million households), which was 35 percent lower than ratings for the 1996 Olympic Games in Atlanta.

NBC officials blamed the low viewership on the long time delay between the United States and Australia, which allowed Internet and cable news channels to reveal results before the network could broadcast its taped coverage of the events. Some analysts claimed the fault lay with NBC's coverage, which they said included too many sentimental features and self-promotional inserts.

The new fall season featured film stars in TV sitcoms. Actress and singer Bette Midler played a fictional version of herself in the CBS series "Bette." On ABC, actor Gabriel Byrne portrayed a divorced father in "Madigan Men," while actress Geena Davis starred as a career woman who moves in with a widower and his children on "The Geena Davis Show."

Two Fox series without big stars received critical acclaim in 2000. Critics applauded "Dark Angel," a science fiction drama developed by James Cameron, for its sleek futuristic style. Critics and audiences alike enjoyed "Malcolm in the Middle," an offbeat comedy about a young boy with a high IQ coping with his unpredictable family.

☐ Troy Segal

Tennessee. See **State government.**

Tennis. Pete Sampras and Venus Williams of the United States netted historic victories at Wimbledon in Great Britain in July 2000. Sampras's triumph at Wimbledon made him the most successful player in Grand Slam history, with a record 13 Grand-Slam wins. Williams's seven match victories at Wimbledon, which resulted in her first Grand Slam title, launched a 35-match winning streak. The streak included a straight-set victory in the U.S. Open in September, making Williams the only multiple Grand-Slam winner of 2000. Lindsay Davenport, of the United States, finally managed to snap Williams's winning streak in October in a tournament in Austria.

Australian Open. Lindsay Davenport fought off a furious comeback by Martina Hingis, of Switzerland, on Jan. 29, 2000, to take the Australian Open in Melbourne. Davenport ended Hingis's three-year grip on the Australian Open, winning 6-1, 7-5 and adding the title to the Wimbledon championship Davenport had won in 1999 and the U.S. Open title she won in 1998. Davenport held one of the most lopsided leads in Grand Slam history as she served for the match at 6-1, 5-1, 30-15, but Hingis fought back to 5-5. Davenport swept through the next two games, breaking Hingis at love in the final game.

Top-rated U.S. television series

The following were among the most-watched television series for the 1999-2000 regular season, which ran from Sept. 20, 1999, to May 24, 2000.

1. "Who Wants to Be a Millionaire?" (Tuesday) (ABC)
2. "Who Wants to Be a Millionaire?" (Thursday) (ABC)
3. "Who Wants to Be a Millionaire?" (Sunday) (ABC)
4. "E.R." (NBC)
5. "Friends" (NBC)
6. "NFL Monday Night Football" (ABC)
7. "Frasier" (NBC)
8. "Frasier" (9:30 p.m. rerun) (NBC)
9. "60 Minutes" (CBS)
10. "The Practice" (ABC)
11. "Touched by an Angel" (CBS)
12. (tie) "Everybody Loves Raymond" (CBS)
    "Law and Order" (NBC)
    "NFL Monday Showcase" (ABC)
15. "Jesse" (NBC)
16. (tie) "CBS Sunday Movie" (CBS)
    "Daddio" (NBC)
18. "Stark Raving Mad" (NBC)
19. "NYPD Blue" (ABC)
20. "Dharma & Greg" (ABC)

Venus Williams returns a serve to Lindsay Davenport during the final match at Wimbledon in July 2000. In addition to winning the singles title, Venus and her sister, Serena, became the first sisters to win the Wimbledon doubles title.

Andre Agassi, of the United States, won his second Australian Open and sixth Grand Slam title January 30 in a bruising victory over Russia's Yevgeny Kafelnikov. Agassi used delicate drop shots and dozens of powerful groundstrokes to defeat Kafelnikov 3-6, 6-3, 6-2, 6-4.

French Open. Mary Pierce, a French citizen born in Canada and raised in Florida, became the first French woman in 33 years to win the French Open. Pierce defeated Conchita Martinez on June 10, 2000, in Paris, winning the title 6-2, 7-5. Gustavo Kuerten, of Brazil, won the men's title on June 11, defeating Magnus Norman, of Sweden, 6-2, 6-3, 2-6, 7-6 (7-6). It was the second time Kuerten had won the French Open men's singles title.

Wimbledon. On July 9, Sampras finished a match delayed three times by rain with a serve that Australia's Patrick Rafter could not return. Rafter's forehand went wide, making Sampras a 6-7 (10-12), 7-6 (7-5), 6-4, 6-2 winner. The win was Sampras's 28th straight at Wimbledon and the 53rd in his last 54 matches.

Sampras's seven Wimbledon titles, four U.S. Opens, and two Australian Opens since 1990 made him the all-time leader in Grand Slam titles. Sampras also tied William Renshaw for the most Wimbledon titles, but Renshaw had to play just one match in five of the tournaments he won from 1881 through 1889.

Two days after defeating her sister, Serena, in the semifinals, Venus Williams defeated fellow American Lindsay Davenport in straight sets on July 8, 2000. Williams played aggressively in her 6-3, 7-6 (7-3) victory against Davenport, clocking serves in excess of 110 miles (177 kilometers) per hour throughout the match.

Two days after winning her first Grand Slam title at Wimbledon, Williams teamed with her sister, Serena, to beat Ai Sugiyama and Julie Halard-Decuguis 6-3, 6-2 on July 10. The victory was the first for sisters in the history of women's doubles at Wimbledon.

U.S. Open. Two months after beating Lindsay Davenport at Wimbledon for her first Grand Slam title, Williams rallied from being down 4-1 in the first set to top Davenport 6-4, 7-5 to win the U.S. Open on September 9. Williams defeated Martina Hingis, of Switzerland, in the semifinals on September 8 to reach the finals.

In the men's U.S. Open tournament, Sampras appeared to have a good chance to add to his 13 Grand-Slam victories. However, he was stopped cold in the title match on September 10, suffering the worst Grand Slam defeat of his career at the hands of Marat Safin. Safin, a 20-year-old Russian, beat Sampras 6-4, 6-3, 6-3, in part because of Safin's 130-mile- (209-kilometer-) per-hour serves. □ Michael Kates

See also **People in the news** (Williams, Venus)

Terrorism. Incidents of terrorism increased throughout the world in 2000, as terrorism continued to be a vehicle for dissatisfied ethnic, cultural, and religious communities seeking recognition, independence, or revenge.

Middle East. On October 12, a small boat packed with explosives rammed into the side of the U.S.S. *Cole*, a Navy destroyer, which was refueling in the Yemeni port of Aden. The explosion ripped a 40-by-40 foot (12-by-12 meter) hole in the hull of the 505-foot (154-meter) ship, killing 17 U.S. sailors and injuring 39 others.

The U.S. Department of Defense subsequently placed U.S. troops stationed in Turkey, Saudi Arabia, Bahrain, and Qatar on the highest alert because of the threat of terrorist attack. Defense officials believed that the attack may have been the work of al Qaeda, a terrorist organization headed by Saudi millionaire Osama bin Laden.

Russia. A wave of bombings, many connected to the violent conflict between the Russian government and the independence-minded province of Chechnya, rocked Russia in the summer of 2000. On July 9, 6 people died and 22 others were injured when a bomb exploded in Vladikavkaz, the capital of Northern Ossetia, which had supported Russia in the 1994-1996 Chechen war of independence. Chechen terrorists were also blamed for a bomb blast in a Moscow pedestrian walkway on Aug. 8, 2000, that killed 11 people and injured nearly 100 others.

South Asia. The tension between India—where the majority of people are Hindu—and Pakistan—where the population is primarily Muslim—over the state of Jammu and Kashmir escalated during 2000. Two-thirds of Kashmir, whose people are primarily Muslims, became part of India in 1947, while Pakistan took control of one-third of the state. Separatist groups waged a violent campaign for Kashmir to withdraw from India throughout the 1990's.

In July 2000, the Hizbul Mujahideen, a militant group that wants Kashmir to become part of Pakistan, called a ceasefire. However, the truce collapsed 15 days later. In August, a series of explosions in Kashmir claimed the lives of nearly 100 people. Separatist groups opposed to the truce claimed responsibility for the attacks. The Hizbul Mujahideen assumed responsibility for a car bomb that exploded on August 10 outside the State Bank of India, killing 12 people and injuring dozens more. On August 14 in northern India, 10 people were killed and 37 injured in a bomb explosion on a train. In September, a bomb in an open-air market in Islamabad, Pakistan, killed 19 people and injured more than 80 others.

Southeast Asia. During the summer of 2000, a series of bomb attacks in Vientiane, the capital

Firefighters remove a victim from a pedestrian walkway under Pushkin Square in central Moscow after a bomb exploded on August 8, killing 11 people and injuring nearly 100 others. Authorities attributed the attack to Chechen terrorists.

of Laos, injured at least 40 people. Laotian authorities blamed the explosions on antigovernment elements within the Hmong, an ethnic group that had supported U.S. forces during the Vietnam War (1957-1975) and have been battling the Communist Laotian government intermittently since.

In Indonesia, a car bomb ripped through an underground garage in the Jakarta Stock Exchange building on Sept. 13, 2000, killing 15 people and injuring 20 others. The blast followed a series of explosions that coincided with major developments in the investigation into allegations of corruption by former president Suharto, who ruled Indonesia for 32 years until 1998.

Western Europe. After a breakdown in peace talks between the Spanish government and Basque separatists in 1999, the separatist group ETA launched a series of bombings across Spain in 2000 that left 20 people dead. ETA stands for Basque Homeland and Freedom in the Basque language. On October 30, a car bomb exploded in Madrid, killing a Supreme Court justice, his driver, and his bodyguard, and wounding 35 people. Tens of thousands of people protested in the streets of Madrid against the violence.

□ Richard E. Rubenstein

See also **India; Middle East; Russia; Spain.**

Texas. See Dallas; Houston; State government.

Thailand. The National Counter Corruption Commission (NCCC), an investigative body created by the Thai government under the 1997 reformist constitution, began to affect politics in Thailand in 2000. The commission was designed to clean up the political system, which had long been driven by patronage and illegal money.

In 2000, a Thai politician was convicted of corruption. The NCCC revealed that Sanan Kachornprasart, the interior minister and secretary-general of the Democratic Party, had falsified a $1.2-million loan. Kachornprasart resigned as interior minister and as secretary-general.

Thailand held elections in March for the upper house of the parliament, whose members had been appointed prior to the adoption of the 1997 constitution. The election took 145 days to complete and cost $57.5 million after Thailand's election commission rejected a third of the elected politicians for buying votes.

Economic growth in Thailand slowed in 2000 but continued its recovery from the 1997 Asian recession. In 2000, small companies continued to have difficulty raising money for expansion, and one-quarter of all bank loans had not been repaid. However, this situation was an improvement over 1999, when nearly one-half of all loans went unpaid. □ Henry S. Bradsher

See also **Asia.**

Theater. Many theatergoers in 2000 felt a clear sense that an era had come to an end with the deaths of three giants of the theater; the closing of two of the most successful Broadway musicals in history; and the continuing rise of corporate producers. In 2000, more legitimate plays were produced on the Broadway stage than musicals for the first time in recent memory.

Deaths in the theater world. The British theater suffered a major loss in 2000 with the death of 96-year-old Sir John Gielgud on May 21. Gielgud was the last survivor of a great triumvirate of British actors that included Sir Ralph Richardson and Sir Laurence Olivier. Critics considered Gielgud one of the greatest Shakespearean actors of the 1900's. He had also enjoyed a late-blooming career in film and television in such varied fare as the popular film *Arthur* (1981) and art-house favorite *Elizabeth* (1998).

Two of the most influential independent U.S. producers of the 1900's died within days of each other in 2000. Alexander H. Cohen, a highly prolific producer on Broadway and to a lesser extent in London's West End, died on April 22 at age 79. Cohen produced some 100 shows, which displayed a remarkably broad range, from Richard Burton as *Hamlet* in 1964 to a British comedy team in *Beyond the Fringe* in 1962.

David Merrick died on April 25, 2000, at age 88. During his long career, he produced more than 80 shows and won six Tony awards and two special Tony awards for his contributions to Broadway. Merrick, who produced such blockbusters as *Hello Dolly* (1964) and *42nd Street* (1980), was known to stop at nothing to see his shows succeed. Merrick's fans called him "The Barnum of Broadway," while his enemies preferred the title, "The Abominable Showman."

Many theater insiders agreed that Cohen's and Merrick's deaths had brought to an end the age of the independent producer, the individual who controlled all aspects of bringing a show to the stage. The independent producer had been replaced by corporate producers or by groups banded together to raise the ever-escalating amounts of capital needed to mount shows.

Corporate involvement in Broadway productions became particularly evident in 2000. In July, the booming, Manhattan-based Roundabout Theater Company opened its latest performance space, the American Airlines Theater, named for one of its major sponsors. The theater was actually the renovated, historic Selwyn Theater, located on 42nd Street, a neighbor of two other venerable Broadway theaters that in 1998 had been joined and renamed for another corporate sponsor, the Ford Motor Company.

In February 2000, Miramax film company entered the world of commercial theater produc-

Brian Stokes Mitchell stars with Marin Mazzie in the 2000 Broadway production of Cole Porter's 1948 classic musical *Kiss Me, Kate*. The production won five Tony awards, including Best Direction of a Musical for Michael Blakemore and Best Leading Actor in a Musical for Mitchell.

tion for the first time, becoming one of several coproducers of the Broadway transfer of Tom Stoppard's *The Real Thing*.

The Walt Disney Company of Burbank, California, continued in 2000 to be the most important corporate presence in theater. Disney mounted its third Broadway musical, *Aida*, in March. The musical retold the story of Verdi's opera about love and intrigue in ancient Egypt. However, Disney's *Aida* was not nearly as successful with critics as Disney's previous musical, *The Lion King*, which continued a successful run on Broadway and also opened in London. Despite its mixed critical reception, *Aida* won four Tony awards and proved popular with audiences.

Tony awards. Controversy surrounding the Tony awards was one Broadway tradition that did not change in 2000. The fuss in 2000 focused around a production called *Contact*, which had premiered at Lincoln Center's small downstairs theater, the Mitzi E. Newhouse Theater, in late 1999. In March 2000, the producers transferred the musical to Lincoln Center's Vivian Beaumont Theater. *Contact* earned rave reviews and was nominated for several Tonys in the new musicals category. This raised the ire of Local 802 of the musicians' union and a group of Broadway orchestrators, who protested the show's classification as a musical. They argued that the produc-

Tony Award winners in 2000

Best Play, *Copenhagen*, by Michael Frayn

Best Musical, *Contact*

Best Play Revival, *The Real Thing*

Best Musical Revival, *Kiss Me, Kate*

Leading Actor in a Play, Stephen Dillane, *The Real Thing*

Leading Actress in a Play, Jennifer Ehle, *The Real Thing*

Leading Actor in a Musical, Brian Stokes Mitchell, *Kiss Me, Kate*

Leading Actress in a Musical, Heather Headley, *Aida*

Featured Actor in a Play, Roy Dotrice, *A Moon for the Misbegotten*

Featured Actress in a Play, Blair Brown, *Copenhagen*

Featured Actor in a Musical, Boyd Gaines, *Contact*

Featured Actress in a Musical, Karen Ziemba, *Contact*

Direction of a Play, Michael Blakemore, *Copenhagen*

Direction of a Musical, Michael Blakemore, *Kiss Me, Kate*

Book of a Musical, Richard Nelson, *James Joyce's The Dead*

Original Musical Score, Elton John and Tim Rice, *Aida*

Orchestration, Don Sebesky, *Kiss Me, Kate*

Scenic Design, Bob Crowley, *Aida*

Costume Design, Martin Pakledinaz, *Kiss Me, Kate*

Lighting Design, Natasha Katz, *Aida*

Choreography, Susan Stroman, *Contact*

Regional Theater, The Utah Shakespearean Festival, Cedar City

Special Awards, T. Edward Hambleton and *Dame Edna: The Royal Tour*

Tony Honors for Excellence in Theater, Eileen Heckart, Sylvia Herscher, and *City Center Encores*

tion featured no new musical compositions nor live musical performances. Instead, the show revolved around a series of dance numbers performed to prerecorded, preexisting tunes. The show was eventually allowed to compete and won four Tonys, which included the all-important Best Musical award.

British shows and artists dominated the Tony awards in June. Veteran director Michael Blakemore (who was born in Australia but made his career in England) made history by becoming the first director to win directing awards for both a play, *Copenhagen*, and a musical, *Kiss Me, Kate*, in a single year. *Copenhagen*, which originated at Britain's Royal National Theater, also won Best New Play honors. Tom Stoppard's *The Real Thing*, which transferred from London's Donmar Warehouse Theater to the Ethel Barrymore Theater in April, won the two top acting awards for plays.

London theater continued to boom in late 2000, the busiest time on the London stage in recent memory. High-profile productions included the West End hit *Madame Melville*, by U.S. expatriate Richard Nelson, about an unlikely liaison between a young student, played by 1990's child film star Macaulay Culkin, and his music teacher. Other well-received plays included a production of Chekhov's *The Cherry Orchard* at the Royal National Theatre, featuring Vanessa and Corin Redgrave, and a West End revival of Harold Pinter's *The Caretaker* with Michael Gambon, who reaffirmed his reputation as the finest British actor of his generation.

Broadway closings. Two of the most important figures in world theater, particularly musical theater—Lord Andrew Lloyd Webber and Sir Cameron Mackintosh—saw their empires shifting in 2000 with the closing on Broadway of two of their flagship hits. Lloyd Webber's *Cats*, the longest-running show in Broadway history, closed in September after nearly 18 years at the Winter Garden Theater. On December 31, Mackintosh's *Miss Saigon* played its last performance at the Broadway Theater after a nearly 10-year run. Both shows had waned at the box office in recent years. While Lloyd Webber and Mackintosh remained active in the field—both premiered new musicals in London during the summer of 2000—the closing of these two productions seemed to signal that the age of the *megamusical* (elaborately produced musicals with large marketing schemes) was coming to an end.

Broadway plays. A significant increase in the production of legitimate plays appeared to signal a new trend in the New York City theater scene in 2000. While critics in the 1980's and early 1990's predicted the death of the legitimate play on Broadway, there were more new legitimate plays in 2000 than there were musicals. Sam

Shepard's *True West*, featuring acclaimed film actors Philip Seymour Hoffman and John C. Reilly alternating the leading roles of two brawling brothers was the biggest hit of the year. Other significant productions of 2000 included David Auburn's *Proof*, about the tangled emotional relationship between a recently deceased mathematician and his unstable daughter, and *The Tale of the Allergist's Wife,* a warm comedy by Charles Busch, which proved to be a star vehicle for Linda Lavin. Both plays had been produced by the nonprofit Manhattan Theater Club and later transferred to Broadway.

Actors Theatre of Louisville. Jon Jory, the producing director of the Actors Theatre of Louisville (ATL), retired in 2000, closing another era in American theatre. Jory ran the Kentucky theatre for 31 years and created its Humana Festival of New American Plays, an annual staging of new works that attracts the best and the brightest theatre artists and professionals from all over the United States. Jory also taught four hours a week for 20 years in ATL's acting classes. In 2000, he took a position teaching acting and directing at the University of Washington in Seattle, where he previously conducted master classes.

☐ Karen Fricker

See also **Deaths.**

Togo. See Africa.

Toronto. Canadian Prime Minister Jean Chretien and Ontario Premier Mike Harris joined Toronto Mayor Mel Lastman in announcing on Oct. 20, 2000, that each level of government planned to contribute $500 million (all amounts in Canadian dollars) for the rehabilitation of Toronto's waterfront. The city's contribution primarily consisted of waterfront land.

The announcement was the first step in a $12- billion plan developed by Toronto-based financier Robert Fung. His plan called for the cleanup of polluted land and the creation of a network of parks and housing along the waterfront.

Olympic hopefuls. The Fung plan included proposed sites for the 2008 Summer Olympic Games, for which the Toronto City Council decided in February 2000 to bid. Premier Harris flew to the Sydney games in Australia in September to lobby the Lausanne, Switzerland-based International Olympic Committee for Toronto as a possible host of the 2008 games.

Expansion. Greater Toronto experienced enormous expansion in 2000. More than 42,200 housing units, almost all of which were single family dwellings, were built in Greater Toronto, which consists of the city and four surrounding urban regions—Halton, Peel, York, and Durham.

The impact of growth became a major political issue in 2000, when a consortium of developers announced plans to build some 12,000 houses on the Oak Ridges Moraine near the small city of Richmond Hill, located immediately north of Toronto. The moraine is a ridge of glacial silt and gravel that cuts 99 miles (160 kilometers) across the northern region of the Greater Toronto area. Conservationists protested that the moraine was responsible for absorbing water and feeding the headwaters of 30 rivers and streams that flowed south to Lake Ontario and north to Lake Simcoe.

On February 23 and again on April 6, the council of Richmond Hill was forced to rent a hotel ballroom to accommodate all the people who wanted to speak out against proposals. The Richmond Hill Council turned the housing proposal down in April, and the provincial government proposed a corridor that would protect the moraine. In response, five development companies appealed to the Ontario Municipal Board (OMB), an independent provincial agency with the power to overrule local councils on planning matters. A two-member panel of the municipal board began hearing the developers' appeal at the end of May. The hearing was expected to last until the spring of 2001.

Adams mine. Concern about urban impact on the environment in 2000 drove the Toronto City Council into a rowdy four-day debate on garbage disposal in October. Toronto proposed sending garbage by train 250 miles (402 kilometers) north to the Adams Mine, an abandoned open-pit site near the gold-mining town of Kirkland Lake. Protestors filled the Toronto Council chamber, claiming that the use of the open-pit site might jeopardize the environment.

On October 11, the City Council approved the Adams mine by a vote of 32 to 24. However, the private consortium that won the garbage contract, Rail-Cycle North, objected to the stripping of a clause that had held the taxpayers responsible for any "unavoidable costs."

Municipal elections. On Nov.13, 2000, Toronto and other Ontario cities held municipal elections to reduce the number of councillors from 57 to 44, as mandated by the provincial government. The reduction in seats meant that many of the councillors had to choose which new ward to run in. Six councillors decided not to retire. In five other wards, political veterans were pitted against each other.

Mayor Mel Lastman cruised to an easy victory, winning 80 percent of the popular vote. However, the newly elected council was more liberal than the previous one and political analysts predicted that Lastman would face increased opposition in his new term.   □ David Stein

See also **Canada; Canadian provinces; City; Montreal.**

Toys and games. Retail toy sales in the United States in 2000 rose only 3 percent over 1999 sales, as analysts had expected. In 1999, sales had increased by an exceptionally high 8 percent over 1998 sales. The average yearly growth in the toy industry is 2 to 5 percent. On-line toy sales continued to climb, especially during the fourth quarter of 2000, with nearly 10 million consumers spending approximately $600 million on toys, games, and family entertainment products. The holiday season traditionally accounts for about 53 percent of all toy sales.

On a roll. Scooters proved to be the hottest trend in playthings in the United States in 2000, despite the fact that companies such as Radio Flyer, Incorporated, of Chicago had marketed the foot-powered vehicles as early as the 1930's. Children and adults alike hopped on the scooter fad, with sales in 2000 topping 5 million units, or more than $500 million at retail cost. The scooter-riding craze began as urban commuters opted for the lightweight vehicles as an alternative mode of transportation on crowded city streets. The trend spread to college campuses nationwide and then ultimately to the children's market. The Razor, made by Razor USA of Cerritos, California, and the Micro Scooter, manufactured by the Huffy Corporation's Huffy Bicycle Company division, based in Miamisburg, Ohio, were the two most popular models.

Short circuits. One of the most eagerly anticipated new products of the year, the PlayStation 2 video game manufactured by Sony Corporation of Tokyo, Japan, proved to be in short supply for the 2000 holidays. Because of a components shortage, the number of units delivered to retail stores was severely reduced, leaving consumers standing in long lines in hopes of purchasing one of the state-of-the-art machines. In addition to video games, the PlayStation 2's drive enabled users to play DVD movies and audio CD's and to access the Internet.

A shortage of electronic microprocessor "chips" also affected the shipment of some high-tech toys from other manufacturers, including Mattel Incorporated of El Segundo, California, and Hasbro Incorporated of Pawtucket, Rhode Island, the two largest toy companies, respectively, in the United States.

Virtual Fido. Proving that toy manufacturers were barking up the right tree, consumers fell in love with the year's newest high-tech trend—robotic pets. Best sellers included Poo-Chi, from Tiger Electronics Limited of Vernon Hills, Illinois, and Tekno, produced by Manley Toy Quest of New York City. The electronic Poo-Chi could stand, sit, dance on its tiptoes, bark, sing six different songs, and respond to voice commands. He could move his head, eyes, ears, legs, and tail.

Poo-Chi's reactions were made to adapt and change the more a child played with the toy. Tekno the Robotic Puppy could walk, bark, talk and cry, and wag his tail. His sensors allowed him to "experience" and respond appropriately to dark, light, and noise. Both toys sold at retail for under $40.

Millionaires and magic. Licensed merchandise accounted for 47 percent of all toy sales in the United States in 2000. The most popular of these products were related to the top-rated television show "Who Wants to Be a Millionaire?" and best-selling Harry Potter novels. The Pressman Toy Corporation of New York City translated the TV quiz show that captured America's fancy, "Who Wants to Be a Millionaire?," into a best-selling board game. And with more than 40 million books sold worldwide, Harry Potter toys, gifts, and novelties were must-haves for fans of the bespectacled hero.

The silly season. There was no upstream fight for a singing, wall-mounted plastic fish named Big Mouth Billy Bass. Fishermen, kids, and adults reeled in this goofy charmer of a novelty item in 2000. At the touch of a button, Billy Bass, manufactured by Gemmy Industries Corporation of Irving, Texas, flapped his tail and turned his head while singing "Take Me to the River" and "Don't Worry, Be Happy."   □ Diane P. Cardinale

Track and field. The most anticipated highlight of the pre-Olympic track and field season in 2000 turned into the most disappointing. Sprinters Maurice Greene and Michael Johnson, both world-record holders, enjoyed more success with their war of words off the track than they did competing in the 200-meter sprint at the U.S. Olympic trials, held in July in Sacramento, California. After weeks of boasting in the media, both men injured themselves during the final qualifying race and failed to finish. In other track and field highlights of 2000, Elijah Lagat of Kenya won the closest Boston Marathon in history, and world records were set in the women's javelin and the women's 800-meter relay.

Sprinter wars. The much-hyped showdown between sprinters Maurice Greene and Michael Johnson in the final Olympic qualifying heat in the 200-meter sprint at the U.S. Olympic trials in July—the most anticipated race of the year—became one of the year's most anticlimactic sporting events. Leading up to the final, Greene and Johnson had engaged in a verbal sparring match for weeks in the press. The two had begun feuding publicly in 1999 when Greene's manager, Emanuel Hudson, suggested that Johnson was avoiding head-to-head competition with Greene. Johnson had not competed against Greene at the 1999 U.S. Championships due to a leg injury.

A modern, collapsible version of the classic scooter proved to be the hottest toy of 2000, with more than 5 million of the lightweight vehicles sold in the United States alone.

Michael Johnson of the United States collapses with a hamstring injury during the 200-meter sprint at the Olympic trials in July. Both Johnson and competitor Maurice Greene failed to qualify for the event.

World outdoor track and field records established in 2000

Event	Holder	Country	Where set	Date	Record
Men indoor					
1,000 meters	Wilson Kipketer	Denmark	Birmingham, England	February 20	2:14.96
Women indoor					
Pole vault	Stacy Dragila	USA	Atlanta, Georgia	March 3	15' 1¾" 4.62m
Men outdoor					
No new world records were set in 2000.					
Women outdoor					
20,000 meters	Tegla Loroupe	Kenya	Borgholzhausen, Germany	September 3	1:05:26.6
3,000-meter steeplechase	Cristina Iloc-Casandra	Romania	Reims, France	August 30	9:40.20
Pole vault	Stacy Dragila	USA	Sacramento, California	July 23	15' 2" (4.63 m)
Javelin throw	Trine Solberg-Hattestad	Norway	Oslo, Norway	July 28	227' 11" (69.48m)
20,000-meter walk	Rossella Giordano	Italy	Almada, Portugal	August 4	1:30:48.3

m = meters

Source: International Amateur Athletic Federation (IAAF).

Even before the final heat, Greene, the world record holder in the 100-meter sprint, made a taunting gesture toward Johnson, the world-record holder and reigning Olympic champion at 200 and 400 meters. The taunt may have had an effect on Johnson, who injured his right quadriceps muscle during his own heat.

This was only a prelude to the 200-meter final. Seconds after the race began, Johnson grabbed his left hamstring and stumbled. Seconds after Johnson fell, Greene also grimaced, hobbled a few steps, and stopped running. Johnson had to be wheeled off of the track, while Greene walked away under his own power. Neither man qualified to run in the 200-meter event at the Olympic games in Sydney, Australia.

Marathons. Kenyan Elijah Lagat won the men's division of the Boston Marathon on April 17, 2000, making it the 10th consecutive Boston Marathon won by a Kenyan runner. Lagat outlasted Ethiopia's Gezahenge Abera and fellow Kenyan Moses Tanui in the closest finish in the race's 104-year history. Lagat and Abera both recorded the same official time of 2 hours 9 minutes 47 seconds, but Lagat broke the tape first.

In the women's division, Catherine Ndereba became the first Kenyan woman to win the event. Ndereba, who finished with a time of 2 hours 26 minutes 11 seconds, thwarted the bid of Ethiopia's Fatuma Roba to become the first participant—male or female—to win the race four consecutive times. Like the men, the women's finish in 2000 was the closest in history.

Penn Relays. The U.S. relay teams, with star sprinters Marion Jones, Maurice Greene, and Michael Johnson running sizzling anchor legs, swept the men's and women's 400-, 800-, and 1,600-meter events at the Penn Relays on April 29 in Philadelphia. The women's U.S. team set a new world record of 1 minute 27.46 seconds in the 800-meter event.

World records. Norway's Trine Hattestad broke the women's javelin world record on July 28 at the Bislett Games in Oslo, Norway, with a throw of 69.47 meters. Hattestad made her big throw in the last round of the competition. Hattestad set the old mark of 68.22 meters at the Golden Gala meet in Rome on July 2.

Stacy Dragila of the United States tied the world outdoor record in the women's pole vault at the Modesto Relays in Modesto, California, on May 13 by clearing 4.60 meters. Dragila also set a new world indoor pole vault record for the third time in the 2000 season. She cleared 4.61 meters on March 3, during the U.S. Track and Field Championships at the Georgia Dome in Atlanta.

□ Michael Kates

See also **Olympics: A Special Report.**
Transit. See Transportation.

Transportation. In July 2000, the Burlington Northern Santa Fe Corporation (BNSF) of Fort Worth, Texas, and the Canadian National Railway Company (CN) of Montreal, Canada, announced their decision to abandon a December 1999 proposal to create the largest railroad in North America. The $62-billion merger would have formed a company that spanned Canada, the western United States, and the Mississippi Valley with 50,000 miles (80,467 kilometers) of track. The cancellation came in the wake of a decision by the Surface Transportation Board (STB) to impose a 15-month moratorium on new merger proposals. The Washington, D.C.- based STB is an agency that regulates the business practices of the railroad industry in the United States. The board called the moratorium in response to complaints of difficulties caused by previous mergers, including disruption and poor service. On October 3, the STB, attempting to prevent future monopolies, proposed new rules that would make mergers more difficult for major railroads.

Train whistles. In January, a proposal from the Federal Railroad Administration (FRA) recommended that trains in the United States be required to sound their horns at every highway railroad crossing, except where gates that blocked the entire road had been erected. The Washington, D.C.-based FRA sets railroad safety standards and inspects locomotives, cars, tracks, and signal systems. Approximately 400 people were killed annually at crossings in the United States during the 1990's. Fearing that they would not qualify under the new rules, residents of some Illinois and Wisconsin communities that had previously banned the sounding of train whistles lobbied Congress to amend the proposal.

Amtrak. The first high-speed train in the United States, the Acela Express, made its maiden run from Washington, D.C., to Boston on Nov. 16, 2000. The train hit 150 miles (240 kilometers) per hour on the run between New York City and Boston. Amtrak, a semipublic corporation that operates intercity passenger trains in the United States, planned high-speed trains in three other rail corridors—from Chicago to Detroit; Chicago to Minneapolis, Minnesota; and Chicago to St. Louis, Missouri. Technical problems delayed the introduction of the new Acela train by more than a year.

Truck driver hours. On April 25, officials with the U.S. Department of Transportation (DOT) announced proposals for the first changes since the 1930's in the number of hours that truck drivers can legally remain on the road. DOT is an executive department of the U.S. government that works to guarantee the availability of safe, economical, and efficient transportation in the United States. Under DOT's new

Construction continues in 2000 on Boston's Big Dig, a subterranean system designed to reroute automobile traffic underground and under Boston Harbor. Officials expected the public works project, one of the largest in U.S. history, to be completed in 2004.

proposal, drivers must have 10 hours of continuous rest each day and take an additional 2 hours in breaks. Officials suggested that the new rules were more appropriate to a human being's *circadian rhythm* (natural rhythms timed to the cycle of day and night) than were the old rules. However, industry opposition led the U.S. Congress to delay implementation by at least a year.

Transit strike. Residents of Los Angeles were without bus and commuter service for 4 ½ weeks in September and October 2000 due to a strike by drivers. The strike began September 16 and lasted for 32 days, stranding an estimated 450,000 commuters. The dispute was settled on October 17, with pay raises and improved pensions. The union agreed to allow the hiring of more part-time employees.

Gas prices increased substantially in the United States in May and June 2000, particularly in the Midwest. The increases were due to a combination of factors, including attempts by oil-producing countries to increase the price of crude oil, and the introduction of a new type of less-polluting gasoline. In June, prices exceeded $2 a gallon in some parts of the country.

Congestion pricing. The mayor of London, Ken Livingstone, proposed in July that all drivers entering central London between 7:00 a.m. and 7:00 p.m. on weekdays be charged five pounds. The mayor hoped the tariff would reduce road congestion and provide revenue for modernizing the public transportation system. In 2000, only Singapore and three cities in Norway had adopted such a system.

Suez Canal. In August, the government of Egypt announced that it would widen and deepen the Suez Canal to permit the passage of super tankers. The canal connects the Mediterranean and Red seas, allowing ships to move between Asia and Europe without traveling around Africa. Engineers planned to increase the width of the canal from 380 to 440 yards (345 to 400 meters) and the depth from 72 to 82 feet (22 to 25 meters). The increases will allow the canal to accommodate most contemporary ships.

Pollution standards. U.S. President Bill Clinton in December approved new rules to reduce levels of diesel pollutants by 2010. Under the rules, manufacturers must remove sulfur from all diesel fuel used for heavy-duty trucks and buses by 2010. The rules also required engine manufacturers to reduce the emission of nitrogen oxide and soot within the next 10 years. The regulations were scheduled to begin in 2006.

☐ Ian Savage

See also **Automobile; Public health and safety.**

Trinidad and Tobago. See West Indies.

Tunisia. See Middle East.

Turkey. A major scandal rocked Turkey in 2000 after police discovered evidence that security forces of the *secular* (nonreligious) government had collaborated with the radical Islamic group Hizbullah to eradicate the Kurdish Workers Party (PKK) during the early 1990's. The PKK was a guerrilla group that had waged a war for self-rule for Kurds against Turkey since 1984. Kurds are an ethnic group living in mountainous regions of southwestern Asia. Hizbullah sought to establish an Islamic government in Turkey.

The scandal emerged in January 2000, after police began a series of raids on Hizbullah hideouts to search for some 200 missing individuals, mainly Kurdish businessmen opposed to militant Islam. Investigators soon discovered the mutilated bodies of a number of missing persons buried beneath various hideouts. By April, approximately 65 bodies had been recovered. Turks were stunned to learn that one of the victims had been Konca Kuris, a well-known Muslim feminist and intellectual.

After the discovery of the bodies, many politicians and news commentators charged that some members of the Turkish military may have collaborated with Hizbullah and encouraged members of the group to kill Kurds. Critics alleged that the government of the early 1990's aided Hizbullah because it regarded the PKK as a greater security threat. Turkish officials have viewed the PKK as less of a threat since the group's leader, Abdullah Ocalan, was arrested in 1999.

Limits to democracy. Former Prime Minister Necmettin Erbakan was sentenced in March 2000 to one year in prison for a 1994 speech, triggering a heated debate in Turkey about democracy. Erbakan, an Islamist, was sentenced under a law that forbade public "incitement" on religious or ethnic grounds. On Feb. 28, 2000, three Kurdish mayors, who had been arrested a week earlier on charges of supporting terrorism, were released from prison pending trial. Some Europeans viewed the mayors as members of a nonviolent Kurdish movement. In December 1999, the European Union had urged Turkey to support human rights reforms as a condition for membership. However, Turkey's hardliners argued that greater social freedom would lead to unrest.

Greek relations. The abrupt withdrawal in October 2000 of Greek forces from a North Atlantic Treaty Organization military exercise dealt a setback to Turkish-Greek relations. The withdrawal took place after the Turkish military blocked Greek warplanes from flying over a contested region of the Aegean Sea. In January, Turkish and Greek officials had signed a series of accords to end decades of tension.

☐ Christine Helms

See also **Greece; Middle East.**

Turkmenistan. See Asia.

Uganda. Ugandan authorities reported that between 330 and 530 members of the Movement for the Restoration of the Ten Commandments of God died on March 17, 2000. Police initially believed the individuals had died in a mass suicide, setting themselves on fire in a sealed chapel in Kanungu, located in southwestern Uganda.

Later in March, the authorities unearthed seven mass graves containing approximately 450 bodies at compounds across southwestern Uganda. Many of the exhumed bodies, which police estimated to have been dead for a month or longer, showed signs of strangling, poisoning, or stabbing. The discoveries prompted the police to announce that they were treating the hundreds of deaths as mass murder. Police believed that the killings may have begun after a prophesy by cult leaders Joseph Kibwetere and Cledonia Mwerinde that the world would end on Dec. 31, 1999, failed to take place. Investigators speculated that Kibwetere and Mwerinde may have begun killing sect members when members demanded the return of valuables they had donated to the cult. Police sources believed that many more corpses remained undiscovered and that the true number of killings may never be known nor the killers apprehended.

Referendum. In a national referendum on June 29, 2000, on whether Uganda should return to multiparty politics, 88 percent of voters supported the "no-party" National Resistance Movement that was set up by President Yoweri Museveni after he seized power in 1986. Supporters of multiple parties responded that the low referendum turnout—51 percent—proved their call for a referendum boycott had succeeded. Museveni argued that the voters had heeded his warning that a *pluralist* (multiparty) constitution would unleash the religious and tribal violence that plagued Uganda from 1971 to 1986.

Debt relief. In April 2000, the International Monetary Fund (IMF) and the World Bank agreed to help Uganda under the Heavily Indebted Poor Countries debt relief program. The IMF is an organization affiliated with the United Nations (UN) that provides short-term credit to member nations. The World Bank, a UN agency, provides long-term loans to countries for development.

Ebola virus. In September, the Ugandan Health Ministry confirmed an outbreak of the Ebola virus in Uganda. Health ministry officials announced on December 5 that the disease had killed more than 150 people, including 14 health workers. The Ebola virus, which is transmitted through bodily fluids, causes fever and severe hemorrhaging and kills 50 percent to 90 percent of its victims. Health officials diagnosed more than 390 cases by December.   □ Simon Baynham

See also **Africa; Congo (Kinshasa).**

Ukraine. Prime Minister Viktor Yushchenko's newly formed government renewed efforts in 2000 toward economic reforms. Yushchenko, who had previously headed the Ukrainian central bank, was nominated for the premiership in late 1999 by newly reelected President Leonid Kuchma after the parliament refused to reconfirm the incumbent prime minister, Valery Pustovoitenko. After taking office, Yushchenko and his cabinet moved quickly to revive Ukraine's stalled privatization program, to reform government administration, and to balance the budget.

Yushchenko took office with the support of a coalition of 11 centrist and right-wing parties that formed in early January. Led by former president Leonid Kravchuk, the coalition voted on January 21 to replace the leftist Speaker of Parliament Oleksandr Tkachenko. When Tkachenko refused to step down, deputies of the progovernment coalition stormed out of the parliament. Since the progovernment group included a majority of the parliament's deputies, it elected Ivan Plyushch as the new speaker of the parliament before returning to the parliamentary chamber in early February.

Strengthening the presidency. To prevent further parliamentary stalemates, President Kuchma held a referendum on April 16 aimed at strengthening the presidency at the expense of the parliament. He proposed making the parliament smaller, creating a second parliamentary chamber, stripping deputies of parliamentary immunity, and giving the president more powers to disband parliament and call new elections. Voters overwhelmingly approved the measures, and in late April, Kuchma introduced constitutional amendments based on the referendum. The parliament accepted an initial version of Kuchma's reforms in July but by a margin well below the two-thirds needed to amend the constitution.

Chernobyl. In December, Kuchma ordered the Chernobyl nuclear power plant shut down. The Chernobyl plant, in northwest Ukraine, was the site of the 1986 nuclear accident, which killed 31 people and released radioactive chemicals that drifted across northern and central Europe.

Economy. By autumn 2000, Yushchenko's economic reforms had become stalled by the debate over changing the constitution. Nevertheless, Ukraine's economy recorded its first full year of economic growth since independence in 1991, boosted by the economic recovery of neighboring Russia. From January to September 2000, Ukraine's *gross domestic product* (the value of all goods and services produced in a country in a given year) grew by 5 percent.   □ Steven L. Solnick

See also **Europe; Russia.**

United Arab Emirates. See Middle East.

During 2000, the economy of the United Kingdom remained strong. The government controlled inflation and reduced unemployment to just over 1 million people, the lowest level since 1979. However, public confidence in the government fell toward the end of 2000, particularly in September, when the cost of gasoline jumped to an all-time high.

Prime Minister Tony Blair's Labour government experienced its most turbulent year since taking office in 1997. Blair's government had previously enjoyed unprecedented levels of popularity. Widespread flooding in October and November 2000 and a major railway accident also contributed to Blair's problems. Nevertheless, Labour generally maintained its lead over the opposition, Britain's Conservative Party, in the opinion polls throughout the year.

Wales and Scotland. The Welsh Assembly and the Scottish Parliament, both formed in 1999, experienced considerable turmoil in 2000. On February 9, Alun Michael of the Labour Party, who had been elected leader of the Welsh Assembly, was forced to resign after a no-confidence vote following his failure to secure a grant for regional aid from the European Union. Many assembly members considered Michael too subservient to Blair's government. Another Labour Party member, Rhodri Morgan—who did not enjoy a cordial relationship with Blair—was sworn in as leader of the Welsh Assembly on February 15. Michael retired from the assembly on March 16 but remained a member of the United Kingdom's House of Commons.

In the Scottish Parliament, Alex Salmond, the leader of the Scottish Nationalists, the main opposition party, resigned on July 17 and was replaced by John Swinney. Scotland's first (prime) minister, Donald Dewar of Labour, who was instrumental in establishing the Scottish Parliament and had often been called the father of Scotland, died on October 11. Henry McLeish replaced Dewar as first minister on October 26.

Mayor for London. The Labour Party in 2000 fulfilled a promise made in 1998 to give London, the capital, a new government, including a mayor and an elected local assembly. Previous mayors of London had been appointed by the crown. The Conservatives had abolished London's elected council in 1985.

In elections held on May 4, 2000, Ken Livingstone, a former Labour Member of Parliament (MP) who ran as an independent, was elected mayor. Livingstone's victory was an embarrassment for Blair, because Blair had supported Health Minister Frank Dobson as the Labour Party's candidate. In an initial election on February 20 to choose the Labour Party candidate, Dobson narrowly defeated Livingstone, who had criticized the Labour government's plan to partially privatize the London Underground railway system. When Livingstone declared himself an independent candidate for mayor of London, Labour expelled Livingstone from the party although he remained an MP.

In the May 4 election for mayor, Dobson came in third, behind Steven Norris, the Conservative candidate and a former transportation minister. The Conservatives had nominated Norris on January 17. He had been runner-up to Jeffrey Archer in an earlier contest for the position. Archer, a popular novelist and former deputy chairman of the Conservative Party, had withdrawn from the race in 1999 after evidence emerged that he had lied in a 1987 libel trial involving allegations that he had had sex with a prostitute. Archer was formally charged with perjury in October 2000.

Labour and the Conservatives won roughly equal numbers of votes in the May 2000 election for the Greater London Assembly. The Labour group of representatives agreed to cooperate with Livingstone, and Labour's Nicky Gavron became deputy mayor for a one-year term.

The economy. Chancellor of the Exchequer Gordon Brown signaled a shift toward increased government expenditure on public services in 2000, after maintaining strict limits on public spending since taking office in 1997. Brown's previous strategy had been to concentrate on sound financial management to demonstrate Labour's ability to run the economy. Brown's budget, announced on March 21, 2000, increased spending by 2.5 percent. The increase came in response to widespread complaints about the underfunding of public services following a flu crisis during the winter of 1999 and 2000, when the National Health Service struggled to cope. The 2000 budget allocated 4.9 billion pounds ($7.2 billion) for the health service, using funds from a government revenue surplus. Brown forecast that the United Kingdom's *gross domestic product* (the value of all goods and services produced in a country in a year) would rise between 2.75 and 3.25 percent during 2000.

Brown also increased funding for a public program designed to find work for people on wel-

The Tate Modern, which showcases contemporary art, opens in London in May 2000 with three sculptures by French artist Louise Bourgeois dominating the great hall. A branch of Tate Britain, the new museum is housed in what had originally been an electrical generating plant.

Members of the British House of Commons

Queen Elizabeth II opened the 2000-2001 session of Parliament on Dec. 6, 2000. At that time, the House of Commons consisted of the following members: 415 Labour Party, 160 Conservative Party, 47 Liberal Democrats, 9 Ulster Unionists, 6 Scottish National Party, 4 Plaid Cymru, 3 Social Democratic and Labour Party, 3 Ulster Democratic Unionist Party, 2 Sinn Fein, 1 United Kingdom Unionist, 1 Independent, 1 Scottish Labour, 1 Member of Parliament for Brent East (Ken Livingstone), and one vacancy. In addition, the unaffiliated speaker and 3 deputies attend sessions but do not vote. This table shows each legislator and party affiliation. An asterisk (*) denotes those who served in the Parliament at some time before the 1997 general election.

A
Diane Abbott, Lab.*
Gerry Adams, S.F.*
Irene Adams, Lab.*
Nick Ainger, Lab.*
Peter Ainsworth, Con.*
Robert Ainsworth, Lab.*
Douglas Alexander, Lab.
Richard Allan, L.Dem.
Graham Allen, Lab.*
David Amess, Con.*
Michael Ancram, Con.*
Donald Anderson, Lab.*
Janet Anderson, Lab.*
James Arbuthnot, Con.*
Hilary Armstrong, Lab.*
Paddy Ashdown, L.Dem.*
Joe Ashton, Lab.*
Candy Atherton, Lab.
Charlotte Atkins, Lab.
David Atkinson, Lab.*
Peter Atkinson, Con.*
John Austin, Lab.*

B
Adrian Bailey, Lab.*
Norman Baker, L.Dem.
Tony Baldry, Con.*
Jackie Ballard, L.Dem.
Tony Banks, Lab.*
Harry Barnes, Lab.*
Kevin Barron, Lab.*
John Battle, Lab.*
Hugh Bayley, Lab.*
Nigel Beard, Lab.
Margaret Beckett, Lab.*
Anne Begg, Lab.
Roy Beggs, U.U.*
Alan Beith, L.Dem.*
Martin Bell, Ind.
Stuart Bell, Lab.*
Hilary Benn, Lab.*
Tony Benn, Lab.*
Andrew Bennett, Lab.*
Joe Benton, Lab.*
John Bercow, Con.
Sir Paul Beresford, Con.*
Gerald Bermingham, Lab.*
Roger Berry, Lab.*
Harold Best, Lab.
Clive Betts, Lab.*
Liz Blackman, Lab.
Tony Blair, Lab.*
Hazel Blears, Lab.
Bob Blizzard, Lab.
David Blunkett, Lab.*
Crispin Blunt, Con.
Paul Boateng, Lab.*
Sir Richard Body, Con.*
David Borrow, Lab.
Tim Boswell, Con.*
Peter Bottomley, Con.*
Virginia Bottomley, Con.*
Keith Bradley, Lab.*
Peter Bradley, Lab.
Ben Bradshaw, Lab.
Graham Brady, Con.
Tom Brake, L.Dem.
Peter Brand, L.Dem.
Julian Brazier, Con.*
Colin Breed, L.Dem.
Helen Brinton, Lab.
Peter Brooke, Con.*
Gordon Brown, Lab.*
Nick Brown, Lab.*
Russell Brown, Lab.
Desmond Browne, Lab.
Angela Browning, Con.*
Ian Bruce, Con.*
Malcolm Bruce, L.Dem.*
Karen Buck, Lab.
Richard Burden, Lab.*
Colin Burgon, Lab.

John Burnett, L.Dem.
Simon Burns, Con.*
Paul Burstow, L.Dem.
Christine Butler, Lab.
John Butterfill, Con.*
Stephen Byers, Lab.*

C
Vincent Cable, L.Dem.
Richard Caborn, Lab.*
Alan Campbell, Lab.
Anne Campbell, Lab.*
Menzies Campbell, L.Dem.*
Ronnie Campbell, Lab.*
Dale Campbell-Savours, Lab.*
Jamie Cann, Lab.*
Ivor Caplin, Lab.
Roger Casale, Lab.
William Cash, Con.*
Martin Caton, Lab.
Ian Cawsey, Lab.
Ben Chapman, Lab.*
Sir Sydney Chapman, Con.*
David Chaytor, Lab.
David Chidgey, L.Dem.*
Malcolm Chisholm, Lab.*
Christopher Chope, Con.*
Judith Church, Lab.*
Michael Clapham, Lab.*
James Clappison, Con.*
David Clark, Lab.*
Lynda Clark, Lab.
Michael Clark, Con.*
Paul Clark, Lab.
Charles Clarke, Lab.
Eric Clarke, Lab.*
Kenneth Clarke, Con.*
Tom Clarke, Lab.*
Tony Clarke, Lab.
David Clelland, Lab.*
Geoffrey Clifton-Brown, Con.*
Ann Clwyd, Lab.*
Vernon Coaker, Lab.
Ann Coffey, Lab.*
Harry Cohen, Lab*
Iain Coleman, Lab.
Tim Collins, Con.
Tony Colman, Lab.
Michael Connarty, Lab.*
Frank Cook, Lab.*
Robin Cook, Lab.*
Yvette Cooper, Lab.
Robin Corbett, Lab.*
Jeremy Corbyn, Lab.*
Sir Patrick Cormack, Con.*
Jean Corston, Lab.*
Brian Cotter, L.Dem.
Jim Cousins, Lab.*
Tom Cox, Lab.*
James Cran, Con.*
Ross Cranston, Lab.
David Crausby, Lab.
Ann Cryer, Lab.
John Cryer, Lab.
John Cummings, Lab.*
Lawrence Cunliffe, Lab.*
Jack Cunningham, Lab.*
Jim Cunningham, Lab.*
Roseanna Cunningham, S.N.P.
David Curry, Con.*
Claire Curtis-Thomas, Lab.

D
Tam Dalyell, Lab.*
Alistair Darling, Lab.*
Keith Darvill, Lab.
Edward Davey, L.Dem.
Valerie Davey, Lab.
Ian Davidson, Lab.*
Denzil Davies, Lab.*
Geraint Davies, Lab.
Quentin Davies, Con.*
Ronald Davies, Lab.*
David Davis, Con.*

Terry Davis, Lab.*
Hilton Dawson, Lab.
Stephen Day, Con.*
Janet Dean, Lab.
John Denham, Lab.*
Andrew Dismore, Lab.
Jim Dobbin, Lab.
Frank Dobson, Lab.*
Jeffrey Donaldson, U.U.
Brian H. Donohoe, Lab.*
Frank Doran, Lab.*
Stephen Dorrell, Con.*
Jim Dowd, Lab.*
David Drew, Lab.
Julia Drown, Lab.
Alan Duncan, Con.*
Iain Duncan Smith, Con.*
Gwyneth Dunwoody, Lab.*

E
Angela Eagle, Lab.*
Maria Eagle, Lab.
Huw Edwards, Lab.*
Clive Efford, Lab.
Louise Ellman, Lab.
Sir Peter Emery, Con.*
Jeff Ennis, Lab.*
Bill Etherington, Lab.*
Nigel Evans, Con.*
Margaret Ewing, S.N.P.

F
David Faber, Con.*
Michael Fabricant, Con.*
Michael Fallon, Con.*
Ronnie Fearn, L.Dem.*
Frank Field, Lab.*
Mark Fisher, Lab.*
Jim Fitzpatrick, Lab.
Lorna Fitzsimons, Lab.
Howard Flight, Con.
Caroline Flint, Lab.
Paul Flynn, Lab.*
Barbara Follett, Lab.
Eric Forth, Con.*
Derek Foster, Lab.*
Don Foster, L.Dem.*
Michael J. Foster, Lab.
Michael Jabez Foster, Lab.
George Foulkes, Lab.*
Sir Norman Fowler, Con.*
Liam Fox, Con.*
Christopher Fraser, Con.
Maria Fyfe, Lab.*

G
Sam Galbraith, Lab.*
Roger Gale, Con.*
George Galloway, Lab.*
Mike Gapes, Lab.*
Barry Gardiner, Lab.
Edward Garnier, Con.*
Andrew George, L.Dem.
Bruce George, Lab.*
Neil Gerrard, Lab.*
Nick Gibb, Con.
Ian Gibson, Lab.
Sandra Gidley, L.Dem.
Christopher Gill, Con.*
Cheryl Gillan, Con.*
Linda Gilroy, Lab.
Norman A. Godman, Lab.
Roger Godsiff, Lab.*
Paul Goggins, Lab.
Llin Golding, Lab.*
Eileen Gordon, Lab.
Teresa Gorman, Con.*
Donald Gorrie, L.Dem.
Thomas Graham, S.Lab.*
James Gray, Con.
Damian Green, Con.
John Greenway, Con.*
Dominic Grieve, Con.
Jane Griffiths, Lab.

Nigel Griffiths, Lab.*
Win Griffiths, Lab.*
Bruce Grocott, Lab.*
John Grogan, Lab.
John Gummer, Con.*
John Gunnell, Lab.*

H
William Hague, Con.*
Peter Hain, Lab.*
Mike Hall, Lab.*
Patrick Hall, Lab.
Sir Archie Hamilton, Con.*
Fabian Hamilton, Lab.
Philip Hammond, Con.
Mike Hancock, L.Dem.*
David Hanson, Lab.*
Harriet Harman, Lab.*
Evan Harris, L.Dem.
Nick Harvey, L.Dem.*
Sir Alan Haselhurst, Deputy*
Nick Hawkins, Con.*
John Hayes, Con.
Sylvia Heal, Deputy*
Oliver Heald, Con.*
John Healey, Lab.
David Heath, L.Dem.
Sir Edward Heath, Con.*
David Heathcoat-Amory, Con.*
Doug Henderson, Lab.*
Ivan Henderson, Lab.
Mark Hendrick, Lab.*
Stephen Hepburn, Lab.
John Heppell, Lab.*
Michael Heseltine, Con.*
Stephen Hesford, Lab.
Patricia Hewitt, Lab.
Keith Hill, Lab.*
David Hinchliffe, Lab.*
Margaret Hodge, Lab.*
Kate Hoey, Lab.*
Douglas Hogg, Con.*
John Home Robertson, Lab.*
Jimmy Hood, Lab.*
Geoffrey Hoon, Lab.*
Phil Hope, Lab.
Kelvin Hopkins, Lab.
John Horam, Con.*
Michael Howard, Con.*
Alan Howarth, Lab.*
George Howarth, Lab.*
Gerald Howarth, Con.*
Kim Howells, Lab.*
Lindsay Hoyle, Lab.*
Beverley Hughes, Lab.
Kevin Hughes, Lab.*
Simon Hughes, L.Dem.*
Joan Humble, Lab.
John Hume, S.D.L.P.*
Andrew Hunter, Con.*
Alan Hurst, Lab.
John Hutton, Lab.*

I
Brian Iddon, Lab.*
Eric Illsley, Lab.*
Adam Ingram, Lab.*

J
Michael Jack, Con.*
Glenda Jackson, Lab.*
Helen Jackson, Lab.*
Robert Jackson, Con.*
David Jamieson, Lab.*
Bernard Jenkin, Con.*
Brian Jenkins, Lab.*
Alan Johnson, Lab.
Melanie Johnson, Lab.
Sir Geoffrey Johnson Smith, Con.*
Barry Jones, Lab.*
Fiona Jones, Lab.*
Helen Jones, Lab.*
Ieuan Wyn Jones, P.C.*
Jenny Jones, Lab.

Jon Owen Jones, Lab.*
Lynne Jones, Lab.*
Martyn Jones, Lab.*
Nigel Jones, L.Dem.*
Tessa Jowell, Lab.*

K
Gerald Kaufman, Lab.*
Sally Keeble, Lab.
Alan Keen, Lab.*
Ann Keen, Lab.
Paul Keetch, L.Dem.
Ruth Kelly, Lab.
Fraser Kemp, Lab.
Charles Kennedy, L.Dem.*
Jane Kennedy, Lab.*
Robert Key, Con.
Piara S. Khabra, Lab.*
David Kidney, Lab.
Peter Kilfoyle, Lab.*
Andrew King, Lab.
Oona King, Lab.
Tom King, Con.*
Tess Kingham, Lab.*
Julie Kirkbride, Con.
Archy Kirkwood, L.Dem.*
Ashok Kumar, Lab.*

L
Stephen Ladyman, Lab.
Eleanor Laing, Con.
Jacqui Lait, Con.*
Andrew Lansley, Con.
Jackie Lawrence, Lab.
Bob Laxton, Lab.
Edward Leigh, Con.*
David Lepper, Lab.
Christopher Leslie, Lab.
Oliver Letwin, Con.
Tom Levitt, Lab.
Ivan Lewis, Lab.
Julian Lewis, Con.
Terry Lewis, Lab.*
Helen Liddell, Lab.*
David Lidington, Con.*
Peter Lilley, Con.*
Martin Linton, Lab.
Ken Livingstone
Richard Livsey, L.Dem.*
Sir Peter Lloyd, Con.*
Tony Lloyd, Lab.*
Elfyn Llwyd, P.C.*
David Lock, Lab.
Michael Lord, Deputy*
Tim Loughton, Con.
Andrew Love, Lab.
Peter Luff, Con.*
Sir Nicholas Lyell, Con.*

M
John McAllion, Lab.*
Thomas McAvoy, Lab.*
Steve McCabe, Lab.
Chris McCafferty, Lab.
Ian McCartney, Lab.*
Robert McCartney, U.K.U.*
William McCrea, U.D.U.P.
Siobhain McDonagh, Lab.
Calum MacDonald, Lab.*
John McDonnell, Lab.
John McFall, Lab.*
Eddie McGrady, S.D.L.P.*
John MacGregor, Con.*
Martin McGuinness, S.F.
Anne McGuire, Lab.
Anne McIntosh, Con.
Shona McIsaac, Lab.
Andrew Mackay, Con.*
Rosemary McKenna, Lab.
Andrew Mackinlay, Lab.*
David MacLean, Con.*
Henry B. McLeish, Lab.*
Robert Maclennan, L.Dem.*
Patrick McLoughlin, Con.*
Kevin McNamara, Lab.*
Tony McNulty, Lab.
Denis MacShane, Lab.*
Fiona Mactaggart, Lab.
Tony McWalter, Lab.
John McWilliam, Lab.*
Sir David Madel, Con.*
Ken Maginnis, U.U.*

Alice Mahon, Lab.*
John Major, Con.*
Humfrey Malins, Con.*
Judy Mallaber, Lab.
Seamus Mallon, S.D.L.P.*
Peter Mandelson, Lab.*
John Maples, Con.*
John Marek, Lab.*
Gordon Marsden, Lab.
Paul Marsden, Lab.
David Marshall, Lab.*
Jim Marshall, Lab.*
Robert Marshall-Andrews, Lab.
Michael Martin, Speaker*
Eric Martlew, Lab.*
Michael Mates, Con.*
Francis Maude, Con.*
Sir Brian Mawhinney, Con.*
John Maxton, Lab.*
Theresa May, Con.
Michael Meacher, Lab.*
Alan Meale, Lab.*
Gillian Merron, Lab.
Alun Michael, Lab.*
Bill Michie, Lab.*
Ray Michie, L.Dem.*
Alan Milburn, Lab.*
Andrew Miller, Lab.*
Austin Mitchell, Lab.*
Laura Moffatt, Lab.
Lewis Moonie, Lab.*
Michael Moore, L.Dem.
Margaret Moran, Lab.
Alasdair Morgan, S.N.P.
Julie Morgan, Lab.
Rhodri Morgan, Lab.*
Elliot Morley, Lab.*
Estelle Morris, Lab.*
Sir John Morris, Lab.*
Malcolm Moss, Con.*
Kali Mountford, Lab.
Marjorie Mowlam, Lab.*
George Mudie, Lab.
Chris Mullin, Lab.*
Denis Murphy, Lab.
Jim Murphy, Lab.
Paul Murphy, Lab.*

N
Douglas Naysmith, Lab.
Patrick Nicholls, Con.*
Archie Norman, Con.
Dan Norris, Lab.

O
Mark Oaten, L.Dem.
Bill O'Brien, Lab.*
Mike O'Brien, Lab.*
Stephen O'Brien, Con.*
Eddie O'Hara, Lab.*
Bill Olner, Lab.*
Martin O'Neill, Lab.*
Lembit Opik, L.Dem.
Diana Organ, Lab.
Sandra Osborne, Lab.*
Richard Ottaway, Con.*

P
Richard Page, Con.*
James Paice, Con.*
Ian Paisley, U.D.U.P.*
Nick Palmer, Lab.
Owen Paterson, Con.
Ian Pearson, Lab.*
Tom Pendry, Lab.*
Linda Perham, Lab.
Eric Pickles, Con.*
Colin Pickthall, Lab.*
Peter Pike, Lab.*
James Plaskitt, Lab.
Kerry Pollard, Lab.
Chris Pond, Lab.
Greg Pope, Lab.
Michael Portillo, Con.
Stephen Pound, Lab.
Sir Raymond Powell, Lab.*
Bridget Prentice, Lab.*
Gordon Prentice, Lab.*
John Prescott, Lab.*
Dawn Primarolo, Lab.*
David Prior, Con.

Gwyn Prosser, Lab.
Ken Purchase, Lab.*

Q
Joyce Quin, Lab.*
Lawrie Quinn, Lab.

R
Giles Radice, Lab.*
Bill Rammell, Lab.
John Randall, Con.
Syd Rapson, Lab.
Nick Raynsford, Lab.*
John Redwood, Con.*
Andrew Reed, Lab.
John Reid, Lab.*
David Rendel, L.Dem.*
Andrew Robathan, Con.*
John Robertson, Lab.*
Laurence Robertson, Con.
Geoffrey Robinson, Lab.*
Peter Robinson, U.D.U.P.*
Barbara Roche, Lab.*
Marion Roe, Con.*
Allan Rogers, Lab.*
Jeff Rooker, Lab.*
Terry Rooney, Lab.*
Ernie Ross, Lab.*
William Ross, U.U.*
Andrew Rowe, Con.*
Ted Rowlands, Lab.*
Frank Roy, Lab.
Chris Ruane, Lab.
Joan Ruddock, Lab.*
David Ruffley, Con.
Bob Russell, L.Dem.
Christine Russell, Lab.
Joan Ryan, Lab.

S
Nick St. Aubyn, Con.
Alex Salmond, S.N.P.*
Martin Salter, Lab.
Adrian Sanders, L.Dem.
Mohammad Sarwar, Lab.
Malcolm Savidge, Lab.
Phil Sawford, Lab.
Jonathan Sayeed, Con.*
Brian Sedgemore, Lab.*
Jonathon Shaw, Lab.
Barry Sheerman, Lab.*
Robert Sheldon, Lab.*
Gillian Shephard, Con.*
Richard Shepherd, Con.*
Debra Shipley, Lab.
Clare Short, Lab.*
Alan Simpson, Lab.*
Keith Simpson, Con.
Marsha Singh, Lab.*
Dennis Skinner, Lab.*
Andrew Smith, Lab*
Angela Smith, Lab.
Chris Smith, Lab.*
Geraldine Smith, Lab.
Jacqui Smith, Lab.
John Smith, Lab.*
Llew Smith, Lab.*
Sir Robert Smith, L.Dem.
W. Martin Smyth, U.U.*
Peter Snape, Lab.*
Nicholas Soames, Con.*
Clive Soley, Lab.*
Helen Southworth, Lab.
John Spellar, Lab.*
Caroline Spelman, Con.
Sir Michael Spicer, Con.*
Richard Spring, Con.*
Rachel Squire, Lab.*
Sir John Stanley, Con.*
Phyllis Starkey, Lab.
Anthony Steen, Con.*
Gerry Steinberg, Lab.*
George Stevenson, Lab.*
David Stewart, Lab.
Ian Stewart, Lab.
Paul Stinchcombe, Lab.
Howard Stoate, Lab.
Gavin Strang, Lab.*
Jack Straw, Lab.*
Gary Streeter, Con.*
Graham Stringer, Lab.

Gisela Stuart, Lab.
Andrew Stunell, L.Dem.
Gerry Sutcliffe, Lab.*
Desmond Swayne, Con.
John Swinney, S.N.P.
Robert Syms, Con.

T
Sir Peter Tapsell, Con.*
Ann Taylor, Lab.*
Dari Taylor, Lab.
David Taylor, Lab.
Ian Taylor, Con.*
John D. Taylor, U.U.*
John M. Taylor, Con.*
Matthew Taylor, L.Dem.*
Sir Teddy Taylor, Con.*
Peter Temple-Morris, Lab.*
Gareth Thomas, Lab.
Gareth R. Thomas, Lab.
Simon Thomas, P.C.
William Thompson, U.U.
Stephen Timms, Lab.*
Paddy Tipping, Lab.*
Mark Todd, Lab.
Jenny Tonge, L.Dem.
Don Touhig, Lab.*
John Townend, Con.*
David Tredinnick, Con.*
Michael Trend, Con.*
Jon Trickett, Lab.*
David Trimble, U.U.*
Paul Truswell, Lab.
Dennis Turner, Lab.*
Desmond Turner, Lab.
George Turner, Lab.
Neil Turner, Lab.*
Derek Twigg, Lab.
Stephen Twigg, Lab.
Paul Tyler, L.Dem.*
Bill Tynan, Lab.*
Andrew Tyrie, Con.

V
Keith Vaz, Lab.*
Peter Viggers, Con.*
Rudi Vis, Lab.

W
Cecil Walker, U.U.*
Jim Wallace, L.Dem.*
Joan Walley, Lab.*
Robert Walter, Con.
Claire Ward, Lab.
Charles Wardle, Con.*
Robert Wareing, Lab.*
Nigel Waterson, Con.*
Dave Watts, Lab.
Steven Webb, L.Dem.
Bowen Wells, Con.*
Andrew Welsh, S.N.P.*
Brian White, Lab.*
Alan Whitehead, Lab.
Sir Raymond Whitney, Con.*
John Whittingdale, Con.*
Malcolm Wicks, Lab.*
Ann Widdecombe, Con.*
Dafydd Wigley, P.C.*
John Wilkinson, Con.*
David Willetts, Con.*
Alan Williams, Lab.*
Alan W. Williams, Lab.*
Betty Williams, Lab.
Phil Willis, L.Dem.
Michael Wills, Lab.
David Wilshire, Con.*
Brian Wilson, Lab.*
David Winnick, Lab.*
Ann Winterton, Con.*
Nicholas Winterton, Con.*
Rosie Winterton, Lab.
Mike Wood, Lab.
Shaun Woodward, Lab.
Phil Woolas, Lab.
Tony Worthington, Lab.*
James Wray, Lab.*
Tony Wright, Lab.*
Tony Wright, Lab.
Derek Wyatt, Lab

Y
Tim Yeo, Con.*
Sir George Young, Con.*

fare. However, he barely increased the basic state pension. Pensions were linked to the rate of inflation and, therefore, rose by less than one pound a week in 2000, when inflation was quite low. The low increase caused an uproar among pensioners, though Brown's measures, including a large raise in the winter fuel allowance, were intended to help the poorest of senior citizens. Blair was later forced to admit that his government had failed to respond to pensioners, and Brown increased the pension in November by about 5 pounds ($7) a week—8 pounds ($12) for couples. In a surprise move, he also increased the payment to pensioners for winter fuel by 50 pounds ($74)—to about 200 pounds ($294).

Euroskepticism. Public support for joining the single European currency, the euro, plummeted in the United Kingdom during 2000. A poll taken on November 8 revealed that support in Britain had fallen to 18 percent, a record low.

Following a referendum in Denmark in September, in which voters rejected a proposal to join the euro, Blair, who favored the euro, indicated Britain would not join any time soon.

Elitism in education. On May 25, Chancellor of the Exchequer Brown charged Britain's two most famous universities, Oxford and Cambridge, with elitism and failure to recruit students from state-funded schools. Brown cited the case of Laura Spence, who attended a *comprehensive* (state school) and was denied admission to a medical program at Oxford despite indications that she would score high marks in her exams. The universities claimed they were making great efforts to recruit students from state schools and that the chancellor's remarks would only hamper their efforts. In August, Spence accepted a scholarship at Harvard University in the United States.

The David Shayler affair. The government took legal action in February against a former MI5 (British Secret Service) agent, David Shayler, for breaking the Official Secrets Act. Shayler, who had fled to France in 1997, alleged that the Secret Service had attempted to assassinate Libyan leader Muammar al-Qadhafi of Libya in 1996 and had bugged the phones of Labour MP's in the 1970's. Shayler returned to Britain in August 2000, as part of an agreement in which he would be freed on bail immediately after his arrest. He later pleaded not guilty to the charges.

The fuel crisis. In September, transportation in Britain was brought to a standstill by protests against the high costs of gasoline and diesel fuel. Fuel costs in Britain—as well as throughout Europe—were among the highest in the world in 2000. A rise in world oil prices and, the government's high level of taxes added to the retail cost.

On September 7, truckers and farmers in Britain blockaded oil refineries to protest the high prices. The blockade led to panic buying by motorists. By September 12, most gas stations were out of gasoline, and fuel was restricted to emergency service vehicles. The shortage affected deliveries of food to supermarkets, where shelves were soon empty of basic foodstuffs. Although backed by huge public support, the protestors called off the blockade after eight days but threatened further action if the cost of fuel was not cut dramatically. On November 8, Chancellor of the Exchequer Brown froze taxes on fuel, cut the price of a liter of environmentally friendly low-sulphur fuel, and reduced the road tax for trucks.

Declining auto sales. Despite the overall strength of the British economy, the manufacturing sector was hurt in 2000 by the strength of

The Cabinet of the United Kingdom*

Tony Blair—prime minister; first lord of the treasury; minister for the civil service

John Prescott—deputy prime minister; secretary of state for the environment, transport, and the regions

Gordon Brown—chancellor of the exchequer

Robin Cook—secretary of state for foreign and Commonwealth affairs

Lord Irvine of Lairg—lord chancellor

Jack Straw—secretary of state for the home department

David Blunkett—secretary of state for education and employment

Margaret Beckett—president of the Privy Council and leader of the House of Commons

John Reid—secretary of state for Scotland

Ann Taylor—chief whip of the House of Commons

Chris Smith—secretary of state for culture, media, and sport

Marjorie Mowlam—minister for the cabinet office; chancellor of the Duchy of Lancaster

Clare Short—secretary of state for international development

Alistair Darling—secretary of state for social security

Nick Brown—minister of agriculture, fisheries, and food

Baroness Jay of Paddington—lord privy seal; leader of the House of Lords; minister for women

Stephen Byers—secretary of state for trade and industry

Alan Milburn—secretary of state for health

Paul Murphy—secretary of state for Wales

Peter Mandelson—secretary of state for Northern Ireland

Geoff Hoon—secretary of state for defence

Andrew Smith—chief secretary to the treasury

*As of Dec. 6, 2000.

the pound, which made British goods expensive to sell abroad. In March, German automobile manufacturer BMW announced it would sell the Rover car factory at Birmingham to the Alchemy Partners investment group because of declining sales. Alchemy planned to phase out production of the Rover and begin manufacturing new models under the MG name, eliminating many jobs. After thousands of workers protested, BMW instead sold Rover in May to the Phoenix Consortium, a group of British business leaders who planned to continue producing the Rover. Ford Motor Company of Dearborn, Michigan, announced in May that the company planned to close its plant at Dagenham, London.

The Queen Mother celebrated her 100th birthday in August. Celebrations were held in her honor throughout the country, and immense affection was directed toward Queen Elizabeth, the Queen Mother, who is generally regarded as the most popular member of the British Royal Family.

British Museum renovation. On December 6, Queen Elizabeth II inaugurated the new Great Court at the British Museum in London. The court, a major renovation to the building designed in 1853, featured a 65,000-square-foot- (6,039-square-meter-) roof of glass and steel. The roof transformed the museum's original, open-air main courtyard with its assortment of outbuildings into an interior space that allowed visitors to access all four museum wings. The museum's famous 150-year-old round Reading Room at the center of the courtyard was opened to the public, after its extensive collections were moved to the new British Library in London. The Reading Room was originally open only to scholars.

Holocaust denial trial. On April 11, 2000, right-wing British historian David Irving lost the legal case he had brought in a British court against Deborah Lipstadt, a professor at Emory University in Atlanta, Georgia. Irving had sued Lipstadt for libel because she had denounced Irving in print as a Holocaust denier. (The Holocaust was the systematic killing of millions of Jews and other people considered undesirable by Germany's Nazi government during World War II, 1939-1945.) The trial centered on Irving's numerous books about the Third Reich. The judge ruled that Irving had falsified history to dispute the Holocaust.

The Tony Martin affair. Britons were outraged on April 19, 2000, when Tony Martin, a farmer who allegedly shot and killed a 16-year-old burglar who was robbing Martin's house, was convicted of murder and sentenced to life imprisonment. (In Britain, the use of firearms is illegal.) Many people asserted that Martin was simply defending his property.

Nail bomber. On June 30, David Copeland was sentenced to life imprisonment for setting off three nail bombs in London in April 1999. Copeland detonated bombs in two areas of London with large black and Asian populations, causing damage but no fatalities. His third bomb, planted in a pub with a gay clientele in the London neighborhood of Soho, caused 3 deaths and injured more than 100 people. Copeland was a member of several far-right organizations. He was identified from pictures from closed-circuit cameras that showed he apparently acted alone.

Pedophile protests. Britons were shocked on July 1, 2000, by the abduction and subsequent murder of an 8-year-old girl, Sarah Payne, by an unknown assailant. In response to the crime, the tabloid newspaper *News of the World* began to publish the photographs, names, and addresses of convicted pedophiles. In towns and villages throughout the country, angry protestors staged vigilante attacks on the houses of suspected pedophiles and set cars on fire. In a number of cases, innocent families were driven from their houses. On August 4, *News of the World* agreed to end its two-week campaign. By the end of 2000, the murderer of Sarah Payne remained at large.

The Hatfield rail crash. A train derailment caused by a damaged rail near Hatfield, Hertfordshire, on October 17 led to the deaths of four people and triggered chaos in Britain's railway system. Formerly a nationalized industry, the railways had been privatized by the Conservatives. Railtrack, a private business, was placed in charge of maintaining the track. The Hatfield crash highlighted the poor quality of many rails and raised issues of passenger safety. A study revealed that 1,800 rails in the system had cracks similar to those that caused the derailment in Hatfield. Railtrack embarked on a massive program of repair, which involved canceling trains and introducing severe speed restrictions so that most train journeys around the country took far longer and were often delayed.

Floods. Severe rain on October 29 and continued severe weather conditions in November caused flooding throughout Britain. In York, the River Ouse burst its banks, subjecting the ancient city center with its worst flooding since 1625. Elsewhere in Britain, the Severn, Avon, and more than 25 other rivers flooded. By early November, about 5,000 houses were under water. John Prescott, the deputy prime minister, announced that 51 million pounds ($75 million) would be allocated toward flood control over the next four years.   ☐ Rohan McWilliam

See also **Europe; United Kingdom: A Special Report.**

The Queen Mother:

Creator of the Modern Monarchy

By Rohan McWilliam

The Queen Mother, who is known for her strength, vitality and perseverance, celebrates her 100th birthday.

The United Kingdom's queen mother celebrated her 100th birthday on Aug. 4, 2000. The celebration was relatively simple, compared with the festivities that preceded it, which included a thanksgiving service at St. Paul's Cathedral; a gala with 8,000 participants; a *tattoo* (an elaborate military parade); and a banquet and birthday ball at Windsor Castle. On the queen mother's actual birthday, a military band played "Happy Birthday to You" outside the gates of her London residence, Clarence House. Immediately afterward, a postman presented her with a special delivery letter. Inside was a card from her daughter, Queen Elizabeth II, the same special card that the queen sends to every citizen of the United Kingdom on the occasion of their 100th birthday.

At noon, the queen mother set off with her grandson, the Prince of Wales, in a horse-drawn carriage. The procession traveled down the Mall to Buckingham Palace, where the queen and other members of the royal family received her. Finally, the queen mother, smiling and waving, stepped out onto the balcony at Buckingham Palace to acknowledge the cheers of the enormous crowds below. At 100, she remained the most popular member of the royal family, a beloved figure connecting Britain's present with its past.

The life of the queen mother reads, in part, like a fairy tale. She was a *commoner* (not a member of a royal family) who married a prince and became the Duchess of York. In the 1920's and 1930's, the public adored her in the way that Princess Diana would be adored half a century later. She became the mother of two princesses and presided over a happy and secure family. Her story, however, is also that of a woman who never expected to become queen. The role was thrust upon her in the wake of a national crisis that profoundly rocked Britain and the British monarchy. As the wife of the new king, she helped him cope with his new position and with his limitations. As *queen consort* (wife of a king), she helped the nation cope with the trials of World War II. She was widowed at age 51 and forced to assume a new role, one that she has played for nearly a half century.

The Queen Mother's childhood

Lady Elizabeth Bowes-Lyon was born in Scotland on Aug. 4, 1900, the ninth child of Lord Glamis, the 14th Earl of Strathmore and Kinghorne. In 1900, Victoria still reigned as queen of the British Isles and empress of India. The United Kingdom was the world's leading superpower with an ever-expanding empire that covered approximately one-third of the world's surface. Though the United States and Germany were beginning to challenge Britain's economic might, Great Britain continued to dominate many of the world's markets. The country was not yet a full democracy. The influence of the aristocracy on government remained strong, and many of the nation's men, and all of its women, were barred from voting in parliamentary elections.

Lady Elizabeth grew up in Scotland, at Glamis Castle, the oldest inhabited dwelling in Britain. She did not attend school but was educated by tutors at home, which was common among the aristocracy at the time. With the outbreak of World War I (1914-1918), her childhood came to an abrupt halt. In 1915, the war took a sharp, personal turn when one of her brothers was killed at the Battle of Loos in France. Glamis Castle was converted into a hospital for wounded soldiers. Although Lady Elizabeth was too young to work as a nurse, she assisted the nurses and entertained patients.

After the war, Lady Elizabeth became a popular debutante among Britain's high society. People commented upon her sense of fun and her ease among strangers. She was considered "a catch" on the marriage market that then existed among members of the British upper class. In time, she caught the eye of Albert, Duke of York, who was called "Bertie" by his friends and family. The duke was the second son of King George V and second in line to the throne after his brother, Edward, the Prince of Wales. When the duke first proposed marriage to Lady Elizabeth, she declined his offer for reasons that remain unclear. However, the duke's mother, Queen Mary, approved of the match and encouraged him to persist. In January 1923, Lady Elizabeth accepted his proposal. King George V approved of his son's choice and gave his consent.

Lady Elizabeth Bowes-Lyon, the future Queen Mother, at age seven

Marriage and family

When the royal family announced the engagement, the press discovered Lady Elizabeth, and she gave the only newspaper interview of her life, happily describing her wedding plans. Newspapers detailed the places she visited, to whom she spoke, and what she wore. After this interview, the royal family, which did not speak to the press, persuaded Lady Elizabeth to keep her private life out of the newspapers. She was, in a sense, marrying not just Bertie, but the whole royal family, which at the time, was considered remote and extremely formal. Later, George V would attempt to combat this perception through radio broadcasts, which allowed him to speak directly to the people. His graceful, new daughter-in-law fitted in perfectly with his plans and would, in effect, complete her father-in-law's strategy to modernize the institution of monarchy.

After the wedding, which took place on April 26, 1923, at Westminster Abbey, the duke relied heavily on his wife's support and advice. He was a nervous, extremely shy man with a terrible stammer and an aversion to public life. At her insistence, he consulted a speech therapist. The therapist was not able to entirely cure the duke's stammer but gave the duke lessons that enabled him to control it. This helped the Duke of York get through the few speaking engagements that were expected of him at the time.

The couple's first daughter, Princess Elizabeth, was born on April 21, 1926, and was third in line to the throne. Few people, however, thought the young princess would ever become queen. Lady Elizabeth gave birth to a second child, Princess Margaret Rose, Aug. 21, 1930, at Glamis Castle. In the 1930's, the British people regarded the Duke and Duchess of York and their daughters as a model family. As part of the strategy to popularize the monarchy, newsreels in cinemas showed the family playing together, revealing a different, less formal royal family for a new, democratic age.

The loving family life of the duke and duchess contrasted sharply with the lifestyle of the Prince of Wales. Although he was first in line to the throne, Prince Edward was a carefree figure who enjoyed a bachelor lifestyle. Unlike the Duke of York, the Prince of Wales possessed self-confidence and enjoyed life in the public eye.

Abdication crisis

On Jan. 20, 1936, George V died, and the Prince of Wales became King Edward VIII. He would, however, never be crowned king.

Edward had fallen in love with and wanted to marry an American, Wallis Warfield Simpson, who had been married twice before. The British government and most British and colonial leaders frowned on the match for two reasons. Wallis Warfield Simpson was neither royal nor a member of the British aristocracy, and more importantly, she was a divorcee. When Edward informed the prime minister that he hoped to marry Mrs. Simpson before the coronation so that she could be crowned with him, the government informed him that this was unacceptable. He was given a choice between the crown and the marriage. Edward chose to be with the woman he loved and *abdicated* (formally renounced) the throne on Dec. 11, 1936. His brother, the Duke of York, became king, taking the name

The author:
Rohan McWilliam is a senior lecturer in history at Anglia Polytechnic University, Cambridge, England.

George VI. When the former king and Mrs. Simpson married in June 1937, George VI granted the couple the titles Duke and Duchess of Windsor.

George VI considered his accession to the throne to be a calamity for himself and for the nation. He had not been raised for the throne, as had his brother Edward. With his stammer and lack of self-confidence, the new king was uncomfortable appearing before the public. He had never even read a government document.

The new queen was as deeply unhappy as her husband about his accession and allegedly resented Wallis Simpson for making it happen. According to various biographers, it was the new queen who decided that the Duchess of Windsor should be denied the title "Her Royal Highness." Edward and Wallis took this as a deliberate insult. Historians have also suggested that the new queen was behind the decision to exclude the duke and duchess from participating in public life in Great Britain, which in effect compelled the couple to live abroad for the rest of their lives. The queen mother later blamed the Duchess of Windsor for George VI's untimely death at age 56, which she believed was the result of the stresses of kingship.

Reinventing the monarchy

Immediately following the abdication of Edward VIII, public discussion about whether the monarchy had a future raged across Britain, its colonies, and the nations of the empire. The debate largely ended with the coronation of George VI, which took place on May 12, 1937. People in the streets and those in attendance at the ceremony at Westminster Abbey were inspired by the apparent self-possession of the new king and the serenity of his queen. The new monarchs arranged to have the coronation broadcast throughout the nation by radio as a way to reassure the nation after the ab-

Lady Elizabeth Bowes-Lyon leaves for her wedding to Albert, Duke of York, on April 26, 1923.

King George VI and Queen Elizabeth ride in a royal procession through London before their coronation at Westminster Abbey on May 12, 1937.

dication and to connect themselves with the people. Like her fa-ther-in-law before her, the queen understood the power of the then-new medium.

Determined that the embarrassment of the abdication should be forgotten as soon as possible, the queen set out to craft a new kind of monarchy. Where royals in the past had stood aloof and unre-sponsive, she won people over with her charismatic smile and ease with the public. According to her biographers, the new queen gen-uinely liked people, and it showed. She also instinctively under-stood that image is an important element of leadership and wanted to present an image of grandeur without ostentation. She wished to forge a monarchy that had a magical quality and yet was human enough that ordinary people could identify with it. She began with herself. Establishing relationships with important dress designers of the day, the queen became fashionable, but not too fashionable, wearing clothes and hats that were highly flattering to a woman who was approaching middle age. She also commissioned portraits of the royal family by artists and photographers who understood her ambitions. Among these was the noted designer and photogra-pher Cecil Beaton, who completed a series of glamorous portraits of the queen and young princesses in the early years of the reign. The widely distributed Beaton photographs helped create the magi-cal image that Queen Elizabeth wanted to convey. Upon complet-ing the assignment Beaton noted, "There is something of the great actress about her."

In May 1939, the king and queen embarked on a royal tour of Canada and the United States, the first British monarchs to do so. In Canada, she enjoyed one of her great public relations triumphs, inventing what would later be termed the "royal walkabout." In Ottawa, she broke protocol by leaving the official party and wad-ing into a crowd of 70,000 people. The response was immediate and enormous. The people loved her. Newspapers reported the in-cident around the world.

King George VI and Queen Elizabeth visit President Franklin Delano Roosevelt (far right) and First Lady Eleanor Roosevelt (far left) at Hyde Park, New York, in 1939. President Roosevelt's mother, Sarah Roosevelt, is seated between the king and queen.

In the United States, the king and queen met President Franklin Delano Roosevelt and First Lady Eleanor Roosevelt, establishing a relationship that would prove to be important during World War II (1939-1945). Photographers and newsreel cameramen captured the queen eating a hot dog during a picnic at the Roosevelt estate at Hyde Park, New York.

Royal missteps

The new king and queen also made decisions during the prewar period of the late 1930's that were later perceived as mistakes. They both publicly supported Prime Minister Neville Chamberlain's appeasement policy of trying to prevent war by meeting German Chancellor Adolf Hitler's demands. Many historians have judged the royal family's support of Chamberlain's policies to have been a dangerous move for a constitutional monarch required to remain aloof from politics. In addition, the king and queen did not trust Winston Churchill, appeasement's greatest critic. They did not hide their preference for a government led by Lord Halifax, Chamberlain's foreign secretary, over Churchill when Chamberlain's government collapsed in 1940. Both the king and queen felt Churchill had been too sympathetic to Edward VIII during the abdication crisis. Despite the king and queen's preferences for Lord Halifax, Churchill became prime minister.

King George VI and Queen Elizabeth tour bombed areas of London during World War II (1939-1945). Many British people admired the king and queen because they stayed in London during the bombings.

World War II

Germany invaded Poland in September 1939, setting off World War II. When Germany began bombing the United Kingdom in 1940, many people assumed that the royal family would go into hiding for safety. The government suggest-

The Beatles are presented to Queen Elizabeth, the Queen Mother after a November 1963 Royal Variety Show at the Prince of Wales Theatre in London.

ed that the princesses be sent to Canada where they would be out of danger. The queen vetoed the idea saying, "The princesses would never leave without me, and I couldn't leave without the king, and the king would never leave." George VI made the crucial decision to remain in London, though the princesses moved to Windsor Castle outside London, which was a less likely target for bombs.

This was a major propaganda victory. The people perceived that the royals were willing to suffer the devastation of war alongside them.

During the war, the royal family lived on the same food rations as other people did. They learned how to handle firearms, and they toured dangerous, bombed-out areas. There were times early in the war when people dispossessed by the bombings booed the royals as they toured the devastation. This changed, however, after a bomb hit Buckingham Palace, the king and queen's London residence. In the most famous pronouncement of her career, Queen Elizabeth said, "I'm glad we've been bombed. It makes me feel I can look the East End [of London] in the face."

During the war, the queen became Commandant-in-Chief for the Army and Air Force Women's Services and for women in the Royal Navy. When the Germans bombed the city of Coventry and many British people found themselves homeless, the queen supervised convoys of women drivers to take food to the deprived city and donated unused furniture from palace attics. In 1944, she told women civil defense workers: "I believe strongly that when future generations look back on this terrible war they will recognize as one of its chief features the degree to which women were actively concerned in it. I do not think it is any exaggeration to say that in this country at any rate, the war could not have been won without their help."

When the war in Europe was finally over in May 1945, crowds flocked to Buckingham Palace to celebrate. The royals and Prime Minister Winston Churchill, standing on the palace balcony, received the cheers of the crowds delighted that the war was over. There were very few calls after the war to abandon the monarchy, even when the Labour Party, which historically was ambivalent about the monarchy, took control of the government in 1945. The monarchy provided romance for the British people who were still living in a period of austerity. (Food continued to be rationed until 1953.)

A new queen

The young Princess Elizabeth married Philip Mountbatten of the Greek royal family on Nov. 20, 1947. Their son, Prince Charles, was born a year later, on Nov. 14, 1948, the first of four children.

Unfortunately, the strain of leading Britain during the war and afterward took its toll on George VI, and his health began to fail. He died on Feb. 6, 1952, after a struggle with lung cancer. His daughter, Elizabeth, was crowned queen on June 2, 1953.

The Queen Mother reinvents herself

It was unclear what the new queen's mother would do. Her official title was *queen dowager* (widow of the former king), and many people assumed that she would go into retirement, leaving public duties to her daughter. The new widow also had to leave Buckingham Palace for a new residence, Clarence House, which she reportedly did not much like. However, retirement was not on her mind. She gave herself a new title by insisting that she be called "Queen Elizabeth the Queen Mother," and she assumed the role of unofficial ambassador for the British monarchy and for Britain itself. Quoting her own mother, the queen mother noted, "Duty is the rent you pay for your life."

Between 1953 and 1989, the queen mother visited 40 countries, including a visit to Canada marking the 50th anniversary of her trip there with the king in 1939. She became patron to more than 350 charities, organizations, and veterans groups. She sponsored *regiments* (collection of army troops), including the Queen's Own Hussars, the Black Watch, and the Gordon Highlanders. She also served as Chancellor of the University of London from 1955 to 1981.

The Queen Mum

The appearance of the queen mother on the balcony at Buckingham Palace on her 100th birthday triggered memories of other such appearances, particularly the king and queen and Churchill waving at the crowds the day World War II ended in Europe. Social historians have suggested that her unprecedented prestige is based on the fact that she is so closely associated with the war and with the selflessness it inspired. The queen mother is the last important public figure of World War II who remains alive. Hitler, who had her on a "hit list," labeled her "the most dangerous woman in Europe" for her ability to inspire and boost public morale. The British monarchy, according to many historians, was an integral part of Churchill's war plan, and the queen was the backbone of that monarchy.

The queen mother was also the moving force in remolding the monarchy for a democratic age. With an uncanny sense of public relations and an inspiring sense of duty, she dragged it out of the age of Queen Victoria and into the modern era.

The ultimate result was a national institution, which the press came to label the "Queen Mum." She became, in effect, the entire nation's beloved grandmother. ■■■

The Queen Mother, accompanied by (clockwise from left) Prince Charles, Prince Harry, Prince William, and Prince Philip, attends a thanksgiving service in July 2000 at St. Paul's Cathedral in London. The service was part of the Queen Mother's 100th birthday celebration.

United Kingdom, Prime Minister of.

Public confidence in the government of Prime Minister Tony Blair fell in 2000. After a crisis in September over the price of gasoline, the main opposition party—the Conservatives—led in the opinion polls. Blair's worst moment, however, came in June, when he addressed the Women's Institute, a group devoted to family issues, only to have his speech drowned by heckling and an exodus by some delegates. Several of Blair's allies suggested that the government was out of touch with its supporters, but by December, Blair's lead in the polls had been restored.

Blair also suffered political embarrassment when his choice for mayor of London—Health Minister Frank Dobson—came in third in the three-way race. Ken Livingstone, a Member of Parliament and a former Labour Party member who ran as an independent, won the post in the May election. Livingstone had served as leader of the Greater London Council before it was abolished by the Conservatives in 1986.

On May 21, 2000, Blair's wife, Cherie, gave birth to a son, Leo, their fourth child. Cherie Blair, a leading attorney, had publicly supported the principle of paternity leave, and her husband took 14 days leave after the birth. The prime minister was later embarrassed when police on July 6 detained his 16-year-old son, Euan, for public drunkenness. Euan Blair was cautioned by the police but not formally charged.

☐ Rohan McWilliam

United Nations.

The largest single gathering of heads of state or government leaders ever assembled in the world—150 men and women—attended a United Nations (UN) Millennium Summit between Sept. 6 and Sept. 8, 2000, at UN Headquarters in New York City. UN Secretary-General Kofi Annan called the summit "a unique opportunity and, therefore, a unique responsibility" to revitalize the UN and to address the challenges facing the organization in the coming century.

The leaders at the summit adopted a declaration promising, by 2015, to cut by half the number of the world's people who live on less than $1 per day; to halt and reverse the spread of HIV, the virus that causes AIDS; and to send every child in the world to elementary school. They also promised to pay greater attention to the needs of African countries, many of which are plagued by protracted conflicts and rampant diseases.

Leaders of the 15 countries that belong to the UN Security Council met on Sept. 7, 2000, as part of the Millennium Summit. They agreed on plans to strengthen UN peacekeeping operations around the world by providing better financing, personnel resources, and enforceable mandates.

The UN General Assembly opened the 55th annual session on September 5, electing former Finnish Prime Minister Harri Holkeri as president.

The assembly's main task was to translate pledges made by world leaders at the Millennium Summit into concrete programs.

In September, the assembly admitted Tuvalu, a group of nine small *atolls* (coral islands) in the South Pacific with about 10,000 inhabitants, as the 189th member of the organization. In November, the assembly readmitted Yugoslavia. Yugoslavia was banned from the UN in 1992, when its leader, Slobodan Milosevic, refused to withdraw his support for the Serbs' ethnic cleansing campaign against Muslims in Bosnia-Herzegovina. Milosevic fell from power in October 2000.

Security Council. On October 10, the General Assembly elected five new members—Colombia, Ireland, Mauritius, Norway, and Singapore—to the Security Council to replace five outgoing countries. The five new members began their two-year term on Jan. 1, 2001, joining Bangladesh, Jamaica, Mali, Tunisia, Ukraine, and the five permanent members of the council—China, France, Russia, the United Kingdom, and the United States.

The Security Council adopted several declarations in the first six months of 2000 specifying measures to protect civilians, particularly children, caught in armed conflicts. On July 17, the council adopted a resolution urging member nations serving in UN peacekeeping operations to train their personnel to prevent and combat AIDS in the countries in which they are stationed. The council called for voluntary testing and confidential treatment of HIV, the virus that causes AIDS, in UN personnel on peacekeeping missions.

Africa. Wars in Angola, Sierra Leone, and Congo (Kinshasa) occupied much of the Security Council's agenda in 2000. In January, the council held a series of meetings to debate the conflicts in Africa, culminating in a conference attended by seven African heads of state and dozens of high-level government delegations.

The illicit sale of rough diamonds by armed rebel groups to raise money to fuel the conflicts was a primary topic during the meetings. On July 21, the World Diamond Congress and other diamond industry organizations in Antwerp, Belgium, agreed to cooperate with the UN in an effort to end the diamond traffic with rebel groups, depriving them of resources to finance wars. Canada led the campaign. In late July, the council adopted strict measures and severe penalties to end the illicit traffic.

In Sierra Leone, rebel troops captured some 500 UN peacekeepers in May and seized their weapons, breaking a peace agreement with the Sierra Leone government. Although the troops freed some of the peacekeepers, 233 UN soldiers remained in custody until July 15, when they were rescued during a raid by other UN forces. In

August, the Security Council agreed to increase the number of UN troops beyond the 13,000 already in place in order to restore stability. The council also approved a resolution in August to set up a war crimes tribunal to try those individuals responsible for atrocities against civilians in Sierra Leone.

Middle East. On June 18, the UN confirmed the complete withdrawal of Israeli Defence Forces from southern Lebanon, which Israel had occupied since 1978. UN peacekeeping forces, later joined by Lebanese government troops, replaced the Israeli forces. However, border skirmishes involving Hezbollah, an Islamist guerrilla group, continued in 2000.

Iraq. The stalemate between Iraq and the UN continued in 2000 as Iraq refused to allow UN arms inspectors into the country. On March 1, Hans Blix of Sweden, an arms specialist, was appointed to head a disarmament commission in Iraq, but he was also refused entry.

The UN humanitarian program known as oil-for-food continued in 2000. Under the program, Iraq sold $6.2 billion worth of oil from June to October and used the profits to purchase medical and food supplies for Iraqi civilians.

☐ J. Tuyet Nguyen

See also **Africa: A Special Report; AIDS; Middle East; Yugoslavia.**

United States, Government of the.

Texas Governor George W. Bush, the Republican candidate in the November 2000 presidential election, claimed victory over his Democratic opponent, Vice President Al Gore, on December 13, five weeks after the November 7 election. The election was one of the closest in U.S. history and was ultimately decided by the U.S. Supreme Court on December 12. Gore conceded after the court ruled that the continued manual recounts in various Florida counties would violate the U.S. Constitution.

Budget surplus. The U.S. government ended fiscal year 2000 on September 30 with a record budget surplus. President Bill Clinton announced that the surplus totaled approximately $230 billion. The surplus surpassed the former record, $122.7 billion set in fiscal year 1999. Fiscal 2000 was the third year in a row that the federal government took in more money than it spent. President Clinton estimated in 2000 that the total government surplus could reach nearly $5 trillion by 2010 if government income and spending continued at the current rates. The president also announced that in 2000 the federal government paid down the national debt by $223 billion. Fiscal 2000 was also the third consecutive year in which the national debt was reduced, an accomplishment that last occurred in 1949.

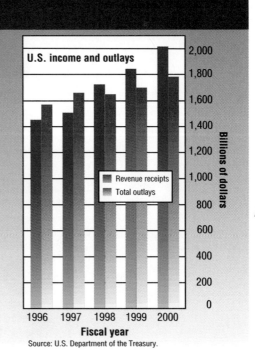

Federal spending
United States budget for fiscal 2000*

Billions of dollars

National defense	293.9
International affairs	17.3
General science, space, technology	19.7
Energy	–1.0
Natural resources and environment	23.3
Agriculture	38.5
Commerce and housing credit	3.3
Transportation	46.2
Community and regional development	11.7
Education, training, employment, and social services	58.4
Health	154.2
Social security	409.4
Medicare	197.1
Income security	247.4
Veterans' benefits and services	47.1
Administration of justice	27.7
General government	13.7
Interest	222.8
Undistributed offsetting receipts	–42.6
Total budget outlays	**1,788.1**

*Oct. 1, 1999, to Sept. 30, 2000.
Source: U.S. Department of the Treasury.

U.S. income and outlays

Revenue receipts
Total outlays

Billions of dollars

Fiscal year

Source: U.S. Department of the Treasury.

In 2000, the U.S. Department of the Treasury issued five newly designed quarters and redesigned $5 and $10 bills.

The U.S. Mint distributed five redesigned quarters in 2000 honoring the states of Maryland, Massachusetts, New Hampshire, South Carolina, and Virginia. The Treasury Department also introduced redesigned $5 and $10 bills with larger portraits of Abraham Lincoln and Alexander Hamilton and various features designed to deter counterfeiters.

National security. Wen Ho Lee, a nuclear scientist who worked for the U.S. government, pleaded guilty on Sept. 13, 2000, to one count of mishandling nuclear secrets following a five-year investigation into whether he had been involved in espionage. The federal government had imprisoned Lee for nine months, suspecting that he had leaked nuclear secrets while working at the Los Alamos Nuclear Laboratory in New Mexico. Lee was fired in March 1999 and arrested in December 1999. Although the U.S. Department of Justice did not charge Lee with espionage, it did charge him with 59 counts of taking classified information to help a foreign government.

The Justice Department alleged that Lee had violated security rules at Los Alamos by copying nuclear secrets onto computer tapes, some of which could not be found. Lee contended that he destroyed the tapes containing the data. A subsequent investigation revealed that most of the material was not classified.

As part of the agreement to plead guilty, Lee was sentenced to the 278 days in prison that he had already served. Supporters argued that the federal government had unfairly targeted Lee because of his Chinese heritage. Lee was born in Taiwan but became a naturalized U.S. citizen. U.S. District Judge James A. Parker dismissed the charges against Lee and criticized the government's handling of the case, saying it had dragged on too long and that officials misled the judge into believing that Lee should be kept in jail because he was a threat to national security.

Missing computers. In another security problem at the Los Alamos laboratory, officials reported on May 31, 2000, that two computer hard drives containing nuclear secrets were missing. The hard drives belonged to the U.S. Department of Energy's Nuclear Emergency Search Team, which is in charge of making sure that nuclear weapons are safe in the event of a nuclear emergency or terrorist threat. The hard drives, which had been missing since May 7, were supposed to be stored in a vault. On June 16, they were discovered behind a copy machine.

Greenspan nomination. On January 4, President Clinton nominated Alan Greenspan to serve a fourth four-year term as chairman of the U.S. Federal Reserve System (the Fed), the central bank of the United States. President Ronald Reagan first appointed Greenspan to the post in August 1987. On Feb. 3, 2000, the U.S. Senate voted 89 to 4 to confirm Greenspan's reappointment.

Dursban ban. The Environmental Protection Agency (EPA), an independent agency of the U.S. government that protects the nation's environment from pollution, announced on June 8 that use of the pesticide Dursban would be greatly restricted. Under the EPA ban, the pesticide could no longer be made for home use on lawns or gardens or by pest exterminators. The EPA reported that the chemical posed a health risk to humans, especially children. Under the ban, stores were required to stop selling products containing Dursban by the end of 2001.

Nixon documents. The U.S. Department of Justice announced on June 12, 2000, that it had agreed to pay $18 million to former President Richard M. Nixon's estate for a large collection of documents, photographs, and audio tapes dating from his administration. Nixon was president from 1969 until August 1974. Representatives of Nixon's estate had argued that the items were private property worth about $200 million. The government had possession of the materials at the time of Nixon's resignation because the House of Representatives had been debating whether to impeach Nixon over the Watergate scandal, which involved a cover-up of illegal activities by Nixon and his aides.

The settlement was paid to the estate's lawyers; the Nixon Foundation, which operates his presidential library in Yorba Linda, California; the Nixon Center, a Washington, D.C., foreign affairs research institute; and Nixon's two daughters, Julie Nixon Eisenhower and Tricia Nixon Cox.

"Slamming" settlement. Clinton, Mississippi-based MCI WorldCom, Inc., the second-largest long-distance telephone company in the United States, in June 2000 agreed to pay the federal government $3.5 million in fines stemming from customers' claims that MCI had switched their long-distance service without their permission. The agreement, announced on June 6, settled an investigation by the Federal Communications Commission (FCC). In 1999, the FCC received 2,900 complaints of "slamming" by WorldCom. Slamming is the illegal, unauthorized switching of a phone customer's long-distance carrier.

Branch Davidians. On July 14, 2000, a five-person federal advisory jury ruled that federal law enforcement agents did not act improperly in their handling of a 51-day standoff in 1993 against the Branch Davidian sect, a religious cult near Waco, Texas. The jury concluded that the government should not pay millions of dollars in a wrongful-death lawsuit filed as a result of the deaths of about 80 Branch Davidians, including the cult's leader, David Koresh, in a fire that destroyed the cult's headquarters on April 19, 1993. The cause of the fire was never determined. The Federal Bureau of Investigation (FBI) admitted in 1999 that the bureau's agents may have used explosive tear gas grenades in the confrontation with the Branch Davidians but maintained that the canisters bounced off a concrete structure within the compound and did not cause the blaze.

Selected agencies and bureaus of the U.S. government*

Executive Office of the President

President, Bill Clinton
 Vice President, Albert Gore, Jr.
 White House Chief of Staff, John D. Podesta
 Presidential Press Secretary, Jake Siewert
 Assistant to the President for Domestic Policy, Bruce N. Reed
 Assistant to the President for National Security Affairs,
   Samuel R. Berger
 Assistant to the President for Science and Technology,
   Neal F. Lane
 Council of Economic Advisers—Martin Neil Baily, Chair
 Office of Management and Budget—Jacob J. Lew, Director
 Office of National Drug Control Policy—
   Barry R. McCaffrey, Director
 U.S. Trade Representative, Charlene Barshefsky

Department of Agriculture

Secretary of Agriculture, Daniel R. Glickman

Department of Commerce

Secretary of Commerce, Norman Y. Mineta
 Bureau of Economic Analysis—J. Steven Landefeld, Director
 Bureau of the Census—Kenneth Prewitt, Director

Department of Defense

Secretary of Defense, William S. Cohen
 Secretary of the Air Force, F. Whitten Peters
 Secretary of the Army, Louis Caldera
 Secretary of the Navy, Richard J. Danzig
 Joint Chiefs of Staff—
   General Henry H. Shelton, Chairman
   General Michael E. Ryan, Chief of Staff, Air Force
   General Eric K. Shinseki, Chief of Staff, Army
   Admiral Vern Clark, Chief of Naval Operations
   General James L. Jones, Jr., Commandant, Marine Corps

Department of Education

Secretary of Education, Richard W. Riley

Department of Energy

Secretary of Energy, Bill Richardson

Department of Health and Human Services

Secretary of Health and Human Services, Donna E. Shalala
 Office of Public Health and Science—
   David Satcher, Assistant Secretary
 Centers for Disease Control and Prevention—
   Jeffrey P. Koplan, Director
 Food and Drug Administration—
   Jane E. Henney, Commissioner
 National Institutes of Health—Ruth L. Kirschstein,
   Acting Director
 Surgeon General of the United States, David Satcher

Department of Housing and Urban Development

Secretary of Housing and Urban Development,
   Andrew M. Cuomo

Department of the Interior

Secretary of the Interior, Bruce Babbitt

Department of Justice

Attorney General, Janet Reno
 Bureau of Prisons—Kathleen Hawk Sawyer, Director
 Drug Enforcement Administration—
   Donnie R. Marshall, Administrator
 Federal Bureau of Investigation—Louis J. Freeh, Director
 Immigration and Naturalization Service—
   Doris M. Meissner, Commissioner
 Solicitor General, Seth P. Waxman

Department of Labor

Secretary of Labor, Alexis M. Herman

Department of State

Secretary of State, Madeleine K. Albright
 U.S. Ambassador to the United Nations, Richard C. Holbrooke

Department of Transportation

Secretary of Transportation, Rodney E. Slater
 Federal Aviation Administration—
   Jane F. Garvey, Administrator
 U.S. Coast Guard—Admiral James M. Loy, Commandant

Department of the Treasury

Secretary of the Treasury, Lawrence H. Summers
 Internal Revenue Service—Charles O. Rossotti, Commissioner
 Treasurer of the United States, Mary Ellen Withrow
 U.S. Secret Service—Brian L. Stafford, Director
 Office of Thrift Supervision—Ellen S. Seidman, Director

Department of Veterans Affairs

Acting Secretary of Veterans Affairs, Hershel W. Gober

Supreme Court of the United States

Chief Justice of the United States, William H. Rehnquist
 Associate Justices—
   John Paul Stevens   David H. Souter
   Sandra Day O'Connor   Clarence Thomas
   Antonin Scalia   Ruth Bader Ginsburg
   Anthony M. Kennedy   Stephen G. Breyer

Congressional officials

President of the Senate pro tempore, Strom Thurmond
 Senate Majority Leader, Trent Lott
 Senate Minority Leader, Thomas A. Daschle
 Speaker of the House, J. Dennis Hastert
 House Majority Leader, Richard K. Armey
 House Minority Leader, Richard A. Gephardt
 Congressional Budget Office—Dan L. Crippen, Director
 General Accounting Office—David M. Walker, Comptroller
   General of the United States
 Library of Congress—James H. Billington, Librarian of Congress

Independent agencies

Central Intelligence Agency—George J. Tenet, Director
Commission on Civil Rights—Mary Frances Berry, Chairperson
Commission of Fine Arts—J. Carter Brown, Chairman
Consumer Product Safety Commission—
   Ann Winkelman Brown, Chairman
Corporation for National Service—
   Harris Wofford, Chief Executive Officer
Environmental Protection Agency—
   Carol M. Browner, Administrator
Equal Employment Opportunity Commission—
   Ida L. Castro, Chairwoman
Federal Communications Commission—William E. Kennard, Chairman
Federal Deposit Insurance Corporation—
   Donna A. Tanoue, Chairman
Federal Election Commission—Darryl R. Wold, Chairman
Federal Emergency Management Agency—James Lee Witt, Director
Federal Reserve System Board of Governors—
   Alan Greenspan, Chairman
Federal Trade Commission—Robert Pitofsky, Chairman
General Services Administration—David J. Barram, Administrator
National Aeronautics and Space Administration—
   Daniel S. Goldin, Administrator
National Endowment for the Arts—William J. Ivey, Chairman
National Endowment for the Humanities—
   William R. Ferris, Chairman
National Labor Relations Board—John C. Truesdale, Chairman
National Railroad Passenger Corporation (Amtrak)—
   George D. Warrington, President & CEO
National Science Foundation—Rita R. Colwell, Director
National Transportation Safety Board—James E. Hall, Chairman
Nuclear Regulatory Commission—Richard A. Meserve, Chairman
Peace Corps—Mark L. Schneider, Director
Securities and Exchange Commission—Arthur Levitt, Jr., Chairman
Selective Service System—Gil Coronado, Director
Small Business Administration—Aida Alvarez, Administrator
Smithsonian Institution—Lawrence M. Small, Secretary
Social Security Administration—Kenneth S. Apfel, Commissioner
U.S. Postal Service—William J. Henderson, Postmaster General

*As of Dec. 31, 2000.

U.S. District Judge Walter Smith, Jr., accepted the jury's recommendation and ruled in September 2000 that the federal government owed nothing to Branch Davidian survivors or their families. Smith also ordered the plaintiffs to pay all court costs in the case.

John Danforth, a former Republican senator from Missouri who was appointed in 1999 to investigate the incident, issued an interim report in July 2000 claiming that the Branch Davidians were responsible for the tragedy. Danforth's investigation also found that there was no government conspiracy to cover up the cause of the fire and that the government did not start the fatal blaze. However, Danforth said that the FBI and government lawyers had failed to reveal that three canisters of tear gas had been fired into an area near the Branch Davidian compound. He added that the devices were fired four hours prior to the fire. Danforth reported that he would continue to examine why the Justice Department had failed to disclose the use of the devices.

Abortion drug. The U.S. Food and Drug Administration (FDA) on September 28 approved the sale of RU-486, a prescription drug that can induce the abortion of a fetus in the first seven weeks of pregnancy. RU-486, which was developed by French researchers in 1980 and marketed in Europe under the name mifepristone, was the first abortion drug legally available in the United States.

Clean water rules. The EPA in July 2000 issued new water pollution rules requiring states to restrict the runoff into waterways of fertilizer, animal waste, and lawn herbicides. The new rules, scheduled to take effect in October 2001, required state and local governments to work with the EPA in setting allowable levels of emissions. The EPA's ultimate goal was to make all U.S. bodies of water suitable for such recreational activities as fishing and swimming. The EPA had previously concentrated on restricting runoff from sewage treatment plants and factories.

Combating AIDS. The U.S. Export-Import Bank, an independent government agency financed by Congress, announced in July 2000 a $1-billion loan program to help African nations purchase drugs and medical services to combat AIDS. In 2000, public health experts reported that Africa had some 24.5 million people who were infected with HIV, the virus that causes AIDS. Public health agencies in less-developed nations were unable to buy the expensive drugs that help to fight the syndrome's medical complications and stem the disease's spread. Most of the loans would be made at the commercial interest rate, which at the time of the program's announcement stood at roughly 7 percent.

Media violence. The Federal Trade Commission (FTC) on September 11 released a report alleging that entertainment industry executives were consciously marketing violent entertainment to children as young as 12 years old. The FTC report, which was the result of a yearlong study, concluded that most of the best-selling music compact discs (CD's), video games, and films rated for mature audiences had been marketed with advertising aimed at young people. The FTC reported that the motion picture, music, and electronic game industries "routinely market to children the very products that have the industries' own parental warnings or ratings with age restrictions due to their violent content."

Medal of Honor recipients. President Bill Clinton on June 21 presented the Medal of Honor to 22 Asian Americans, most of them of Japanese heritage, for their heroism with serving in the U.S. Army during World War II (1939-1945). The Medal of Honor is the highest military decoration that the United States grants to members of its armed forces. Senator Daniel K. Inouye (D., Hawaii) was among the recipients.

☐ Linda P. Campbell and Geoffrey A. Campbell

See also **Africa: A Special Report; Congress of the United States; Courts; Crime; Democratic Party; Elections; Republican Party; Special Election 2000 Supplement; State government; Supreme Court of the United States.**

United States, President of the.

In July 2000, President Bill Clinton hosted a summit between Israeli Prime Minister Ehud Barak and Palestinian leader Yasir Arafat in an effort to reach a final peace agreement in the Middle East. The leaders met at Camp David, the presidential retreat in Maryland. Clinton had hoped to reach an accord to end the often violent conflict between Israelis and Palestinians. However, the summit ended when neither side could resolve such issues as the division of Jerusalem, which both sides claim as their capital; the fate of Palestinian refugees; and how much land Israel would cede to a Palestinian state in exchange for areas of the West Bank with large Jewish settlements.

Presidential visits. In November, President Clinton visited Vietnam. The trip was the first by a U.S. president since Richard Nixon visited U.S. troops stationed in South Vietnam during the Vietnam War (1957-1975). During his three-day stay, President Clinton encouraged Vietnamese leaders to further open their economy to trade with the West.

In August 2000, the president visited Nigeria, Tanzania, and Egypt. While in Egypt, President Clinton met with President Hosni Mubarek to discuss the Israeli-Palestinian conflict.

From May 30 to June 5, the president visited Portugal, Germany, and Ukraine. The trip included a three-day summit with Russian President Vladimir Putin in Moscow. In March, President Clinton conducted a six-day tour of Asia, which included stops in India, Bangladesh, and Pakistan. In India, the president signed a trade agreement with Indian Prime Minister Atal Vajpayee.

Marriage penalty veto. President Clinton vetoed a bill in August 2000 that would have cut taxes for married couples in the United States. The president said that the legislation provided a larger tax cut to wealthy families than middle-income families.

New national monuments. In January, the president signed proclamations creating three national monuments. He doubled the amount of federally protected land at the Grand Canyon in Arizona by designating 1,500 square miles (3,890 square kilometers) on its northern rim as the Grand Canyon-Parashant National Monument. He also added land to the Pinnacles National Monument east of Salinas, California, and gave federal protection to Agua Fria, land containing prehistoric ruins north of Phoenix. In 2000, Clinton put more than 135,0000 square miles (350,000 square kilometers) of land under federal protection.

☐ Linda P. Campbell and Geoffrey A. Campbell

See also **Congress of the United States; Conservation; Israel; Middle East; Taxation; United States, Government of the; Vietnam.**

Uruguay. Jorge Batlle, of Uruguay's incumbent Colorado Party, was sworn to a five-year term as president on March 1, 2000. Batlle, a lawyer, promised to address Uruguay's 11-percent unemployment rate and other serious economic problems.

Batlle also pledged to work toward continental unity among South American countries. In September, he and Luis Gonzalez Macchi, the president of Paraguay, urged Mercosur—an international trade organization based in Montevideo, the Uruguayan capital—to grant Chile and Bolivia "greater participation." Uruguay, Paraguay, Argentina, and Brazil were full members of Mercosur, while Chile and Bolivia were associate members.

Government statistics indicated that visitors from Mercosur nations boosted tourism in Uruguay 25 percent between 1994 and 1999.

In November 2000, Batlle presided at a ceremony in Montevideo to launch construction of the Cruz del Sur pipeline, scheduled to deliver natural gas from Argentina to Uruguay by 2002. The pipeline was to eventually extend into Brazil. Batlle noted that the project continued "a process of energy integration" in South America.

☐ Nathan A. Haverstock

See also **Latin America.**

Utah. See State government.

Uzbekistan. Islam Karimov was reelected president on Jan. 9, 2000. He won 92 percent of the vote with a reported turnout of 95 percent. Karimov's sole opponent, Abdulhafiz Jalolov, cast his vote publicly for Karimov. The Organization for Security and Cooperation in Europe (OSCE), an international security group that monitors elections, refused to send observers to the election, claiming the event offered voters "no genuine choice." Karimov's supporters also had captured every parliamentary seat in noncompetitive elections in December 1999.

In August 2000, guerrillas from the Islamic Movement of Uzbekistan (IMU) crossed the border from Tajikistan and attacked rural targets in Uzbekistan. The Uzbek government pressured Tajikistan to take action against IMU bases on Tajik territory. In September, the United States added the IMU to its list of terrorist groups, alleging that the IMU had ties to Saudi Arabian terrorist Osama bin Laden.

Drought and the collapse of global prices for gold and cotton, Uzbekistan's primary exports, shook the Uzbek economy in 2000. The economic crisis led to a 50-percent devaluation of the som, Uzbekistan's main unit of currency, over the course of 2000. ☐ Steven L. Solnick

See also **Afghanistan; Asia.**

Vanuatu. See Pacific Islands.

Venezuela. President Hugo Chavez Frias was sworn in to a new term as Venezuela's president on Aug. 19, 2000, despite allegations of election irregularities. Originally taking office in December 1999, Chavez had launched initiatives to rewrite the country's constitution in order to overhaul political institutions and rid the government of what he said was massive corruption.

As part of his goal to achieve an "economic revolution," Chavez moved against the Venezuelan Workers' Confederation (CTV), a trade-union coalition with more than 1 million members. In December 2000, Venezuelans approved a referendum backed by Chavez to suspend the leaders of the CTV and replace them within six months. Many international labor groups condemned the vote. The new Venezuelan constitution called for a single, government-dominated union.

Revitalizing OPEC. In the days leading up to his inauguration, Chavez visited 10 nations belonging to the Organization of Petroleum Exporting Countries (OPEC), a group of 12 oil-exporting nations, including Venezuela. On August 10, Chavez became the first head of state to meet with Iraqi President Saddam Hussein since the Persian Gulf War (1991), in which United States forces led a coalition of nations to push Iraqi troops out of Kuwait. The U.S. State Department characterized the visit as "particularly galling."

In March 2000, OPEC ministers elected Venezuela's Minister of Energy, Ali Rodriguez Araque, president of OPEC in reward for engineering a steep rise in oil prices by persuading OPEC members to adhere to production quotas. These price increases led to record Venezuelan oil revenues of $21 billion in 2000. In September, the Venezuelan capital, Caracas, hosted the first summit meeting of government leaders of OPEC nations since 1975. Officials at the summit worked to develop solidarity among the often divided OPEC members.

Dispute with Guyana. Referring to a disputed region believed to be rich in minerals on Venezuela's border with neighboring Guyana, President Chavez claimed in August 2000, "that territory is ours." Venezuela had long claimed the area, but Chavez was prompted to bring the matter up again because of a May agreement between the Guyanese government and Beal Aerospace Technologies, Incorporated, of Frisco, Texas. Chavez maintained that the agreement, which concerned the construction of a spaceport within the region to launch satellites, masked U.S. government intentions to establish a military presence along Venezuela's eastern border.

☐ Nathan A. Haverstock

See also **Energy supply; Iraq; Latin America.**

Vermont. See State government.

Vietnam. United States President Bill Clinton visited Vietnam on Nov. 16, 2000. The visit was the first by a U.S. president since Richard Nixon visited South Vietnam during the Vietnam War (1957-1975). The war ended with 58,000 Americans dead and the defeat of the U.S.-backed regime in South Vietnam.

On June 13, 2000, Trade Minister Vu Khoan signed a trade agreement with the United States that opened U.S. markets to Vietnamese exports under the same conditions extended to countries with "most-favored-nation" status. Some top Communist leaders opposed the agreement, but other Vietnamese officials believed it would help improve the economy. The U.S. Congress ended its 2000 session without ratifying the agreement.

In June, the chief ideologue of Vietnam's ruling Communist Party, Nguyen Duc Binh, and 15 other senior officials attended a seminar in China on how to reform a socialist economy. The seminar was hosted by the Chinese party's leadership, whose moves toward world trade put pressure on Vietnam to compete for those markets.

Pham Van Dong, the premier of North Vietnam for 33 years, died on April 29 at age 94.

☐ Henry S. Bradsher

See also **Asia.**

Virginia. See State government.
Vital statistics. See Census; Population.

U.S. President Bill Clinton stands before a bust of the Vietnamese revolutionary leader Ho Chi Minh during a welcoming ceremony in Hanoi in November 2000. Clinton was the first U.S. president to visit Vietnam since the Vietnam War ended in 1975.

An artist's rendering of the World War II memorial, for which ground was broken in November, highlights the monument's neoclassical design. Both the design and the memorial's location—between the Lincoln Memorial and the Washington Monument—sparked controversy.

Washington, D.C., underwent a major resurgence in 2000. Business leaders gave much of the credit for the turnaround to Mayor Anthony A. Williams, who made economic development—particularly the attraction of new businesses and residents to the city—the focus of his administration after taking office in 1999.

Growth in the city's population, which had been reported by the United States Census Bureau in late 1999, continued in 2000, after decades of decline. Analysts attributed the increase, in part, to a tax cut passed in 1999 and a $5,000 tax credit for first-time home buyers. In addition, city officials reported in September 2000 that Washington, D.C., had balanced its budget for the fourth year in a row and had improved its *bond rating* (eligibility to borrow money). Both achievements were requirements set by the D.C. control board, an agency created by Congress in 1995 to run the city. After regulators complete verification of the city's economic standing—a process that was expected to be completed by February 2001—the board was to return full governing powers to the mayor and city council.

Revitalization. A number of construction and redevelopment projects were launched in 2000 that business leaders expected would help revitalize the city. Mayor Williams announced in August that 81 small, disadvantaged businesses

had been awarded contracts for work on a new convention center, located in Mount Vernon Square. Completion of the center was scheduled for 2003. The San Francisco-based Kimpton Hotel & Restaurant Group, Incorporated, began renovation in early 2000 of the U.S. Tariff Commission Building. The company planned to turn the structure into a 172-room luxury hotel. The popular Newseum, a media museum located in the Virginia suburb of Rosslyn, announced plans in July 2000 to move to a site in Washington, D.C., on Pennsylvania Avenue. In September, the city government and a private developer announced an agreement to build a major retail complex near Capitol Hill. The new center represented a victory for the neighborhood and the city, as the great number of shopping options that characterize America's suburbs have long been unavailable to D.C. residents.

Infrastructure and taxes. Despite the boom, Washington, D.C., lagged behind the rest of the region in economic growth and development. According to city planners, much of the city's infrastructure—its bridges, roads, water and gas systems, sewers, and telephones—were at or near the end of their useful lives, hampering economic growth. The deterioration came to light in spring and summer 2000 as the city laid the fiberoptic cable networks necessary to attract

hi-tech workers and businesses. The D.C. control board estimated in June 2000 that an upgrade of the city's infrastructure could cost $5 billion.

In 2000, the city government again took up the issue of taxing commuter workers. Government officials estimated that two-thirds of the people who work in D.C. actually live in Virginia and Maryland. Although most U.S. states levy income taxes on anyone who earns money in the state, Washington, D.C., cannot. D.C.'s congressional delegate, Eleanor Holmes Norton, proposed in April that a 2 percent tax be levied on commuter workers' salaries. The tax would not be an additional tax but rather would be redirected from workers' federal income taxes. Such a tax would raise about $400 million annually.

Memorial. On November 11, ground was broken for a memorial to the U.S. soldiers who fought in World War II (1939-1945), despite the fact that the chosen site—a location on the Mall between the Lincoln Memorial and the Washington Monument—sparked controversy. Many critics claimed the memorial would destroy the open nature of the Mall, while others believed the location should be preserved as the site of Marian Anderson's 1939 concert and Martin Luther King, Jr's., "I Have a Dream" speech during the March on Washington in 1963.   ☐ Robert Messenger

See also **City.**

Weather. Extremes characterized weather patterns in many areas of the world in 2000. The United States had the warmest winter since record-keeping began in 1895. In Europe, a summer heat wave triggered fires in Italy, Greece, and the Balkans, while autumn rains caused record-breaking floods in the United Kingdom and France. Unseasonably heavy rains also produced floods in Africa and southeast Asia.

Floods in Africa. Deadly flooding plagued southeastern Africa in February and March. Two tropical cyclones, Eline and Gloria, dropped vast amounts of rain on already swollen rivers. An area of Madagascar received more than 55 inches (140 centimeters) of rain in the two-month period. The floods affected more than 1 million people, many of whom contracted malaria and cholera in the wake of the flooding.

Heat and floods in Europe. A heat wave scorched southeast Europe in early July when a ridge of high pressure swept in from the Sahara and stalled above Turkey, Bulgaria, Greece, Romania, and Italy, where temperatures reached as high as 113 °F (45 °C). By mid-July, the continuing heat had sparked hundreds of fires. More than 28,000 acres (11,500 hectares) of crops and forests were destroyed.

In early November, heavy rains caused the worst flooding in more than 50 years in Great

Extremes—especially floods and droughts—dominated weather patterns worldwide in 2000.

Residents of Bucharest, Romania (above), fish in the bed of the Dambovita River, which went dry during the heat wave that scorched southeastern Europe in early July. A ridge of high pressure swept in from the Sahara and stalled, causing record-breaking high temperatures.

A Texas cattle rancher (below) surveys his dried-up stock pond in August. On August 29, U.S. Agriculture Secretary Dan Glickman designated 153 Texas counties disaster areas, as the state experienced its driest July and August on record.

Shattered windows in a skyscraper attest to the power of two tornadoes that devastated downtown Fort Worth, Texas, on March 28, killing five people.

A woman passes near the gates of the Old City of Jerusalem during a storm that buried the city under more than 12 inches (30 centimeters) of snow in January.

A U.S. Forest Service worker monitors a fire in a canyon at Burgdorf Junction, Idaho, in August. By late September, wildfires had burned almost 1 million acres (405,000 hectares) throughout Idaho and Montana.

Britain. France, Italy, and Spain were also flooded, as the storm stalled over Europe. Six people were killed and thousands of houses destroyed.

Flooding in Asia. Heavy rains that began in July—weeks before the normal start of the monsoon season—caused flooding in Cambodia, Vietnam, Laos, and Thailand through October. Government officials reported that the Mekong River reached its highest level in 70 years. More than 250 people were killed, and 4.5 million people were displaced by the floods. Late monsoons in mid-September in the Indian state of West Bengal caused devastating floods that continued into October. The flood waters swept into neighboring Bangladesh, causing serious flooding.

United States. The year 2000 began with unusually mild weather across the United States. In the Northeast, a pattern of sparse snowfall, which started in 1999, continued into early January 2000. Boston ended a record-breaking 303 consecutive days without measurable snow with a 5.6-inch (14.2-centimeter) accumulation on January 13.

On January 22 and 23, parts of the Southeastern United States were engulfed by a severe ice storm. Areas of northern Georgia and western South Carolina had more than 2 inches (5 centimeters) of rain with temperatures below freezing. In the Atlanta area, more than 500,000 utility customers lost power because of the storm.

Heavy snow fell from the Carolinas to New England on January 24. The snowstorm was the worst in more than 100 years in central North Carolina. Raleigh, the state capital, received a total of 20.3 inches (51.6 centimeters), a new city record for a single storm.

Weather in February was exceptionally warm throughout the United States. Mid-month, all-time high temperatures for February set records in the Middle West and Northeast, including International Falls, Minnesota (58 °F, 14 °C), Green Bay, Wisconsin (61 °F, 16 °C), and Buffalo, New York (71 °F, 22 °C). The warm temperatures contributed to the mildest winter season in the United States since record keeping began in 1895.

Spring storms. A fierce storm brought heavy rain to the Southwestern United States in March 2000. Phoenix had 1.53 inches (3.89 centimeters) on March 6, the city's second-wettest March day on record. The storm swept toward the Great Lakes on March 8, triggering the earliest tornado ever observed in Milwaukee County, Wisconsin. On March 28, two tornadoes tore through Fort Worth, Texas, marking the fourth time in two years that a large U.S. metropolitan area had been directly hit by a tornado. Five people in Fort Worth died, including a person who was hit in the head by a baseball-sized hailstone, the first death by hail in the United States since 1979.

Drought and fire. In spring 2000, abundant sunshine and modest rainfall in much of the interior West and South foreshadowed a summer of drought and fires. Florida had its driest May on record with statewide average rainfall only 23 percent of normal. The dryness fueled wildfires across Florida with the state forestry division reporting over 100,000 acres (40,500 hectares) burned since the beginning of 2000. In early May in New Mexico, strong winds sent a fire, set by the National Park Service to clear underbrush, out of control. The fire consumed 48,000 acres (19,440 hectares) and destroyed over 200 houses near Los Alamos, New Mexico. Federal officials estimated the damage at more than $1 billion.

Record heat affected parts of the Southwest in May and June. A new heat record in the United States for May was set at Death Valley, California, on May 29 when the temperature reached 122 °F (50 °C). New state temperature records for May were set at Frederick, Oklahoma (112 °F, 44 °C), and Carlsbad, New Mexico (110 °F, 43 °C). In mid-June, San Francisco had its hottest day on record, when the mercury touched 103 °F (39 °C).

During much of the summer, a stagnant, upper-level high pressure system centered near Texas contributed to a heat wave and drought that affected the Southern Plains and parts of the interior West. The federal government declared Georgia, Alabama, and Texas disaster areas because of agricultural losses, which exceeded $600 million in both Texas and Georgia. Texas suffered the driest July and August on record. Dallas went 84 days without measurable precipitation, smashing the old record of 58 days set in both 1950 and 1934. The record heat reached a crescendo in early September 2000 when the highest temperatures ever recorded for that month were either tied or exceeded in Houston (109 °F, 43 °C); Dallas (111 °F, 44 °C); New Orleans, Louisiana (101 °F, 38 °C), Fort Smith, Arkansas (109 °F, 43 °C), Tucson, Arizona (107 °F, 42 °C); Salina, Kansas (110 °F, 43 °C); and Lincoln, Nebraska (106 °F, 41 °C). Drought also plagued the region.

Fire in the West. The continuing dry weather in the United States fueled widespread fires across the interior West. By late September, close to 1 million acres (405,000 hectares) had burned in Idaho and Montana. Nationally, nearly 7 million acres (2,835,000 hectares) were charred, the largest area to burn since 1988. In parts of the northern Rockies, the summer of 2000 was the worst fire season in 50 years.

Cool summer in the Northeast. Much of the summer in the Northeast was exceptionally cool. July was the coolest on record in both Pennsylvania and West Virginia. In July, Albany, New York, failed to reach 85 °F (29 °C) for the first time on record, while in New York City, the temperature did not reach 90 °F (32 °C) for only the second time in 100 years.

Hurricane season. The first hurricane of the Atlantic season was born on August 4 near the Cape Verde Islands and moved into the central Atlantic. Hurricane Alberto remained on weather maps through August 23 but never threatened land. Alberto was the longest-lived August hurricane on record. None of the other 11 named hurricanes or tropical storms of the 2000 season had a major impact on North America.

Snow and cold. An early snowstorm hit the northern Rockies on September 23 and 24. Cheyenne, Wyoming, had its snowiest September day on record when 6.4 inches (16. 3 centimeters) fell on September 24.

An early discharge of Arctic air poured into parts of the Northern states in November. On November 12, the mercury plummetted to –18 °F (–28 °C) in Wheatland, Wyoming, and –14 °F (–26 °C) in Alliance, Nebraska, establishing record-low temperatures for November at both locations. On November 20, an intense snowstorm buried Buffalo, New York, when cold air sweeping across Lake Erie brought 24.9 inches (63.2 centimeters) of snow, the highest 24-hour November total on record there. □ Fred Gadomski and Todd Miner

See also **Africa; Asia; Disasters; Europe.**

Weightlifting. See Sports.

Welfare. The United States Department of Health and Human Services (HHS) announced on Aug. 22, 2000, that welfare caseloads had decreased to 6.3 million recipients in December 1999, a 56 percent decline since 1993. The number of welfare recipients as a proportion of the U.S. population stood at 2.3 percent in 1999, the lowest level since 1965. Government officials attributed the decrease primarily to the Personal Responsibility and Work Opportunity Reconciliation Act, a law signed by President Bill Clinton in 1996. The act required welfare recipients to work in exchange for time-limited public assistance.

The law also mandated a schedule requiring states to meet employment goals for welfare recipients, commonly referred to as welfare-to-work participation rates. HHS Secretary Donna E. Shalala and President Clinton announced in August 2000 that all 50 states and the District of Columbia met the overall 1999 participation rates required by the law, the third year in a row that all states had fulfilled the requirement. States achieved a total work participation rate of over 38 percent, an increase of 9 percent from 1999.

Help for municipalities. On June 1, 2000, President Clinton announced that HHS, the U.S. Department of Labor, and the U.S. Department of Transportation had released new guidance on how states and communities could coordinate federal assistance to address transportation problems for people moving from welfare to work. Among other suggestions, the departments offered strategies ranging from making public transporation more available for weekend and evening shifts to helping people lease, purchase, or repair automobiles.

State hoarding. Forty-five states and the District of Columbia held more than $7.3 billion in federal welfare money in reserve at the end of 1999, according to a study released Feb. 24, 2000, by the National Campaign for Jobs and Income, a group of social welfare organizations, and by the Center on Budget and Policy Priorities, a policy research institute. The study found that, instead of spending the federal money on services designed to help move families off welfare and into paying jobs, some states held on to the money in case of a future economic downturn. In addition, the study indicated that at least six states used federal money to cover state budget cuts for welfare programs.

Responsible fatherhood initiative. President Clinton unveiled a new package of welfare reform proposals on January 26 designed to help fathers find work and meet their child support obligations. Clinton called the proposals an important next step in welfare reform.

□ Linda P. Campbell and Geoffrey A. Campbell

West Indies. Rafael Hipolito Mejia Dominguez, of the center-left Dominican Revolutionary Party, was sworn in to a four-year term as president of the Dominican Republic on Aug. 16, 2000. The same day, Milagros Ortiz Bosch became the Dominican Republic's first female vice president. Bosch was a niece of the late Juan Bosch, who in 1963 became the first democratically elected president of the Dominican Republic.

Mejia Dominguez promised special attention to the "hungry masses," the many Dominicans who had been left behind by modernization. He pledged to boost government spending on health care, education, housing, and the concerns of farmers, many of whom were in financial distress as a result of recent privatization of the previously state-owned sugar business.

Dominica. On Jan. 31, 2000, Roosevelt Douglas, of the Dominica Labour Party, was elected prime minister of the eastern Caribbean Commonwealth of Dominica. His party ousted the ruling United Workers Party of Prime Minister Edison James by a narrow margin. On October 1, Douglas suddenly died at age 58. Communications Minister Pierre Charles was named acting prime minister.

St. Kitts and Nevis. On March 6, voters of the two-island nation of St. Kitts and Nevis expanded the incumbent Labour Party's parliamentary majority and gave Prime Minister Denzil Douglas a second five-year term. Shortly before the election, in a move that proved popular with the electorate, the government *extradited* (gave up to another nation) Charles "Little Nut" Miller to the United States, where the St. Kitts resident was wanted on charges of smuggling cocaine.

AIDS. At a September conference in Bridgetown, the capital of Barbados, several international donors promised $120 million to the nations of the Caribbean to fight AIDS. The World Bank, a United Nations (UN) financial agency based in Washington, D.C., that provides loans for development and other purposes, pledged to furnish the bulk of the funds. Other donors included the governments of Canada and the Netherlands and the World Health Organization, a UN agency based in Geneva, Switzerland.

Government officials of various Caribbean nations estimated in 2000 that 360,000 people in the Caribbean suffered from AIDS or were infected with HIV, the virus that causes AIDS. Many health experts, however, said the actual number of AIDS cases in the region exceeded 500,000.

☐ Nathan A. Haverstock

See also **AIDS; Latin America.**

West Virginia. See **State government.**
Wisconsin. See **State government.**
Wyoming. See **State government.**

Yugoslavia. On Oct. 7, 2000, Vojislav Kostunica, a constitutional law professor who previously had not been active in politics, became president of Yugoslavia after Slobodan Milosevic resigned. Milosevic had been president since 1997 and had been indicted in 1999 as a war criminal by the International Tribunal for War Crimes for his role in various wars in the 1990's involving former units of Yugoslavia. In 2000, Yugoslavia consisted of Serbia and Montenegro.

Milosevic had scheduled presidential elections for September 24, reportedly to build political support. After the election, Kostunica's supporters claimed he had won with more than 50 percent of the vote. The government, controlled by Milosevic, claimed that neither candidate had won a majority and ordered a runoff election, which was scheduled for October. The opposition refused to accept that Kostunica had not defeated Milosevic outright, and they organized demonstrations and strikes to demand that Kostunica be declared president.

On October 5, several hundred thousand people from across Serbia converged on the capital, Belgrade, and stormed parliament and the state broadcasting center, demanding that Milosevic resign. During a gun battle, protesters set fire to several buildings and Serb police could do little to stop the crowd. Milosevic resigned on October

6, and Kostunica was sworn in as president of Yugoslavia on October 7.

Many international observers were shocked by Milosevic's downfall, which was brought about by the huge public demonstrations against him. Opposition groups had been trying for years to remove Milosevic from office. However, he had managed to hold on to power for 13 years through four wars and isolation from the international community that his racist policies of *ethnic cleansing* (killing or forcing people of a certain race out of a country) had caused.

Transitional government. On October 16, leaders of Yugoslavia's Socialist Party, which Milosevic still headed, agreed to join with two major opposition parties to form a transitional government. However, though Kostunica had the support of the people, the Socialist Party leaders still controlled many parts of the government, including the police and the court system.

Serbian elections. The democratic coalition led by President Kostunica won 64.5 percent of the vote in Serbian parliamentary elections held on December 23. The coalition won 176 of 250 seats, dealing a final blow to the Socialist Party led by Slobodan Milosevic, which won just 37 seats.

Kosovo. In October 2000, the moderate Democratic League of Kosovo, led by Ibrahim Rugova, won approximately 60 percent of the vote in local elections held in Kosovo, a semiautonomous province of Yugoslavia. Parties led by previous commanders of the Kosovo Liberation Army (KLA), a guerrilla group involved in the violence in Kosovo in the 1990's, came in second and third. All three parties favored independence for Kosovo. Despite the fact that international observers declared the election free and fair, Kostunica invalidated the results because many Serbs had boycotted the election.

Kostunica's election left the future of Kosovo in dispute. In 1999, the North Atlantic Treat Organization (NATO) conducted a bombing campaign in Serbia to stop violent clashes between the Serbian military and the KLA. In October 2000, Kostunica conceded that Serbs had committed atrocities against ethnic Albanian citizens in Kosovo in the 1990's. However, he had opposed independence for Kosovo and had strongly disagreed with the NATO bombing campaign.

Montenegro. Montenegran voters boycotted the Yugoslav presidential election in September 2000. Members of the Democratic Party of Socialists, the ruling party of Montenegro, began preparations in November for a referendum declaring Montenegro's independence from Yugoslavia. However, they agreed not to take any action until early in 2001.

Foreign affairs. Yugoslavia's new leaders moved quickly to begin to improve relations with

Yugoslav demonstrators in Belgrade, the Yugoslav capital, celebrate Vojislav Kostunica's apparent election victory over President Slobodan Milosevic on Sept. 27, 2000. Kostunica became president on October 7, after Milosevic resigned in the face of growing public hostility to his regime.

neighboring countries and overcome the international isolation that had developed under Milosevic. On Nov. 2, 2000, Yugoslavia was readmitted as a full member of the United Nations (UN). Officials of Yugoslavia and the European Union (EU) in November signed an agreement designed to help stabilize the region.

Kostunica also met with Bosnian leaders in November and pledged to work to establish better diplomatic relations. In November, Kostunica traveled to Moscow for talks with Russian President Vladimir Putin concerning energy supplies.

On October 12, the United States lifted its oil embargo and ban on airline flights to Yugoslavia and pledged $100 million in aid. The United States reestablished formal diplomatic ties with Yugoslavia on November 17. Yugoslav officials in November also reestablished diplomatic relations with Great Britain, France, and Germany. In October, officials from the International Monetary Fund, a UN-affiliated organization that provides short-term credit to member nations, visited Belgrade to assess Yugoslavia's economic situation and its ability to begin to repay its sizable debts.

☐ Sharon L. Wolchik

See also **Europe.**

Yukon Territory. See Canadian territories.
Zambia. See Africa.

Zimbabwe. President Robert Mugabe's authority was shaken severely in 2000, as Zimbabwe confronted its toughest political and economic crisis since independence from British rule in 1980. A terror campaign, waged by Mugabe's ruling Zimbabwe African National Union-Patriotic Front (ZANU-PF) before June 2000 parliamentary elections, claimed dozens of lives. The campaign began in February, when black squatters, apparently with government backing, illegally invaded more than 1,000 white-owned farms.

Referendum. Mugabe suffered the first electoral defeat of his 20-year rule in February 2000, when voters rejected a new constitution that would have entrenched his powers and allowed the government to seize white-owned land for redistribution to blacks without paying compensation. According to political analysts, unemployment, fuel shortages, and corruption caused discontent among voters, who rejected the new constitution by 54.7 percent to 45.3 percent.

Land invasions. In 2000, armed squatters, many claiming to be veterans of the pre-1980 guerrilla war against white rule, occupied about 1,600 of Zimbabwe's 4,500 white-owned commercial farms. These farms made up 70 percent of Zimbabwe's most fertile land. At least 47 people were killed and thousands injured in the widespread intimidation of white owners and

Armed with farm tools, black squatters occupy a white-owned farm in Zimbabwe in April 2000. Squatters, demanding land reforms, illegally invaded more than 1,000 farms during Zimbabwe's 2000 presidential election campaign.

their black workers that accompanied the occupations. Human rights activists claimed that Mugabe was orchestrating the violence to scare opposition supporters away from the polls. The land invasions severely disrupted agriculture, the backbone of the economy, which in 2000 was shrinking faster than any other economy in Africa.

General election. Against overwhelming odds, Morgan Tsvangirai's opposition Movement for Democratic Change (MDC) captured 57 of the National Assembly's 120 elective seats in bitterly fought elections on June 24 and 25. Mugabe's ZANU-PF won 62 seats. One seat went to an independent. The constitution allowed the president to appoint 30 additional parliamentary members, giving ZANU-PF 92 of the 150 seats—a sharp drop from the 147 held prior to the election.

On July 15, President Mugabe announced his new cabinet, reduced from 27 full ministers to 19. Many of Mugabe's long-serving ministers were cast aside in favor of younger business executives. However, on September 29, the MDC announced a campaign of strikes and demonstrations to force Mugabe's resignation. On Sept. 30, 2000, Tsvangirai warned Mugabe, "If you don't want to go peacefully, we will remove you violently."

□ Simon Baynham

See also **Africa; Congo (Kinshasa).**

Zoology. See **Biology.**

Zoos. The South Carolina aquarium in Charleston, South Carolina, opened on May 19, 2000. Visitors took a journey through the state's aquatic habitats, from the Blue Ridge Mountains to the Atlantic Ocean. The aquarium consists of five galleries with more than 60 exhibits and approximately 10,000 creatures. The tour begins in a forested mountain ravine with free-flying birds—Carolina wrens, chickadees, warblers, and woodpeckers—darting through the trees. Waterfalls cascade down wooded slopes into a deep pool with river otters. Foothill streams, brooks, and a headwaters habitat feature fish of the southern Appalachian Mountains.

Visitors also learn about the rippling valleys and hills of the "Piedmont Plateau," where free-flowing rivers are commonly dammed to form reservoirs. The "Coastal Plain" exhibit features freshwater swamps and marshes. Special effects reproduce a misty cypress-tupelo blackwater swamp at dusk. Fiberoptic lights give the effect of twinkling fireflies. The ground is soft and spongy, like a real swamp, with machine-made fog hugging the ground and Spanish moss on the tree branches hanging overhead. In the dim light, visitors see several Atlantic sturgeon and American eels as well as frogs, turtles, and crayfish.

The "Coastal Gallery" exhibit features salt marsh planted with vegetation that hosts clapper

America, with a wingspan of nearly 10 feet (3 meters)—is the focus of a captive-breeding recovery program. Several condors hatched at the Wild Animal Park and been released to the wild.

Lion kings and queens. In late May, the Sedgwick County Zoo in Wichita, Kansas, premiered "Pride of the Plains," an exhibit where African trees, shrubs, and grasses recreate the look of a savannah. Visitors find a colony of meerkats in perpetual motion. Several warthogs root about the grassland, and a pride of lions wait around the corner. Large glass panels allow visitors to get within 1 inch (2.54 centimeters) of the big cats. At the end of the trail, a pack of African hunting dogs roam along a stream.

Wild Pacific. The Oregon Zoo in Portland expanded its Great Northwest section with the opening in July of "Steller Cove," an exhibit devoted to Oregon's coastal environment. The Steller sea lions, for which the exhibit is named, are among the largest seals in the world. Males reach 11 feet (3.35 meters) in length and weigh more than 2,000 pounds (907.1 kilograms). When they are not lounging, the giant Steller sea lions featured in the exhibit paddle around a 198,000-gallon (750,000-liter) pool. Visitors can see the sea otters from above and below the water's sur-

rails, sandpipers, marsh wrens, and painted buntings. Baby sharks, shrimp, stingrays, crabs, red drum, and terrapins inhabit the gallery's pools. A freshwater marsh is inhabited by alligators that appear above and below the water's surface.

The tour concludes at the sea where a two-story, 322,000-gallon (1.2 million-liter) "Great Ocean" exhibit gives several perspectives. The sandy sea floor reveals skates and stingrays and a reef that is inhabited by small fishes, sponges, and octopus, nestled among crevices. The "Deep Sea" provides the feeling of sitting on the edge of the Continental Shelf while sharks, sea turtles, and schools of fish prowl the water.

American wilderness. The San Diego Wild Animal Park in California, features some of the most endangered species in the United States at the "Condor Ridge" exhibit, which opened in May. The tour begins at a pine forest alive with thick-billed parrots. In a grassland habitat, small aplomado falcons fly overhead. Visitors to a series of prairie ecosystem exhibits encounter black-tailed prairie dogs, black-footed ferrets, burrowing owls, desert tortoises, Harris hawks, and American magpies. An observation deck offers close-up views of a herd of rare desert bighorn sheep. The deck overlooks a six-story aviary where California condors glide about artificial cliffs. The condor—the largest bird of North

Zoo and aquarium attractions

Additional zoo and aquarium exhibit openings in 2000

Cincinnati Zoo, Cincinnati, OH. "Vanishing Giants," which opened in May, focuses on the conservation of threatened large mammals, including Asian elephants, Maasai giraffes, and the okapi.

Cleveland Metroparks Zoo, Cleveland, OH. "Australian Adventure," which opened in June, is an Australian-themed children's zoo with koalas, a tree kangaroo, a lorikeet (parrot) aviary, and wallaby and kangaroo species.

Detroit Zoological Institute, Detroit, MI. "Amphibiville," which opened in June, features hundreds of amphibians in a variety of habitats.

Monterey Bay Aquarium, Monterey, CA. "Splash Zone," which opened in April, features two coastline habitats and live animals with "hands-on" displays.

National Aquarium, Baltimore, MD. "Amazon River Forest," which opened in March, focuses on a black water Amazon tributary and the forest it floods during the rainy season.

New England Aquarium, Boston, MA. "Nyanja! Africa's Inland Sea," which opened in April, examines the ecology and conservation of Lake Victoria, the world's second-largest lake.

Oregon Coast Aquarium, Newport, OR. "Passages of the Deep," which opened in May, features a 2-million-gallon (7.6-million liter) tank divided into three large ocean habitats.

Visitors to the South Carolina Aquarium in Charleston, enjoy the 322,000-gallon (1.2-million-liter) Great Ocean Tank. Hundreds of animals and plants inhabit the exhibit, which visitors can view from three enormous windows.

face. Inside a rocky cave, visitors observe small fish and invertebrates among swaying branches in an underwater forest of giant kelp.

Aquatic launch. The Pittsburgh Zoo in Pennsylvania opened a new aquarium in May, based on state-of-the-art technology. The "Diversity of Water" exhibit features five galleries housing more than 40 exhibits that showcase nearly 4,000 aquatic animals of 500 different species. A 500-gallon (1,900-liter) tank revolves 360 degrees for a view of the coral reef-and-fish ecosystem within.

A two-story, 100,000-gallon (380,000-liter) tank provides five views of the saltwater ecosystem inhabited by sharks and other fish. King and rockhopper penguins toddle about or swim gracefully underwater. Specialized lighting repro-

duces the day-night cycle of their natural environment, encouraging breeding. A special window allows visitors to walk underwater with cold water fish swimming overhead. Children can navigate a crawl-through tunnel with stingrays swimming above and alongside. A rainforest exhibit offers underwater viewing of a rare Amazon River dolphin. A trio of waterfalls amid hundreds of plants supply a tropical atmosphere as tiny golden lion tamarins explore the vegetation.

Two young giant pandas arrived at the National Zoo in Washington, D.C., in December. The government of China sent Mei Xiang, a 2-year-old female, and Tian Tian, a 3-year-old male, in exchange for a $10-million donation to aid panda conservation in China.   □ Eugene J. Walter, Jr.

WAR FOR THE WHITE HOUSE: A LEGACY OF THE U.S. CONSTITUTION

A down-to-the-wire battle for the presidency rivets the nation's attention and raises questions about a once-obscure institution, the Electoral College.

By David Dreier

"Too close to call." That was the virtually unanimous conclusion of American pollsters and political analysts as the 2000 presidential campaign entered its final hours on the eve of Election Day, November 7. Polls showed the two main contenders—Republican Governor George W. Bush of Texas and Democratic Vice President Al Gore—locked in a statistical dead heat. One thing seemed certain, however: By the morning of November 8, the nation would know who its next president was. No one expected that they were about to witness election history in the making.

The election, in fact, remained too close to call even after all the votes were in. For the first time in almost 125 years, the outcome of a United States presidential election remained unknown in the days and weeks following the balloting. Though Gore defeated Bush by a narrow margin in the nationwide popular vote, he had not amassed enough of the votes that matter most—electoral votes. In the 2000 election, a presidential candidate needed at least 270 electoral votes to win the presidency. The popular vote in each state determines who gets the state's electoral votes. In the states of Florida, New Mexico, and Oregon, the popular tally was so close that the states' electoral votes remained in limbo.

Of those three states, Florida, with 25 electoral votes, was the key to the election. Both Bush, with 246 electoral votes, and Gore, with 255, needed Florida's 25 votes to reach the magic number of 270. Despite an Election Day turnout in Florida of more than 6 million voters, only a few hundred votes separated the two candidates, with Bush in the lead. Weeks of ballot recounts, angry disputes, and legal challenges, including appeals to the Florida Supreme Court and the Supreme Court of the United States, followed as the two camps strove to win that vital state. In the end, Bush prevailed, and on December 13 Gore conceded the election.

The battle for Florida's electoral votes highlighted the central role of a little-understood institution, the Electoral College, in U.S. presidential elections. Gore's situation brought home to Americans a peculiarity of the Electoral College system that most had learned in high-school civics class but had not given much thought to since: It is possible for a presidential candidate to win the popular vote but lose the election. That fact struck many people as unfair, and in the aftermath of the 2000 election a growing number of Americans felt that the time had come to abolish the Electoral College.

The Founding Fathers debate a difficult question

The Electoral College was a creation of the 1787 Constitutional Convention in Philadelphia, at which representatives of the 13 original states labored to establish a stronger national government for the United States of America. Of the many issues that the representatives grappled with, none proved more troublesome than the question of how to elect the president.

Some delegates favored direct election by popular vote. Delegate James Wilson of Pennsylvania, who put forth the first proposal for direct election, argued that the office of the presidency would be

Previous page: Supporters of Democratic Vice President Al Gore and Republican Governor George Bush of Texas, the main candidates in the 2000 presidential election, exchange heated words in Palm Beach, Florida, after the November 7 balloting. As votes in Florida's extremely close popular ballot were recounted and the state's electoral votes remained undecided, each side accused the other of trying to steal the election.

The electoral-vote situation on Nov. 8, 2000

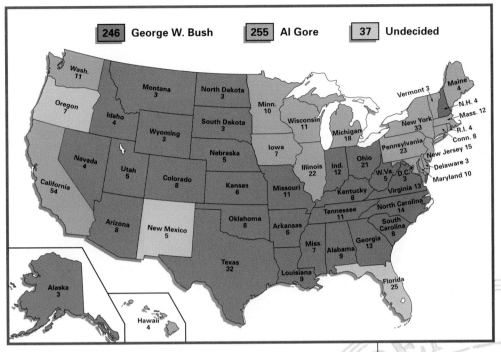

246 George W. Bush   **255** Al Gore   **37** Undecided

weak unless its power "flowed from the people at large." But popular election was strongly opposed by many others at the convention. One objection they put forth was that the people of a particular state would not know enough about presidential candidates from other states to make an informed decision. Furthermore, they argued, voters would naturally tend to prefer candidates from their own states, so candidates from the largest, most populous states would always win. Beyond those arguments, there was a general mistrust among many of the delegates of pure democracy, which the nervous gentry of the new nation equated with mob rule.

Another proposal called for letting Congress choose the president. The delegates rejected that system as well, largely because it would make the executive branch of the government subordinate to the legislative branch and would invite intrigue and corruption. Some representatives even suggested that the state legislatures elect the president. However, because the whole purpose of the new Constitution was to strengthen the national government, this idea had few takers.

Finally, exasperated with their inability to settle the matter, the delegates referred the election issue to a special committee. The solution the committee arrived at, which the convention accepted with almost no argument, was the elector system, later known as the Electoral College.

Under the elector system, each state was allotted a number of electoral votes equal to the combined total of the state's representatives and senators. The votes were to be cast by designated electors. A state was free to choose its slate of electors in any way it pre-

On Nov. 8, 2000, Gore had a slight lead in the nationwide popular vote but neither he nor Bush had garnered the 270 votes in the Electoral College needed for election. The electoral votes of three states—Florida, New Mexico, and Oregon—remained in question. Gore with 255 electoral votes and Bush with 246 both needed Florida's 25 electoral votes to win the presidency.

The author:

David Dreier is a contributing editor of the *Year Book*.

Electoral controversies of the past

The 2000 election was hardly the first one in which the Electoral College system caused problems. In the 1800's, four elections either wound up being decided by Congress or resulted in the election of a president who had not received the most popular votes.

Rutherford B. Hayes

John Quincy Adams

Thomas Jefferson

In 1800, it took 36 ballots in the House of Representatives to elect Thomas Jefferson. The election of 1824 was also decided by the House, which chose John Quincy Adams, even though Andrew Jackson had received more popular votes. After a disputed election in 1876, a congressional commission awarded 20 contested electoral votes to Rutherford B. Hayes, giving him the presidency. Despite losing the popular vote in the 1888 election, Benjamin Harrison was the victor, winning a majority in the Electoral College.

ferred. The electors were to meet in their respective state capitals at a specified time and cast two votes for president, one of which had to be for a candidate from outside the state. The votes were then to be sent to the U.S. capital, where they would be counted in the presence of both houses of Congress. The candidate receiving the most votes would be elected president, and the candidate with the second-most votes would become vice president.

In the event of a tie, or of any one candidate failing to receive a majority of the electoral votes, the election would be decided by the House of Representatives. The members of the House from each state would vote among themselves for the president. Then each state's representatives, acting as a group, would cast one vote for the candidate who had received the most ballots. The delegates actually saw election by the House as the likely outcome of most elections, because they thought that few presidential candidates would have enough support to win a majority of electoral votes.

The rise of political parties brings changes

The elector system was awkward, but it worked for a while. In the first two presidential elections, in 1789 and 1792, George Washington won votes from all the electors. John Adams received a smaller majority of electoral votes in these elections and became vice president. However, a weakness in the system became clear in the election of 1796, when Adams and Thomas Jefferson were elected president and vice president, respectively, even though they belonged to opposing political parties. Adams, a Federalist, favored a strong central government. Jefferson, a Democratic-Republican, was wary of governmental power, placing his faith in the people.

The elector system broke down completely in 1800. By that time, political parties had become more important in elections than the candidates' home states. In the election of 1800, Jefferson was the presidential choice of the Democratic-Republican Party, and Aaron Burr was the party's choice for vice president. They ran against Adams and Charles C. Pinckney, the Federalist candidates for president and vice president.

Benjamin Harrison

Although Jefferson was confident of a Democratic-Republican victory, he worried that the party's electors would inadvertently cast equal numbers of votes for both him and Burr, which would throw the election into the House. Jefferson received assurances that two or three Democratic-Republican electors planned to cast their second votes for candidates other than Burr to ensure that Jefferson would be elected president. However, that did not happen, perhaps because of secret maneuvering by Burr and his allies. When the electoral votes were counted, Jefferson and Burr had ended Adams's hope for a second term, but they were tied with 73 votes each.

Burr refused to defer to Jefferson, so the election moved to the House, where it took 36 ballots before Jefferson was finally elected president.

To prevent that kind of deadlock from ever recurring, Congress in 1803 passed the 12th Amendment, changing the Electoral College procedures. The amendment, ratified by the states in 1804, stipulated that electors would cast a vote for president and a separate vote for vice president.

By that time, the states themselves had begun to alter the way they determined their electoral votes. One major change involved procedures for choosing electors. Originally, most states left the selection of electors up to their legislatures, but after 1800 an increasing number of states chose electors through popular elections. By the mid-1830's, that system was being used in all but one state, South Carolina, which finally adopted it in the 1860's.

But even with the popular selection of electors, there was a big problem in the first decades of the 1800's, because groups within a political party might support different candidates for president. In 1824, the presidential election again wound up in the House when four Democratic-Republican candidates—John Quincy Adams, Henry Clay, William H. Crawford, and Andrew Jackson—split the electoral vote, with none receiving a majority. Jackson, who received the most electoral votes and the most popular votes, considered himself the rightful president. But in the political maneu-

SPECIAL ELECTION 2000 SUPPLEMENT ★ ★ ★   ★ ★ ★

vering that followed, Clay threw his support to Adams, who was then chosen president by the House.

Elections became more orderly later in the 1800's when parties began to run a single presidential ticket in all the states. In each state, the party put forth a slate of electors pledged to cast ballots for that party's candidates in the Electoral College vote. With this change, the individual electors became less important, and eventually their names disappeared from most ballots, giving voters the mistaken impression that they were voting directly for the candidates.

Another important change was a move to the "winner-take-all" method of allocating electoral votes. In that system, which is used today by every state except Maine and Nebraska, all of a state's electoral votes go to the presidential and vice presidential candidates who capture the most popular votes within that state.

Other troubled elections

Despite the changes made to Electoral College procedures over the years, it remained a problematic way of choosing a president. The system's flaws were on display once again in the presidential election of 1876, one of the most chaotic elections in United States history. The Democratic presidential candidate, Samuel J. Tilden, defeated Republican Rutherford B. Hayes by about 250,000 popular votes out of some 8.3 million cast. But Tilden's apparent victory was thrown into doubt when Oregon and three deeply divided Southern states—Florida, Louisiana, and South Carolina—submitted two sets of electoral votes, one from the Democrats and one from the Republicans. Twenty electoral votes from those states were disputed in Congress, and until those votes could be sorted out, both candidates were short of an electoral majority. Tilden, with 184 votes, was just one vote short of the 185 electoral votes required for election. Hayes, with 165 votes, needed all 20 votes to win.

In January 1877, Congress appointed a special 15-member commission to settle the issue. The commission, however, was dominated by Republicans, so it ruled in favor of Hayes on every disputed electoral vote. As the commission deliberated, members of the two parties argued bitterly, and some hotheads threatened to seize the government by force.

Hayes was finally awarded all 20 of the contested votes, but even then the crisis was not over. The commission's report had to be accepted by both houses of Congress, and the House of Representatives had a Democratic majority. A group of Southern Democrats in Congress then made a private deal with the Republicans. They agreed not to oppose the

Al Gore campaigns in Pennsylvania in the final days of the 2000 presidential campaign. Pennsylvania was a so-called battleground state, one in which preference polls indicated that either candidate could win the popular vote and thus take all of the state's electoral votes.

decision of the commission in return for a Republican vow to end *Reconstruction* (Northern control of the South after the Civil War [1861-1865]). On March 2, 1877—just 56 hours before Inauguration Day—the Southern Democrats voted with the Republicans to accept the commission's report. Hayes was declared the winner of the election, but he was so tainted by the whole process that he was openly derided as His Fraudulency.

Another controversial election occurred just 12 years later, in 1888. In that contest, incumbent President Grover Cleveland, a Democrat, defeated Republican Benjamin Harrison in the popular ballot by more than 90,000 votes out of about 11 million cast and won the electoral votes of 19 states. Harrison also won 19 states, but those states had enough electoral votes to give Harrison an Electoral College majority of 233 votes to 168. Thus, even though Cleveland won the popular vote, he lost the election.

George W. Bush addresses workers at a General Motors plant in Michigan, another battleground state. Many political observers argue that the need for presidential contenders to spend most of their time and resources fighting for such states, while largely ignoring states where one candidate is far ahead of the other, is a major weakness of the Electoral College system.

A flawed system, but perhaps a needed one

Clearly, the Electoral College system has its faults. Besides its potential for denying the presidency to the winner of the popular vote, it skews presidential campaigns. Because of the winner-take-all arrangement in all but two states, candidates conduct intensive campaigns in so-called battleground states in which either ticket has a reasonably good chance of winning the popular vote. Conversely, candidates mostly ignore states in which preference polls have revealed that voters favor one ticket over the other by a large margin. It makes no sense for candidates to campaign in a state where they have no chance of winning enough popular votes to claim the state's electoral votes. The popular ballots in a state do not count for anything outside the state. That fact also makes it pointless for the likely winner in a state to seek to increase the margin of victory in the state's popular vote.

The biggest problem with the Electoral College system, however, is that it can result in political train wrecks such as the ones that occurred in 1876 and 2000. After the 2000 election, there were renewed calls for the Electoral College to be abolished in favor of direct popular election of the president. But would that really be a good idea? Political experts have differing opinions.

Those in favor of abolishing the Electoral College argue that, in addition to affecting presidential campaigns and sometimes deny-

ing the presidency to the winner of the popular vote, the system depresses voter turnout. They claim that if a candidate is an almost sure winner in a state, many voters there will feel that there is little point in going to the polls, since their votes will mean nothing beyond the state.

Opponents of the Electoral College system also point out that it tends to overrepresent the interests of small states. That occurs because of the way electoral votes are apportioned, with every state getting an electoral vote for each of its representatives in the House as well as a vote for each of its two senators. A senator in a small or sparsely populated state represents far fewer people than a senator in a populous state. Thus, an electoral vote in New York represents 550,000 people, while an electoral vote in South Dakota represents 232,000.

Another argument against the Electoral College is that it discourages third parties. Because of the winner-take-all system, a third-party presidential ticket can attract a reasonably large number of popular votes throughout the nation but collect not a single electoral vote.

There is also the issue of so-called faithless electors, electors who vote for candidates other than the ones they are pledged to. Though a few electors have jumped ship over the years, they have never influenced the outcome of an election. Nonetheless, electors who cast surprise votes could conceivably be a factor in a very close election.

Supporters of the Electoral College system see most of its sup-

---

Arguments against and for the Electoral College

Against

★ In a tight presidential race, a close popular vote in one or more key states can lead to a fierce post-election battle—recounts and legal challenges—resulting in a possible constitutional crisis if no clear winner emerges.

★ A candidate who receives a majority of the nationwide popular vote can lose the election.

★ Candidates campaign heavily in states where either candidate stands a good chance of winning the popular vote and mostly ignore other states.

★ Voter turnout may be depressed in states where preference polls have indicated that one candidate is strongly ahead of the other.

★ The growth of third parties is discouraged because it is very difficult for their candidates to earn electoral votes.

★ The system is unfair, because an electoral vote in smaller or less populous states represents fewer people than an electoral vote in a large, heavily populated state.

★ An election that results in a close electoral victory could be overturned by "faithless electors" who do not vote for their party's candidate.

For

★ The system strengthens national unity by forcing candidates to campaign in smaller and less populous states rather than just seeking masses of popular votes in large urban centers.

★ Third parties are encouraged to moderate their views and join with one of the two major parties, which contributes to the political stability of the nation.

★ Candidates must address the interests of minority groups because minority ballots may be needed to win a state's popular vote and thus its electoral votes.

★ The system preserves the federal power-sharing arrangement established by the Founding Fathers between the states and the federal government.

posed weaknesses as strengths. They argue that while it is unfortunate for the winner of the popular vote to lose an election, the system protects the interests of smaller states by making it necessary for candidates to campaign nationwide. A candidate in a close race cannot afford to ignore small or less populous states that could go either way. If the presidency were determined by the popular vote alone, candidates would tend to concentrate their efforts in a handful of metropolitan areas with huge populations. In addition, candidates must pay attention to the interests of minority groups, because the ballots of minorities can make the difference between winning or losing a key state. Therefore, the Electoral College's proponents contend, the system strengthens the cohesiveness and stability of the nation.

Furthermore, supporters contend that our present method of electing presidents, by making it difficult for third parties to succeed, persuades splinter groups to moderate their stands and join with one of the two major parties. In this view, a two-party system, whatever its faults, is better than a proliferation of parties representing ever-smaller segments of the population.

Finally, advocates of the Electoral College argue, the system preserves the federal power-sharing arrangement established by the Founding Fathers between the states and the central government. They caution that we should be wary of tampering with that delicate balance.

They add that the problem of faithless electors could be overcome by eliminating actual electors. Each state's electoral votes would then be just a numerical total that is automatically assigned to the winner of the state's popular vote. But this change, as with eliminating the Electoral College altogether, would require a constitutional amendment.

The Electoral College issue is undeniably a thorny one. As the election of 2000 played itself out, many people thought that the obvious solution for preventing similar electoral crises in the future was to simply junk this aging institution and rely on the will of the people. Some political experts agreed, but others cautioned against a rush to judgment. The Founding Fathers, they pointed out, did not think that a system for electing the president was a simple matter in 1787, and it may not be so simple today either. ■ ■ ■

For further information:

Books

Best, Judith A. *The Choice of the People?: Debating the Electoral College.* Rowman & Littlefield, 1996.

Longley, Lawrence D. *The Electoral College Primer.* Yale University Press, 1996.

Web sites

U.S. Electoral College—www.nara.gov/fedreg/elctcoll (the official home page of the Electoral College)

Federal Election Commission—www.fec.gov (extensive information about U.S. elections and the Electoral College)

Careers

2001 WORLD BOOK SUPPLEMENT

Cleveland
Conservation
Family
Vietnam War

© David R. Frazier

Choosing a career is an important decision that will affect a person's life in many ways. A person should choose a career that suits his or her abilities, interests, and values. Attending job fairs like the one shown here can help a jobseeker learn about career fields and employment opportunities.

Careers

Careers are the patterns of work and work-related activities that people develop throughout a lifetime. A career includes the job or series of jobs a person has until retirement. Careers vary greatly in the type of work involved and in the ways they influence a person's life.

Almost every adult has a career of some kind. Most people build a career to help them satisfy certain goals. Such goals might include earning a living or helping society. The best-known career pattern develops around work for pay. Most workers in such a career hold a job to support themselves and their family. However, some people build a career around activities for which they receive no money. For example, many people's careers are caring for their families and their homes. Others volunteer their time to help others.

The kind of career you have can affect your life in many ways. For example, it can determine where you live, the friends you make, and the amount of money you earn. Your career can also affect how you feel about yourself and the way other people act toward you. By making wise decisions concerning your career, you can help yourself build the life you want.

Duane Brown, the contributor of this article, is Professor of Education at the University of North Carolina at Chapel Hill. He is the coauthor of the books Career Choice and Development *and* Career Counseling Techniques.

Important career decisions include choosing a career field and deciding how you want your career to develop. Other decisions involve selecting the educational and job opportunities that will advance your career. Knowing your abilities, interests, values, and goals gives you a foundation on which to base your career decisions. Also, a broad knowledge of the world of work can help you discover career possibilities that you did not know existed.

This article discusses careers based on work for pay. It provides information that can help you choose and plan a career. It also describes skills that can be useful in getting a job. In addition, the article discusses major career fields and many occupations within each field.

Choosing and planning a career

To make wise career decisions and plans, you need as much information as possible. The more you know about yourself and career opportunities, the better able you will be to choose a satisfying career.

Discovering the world of work. Most people begin to discover the world of work in early childhood. Even before children enter school, they become aware that people work in various occupations. Most children also start to form ideas about life and about themselves as individuals. A realistic view of themselves and the world of work can help children prepare to make successful career choices.

Adults can help children discover the world of work in many ways. For example, parents and teachers can encourage children to notice and talk about different jobs in the community. They might also read and discuss stories that deal with different kinds of workers.

Teachers can ask students to select an occupation and give a report on it. Students may watch workers perform their duties during field trips. Teachers may also invite workers into the classroom to discuss their jobs.

Learning about oneself. Students should begin to explore career fields when they are in middle or junior high school. High school students should become involved in activities that relate to their career interests.

At the high school level, students should think about their life and career goals. To do this, students should determine their (1) aptitudes, (2) interests, (3) personal characteristics, and (4) values. Most workers are happiest and most successful when their jobs match their strengths, personality, and beliefs.

Aptitudes are a person's natural talents. Aptitudes indicate how easily a person can acquire certain skills or be trained for a specific career. An aptitude is sometimes known as an *ability.* However, the term *ability* can also refer to a skill—such as reading or speaking a foreign language—that a person has learned.

One of the most important aptitudes is *scholastic aptitude.* People who have high scholastic aptitude tend to succeed more easily in school than those who do not. Scholastic aptitude plays a major role in determining a person's career choice.

Many special aptitudes besides scholastic aptitude are related to success in various jobs. For example, people with *numerical reasoning aptitude* can easily become skilled in using numbers to solve mathematical problems. *Spatial relations aptitude* can help you imagine objects in two and three dimensions. *Mechanical reasoning aptitude* can help you understand mechanical concepts that relate to repairing and assembling machines. Thinking and reasoning with words involves *verbal reasoning aptitude.* *Abstract reasoning aptitude* can help you reason with symbols other than words and numbers.

Before you make a career choice, you should determine if performing that job requires any special aptitudes. To succeed in engineering, for example, you should have aptitudes for verbal reasoning, numerical reasoning, and spatial relations.

Aptitude tests can predict your ability to learn certain skills. How well you do in recreational activities, such as playing computer games or building model cars, and in various school subjects may also indicate aptitude.

You should remember, however, two important factors about aptitudes. First, people may not realize they have certain aptitudes unless they get an opportunity to develop them. Second, if you have relatively low aptitude in a given area, you can still develop the skills and abilities needed to perform successfully in that area. For example, people with low mechanical aptitude can learn to skillfully perform mechanical tasks. However, they may have more difficulty in learning mechanical skills and concepts than they would if they had more aptitude.

Interests are likes or preferences. The subjects that you like in school and the leisure activities you prefer are indications of your interests. Many people have interests in artistic, mechanical, outdoor, or scientific activities. Other interests include collecting various objects, such as rocks or stamps, or reading books.

Many people base their career choices on their interests. For many workers, job performance and job satisfaction depend on how much their work relates to their interests. It is therefore helpful to identify your strongest interests before you select a career field. To find out what your interests are, examine the kinds of school subjects and activities you have enjoyed. Such activities might include clubs, hobbies, and sports. The activities you enjoy most may represent your strongest interests.

Personal characteristics can contribute to success in a career. They may even be essential elements of some careers. Many employers look for workers who are ambitious, reliable, and trustworthy. In addition, your personality can help you decide what kind of job you want. If you are independent, you might be happiest in a job where you work alone, not as a member of a team. These kinds of characteristics are difficult to measure. However, a serious look at your past behavior can help you find out your qualities.

Values are deeply held beliefs that influence the way people think, act, and feel. They reflect what people consider to be important and greatly affect the goals people set for themselves. Each person has many values, which vary in strength. For example, money is the strongest value for some people—that is, wealth is more important to them than anything else. As a result, they focus their thoughts, behavior, and emotions on the goal of earning a high income. Other values include devotion to religion and helping others. People should understand their values prior to making a career decision.

You can develop an understanding of your values by asking yourself what is most important to you and by examining your beliefs. For example, if it is important to you to spend time with your family, you should find a job that requires little travel or overtime work.

What to look for in career fields. For most workers, job satisfaction depends on how well the various characteristics of a job satisfy their interests and values. In exploring an occupation, you should therefore consider the following job characteristics.

The nature of the work. Some jobs chiefly involve working with things, and others mainly require dealing with people or information. Most jobs combine a variety of work activities. You should look for an occupation that involves activities you enjoy and can do well.

Working conditions mean the environment in which a particular job is performed. A work environment might be indoors or outdoors. Some jobs involve high levels of dust or noise, physical hazards, or mental stress. Other conditions to consider include the number of hours employees work each week and whether employees work alone or in groups.

Special abilities required. Some jobs call for more mechanical aptitude, artistic talent, or other abilities than most people possess. You should therefore be aware of any special requirements in the jobs you consider.

Physical demands. Some occupations make special physical demands on workers. For example, jobs that involve carrying or lifting objects require strength. Some occupations require workers to perform repetitive tasks. Other occupations might require workers who have keen vision or who can stand for long periods. When you consider a job, be sure that you can meet any physical demands the work might make on you.

Preparation needed. The amount of preparation required to enter an occupation varies from job to job. It can range from a few hours of training to more than 10 years of education beyond high school. In addition, workers in many occupations must continue their education to keep their jobs or to advance in them. Some occupations require several years of experience and preparation at lower-level jobs. You should thus consider how much time and money you might have to invest in the careers that interest you.

Chances for employment. Before you choose a career field, you should consider your chances for getting a job in that field. In businesses and industries with steady or decreasing employment, workers are hired only to replace employees who have left their jobs. In growing businesses and industries, however, additional workers are needed. The introduction of new products and advanced technologies affect employment opportunities. Government spending and economic conditions also alter job opportunities.

Probable earnings. In exploring an occupation, you will want to know how much money you can expect to earn. Government, professional, and trade publications supply information on probable earnings for various occupations. Pay scales vary with location and employers, however. Union agreements and the amount of experience and education required also affect salaries and wages. Many employers provide insurance coverage, paid vacations, and other such *fringe benefits,* which you should consider in addition to probable earnings.

Chances for advancement. In exploring various occupations, you should examine possible patterns of promotion, known as *career ladders* or *career paths.* In some occupations, workers are promoted to higher positions based on their ability and experience. However,

some employers hire people from outside the company to fill high-level openings. If employers consistently do this, workers can advance only by changing jobs. Some occupations allow only limited advancement. Workers in such fields must obtain additional education or training or change occupations if they wish to advance.

Social status is a person's position or rank in society. Many people believe that certain jobs have higher social status than others do. Some people who value status seek it through choosing highly regarded occupations. You must decide for yourself how important social status is in making your career choices.

Sources of information. A number of sources supply information that can help you explore career fields. Government agencies, industries, professional organizations, and many employers maintain Web sites and publish materials that describe various occupations.

Many schools offer career courses and clubs to help students learn about job opportunities. Teachers often supplement class discussions with interactive career guidance software available on personal computers.

Career information is also available from career and guidance counselors. These experts work in high schools, community agencies, employment offices, and college career development and placement centers. Counselors can help you identify your immediate and future career goals. They can also administer tests that identify the qualities you have to offer an employer. Counselors can then assist you in determining the right occupation for you. They can also advise you on how to prepare for and obtain a job in your chosen field.

You can learn about individual jobs by interviewing workers in those positions. In addition, you can gain firsthand information about an occupation through part-time jobs and volunteer work. For example, a person considering a career in medicine might volunteer at a hospital. *Job shadowing*—that is, observing a worker performing his or her job for a few hours or a day—can also give you firsthand career information.

Preparing for a career. Career preparation involves learning a variety of skills. Some skills, such as being able to accept supervision and knowing how to get along with others, are learned though everyday experiences in school and in the community. Others require specialized training.

High school courses and experiences are the most important preparations for some careers. In high school, students develop basic verbal and numerical skills, study habits, and other practical abilities. These skills provide the foundation for future learning.

Some people begin specialized career preparation in high school. Business and vocational courses prepare high school students to enter an occupation immediately after graduation. These courses teach skills used in such fields as business, construction, and manufacturing. Most high schools also offer college preparatory courses for students who plan to go to college. Many high schools offer *cooperative education programs* or *school-to-work programs* that help students prepare to enter the work force. Under these programs, students continue their classroom education while they experience the world of work through an internship, volunteer work, or a part-time job.

Certain occupations require only a high school educa-

Average starting salaries in the United States

This graph shows average annual starting salary offers for new college graduates in selected disciplines. Figures are by curriculum only; some graduates find work in unrelated fields.

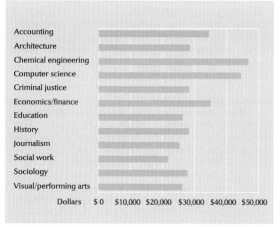

| | Dollars | $0 | $10,000 | $20,000 | $30,000 | $40,000 | $50,000 |

Accounting
Architecture
Chemical engineering
Computer science
Criminal justice
Economics/finance
Education
History
Journalism
Social work
Sociology
Visual/performing arts

Figures are for 1999.
Source: National Association of Colleges and Employers; American Federation of Teachers.

tion. But most jobs call for additional training. This section briefly describes the major kinds of career preparation programs.

On-the-job training means that a worker is taught job skills after being hired. In most cases, an experienced worker trains and supervises the beginner. The training may last a few hours or many months.

Apprenticeships are structured programs of training that combine classroom instruction and on-the-job training. They require two or more years of job experience and instruction. Every apprenticeship is based on a written agreement between the employer and the apprentice. Most apprenticeships train workers for skilled occupations in construction and production.

Vocational schools, also called *trade schools,* offer courses in restaurant cooking, automobile repair, and many other skills. Some trade schools specialize in training such workers as dental assistants, hairstylists, and travel agents. Courses range from several months to two years. Most vocational schools prepare students to meet any licensing requirements needed to enter a trade or profession. Many also award certificates to graduates.

Armed forces schools provide career education opportunities for people in military service. These opportunities range from on-the-job training and short courses to college and graduate school. In most cases, the training is designed for jobs in military career fields. However, many skills used in military occupations can be applied to civilian jobs.

Distance learning programs enable people to learn skills anywhere at anytime. Instructors may give lectures on television, or present lessons on the Internet, a global network of computers. Students can also listen to or watch lectures on audiotapes or videocassettes when it is convenient for them. They can also communicate with other students in forums on the Internet called *chat rooms*. Students receive assignments, course materials, study guides, and examinations through the mail, by e-mail (electronic mail), or by fax transmission. They return the completed work to the instructor for grading.

Technical institutes provide advanced, specialized training in such areas as electronics, engineering, computer science, and metalworking. Many graduates of these schools become *technicians*—that is, workers who assist engineers, scientists, and other highly trained specialists. Most technical institutes have two- or three-year programs, and many are associated with a hospital, university, or other institution.

Community colleges provide two years of college-level education. They prepare some students to transfer to a four-year college. They train other students for jobs as technicians and for such occupations as nursing, office management, and law enforcement.

Colleges and universities offer four-year programs that lead to a bachelor's degree. For the first two years, students study a variety of subjects. For the last two, most students take courses in their chosen career fields. College students learn skills for a range of professions, such as architecture, journalism, science, and teaching.

Professional and graduate schools. Such professions as dentistry, law, and medicine require education beyond college at a professional school. In addition, many students in business, education, science, and other fields attend graduate school for advanced study in their subject areas. Most professional and graduate schools are part of large universities.

Getting a job

The first step in advancing a career plan is writing a good *resume* (pronounced REHZ u MAY or REHZ uh may), a document that describes your background and qualifications. You must also find job openings, apply for them, and convince employers that you are the best applicant. An employer can tell a lot about potential employees by the way they present their qualifications and apply for a job. Therefore, you should know how to contact employers, how to complete job applications, and how to make a good impression in interviews. All these skills can improve your chances for employment. However, do not be discouraged if you are not offered the first job you apply for. Most employers consider several applicants for each opening, and many people apply for numerous jobs before they are hired.

Writing a resume. A resume can be a paper or an electronic document. A good resume is neat, well organized, and easy to read.

All resumes should include the same basic information. Begin your resume with your name, address, and telephone number. You could also include your e-mail address if you have one. Most jobseekers include an objective, or career goal, on their resume. Next list your employment history, starting with the most recent job. Give the names and locations of past employers, dates of employment, job titles, and a description of your duties. You can also include any related volunteer work if you are a recent graduate or have not held many jobs.

Next, list the names and locations of all schools and training programs you have attended since high school. Include your attendance dates and major subjects plus any degrees, diplomas, certificates, and honors you received. You can also list any special skills, such as languages you speak or computer programs you can use, that would relate to the job you are seeking. Some jobseekers list their education and skills before their employment history. Some jobhunters also list their hobbies, travel experience, or awards on their resume.

Finally, many employers ask for the names and addresses of *personal references*—that is, people the employer may contact to learn more about you.

Finding job opportunities. One of the most common ways to learn about job opportunities is by word-of-mouth. Many jobs are filled by people who have heard of the job opening from professional associates, friends, relatives, teachers, and acquaintances. You should tell the people you know and meet that you are looking for certain kinds of job opportunities. This process is known as *networking.*

Another common way to locate job opportunities is through the help-wanted section of newspapers. Many professional and union newsletters, journals, and other trade publications also carry advertisements for job openings. Most help-wanted ads briefly describe the job responsibilities and provide other information that can help you decide to apply for the position.

Increasingly, people find job opportunities on the Internet. Jobseekers may search the databases of career-related Web sites for job openings and apply for the positions online. They may also *post* (enter) resumes at

```
Jerry Williams                              123 Oak Street
                                       Chicago, Illinois 60123
                                              312/123-4567
                                     jwilliams@mymailbox.com

OBJECTIVE:        To obtain an editorial position where I can apply
                  my talents and experience in a challenging and
                  progressive environment.

EDUCATION:        Northern Illinois University, De Kalb, Illinois
                  Bachelor of Arts in Communication, May 1998
                  Major GPA: 3.8/4.0

SKILLS:           Adobe PageMaker, Adobe Photoshop, Microsoft
                  Word, Netscape Communicator, QuarkXPress

EMPLOYMENT:       Acme Publishing Company, Chicago, Illinois
1999 to present   Assistant Editor
                  Responsibilities include copy editing manuscripts
                  for company s line of children s books.
                  Coordinate work for in-house and free-lance
                  typesetters and free-lance proofreaders.
                  Proofreading as required.

1998 to 1999      Jacobs Company, Chicago, Illinois
                  Corporate Communications Intern
                  Wrote, designed, and produced Jacobs
                  Company s monthly employee newsletter.

ACTIVITIES        Golden Key National Honor Society
AND AWARDS:       Member of Society for Professional Journalists
                  Member of Illinois Newspaper Association
                  Northern Illinois Newspaper Association
                      Scholarship Recipient
                  Volunteer for United Way/Crusade of Mercy, Inc.

REFERENCES:       Available upon request.
```

WORLD BOOK illustration

A traditional resume describes a jobseeker's work experience and education. It can be mailed or faxed to potential employers.

```
Jerry Williams
123 Oak Street
Chicago, Illinois 60123
312/123-4567
jwilliams@mymailbox.com

OBJECTIVE:
To obtain an editorial position where I can apply my tal-
ents and experience in a challenging and progressive
environment.

EDUCATION:
Northern Illinois University, De Kalb, Illinois
Bachelor of Arts in Communication, May 1998
Major GPA: 3.8/4.0

SKILLS:
Adobe PageMaker, Adobe Photoshop, Microsoft Word, Netscape
Communicator, QuarkXPress

EMPLOYMENT:
Acme Publishing Company, Chicago, Illinois
1999 to present, Assistant Editor
Responsibilities include copy editing manuscripts for comp-
any's line of children's books. Coordinate work for in-
house and free-lance typesetters and free-lance proofreaders.
Proofreading as required.

Jacobs Company, Chicago, Illinois
1998 to 1999, Corporate Communications Intern
Wrote, designed, and produced Jacobs Company's monthly
employee newsletter.

ACTIVITIES AND AWARDS:
Golden Key National Honor Society
Member of Society for Professional Journalists
Member of Illinois Newspaper Association
Northern Illinois Newspaper Association Scholarship
Recipient
Volunteer for United Way/Crusade of Mercy, Inc.

REFERENCES:
Available upon request.
```

WORLD BOOK illustration

An electronic resume can be sent to employers by e-mail. It provides the same type of information as a traditional resume.

many of these sites for potential employers to review. In addition, companies and organizations often announce job opportunities on their Web sites.

Information about job openings is also available from employment agencies. Public employment agencies are run by the government and their services are free. Private agencies charge jobseekers or employers a fee if a person is hired as a result of their efforts. Many high schools, colleges, and other schools have *placement offices,* which help students and graduates find jobs.

Jobseekers may also contact employers to learn about openings. Telephone directories and other publications list the names, addresses, and phone numbers of employers in various fields.

Contacting employers. Your first contact with an employer will be either to apply for a known job opening or to find out if any jobs are available. The most common ways of contacting employers are by mail or fax transmission, by e-mail, by telephone, and by personal visit to an employer's office.

If jobseekers contact employers by mail or fax, they should write a letter to an employer, called a *cover letter.* This type of letter introduces the applicant to the employer. If you are responding to a known opening, indicate the position you are applying for and how you became aware of the opening. Briefly indicate your qualifications and accomplishments that would benefit the employer. Finally, state when you would be available for an interview or when you will call the employer to discuss your qualifications. Be sure to include your mailing address, e-mail address, and telephone number so that the employer can reach you. A resume should be faxed or mailed with the cover letter.

If you contact an employer by e-mail, provide the same information that you would include in a cover letter. If possible, include an ASCII (American Standard Code for Information Interchange) or text-only version of your resume in the body of the e-mail, or as a separate text file. These formats ensure that employers will be able to read your resume.

Some jobseekers contact employers by telephone. These applicants may be responding to help-wanted ads. Others call employers to find out if there are any jobs available. In any situation, you should briefly state your qualifications and try to arrange an interview.

Completing job applications. Most employers ask applicants to fill out an application. Applications help employers find out about your qualifications. Most applications request the same kinds of information. Much of the information will already appear on your resume.

Many companies ask applicants to complete paper application forms. Other employers prefer applicants to complete electronic applications. Applicants may enter their information using computer terminals in a company's office or online at a company's Web site. Some businesses use automated telephone systems that enable applicants to apply for jobs over the phone.

All types of applications ask for your address, telephone number, and the title of the job for which you are applying. In many countries, applications request an identification number, such as a social security or other national insurance number, or a national identification number. Most applications also ask about your previous employment, including employers' and supervisors' names, the dates of your employment, your duties, and your wages. Applications also request that you list the schools you attended, the dates you attended them, and any degrees, diplomas, and certificates you received. Many applications request additional information, such as your military experience or hobbies. They may also ask for personal references. Many companies check the accuracy of information included on job applications.

Being interviewed. If your resume or application indicates you are qualified, the employer may request an interview. The interview enables you to learn more about the job opening. It also helps the employer find out if you are the best person to hire for the job.

Many people prepare for an interview by learning about the employer's business. They find out about the kinds of products the company manufactures or the services it provides. You can find such information in an organization's annual report or on its Web site. This kind of knowledge can help you ask intelligent questions during your interview. It also shows the interviewer that you are interested in the employer's business.

Most interviewers pay close attention to the way an applicant acts, dresses, and answers questions. You can make a good impression by arriving on time and by being confident, prepared, and well organized. Your clothing should be clean, comfortable, and professional. Wear the kinds of clothes appropriate to the company, unless the workers wear uniforms.

The interviewer will probably ask about your interests, your work experience, and your goals. Common questions also include your reasons for applying for the job and what you believe you can contribute to the success of the employer's business. Answer all questions briefly. You might find it helpful to think out your answers to such questions before an interview. You should also prepare questions to ask the interviewer about the company and the position you are seeking.

Send a follow-up letter to everyone who interviewed you no later than two days after the interview. In the letter, thank the interviewer for the time spent discussing the position with you. Let the interviewer know if you are still interested in the job.

The world of work

The world of work is vast and constantly changing. Scientific advances and other developments constantly eliminate some jobs and create new ones. Anyone selecting a career should explore all the possibilities. People who research a variety of jobs may find that they are interested in a career they may not have considered.

Teachers and career counselors use a variety of sources to help jobseekers learn about occupations. Many of these sources use different classification systems to arrange career information. However, each system groups career fields that are similar in some way. This article divides many of the most common occupations into 17 career groups. These groups are (1) administrative support; (2) art, design, and communications; (3) community and social services; (4) construction, maintenance, and repair; (5) farming, fishing, and forestry; (6) health care; (7) law; (8) life, physical, and social sciences; (9) management; (10) personal services; (11) production; (12) sales; (13) sports and entertainment; (14) teaching; (15) technical and mathematical occupations; (16) tourism

and hospitality; and (17) transportation. Occupations within each group have similar interests and job duties.

The following sections contain the characteristics of the occupations of each group. They describe what the workers do, the working conditions, and the training required to perform the occupations. However, these examples provide only a general guide. Responsibilities, working conditions, and preparation requirements vary.

Administrative support. Businesses, governments, industries, and other organizations need workers to help them run smoothly and efficiently. Almost every organization employs workers to perform such tasks as filing, answering telephones, operating office machines, receiving payments, and distributing mail. They also need employees to produce, organize, and analyze documents, letters, reports, and other records.

Secretaries and administrative assistants provide support for managers or executives. They may keep records; compose and edit documents, letters, and reports; schedule meetings; and supervise other office-support workers. Data entry operators process information. They may use computers or scanners to record data, such as information about a customer.

Specialists in the area of records systems gather and analyze information. Bookkeeping clerks record the financial transactions of a business or organization. Accounting clerks assist accountants by performing calculations and preparing other information needed for financial reports. Auditing clerks verify an organization's financial records. Billing clerks prepare customers' bills for various goods or services. Timekeeping clerks review employee timecards and calculate how many hours each employee has worked. Payroll clerks calculate employees' pay and prepare paychecks.

Many administrative and office support workers work directly with customers. Telephone operators assist callers with telephone calls. They may search for phone numbers, handle emergency calls, and transfer calls. Customer service representatives answer customers' questions, help them solve problems, and resolve com-

WORLD BOOK photo by Steven Spicer

Customer service representatives spend most of their workday on the telephone. They help answer customers' questions, solve problems, take customers' orders, and resolve complaints.

plaints. Receptionists greet an organization's visitors. They may also answer telephones and provide information about the organization. Bank tellers assist customers with their banking transactions. They may cash customers' checks or take their deposits or payments.

Other workers are concerned with the delivery of letters, packages, and other items. Shipping clerks keep records of all shipments that leave an organization. They may prepare items for shipment by calculating the shipping costs and making mailing labels. Receiving clerks keep records of all shipments that an organization receives. They verify the contents of each shipment and make sure the items were not damaged during delivery. Postal service clerks perform many duties, such as selling stamps, sorting mail, and checking items for correct postage. Mail carriers deliver mail on assigned routes.

Working conditions. Many workers in this group work in an office. They may sit for long periods at a desk, often repeating the same kinds of tasks. Mail carriers often work outdoors in all kinds of weather. Shipping and receiving clerks may work in warehouses or stockrooms and often lift or carry heavy packages.

Training and education. Most administrative support workers have a high school education, but many employers prefer to hire candidates with some college experience. Many business and vocational schools and community colleges offer training classes.

Art, design, and communications occupations deal with the expression of ideas, feelings, and thoughts. Some workers in this group express themselves while adding beauty to people's lives. Others express thoughts and ideas by processing and delivering information.

Artists express themselves through various creative activities. Such artists as painters, photographers, and sculptors create original pieces of work. They may sell their artwork to clients or display it in galleries or museums. Illustrators produce pictures for books, posters, and other products. Multimedia artists use computers to create animation, special effects, and other images for advertisements, movies, and video games.

Designers help clients express their own ideas and style. Fashion designers study colors, fabrics, and trends before they develop a collection of clothing and accessories. Interior designers plan and furnish indoor areas of homes, hotels, offices, and other buildings. Graphic designers use color, image, and text elements to create art that communicates a message. They may design a company's logo, a layout for a magazine, or a store display for a new product. Industrial designers use product research and their artistic ability to develop or redesign products, such as automobiles, furniture, and toys.

Communications workers deliver ideas to the public. Authors write such materials as articles and novels. Reporters use interviews, investigative techniques, and research to gather information for their stories. Editors review and revise material and prepare it for publication or broadcast. Radio announcers select and introduce music, read the news and weather, and interview guests. Television anchors present news stories and introduce live or taped reports from reporters. Public relations specialists provide information to the public about their clients. Translators and interpreters convert speech and written text from one language to another.

Working conditions differ for various occupations in the art, design, and communications group. Many workers perform their duties in offices or studios. Most journalists work long hours to meet their deadlines. Artists may work at their own pace.

Education and training. Most artists and designers have natural artistic abilities. Some artists have not had

WORLD BOOK photo by Steven Spicer

Workers in the art, design, and communications field often work with one another. The graphic designer shown here is discussing her proposed layout of a children's book with the editor who wrote the text.

any formal training, but others have a degree in fine arts from a college, university, or school of art. Most designers have a college degree. Most employers in the communications field require employees to have a bachelor's or master's degree.

Community and social services workers provide assistance to society. People depend on these workers to help meet their needs and improve the quality of life in their community.

Some workers in this group help individuals, groups, and families solve problems. Counselors help people identify their problems and find solutions. They may help people discover their career interests, work out problems in their marriage, or recover from mental illnesses. Social workers provide counseling, support, guidance, and other services to people in need. For example, they may help people with disabilities, the homeless, or the unemployed.

Members of the clergy, such as ministers, priests, rabbis, and imams, lead religious services and perform rituals. These people also provide counseling to their congregation and participate in community activities.

Other workers in the community and social services group are concerned with the organization and preservation of ideas. Librarians provide information. They may select the materials, such as books and magazines, found in libraries; organize and maintain the materials; and help people with research or questions. Curators oversee museum collections. They plan collections, acquire the items, and prepare them for display.

Some workers in this group safeguard citizens and their possessions. Police officers enforce the law, maintain order, and protect life and property. Police detectives work to solve or prevent crimes. Firefighters put out fires and help people in other emergency situations. They also teach fire prevention.

Military personnel also protect citizens. They stand ready to defend their country. Armored vehicle crew members drive tanks and other armored vehicles. Infantry soldiers fight enemy forces on land. They may use such handheld weapons as grenades, rifles, and machine guns to seize, occupy, and defend land areas. Artillery personnel support the infantry. They aim and fire such heavy weapons as cannons and missiles.

Some employees in the community and social services group work with people who break the law. Parole officers supervise people who have received an early release from prison. Correctional officers guard people who are waiting for a trial or prisoners in jail.

Working conditions. Counselors and social workers may be called at any time to handle emergencies. Members of the clergy work long hours, often on weekends and on holidays. Librarians and curators usually work in quiet settings. Firefighters, police and corrections officers, and military personnel often work in dangerous situations.

Education and training. All branches of the armed forces and most police departments, fire stations, and correctional institutions require applicants to have at least a high school education. Most social workers and parole officers have at least a bachelor's degree. Members of the clergy generally study at a seminary after going to college. Most counselors, librarians, and curators have a master's degree.

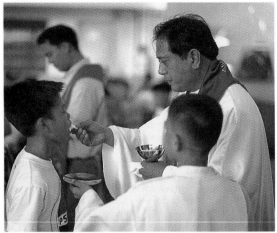

WORLD BOOK photo by Mark Downey

A Roman Catholic priest gives Holy Communion, a sacred ceremony, to a boy in the Philippines. Members of the clergy also lead religious services and counsel their congregations.

Construction, maintenance, and repair. Workers in construction build, modernize, and repair bridges, factories, highways, houses, and other buildings and structures. Maintenance workers help keep buildings and homes in good condition. Mechanics and technicians maintain automobiles, computers, and other machinery and fix them when they do not work properly.

Most construction workers specialize in certain building materials. For example, carpenters use wood to construct the framework of buildings and such features as hardwood floors, cabinets, and stairways. Bricklayers use bricks and other similar materials to build arches,

AP/Wide World

Construction workers build, modernize, and repair buildings and other structures. They often work outdoors in dangerous situations, such as these workers installing the roof of a building.

walls, fireplaces, and other structures. Concrete masons build sidewalks, roads, and other structures made of concrete. Electricians install wiring and electrical fixtures that supply light, heat, air conditioning, refrigeration, and communications systems. Plumbers install water, gas, and sewer systems. They can also install such fixtures as bathtubs and sinks, and unclog drains. Roofers cover the roofs of buildings with such materials as shingles, tar, rubber, or metal.

Some construction workers do the finishing work on a building. Carpet installers lay down padding and carpet on floors. Tile and marble setters apply decorative tile or marble to walls, floors, and other surfaces. Painters prepare surfaces, such as walls and ceilings, to be painted and then apply paint to the surfaces.

Maintenance workers care for apartment and office buildings, houses, and other types of buildings and properties. Janitors make sure that buildings are clean and in working order. They may wash floors, empty the garbage, or perform minor repairs. Maids and housekeepers clean such places as houses, hotels, and hospitals. They may dust, vacuum, or make beds. Exterminators make sure that houses and buildings are free from insects or other pests. They set traps or spray chemicals to kill the pests. Landscape workers and groundskeepers care for the lawns of houses, grounds of offices and parks, and other outdoor areas. They may mow grass, trim bushes and shrubs, and plant flowers.

Repair workers, such as mechanics and technicians, make sure that machines and other items work as they should. If equipment is not operating properly, these workers will fix it. Most repairers specialize in one area. Computer and office machine technicians install, repair, and maintain computers and electronic office machines, such as fax and photocopying machines. Aircraft mechanics work on all types of aircraft. Some aircraft mechanics perform regular maintenance after a plane has flown a certain distance. Others may inspect aircraft before a flight. Automobile mechanics maintain and repair automobiles. They may perform routine maintenance or diagnose and fix a problem. Locksmiths install, repair, and open locks. They may also make keys and change locks. Other repair workers include those that fix electronic equipment; heating, air conditioning, and refrigeration systems; household appliances; and telephones.

Working conditions. Many construction workers perform their jobs outdoors or in partly completed buildings. Construction workers are more likely to be injured on the job than are most other kinds of workers. Janitors, housekeepers, and exterminators usually work indoors. Mechanics and technicians may need to lift heavy parts and work in awkward positions to make repairs.

Education and training. Most workers in this group have a high school education. Many construction workers learn their trade through apprenticeship programs. Many repair workers complete training programs offered by their employers or at vocational or technical schools or community colleges. Most maintenance workers learn their skills through on-the-job training.

Farming, fishing, and forestry. Workers in this group help to produce our basic needs. They raise much of the food we eat and many of the materials used to make our clothes and build our homes.

Farmers oversee the entire operation of a farm. They may decide which crops to plant; raise and market livestock; hire, train, and supervise farmworkers; and keep track of the farm's finances.

Farmworkers help farmers. Farmworkers may plant, care for, and harvest crops. They may plow and fertilize the soil, spray the crops with *pesticides* (chemicals that kill insects and other pests), and pack the harvested crops for shipment to markets. Other workers may feed farm animals, clean their living areas, and give medications. Agricultural equipment operators run a variety of farm equipment. They may drive tractors to plant, fertilize, and cultivate crops. Some operate balers to gather and tie hay.

Animal breeders work to improve the quality of livestock by selecting superior animals for reproduction. For example, they may choose to breed animals that produce large quantities of eggs, meat, or milk. Animal breeders also keep records of such information as an animal's *pedigree* (list of ancestors) and *heat cycles* (times when a female animal is sexually receptive).

Agricultural inspectors make sure farm products meet certain standards. They give products a grade after

© Jim Foster, The Stock Market

Farmers produce much of the food we eat. Members of a family, such as the father and son harvesting corn in this photo, often own and operate their own farms.

AP/Wide World

Foresters manage and protect forests, woodlands, and parks. This forester is talking to visitors in a recreational area of a national park.

they check certain characteristics, such as color, condition, and size. Some inspectors also ensure that agricultural workers are following health and safety regulations.

Fishing crews use a variety of equipment, such as nets, hooks, and harpoons, to catch fish. Fish farmers raise fish in ponds, lakes, or artificial enclosures.

Forestry workers include foresters, forest technicians, fallers, and log graders. Foresters manage and protect forests and woodlands. They may decide which trees should be cut for timber, direct the planting of new trees, and protect forests from diseases and pests. Forest technicians work under the direction of foresters. They may gather data on such characteristics as the size and condition of various forest resources, maintain campsites and recreation areas within a forest, and train and supervise other forest workers. Fallers cut down trees with axes or chainsaws. Log graders evaluate logs cut from trees. They give each log a grade after they have calculated its size and looked for defects.

Working conditions. Most workers in this group work outdoors. Many of the jobs are physically demanding. Some of the work is dangerous. Some fishing crews are away from home for weeks or months.

Education and training. There are no formal educational requirements for many occupations in this group. Many of these workers learn their skills on the job. Animal breeders, log graders, and farmers need at least a high school education. Most foresters and agricultural inspectors have a bachelor's degree.

Health care. Workers in this group help people live healthier and happier lives. The services they provide range from teaching children how to brush their teeth to performing a kidney transplant.

Physicians diagnose, treat, and prevent diseases and conditions. Primary care physicians treat general medical problems, but many physicians specialize in one area of medicine. For example, dermatologists diagnose and treat diseases and disorders of the skin, hair, and nails; and surgeons perform operations.

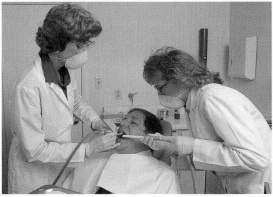

© Jim Pickerell, Stone

A dentist, *left,* uses a drill to remove decay from her patient's tooth before filling a cavity. A trained dental assistant, *right,* helps the dentist during the procedure.

WORLD BOOK photo

A veterinarian cares for family pets, livestock, and other animals. These doctors prevent, diagnose, and treat illnesses in animals. This veterinarian is examining the eyes of a dog.

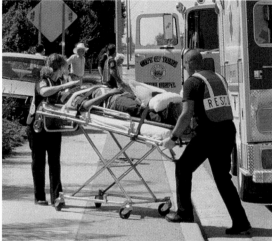

© Tony Freeman, PhotoEdit

Emergency medical technicians provide emergency care to critically ill or injured people. These technicians are preparing to transport a patient to a medical facility for further treatment.

Other types of doctors include chiropractors, dentists, optometrists, podiatrists, and veterinarians. Chiropractors treat diseases and conditions by manipulating or adjusting the spine and other parts of the body. Dentists diagnose, treat, and prevent diseases and other problems of the teeth, jaws, and gums. Optometrists diagnose vision problems and diseases. They may prescribe and fit eyeglasses and contact lenses. Podiatrists diagnose, treat, and prevent diseases and conditions of the foot and lower leg. Veterinarians treat animals.

Other health care professionals also provide medical care. Physician assistants provide basic medical care under the supervision of a physician. They may examine patients or order tests. Some physician assistants prescribe medication. Nurses take care of sick and injured people and people with disabilities. They also help healthy people stay well. Registered nurses may assist physicians during treatments and examinations, monitor patients' conditions, give medications and vaccinations, and keep patients' medical records up to date. Advanced practice nurses, such as nurse practitioners and certified nurse midwives, are registered nurses who have completed specialized training. Licensed practical nurses, also called licensed vocational nurses, assist registered nurses by providing routine patient care.

Some health care professionals provide treatments recommended by physicians. Dietitians, also called nutritionists, plan balanced diets for individuals or groups. Pharmacists fill prescriptions written by physicians and other health practitioners. They also provide patients with instructions on how to take the medication and inform them of possible side effects. Speech-language pathologists work with people with speech and language problems, such as stuttering. They identify a patient's problem and organize a treatment plan. Audiologists detect and diagnose hearing problems. They may also fit patients for hearing aids. Occupational therapists work with people with disabilities or illnesses. They plan a program of activities that help their patients recover, develop, or maintain practical skills. Physical therapists use such rehabilitation treatments as heat, cold, and exercise to relieve pain or correct injuries or diseases.

Many health care workers perform tests and procedures that help doctors diagnose and treat diseases and conditions. Cardiovascular technologists conduct or assist in tests and procedures to diagnose disorders of the heart and blood vessels. Medical laboratory technicians perform tests on patients' blood and other body fluids or tissues. Radiologic technologists prepare patients for imaging procedures, such as X rays. They also operate the equipment used during the procedures. Dental hygienists help patients maintain good oral health. They clean and polish teeth, examine the mouth for signs of disease, and take X rays of the teeth and jaws. They may also teach their patients how to properly brush and floss their teeth.

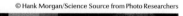
© Hank Morgan/Science Source from Photo Researchers

Physical therapists and patients work together to improve the patients' health. Physical therapists use rehabilitation treatments, such as exercise, to help patients relieve pain or correct injuries or disease.

A lawyer protects and preserves the rights and freedoms of clients. A lawyer also offers advice on legal matters and represents clients in courts of law.

© Robert E. Daemmrich, Stone

Other workers play an important role in patient care. Emergency medical technicians drive ambulances or fly specially equipped helicopters to the scenes of accidents or other emergencies. They provide urgent medical care to critically ill or injured people and transport them to medical facilities. Medical records technicians organize, file, and track patients' health information.

Working conditions. Many health care professionals work weekend, evening, or late-night shifts. Some deal with seriously ill or injured patients and may be exposed to various diseases. Many of these workers may be called in to work at any time to handle emergencies. However, taking care of sick people can be rewarding.

Education and training. Preparing for a health care career can take many years of study. Most chiropractors, dentists, optometrists, physicians, podiatrists, and veterinarians earn a bachelor's degree before they begin their medical training. Audiologists, physical therapists, and speech-language pathologists must have at least a master's degree. Dietitians, medical technicians and technologists, occupational therapists, pharmacists, and most physician assistants have a bachelor's degree. Other health care workers usually need an associate's degree.

Law. Legal occupations are important in every society. Workers in this field help people protect and preserve their rights and freedoms.

Lawyers, also called attorneys, represent clients in a court of law. They also advise their clients on legal matters and draw up legal documents, such as wills or divorce agreements. Judges are public officials that preside over law courts. They may advise lawyers, give instructions to a jury, or determine the punishment for people found guilty of a crime.

Paralegals, also called legal assistants, perform routine legal tasks under a lawyer's supervision. Paralegals may do preparatory work for lawyers, conduct legal research, and assist lawyers during trials. Court reporters document all words spoken during trials, hearings, and other official proceedings.

Working conditions. Most workers in legal occupations work in courtrooms, offices, and law libraries.

Many lawyers and paralegals work long hours while they prepare for a case.

Education and training. Most lawyers have a college education and a degree from a law school. Most judges have been lawyers. Paralegals usually have an associate's or a bachelor's degree and have completed a paralegal training program. Employers often require court reporters to complete a training program offered by many technical and vocational schools.

Life, physical, and social sciences. Workers in this group, called scientists, explore the workings of the world. Their discoveries can range from developing new drugs to finding better ways to prevent pollution.

Life scientists study living matter. Specialists in the life sciences include agricultural scientists, biochemists, microbiologists, zoologists, and epidemiologists.

Agricultural scientists study the relationship of animals and crops to their environment. They develop ways to improve the quality and quantity of crops and the breeding and raising of livestock. Some agricultural scientists specialize in farm animals. They may research animal nutrition and how it affects the quality of meat and other animal products. Other scientists may specialize in soil and plants. They may study how to make crops resistant to pests or how to improve soil conditions.

Biochemists study the chemical processes of living things. They examine the composition and function of molecules in cells and tissues. Biochemists may use this information to solve biological problems, such as determining the effectiveness of new medications.

Microbiologists study microscopic organisms, often called microbes. Many microbiologists investigate the relationships between microbes and human beings, animals, and plants. Medical microbiologists analyze the relationship between microbes and disease and search for cures. Others may specialize in agricultural, environmental, food, and industrial microbiology.

Zoologists study animals. They may investigate how animals *evolved* (changed over long periods), how they interact with human beings and other animals, and the characteristics that many animals have in common. Most

A cultural anthropologist might travel the world to study the origin and development of human cultures. This cultural anthropologist is learning about a community in Indonesia by living with the people and participating in their daily lives.

© Arne Hodalic, Saola from Liaison Agency

zoologists specialize in a certain type of animal. For example, entomologists study insects.

Epidemiologists study outbreaks of diseases. They first try to figure out what caused the outbreak. They then try to control the disease and prevent its spread.

Physical scientists study nonliving matter. Specialists in the physical sciences include astronomers, physicists, chemists, geoscientists, meteorologists, and environmental scientists.

Astronomers study the universe and comets, planets, stars, and other celestial bodies. They investigate the size, composition, shape, position, and movement of objects in the universe. Their findings help us to understand the origins of the universe and predict future events. They also help plan space missions. Astronauts may conduct experiments and do research in space. Their work may focus on a particular area of science, such as astronomy or biology.

Physicists study the properties and behavior of matter and energy. Some physicists perform experiments. Based on what they observe, these physicists develop laws and theories. Other physicists use this knowledge to solve problems in other fields.

Chemists investigate the characteristics of substances. They study how substances behave under different conditions. Many chemists work to improve and create new products, such as medications and artificial fibers.

Geoscientists, also called geologists and geophysicists, study the composition, structure, and history of the earth. Geologists research how the earth was formed and how it changes. They may study fossils, rocks, and soils or explore the earth for oil, gas, coal, ground water, and other natural resources. Geophysicists use physics to research the earth's physical properties and processes. They may study earthquakes and tremors, glaciers, volcanoes, oceans, and mountains.

Meteorologists study the earth's atmosphere and the conditions that produce weather. Weather satellites and balloons, radar, and computers measure the wind, temperature, air pressure, and other conditions. Meteorologists use this information to predict the weather.

Environmental scientists work to protect the environment. They perform research to determine the causes of air, water, soil, and noise pollution. They investigate possible ways to prevent and control these problems.

Social scientists study human society. Specialists in the social sciences include anthropologists, economists, psychologists, sociologists, and political scientists.

Anthropologists active in *cultural anthropology* study the origin and development of human cultures. They compare the arts, beliefs, customs, daily life, inventions, languages, social relationships, and values of cultures throughout the world. Another type of anthropology, *physical anthropology,* studies changes and variations in the human body.

Economists study how people produce, distribute, and use goods and services. They conduct research and analyze data on economic trends and issues. Economists can then determine how various economic systems work and predict how changes will affect the systems.

Psychologists study mental processes and behavior. They observe people and groups, perform experiments, conduct interviews, and administer tests. The information they obtain helps psychologists understand why people act, think, and feel as they do. Many psychologists provide counseling to individuals, couples, and groups.

Sociologists study behavior in groups. They observe groups and other social institutions. They study how groups are formed, how people interact in groups, and how groups influence the behavior of their members.

Political scientists study political systems. They research the origin and operation of various forms of government. Political scientists study political parties, elections, public policies, and other political activities. They also measure peoples' opinions about political topics.

Working conditions. Some life, physical, and social scientists work long hours. Many scientists work in an office or in a laboratory. Some scientists, however, such as soil and plant scientists and anthropologists, may do

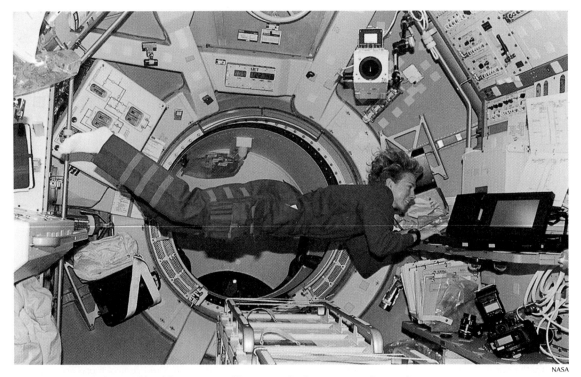

NASA

An astronaut works in Spacelab, a laboratory carried by a space shuttle. Astronauts often conduct scientific experiments in space. Many astronauts have degrees in biological or physical sciences.

much of their work outdoors. Some workers, including chemists, must take safety precautions while they work.

Education and training. Life, physical, and social scientists who plan to do research or teach at a four-year college or university must have a doctor's degree. Graduates with a bachelor's degree can teach at elementary, middle, and high schools. Employers may hire applicants with a bachelor's degree for some entry-level positions. Workers with a master's degree may teach at community or junior colleges or assist with research.

Management workers, called managers, are the leaders of organizations and businesses. All businesses and organizations need managers to plan and administer activities and policies and to train and supervise other employees. Mayors of cities, governors, state representatives, presidents of countries, and other elected officials are also managers. They develop laws and direct government activities.

A business or organization usually has three levels of managers. Each level has a different amount of authority or responsibility. Upper managers, such as chief executive officers and presidents or vice presidents of a company, have the most authority. They usually determine company policies and the long-term strategies for an organization. Middle managers may be in charge of a specific department in an organization, such as accounting. They report to upper managers and are responsible for making decisions about how the company should operate over the short term. Supervisory managers, such as foremen and forewomen in a factory, have the least authority. They may make decisions that relate to the daily operation of an organization.

Managers work in all fields. They may have worked in a certain field for a time before they were promoted to a managerial position. For example, a publisher of an encyclopedia may have begun his or her career as an editor or a writer. A principal probably started as a teacher.

© David R. Frazier

A plant foreman, *center,* discusses a project with workers in a factory. Foremen and forewomen supervise groups of workers. They may monitor rates of production and train new employees.

Managers may perform different duties that are specific to their industry. Managers have many responsibilities in common, however. Managers make plans, such as setting long- and short-term goals for their business or organization. They make sure that employees use their skills effectively. Managers also make sure that the organization's goals are being met. They let their employees know how well they are doing their job. They should also make their employees' jobs rewarding.

Human resources, also called personnel management, is a special field of management. Managers in this field may interview and recommend applicants to fill job openings. They may also coordinate employee benefits, such as health insurance and retirement savings programs, evaluate compensation programs, direct training programs, and help solve work-related problems.

Businesses and organizations hire management analysts and consultants when they have a problem. For example, a company may want to cut costs. Analysts and consultants evaluate the problem and suggest solutions.

Working conditions. Many managers work long hours in an office setting. Some managers may feel stress if they are asked to meet specific goals within a short time. Management analysts and consultants frequently travel to their clients' offices.

Education and training. Most managers, elected officials, and management analysts and consultants are college graduates, and many have advanced degrees. Courses in business administration are helpful. Many elected officials have been lawyers. Some organizations offer formal training programs for their managers.

Personal services. Workers in this category perform personal tasks for people. Many personal services include tasks that most people could do themselves. But some people have workers do these tasks because the jobs may be difficult or time consuming. Some personal services require special skills that many people lack.

Some workers in this field help people to look and feel their best. Cosmetologists take care of the hair and skin. Some, known as hairdressers, shampoo, cut, style, and apply color to women's hair. Some give facials and head and neck massages and remove unwanted hair from a client's face or body. Others, called manicurists and pedicurists, clip, shape, and polish their client's nails. Barbers usually work on men's hair and may also shave or trim beards and mustaches. Fitness trainers teach people how to exercise. They may design individual workout programs and show their clients how to use proper techniques while they exercise.

Other personal services workers provide care for family members. Child-care workers and nannies take care of children while their parents are at work or away from home. They feed and dress the children and organize play activities. Home-care aides help elderly or disabled adults with personal care and household chores. They may make beds, clean house, or help their client bathe and dress. Some workers take care of people after they have died. Embalmers prepare bodies for funerals. Funeral directors help families plan and arrange funeral services. Some people also need workers to care for their pets. Animal trainers teach animals to obey commands. They also prepare animals for competitions. Animal caretakers feed, groom, and exercise pets.

Flight attendants look after the safety of airline passen-

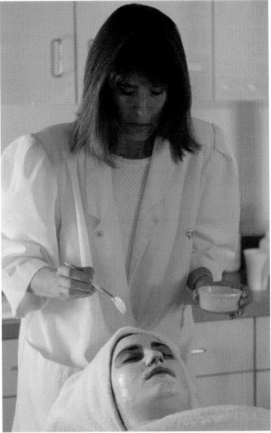

© Patrick Bennett, Corbis

A cosmetologist helps people look and feel their best. This cosmetologist is giving her client a facial treatment. Many cosmetologists also provide hair care services and give massages.

gers. They teach the passengers emergency procedures and make sure they are comfortable during the flight.

Concierges arrange personal services for such clients as hotel guests, apartment residents, and office tenants. They may make dinner and theater reservations, arrange leisure activities, or run errands.

Working conditions. Many cosmetologists and barbers work on weekends and spend much of their time standing. Nannies, child-care workers, and home-care aides usually work in their employer's home. Funeral directors may be called into work at any time. Pets sometimes bite or scratch animal trainers and caretakers. Flight attendants travel to other cities and countries and may spend time away from home between flights. Concierges may work with many people in busy lobbies or independently with personal clients.

Education and training. Some employers in this field require that applicants have at least a high school education. Cosmetologists and barbers must graduate from a cosmetology or barber school. Other workers, including animal trainers and caretakers, receive on-the-job training. Requirements vary for nannies, child-care workers, and home-care aides. Some employers require these workers to have formal training.

Many airlines prefer to hire flight attendants who

have a college degree. A majority of flight attendants receive specialized training in safety procedures and customer service. Funeral directors and embalmers usually need an associate's or bachelor's degree.

Production. Workers in this group are involved in making or preparing goods by hand or machine. These products range from simple wooden objects, such as tables and chairs, to complex computer parts.

Some production workers are involved in food processing. Bakers produce bread, pies, cakes, and pastries. Meat dressers kill animals, such as cattle and hogs, and prepare the meat. After they have slaughtered the animal, they use knives and other equipment to divide the meat into large cuts. Butchers cut and trim these cuts into meal-sized portions and sell them to consumers.

Apparel, textile, and upholstery workers make clothes, fabrics, and furniture. Tailors and dressmakers take a person's measurements and make clothing to fit. They also repair or alter clothing. Textile machinery operators run machines that manufacture a variety of fabrics. Upholsterers make new upholstered furniture or replace the worn coverings on existing furniture.

Assemblers put together parts to make finished products, such as automobiles and radios. Precision assemblers construct particularly complex goods, such as aerospace and computer equipment.

Other production occupations deal with metals. Machinists operate the power-driven machines, called *machine tools,* that are used to shape or cut metal. Tool-and-die makers are skilled machinists. They produce the precision parts and devices used by machine tools. Welders operate a variety of equipment that uses heat, pressure, or both to permanently join pieces of metal.

Other occupations in this group are in the printing industry. Prepress workers prepare materials for printing. Their responsibilities may include typesetting text, making negatives of illustrations, or preparing customer-supplied computer files for printing. Printing press operators run printing presses that reproduce words and images on paper and other materials. Bindery workers operate machinery that transforms printed materials into finished products. The machines may fold paper into pamphlets or fasten loose pages into books.

Woodworkers make various items out of wood. Some woodworkers operate machines that cut logs into boards. Others run machinery that cuts and shapes wood into parts that are later assembled to form such products as tables and chairs.

Jewelers make jewelry from precious metals, such as gold, silver, and gemstones. Jewelers may also repair and *appraise* (determine the value of) jewelry.

Mine workers are also included in the production group. Mining machine operators use specialized machines to cut coal and minerals, such as copper, iron, and silver, from the earth.

Working conditions. Most employees in the production industry work in factories or shops. Common working conditions include high levels of dust, heat, or noise. Some factory jobs require great strength or standing for long periods. Other jobs involve repetitive tasks.

Education and training. Most employers in this group prefer to hire workers with at least a high school education. Most bakers, meat dressers, butchers, bindery workers, and woodworkers receive on-the-job training. Other workers, such as tool-and-die makers, participate in apprenticeship programs or study at college or at vocational or technical schools.

Sales. Workers in sales inform people about products or services and persuade them to buy. Most sales workers sell their products in stores, but others may sell over the telephone or inside people's homes.

Retail salespeople work in retail stores, such as department, discount, or grocery stores, and sell merchandise directly to the consumer. Retail salespeople may help consumers find what they are looking for, demonstrate how a product works, or answer questions.

Many workers in this group are sales representatives. Wholesalers buy large quantities of an item from several manufacturers. Sales representatives for wholesalers then try to sell smaller amounts of that item to retail stores. Manufacturers' representatives sell goods to other manufacturers, to wholesalers, or to retail stores.

Other sales representatives sell services. Insurance sales agents sell various types of insurance policies, including automobile, health, and life insurance. Stockbrokers buy and sell *securities* (stocks and bonds). They determine their clients' investment goals and then advise them about which securities to buy or sell. Financial services sales representatives sell banking services, such as certificates of deposit and financial planning. Real estate agents help their clients buy, sell, or rent buildings and land. They may determine the value of a property a client wants to sell and prepare advertise-

© David R. Frazier

A baker in a large commercial bakery follows recipes to produce bread, cakes, pastries, pies, and other baked goods in large quantities. This baker is making loaves of bread.

© Paul Barton, The Stock Market

A real estate agent discusses the features of a house for sale with prospective home buyers. Real estate agents help their clients buy, sell, or rent buildings and land.

© David R. Frazier

Athletes competing in team sports may draw large crowds of fans. Jobs in the sports field often require both natural talent and many hours of practice and can be physically demanding.

ments describing the house, building, or land.

Advertising sales representatives sell advertising time for commercials on TV or radio or advertising space in newspapers or magazines. They may also sell ad space on Web sites on the Internet, on the sides of buses and buildings, or on outdoor facilities, including billboards and benches.

Other types of sales workers include telemarketers and fashion models. Telemarketers call customers over the telephone and persuade them to buy goods or services. Models promote the sale of clothing and accessories. They may wear these items at fashion shows or may pose for photographs that appear in advertisements on TV or in catalogs, magazines, and newspapers.

Working conditions. Many workers in this group work long hours, often in the evening or on weekends. Some travel to meet with potential customers and may be away from home for some time. Other sales workers have flexible hours and work when they want. Some sales workers feel stress because they are expected to sell a certain amount of product in a specified time.

Education and training. Most employers prefer retail sales workers to have at least a high school education. They usually receive on-the-job training or participate in formal training programs. Real estate agents must have at least a high school education. Some models have taken courses from modeling schools. Most insurance sales agents, stockbrokers, and financial services sales representatives have a college education. Employers also prefer to hire wholesale and manufacturing sales representatives who have a college degree.

Sports and entertainment. Workers in sports and entertainment perform in activities that amuse or interest audiences. Millions of people watch sporting events and enjoy the excitement of the competition. Others like the beauty of a ballet, concert, or other performance.

Workers in the sports field participate in organized athletic activities. Athletes compete in individual sporting events or team sports. Coaches instruct individual

athletes or teams. They help to improve the athletes' techniques and plan strategies for competition. Scouts observe athletes during practice and competition and evaluate their performance. They then try to recruit talented athletes to play for their team. Umpires, referees,

© Dan Nelken, Liaison Agency

Performing artists work to entertain audiences. This singer, *left,* and composer, *right,* are working in a recording studio to make an album of music for listeners to enjoy.

and other sports officials make sure the athletes follow the rules of the sport. They must know the rules, watch for violations, and determine the correct penalties.

Many workers in the entertainment field participate in the performing arts. Actors and actresses pretend to be characters in stage plays and movies and on television and radio. Dancers perform dances. They use their bodies to express emotions, tell a story, or set a mood. Instrumental musicians play such instruments as piano, drums, or guitar. They often perform alone or in groups, including rock bands or orchestras. Some musicians record their music. Singers are musicians who produce musical tones using their voices. Conductors direct musical groups, such as orchestras and choirs.

Other workers in the performing arts work behind the scenes. Producers are the business managers of a production. They may select scripts, raise money to finance the production, and set a budget. Directors make creative decisions for a production, such as interpreting the script, casting and rehearsing performers, and working with set and costume designers. Choreographers create new dance routines and teach them to dancers. Composers write music for musicians to play.

Working conditions. Many workers in this group, such as actors, musicians, and singers, work long hours. They may have difficulty finding steady work. Others, including producers and directors, may need to work under deadlines. Dancers and athletes must practice many hours. Their work is physically demanding. Coaches need to make quick decisions during competitions.

Training and education. There are no specific educational requirements for many careers in the sports and entertainment group. Almost all workers in this field have natural talent and must practice or train many hours every day. However, many athletes earn a degree while they compete in college athletic programs. Many coaches and sports officials begin their careers as athletes. Singers, dancers, musicians, and actors and actresses may have studied with private teachers for years. Others have attended schools for the performing arts. Almost all

choreographers begin as dancers. Composers and conductors may have attended a *conservatory* (specialized music school) or studied music at a college or university.

Teaching. Workers in this group help other people learn. They teach many kinds of skills and transmit cultural values to students of all ages.

Preschool teachers use a variety of play activities to develop the intellectual, physical, and social skills of children up to 6 years old. Teachers may read stories, create learning opportunities, and care for children.

Kindergarten teachers prepare children who are 4 to 6 years old for elementary school. They use activities, such as group discussion, games, and storytelling, to teach basic subjects. Some kindergarten teachers offer instruction in reading and writing.

Elementary school teachers teach basic academic and social skills to students from ages 5 or 6 to age 12, 13, or 14. They usually teach many subjects to one class of students who are the same age. These teachers also emphasize communication and mathematical skills and personal development.

Middle school teachers teach basic subjects to students in sixth, seventh, and eighth grade. They prepare their students for high school. Middle school teachers also help young people understand the physical, social, and emotional changes they are going through.

High school teachers cover subjects in more detail than what was taught in elementary school. They prepare students for college or for a job after graduation.

Special education teachers provide instruction for disabled or gifted children. They use special equipment or programs to help children with physical or mental disabilities learn. They coach gifted children and help them develop their talents.

College and university faculty teach advanced courses. They specialize in one area, such as business or English, and teach a variety of courses in that field. Most college and university teachers also conduct research.

Many kinds of teachers hold classes for adults. Some teachers may provide remedial education courses in ba-

© Pablo Bartholomew, Liaison Agency

Teachers use a variety of methods to help their students learn. This teacher helps her student master new skills by using a computer to tap into information resources on the Internet.

sic skills, such as reading and writing. Continuing education teachers lead classes for adults who want to continue to learn. They may teach personal interest courses, such as cooking or photography, or help people learn new job skills. Vocational education teachers prepare students for occupations that do not require a college degree, such as automobile repair.

Teacher aides work under the supervision of teachers. They help with classroom activities. Aides may also grade tests and homework, provide individual attention to students, and help answer parents' questions.

Working conditions. Working with students and watching them learn new skills can be rewarding. But teachers may experience stress if classrooms become overcrowded. Many teachers work only during the school year. Long summer vacations enable them to travel, take continuing education classes, or pursue other interests.

Education and training. Almost all teachers need a bachelor's degree. Most also need to complete a professional training program before they can teach. Some preschool teachers and teacher aides do not need a degree. Many high school teachers and most college and university faculty have advanced degrees.

Technical and mathematical occupations. Workers in this group use technology and mathematics to prepare or analyze a variety of complicated procedures. Businesses and other organizations could not function efficiently without these workers.

Some workers in this group are computer specialists. Computer hardware engineers design *hardware* (the physical parts of computer systems), such as memory chips and microprocessors. Computer software engineers design *software* (programs, or sets of computer instructions and information). They may create *specifications* (detailed plans) for programs for general use or customize programs for clients.

Computer systems analysts design or modify computer systems to meet the needs of an organization. Analysts first evaluate an organization's requirements. They then prepare detailed specifications, which may include modifying software or hardware.

Computer programmers write programs. They break down the program specifications into logical steps. They then write these steps into instructions the computer can follow using various computer languages. They may work with systems analysts and software engineers to create new programs or modify existing programs. Some programmers also design Web sites.

Computer network administrators maintain an organization's *network* (system of two or more computers connected by communications lines). They also maintain the network's software and hardware. Database administrators use special software to manage *databases* (large, searchable bodies of information). They supervise the operation of databases and make sure the information is kept up to date. Computer support specialists help computer users. They may answer users' questions about hardware, such as printers, or software, such as word processing applications.

Some workers in this group are mathematics specialists. They use their knowledge to conduct research, develop new theories, or predict future developments. Mathematicians may develop new mathematical theo-

© David R. Frazier

A computer programmer writes sets of coded computer instructions called *programs* using various programming languages. This programmer is checking his code for errors.

ries, relationships, and principles. Other mathematicians use existing techniques to solve problems in other fields. Statisticians use statistical methods to collect, organize, analyze, and interpret data. Their findings provide information that enables others to draw conclusions and make decisions. For example, a statistician may predict the change in population for a specific area. Actuaries are mathematicians who calculate future risk. Some actuaries work for insurance companies. They analyze data to calculate the probability of such occurrences as accidents and death. They then help design policies, calculate premium rates, and determine insurance company reserves to ensure payment of claims.

Financial specialists use mathematics to keep track of money. Accountants gather, analyze, and summarize their clients' financial information. They prepare statements and reports and provide advice to help their clients make decisions and plan for the future. They also design systems and procedures to track financial information. Budget analysts prepare an organization's financial plan that determines how money will be spent.

Specialized occupations in the technical and mathematical group include cartographers, architects, drafters, and surveyors. Cartographers use such information as

© Lawrence Manning, Stone

Architects combine artistic and engineering skills in designing offices, museums, churches, houses, and other buildings. These architects are examining a model of a part of a structure.

© Frank Cezus, Stone

A surveyor uses special equipment to take measurements of various boundaries. Many surveyors work at construction sites to check the positioning of a wall or other architectural feature.

statistical data, photographs taken from airplanes, and satellite images to produce maps. Architects design buildings and other structures. They prepare plans for every detail of the structure, such as plumbing and air-conditioning systems. They must make sure the structure meets safety and design regulations. Drafters prepare technical drawings and plans. These drawings and plans provide precise information on how to build products and structures. Surveyors take measurements to determine land, air space, and water boundaries. They may also gather information about such characteristics of land features as elevation and shape.

Other professionals in the technical and mathematical group have careers in engineering. Engineers use scientific knowledge to solve practical problems. They specialize in a particular field of engineering, including aerospace, biomedical, chemical, civil, electrical, industrial, materials, mechanical, nuclear, mining and geological, and petroleum engineering.

Aerospace engineers design, produce, and test aircraft, guided missiles, and spacecraft. Biomedical engineers use engineering methods to solve medical problems. For example, they may design artificial limbs or hearing aids. Chemical engineers design chemical factories and equipment used to process chemicals and chemical products for industrial and consumer uses. Civil engineers plan and supervise the construction and maintenance of large structures and facilities, such as bridges, dams, highways, and sewer systems.

Electrical engineers develop, produce, and test electrical devices and equipment. For example, they may design the equipment used to generate and transmit power for electric companies. Electronics engineers specialize in designing electronic equipment, such as communications gear. Industrial engineers determine the most economic and efficient ways to use people, machines, and materials to produce goods and services.

Materials engineers work with various materials, such

as metals, ceramics, and plastics. They evaluate the properties, structure, and production methods of materials. They then work to develop new materials or new uses for existing materials.

Mechanical engineers plan, design, and test all kinds of machines that produce and use power, such as air-conditioning equipment, elevators, engines, and machine tools. Nuclear engineers study the production and use of nuclear energy and radiation. Most nuclear engineers design, develop, and operate nuclear power plants that generate electric power.

Mining engineers find deposits of minerals, such as copper and tin, and determine the best way to remove the *ore* (mineral-bearing material). They design mines, supervise the construction of shafts and tunnels, and select the mining machinery. Petroleum engineers locate petroleum and natural gas deposits and develop methods to drill and recover the oil and gas from the earth.

Working conditions. Most workers in the technical and mathematical group work in offices, laboratories, or industrial plants. Other workers, such as surveyors and mining and petroleum engineers, perform some or all of their duties outdoors. Many workers in this group need to work extra hours to meet deadlines. Some workers, especially computer specialists, can *telecommute*—that is, use computers to do some or all of their work from home.

Education and training. Employers prefer to hire drafters who have a high school education and have completed training programs offered at technical institutes, community colleges, and universities. Computer programmers, architects, surveyors, and cartographers need a bachelor's degree. Most other occupations in the technical and mathematical group require at least a bachelor's degree. Many of these workers have advanced degrees. Workers who want to participate in research or teach at an institution of higher education should have a doctor's degree.

© Michael Newman, PhotoEdit

A travel agent shows her client brochures and helps him decide on a destination. Travel agents handle hotel and transportation reservations. Most agents get discounts on their own travel.

© Nik Wheeler, Corbis

A chef adds a decorative touch to a dish while he teaches students how to prepare fish. Most chefs plan menus and cook food, but one of their main duties is to supervise cooks.

Tourism and hospitality. Workers in the field of tourism and hospitality provide services that help people enjoy their leisure time. Some plan activities, while others make sure that their guests are happy and enjoying the service and surroundings.

Travel agents help people plan vacations and business trips. They help their clients decide on a destination and provide information about restaurants, transportation, and hotels and other accommodations. They also make airline and hotel reservations and other travel arrangements. Tour guides take tourists on sightseeing excursions or to places of interest. They also help tourists learn about the areas they visit.

When people are away from home, many kinds of workers help make them comfortable. These workers include employees who provide lodging in hotels, motels, and similar establishments. Front desk clerks greet guests and assign them rooms to sleep in. They also take and confirm room reservations and help guests check out when they are ready to leave.

Other workers prepare or serve food and drinks in restaurants and bars. Restaurant hosts and hostesses greet guests, seat them at tables, and give them menus. Waiters and waitresses take guests' orders and serve

AP/Wide World

A tour guide takes visitors to places of interest. This guide leads tourists in a ceremony at the grave of President George Washington. She wears clothing from the 1700's to help visitors learn about the history of the site.

their food and drinks. Bartenders prepare drinks. Cooks prepare meals. Chefs supervise the cooks and other kitchen workers, plan the menu, and order supplies. They may also prepare and cook food.

Working conditions. Many workers in the tourism and hospitality group work evenings, weekends, and on holidays. Travel agents do most of their work on computers. Chefs and cooks work long hours near hot ovens and grills. Waiters and waitresses spend many hours standing and often carry heavy trays of food.

Education and training. Most tourism and hospitality workers need at least a high school education. Many employers prefer to hire travel agents who have completed travel courses at vocational schools, community colleges, or universities. Some bartenders receive training at bartending, vocational, or technical schools. Many cooks and chefs learn their skills through vocational and ap-

prenticeship programs or take college courses.

Transportation. Industrialized societies need fast, safe, and dependable methods for moving people and goods from one place to another. Workers in the transportation field help passengers and goods travel by air, land, and water.

Pilots and air traffic controllers are two of the best-known air transportation workers. Pilots operate and navigate aircraft and are responsible for the safety of their aircraft, passengers, crew, and cargo. Air traffic controllers help provide safe air transportation. They direct the movement of aircraft preparing to take off or land. They also make sure that all aircraft are clear from other traffic in the air.

Land transportation workers can be divided into two groups: (1) road and highway and (2) rail. Road and highway transportation moves goods and people by automobile, bus, or truck. Taxi drivers and chauffeurs operate such motor vehicles as automobiles, vans, and limousines and take passengers wherever they need to go. Bus drivers operate buses, usually on a fixed route. They may provide transportation for passengers traveling from one city to another or within a city. Other bus drivers carry students to and from school. Truckdrivers operate trucks to pick up, transport, or deliver packages and other goods. They may drive short distances within a specific area or long distances across many states.

Rail transportation moves freight and passengers by trains, streetcars, and subways. Locomotive engineers operate trains. Conductors supervise the crew on passenger and freight trains. On passenger trains, they may collect tickets and inform the engineer when it is safe to leave a station after a stop. On freight trains, they may check the contents of each car and make sure the appropriate cars are removed or added at each stop.

Water transportation involves barges, general cargo ships, passenger liners, riverboats, tankers, and a wide variety of other vessels. Captains are the top officers on ships. They are responsible for their ship, passengers, crew, and cargo. Officers called mates assist the captain. They navigate the ship and supervise other crew members. Marine engineers design ships and their machinery. They also make sure the machinery is working properly and make any needed repairs. Pilots guide ships through harbors and difficult waters.

Working conditions. Most transportation workers travel as a part of their job. Workers assigned to long-distance trips may be away from their homes for long periods. Some transportation employers, such as airlines, allow employees to travel at no cost or at reduced fares.

Education and training. Employers prefer to hire road and highway transportation workers who have a high school education. These workers often receive on-the-job training. Railroad conductors must have at least a high school education. Locomotive engineers usually participate in a formal training program. Many airlines prefer to hire pilots who have a bachelor's degree. All pilots, however, must have attended a flight school or received armed forces training. Air traffic controllers receive formal and on-the-job training. Many also have a college degree. Many water transportation workers have a bachelor's degree from a nautical school or marine academy.   Duane Brown

AP/Wide World

A truckdriver uses a truck to transport packages and other goods. This truckdriver works for a package delivery service. He drives a short distance each day on a specific route.

© James Blank, The Stock Market

Cleveland, an Ohio city on Lake Erie, is a leading industrial center and an important Great Lakes port. Shown here is a view of downtown Cleveland from Edgewater State Park on the lakefront.

Cleveland is the largest metropolitan area in Ohio and one of the leading industrial centers of the United States. Cleveland lies on the southern shore of Lake Erie, at the mouth of the Cuyahoga River. These waterways and the city's location near huge supplies of coal and iron ore helped make Cleveland an important steel producer. The city also ranks as a transportation, medical, and cultural center of the Midwest and a chief port of the Great Lakes.

Moses Cleaveland, a surveyor, founded Cleveland in 1796. The village was named for Cleaveland, but a newspaper printer misspelled the name in 1831 and it has been known as Cleveland ever since.

The city

A valley formed by the Cuyahoga River divides the city of Cleveland into an East Side and a West Side. Iron and steel mills and other plants operate in the valley, which is known as the Flats. The part of the Flats near where the Cuyahoga flows into Lake Erie has been redeveloped into a thriving entertainment district.

Downtown Cleveland. The layout for Cleveland's downtown area was part of a plan developed in the early 1900's by a commission headed by architect and city planner Daniel Burnham. In keeping with the commission's plan, Cleveland's public buildings border a large green space called the Mall. These buildings include the Cuyahoga County Court House, City Hall, the Cleveland Convention Center, and the Public Library.

Public Square, which lies near the Mall, covers about 10 acres (4 hectares). The city's founder, Moses Cleaveland, had set aside the land for use as a town square. A statue of Cleaveland stands in the square, along with the Civil War Soldiers and Sailors Monument and a statue of Tom L. Johnson, a progressive mayor of the early

---

Facts in brief

Population: *City*—505,616. *Metropolitan area*—2,202,069. *Consolidated metropolitan area*—2,859,644.

Area: *City*—76 sq. mi. (197 km²), excluding inland water. *Metropolitan area*—2,708 sq. mi. (7,014 km²), excluding inland water. *Consolidated metropolitan area*—3,613 sq. mi. (9,358 km²).

Altitude: 660 feet (201 meters) above sea level.

Climate: *Average temperature*—January, 27 °F (−3 °C); July, 73 °F (23 °C). *Average annual precipitation* (rainfall, melted snow, and other forms of moisture)—32 inches (81 centimeters). For the monthly weather in Cleveland, see **Ohio** (Climate).

Government: Mayor-council. *Terms*—4 years for the mayor and the 21 council members.

Founded: 1796. Incorporated as a city in 1836.

Largest communities in the Cleveland area

Name	Population	Name	Population
Cleveland	505,616	Strongsville	35,308
Parma	87,876	North Olmsted	34,204
Lakewood	59,718	East Cleveland	33,096
Euclid	54,875	Garfield Heights	31,739
Cleveland Heights	54,052	Shaker Heights	30,955

Source: 1990 Census.

Symbols of Cleveland. The city's red, white, and blue flag was adopted in 1895. It bears a shield that resembles the city seal. The seal includes Cleveland's founding date and symbols of its industry and its waterways.

City of Cleveland

Cleveland lies on Lake Erie in northeastern Ohio. The map at the right shows the metropolitan area of Cleveland. The map below shows the city and its major points of interest. The Cuyahoga River divides Cleveland into two parts.

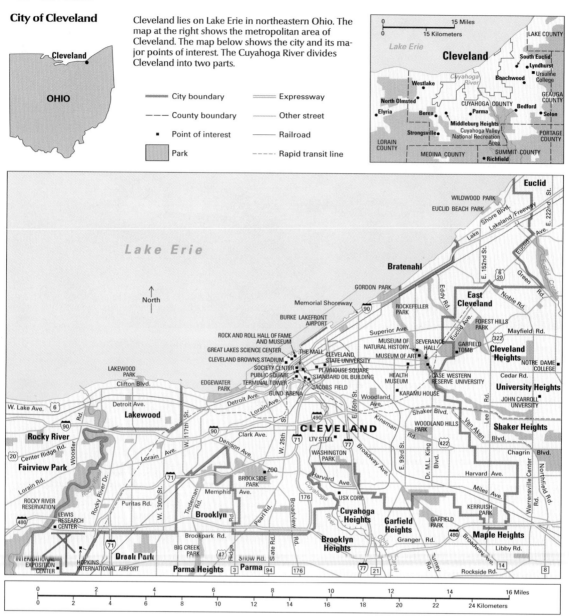

▬▬ City boundary	▬▬ Expressway
▬ ▬ County boundary	▬▬ Other street
▪ Point of interest	▬▬ Railroad
▨ Park	▬ ▬ Rapid transit line

WORLD BOOK maps

1900's. During the winter holidays, the square features an ice skating rink and colorfully lighted displays. During the summer, it serves as a site for outdoor entertainment events.

Public Square is framed by high-rise office buildings, including the Terminal Tower Building, a city landmark. The Terminal Tower Building rises 708 feet (216 meters) at the southwest corner of the square. Tower City Center, a part of the Terminal Tower complex, includes shops, restaurants, motion-picture theaters, a hotel, and offices. It is also a hub for the rapid transit system.

Cleveland's downtown lakefront underwent extensive redevelopment in the late 1900's. The lakefront attractions include a sports stadium, a science museum, and

the Rock and Roll Hall of Fame and Museum.

The neighborhoods. Cleveland has about 35 neighborhoods. These residential areas spread outward from the downtown district. Like many other cities, Cleveland began experiencing decline in its neighborhoods in the mid-1900's. The decline continued for many years. But in the late 1900's, Cleveland's neighborhoods became the focus of redevelopment and revitalization efforts. These efforts included building new housing and neighborhood shopping centers, and resurfacing neighborhood streets.

The metropolitan area of Cleveland extends over six counties—Ashtabula, Cuyahoga, Geauga, Lake, Lorain, and Medina. The United States Bureau of the Census calls it the Cleveland-Lorain-Elyria metropolitan area. The Census Bureau groups the metropolitan area of Cleveland-Lorain-Elyria with that of Akron to form the Cleveland-Akron Consolidated Metropolitan Statistical Area.

The Cleveland metropolitan area began to form in the early part of the 1900's, when middle- and upper-income families moving outward from the central city established a ring of suburbs around Cleveland. These communities included Cleveland Heights, East Cleveland, Euclid, Garfield Heights, Lakewood, Parma, and Shaker Heights. After World War II ended in 1945, the outward migration increased, and additional rings of suburbs were developed. Such communities as Beachwood, Solon, Strongsville, and Westlake grew rapidly. In the late 1900's, the sprawl of growth extended into the neighboring counties of Lorain, Medina, Geauga, and Lake.

The people

Ethnic groups. Cleveland's diverse population includes more than 80 nationalities. About half of the people have European ancestry, and most of the rest are African Americans. Other residents include people of Hispanic, Asian, or American Indian background.

Education. The mayor of Cleveland has responsibility for the public school system. The mayor selects the superintendent of schools, who serves as the school district's chief executive officer. A school board, consisting of nine members, sets school policy. The mayor appoints the board members, who serve a four-year term.

Institutions of higher learning in Cleveland include Case Western Reserve University, the Cleveland Institute of Art, Cleveland State University, Cuyahoga Community College, John Carroll University, Notre Dame College, and Ursuline College.

Social problems. Cleveland's ethnic diversity presents the city's people with the challenge of developing respect and tolerance for one another. Cleveland experienced racial tensions in the 1960's. Riots occurred in the African American neighborhoods of Hough and Glenville on the West Side.

After the riots, city programs helped to ease the tensions. For example, a fund-raising program called Cleveland: Now helped finance projects to train the unemployed and find jobs for them. The city also set up child day-care centers and helped African Americans develop their own businesses. In 1982, Cleveland-area leaders established a multicultural, multiracial organization called the Greater Cleveland Roundtable to help resolve human-relations problems facing the city. The organization has opened lines of communication among community leaders and has provided a forum for the discussion of issues and the development of solutions.

A large number of the city's African Americans have been elected to local, state, and national offices, and they have assumed leadership roles in local businesses and organizations. But the level of unemployment among African Americans remains a problem. The Urban League and other civic organizations have been making efforts to reduce that level.

Cultural life and recreation

The arts. The world-famous Cleveland Orchestra performs in Severance Hall. The orchestra gives outdoor summer concerts in the Blossom Music Center near Cuyahoga Falls. The Cleveland Ballet and two opera companies also make their home in Cleveland.

The Cleveland Play House is the country's oldest regional theater. It produces plays at four theaters in the same building—the Bolton, Brooks, Drury, and Studio One theaters. Karamu House opened in 1915 as an ex-

© Superstock

The Rock and Roll Hall of Fame and Museum, on Cleveland's lakefront, features exhibits on rock music performers. American architect I. M. Pei designed the striking building.

periment in racial understanding through the arts. Today, its two theaters present integrated casts in dance and drama programs. The Playhouse Square Center, originally built in the 1920's, was renovated in the late 1900's. This downtown complex, which includes five theaters, is one of the largest performing arts centers in the country. Its presentations include plays, dance performances, and operas.

Museums and libraries. The city has a wide range of museums. The Cleveland Museum of Art owns one of the nation's finest collections of American, Asian, and European paintings and sculpture. The Cleveland Museum of Natural History has exhibits on the development of life on the earth. The Museum of Natural History also has a planetarium.

The Health Museum of Cleveland, which opened in 1940, was the first permanent health museum in the United States. The Rock and Roll Hall of Fame and Museum features costumes and instruments used by rock music performers, original song manuscripts, and films of rock music performances. The Great Lakes Science Center has exhibits on science, technology, and the environment, and a theater for science films.

The Cleveland Public Library is one of the largest public research libraries in the country. It has one of the nation's most extensive collections of books on open shelves. During the 1880's, the library became one of the first in the United States to adopt the open-stacks plan. This plan allows library users to select books directly from the shelves. The landmark 1920's building that is the home of the library was renovated during the 1990's, and the Louis Stokes Wing was constructed. Stokes, for whom the addition is named, served as a U.S. representative from Ohio from 1969 to 1999.

Recreation. Cleveland's largest park, 273-acre (110-hectare) Rockefeller Park, was given to the city by the industrialist John D. Rockefeller, Sr. It includes the Cleveland Cultural Gardens, a series of gardens that represent the city's nationality groups. Brookside Park is the site of the Metroparks Zoo. Parks linked by parkways surround the city in a ring about 100 miles (160 kilometers) long. Biking and walking trails run through most of the parks and parkways. The ring of parklands is referred to as the Emerald Necklace because it encircles the city with green space.

Cleveland has several professional sports teams. It is the home of the Cleveland Browns of the National Football League, the Cleveland Cavaliers of the National Basketball Association, and the Cleveland Indians baseball team of the American League.

Economy

Manufacturing is the backbone of the local and regional economy. It employs about a fifth of the the city's workers. Motor vehicle parts and steel are the city's most important products. Companies also produce biotechnology, chemicals, electronics, fabricated metal products, machine tools, and plastics.

Cleveland is an important center of new-product research and development. One focus of the city's many research institutes has been to improve the productivity and competitiveness of the older manufacturing industries. These industries have experienced major increases in productivity without increasing employment.

Service industries are an increasingly significant part of Cleveland's economy. Hospitals, colleges and universities, law firms, banks, and a wide range of service companies provide jobs for many workers. The Cleveland area is an important health care center. The Cleveland Clinic Foundation ranks as one of the leading medical institutions in the United States and is especially known for its advanced treatment of heart and kidney disease. The foundation is one of the city's largest employers. Tourism is growing as a source of income and employment.

Shipping. Cleveland's harbor is one of the busiest on the Great Lakes. From 1940 to 1959, the city spent over $20 million to widen, deepen, and straighten the Cuyahoga River. Today, ore and coal vessels travel more than 5 miles (8 kilometers) inland to steel mills. The opening of the St. Lawrence Seaway in 1959 made Cleveland an international seaport. Oceangoing ships sail the seaway from the Atlantic Ocean to the Great Lakes.

Transportation. Cleveland Hopkins International Airport lies in the southwestern section of the city, and Burke Lakefront Airport is near downtown Cleveland. Passenger and freight rail lines serve Cleveland. The Regional Transit Authority provides the chief means of local transportation. Its buses and rapid-transit lines serve the city and many suburbs. In 1968, Cleveland opened a rapid-transit line between the downtown area and Hopkins Airport. It was the first U.S. city to offer downtown-to-airport train service.

Communication. Cleveland has one daily newspaper, *The Plain Dealer*. WHK, Ohio's oldest radio station, began in Cleveland in 1922. The state's first television station, WEWS-TV, opened in Cleveland in 1947.

Government

Cleveland has a mayor-council form of government. The voters elect the mayor and the 21 members of City Council—all to four-year terms.

Like most big cities, Cleveland has difficulty raising enough money to pay for increasingly costly city services. In 1967, the city began to tax the incomes of everyone—including suburbanites—who worked there. This tax is Cleveland's largest single source of revenue. Other sources include property taxes, local bond issues, and federal grants.

History

Early settlement. The Chippewa, Erie, and Iroquois Indians lived in the Cleveland region before the first European settlers arrived. In 1796, Moses Cleaveland, a surveyor for the Connecticut Land Company, led a group of Connecticut settlers to the site of what became Cleveland. Connecticut had held claim to a strip of land in northeastern Ohio called the Western Reserve since receiving a royal charter for it in 1662. In 1795, the Connecticut Land Company bought most of the Western Reserve, including the site of Cleveland. During the early 1800's, more settlers from New England came to the area. Cleveland became the seat of Cuyahoga County in 1810 and was incorporated as a village in 1814.

Industrial growth. The opening of the Erie Canal in 1825 provided a cheap transportation route for manufactured goods traveling to the Northwest and for raw materials going to the East. The canal helped Cleveland be-

Industry along the Cuyahoga River contributed greatly to Cleveland's growth. At the left in this photo, Terminal Tower, still a landmark, looms over downtown in the first part of the 1900's.

© Corbis

come a commercial center. In 1836, the Ohio legislature granted Cleveland a city charter. The city had a population of about 6,000 at that time.

During the last half of the 1800's, Cleveland changed from a commercial to an industrial center. The first railroad came to the city in 1851 and connected it with Columbus, the state capital. In 1852, the first boatload of iron ore from the Lake Superior region entered Cleveland's harbor. Shipments of iron ore from Minnesota and coal from Pennsylvania helped the city become a major producer of locomotives and other iron products. Between 1850 and 1870, Cleveland's population grew from 17,034 to 145,281. The city also became the chief refiner for Pennsylvania oil. In 1870, John D. Rockefeller organized the Standard Oil Company in Cleveland.

During the 1880's and 1890's, the city's rapid industrial growth attracted many settlers from other countries. Most came from Hungary, Lithuania, Poland, or Russia. By 1900, 381,768 people lived in Cleveland.

Continued growth and progress. During Tom L. Johnson's term as mayor, from 1901 to 1909, Cleveland became one of the best-governed cities in the United States. Johnson improved the police department, and he brought about lower streetcar fares. He also developed a system of taxing owners of commercial property at a higher rate than homeowners.

The development of the automobile industry during the early 1900's greatly aided steel manufacturing in Cleveland. After the United States entered World War I in 1917, the city made airplanes, ships, and tanks for the Allies, the countries opposing Germany and its partners. The rapid growth of the steel industry after the war helped Cleveland's population hit 900,429 by 1930.

During World War II (1939-1945), the city again produced war materials. Thousands of people from other parts of the United States, including great numbers of African Americans from the South, came to Cleveland seeking work in the city's defense industries. By 1950, Cleveland's population had risen to 914,808.

Downturn and racial tensions. A trend toward suburban living developed during the 1950's, and thousands of white middle-class Clevelanders moved to newly built areas outside the city. Cleveland's population fell to 876,050 by 1960.

The city faced serious racial problems in the 1960's. In July 1966, four people were killed during a five-day riot in the Hough area. Racial tension decreased in 1967 after voters elected Carl B. Stokes mayor. Stokes, a Democrat, was the first black mayor of a major U.S. city. He served until 1971. Another riot occurred in the Glenville area in July 1968. It resulted in 11 deaths.

Cleveland's population declined dramatically in the 1960's and 1970's. By 1980, it had fallen to less than 574,000. During this period, the city lost thousands and thousands of jobs as industries declined or moved to the suburbs or other regions.

Financial problems. Cleveland encountered severe financial difficulties during the 1970's. In 1978, Cleveland became the first major U.S. city since the Great Depression of the 1930's to *default on* (fail to pay when due) its loans. In 1979, voters approved an increase in the city income tax to help raise funds. Cleveland emerged from default in 1980 after city leaders and eight banks reached an agreement that enabled the city to repay its overdue loans.

Comeback City. In the 1980's, Cleveland worked to recover from its financial problems. The city's efforts led to its being called the Comeback City.

To help achieve fiscal stability, the city government eliminated hundreds of city jobs, and voters approved another income tax increase. To improve political stability, voters approved a reduction of the City Council from 33 to 21 members and changed the terms of the mayor and council members from two years to four years. The number of jobs in manufacturing continued to drop, but service industries began to develop. Cleveland's population loss slowed during the 1980's. In 1990, the population leveled off at about 500,000.

The downtown area, including the lakefront, was the site of many redevelopment projects during the 1980's and 1990's. These projects included the development of the Tower City Center with its many retail and entertainment facilities, the renovation of Playhouse Square into a major performing-arts complex, and the development of the Gateway complex, which includes a sports stadium and a sports arena. Several new apartment and condominium complexes provided additional housing in the downtown area. The North Coast Harbor project transformed the lakefront with a harbor, a park, a sports stadium, and two museums.

Despite Cleveland's economic comeback, the school system remained a source of concern. In 1995, after years of financial problems, the city's school system was put under state control. But in 1997, the Ohio governor signed into law a bill giving responsibility to the Cleveland mayor, who officially took control in 1998. Goals for the school system included improving student scores on state tests, increasing parent involvement, and improving school safety.

Recent developments. Cleveland emerged in the 2000's with a substantially changed skyline and a new label, the New American City. But certain human issues continued to need attention, including race relations, public school reform, and job training for the unemployed.　　David C. Sweet

See also **Stokes, Carl B.; Western Reserve.**

Conservation

Conservation is the management, protection, and wise use of natural resources. Natural resources include all the things that help support life, such as sunlight, water, soil, and minerals. Plants and animals are also natural resources.

The earth has limited supplies of many natural resources. Our use of these resources keeps increasing as the population grows and our standard of living rises. Conservationists work to ensure that the environment can continue to provide for human needs. Without conservation, most of the earth's resources would be wasted, degraded, or destroyed.

Conservation includes a wide variety of activities. Conservationists work to keep farmlands productive. They manage forests to supply timber, to shelter wildlife, and to provide people with recreational opportunities. They work to save wilderness areas and wildlife from human destruction. They try to find ways to develop and use mineral resources without damaging the environment. Conservationists also seek safe, dependable ways to help meet the world's energy needs. In addition, they work to improve city life by seeking solutions to air pollution, waste disposal, and urban decay.

Conservationists sometimes divide natural resources into four groups: (1) inexhaustible resources, (2) renewable resources, (3) nonrenewable resources, and (4) recyclable resources.

Inexhaustible resources, such as sunlight, cannot be used up. Conservation experts consider water an inexhaustible resource because the earth will always have the same amount of water. But water supplies vary from one area to another, and some areas have shortages of clean, fresh water. The supplies of salt and some other minerals are so abundant that they are not likely to be used up.

Renewable resources can be used and replaced. They include plants and animals, which reproduce and so replace themselves. Most renewable resources cannot be stored for future use. For example, old trees rot and become useless for timber if they are not cut down, though rotting trees can serve such important purposes as providing habitat for wildlife. In addition, because most renewable resources are living things, they interact with one another. Thus, the use of one such resource affects others. For example, cutting down trees affects many plants and animals, as well as soil and water resources. Soil may be considered a renewable resource because crops can be grown on the same land for years if farmers care for the soil properly. But if farmers allow the soil to wash or blow away, it will take hundreds of years to replace.

Nonrenewable resources, such as coal, iron, and petroleum, cannot be replaced. They take thousands or millions of years to form. People deplete supplies of these resources faster than new supplies can form. We can store most nonrenewable resources for future use. Mining companies sometimes leave minerals in the ground

Daniel Simberloff, the contributor of this article, is Nancy Gore Hunger Chair of Excellence in Environmental Studies at the University of Tennessee.

to save them for the future. Little interaction occurs among most nonrenewable resources, so using one nonrenewable resource has little effect on another.

Recyclable resources, such as aluminum and copper, can be used more than once. For example, aluminum can be used to make containers and then be reprocessed and reused.

People have practiced some kinds of conservation for hundreds of years. As a popular movement, however, conservation began in the United States during the early 1900's. The word *conservation* was probably first used by Gifford Pinchot, head of the U.S. Forest Service during President Theodore Roosevelt's administration. The term comes from two Latin words—*servare,* which means *to keep* or *to guard,* and *con,* which means *together.* During the early 1900's, American conservationists worked chiefly to preserve the nation's forests and wildlife. Today, conservationists work in many fields, including forestry, geology, range ecology, soil science, wildlife biology, and urban planning. Conservationists are also called *environmentalists.*

One of the most difficult challenges of conservation is to reconcile two, sometimes conflicting, goals—(1) to protect the environment and (2) to maintain or increase agricultural and industrial production. For example, the agricultural use of some chemical fertilizers and pesticides pollutes the environment but also greatly increases crop yields. Thus, most farmers do not want to stop using these chemicals, even though it would be best for the environment. Only the combined efforts of many people can solve such problems. Business leaders, government officials, scientists, and individuals must all work together to conserve natural resources.

The importance of conservation

Conservation is important for many reasons. Farmers may practice conservation to prevent erosion and to maintain the quality of the soil. City dwellers may be chiefly concerned about air pollution, inadequate parks, and decaying neighborhoods. Nature lovers appreciate the beauty and other values of wildlife and landscapes. Business executives may promote conservation to help ensure continuous supplies of minerals and other resources on which their industries depend. But in general, conservation is important for two basic reasons: (1) to meet demands for natural resources and (2) to maintain the quality of life.

To meet demands for resources. The demand for natural resources has steadily increased as a result of the growth of the world population and the rise in standards of living in many countries. While the demand for resources has increased, the supply has not, and some resources are being used up rapidly.

From A.D. 1 to about 1800, the world population quadrupled from about 300 million to 1 billion. But since then, the population has multiplied six times to about 6 billion. Although the rate of growth is slowing, the world is expected to have approximately 11 billion people by 2100. Such a large increase in population will result in even greater demands for natural resources. People will need more land for homes and agriculture. They will require more fuel and fresh water. No one knows how many people the earth can support. But most conservationists believe the rate of population growth must be reduced to keep from depleting many of our natural resources.

The rise in the standard of living in industrialized nations has created further demands for natural resources. Such industrialized nations as the United States, Canada, Australia, and Switzerland have high living standards, and they use a disproportionately large share of the world's natural resources. In addition, many less developed countries are working to raise their living standards and are increasing their demands for resources.

The high living standards in the United States and many other nations are supported largely by the growth of industry. Industry uses huge amounts of fuel and other resources, and it depends on continuous supplies of these resources. Unless people practice conservation, shortages of some resources may develop within the next 100 years.

In many cases, meeting demands for one resource makes it difficult to conserve another. The same land that is needed to produce food, wood, or fuel is often valued for its wildlife, recreational opportunities, or beautiful scenery. For example, the construction of a dam may provide water to irrigate farmland or to produce electric power. But it may also destroy scenic lands and wildlife habitats.

To maintain the quality of life. Conservationists use the term *quality of life* to refer to the health of the environment. Such factors as clean air and water, uncluttered living areas, and unspoiled scenic lands contribute to the quality of life.

Industrial development has created a high standard of living for many people. But it has also damaged the environment in ways that impair the quality of life. For example, many factories release smoke and other pollutants into the air and empty waste products into lakes and streams. As a result, the air in many cities is unhealthy to breathe, and the water in many lakes and streams is unsafe to drink or to swim in. Some methods of mining also cause pollution and may leave the land barren. In addition, the use of certain industrial products contributes to pollution. For example, the exhaust fumes from automobiles are a major source of air pollution.

To maintain or improve the quality of life, we must use

© Renee Lynn, Photo Researchers

Conservation includes the efforts of individual people to preserve natural resources. These student volunteers preserve live Christmas trees by planting them at their school.

natural resources in ways that cause the least possible damage to the environment. In addition, we need to preserve some places in their natural state and protect them from any form of development. Certain species can survive only in natural environments, such as prairies, wetlands, and forests. These habitats provide homes for many kinds of wildlife. Preserving such habitats contributes to the *biological diversity,* or *biodiversity,* of the earth—that is, its variety of plant and animal species. If we do not preserve such environments, large areas of the earth will support only a few species of plants and animals.

The number of species has already declined greatly in many parts of the world. For example, corn and wheat fields have replaced most of the prairies of North America. As a result, such wildlife as pronghorns and prairie

© Robert C. Fields, Animals Animals

Wildlife conservation requires setting aside areas where animal habitats are not disturbed. Mallards and other birds nest in Lower Klamath National Wildlife Refuge in California, *shown here.*

chickens, once plentiful on the prairies, are no longer abundant throughout their former ranges. Such prairie plants as Pitcher's thistle and running buffalo clover have also become threatened. Conservationists are working to protect the few remaining prairies and to preserve other natural environments.

Kinds of conservation

This section divides the broad field of conservation into nine main categories. They are (1) biodiversity conservation, (2) water conservation, (3) ocean conservation, (4) soil conservation, (5) conservation of grazing lands, (6) forest conservation, (7) mineral conservation, (8) energy conservation, and (9) urban conservation.

Each kind of conservation has different problems and solutions. Often, however, the management of one resource affects several other resources. For example, the conservation of forests helps conserve biodiversity, water, and soil. Forests absorb rain water and so keep it from running off the land too rapidly. They thus help prevent rain water from washing away the soil. Forests also provide homes for animals, plants, and other living things. In fact, a forest constitutes an *ecosystem,* a group of living organisms interacting with one another and with their physical environment.

This section deals mainly with conservation problems and practices in the United States. But much of the information applies to other countries as well. The section *Conservation around the world* discusses specific conservation concerns in other countries.

Biodiversity conservation. Biodiversity, also called biological diversity, refers to the great variety of the world's living creatures. Animals, plants, and other living things make up an essential feature of nature, and they contribute to the beauty and wonder of life. Although biologists cannot agree on the true number of species on the earth, scientists have classified between 1,400,000 and 1,700,000 species. Most specialists, however, believe at least 4 million other species remain unstudied, and some scientists speculate that that number may be more than 30 million. Different populations of a single species may also differ *genetically* from one another. That is, they possess different *genes,* the biological structures that carry specific traits from one generation to the next. Genetic differences add to biodiversity.

Through the ages, human activities have contributed to the extinction of numerous animal and plant species. Such extinct species include the passenger pigeon of North America and the Tasmanian tiger of Australia. Today, human activities threaten the survival of other animals and plants. Conservationists classify more than 8,000 species around the world as *endangered* (near extinction), and many other species that have been poorly studied may be equally in peril.

In the past, uncontrolled hunting was a major cause of endangerment and extinction. But today, many countries have laws that protect animals by regulating hunting and fishing. The destruction of habitat is the major threat to both animals and plants today. Although such legislation as the U.S. Endangered Species Act of 1973 protects the habitat of species listed as endangered or threatened, no laws protect the habitats of many other species whose numbers are dwindling. Development of land for homes, farms, industries, and transportation leaves fewer areas where wild animals and plants can live and reproduce. Pollution also damages natural habitats. Chemicals from sewage, industrial wastes, fertilizers, and pesticides build up in lakes and streams and in the soil.

Human beings also bring species of plants and animals from their native regions to other areas of the world. These *nonindigenous species* present a major threat to biodiversity. They often lack natural enemies in their new homes, enabling them to multiply quickly and drive out native animals and plants. The South American banana poka plant, for instance, has disrupted the native ecosystem of Hawaii. It has killed off many native trees and now dominates vast tracts of land. By destroying native trees, the banana poka threatens the existence of native animals that rely on these trees. Nonindigenous species can also harm people. One example, the South American red imported fire ant, has spread to North America and caused vast agricultural damage. In addition, many introduced species of animals and plants carry diseases that devastate native species.

A chief goal of conservation is to ensure the survival of animal and plant species. Conservation thus includes the enforcement of hunting and fishing laws, as well as laws protecting endangered species and regulating the importation of nonindigenous species. In many cases, an entire habitat requires protection and management. Some areas must then be set aside as national parks, state parks, nature reserves, and wildlife refuges. Farmers can help conserve such wildlife as rabbits and quail by leaving strips of natural vegetation along the edges of their fields. They can also reduce the use of harmful pesticides and fertilizers.

The populations of some species of animals and plants have dwindled to the point that they cannot survive in their natural environments. Zoos, botanical gardens, and other facilities attempt to breed these species in *captive breeding* programs. Sometimes they produce a large enough population for release into a protected area.

Water conservation. People require clean, fresh drinking water. People also use water for bathing, cooking, and cleaning. Farmers need water to irrigate dry croplands. Industries use water to produce electric power and in the manufacture of many products. Water is also important in recreation and transportation.

The demand for water constantly increases as a result of population growth and the expansion of agriculture and industry. The earth has an abundant supply of water, but the water is unevenly distributed. Some areas do not receive enough rainfall, while others get more than they need.

Many dry regions of the world, such as the Middle East, North Africa, and parts of western and central North America, face serious water shortages. In some areas, people obtain water by drilling wells to tap underground supplies. But in parts of the western and central United States, farmers have drilled so many wells to provide water for irrigation that the level of the ground water has been greatly lowered. Many cities have also used up much of their ground water. In some cases, underground reservoirs can be refilled by pumping in water during periods of heavy rainfall.

Some rural areas and cities obtain water by damming rivers to create reservoirs. Engineers also built dams to control flooding. But in many cases, the construction of new dams to meet ever-increasing demands for water or to reduce flooding threatens wildlife. For example, during the late 1970's, conservationists opposed the construction of the Tellico Dam on the Little Tennessee River because of its possible harmful effect on a rare species of fish called the snail darter. The dam was completed in 1979, and some snail darters were transferred to the Hiwassee River in Tennessee in an attempt to ensure their survival.

A dam may harm certain fish because it reduces the flow of water. Dams can also prevent such migrating fish as salmon from reaching their breeding grounds. As the land behind a dam becomes flooded, the water destroys some wildlife habitats. Certain streams should not be dammed because they carry too much silt. On such streams, reservoirs quickly fill up with silt and can no longer store water.

People also deplete lakes to provide water for irrigation. Such irrigation practices have caused the Aral Sea, a saltwater lake in central Asia, to shrink to about 40 percent of its original size.

Water supplies for cities and farms can be increased partly through *watershed management* (the management of vegetation to prevent rapid runoff of rain and melting snow). Trees and other plants keep water from running off the land and so enable it to filter into the ground. The water thus refills underground supplies and flows through underground channels into lakes and streams. The destruction of plant cover disturbs this natural cycle. Rain water runs off the land rapidly instead of filtering into the ground. Watershed management also helps reduce flooding and soil erosion.

Some cities near seacoasts meet part of their water needs by desalting seawater. This process, called *desalination,* requires massive amounts of energy and is thus expensive. For this reason, desalination is not yet practical on a large scale. But solar energy may one day provide enough cheap power for large-scale desalination.

Many communities have problems with water pollution. The disposal of sewage, industrial chemicals, and other wastes into lakes and streams makes the water unhealthy for wildlife and human beings. Even bodies of water as large as Lake Erie have become seriously polluted. Cities and industries can reduce pollution by removing harmful substances from wastes before emptying the

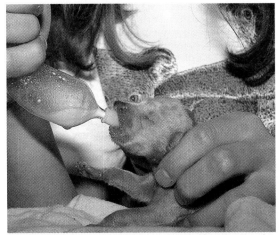

© Terry Whittaker, Photo Researchers

Biodiversity conservation includes raising endangered animals in captivity. This conservationist is feeding a bush dog pup at Port Lympne Wild Animal Park in the United Kingdom.

wastes into lakes and streams. But waste treatment is expensive, and the job of cleaning up lakes and streams will take years. See **Water pollution.**

Ocean conservation. The oceans make up more than 70 percent of the earth's surface and provide homes to vast numbers of living species. They also help keep the world's climate from becoming too warm. Oceans do this by storing carbon dioxide gas and preventing too much of the gas from entering the atmosphere. Atmospheric carbon dioxide warms the earth by absorbing heat from the sun.

People catch millions of tons of ocean fish and shellfish each year. This catch yields a major source of animal protein in many countries. Increasingly, people also eat such ocean species as seaweed, sea urchins, and other marine organisms. Medical science uses chemicals from some marine organisms to fight cancer and other diseases. In addition, oceans and their shores provide people with recreational activities, including boating, fishing, and swimming.

The oceans receive ever greater amounts of pollution

© Bob Edwards/SPL from Photo Researchers

Water conservation aims to preserve supplies of clean, fresh water. This scientist in India is collecting samples of polluted water, which has turned yellow because of chemical contamination. A factory is dumping this water into a ditch. Such water could harm many kinds of living things, including animals that drink it.

as human population grows and shipping increases. Industrial wastes often find their way into the oceans, either directly or indirectly through rivers. Single accidents involving large oil tankers can foul an entire coastal region, killing thousands of living things. Underwater mining and excavation spills such toxic materials as heavy metals and pesticides into ocean waters. Every year, people also throw millions of tons of litter into the oceans from ships. Millions of seabirds, turtles, fish, and marine mammals die annually from becoming entangled in or consuming discarded plastic items in the litter. Concentration of pollutants also renders beaches unsafe for people.

Overharvesting ranks as the other major threat to marine biodiversity. With the advent of mechanized fishing boats, overfishing increased dramatically. Many formerly productive fishing areas, including those for cod and haddock, declined greatly. Many sea creatures become *by-catch*—that is, species caught accidentally in nets set for other species. Nets used to catch shrimp, for example, also trap endangered marine turtles. Globally, overfishing and pollution have combined to cause a sharp decline in the total number of fish caught in the ocean since 1989. The total fish harvest increased, however, because of increases in *aquaculture,* also called fish farming.

Many international conservation problems involve marine animals and other ocean resources. International agreements and rigorously enforced limits on catch have saved certain international fishing areas, such as those for Pacific halibut. On the other hand, the commercial hunting of whales remains an international problem. Because of overhunting, several species of whales verge on extinction. The International Whaling Commission (IWC), an organization devoted to conserving whales, recommends that all nations should completely stop commercial whale hunting. But not every country has agreed with this recommendation.

Soil conservation. Soil is essential for the growth of plants, which in turn provide food for animals and human beings. Soil consists chiefly of minerals mixed with *organic* (plant and animal) matter. Soil forms from rocks and similar materials that are broken up into smaller particles by physical and chemical processes called *weathering.* The particles become mixed with *humus,* a substance formed from plant and animal remains. Bacteria in the soil break down the humus into nutrients needed by plants.

The thin layer of fertile soil that covers much of the land was formed by natural processes over thousands of years. But in many areas, careless human practices have destroyed the soil in just a few years.

Rain, wind, and other natural forces gradually wear away the soil. This process, called *erosion,* normally occurs slowly. But people have greatly increased the rate of soil erosion by removing natural vegetation to clear land for construction projects, mines, or farmland. Plants protect soil from rain and wind. Their roots form an underground network that holds soil in place. Plants also absorb some rain water so that less runs off the land. Thus, fewer soil particles are washed away.

Soil erosion has long been a major conservation problem, especially on croplands. In the United States, soil erosion has severely damaged millions of acres or hectares of land. Much of the soil eroded each year ends up in lakes, streams, and rivers.

Farmers can reduce soil erosion by planting trees and leaving patches of natural vegetation between their fields and on other unplowed areas. The trees serve as windbreaks, and the plant cover slows the runoff of rain water. Many farmers also practice such soil conservation methods as *contour plowing, strip cropping, terracing,* and *minimum tillage.*

Contour plowing is practiced on sloping land. Farmers plow across a slope, instead of up and down. The plowed soil forms ridges across the slope. The ridges help slow the flow of rain water.

Strip cropping also helps slow the flow of rain water down a slope. Farmers plant grass, clover, or other close-

© Andy Levin, Photo Researchers

Ocean pollution can damage shorelines as well as the oceans themselves. These conservation workers are cleaning up an oil spill along a coastal area in Puerto Rico.

growing plants in strips between bands of corn, wheat, or other grain crops. Grass and clover hold water and protect the soil better than grain crops do.

Terracing helps prevent soil erosion on hillsides. Farmers build wide, flat rows called *terraces* on the hillsides. A terraced hillside resembles a large staircase. The terraces hold rain water and so prevent it from washing down the hillside and forming gullies.

Minimum tillage, also called *conservation tillage,* consists of several methods of reducing the number of times a field must be tilled. Normally, farmers till their fields three or more times each growing season. One form of minimum tillage is called *zero-tillage* or *no-till.* After harvesting a crop, farmers leave the *residues* (remains) from the crop on the field as a covering for the soil, instead of plowing them under. During the next planting, the farmer prepares the seedbed with a device that leaves the residues between the crop rows. Zero-tillage not only provides cover for the soil but also conserves tractor fuel.

Another major conservation problem on farmlands is declining soil fertility, which is caused partly by planting the same crop in a field year after year. Corn, wheat, and other grain crops drain the soil of an essential chemical called *nitrogen* if they are grown on the same field for several years. Farmers can maintain the fertility of the soil by practicing *crop rotation,* in which crops are alternated from year to year. The rotation crop is usually a *legume,* such as alfalfa or soybeans. Unlike corn and wheat, legumes restore nitrogen to the soil.

Some farmers add plant remains or *manure* (animal wastes) to their fields to enrich the soil. Many use chemical fertilizers for this purpose. Excessive use of some chemical fertilizers, however, may decrease the ability of bacteria to decay humus and produce nutrients naturally. As a result, the soil may gradually harden and lose much of its ability to absorb rain water. The soil then erodes more easily. In addition, the chemicals from fertilizers may wash out of the soil and enter lakes, streams, and even wells, polluting the water. Excessive use of pesticides causes similar problems.

A common problem on irrigated farmland is the build-up of various chemical salts in the soil. Most irrigation water contains small amounts of these salts. In time, the salts accumulate in the soil and may reduce plant growth and ruin cropland.

Grant Heilman

Soil conservation techniques include *contour plowing,* in which farmers plow across a slope, and *strip cropping,* in which farmers alternate strips of close-growing plants and grain crops.

Conservation of grazing lands. Grazing lands, also called *ranges,* are grass-covered areas too dry to support farms or forests. These lands provide homes for many wild animals, including pronghorns and mule deer. Numerous grasses and such flowering plants as goldenrods and sunflowers grow there. Ranges also provide pasture for cattle, horses, and sheep. Some of the world's largest grazing lands lie in western North America, southern South America, and Australia.

© Jean-Claude Lejeune, Black Star

Terracing helps check soil erosion on hillsides. The terraces hold rain water and prevent it from washing down a hillside and forming gullies.

Georgia Pacific (Designer Photo)

A tree nursery supplies seedlings for replanting forests that have been cut down for timber. Seedlings grow in a nursery for one to four years before being transplanted in a forest.

The chief conservation problem on ranges is overgrazing, which results when too many animals graze an area or when the animals stay in one place too long. The grasses then die and are replaced by weeds and poisonous plants, which provide poor pasture for livestock.

Overgrazing also results in increased runoff of water, which causes soil erosion. Overgrazing also ruins wildlife habitats. For example, it often occurs on the fertile areas that border a stream. Livestock trample on stream banks and kill plant life. This results in increased erosion along the stream bank and may cause the stream to become too muddy to support fish and other aquatic life.

Grazing lands, many of which are owned by national governments, must be carefully managed to ensure a continuous supply of *forage* (plant food) for wildlife and for livestock. To prevent overgrazing, range conservationists must determine the *carrying capacity* of the land. The carrying capacity is the largest number of animals that an area of land can support without destruction of plant life. Range conservationists limit the number of livestock on a range so that the carrying capacity is not exceeded. Livestock managers must move the herds from time to time so that the grasses can regrow.

To improve the vegetation on grazed lands, range managers sometimes practice *prescribed burning*. That is, they set fires to help control brush and poisonous plants. When properly controlled, such burning will not harm native plants. Many of these native plants have become adapted to frequent, low-intensity fires. Herbicides can also eliminate undesirable plants. But many conservationists oppose the use of chemical herbicides because the chemicals in them may harm animals.

Another problem on grazing lands is the control of such animals as bobcats, coyotes, and mountain lions, which sometimes prey on livestock. Many ranchers want these predators killed or removed. But most conservationists want to protect the animals.

Forest conservation. Forests serve as sources of timber and as habitats for many animals and plants. They also provide recreational areas for campers, hikers, and hunters. In addition, forests are important as watersheds. They absorb large amounts of rain water, preventing the rapid runoff of water that causes erosion and flooding.

Many forests are owned by national governments. In the United States, the U.S. Forest Service manages these national forests under the principle of *multiple use,* which means they provide several benefits at once. For example, the Forest Service manages woodlands to furnish timber, shelter wildlife, provide recreational space, and conserve water. Timber production, however, may conflict with the need to conserve wildlife, water, and other resources.

Oxford Scientific Films

Grazing lands provide pasture for livestock. But improper management may result in overgrazing, which destroys the vegetation on the land. In this picture, the land on the left has been overgrazed, and the land on the right has been properly grazed.

Prescribed burning is one way to improve the vegetation on overgrazed land. The fire destroys weeds and other undesirable plants, and grasses can then regrow.

Steve Bunting

Also, the use of prescribed burning in forests, often done to maintain native species that are adapted to frequent fires, can conflict with concern over smoke and the danger of fire in adjacent areas.

The conservation of forests used to produce timber depends on replacing trees that are cut down so that the forest has a *sustained yield*. Sustained yield is an approximate balance between the annual harvest and the annual growth of wood. The **Forestry** article in *World Book* describes methods of harvesting trees to achieve sustained yield. It also describes how forest resources other than trees are managed and how forests are protected from diseases and insect pests.

For centuries, people have cut down forests to clear land for farms and cities. Today, forest destruction in the United States and other industrialized countries has slowed, though many forest-dwelling species remain threatened. In many other countries, however, especially those in tropical areas, forest destruction continues at a rapid pace. The reduction of tropical rain forests has put at risk the survival of the richest and most diverse ecosystems in the world.

Mineral conservation. Minerals include such substances as copper, gold, iron, lead, and salt. Industries use minerals to manufacture countless products.

The use of many minerals has increased greatly throughout the world. The use of aluminum, for example, has increased about five times since 1960. The use of nickel has more than doubled during this period. Some minerals, such as *bauxite* (the mineral from which aluminum is obtained) and salt, are plentiful. But the proved reserves of such minerals as copper, lead, nickel, and zinc may be depleted within 100 years.

Mining companies can profitably extract most minerals only where they occur in large deposits. Industries first develop the highest-grade and most easily minable ores. When these are depleted, mining companies turn to lower-grade and harder-to-mine ores. Many such deposits require advanced technology and large amounts of energy

to mine. Some take so much energy to mine and refine that they cannot be profitably developed.

Deposits of minerals are unevenly distributed around the world. This uneven distribution of minerals has played a major role in history. For example, the ancient Romans battled the Celts for control of the tin mines in southern England. A desire for gold was largely responsible for the Spanish explorations and conquests of many parts of the New World.

The need for minerals continues to influence international relations today. Many countries must import large amounts of various minerals. The United States, for example, imports almost all of the sheet mica and strontium it uses. In addition, the United States imports more than half of its chromium, cobalt, fluorine, manganese, nickel, platinum, and tin.

Mining and refining minerals often destroys scenic lands and habitats for animals and plants. It can also pollute air and water. One method of copper mining, for example, leaves large open pits on the surface of the land. Fumes from copper smelters, iron and steel mills, and other refineries pollute the air and kill many plants. Some refineries discharge wastes in lakes and streams.

We can conserve minerals in a number of ways. Industries can reduce waste by using more efficient mining and processing methods. In some cases, industries can substitute plentiful materials for scarce ones. Some mineral products can be recycled. Aluminum cans are commonly recycled. Although bauxite is plentiful, it can be expensive to refine. Recycling aluminum products does not require the large amounts of electric power needed to refine bauxite. Products made from many other minerals, such as nickel, chromium, lead, copper, and zinc, can also be recycled.

Energy conservation. All industries require energy to operate. Energy is also used in transportation and recreation. In addition, we use energy to warm and cool our homes, to cook food, to provide lighting, and to operate many appliances.

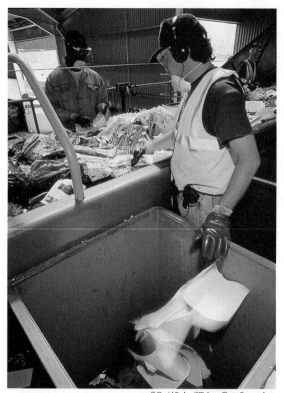

© David Parker/SPL from Photo Researchers

Recycling is an important conservation activity. Workers at this waste transfer station remove plastics and other recyclable materials from household trash. Industries then reuse the materials.

Materials recycled in the United States

Recycling is a way to conserve important resources. This pie graph shows the substances that make up the total amount of recycled materials in the United States. The bar graph shows the percentages of various discarded items that are recycled.

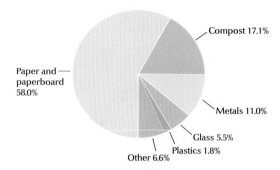

Types of recycled materials

Compost 17.1%

Paper and paperboard 58.0%

Metals 11.0%

Glass 5.5%

Plastics 1.8%

Other 6.6%

Percentage of some common items recycled

	Amount recycled	Amount not recycled
Lead-acid batteries	94%	6%
Steel cans	58%	42%
Aluminum packaging	52%	48%
Paper and paperboard	41%	59%
Yard waste	39%	61%
Glass containers	29%	71%
Plastic containers	23%	77%
Tires	19%	81%

Figures are for 1996.
Source: U.S. Environmental Protection Agency.

About 95 percent of the energy used throughout the world comes from oil, coal, and natural gas. These substances are called *fossil fuels* because they developed from fossilized remains of prehistoric plants and animals. Large deposits of fossil fuels take millions of years to form. The earth has a limited supply of fossil fuels. But the worldwide use of fossil fuels has nearly doubled every 20 years since 1900. As the supply dwindles, the cost of fossil fuels keeps rising.

Many nations are working to develop other sources of energy to reduce their dependence on fossil fuels. But every source of energy has some disadvantages that make its development difficult. The **Energy supply** article describes such sources of energy as nuclear energy, solar energy, and geothermal energy.

Until other sources of energy are further developed, nations must conserve fossil fuels to make the supply last as long as possible. Most of the responsibility for conservation rests with industrialized nations because they consume the majority of the world's energy. The United States alone uses about 25 percent of the world's energy, and it produces only about 20 percent. Higher fuel prices and periodic fuel shortages have forced the United States and many other industrialized nations to develop better conservation programs.

Industries and individuals can conserve energy in many ways. Improved mining and manufacturing techniques can make the industrial use of fuel more efficient. Individuals can save fuel in their homes by installing insulation,

which reduces the amount of fuel used for heating and air conditioning. People can set their thermostats at or below 68 °F (20 °C) in winter and at or above 78 °F (26 °C) in summer. These thermostat settings are required in most public buildings by the federal government. People can also conserve energy by using less hot water and turning off unnecessary lights. Motorists can save gasoline by driving smaller cars and by forming car pools. Much gasoline would be saved if more people used public transportation.

The development and use of energy causes many environmental problems. For example, strip mining of coal destroys plant life and exposes the land to erosion. Blowouts of offshore oil wells and leaks from tankers produce oil spills that pollute the oceans. The burning of fossil fuels pollutes the air and results in the formation of *acid rain,* rain and other precipitation polluted mainly by sulfuric and nitric acid. Acid rain can kill fish in lakes and streams. Sound conservation practices, such as restoring strip-mined land as closely as possible to its original condition, can help reduce environmental damage.

Urban conservation. About half of the world's people live in or near cities. Since the 1800's, many cities have grown so rapidly that public services have not kept up with population increases. Cities thus have such problems as overcrowding, traffic jams, and inadequate public transportation. Most large cities are also noisy and suffer from air pollution, partly because of the many motor vehicles in use. In addition, many cities lack sufficient parks and other recreational facilities. The urban landscape consists largely of pavement and buildings.

Because of the drawbacks of city life, many people and businesses have moved to the suburbs. As suburbs nearest the city become crowded, people move farther and farther out, creating a condition known as *urban sprawl.* When businesses and upper- and middle-class people move to the suburbs, the cities lose tax money needed to maintain city services and neighborhoods. Many cities are left with a large population of poor people living in crowded, run-down housing. The hearts of many cities consist of large slum areas, a condition known as *urban blight.* In addition, much prime farmland has been lost to urban sprawl, and wildlife habitat has been damaged.

The goal of urban conservation is to improve the quality of life in cities and to make them more attractive and pleasant places to live. Many cities have *urban renewal projects,* which demolish run-down buildings and replace them with public housing or other developments. In some cities, developers restore old houses and apartment buildings instead of tearing them down. Many cities try to enhance their environments by developing strips of grass or trees called *greenbelts.* Some cities try to reduce traffic problems and air pollution by improving public transportation systems and encouraging their use. Most cities also need to develop more parks and recreational facilities.

Early history of conservation

Prehistoric times. During early prehistoric times, there were not enough people on earth to use a large amount of natural resources or to damage the environ-

Steve Hale
Urban conservation includes efforts to restore houses and so maintain the attractiveness of old neighborhoods in cities.

ment significantly. Early prehistoric people thus had little need to practice conservation.

About $1\frac{1}{2}$ million years ago, people learned how to make fire. They built fires to cook food, to keep warm, and, later, to kill animals. The fires drove the animals over

© Bruce M. Wellman, Tom Stack & Associates

Solar collectors can be used to help heat houses and many other buildings. The development of new energy sources reduces our dependence on the dwindling supplies of fossil fuels.

cliffs or into traps. In addition, people have used fire for thousands of years to clear forests and encourage the growth of food plants. Some scientists believe Africa's *savannas* (grasslands with widely scattered trees and shrubs) resulted from burning of forests.

The rise of civilization. A number of civilizations arose around the Mediterranean Sea from at least 3500 B.C. to the A.D. 400's. Many people of the region tended large flocks of sheep and goats, which severely overgrazed the land. In time, the shallow soils of the region eroded. The grassy pastures turned to wastelands, and large areas became desertlike. Much of the land in the Mediterranean region remains in poor condition today.

Although ancient civilizations in the Mediterranean region damaged the land, they also developed some conservation practices to keep farmlands productive. For example, the Phoenicians, whose culture peaked about 1000 B.C., developed techniques of terracing hillsides to prevent soil erosion. The Greeks introduced the practice of crop rotation sometime before the 300's B.C. The Romans, whose empire reached its greatest size in the A.D. 100's, brought knowledge about irrigation practices to the lands they conquered. Many conservation techniques later spread to northern Europe and formed the basis for wise land management there.

The Industrial Revolution was a period during the 1700's and early 1800's when industrialization developed in western Europe and the northeastern United States. During this period, power-driven machines were invented and factories were organized. Machine-made goods produced in factories replaced handmade goods produced at home. Manufacturing, mining, and construction industries expanded rapidly. The Industrial Revolution resulted in increased production of many kinds of goods. It changed most Western nations from rural, agricultural societies to urban, industrial societies. It also brought many environmental problems.

During the Industrial Revolution, burning coal provided power for factories and to heat homes. As a result, smoke and soot polluted the air over London and other industrial cities. Iron smelting and other industries dumped wastes into lakes and rivers. The crowded cities also discharged large amounts of raw sewage into the water. Power-driven machines and improved tools increased people's ability to change the environment. They dammed rivers, cleared thick forests, turned vast prairies into cropland, and drained marshes.

During and after the Industrial Revolution, wildlife and native plant populations decreased rapidly. With improved guns and traps, commercial hunters killed many animals. As more and more people traveled to new lands, they brought animals, plants, and disease organisms that harmed native species, especially on islands. Rats escaped from ships and preyed on birds and their eggs. Goats, sheep, and other livestock overgrazed land, destroying the food supply of wild animals. Introduced Asian and European plants replaced native American grasses that could not tolerate overgrazing by livestock. Wildlife habitats were destroyed as people cleared forests and drained marshes. Habitat destruction dramatically reduced wildlife populations, and it continues to be the major threat to wildlife. Since 1600, more than 400 species of animals have become extinct, and many more have dwindled in number.

Conservation in the United States

Early conservation problems. When the European settlers came to North America, they found a vast land rich in natural resources. But they had to struggle to provide food and shelter for themselves. They regarded nature as a force that they had to fight and conquer. They cleared forests to provide logs for cabins and to establish farms. But most settlers did not follow sound agricultural practices. When the soil eroded or lost its fertility, they moved on to new lands. The settlers had little concern for conservation because they thought the frontier extended so far that it would last forever. Although many colonies passed hunting laws to conserve game animals, the laws were not well enforced.

In the early 1800's, such explorers as Meriwether Lewis and William Clark helped open up the western United States. Many people believed that an unlimited supply of natural resources awaited use by the young nation. Trappers came to hunt animals for their furs. Beaver skins were especially valuable during the 1800's because men's hats were made from the fur. Trappers believed the supply of beavers was inexhaustible, and they trapped too many of the animals. They then had to travel farther west to find more beavers.

The millions of *bison* (American buffalo) that roamed the plains represented another valuable resource. Their hides made warm robes, and their bones were used in fertilizer. During the late 1800's, commercial hunters slaughtered millions of bison. By 1889, only 541 bison could be found alive in the United States. Only the enforcement of game laws and other protective measures saved the bison from extinction. By 2000, the population had grown to about 300,000.

Such careless misuse of many of the country's natural resources aroused some people to the need for conservation. The first national park in the world—Yellowstone National Park—was established in 1872 to preserve the area's unusual natural features and scenic beauty. American naturalists, including John James Audubon, Henry David Thoreau, George Perkins Marsh, and John Muir, promoted conservation measures. Audubon's paintings of birds and other animals aroused public interest in the nation's wildlife. In his book *Walden* (1854), Thoreau discussed his belief that people should live in harmony with nature. Marsh wrote *Man and Nature* (1864), one of the first textbooks to discuss ecology and conservation. It was later retitled *The Earth as Modified by Human Nature.* Muir influenced Congress to establish Sequoia National Park and Yosemite National Park.

The rise of the conservation movement. During the early 1900's, conservation began to develop as a national movement. Its dominant theme was the wise use of natural resources, including plants and animals, for human benefit. The federal government took many steps to preserve these resources, and conservationists sought to avoid waste at all cost. Throughout this period, however, people considered plants and animals primarily as instruments to increase human welfare, rather than as independent species with their own rights.

Congress passed a conservation law called the Lacey Bird and Game Act of 1900. The act, named for its sponsor, Representative John F. Lacey of Iowa, made it a federal crime to transport illegally killed animals across state borders. It also set controls on the trade in bird feathers, the importation of animals, and the commercial killing of game.

President Theodore Roosevelt made many important contributions to the conservation movement. In 1903, he established the first federal wildlife refuge at Pelican Island, Florida. At the urging of Gifford Pinchot, the head of the U.S. Forest Service, and other conservation leaders, Roosevelt added more than 140 million acres (57 million hectares) to the nation's forest reserves.

In 1908, President Roosevelt brought together governors, federal officials, scientists, business executives, and conservation leaders for a White House conference to adopt national policies for the use of natural resources. The conference approved the principle of multiple use in the management of national forests and parks. The principle of multiple use provided that public lands be managed to serve many benefits. It thus protected these lands from being used solely or primarily for commercial development.

The 1908 conference had far-reaching effects. Within a few years, 41 governors established conservation commissions in their states. The National Conservation Commission was formed, and Gifford Pinchot became its chairman. The commission made the first inventory of the nation's natural resources. Based on the commission's recommendations, President Roosevelt later set aside some public lands as natural resource reserves to be used for scientific studies. In 1911, Congress passed the Weeks Act, named for its sponsor, Representative John W. Weeks of Massachusetts. The Weeks Act formally established the policy of multiple use in the management of national forests and other public lands.

Many conservation projects were begun during the Great Depression of the 1930's, partly to provide jobs for the unemployed. In 1933, President Franklin Roosevelt formed the Civilian Conservation Corps (CCC). Workers in the CCC planted trees, fought forest fires, made paths in national forests and parks, and built dams to control floods. Also in 1933, Congress established the Tennessee Valley Authority (TVA) to conserve the resources of the Tennessee Valley. The region suffered from serious soil erosion and from flooding. The TVA planted trees to restore the region's forests. It built several large dams to control flooding and to provide cheap electric power to rural areas.

The tragedy of the Dust Bowl in the early 1930's dramatized the need for soil conservation in the United States. The Dust Bowl was the name given to parts of the Great Plains where windstorms carried away the topsoil. A severe drought and poor farming and ranching practices had damaged the land. The Dust Bowl covered about 50 million acres (20 million hectares). Many farm families suffered great hardships and had to leave the area. In 1935, President Franklin D. Roosevelt established the Soil Conservation Service to promote soil conservation practices among farmers and ranchers.

In 1937, Congress passed the Federal Aid in Wildlife Restoration Act, which levied a federal tax on sporting arms and ammunition. The federal government distributes tax money to the states for use in wildlife management and research.

Aldo Leopold, an American naturalist, was one of the most influential leaders in the conservation movement during the mid-1900's. He wrote *Game Management* (1933), the first textbook on wildlife management. Leopold promoted the active management of wildlife.

Renewed interest in conservation. The 1960's and 1970's brought renewed interest in conservation. Scientific discoveries about various forms of pollution had a major impact on the conservation movement during the 1960's and 1970's. Rachel Carson, a marine biologist, wrote about the destructive effects of DDT and other pesticides in her book *Silent Spring* (1962). She pointed out that pesticides poison the food supply of wild animals and could also contaminate the food supply of human beings. Beginning in 1972, DDT was gradually phased out.

Publicity about DDT and other pollutants led to increased public concern about environmental health. Membership in conservation organizations rose, and people urged Congress to pass laws to protect the health of the environment.

Corbis/Bettmann

Serious pollution problems accompanied the development and spread of the Industrial Revolution during the 1700's and early 1800's. The air in Sheffield, England, *pictured here,* and many other cities became clouded with smoke and soot from coal-burning factories.

The slaughter of buffaloes for their hides almost resulted in the extinction of the animal in the United States in the late 1800's. Buffalo hides awaiting shipment east were piled high at Dodge City, Kansas, *shown here.* Strict conservation measures were required to save the buffalo from extinction.

Kansas State Historical Society, Topeka

Congress passed the National Environmental Policy Act in 1969. The act requires that a study called an *environmental assessment* be prepared for all federally funded construction projects or other activities that might affect the environment.

The act also requires preparation of an *environmental impact statement* if experts review the assessment and find the project or activity to have environmental significance. Environmental impact statements are reports that describe how proposed highways, dams, power plants, or other construction projects would affect the environment. Conservationists can use environmental impact statements in court to challenge projects that may be environmentally harmful. In some cases, a court may order that projects be stopped or redesigned to minimize environmental damage.

In 1970, Congress established the Environmental Protection Agency (EPA). The EPA sets and enforces pollution control standards and assists state and local governments in pollution control.

In 1973, Congress passed the Endangered Species Act, which provided more protection for threatened and endangered species of wildlife than earlier laws had. The act prohibits federal projects that would destroy the habitat of an endangered species. In 1978, Congress amended the act to allow exemption of certain projects that serve the best interests of a region or of the nation. In 1995, the Supreme Court of the United States ruled that deliberate destruction of habitat of an endangered species is also prohibited on private property.

During the 1970's, the United States experienced periodic fuel shortages, which led to higher prices for gasoline and home heating fuel. The fuel shortages helped dramatize the need for energy conservation. In 1977, Congress created the Department of Energy, which was given responsibility to develop and promote new sources of energy and ways to save existing supplies.

One project called for the production of synthetic fuels, or fuels that can be substituted for crude oil and natural gas. Synthetic fuels, also called *synfuels*, are gases or liq-

uids produced from coal, *oil shale* (a rock that yields oil when heated), *bituminous sands* (sands that also contain a substance from which oil can be obtained), and *biomass* (organic matter, such as wood, garbage, and animal manure). Synfuels are expensive to make and not widely used. But if oil prices rise greatly, synfuels may become an important energy alternative.

Beginning in the 1970's, private conservation organizations, such as the Nature Conservancy, the World Wildlife Fund, and the Environmental Defense Fund, became more prominent. These organizations publicize the plight of endangered species and the scale of habitat destruction. They also promote conservation legislation in both federal and state governments.

Corbis/Bettmann

Vast areas were set aside as national parks during the late 1800's and early 1900's. Yosemite National Park, *pictured here,* was created largely through the efforts of the American naturalist John Muir, *right,* shown standing with President Theodore Roosevelt, who was also an avid conservationist.

The Civilian Conservation Corps employed workers to plant trees in national forests and to perform various other conservation tasks. President Franklin D. Roosevelt formed the Civilian Conservation Corps in 1933.

Corbis/Bettmann

Recent developments. In 1993, Congress established the Office on Environmental Policy. It coordinates environmental policy within the federal government. Such policy increasingly attempts to manage entire ecosystems for the benefit of all the species within them, rather than producing individual management plans for each species as it becomes threatened.

Since the late 1900's, a different kind of conservation philosophy has begun to emerge. Many environmentalists and philosophers now believe that nonhuman species have inherent rights of existence. This movement, foreshadowed in the writings of Henry David Thoreau and John Muir, seeks to give conservation a deeper respect for nature and to make such respect the cornerstone of conservation laws.

Conservation around the world

Many countries have conservation problems similar to those of the United States. Almost all industrialized nations, for example, face such problems as air and water pollution, urban crowding, and shortages of fossil fuels. This section chiefly deals with land management and wildlife conservation in Canada, Latin America, Europe, Asia, Australia, and Africa. It also discusses international conservation problems.

Canada has a large land area and a fairly small population. Most of the people live in the southern part of the country. Canada's interior is only sparsely settled. The country has bountiful supplies of natural resources. Evergreen forests, prairies, and tundra cover much of the country. Canada has many rivers and lakes, most of which are not seriously polluted. The country also has rich deposits of copper, uranium, zinc, and other minerals, many of which lie in remote areas of the interior.

Large areas of Canada remain undeveloped. Thus, many kinds of wildlife are as abundant as they were before the country was settled by Europeans. Canada has plans to develop some of the mineral resources of its interior, however. Unless such development is carefully planned and managed, the growth of the mining industry may result in destruction of wildlife habitats and a de-

crease in animal populations.

The drainage of wetlands in agricultural areas of Alberta, Saskatchewan, and western Manitoba has destroyed many wildlife habitats. The prairies of these provinces have fertile soil and are intensively farmed to produce cereal grains. Some people want to drain the remaining prairie wetlands, called *prairie potholes,* to increase crop production. But conservationists do not want the wetlands drained because they are important breeding places for ducks and other migratory birds. The wetlands also store runoff water and so help prevent flooding.

Many Canadian forests have been heavily logged. The scale of Canadian *deforestation* (destruction of forests) now compares to that in the United States. Many people

© Curt Gunther, Camera 5

Fuel shortages in the 1970's forced automobile drivers to wait in long lines at the few stations that had gasoline. The gasoline shortages dramatized the need for energy conservation.

in British Columbia and other provinces are greatly concerned about the destruction of original forests and the common practice of *clearcutting* (removing all trees) over large areas.

Canada and the United States have long worked together to protect waterfowl and other wild animals that cross their border. The two countries have treaties that protect migratory birds and other wildlife.

Other issues are not settled, however. Canadians have called for action to prevent the production of harmful chemicals that cross the border in the smoke and other exhausts from U.S. factories. The chemicals mix with water vapor in the atmosphere to form sulfuric and nitric acids. These acids pollute rain, sleet, and snow. The polluted precipitation, commonly called acid rain, kills fish and other wildlife in and around many Canadian ponds and lakes. Most conservationists also believe that acid rain may damage northern forests. They argue that acid rain stops leaves from producing food for trees. Acid rain is thus a major conservation issue in Canada because of its destruction to the environment and the economic hardships it may cause.

Latin America has vast tropical rain forests, where many unique species of plants and animals live. It also has valuable mineral deposits. Mexico, for example, has large deposits of petroleum and natural gas.

Most of Latin America was colonized by the Spanish, who were primarily interested in obtaining gold and other raw materials from the New World. The Spanish generally restricted their settlements to mining centers and areas that had a favorable climate. Thus, until recently, much of Latin America consisted of wilderness areas that were largely undisturbed, though the land around most cities was severely damaged. Parts of Mexico and Central America, however, were more extensively settled and suffered from widespread forest destruction, overgrazing, and soil erosion.

Many nations of Latin America have a rapidly growing population, and most of the people are poor. To raise living standards, a number of countries have begun programs to expand industry and agriculture. The tropical rain forests contain commercially valuable trees, and timber production has increased. Many countries have cut through forests to build roads to reach remote areas where mineral deposits lie. In addition, farmers have cleared forests to provide land for growing crops. The soil of the tropical rain forests, however, does not generally make good farmland. Most tropical soils are not fertile, and few Latin American farmers can afford the large amounts of fertilizers needed to enrich the soil. In addition, tropical soils may harden when they are exposed to direct sunlight. They then become useless for growing crops. As a result, the farmers remove more trees each year to provide new cropland.

The expansion of industry and agriculture in Latin America has thus resulted in destruction of forests and wildlife habitats. Many countries have established national parks to conserve forests and wildlife. But in many cases, the parks are not well protected.

Europe. Much of the land in southern Europe has been severely damaged by the destruction of forests and by overgrazing of livestock. The soil has eroded from hillsides, and the vegetation on grasslands is sparse and of poor quality. Many countries of southern Europe have begun programs to replant trees on hillsides and to improve vegetation on grasslands.

In northern Europe, forests still cover much of the land, and environmental damage is not as great as it is in southern Europe. Northern Europeans were among the first people to recognize the environmental value of trees, and they developed the science of forestry. The forests of northern Europe contain only a few species of trees and a small variety of endangered animals and plants. Thus foresters can clearcut large areas of these forests and still safely replenish them by replanting the same few tree species. Such forestry practices would not work well in environments with greater biodiversity. Northern Europeans also have practiced wildlife conservation for many years. In some countries, much of the land is privately owned, and the landowners take responsibility for protecting wildlife. Most of the countries have also established nature reserves.

Russia, part of which is in Europe and part in Asia, has the world's largest forest reserves. Russia makes considerable commercial use of its forests for logging, and of its wildlife for food and manufactured goods. But the country has also worked to conserve its forests from too much logging and to protect polar bears and other wildlife resources.

Asia has more people than any other continent. Many Asian countries have difficulty conserving natural resources because the land must support so many people.

In Southeast Asia, many forests have been cut down to produce timber and to clear land for farms and industries. The destruction of forests has reduced the living space of wildlife. Much of Asia's wildlife is also threatened by overhunting. Many people kill animals for food or hunt them

WORLD BOOK photo by Werner Braun

Farming in dry regions requires special techniques to conserve water. The almond tree being hoed by these farmers in Israel is surrounded by a bank of soil that helps retain rain water.

Caring for wildlife is one of many ways people can help conserve the world's biodiversity. This worker is helping an elephant bathe in a wildlife sanctuary in India.

© M. Amirtham, Dinodia

to sell to zoos, medical researchers, and pet traders. Because of habitat destruction and overhunting, many large Asian animals, including elephants, rhinoceroses, and tigers, have become endangered.

In China, people have cut down most of the forests for wood, which has caused serious soil erosion. The soil is deposited in rivers and streams, which lowers the quality of the water. The Huang He, or Yellow River, is so named because the light-colored soil gives the water a yellowish color. The soil has also raised the riverbed. As a result, the Huang He often floods, causing great property damage and loss of life along its banks.

In the Middle East, deserts cover much of the land. With irrigation, however, farmers have turned some areas into productive croplands. Israel is especially well known for its irrigation efforts. Some farmland in Israel and a number of other countries, however, has been seriously damaged by the build-up of salts in the soil, a common problem on irrigated land.

Australia. Ranges cover much of Australia, and sheep ranching is widespread. In many dry regions, overgrazing has seriously damaged the vegetation.

Australia's wildlife includes numerous species of mammals called *marsupials.* Kangaroos and some other marsupials are grazing animals. They thus compete for food, water, and living space with the sheep that graze on the ranges. Ranchers have killed many kangaroos because they believe the animals reduce the grass supply for sheep. Hunters have also killed many kangaroos for their hides and to sell their meat. Because the Australian government feared that kangaroos might become extinct, it banned the sale of live kangaroos and of kangaroo hides and meat to other countries in 1973.

The control of predators is a major problem. On ranges, wild dogs called *dingoes* prey on the sheep. Some ranchers have tried to kill the dingoes with poisons. But many conservationists oppose poisoning because they believe it also kills other species of wild animals. Introduced red foxes and cats have devastated populations of native marsupials in much of Australia.

The introduction of European rabbits into the wild in Australia during the 1850's created a major conservation problem that continues today. In Australia, these rabbits had no natural predators or diseases to limit their popula-

tion, and their numbers soared. The rabbits consumed so much forage that many sheep ranchers were forced to reduce the size of their flocks. After other control measures failed, Australian scientists succeeded in reducing the rabbit population in the 1950's by exposing the animals to a viral disease called *myxomatosis,* which affects only rabbits. Later generations of rabbits developed resistance to this virus, however. The rabbits again grew in numbers and again became a problem.

Africa. In northern Africa, many people live by tending herds of sheep and goats. Along the southern edge of the Sahara, overgrazing has severely damaged much of the land. In these arid areas, the sandy soil quickly erodes after the protective covering of vegetation has been removed. The land then becomes desertlike. Overgrazing and droughts have contributed to the expansion of the Sahara, which advances along parts of its southern border up to 30 miles (48 kilometers) a year.

In central and southern Africa, destruction of habitats and overhunting have reduced wildlife populations. People have overhunted many species of African wildlife because they prize the animals as trophies and as sources of valuable products. Elephant tusks provide valuable ivory. Craftworkers use much of the ivory to make beads and bracelets. Fur traders prize leopards for their hides, which are used to make expensive fur coats. Many African nations have passed strict hunting laws, but the laws are difficult to enforce in remote areas. The commercial value of elephant tusks, leopard hides, and other animal products on the world market makes *poaching* (illegal hunting) extremely profitable. In 1989, many nations agreed to end the sale of ivory. But some conservationists believe that poaching will continue as long as people buy ivory. To help protect their wildlife, many African nations have established large national parks and nature preserves.

International problems. The United Nations, the IUCN (International Union for the Conservation of Nature and Natural Resources), and other organizations support worldwide conservation programs. The IUCN gathers information on the world's endangered wildlife and publishes the data in its *Red Data Book.* Other international conservation organizations, such as the International Whaling Commission, work to conserve animal, mineral, and other resources in the oceans.

Conservationists are also concerned about the growing level of carbon dioxide in the atmosphere. Carbon dioxide traps heat in a process called the *greenhouse effect.* The amount of carbon dioxide in the atmosphere is increasing chiefly because of the burning of such fossil fuels as coal, oil, and natural gas. The destruction of forests, which absorb carbon dioxide from the atmosphere, also contributes to an increase in this gas. Some scientists believe significant global warming may alter the earth's ecological balance and cause great changes in rainfall patterns and ocean levels. Conservationists are working to replant forests and decrease fossil fuel use.

Careers in conservation

Most careers in conservation require a college degree. Many people with an interest in the outdoors pursue a career in forestry, wildlife ecology, or soil conservation. Others work in conservation education, urban planning, or various other fields.

Conservation biologists work for government agencies, private conservation organizations, and universities. They study the full range of ways in which living species are threatened, as well as the status of biodiversity worldwide. They also work toward the protection, management, and restoration of biodiversity.

Forestry is one of the oldest conservation professions. Foresters are employed by national and local governments, as well as by logging companies. Some foresters specialize in *silviculture,* the science of growing trees. Others work in such areas as watershed management, insect and disease control, or timber harvesting.

Wildlife biologists may work in national wildlife refuges, nature reserves, rangelands, forest reserves, fish hatcheries, or government agencies responsible for wildlife management. In addition, private consulting firms employ wildlife biologists to prepare environmental impact statements. Many land development companies employ people with wildlife management training.

Soil conservationists are employed by various government agencies to promote the wise management of plant, soil, and water resources. Many agricultural specialties, including *agronomy, range ecology,* and *soil physics,* deal with resource management.

Urban planners and urban geographers work with regional or city planning agencies. These agencies work to improve city services. They also plan urban renewal projects and other city development programs.

Geologists, civil engineers, and scientists in many fields contribute to conservation. They conduct research and seek solutions to many conservation problems, including pollution control and the development of new energy sources.   Daniel Simberloff

Related articles in *World Book* include:

Soil and water conservation

Coal (Strip mining)	Reclamation, Bureau of
Cropping system	Sewage
Dam (What does a dam do?)	Shelterbelt
Drainage	Soil
Erosion	Tennessee Valley Authority
Flood	Water
Ground water	Water pollution
Irrigation	Wetland
Land Management, Bureau of	World Health Organization

Forest and wildlife conservation

Animal (The future of animals)	Fur (Trapping)
Arbor Day	National forest
Biodiversity	National park
Bird (Bird study and protection)	National Park Service
	National Park System
Endangered species	Poaching
Fish and Wildlife Service	Salmon (Salmon conservation)
Fishing industry (Fishery conservation)	Tree farming
	Wildlife conservation
Forestry	

Mineral and energy conservation

Energy supply	Petroleum (Petroleum conservation)
Mineral	

Urban conservation

Air pollution	Housing and Urban Development, Department of
City (City problems)	
City planning	Park
Housing	Urban renewal
	Waste disposal

Conservation organizations

Audubon Society, National	Nature Conservancy
Greenpeace	Sierra Club
Izaak Walton League of America	World Wildlife Fund
National Wildlife Federation	

Conservation leaders

Adamson, Joy	Leopold, Aldo
Audubon, John James	Miner, Jack
Carson, Rachel	Mowat, Farley
Commoner, Barry	Muir, John
Darling, Ding	Pinchot, Gifford
Elton, Charles Sutherland	Roosevelt, Theodore
Fossey, Dian	

Other related articles

Agriculture, Department of	Environmental Protection Agency
Balance of nature	
Earth Day	Food supply
Ecology	Interior, Department of the
Environmental impact statement	Natural resources
	Recycling
Environmental pollution	

Outline

I. The importance of conservation
  A. To meet demands for resources
  B. To maintain the quality of life
II. Kinds of conservation
  A. Biodiversity conservation
  B. Water conservation
  C. Ocean conservation
  D. Soil conservation
  E. Conservation of grazing lands
  F. Forest conservation
  G. Mineral conservation
  H. Energy conservation
  I. Urban conservation
III. Early history of conservation
  A. Prehistoric times
  B. The rise of civilization
  C. The Industrial Revolution
IV. Conservation in the United States
  A. Early conservation problems
  B. The rise of the conservation movement
  C. Renewed interest in conservation
  D. Recent developments
V. Conservation around the world
  A. Canada
  B. Latin America
  C. Europe
  D. Asia
  E. Australia
  F. Africa
  G. International problems
VI. Careers in conservation

A nuclear Russian family

© Jonathan T. Wright, Bruce Coleman Inc.

An extended Indian family

© Gottlieb, Monkmeyer

A single-parent American family

© David R. Frazier

A childless Chinese couple

© Todd Gipstein, Corbis

People of all cultures live in families. These groups range from two people to *extended families,* in which grandparents, parents, and children may share a home. The most common family type in many nations, the *nuclear family,* consists of a mother, a father, and their children.

Family

Family is the basic unit of social organization in all human societies. Since prehistoric times, families have served as the primary institution responsible for raising children, providing people with food and shelter, and satisfying people's need for love and support.

The term *family* generally refers to a group of people related to one another by birth, marriage, or adoption. In contemporary society, people often apply the word *family* to any group that feels a sense of *kinship* (family connection).

Varieties of families

Family types vary in different countries and among different cultures. In Western, industrialized societies, the *nuclear family* ranks as the most common family type. It consists of a father, a mother, and their children. But nuclear families exist alongside many other types of family units. In

Steven Mintz, the contributor of this article, is Professor of History and Associate Dean at the University of Houston. He is the author of Domestic Revolutions: A Social History of American Family Life *and* A Prison of Expectations: The Family in Victorian Culture.

the *single-parent family,* for example, a mother or a father heads the family alone. A *blended family* is formed when a divorced or widowed parent remarries. As divorce rates have risen, the number of single-parent and blended families has increased.

An increasingly common family form in Western societies is the *consensual union,* in which couples live together but remain unmarried. When a homosexual couple decides to live together as a family, they form a *same-sex union.* Although such unions have become more common, most countries do not recognize them as legal families. People often call a married couple whose children have grown up and left home an *empty-nest family.*

In many parts of the world, parents and children live together with other family members under the same roof. These *complex families* usually contain several generations of family members, including grandparents, parents, and children. They may also include brothers or sisters and their families, uncles, aunts, and cousins. Even when relatives do not live together, they still consider themselves members of the same *extended family.* In Latin American and Hispanic American cultures, the extended family, called *la familia,* includes grandparents, uncles, aunts, and cousins.

Some cultures follow a traditional practice called *polygamy,* in which a person can have more than one *spouse* (husband or wife). The two chief forms of polygamy are *polygyny* and *polyandry.* In *polygyny,* a man marries more than one woman. In *polyandry,* a woman has more than one husband.

Since the early 1800's, various *utopian communities* have attempted to create substitutes for the nuclear family. Utopian communities are groups of people who want to create an ideal society in which everyone will be happy. The Oneida community, which flourished in rural New York state from the 1840's to the late 1870's, considered all its adult citizens married to one another. Oneida children were raised by the community as a whole. One of the aims of such utopian communities was to modify the rigid family roles of husband and wife so that women could participate more equally in society.

Family relationships

Family members can be related to one another by *blood*—that is, by birth; by *affinity*—that is, through marriage; or through adoption. Most nuclear families consist of a father, a mother, and their *biological children* (children born to them). When a couple adopt a child, the child becomes a member of their family. Brothers and sisters who share the same parents are *siblings. Half brothers* and *half sisters* share either the same biological mother or biological father. When divorced or widowed parents remarry, the parent's new spouse becomes the children's *stepfather* or *stepmother.* Children from the couple's previous marriages become *stepbrothers* and *stepsisters* to one another.

When people marry, they gain a new set of relatives called *in-laws.* The mother of a person's spouse is called a *mother-in-law,* the brother is called a *brother-in-law,* and so on throughout the rest of the family.

The parents of a person's mother or father are that person's *grandparents. Great-grandparents* are the parents of a person's grandparents. An *aunt* is the sister of a person's mother or father. An *uncle* is the brother of a parent. An uncle's wife is also called aunt, and an aunt's husband is also called uncle. A *first cousin* is the child of a person's aunt or uncle. The child of a first cousin is a person's *first cousin once removed*—that is, removed by one generation. Children of first cousins are *second cousins* to each other.

Some people consider certain friends as part of their family because they feel special affection for them. Although these friends are not true family members, such friends are called *fictive kin,* and family members might call them "aunts" or "uncles." Relatives or close friends of a parent may become *godparents* to that parent's children. Godparents, as sponsors to a Christian baptism, often play more vital roles in the lives of families than other fictive kin. In Latin American and Hispanic American families, godparents, called *compadres,* provide advice, emotional support, and assistance in times of need.

Importance of the family

Family functions. Families perform many necessary functions, both for individual family members and for society as a whole. In virtually all cultures, the family serves as the basic institution for bearing children, caring for them during their early years, and preparing them to function effectively in society. Families around the world must also provide food and clothing to their members. In addition, families meet important psychological needs, such as the need for love, support, and companionship.

The family's duties have changed over time. In the past, families not only cared for the young but also grew their own food, made their own clothing, and provided services for themselves that modern families generally do not provide. Parents taught reading, writing, and craft skills to their children. Families also cared for sick and elderly relatives and often provided financial support for members in need. Since the 1800's, many of these traditional responsibilities have shifted to such institutions as schools, hospitals, insurance companies, and nursing homes.

Roles within the family have also changed. Traditionally, the father was expected to take up an occupation to support his wife and children. The mother, in turn, ran the home and cared for the children. Today, however, both parents commonly work outside the home, and fathers often perform household duties formerly expected of women.

Home life. The home is the center of family activities. These activities include raising children, eating meals, playing games, watching television, keeping house, and entertaining friends. In the home, children learn basic social skills, such as how to talk and get along with others. They also learn health and safety habits there.

A family's home life is influenced by which members live in the home and by the roles each member plays. Home life can also be affected by relatives who live outside the family's home. Traditions, laws, and social conditions help determine who lives in a home and the place each family member holds.

Traditions, which are customs or beliefs that people have followed for a long time, strongly influence family life. For example, some Americans have little contact with relatives outside the nuclear family. But many Chinese families feel strong ties to such relatives and see them often. Aunts, uncles, and cousins traditionally play important roles in the lives of these people.

Laws affect family behavior in various ways. Some laws set forth the legal rights and responsibilities people have as husbands, wives, parents, and children. In many Western nations, laws forbid abuse of children by parents, and of one spouse by the other. Laws also deal with marriage, divorce, and adoption.

Social conditions can also influence family life. For example, in cultures that discourage women from working outside the home, mothers become full-time homemakers, while men act as the sole wage earners.

Development of the family

Ancient families. Most ancient societies had no term exactly the same as our modern word for family. This was because ancient families varied widely in their size and structure depending on social class. The wealthiest households contained dozens of kinsfolk, servants, and slaves. At the same time, slaves and poor free people had no opportunity to establish independent homes.

Ancient families had strict arrangements of higher- and lower-ranking persons. In ancient Roman society, which flourished about 2,000 years ago, the male head of the family, the *paterfamilias,* had absolute authority. Under Roman law, he could sell his children, abandon them, or even put them to death. Male heads of families arranged marriages in most ancient societies. Fathers often contracted daughters to marry at young ages. In ancient Greek culture, which reached its height during the mid-400's B.C., the average marriage age of women ranged from 12 to 15, while many men married at about age 30.

The ancient world permitted a variety of family practices that most people would condemn today. In ancient Greece and Rome, for example, parents could leave handicapped or sickly infants outdoors to die, a practice called *exposure*. In ancient Egypt, which arose about 5,000 years ago, men could marry their sisters. Most cultures today consider such marriages *incest* and prohibit them by law.

Ancient cultures also permitted easy divorce and often practiced polygyny and *concubinage* (the practice of a husband living with a woman who was not his legal wife). Polygyny and concubinage enabled a powerful or wealthy family to have children when the man's first wife failed to produce an *heir*, a child who could inherit the family's wealth.

Development of the Western family. Christianity played a critical role in the emergence of new family patterns. At the beginning of the Christian era, as early as the A.D. 300's, family patterns in Western Europe began to diverge from those in the non-Western world. Western European families placed an emphasis on the bond between husband and wife, as opposed to broader kinship relationships.

The Christian church encouraged young people to remain *celibate* (unmarried) and to enter religious orders. During the early Christian era, a growing number of women in Western Europe never married or bore children. The church also condemned the exposure of infants and opposed concubinage, polygyny, arranged marriages, marriages with close kin, and divorce. The church insisted that marriages could not be dissolved by divorce, helping make the nuclear family more important than in the past.

During the Middle Ages in Europe, which lasted from about the A.D. 400's to the 1500's, the wealthiest households could contain 40 or more people. These inhabitants included such nonrelatives as *pages* (boys from wealthy families in training to become knights) and servants. But the average medieval household was much smaller, containing about four or five members. Most families lived in cramped houses that lacked privacy. Relatives often shared beds and used the same rooms for working, entertaining, cooking, eating, storage, and sleeping.

Medieval households were productive units. Wives cooked, preserved food, made textiles and clothing, tended gardens, and brewed beer. In addition to farming, many husbands engaged in such crafts as carpentry, ironworking, and barrel-making.

Family life in medieval Europe was unstable. Famine, plagues, and other calamities caused a radical decline in population. Because most parents worked much of the day, young children received little supervision from adults. Economic pressures forced many parents to send their children away from home at young ages, often before the age of 8. Numerous children became servants in private homes, apprentices in business, or workers for the church. Because of the high death rate, many people remarried. A large number of marriages involved partners who had been married before. Consequently, numerous medieval families contained stepparents and stepchildren.

During the 1500's, Protestant reformers often criticized the Roman Catholic Church for permitting certain family practices. These practices included allowing young people to marry without parental consent, forbidding clergy to marry, and prohibiting divorce and remarriage when marriages broke down. Many Protestant societies, including those in Puritan New England, required parental consent to make a marriage valid and instituted laws against wife beating and adultery. Protestant countries recognized a right to divorce with remarriage in cases of abandonment, adultery, and extreme physical cruelty.

© Edward S. Ross

Touring places of interest is a popular family activity throughout the world. In Thailand, many families enjoy visiting their country's beautiful temples, such as this one in Bangkok.

Early Western families in America. During America's colonial period, which lasted from the 1500's to 1775, the family served many functions. It educated children, cared for the elderly and sick, taught job skills to the young, and functioned as the economic center of production. Every person was strongly urged to live in a family. In some parts of New England, the government taxed bachelors and imposed other penalties on those who did not marry. Married couples who lived apart from each other had to show good reason.

American families in the 1600's were led by the father. He had to give his legal consent before his children could marry. His control over inheritance kept his grown sons and daughters dependent upon him for years, while they waited for his permission to marry and to establish a separate household.

Early Americans did not consider love a requirement for marriage, and couples assumed that love would follow marriage. Relations between spouses tended to be formal. Husbands and wives treated each other with correct, serious manners rather than the relaxed, friendly way families interact today.

African American families under slavery faced unique problems in early America. Many states refused to recognize slave marriages as legal. Moreover, about a third of all slave marriages were broken by sale, and about half of all slave children were sold from their parents. Even when sale did not break the marriage, slave spouses often resided on separate plantations. On large plantations, a slave father might have a different owner than his wife had, and he could visit his wife and family only with his master's permission.

Despite all these obstacles, enslaved African Americans forged strong family and kinship ties. Most slaves married and lived with the same spouse until death. To sustain a sense of family identity, slaves named their children after parents, grandparents, and other kin. Enslaved African Americans also passed down family names to their children, usually the name of an ancestor's owner rather than that of the current owner. Ties to an immediate family stretched outward to an involved network of extended kin. Whenever children were sold to neighboring plantations, grandparents, aunts, uncles, and cousins took on the functions of parents. Strangers cared for and protected children who had lost their blood relatives.

Changes. During the mid-1700's, family life in colonial America and parts of Europe underwent far-reaching changes. Parents gave children more freedom in selecting their own spouse. This freedom led people to view marriage increasingly as an emotional bond involving love and affection. Spouses displayed affection for each other more openly. In addition, parents became more interested in their children's development. Instead of viewing children as miniature adults, parents regarded children as people with special needs and began to buy them children's books, games, and toys.

During the early 1800's, many middle-class families became able to rely on a single wage-earner, where the husband worked outside the home and the wife served as a full-time homemaker and mother. Many of these families could afford to keep their children home into their late teens, instead of sending them out as servants or apprentices. By the mid-1800's, such family events as the vacation and the birthday party had appeared.

For many working-class families, however, low wages and a lack of year-round employment meant that all family members had to work. All members of a working-class family had to help earn a living. Wives did piecework in the home, took in laundry, or rented rooms to boarders. Many working-class families depended on the labor of children.

By the end of the 1800's, many people in Western societies had become worried about what was happening to the family. The divorce rate was rising. Infant and child death rates were high, with as many as a third of children dying by the age of 15. Meanwhile, more Western women never married, and the birth rate had fallen sharply during the 1800's. Instead of bearing seven or more children, as women had in 1800, a typical middle-class woman in the United States bore only three.

At the beginning of the 1900's, groups of people fought to improve the well-being of families and children. To reduce children's death rate, these reformers lobbied for an end to child labor. They also fought for special *pensions* (government payments) to enable widows to raise their children at home, instead of sending them to orphanages.

As more people grew concerned about strengthening families, a new family ideal became popular by the 1920's. This ideal, called the *companionate family,* held that husbands and wives should be "friends and lovers" and that parents and children should be "pals."

During the Great Depression of the 1930's, unemployment, lower wages, and the demands of needy relatives tore at the fabric of family life. Many people had to share living quarters with relatives, delay marriage, and put off having children. The divorce rate fell because fewer people could afford it, but many fathers deserted their families. Families sought to cope by planting gardens, canning food, and making clothing. Children worked in part-time jobs, and wives worked outside the home or took in sewing or laundry. Many families housed lodgers, and some set up a small grocery store in a front parlor.

World War II (1939-1945) also subjected families to severe strain. During the war, families faced a great shortage of housing, a lack of schools and child-care facilities, and prolonged separation from loved ones. When fathers went to war, mothers ran their homes and cared for their children alone, and women went to work in war industries. The stresses of wartime contributed to an increase in the divorce rate. Many young people became unsupervised "latchkey children," returning from school each day to an empty home, and rates of juvenile delinquency rose.

The late 1940's and 1950's witnessed a sharp reaction to the stresses of the Great Depression and World War II. The divorce rate slowed, and couples married earlier than their parents had. Women bore more children at younger ages and closer together than in the past. The result was a "baby boom."

Since the mid-1900's, families in all Western countries have undergone far-reaching changes. From the 1960's to

Photograph (1908) by Lewis Wickes Hine; International Museum of Photography, Rochester, N.Y.

A family of the early 1900's made artificial flowers in their home to sell. Working as a group to earn a living was an important function of the family everywhere before the Industrial Revolution began in the 1700's. But by the time this photograph was taken, few families in industrial societies still worked together at home to support themselves.

the 1980's, birth rates dropped and divorce rates rose considerably. In addition, mothers entered the labor force in record numbers, and a growing proportion of children were born to unmarried mothers. The pace of familial change slowed during the late 1900's and early 2000's, but family life remains considerably altered from what it was before the 1960's.

Non-Western families. Traditionally, non-Western societies have attached less importance to the nuclear family than to the larger family network. People in this network, which is often called the *lineage, clan,* or *tribe,* trace their descent to a common ancestor. In many parts of the world, kinship ties determine whom one can and cannot marry and where one lives after marriage. Different kinds of societies have produced different extended family traditions. The three major kinds of societies are known as *patrilineal, matrilineal,* and *bilateral kinship.*

In patrilineal societies, including many in India, China, and various African countries, a husband and wife commonly reside with the husband's father and his kin after marriage. In matrilineal cultures, such as the Navajo and the Pueblo of the American Southwest, a husband joins his wife's mother's household. Within matrilineal societies, a mother's older brother often has responsibility for disciplining children and offering advice about marriage. In cultures with a bilateral kinship system, such as that of the Inuit (Eskimos), a couple might join either the husband's father's family or the wife's mother's family, or form an independent household.

Forms of marriage have also differed across cultures. Some societies, including many African cultures, allow men to take more than one wife. In such societies, only the wealthiest males can afford polygyny. Many societies, such as those of China and India, also practiced arranged marriages and *child marriage* (marriage at or before puberty). In addition, numerous non-Western cultures permitted divorce and remarriage long before Western countries legalized such practices. A number of predominantly Catholic countries did not permit divorce and remarriage until the late 1900's.

Since the mid-1900's, families around the world have become more similar. Birth rates are dropping, divorce rates are rising, increasing numbers of homes are headed by women, and more births are taking place outside of marriage. As societies allow more personal choice, such practices as child marriage, arranged marriages, polygyny, and concubinage have become less common.

Challenges and opportunities

Public concern about the family remains high for many reasons. High rates of teen-age pregnancy and births to unmarried mothers force many young women to leave school or abandon career plans. Children from such families often grow up in poverty and will more likely turn to crime. Drug and alcohol use and domestic violence also plague many families and lead to developmental disorders in children.

With both mothers and fathers in many families working, parents struggle to find enough time to spend with their children. Working parents who can afford to may send their children to day care, but such parents often feel guilty that they do not spend enough time with their children. Those who cannot afford to or do not choose to use day care often have to leave their jobs or take cuts in pay. The resulting loss of income makes it harder for them to keep up their

Edward S. Ross

San families in southwestern Africa live much as their ancestors did centuries ago. The women and young children gather wild plants for food, *shown here,* and the men hunt.

standard of living. For poorer parents, such a cut in earnings can be devastating.

Although not a new problem, divorce remains an important challenge for families to overcome. Most men and women who seek a divorce do so because they cannot solve certain problems in their marriage. Such problems may include differences in goals or financial difficulty. If such problems remain unsolved, the marriage often breaks down. Divorce can affect every member of the family deeply. Children, for example, may grow up in a fatherless or motherless home. If one or both of the parents remarry, the children may fail to develop loving relationships with their new stepparents.

Despite the challenges of today's society, however, the family is not a dying institution. In many respects, family life today is stronger than it was in the past. Most people marry and have children. Although divorce rates are higher than in the past, most individuals who do divorce eventually remarry.

Because of declining death rates, more couples now grow into old age together, and more children have living grandparents. These relatives generally live much farther away from each other than they did in the past. However, e-mail and other communications technology may promote greater contact between separated family members.

Meanwhile, parents now make greater emotional and economic investment in their children. Lower birth rates mean that parents can devote more attention and greater financial resources to each child. Fathers especially have become more involved in child rearing.

More than ever before, families in trouble can receive help from a variety of outside sources, such as a family counselor, a social worker, or a psychologist. Such specialists often meet with the entire family to help its members work out problems together. Public welfare agencies and other groups provide economic aid to poor families and assistance to abused spouses or children.

In the future, families will continue to face many challenges, especially the need to balance the demands of work and family life. Working parents must not only care for their young children, but, because of increasing life spans, tend to aging parents as well.   Steven Mintz

Vietnam War was the longest war in which the United States took part. It began in 1957 and ended in 1975. Vietnam, a small country in Southeast Asia, was divided at the time into the Communist Democratic Republic of Vietnam, commonly called North Vietnam, and the non-Communist Republic of Vietnam, commonly called South Vietnam. North Vietnamese and Communist-trained South Vietnamese rebels sought to overthrow the government of South Vietnam and to eventually reunite the country. The United States and the South Vietnamese army tried to stop them, but failed.

The Vietnam War was actually the second phase of fighting in Vietnam. During the first phase, which began in 1946, the Vietnamese fought France for control of Vietnam. At that time, Vietnam was part of the French colonial empire in Indochina. The United States sent France military equipment, but the Vietnamese defeated the French in 1954. Vietnam was then split into North and South Vietnam.

United States aid to France and later to non-Communist South Vietnam was based on a Cold War policy of President Harry S. Truman. The Cold War was an intense rivalry between Communist and non-Communist nations. Truman had declared that the United States must help any nation challenged by Communism. The Truman Doctrine was at first directed at Europe and the Middle East. But it was also adopted by the next three presidents, Dwight D. Eisenhower, John F. Kennedy, and Lyndon B. Johnson, and applied to Indochina. They feared that if one Southeast Asian nation joined the Communist camp, the others would also "fall," one after the other, like what Eisenhower called "a row of dominoes."

The Vietnamese Communists and their allies called the Vietnam War a war of national liberation. They saw the Vietnam War as an extension of the struggle with France and as another attempt by a foreign power to rule Vietnam. North Vietnam wanted to end U.S. support of South Vietnam and to reunite the north and south into a single nation. China and the Soviet Union, at that time the two largest Communist nations, gave the Vietnamese Communists war materials but not troops.

The Vietnam War had several stages. From 1957 to 1963, North Vietnam aided rebels opposed to the government of South Vietnam, which fought the rebels with U.S. aid and advisory personnel. From 1964 to 1969, North Vietnam and the United States did much of the fighting. Australia, New Zealand, the Philippines, South Korea, and Thailand also helped South Vietnam. By April 1969, the number of U.S. forces in South Vietnam had reached its peak of more than 543,000 troops. By July, the United States had slowly begun to withdraw its forces from the region.

In January 1973, a cease-fire was arranged. The last American ground troops left Vietnam two months later. The fighting began again soon afterward, but U.S. troops did not return to Vietnam. South Vietnam surrendered on April 30, 1975, as North Vietnamese troops entered its capital, Saigon (now Ho Chi Minh City).

The Vietnam War was enormously destructive. Military deaths reached about 1.3 million, and the war left much of Vietnam in ruins.

Just before the war ended, North Vietnam helped rebels overthrow the U.S.-backed government in nearby Cambodia. After the war, North Vietnam united Vietnam and helped set up a new government in nearby Laos. The U.S. role in the war became one of the most debated issues in the nation's history. Many Americans felt U.S. involvement was necessary and noble. But many others called it cruel, unnecessary, and wrong. Today, many Americans still disagree on the goals, conduct, and lessons of U.S. participation in the Vietnam War.

Background to the war

The Indochina War. In the late 1800's, France gained control of Indochina—that is, Vietnam, Laos, and Cambodia. Japan occupied Indochina during most of World War II (1939-1945). After Japan's defeat in 1945, Ho Chi Minh, a Vietnamese nationalist and Communist, and his Vietminh (Revolutionary League for the Independence of Vietnam) declared Vietnam to be independent. But France was determined to reclaim its former colonial possessions in Indochina. In 1946, war broke out between France and the Vietminh. It finally ended in 1954, following the conquest of the French garrison of Dien Bien Phu by Vietminh forces in May. In July, the two sides signed peace agreements in Geneva, Switzerland.

The Geneva Accords provided that Vietnam be temporarily divided into northern and southern zones at the 17th parallel. The accords also called for national elections in 1956 to reunify the country.

The United States had provided aid to the French in Indochina since 1950. President Harry S. Truman had been convinced that such assistance was necessary in part because of the Communist take-over of China in 1949. Truman feared a Vietminh victory in Vietnam would lead to a Communist take-over of Indochina as part of a larger Communist plan to dominate Asia. This fear was so great that Truman ignored pleas by Ho for U.S. aid against French colonialism and for an alliance with the United States.

The divided country. After 1954, Ho strengthened the rule of his Communist government in the Democratic Republic of Vietnam, which became known as North Vietnam. He suppressed non-Communist political parties. He also enacted land reforms and established legal equality between men and women. Ho hoped the elections of 1956 would provide him with the means with which to peacefully reunify the country under his revolutionary government. These elections never occurred.

The United States moved to make the division of Vietnam permanent by helping leaders in the southern half to form a non-Communist Republic of Vietnam, also known as South Vietnam. Ngo Dinh Diem, who had once refused a place in Ho's government and vigorously opposed any Communist influence in his country, became president of South Vietnam in 1955. With the approval of the United States, he refused to go along with the proposed nationwide elections scheduled for the following year. He argued that the Communists would not permit fair elections in North Vietnam. Most experts believe, however, that Ho was so popular that he would have won the elections under any circumstances. President Dwight D. Eisenhower provided economic aid and sent several hundred U.S. civilian and military advisers to assist Diem.

Early stages of the war

The Viet Cong rebellion. Diem suppressed all rival political groups in his effort to strengthen his government. But his government never achieved widespread popularity, especially in rural areas, where his administration did little to ease the hard life of the peasants. Diem became in-

The Vietnam War was the longest war in which the United States took part. It lasted from 1957 to 1975. In the war, U.S. and South Vietnamese forces battled against Communist-trained South Vietnamese rebels and North Vietnamese troops. Helicopters often ferried U.S. soldiers, such as these Marines, from one site to another.

Hulton Getty from Liaison Agency

creasingly unpopular in 1956, when he ended local elections and appointed his own officials down to the village level, where self-government was an ancient and honored tradition. From 1957 to 1959, he sought to eliminate members of the Vietminh who had joined other South Vietnamese in rebelling against his rule. Diem called these rebels the Viet Cong, meaning *Vietnamese Communists.* These rebels were largely trained by the Communists, but many were not Communist Party members.

Although North Vietnam had hoped to achieve its goals without a military conflict against the United States or the South Vietnamese government, it supported the revolt against Diem from its early stages. In 1959, as U.S. advisers rushed aid to South Vietnam by sea, North Vietnam developed a supply route to South Vietnam through Laos and Cambodia. This system of roads and trails became known as the Ho Chi Minh Trail. Also, in 1959, two U.S. military advisers were killed during a battle. They were the first American casualties of the war.

By 1960, discontent with the Diem government was widespread, and the Viet Cong had about 10,000 troops. In 1961, they threatened to overthrow Diem's unpopular government. In response, President John F. Kennedy greatly expanded economic and military aid to South Vietnam. From 1961 to 1963, he increased the number of U.S. military advisers in Vietnam from about 900 to over 16,000.

The Buddhist crisis. In May 1963, widespread unrest broke out among Buddhists in South Vietnam's major cities. The Buddhists, who formed a majority of the country's population, complained that the government restricted their religious practices. Buddhist leaders accused Diem, a Roman Catholic, of religious discrimination. They claimed that he favored Catholics with lands and offices at the expense of local Buddhists. The government responded to the Buddhist protests with mass arrests, and Diem's brother Ngo Dinh Nhu ordered raids against Buddhist temples. Several Buddhist monks then set themselves on fire as a form of protest.

The Buddhist protests aroused great concern in the United States. Kennedy urged Diem to improve his dealings with the Buddhists, but Diem ignored the advice. Kennedy then supported a group of South Vietnamese generals who opposed Diem's policies. On Nov. 1, 1963, the generals overthrew the Diem government. Diem and Nhu were murdered.

The fall of the Diem government set off a period of political disorder in South Vietnam. New governments rapidly succeeded one another. During this period, North Vietnam stepped up its supply of war materials and began to send units of its own army into the south. By late 1964, the Viet Cong controlled up to 75 percent of South Vietnam's population.

The Gulf of Tonkin incident. In 1964, President Lyndon B. Johnson approved secret South Vietnamese naval raids against North Vietnam. Just after one of these raids, on Aug. 2, 1964, North Vietnamese torpedo boats attacked the U.S. destroyer *Maddox,* which was monitoring the impact of the raid off the coast of North Vietnam in the Gulf of Tonkin. Johnson warned the North Vietnamese that another such attack would bring "grave consequences." On August 4, he announced that North Vietnamese boats had again launched an attack in the gulf, this time against the *Maddox* and another U.S. destroyer, the *C. Turner Joy.*

Some Americans doubted that the August 4 attack had occurred, and it has never been confirmed. Nevertheless, Johnson ordered immediate air strikes against North Vietnam. He also asked Congress for power to take "all necessary measures to repel any armed attack against the forces of the United States and to prevent further aggression." On August 7, Congress approved these powers in the Tonkin Gulf Resolution. The United States did not declare war on North Vietnam. But Johnson used the resolution as the legal basis for increased U.S. involvement. In March 1965, he sent a group of U.S. Marines to South Vietnam, the first American ground combat forces to enter the war.

The fighting intensifies

The opposing forces. The war soon became an international conflict. United States forces rose from about 60,000 in mid-1965 to a peak of over 543,000 in 1969. They joined about 800,000 South Vietnamese troops and a total of about 69,000 troops from Australia, New Zealand, the Philippines, South Korea, and Thailand. The North Vietnamese and the Viet Cong had over 300,000 troops, but

Important dates in the Vietnam War

1957 The Viet Cong began to rebel against the South Vietnamese government headed by President Ngo Dinh Diem.

1963 (Nov. 1) South Vietnamese generals overthrew the Diem government, and Diem was killed the next day.

1964 (Aug. 7) Congress passed the Tonkin Gulf Resolution, which gave the president power to take "all necessary measures" and "to prevent further aggression."

1965 (March 6) President Lyndon B. Johnson sent U.S. Marines to Da Nang, South Vietnam. The Marines were the first U.S. ground troops in the war.

1968 (Jan. 30) North Vietnam and the Viet Cong launched a major campaign against South Vietnamese cities.

1969 (June 8) President Richard M. Nixon announced that U.S. troops would begin to withdraw from Vietnam.

1973 (Jan. 27) The United States, North and South Vietnam, and the Viet Cong signed a cease-fire agreement.

1973 (March 29) The last U.S. ground troops left Vietnam.

1975 (April 30) South Vietnam surrendered.

the exact number is unknown.

The two sides developed strategies to take advantage of their strengths. The United States had the finest modern weapons and a highly professional military force. Its field commanders were General William C. Westmoreland from 1964 to 1968 and, afterward, Generals Creighton Abrams and Frederick Weyand. The United States did not try to conquer North Vietnam. Instead, American leaders hoped superior U.S. firepower would force the enemy to stop fighting. The United States relied mainly on the bombing of North Vietnam and "search and destroy" ground missions in South Vietnam to achieve its aim.

The United States used giant B-52 bombers as well as smaller planes for the main air strikes against the enemy. American pilots used helicopters to seek out Viet Cong troops in the jungles and mountains. Helicopters also carried the wounded to hospitals and brought supplies to troops in the field.

In contrast, Viet Cong and North Vietnamese leaders adopted a defensive strategy. Their more lightly armed troops relied on surprise and mobility. They tried to avoid major battles in the open, where heavy U.S. firepower could be decisive. The Viet Cong and North Vietnamese preferred guerrilla tactics, including ambushes and hand-laid bombs. Their advantages included knowledge of the terrain and large amounts of war materials from the Soviet Union and China.

Course of the war. From 1965 to 1967, the two sides fought to a highly destructive draw. The U.S. bombing caused tremendous damage, but it did not affect the enemy's willingness or ability to continue fighting. North Vietnam concealed its most vital resources, and the Soviet Union and China helped make up the losses.

American victories in ground battles in South Vietnam also failed to sharply reduce the number of enemy troops there. The U.S. Army and Marines usually won whenever they fought the enemy. But North Vietnam replaced its losses with new troops. Its forces often avoided defeat by retreating into Laos and Cambodia.

Reactions in the United States. As the war dragged on, it divided many Americans into so-called *hawks* and *doves*. The hawks supported the nation's fight against Communism. But they disliked Johnson's policy of slow, gradual troop increases and urged a decisive defeat of North Vietnam. The doves opposed U.S. involvement and

held mass protests. Many doves believed that U.S. security was not at risk. Others charged that the nation was supporting corrupt, undemocratic, and unpopular governments in South Vietnam.

The growing costs of the war, however, probably did more to arouse public uneasiness in the United States than the antiwar movement did. By late 1967, increased casualties and Johnson's request for new taxes helped produce a sharp drop in public support for the war.

The Tet offensive. North Vietnam and the Viet Cong opened a new phase of the war on Jan. 30, 1968, when they attacked major cities of South Vietnam. The fighting was especially fierce in Saigon, South Vietnam's capital, and in Hue. This campaign began at the start of Tet, the Vietnamese New Year celebration. North Vietnam and the Viet Cong hoped the offensive would deal a serious blow to U.S. forces and make the South Vietnamese people lose faith in their government and rise against South Vietnamese leaders. They also hoped that the offensive would convince U.S. officials to enter into peace negotiations with North Vietnamese leaders.

The plan failed to achieve all of its objectives. No widespread uprising of the population occurred in South Viet-

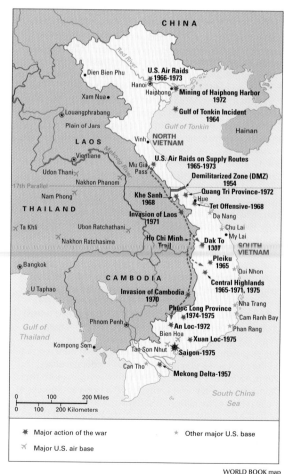

WORLD BOOK map

The Vietnam War was fought mainly in North and South Vietnam from 1957 to 1975. Troops also battled in Laos and Cambodia, and U.S. pilots flew missions from bases in Thailand.

nam. In addition, the United States and South Vietnam quickly recovered their early losses, and the enemy suffered a huge number of casualties. But the Tet attacks stunned the American people and demoralized their war managers. Shortly before the offensive, the U.S. commander in the field, General Westmoreland, had assured the nation that the enemy had already been largely beaten. But the Tet offensive seemed to contradict this statement. As a result of the offensive, Johnson made a number of basic changes in his policies. He cut back the bombing of North Vietnam and rejected Westmoreland's request for 206,000 additional troops. Johnson also called for peace negotiations and declared that he would not seek re-election in 1968. Peace talks opened in Paris in May.

Vietnamization

The U.S. withdrawal begins. The peace talks failed to produce agreement, and more and more Americans became impatient for the war to end. President Richard M. Nixon felt he had to reduce U.S. involvement in the conflict. On June 8, 1969, he announced a new policy known as Vietnamization. This policy called for stepped-up training programs for South Vietnamese forces and the gradual withdrawal of U.S. troops from South Vietnam. The U.S. troop withdrawal began in July 1969.

The invasion of Cambodia. In April 1970, Nixon ordered U.S. and South Vietnamese troops to clear out military supply centers that North Vietnam had set up in Cambodia. Large stocks of weapons were captured, and the invasion may have delayed a major enemy attack. But many Americans felt the campaign widened the war. The invasion aroused a storm of protest in the United States, especially on college and university campuses.

The nation was shocked on May 4, 1970, when National Guard units fired into a group of demonstrators at Kent State University in Ohio. The shots killed four students and wounded nine others. Antiwar demonstrations and riots occurred on hundreds of other campuses throughout May. A move began in Congress to force the removal of the troops from Cambodia. On June 3, Nixon announced the completion of troop withdrawals from Cambodia. That same day, the Senate voted to repeal the Tonkin Gulf Resolution. These actions ended the Cambodian campaign.

Growing protest. Opposition to the war in the United States grew rapidly during Nixon's presidency. Many people claimed that this increased opposition was due to the news media, particularly television coverage, which brought scenes of the war into millions of homes. Most scholars have concluded, however, that media coverage reflected, rather than brought about, America's growing opposition to the war.

In March 1971, the conviction of Lieutenant William L. Calley, Jr., for war crimes raised some of the main moral issues of the conflict. Calley's Army unit had massacred about 400 to 500 or more civilians in 1968 in the hamlet of My Lai in South Vietnam. All of those killed were unarmed women, children, and old men. None had offered any resistance to U.S. forces. Calley was found guilty of the murder of at least 22 Vietnamese and was sentenced to prison. He was paroled in 1974.

Some war critics used Calley's trial to call attention to the large numbers of civilians killed by U.S. bombing and ground operations in South Vietnam. Others pointed to the vast stretches of countryside that had been destroyed

AP/Wide World

Antiwar demonstrations took place throughout the United States in the late 1960's and early 1970's. Thousands of protesters gathered for this demonstration in Washington, D.C., in 1971.

by bombing and by spraying of chemicals. United States forces used such weedkillers as Agent Orange to reveal enemy hiding places in the jungle and to destroy enemy food crops (see **Agent Orange**).

Public distrust of the U.S. government deepened in June 1971, when newspapers published a secret government study of the war called *The Pentagon Papers.* This study raised questions about decisions and secret actions of government leaders regarding the war.

Invasion of the south. In March 1972, North Vietnam began a major invasion of South Vietnam. Nixon then renewed the bombing of North Vietnam and used American airpower against the exposed formations of regular enemy troops and tanks. He also ordered the placing of explosives in the harbor of Haiphong, North Vietnam's major port for importing military supplies. These moves helped stop the invasion, which had nearly reached Saigon by August 1972.

The high cost paid by both sides during the 1972 fighting led to a new round of peace negotiations. The talks were conducted by Henry A. Kissinger, Nixon's chief foreign policy adviser, and Le Duc Tho of North Vietnam. On Jan. 27, 1973, a cease-fire agreement was signed in Paris by the United States, South Vietnam, North Vietnam, and the Viet Cong. The pact provided for the withdrawal of all U.S. and allied forces from Vietnam and for the return of all prisoners—both within 60 days. It also permitted North Vietnam and the Viet Cong to leave their troops in the south. In addition, it called for internationally supervised elections that would let the South Vietnamese decide their political future.

The end of the war. On March 29, 1973, the last U.S. ground forces left Vietnam. But the peace talks soon broke down, and the war resumed. Congress, responding to voters who wished to see an end to the war, opposed further U.S. involvement. As a result, American troops did not return to the war. In mid-1973, Congress began to reduce military aid to South Vietnam.

In late 1974, North Vietnamese and Viet Cong troops attacked Phuoc Long, northeast of Saigon, and won an easy

AP/Wide World

Fleeing from advancing North Vietnamese troops, South Vietnamese civilians scrambled to get aboard a United States evacuation helicopter near the end of the war in April 1975.

victory. In March 1975, the North Vietnamese forced South Vietnamese troops into a retreat from a region known as the Central Highlands. Thousands of civilians—many of them families of the South Vietnamese soldiers—also fled and died in the gunfire or from starvation. This retreat became known as the Convoy of Tears. Although some South Vietnamese army units fought on, few soldiers or civilians rallied in support of the failing South Vietnamese government.

Early in April, President Gerald R. Ford asked Congress for $722 million in military aid for South Vietnam. But Congress, believing defeat was now inevitable, provided only $300 million in emergency aid. The money was mainly for the evacuation of Americans from Saigon, which was threatened by rapidly advancing enemy troops. The war ended on April 30, 1975, when these troops entered Saigon and the South Vietnamese government formally surrendered to them. Saigon was then renamed Ho Chi Minh City.

Results of the war

Casualties and destruction. About 58,000 American military personnel died in the war, and about 300,000 were wounded. South Vietnamese military losses were approximately 224,000 killed and 1 million wounded. North Vietnamese and Viet Cong losses totaled about 1 million dead and 600,000 wounded. Countless numbers of civilians in North and South Vietnam also perished.

The U.S. bombing in the conflict was more than three times as great as the combined U.S.-British bombing of Germany in World War II. The American air strikes destroyed much of North Vietnam's industrial and transportation systems. But South Vietnam, where most of the fighting took place, suffered the most damage. The war made refugees of as many as 10 million South Vietnamese. The bombing and the use of chemicals to clear forests scarred the landscape and may have permanently damaged much of South Vietnam's cropland and plant and animal life.

Other effects in Southeast Asia. In 1976, North and South Vietnam were united into a single nation, which was renamed the Socialist Republic of Vietnam. North Vietnamese leaders then forced their own rigid political culture on people of the south. They imprisoned thousands who had held positions of responsibility in the South Vietnamese army or government. They also waged a campaign against independent businesses, run mainly by Vietnamese merchants of Chinese descent. As a result, over 1 million Vietnamese fled Vietnam between 1975 and the early 1990's, and the economy stagnated. But the harsh social divisions between rich and poor were ended, and literacy rates soared.

North Vietnam had helped establish Communist governments in Laos and Cambodia in 1975. However, the anti-Vietnamese policies of the pro-Chinese Communist Khmer Rouge movement in Cambodia forced Vietnam into a lengthy and costly campaign in that country. China reacted to this evidence of Vietnam's growing influence in the region by briefly invading Vietnam in 1979.

Effects in the United States. The Vietnam War also had far-reaching effects in the United States. The United States spent about $200 billion on the war. Many experts believe that this high cost of the war damaged the U.S. economy for years after the war's conclusion.

The Vietnam War was the first foreign war in which U.S. combat forces failed to achieve their goals. This failure hurt the pride of many Americans and left bitter and painful memories. The Americans most immediately affected included the approximately 2,600,000 men and women who had served in the war, and their families. Most veterans adjusted smoothly to civilian life. But others, particularly those with psychological problems associated with combat stress, encountered difficulties in making the adjustment to postwar American society. These veterans suffered from high rates of divorce, drug abuse, unemployment, and homelessness.

After World Wars I and II, the country viewed its soldiers as heroes. Americans who opposed the U.S. role in Vietnam had embraced those veterans who joined the antiwar movement upon their return from the battlefield, but some criticized or shunned those veterans who felt the war was justified. Many Americans who supported the war came to regard Vietnam veterans as symbols of America's defeat. Some leading hawks opposed expanding benefits to Vietnam veterans to match those given to veterans of earlier wars. These reactions shocked the veterans. Many of them felt that the nation neither recognized nor appreciated their sacrifices.

After the war, Congress and the public became more willing to challenge the president on military and foreign policy. The war also became a standard of comparison in situations that might involve U.S. troops abroad.

Today, Americans still disagree on the main issues and lessons of the war. Some believe U.S. participation was necessary and just. Many of these people say the war was lost because the United States did not use its full military power and because opposition at home weakened the war effort. Others point to the failure of the South Vietnamese government to develop popular support and to its overreliance on the United States. Still others view U.S. involvement as immoral and unwise. Some of them feel U.S. leaders made the war a test of the nation's power and leadership. Some view the conflict as a civil war that had no importance to U.S. security. Since Vietnam, many Americans have argued that the nation should stay out of wars that do not directly threaten its safety or vital interests.　　Marc Jason Gilbert

Index

How to use the index

This index covers the contents of the 1999, 2000, and 2001 editions.

Each index entry gives the edition year and the page number or numbers—for example, **Cleveland Orchestra 01:** 153-154. This means that information on this topic may be found on pages 153 through 154 in the 2001 edition.

When there are many references to a topic, they are grouped alphabetically by clue words under the main topic. For example, the clue words under **Clinton, Bill** group the references to him under several subtopics.

The "see" and "see also" cross-references—for example, **Clothing**—refer the reader to other entries in the index or to Update articles in the volumes covered by the index.

When a topic such as **Colombia** appears in all capital letters, this means that there is an Update article entitled Colombia in at least one of the three volumes covered by this index. References to the topic in other articles may also appear after the topic name.

When only the first letter of a topic, such as **Communist Party,** is capitalized, this means that there is no article entitled Communist Party but that information on this topic may be found in the edition and on the pages listed.

The indication (il.) means that the reference on this page is to an illustration only, as in the pictures relating to **Concorde** on pages 24 and 233 of the 2001 edition.

An entry followed by *WBE* refers to a new or revised *World Book Encyclopedia* article in the supplement section, as in **Conservation 01:** 486. This means that a *World Book Encyclopedia* article on this topic begins on page 486 of the 2001 edition.

Acknowledgments

The publishers acknowledge the following sources for illustrations. Credits read from top to bottom, left to right, on their respective pages. An asterisk (*) denotes illustrations and photographs created exclusively for this edition. All maps, charts, and diagrams were prepared by the staff unless otherwise noted.

6   AP/Wide World; Reuters/Archive Photos; Agence France-Presse
7   AP/Wide World; Reuters/Archive Photos
8   AP/Wide World; Reuters/Archive Photos
9   Reuters/Archive Photos; AP/Wide World; AP/Wide World
10   AP/Wide World; Reuters/Archive Photos
11   Goddard Space Flight Center from NOAA Goes-8 DATA/Hal Pierce/Fritz Hasler/NASA
13   Reuters/Archive Photos
15-22   AP/Wide World
24   Reuters/Archive Photos
26-27   AP/Wide World
28   Agence France-Presse
31-34   AP/Wide World
32-34   AP/Wide World
36   Rendering of planets by Sylvain Korzennik, Harvard University; photograph by Till Credner, Max Planck Institute for Aeronomy
38   Corbis/Bettmann; Brown Bros.
39   Brown Bros.; Granger Collection; Granger Collection
40   Culver; Corbis © Schenectady Museum: Hall of Electrical History Foundation
41   Library of Congress; Corbis
42   Granger Collection
43   Granger Collection; Corbis/Bettmann
44   Culver; Corbis
46   Corbis/Bettmann; Corbis
47   Brown Bros.
48   Hulton Getty/Archive Photos; Corbis/Bettmann
49   Granger Collection; Corbis
50   Granger Collection; Granger Collection; Corbis/Hulton-Deutsch
53   Agence France-Presse
58   © Karin Retief, The Image Works
64   © Thomas White, Liaison Agency
65   © Radhika Chalasani, Sipa Press
66   © Radhika Chalasani, Sipa Press; © Wendy Stone, Liaison Agency
68   © Malcom Linton, Liaison Agency
73   Reuters/Archive Photos
75   University of Chicago
76-81   AP/Wide World
83   Reuters/Archive Photos
87   NASA
88-91   AP/Wide World
94   Reuters/Archive Photos
96   American Honda Motor Company, Inc.; Daimler-Chrysler Corporation; Toyota Motor Sales U.S.A., Inc.
98   © Jon Ferry, Allsport
100   Reuters/Archive Photos
103   © Ronald Martinez, Allsport; © Jed Jacobsohn, Allsport; © Harry How, Allsport
106   Reuters/Archive Photos
110   AP/Wide World
113   Reuters/Archive Photos
114   Agence France-Presse
116   AP/Wide World
119   Reuters/Archive Photos
124-128   AP/Wide World
133   Phil Velasquez © Chicago Tribune
135   Reuters/Archive Photos
140   © Walter Bibikow, FPG
144   AP/Wide World; © Charlie Mayer, Jameson Realty Group
145   AP/Wide World
146   © Bill Cardoni, Liaison Agency; © A. Ramey, PhotoEdit

147   © Steve Dunwell; © Kunio Owaki, The Stock Market
148   AP/Wide World
153   Seattle Opera (photo by Gary Smith)
155   Apple Computer, Inc.
156   Reuters/Archive Photos
162-166   AP/Wide World
168   Carl Juste © The Miami Herald
170   AP/Wide World
173   Corbis/Bettmann
175   Hershey Community Archives; Corbis/Bettmann
176   Corbis/Bettmann
177   Hulton Getty/Archive Photos
178   Corbis/Bettmann
179   © Mark Lewis, Liaison Agency; © Cynthia Carris, Impact Visuals
181   © J.B. McCourtney, Impact Visuals
183   Eifman Ballet (photo by Nina Alovert)
185   Archive Photos; Hulton-Getty/Archive Photos; Archive Photos
186   Archive Photos; AP/Wide World
187   Archive Photos; Hulton-Getty/Archive Photos; AP/Wide World; AP/Wide World; Hulton-Getty/Archive Photos
188   Archive Photos; AP/Wide World; Popperfoto/Archive Photos; AP/Wide World
189   AP/Wide World
190   Archive Photos; AP/Wide World
191   PEANUTS © United Feature Syndicate; AP/Wide World
192-193   PEANUTS © United Feature Syndicate
194   AP/Wide World
196   Archive Photos
201   Reuters/Archive Photos
204   © Superstock
206   © Corbis
207   © Mauro Panci, The Stock Market
209   © William Taufic, The Stock Market; © PhotoDisc, Inc.
210   © Greg Pease, Corbis
213   Knight Ridder © Chicago Tribune
214   Reuters/Archive Photos
216   AP/Wide World
217   Motorola, Inc.
218   © Jeff Darcy, The Plain Dealer
220   AP/Wide World
223   © James Hill, NYT Pictures
226   Reuters/Archive Photos
227   Steven Spicer*
231-233   AP/Wide World
234   © Joseph De Sciose, Brooklyn Botanic Garden
236-244   AP/Wide World
245-248   Agence France-Presse
250   Reuters/Archive Photos
252   AP/Wide World
254-256   Reuters/Archive Photos
258   AP/Wide World
261   Reuters/Archive Photos
262   AP/Wide World
266   Reuters/Archive Photos
268   AP/Wide World
271   © Tim Boyle, Liaison Agency
272   Agence France-Presse
277   AP/Wide World
278   Bibliotheca Alexandrina
283-288   AP/Wide World
291-293   Reuters/Archive Photos
295   AP/Wide World
298   © Fox Searchlight Pictures from Shooting Star; © Dreamworks from Shooting Star; © Miramax from Shooting Star

302   American Museum of Natural History
303   AP/Wide World
304   Reuters/Archive Photos
305   © Keith Meyers, NYT Pictures; National D-Day Museum, New Orleans, LA
306   © Milwaukee Journal Sentinel; Reuters/Archive Photos
310-325   AP/Wide World
326   Agence France-Presse
327-330   AP/Wide World
331   Reuters/Archive Photos
332   AP/Wide World; Reuters/Archive Photos; AP/Wide World
333   Reuters/Archive Photos
334   AP/Wide World
335   Reuters/Archive Photos; AP/Wide World; Reuters/Archive Photos
337   AP/Wide World
339   Agence France-Presse
342   AP/Wide World
344   Reuters/Archive Photos
346   AP/Wide World
347   Knight Ridder © Chicago Tribune
349   AP/Wide World
351   Reuters/Archive Photos
352   Corbis/Reuters; Corbis/AFP
354   Reuters/Archive Photos; AP/Wide World; AP/Wide World
355   AP/Wide World; AP/Wide World; Reuters/Archive Photos
358   AP/Wide World
359-363   Reuters/Archive Photos
365-366   AP/Wide World
371   Reuters/Archive Photos
372   Photofest
373   NASA
374   Photofest; NASA
375   Photofest; NASA
376   Photofest
377   NASA
379   Lockheed Martin Corporation
380   NASA; Lockheed Martin Corporation
383   NASA
384-396   AP/Wide World
397   Agence France-Presse
398   AP/Wide World
402   © ABC from Shooting Star; Photofest
404   AP/Wide World
405   Agence France-Presse
407   © Joan Marcus
410   © Ken Ruinard, Anderson Independent-Mail
411-422   AP/Wide World
423-425   Hulton Getty/Liaison Agency
426   Hulton Getty/Archive Photos
427   Hulton Getty/Liaison Agency; Hulton Getty/Archive Photos
428   Hulton Getty/Liaison Agency
429   © Liaison Agency
432   (coins) U.S. Mint; (bills) U.S. Bureau of Engraving & Printing
437   AP/Wide World
438   Design by Friedrich St. Florian
440   AP/Wide World
441   Reuters/Archive Photos; AP/Wide World; Agence France-Presse
445   Reuters/Archive Photos
446   Agence France-Presse
448   South Carolina Aquarium
449   Reuters/Archive Photos
452-453   Library of Congress
454   AP/Wide World
455   © Bill Pugliano, Liaison Agency
458   WORLD BOOK photo by Steven Spicer